Lecture Notes in Computer Science   1384

Edited by G. Goos, J. Hartmanis and J. van Leeuwen

Springer
Berlin
Heidelberg
New York
Barcelona
Budapest
Hong Kong
London
Milan
Paris
Santa Clara
Singapore
Tokyo

Bernhard Steffen (Ed.)

Tools and Algorithms for the Construction and Analysis of Systems

4th International Conference, TACAS'98
Held as Part of the Joint European Conferences
on Theory and Practice of Software, ETAPS'98
Lisbon, Portugal, March 28 – April 4, 1998
Proceedings

 Springer

Series Editors

Gerhard Goos, Karlsruhe University, Germany
Juris Hartmanis, Cornell University, NY, USA
Jan van Leeuwen, Utrecht University, The Netherlands

Volume Editor

Bernhard Steffen
Universität Dortmund, Lehrstuhl für Programmiersysteme
Fachbereich Informatik
D-44221 Dortmund, Germany
E-mail: steffen@informatik.uni-dortmund.de

Cataloging-in-Publication data applied for

Die Deutsche Bibliothek - CIP-Einheitsaufnahme

Tools and algorithms for the construction and analysis of systems
: 4th international conference ; proceedings / TACAS '98, held as part
of the Joint European Conferences on Theory and Practice of
Software, ETAPS '98, Lisbon, Portugal, March 28 - April 4, 1998.
Bernhard Steffen (ed.). - Berlin ; Heidelberg ; New York ; Barcelona ;
Budapest ; Hong Kong ; London ; Milan ; Paris ; Santa Clara ;
Singapore ; Tokyo : Springer, 1998
   (Lecture notes in computer science ; Vol. 1384)
   ISBN 3-540-64356-7

CR Subject Classification (1991): F.3, D.2.4, D.2.2, C.2.4

ISSN 0302-9743
ISBN 3-540-64356-7 Springer-Verlag Berlin Heidelberg New York

© Springer-Verlag Berlin Heidelberg 1998
Printed in Germany

Typesetting: Camera-ready by author
SPIN 10632045   06/3142 – 5 4 3 2 1 0   Printed on acid-free paper

Foreword

The European conference situation in the general area of software science has long been considered unsatisfactory. A fairly large number of small and medium-sized conferences and workshops take place on an irregular basis, competing for high-quality contributions and for enough attendees to make them financially viable. Discussions aiming at a consolidation have been underway since at least 1992, with concrete planning beginning in summer 1994 and culminating in a public meeting at TAPSOFT'95 in Aarhus.

On the basis of a broad consensus, it was decided to establish a single annual federated spring conference in the slot that was then occupied by TAP-SOFT and CAAP/ESOP/CC, comprising a number of existing and new conferences and covering a spectrum from theory to practice. ETAPS'98, the first instance of the European Joint Conferences on Theory and Practice of Software, is taking place this year in Lisbon. It comprises five conferences (FoSSaCS, FASE, ESOP, CC, TACAS), four workshops (ACoS, VISUAL, WADT, CMCS), seven invited lectures, and nine tutorials.

The events that comprise ETAPS address various aspects of the system development process, including specification, design, implementation, analysis and improvement. The languages, methodologies and tools which support these activities are all well within its scope. Different blends of theory and practice are represented, with an inclination towards theory with a practical motivation on one hand and soundly-based practice on the other. Many of the issues involved in software design apply to systems in general, including hardware systems, and the emphasis on software is not intended to be exclusive.

ETAPS is a natural development from its predecessors. It is a loose confederation in which each event retains its own identity, with a separate programme committee and independent proceedings. Its format is open-ended, allowing it to grow and evolve as time goes by. Contributed talks and system demonstrations are in synchronized parallel sessions, with invited lectures in plenary sessions. Two of the invited lectures are reserved for "unifying" talks on topics of interest to the whole range of ETAPS attendees. The aim of cramming all this activity into a single one-week meeting is to create a strong magnet for academic and industrial researchers working on topics within its scope, giving them the opportunity to learn about research in related areas, and thereby to foster new and existing links between work in areas that have hitherto been addressed in separate meetings.

ETAPS'98 has been superbly organized by José Luis Fiadeiro and his team at the Department of Informatics of the University of Lisbon. The ETAPS steering committee has put considerable energy into planning for ETAPS'98 and its successors. Its current membership is:

André Arnold (Bordeaux), Egidio Astesiano (Genova), Jan Bergstra (Amsterdam), Ed Brinksma (Enschede), Rance Cleaveland (Raleigh), Pierpaolo Degano (Pisa), Hartmut Ehrig (Berlin), José Fiadeiro (Lisbon), Jean-Pierre Finance (Nancy), Marie-Claude Gaudel (Paris), Tibor Gyimothy (Szeged), Chris Hankin (London), Stefan Jähnichen (Berlin), Uwe Kastens (Paderborn), Paul Klint (Amsterdam), Kai Koskimies (Tampere), Tom Maibaum (London), Hanne Riis Nielson (Aarhus), Fernando Orejas (Barcelona), Don Sannella (Edinburgh, chair), Bernhard Steffen (Dortmund), Doaitse Swierstra (Utrecht), Wolfgang Thomas (Kiel)

Other people were influential in the early stages of planning, including Peter Mosses (Aarhus) and Reinhard Wilhelm (Saarbrücken). ETAPS'98 has received generous sponsorship from:

Portugal Telecom
TAP Air Portugal
the Luso-American Development Foundation
the British Council
the EU programme "Training and Mobility of Researchers"
the University of Lisbon
the European Association for Theoretical Computer Science
the European Association for Programming Languages and Systems
the Gulbenkian Foundation

I would like to express my sincere gratitude to all of these people and organizations, and to José in particular, as well as to Springer-Verlag for agreeing to publish the ETAPS proceedings.

Edinburgh, January 1998   Donald Sannella
                                       ETAPS Steering Committee chairman

Preface

This volume contains the proceedings of the 4th TACAS, International Conference on *Tools and Algorithms for the Construction and Analysis of Systems*. TACAS'98 took place at the Gulbenkian Foundation in Lisbon, Portugal, March 31st to April 3rd, 1998, as part of the First European Joint Conferences on Theory and Practice of Software (ETAPS), whose aims, organization, and history are detailed in the separate foreword by Donald Sannella.

It is the goal of TACAS to bring together researchers and practitioners interested in the development and application of tools and algorithms for specification, verification, analysis, and construction of software and hardware systems. In particular, it aims at creating an atmosphere that promotes a cross-fertilization of ideas between the different communities of theoreticians, tool builders, tool users, and system designers, in various specialized areas of computer science. In this respect, TACAS reflects the overall goal of ETAPS under a tool-oriented perspective. In fact, the scope of TACAS intersects with all the other ETAPS events, which address more traditional areas of interest.

As a consequence, in addition to the standard criteria for acceptability, contributions have also been selected on the basis of their conceptual significance in the context of neighbouring areas. This comprises the profile-driven comparison of various concepts and methods, their degree of support via interactive or fully automatic tools, and in particular case studies revealing the application profiles of the considered methods and tools.

In order to emphasize the practical importance of tools, TACAS allows tool presentations to be submitted (and reviewed) on equal footing with traditional scientific papers, treating them as 'first class citizens'. In practice, this entails their presentation in plenary conference sessions, and the integral inclusion of a tool report in the proceedings. The conference, of course, also included informal tool demonstrations, not announced in the official program.

TACAS'98 comprised

- **An invited Lecture** by Randal Bryant, the 'father' of the Binary Decisions Diagrams (BDDs), which have become over the last decade the most prominent data structures for industrially relevant tools, as well as

- **Regular Sessions** featuring 28 papers selected from 78 submissions, ranging from foundational contributions to tool presentations including online demos.

Grown itself out of a satellite meeting to TAPSOFT in 1995, TACAS'98 featured two new satellite events:

- *ACoS'98, International Workshop on Advanced Communication Services*, on April 3 – 4, and
- *VISUAL'98, International Workshop on Visualization Issues for Formal Methods*, on April 4th

selected papers of which appear in Volume 1385 of Springer Verlag's Lecture Notes in Computer Science.

TACAS'98 was hosted by the University of Lisbon, and, being part of ETAPS, it shared the excellent sponsoring and support described in Donald Sannella's foreword. Like ETAPS, TACAS will be continued next year at the University of Amsterdam, and in 2000 at the Technical University of Berlin.

Finally, warm thanks are due to the program committee and to all the referees for their assistance in selecting the papers, to Donald Sannella for mastering the coordination of the whole ETAPS, to José Luiz Fiadeiro and his local team for their brilliant organization, and, last but not least, to Claudia Herbers for her professional assistance during the last months and for her first class support in the preparation of this volume.

Dortmund, March 1998   Bernhard Steffen

Program Committee

Ed Brinksma (NL)
Rance Cleaveland (USA)
Fausto Giunchiglia (I)
Susanne Graf (F)
Tom Henzinger (USA)
Daniel Jackson (USA)
Kurt Jensen (DK)

Kim G. Larsen (DK)
Tiziana Margaria (D)
Jens Palsberg (DK)
Doron Peled (USA)
Scott Smolka (USA)
Bernhard Steffen (D, chair)
Frits Vaandrager (NL)

Referees

Rajeev Alur
Henrik Reif Andersen
Alessandro Armando
Alessandro Artale
Michael von der Beeck
M. Benerecetti
Karen Bernstein
Piergiorgio Bertoli
Ahmed Bouajjani
Marius Bozga
Francesco Calzolari
Søren Christensen
Alessandro Cimatti
Andreas Claßen
Pedro D'Argenio
Luca de Alfaro
Marco Daniele
Rob DeLine
Srinivas Devadas
Yifei Dong
Xiaoqun Du
Ansgar Fehnker
Stephen Garland
Klaus Havelund
Gerard Holzmann

Thierry Jéron
Somesh Jha
Joost Pieter Katoen
Peter Kelb
Nils Klarlund
Josva Kleist
Lars M. Kristensen
Kåre Kristoffersen
Orna Kupferman
Rom Langerak
Markus Müller-Olm
Angelika Mader
Ken McMillan
Michael Mendler
Kjeld Mortensen
Laurent Mounier
Gail Murphy
George Necula
Uwe Nestmann
Mogens Nielsen
Albert Nymeyer
Robert O'Callahan
Florence Pagani
Wojciech Penczek
Anuj Puri

Shaz Qadeer
C.R. Ramakrishnan
Pascal Raymond
Marco Roveri
Vlad Rusu
Theo Ruys
Elmer Sandvad
Roberto Sebastiani
Luciano Serafini
Arne Skou
Oleg Sokolsky
Jan Springintveld
Andrzej Szalas
Jan Tretmans
Stavros Tripakis
Antti Valmari
Moshe Vardi
Kimmo Varpaaniemi
Mandana Vazhiri
Adolfo Villafiorita
Carsten Weise
Hanno Wupper
Husnu Yenigün
Job Zwiers

Contents

Contents

Invited Lecture

Regular Sessions

1. Model Checking

2. Design and Architecture

3. Various Applications

7. Case Studies and Experience

Formal Verification of Pipelined Processors*

Randal E. Bryant

Carnegie Mellon University, Pittsburgh PA 15213, USA

Abstract. Correspondence checking formally verifies that a pipelined microprocessor realizes the serial semantics of the instruction set model. By representing
the circuit state symbolically with Ordered Binary Decision Diagrams (OBDDs),
this correspondence checking can be performed directly on a logic-level representation of the circuit. Our ongoing research seeks to make his approach practical
for real-life microprocessors.

1 Motivation

Microprocessors are among the most complex electronic systems created today. High
performance processors require millions of transistors and employ complex techniques
such as pipelining, multiple instruction issue, branch prediction, speculative and/or
out-of-order execution, register renaming, and many forms of caching. When correctly
implemented, these implementation artifacts should be invisible to the user. The processor should produce the same results as if it had executed the machine code in strict,
sequential order.

Design errors can often lead to violations of the sequential semantics. For example,
an update to a register or memory location by one instruction may not be detected by an
instruction following too closely in the pipeline. An instruction following a conditional
branch may be executed prematurely, modifying a register even though the processor
later determines that the branch is taken. Such *hazard* possibilities increase dramatically
as the instruction pipelines increase in both depth and width.

Historically, microprocessor designs have been validated by extensive simulation.
Instruction sequences are executed, in simulation, on two different models: a high-level
model describing the desired effect of each instruction and a low-level model capturing
the detailed pipeline structure. The results from these simulations are then compared
for discrepancies. The instruction sequences may be taken from actual programs or
synthetically generated to exercise different aspects of the pipeline structure [5].

Validation by simulation becomes increasingly costly and unreliable as processors
increase in complexity. The number of tests required to cover all possible pipeline
interactions becomes overwhelming. Furthermore, simulation test generators suffer from
a fundamental limitation due to their use of information about the pipeline structure
in determining the possible interactions in an instruction sequence that need to be

* This research was supported in part by the Defense Advanced Research Project Agency, Contract DABT63-96-C-0071, and in part by the Semiconductor Research Corporation, Contract
97-DC-068.

simulated. A single conceptual design error can yield both an improperly-designed pipeline and a failure to test for a particular instruction combination.

As an alternative to simulation, a number of researchers have investigated using formal verification techniques to prove that a pipelined processor preserves the semantics of the instruction set model. Formal verification has the advantage that it demonstrates correct execution for all possible instruction sequences. Our interest is in developing automated techniques that apply powerful symbolic evaluation techniques to analyze the behavior of the processor over all possible operating conditions. We believe that high degrees of automation are essential to gaining acceptance by chip designers.

2 Verification Methodology

Our task is to verify that a processor will execute all possible instruction sequences properly. Since there is an infinite number of possible sequences, this condition cannot be proved directly. Instead, we show that each possible individual instruction will be executed correctly, regardless of the preceding and following instruction sequences. The correct execution of a complete sequence then follows by induction on its length. One methodology for proving the correctness of individual instructions is based on proving the invariance of an abstraction function between processor and program states by each instruction execution. A similar methodology was proposed by Hoare for proving the correctness of each operation in the implementation of an abstract data type [4].

We model the processor as having states in the set Q_{pipe}, and the behavior of the processor for each clock cycle of operation by a next-state function $\delta_{\text{pipe}}: Q_{\text{pipe}} \rightarrow Q_{\text{pipe}}$. Similarly, the state visible to the assembly language programmer (typically the main memory, integer and floating point registers, program counter, and other status registers) is modeled by a state set Q_{prog} and the execution of a single instruction by a next-state function $\delta_{\text{prog}}: Q_{\text{prog}} \rightarrow Q_{\text{prog}}$. In our simplified formulation, we we do not consider the input or output to the processor, but rather that the action taken on each step is determined by the program or pipeline state.

Our task is to show a correspondence between the transformations on the pipeline state by the processor and on the program state by the instruction execution model. This correspondence can be described by an *abstraction function Abs*: $Q_{\text{pipe}} \rightarrow Q_{\text{prog}}$ identifying which program state is represented by a given pipeline state. Typically, this corresponds to the effect of completing any instructions in the pipeline without fetching any new instructions. For each pipeline state, there must be a value k indicating the number of clock cycles required after fetching the most recent instruction until the next instruction can be fetched. Our correctness condition states that the effect of fetching and executing a single instruction should match the effect of performing the corresponding instruction on the program state. That is, for all $Q_{\text{pipe}} \in Q_{\text{pipe}}$, there must be a k such that

$$\delta_{\text{prog}}(Abs(Q_{\text{pipe}})) \;=\; Abs(\delta_{\text{pipe}}^{k}(Q_{\text{pipe}})) \tag{1}$$

In addition to the invariance property described in Equation 1, we require Abs to be surjective to guarantee that all program behaviors can be realized. That is, for every program state Q_{prog}, there must be a state Q_{pipe} such that $Abs(Q_{\text{pipe}}) = Q_{\text{prog}}$. Beyond this requirement, the abstraction function can be arbitrary, as long as it satisfies Equation 1.

The validity of the verification is not compromised by an incorrect abstraction function. That is, an invalid abstraction function will not cause the verifier yield a "false positive" result, declaring a faulty pipeline to be correct. We can let user provide us with the abstraction function [1, 6], but this becomes very cumbersome with increased pipeline complexity. Alternatively, we can attempt to derive the abstraction function directly from the pipeline structure [3]. Unlike simulation test generation, using information about the pipeline structure does not diminish the integrity of the verification.

3 Automated Correspondence Checking

Burch and Dill [3] first proposed using the pipeline description to automatically derive its abstraction function. They do this by exploiting two properties found in many pipeline designs. First, the programmer-visible state is usually embedded within the overall processor state. That is, there are specific register and memory arrays for the program registers, the main memory, and the program counter. Second, the hardware has some mechanism for "flushing" the pipeline, i.e., to complete all instructions in the pipeline without fetching any new ones. For example, this would occur when the instruction cache misses and hence no new instructions could be fetched. A symbolic simulator, which can model the behavior of the circuit over symbolically-represented states, can automatically derive the abstraction function. First, we initialize the circuit to an arbitrary, symbolic state, covering all the states in Q_{pipe}. We then symbolically simulate behavior of a processor flush. We then examine the state in the program visible register and memory elements and declare these symbolic values to represent the mapping Abs. Using similar symbolic simulation techniques, we can also compute the effect of the processor on an arbitrary pipeline state δ_{pipe} and the effect of executing an arbitrary program instruction δ_{prog}. Thus, a symbolic simulator can solve the key problems related to verifying pipeline processors.

Burch and Dill use symbolic simulation tools based on a logic of uninterpreted functions with equality, a weakened form of first order predicate calculus. Using this weak form, they can guarantee a complete decision procedure. Using their approach requires having a model of the circuit that abstracts away many details, including the sizes of the memory and register arrays, the bit widths of the data paths, and even the functionality of the data operations. This abstract model allows them to concentrate on the key issues of pipeline structure and control. Unfortunately, it can be difficult and time-consuming to derive such a model from the circuit description and to maintain it as the circuit design evolves. In addition, determining the correctness of some aspects of the circuit behavior require more detailed information about the data operations.

4 Verifying at the Bit-Level

Our recent research has focussed on adapting Burch and Dill's verification methodology to operate directly on a low-level model of the circuit, in which state is explicitly represented by sets of Boolean values and the state transformations are described by Boolean functions over this state. Such a model can be derived directly from a logic-level description of the circuit, avoiding the need to manually create a more abstract model. Instead of manipulating symbolic variables representing abstract state and uninterpreted functions, we use Ordered Binary Decision Diagrams (OBDDs) [2] to represent the symbolic circuit state. OBDDs have the advantage over other approaches to symbolic Boolean manipulation of being canonical as well as reasonably compact for many of the functions encountered in modeling digital circuits.

Many difficult hurdles must be overcome to make bit-level correspondence checking practical. One problem is to find an efficient representation of the initial, but arbitrary pipeline state, given the large number of memory elements found in a processor. A naive approach would be to introduce a distinct Boolean variable for each bit in each register or memory array, but this could require thousands, or even millions of variables. Instead, we have developed techniques to introduce only as many variables as are needed to represent the states of the symbolic locations that are actually accessed during the execution of the instruction sequence [7]. Since the sequences we symbolically simulate are relatively short, this leads to a greatly reduced number of variables. Other problems are related to the OBDD complexities caused when modeling the interactions between successive instructions, such as when the value generated by one instruction becomes the target address by a later jump instruction. We have made some progress in this area, but much more is required before we will be able to handle full scale microprocessors.

References

1. S. Bose, and A. L. Fisher, "Verifying Pipelined Hardware Using Symbolic Logic Simulation," *International Conference on Computer Design (ICCD '89)*, 1989, pp. 217–221.
2. R. E. Bryant, "Symbolic Boolean Manipulation with Ordered Binary Decision Diagrams," *ACM Computing Surveys*, Vol. 24, No. 3 (September, 1992), pp. 293–318.
3. J. R. Burch, and D. L. Dill, "Automated Verification of Pipelined Microprocessor Control," *Computer-Aided Verification (CAV '94)*, LNCS 818, Springer-Verlag, June, 1994, pp. 68–80.
4. C. A. R. Hoare, "Proof of Correctness of Data Representations," *Acta Informatica* Vol. 1, 1972, pp. 271–281.
5. M. Kantrowitz, and L. M. Noack, "I'm Done Simulating; Now What? Verification Coverage Analysis and Correctness Checking of the DECchip 21164 Alpha Microprocessor," *33rd Design Automation Conference (DAC '96)*, 1996, pp. 325–330.
6. K. L. Nelson, A. Jain, and R. E. Bryant, "Formal Verification of a Superscalar Execution Unit," *34th Design Automation Conference (DAC '97)*, June, 1997.
7. M. N. Velev, and R. E. Bryant, "Verification of Pipelined Microprocessors by Comparing Memory Execution Sequences in Symbolic Simulation," *Asian Computer Science Conference (ASIAN '97)*, LNCS 1345, Springer-Verlag, December 1997, pp. 18–31.

Fully Local and Efficient Evaluation of Alternating Fixed Points*
(Extended Abstract)

Xinxin Liu, C. R. Ramakrishnan, and Scott A. Smolka

Department of Computer Science
State University of New York at Stony Brook
Stony Brook, NY 11794 USA

{xinxin,cram,sas}@cs.sunysb.edu
+1 516 632-8334 (fax)

Abstract. We introduce Partitioned Dependency Graphs (PDGs), an abstract framework for the specification and evaluation of arbitrarily nested alternating fixed points. The generality of PDGs subsumes that of similarly proposed models of nested fixed-point computation such as Boolean graphs, Boolean equation systems, and the propositional modal mu-calculus. Our main result is *an efficient local algorithm for evaluating PDG fixed points*. Our algorithm, which we call LAFP, combines the simplicity of previously proposed induction-based algorithms (such as Winskel's tableau method for ν-calculus model checking) with the efficiency of semantics-based algorithms (such as the bit-vector method of Cleaveland, Klein, and Steffen for the equational μ-calculus). In particular, LAFP is simply specified, we provide a completely rigorous proof of its correctness, and the number of fixed-point iterations required by the algorithm is asymptotically the same as that of the best existing global algorithms. Moreover, preliminary experimental results demonstrate that LAFP performs extremely well in practice. To our knowledge, this makes LAFP the first efficient local algorithm for computing fixed points of arbitrary alternation depth to appear in the literature.

1 Introduction

Model checking [CE81, QS82, CES86] is a verification technique aimed at determining whether a system specification possesses a property expressed as a temporal logic formula. Model checking has enjoyed wide success in verifying, or finding design errors in, real-life systems. An interesting account of a number of these success stories can be found in [CW96].

Model checking has spurred interest in evaluating *alternating fixed points* as these are needed to express system properties of practical import, such as those involving subtle fairness constraints. Probably, the most canonical temporal logic for expressing alternating fixed points is the modal mu-calculus [Pra81, Koz83],

---

* Research supported in part by NSF grants CCR-9505562 and CCR-9705998, and AFOSR grants F49620-95-1-0508 and F49620-96-1-0087.

which makes explicit use of the dual fixed-point operators μ (least fixed point) and ν (greatest fixed point). Intuitively, the *alternation depth* of a modal mu-calculus formula [EL86] is the level of nontrivial nesting of fixed points in ϕ with adjacent fixed points being of different type. The term "alternating fixed point," then, refers to such adjacent fixed points.

In this paper, we present a very general framework for specifying and evaluating alternating fixed points. In particular, we introduce *Partitioned Dependency Graphs* (PDGs), whose generality subsumes that of similarly proposed models of nested fixed-point computation, such as Boolean graphs [And94], Boolean equation systems [VL94], the modal mu-calculus, and the equational μ-calculus [CKS92, BC96b]. A PDG is a directed hypergraph G with hyper-edges from vertices to sets of vertices. A PDG vertex x can be viewed as a kind of disjunctive normal form (DNF), with each of x's target sets of vertices representing a disjunct (conjunctive term) of x. Moreover, the vertices of G are partitioned into blocks, each of which is labeled by μ or ν, and the ith block represents the ith-most nested fixed point. A subset A of G's vertices is a proper evaluation of G if it respects the semantics of DNF (i.e., x is in A if one of its target sets is contained in A), and the semantics of the block labeling (i.e., the projection of A onto block i is the least fixed point of an appropriately defined function of A if this block is labeled by μ, and dually for ν).

Our main result is a new local algorithm for evaluating PDG fixed points. Our algorithm, which we call LAFP, combines the simplicity of previously proposed induction-based algorithms (such as Winskel's tableau method for ν-calculus model checking [Win89]), with the efficiency of semantics-based algorithms (such as the bit-vector method of Cleaveland, Klein, and Steffen for equational μ-calculus model checking [CKS92]). LAFP takes as input a PDG G and a vertex x_0 of G and determines, in a need-driven fashion, whether or not x_0 is in the solution of G. LAFP thereby avoids the *a priori* construction of G. In contrast, global algorithms by definition require the a priori construction of a system's state space, which results in good worst-case performance but poor performance in many practical situations. The main features of LAFP are the following:

- Like the algorithm of [VL94], LAFP constructs a stable and complete search space—in the sense that PDG vertices belonging to the search space depend only upon vertices inside the search space—and does so in a need-driven manner. Moreover, it partitions the search space into three blocks I, O, and Q: those vertices currently considered to be inside the solution, those vertices currently considered to be outside the solution, and those whose status is currently unknown, respectively.
- Like most fixed-point algorithms, LAFP computes PDG fixed points iteratively. By carefully accounting for the effects of moving a vertex x from Q to I or Q to O on vertices transitively dependent on x, LAFP avoids unnecessary recomputation when a fixed point is nested directly within the scope of another fixed point of the same type. As a result, the number of iterations required by LAFP to evaluate fixed points in a PDG with vertices V and alternation depth ad is $O((|V|-1)+(\frac{|V|+ad}{ad})^{ad})$. Asymptotically, this matches

the iteration complexity of the best existing global algorithms. Moreover, a prototype implementation of LAFP based on the XMC model checker for the alternation-free modal mu-calculus [RRR+97] and the *smodels* stable models generator [NS96] demonstrates that LAFP performs extremely well in practice.
- Because of the simplicity/abstractness of the PDG framework, the pseudo-code for LAFP is clear and concise, and we provide a completely rigorous proof of the algorithm's correctness.

In terms of related work, LAFP is to our knowledge the first efficient local algorithm for evaluating structures of arbitrary alternation depth to appear in the literature. Tableau-based local algorithms such as [Win89, Cle90, SW91] suffer an exponential blowup even when the alternation-depth is fixed. The "semi-local" algorithm of [RS97] is demonstratably less "local" than LAFP, exploring more vertices than LAFP on certain examples.

Several efficient local methods for various subsets of the μ-calculus have been proposed, including [And94, VL94, BC96a]. The algorithm of [VL94], which deals with Boolean Equation Systems of alternation depth 2, is closest to LAFP when their "restore strategy" no. 4 is used. However, we have found a counterexample to the algorithm's correctness, the details of which can be found in Appendix A. It should also be noted that their algorithm, and their proposed generalization of their algorithm to higher alternation depths, is for a given alternation depth k fixed in advance. We see no obvious way to extend their algorithm to handle equational systems of arbitrary alternation depth.

A number of global algorithms have been devised for the full μ-calculus, the most efficient of which are [CKS92, LBC+94]. The algorithm of [LBC+94] is more efficient time-wise ($O(n^{ad/2})$ vs. $O(n^{ad})$ fixed-point iterations) but requires more space ($O(n^{ad/2})$ vs. $O(n)$). The LAFP algorithm is inspired by a model checking algorithm that appeared in [Liu92].

The structure of the rest of the paper is as follows. Section 2 defines our partitioned dependency graph framework. Section 3 presents LAFP, our local algorithm for PDG evaluation, along with an analysis of its correctness and computational complexity. The XMC-based implementation of LAFP and accompanying experimental results are the topic of Section 4. Finally, Section 5 concludes and identifies directions for future work. Because of space limitations, only proof outlines are given in this extended abstract. Full proofs can be found in http://www.cs.sunysb.edu/~sas/lafp.ps.

2 Partitioned Dependency Graphs

A *partitioned dependency graph* (PDG) is a tuple $(V, E, V_1 \ldots V_n, \sigma)$, where V is a set of vertices, $E \subseteq V \times \wp(V)$ is a set of *hyper-edges*, $V_1 \ldots V_n$ is a finite sequence of subsets of V such that $\{V_1, \ldots, V_n\}$ is a partition of V, and $\sigma :$ $\{V_1, \ldots, V_n\} \rightarrow \{\mu, \nu\}$ is a function that assigns μ or ν to each block of the partition. Let $\theta \in \{\mu, \nu\}$. We shall subsequently write $\sigma(x) = \theta$ if $x \in V_i$ and $\sigma(V_i) = \theta$.

Intuitively, a PDG G represents an equational system (in disjunctive normal form) having n nested, possibly alternating, blocks of boolean equations. V_1 is the outermost block and V_n is the innermost block. For the reader familiar with *nested boolean equation systems* [VL94], a PDG $(V, E, V_1 \ldots V_n, \sigma)$ can be viewed as a (arbitrarily) nested boolean equation system with equation blocks V_i and each $x \in V_i$ having the equation $x = \bigvee_{(x,S) \in E} \bigwedge_{y \in S} y$. Each V_i has the type $\sigma(V_i)$, and they are nested in the order given by $V_1, \ldots, V_n$.

Example 1. Let $G = (V, E, V_1 V_2, \sigma)$ be a PDG where $V = \{x, y, z\}$, $V_1 = \{x, y\}$, $V_2 = \{z\}$, $E = \{(x, \{y\}), (x, \{z\}), (y, \{z\}), (y, \{z\}), (z, \{x, y\})\}$, $\sigma(V_1) = \nu$, $\sigma(V_2) = \mu$. *The corresponding nested boolean equation system is the following:*

$$\nu : \begin{cases} x = y \vee z \\ y = x \vee z \end{cases}$$
$$\mu : \{ z = x \wedge y$$

Let $G = (V, E, V_1 \ldots V_n, \sigma)$ be a PDG. To give a formal semantics to PDGs, first notice that G induces two functions $g, \bar{g} : \wp(V) \to \wp(V)$ such that for $A \subseteq V$,

$$g(A) = \{x \in V \mid \exists (x, S) \in E.\ S \subseteq A\},$$
$$\bar{g}(A) = \{x \in V \mid \forall (x, S) \in E.\ S \cap A \neq \emptyset\}.$$

For $A \subseteq V$ we write $\overline{A}$ for $V - A$. Clearly from the definition, for $A \subseteq V$ it holds that $\overline{g(A)} = \bar{g}(\overline{A})$. It is also clear from the definition that both g and $\bar{g}$ are monotonic functions with respect to set inclusion. In words, a vertex x is in $g(A)$ if x has a target set of vertices contained in A. Dually, x is in $\bar{g}(A)$ if each of x's target sets has an element in A. Thus, g ($\bar{g}$) allows us to interpret PDG vertices as boolean equations of disjunctive (conjunctive) normal forms.

We write $\mathbf{V}_G$ for $\wp(V_1) \times \cdots \times \wp(V_n)$. Define $\phi : \mathbf{V}_G \to \wp(V)$ to be the *flattening function* such that for $\mathbf{v} \in \mathbf{V}_G$, $\phi(\mathbf{v}) = \bigcup_{i=1}^n \mathbf{v}(i)$. Clearly ϕ is in one-one correspondence with its inverse ϕ^- given by $\phi^-(A) = (A \cap V_1, \ldots, A \cap V_n)$ for $A \subseteq \wp(V)$.

For $\mathbf{v} \in \mathbf{V}_G$, we will write $\mathbf{v}[x/k]$ for the updated version of $\mathbf{v}$ in which its kth component is replaced by x, and $\bar{\mathbf{v}}$ for the componentwise complementation of $\mathbf{v}$. We will also write $\bot$ for $(\emptyset, \ldots, \emptyset)$.

With $g, \bar{g}$ defined as above, a PDG further induces the $2n + 2$ functions

$$g_0, \ldots, g_n, \bar{g}_0, \ldots, \bar{g}_n : \mathbf{V}_G \to \mathbf{V}_G$$

such that $g_n = \phi^- \circ g \circ \phi$, $\bar{g}_n = \phi^- \circ \bar{g} \circ \phi$, and for $\mathbf{v} \in \mathbf{V}_G$, $k \in \{1, \ldots, n\}$,

$$g_{k-1}(\mathbf{v}) = \begin{cases} \nu u.g_k(\mathbf{v}[u(k)/k]) & \sigma(V_k) = \nu \\ \mu u.g_k(\mathbf{v}[u(k)/k]) & \sigma(V_k) = \mu \end{cases},$$

$$\bar{g}_{k-1}(\mathbf{v}) = \begin{cases} \nu u.\bar{g}_k(\mathbf{v}[u(k)/k]) & \sigma(V_k) = \mu \\ \mu u.\bar{g}_k(\mathbf{v}[u(k)/k]) & \sigma(V_k) = \nu \end{cases},$$

where $\nu u.g_k(\mathbf{v}[u(k)/k])$ ($\mu u.g_k(\mathbf{v}[u(k)/k])$) is the maximum (minimum) $u \in \mathbf{V}_G$ such that $u = g_k(\mathbf{v}[u(k)/k])$. Following the standard argument,

$\lambda u.g_k(v[u(k)/k])$ is a monotonic function on the complete lattice $(\wp(V_1) \times \ldots \times \wp(V_n), \sqsubseteq)$, with $\sqsubseteq$ being the pointwise inclusion relation. Thus, by the Knaster-Tarski fixed-point theorem, such u do uniquely exist. The well definedness of $\bar{g}_k$ is guaranteed in the same way.

Intuitively, the expression $g_{k-1}(v)$ computes the fixed point of the kth block in environment v. Moreover, $g_0(v)$ gives the solution to the entire equational system. Since G is a *closed* system, the choice of argument to g_0 is irrelevant. Given a distinguished vertex x_0 in V, the problem then of *locally evaluating* G is the one of determining whether $x_0 \in \phi(g_0(\bot))$.

3 LAFP: A Local Algorithm for Evaluating PDGs

The pseudo-code for algorithm LAFP is given in Figure 1. LAFP takes as input a PDG $G = (V, E, V_1 \ldots V_n, \sigma)$ and a distinguished vertex $x_0 \in V$, and decides whether $x_0 \in \phi(g_0(\bot))$; that is, whether x_0 is in the solution to G. Before explaining further the algorithm, we need some additional notation. Let $Q^+ = \{x \in Q \mid x \in V_i \text{ and } \sigma(V_i) = \nu\}$ be the vertices in Q defined in blocks of type ν and, similarly, let $Q^- = \{x \in Q \mid x \in V_i \text{ and } \sigma(V_i) = \mu\}$ be the vertices in Q defined in blocks of type μ. By default, vertices of Q^+ are assumed to be in the solution to G while vertices of Q^- are not. Also, we write $y > x$ when the index of the block containing vertex y is greater than the index of the block containing vertex x; i.e., y is in a block more deeply nested than the block containing x.

Like the algorithm of [VL94], LAFP seeks to construct a stable and complete search space (subset of V) in the sense that PDG vertices belonging to the search space depend only upon vertices inside the search space. Moreover, it partitions the search space into three blocks I, O, and Q. I contains those vertices currently considered to be inside the solution, O contains those vertices currently considered to be outside the solution, and Q is the set of vertices that have been explored but whose status is undetermined.

The algorithm starts with x_0 in Q, terminates when Q is empty, and each iteration of the while-loop is designed to maintain the invariants given in the proof sketch of Theorem 1. In particular, a vertex x is chosen from Q from among those that are most deeply nested (in the block with the largest index). This is to prevent computation in an outer block (relative to x's block) from proceeding with possibly erroneous default values.

In case 1, x is a vertex that belongs in I since one of x's target sets of vertices S is contained in $Q^+ \cup I$. In this case, x is moved from Q to I; the fact that S is only required to be contained in $Q^+ \cup I$ rather than in I reflects the intuition that vertices from a ν-block are assumed to be in the solution set. Subsequently, a check is performed to see if x is from a μ-block. If so, then all nodes in O that transitively depend on the assumption that x is not in the solution (since x is in a μ-block) are moved from O to Q, a process we refer to as our *restore strategy*. For this purpose, we associate with each vertex $y \in I \cup O$ an attribute $y.T$, which is the set of vertices y transitively depends on for being in I or O. $y.T$ is computed by the procedure Closure[1] upon adding y into I.

procedure LAFP(G, x_0)
  initialize $I := \emptyset$, $O := \emptyset$, $Q := \{x_0\}$
  while $Q \neq \emptyset$ **do**
    choose $x \in Q \cap V_k$ where k is the largest k such that $Q \cap V_k \neq \emptyset$
    case
      1. $x \in g(Q^+ \cup I)$:
        $I := I \cup \{x\}$
        $Q := Q - \{x\}$
        choose $(x, S) \in E$ such that $S \subseteq Q^+ \cup I$
        Closure$^1(x, S)$
        if $\sigma(x) = \mu$ **then**
          $Q := Q \cup \{y \mid y \in O, x \in y.T\}$
          $O := \{y \in O \mid x \notin y.T\}$
      2. $x \in \bar{g}(Q^- \cup O)$:
        $O := O \cup \{x\}$
        $Q := Q - \{x\}$
        $T := \emptyset$
        for each $(x, S) \in E$ **do**
          choose $y \in S \cap (Q^- \cup O)$
          $T := T \cup \{y\}$
         Closure$^0(x, T)$
        if $\sigma(x) = \nu$ **then**
          $Q := Q \cup \{y \mid y \in I, x \in y.T\}$
          $I := \{y \in I \mid x \notin y.T\}$
      3. **otherwise:**
        choose $y \in \bigcup\{S \mid (x, S) \in E\}$ such that $y \notin Q \cup I \cup O$
        $Q := Q \cup \{y\}$

procedure Closure$^1(x, S)$
  $x.T := S$
  do the following until $x.T$ stops increasing
    if $y \in x.T$ and $(\sigma(x) = \mu$ or $y > x)$ **then** $x.T := x.T \cup y.T$

procedure Closure$^0(x, S)$
  $x.T := S$
  do the following until $x.T$ stops increasing
    if $y \in x.T$ and $(\sigma(x) = \nu$ or $y > x)$ **then** $x.T := x.T \cup y.T$

Fig. 1. Pseudo-code for algorithm LAFP.

Case 2 is dual to case 1: each of x's target sets has an element in $Q^- \cup O$. In case 3, there is not enough information to place x in I or O, so one of its unexplored successors is added to Q. It is easy to show that case 3 is always executable when both cases 1 and 2 fail to hold.

In procedure Closure^1, the attribute set $x.T$ is constructed. Assume, for the purposes of discussion, that we are computing $x.T$ for some x which has just been added into I (the explanation of Closure^0 is dual if x has just been added to O). Then $x.T$ should contain vertices in I and Q^+ on which x's membership in I depends. (Later, we will see that an invariant property of LAFP is that, in this case, $x.T \subseteq I \cup Q^+$.) Thus if $y \in x.T$ and y is from a μ-block then y must be in I. Also, if $y \in x.T$ and y is from a block more deeply nested than the block containing x, then also y must be in I (otherwise x would not have been evaluated in the first place). In these cases, since $x \in I$ depends on $y \in I$ which in turn depends on all the vertices in $y.T$, $y.T$ must be a subset of $x.T$.

Example 2. Consider PDG G of Example 1. If we want to determine whether $x \in g_0(\bot)$, we run LAFP with $Q = \{x\}$ initially. There are many possible runs of the algorithm on this instance. One of these is as follows: y is added into Q (case 3 on x); x is moved from Q to I (case 1 on x); y is moved from Q to I (case 1 on y); terminate with $I = \{x, y\}, O = \emptyset, Q = \emptyset$.

Another possible run is as follows: z is added into Q (case 3 on x); y is added into Q (case 3 on z); z is moved from Q to I (case 1 on z); y is moved from Q to I (case 1 on y); x is moved from Q to I (case 1 on x); terminate with $I = \{x, y, z\}, O = \emptyset, Q = \emptyset$.

The above example shows that in some cases LAFP may terminate without exploring all the vertices, a characteristic of local algorithms. The next example illustrates LAFP's restore strategy.

Example 3. Let $G = (V, E, V_1 V_2, \sigma)$ be a PDG where $V = \{x, y, z\}$, $V_1 = \{x, y\}$, $V_2 = \{z\}$, $E = \{(y, \{x\}), (y, \{z\}), (z, \{x\}), (z\{y\})\}$, $\sigma(V_1) = \nu, \sigma(V_2) = \mu$. The corresponding nested boolean equation system is the following:

$$\nu : \begin{cases} x = 0 \\ y = x \vee z \end{cases}$$
$$\mu : \{ z = x \vee y$$

If we want to determine whether $z \in g_0(\bot)$, we run the algorithm with $Q = \{z\}$ initially, and the following is a possible execution: x is added into Q (case 3 on z); z is moved from Q to I with $z.T = \{x\}$ (case 1 on z); x is moved from Q to O with $x.T = \emptyset$, and z is moved from I back to Q since $x \in z.T$ (case 2 on x); y is added into Q (case 3 on z); z is moved from Q to I with $z.T = \{y\}$ (case 1 on z); y is moved from Q to I with $y.T = \{y, z\}$ (case 1 on y); terminate with $I = \{z, y\}, O = \{x\}, Q = \emptyset$.

The (partial) correctness of LAFP is guaranteed by the following theorem.

Theorem 1. *When algorithm LAFP terminates, whenever $x \in I$ then $x \in \phi(g_0(\bot))$, and whenever $x \in O$ then $x \in \phi(g_0(\bot))$.*

Proof sketch The proof depends on the following key invariants of the while-loop:

1. if $x \in I$ then $x \in g(x.T)$ and $x.T \subseteq I \cup Q^+$,
2. if $x \in O$ then $x \in \bar{g}(x.T)$ and $x.T \subseteq O \cup Q^-$,

3. if $x \in I \cap V_k$ and $\sigma(V_k) = \nu$ then $x \in g_k(\phi^-(x.T))(k)$,
4. if $x \in I \cap V_k$ and $\sigma(V_k) = \mu$ then $x \in g_{k-1}(\phi^-(x.T))(k)$,
5. if $x \in O \cap V_k$ and $\sigma(V_k) = \mu$ then $x \in \bar{g}_k(\phi^-(x.T))(k)$,
6. if $x \in O \cap V_k$ and $\sigma(V_k) = \nu$ then $x \in \bar{g}_{k-1}(\phi^-(x.T))(k)$.

Now suppose after LAFP terminates $x \in I$. Clearly $x \in g(x.T) \subseteq g(I \cup Q^+)$ by the above invariants. When LAFP terminates $Q = \emptyset$, thus $x \in g(I)$, that is $x \in \phi(g_n(\phi^-(I)))$. Note that $g_0(\phi^-(I)) = g_0(\bot)$. To conclude $x \in g_0(\bot)$ we will show that at termination it holds that $g_k(\phi^-(I)) \sqsubseteq g_{k-1}(\phi^-(I))$ for $k = 1, \ldots, n$. To see this we need to consider two cases. The first is that V_k is a μ-block. In this case for all $y \in \phi^-(I)(k)$ it holds that $y \in g_{k-1}(\phi^-(y.T))(k) \subseteq g_{k-1}(\phi^-(I))(k)$, by invariants 4 and 1. Now $g_k(\phi^-(I)) \sqsubseteq g_k(\phi^-(I)[g_{k-1}(\phi^-(I))(k)/k]) = g_{k-1}(\phi^-(I))$. The second case is that V_k is a ν-block. In this case for all $y \in \phi^-(I)(k)$ it holds that $y \in g_k(\phi^-(y.T))(k) \subseteq g_k(\phi^-(I))(k)$, by invariants 3 and 1. So $g_k(\phi^-(I)) \sqsubseteq g_k(\phi^-(I)[g_k(\phi^-(I))(k)/k])$. This inequality shows that $g_k(\phi^-(I))$ is a pre-fixed point of $\lambda u.g_k(\phi^-(I)[u(k)/k])$, thus $g_k(\phi^-(I)) \sqsubseteq \nu u.g_k(\phi^-(I)[u(k)/k]) = g_{k-1}(\phi^-(I))$.

For $x \in O$, we can similarly show that after termination $x \in \phi(\bar{g}_0(\bot))$. Thus in this case $x \in \phi(g_0(\bot))$ since $\bar{g}_0(\bot) = g_0(\bot)$. □

In analyzing the computational complexity of LAFP, the concept of *alternation depth* plays an important role. Let $G = (V, E, V_1 \ldots V_n, \sigma)$ be a PDG. For $x \in V$, let $\text{succ}(x)$ be the set of vertices that are related to x by the transitive closure of G's hyper-edge relation. More precisely $\text{succ}(x)$ is the smallest set such that if $(x, S) \in E$ then $S \subseteq \text{succ}(x)$ and if $y \in \text{succ}(x)$ and $(y, T) \in E$ then $T \subseteq \text{succ}(x)$. For $x \in V_k$, its alternation depth, $ad(x)$, is defined by

$$ad(x) = 1 + \max\{ad(y) \mid y \in \bigcup_{i=1}^{k-1} V_i, y \in \text{succ}(x), \sigma(x) \neq \sigma(y)\}.$$

We adopt the convention that $\max \emptyset = 0$. Thus clearly for $x \in V_1$, $ad(x) = 1$. Then for the PDG G its alternation depth is the maximum alternation depth of the vertices.

The following theorem gives the fixed-point iteration complexity of LAFP.

Theorem 2. *Let $G = (V, E, V_1 \ldots V_n, \sigma)$ be a PDG with x_0 a distinguished vertex in V. Then the number of iterations taken by the while-loop of LAFP to decide if $x_0 \in \phi(g_0(\bot))$ is bounded by*

$$(|V| - 1) + \left(\frac{|V| + ad}{ad}\right)^{ad}$$

where ad is the alternation depth of G.

Proof sketch Elements of the set $I \cup O$ can be partitioned into the following two subsets:

$$A = \{x \mid x \in I \wedge \sigma(x) = \mu\} \cup \{x \mid x \in O \wedge \sigma(x) = \nu\},$$
$$B = \{x \mid x \in I \wedge \sigma(x) = \nu\} \cup \{x \mid x \in O \wedge \sigma(x) = \mu\},$$

and elements of A and of B are said to be *alternating* and *straight*, respectively. A can be further partitioned into $A_1, \ldots, A_{ad}$, where $A_d = \{x \in A \mid ad(x) = d\}$. The key to the complexity analysis is the pattern by which vertices move among these sets during the execution of LAFP. The pattern is characterized by the following observations:

1. if case 1 or 2 is executed, the size of the set $I \cup O \cup Q$ does not change, whereas if case 3 is executed it increases by 1;
2. if case 3 is executed all $A_1, \ldots, A_{ad}, B$ remain unchanged;
3. if case 1 or 2 is executed, then a new element x is added into $I \cup O$ either as an alternating or as a straight element. If x becomes a straight element of $I \cup O$ then $|B|$ increases by 1 and all $A_1, \ldots, A_{ad}$ remain unchanged, and if x becomes an alternating element of $I \cup O$ then $|A_d|$ increases by 1 and A_i remains unchanged for $i < d$, where $d = ad(x)$.

With these observations, the lexicon order of the array $(|A_1|, \ldots, |A_{ad-1}|, |I \cup O \cup Q| + |B \cup A_{ad}|)$ increases at least by 1 after each iteration. Routine calculation shows that this order is bounded by

$$(|V| - 1) + \left(\frac{|V| + ad}{ad} \right)^{ad}.$$

$\square$

A careful amortized analysis of the *total* execution time of LAFP (in which the time taken during iterations of the while-loop is taken into account) introduces a factor of $|V|^2$ into the bound of Theorem 2. This additional factor is mainly due to the computation performed by procedure Closure, and is the price we pay for being able to perform local model checking on structures of arbitrary alternation depth. However, the complexity of LAFP does not appear to be an issue in practice, as the algorithm performs extremely well on published benchmarks, in particular, those involving formulas of alternation depth 2 (see Section 4).

It is not difficult to see that in the worst case LAFP requires space quadratic in the size of the explored state space; this is due to the maintenance of the $y.T$ attribute sets, each of which can potentially grow to size $O(|V|)$ after performing the Closure operation. In contrast, most existing model checking algorithms for the modal mu-calculus need only linear space. However, we strongly conjecture that there exists a version of LAFP in which the Closure operation is avoided and PDG fixed-points are still computed correctly. Moreover, it should be possible to do so without affecting LAFP's iteration complexity. This would yield the desired linear space complexity bound.

One possible way of achieving this space complexity is by storing S and T in $x.T$ instead of their "closure," in cases 1 and 2 of procedure LAFP, respectively. If these changes are made, then care must be taken to ensure that the restore strategy properly propagates the effect of moving a node from O to Q or from I to Q. To clarify, consider an example. Suppose x is a node in a μ block and $y, z \in O$ with $y.T = \{x\}$, $z.T = \{y\}$. Then, if x turns out to be in I, the restore strategy should not only move y from O back to Q (since $x \in y.T$), but also z since $z.T = \{y\}$ implies that $z \in O$ depends on $y \in O$.

4 Experimental Results

We describe a prototype implementation of LAFP based on the XMC model checker [RRR+97] and the *smodels* stable models generator [NS96]. XMC is an efficient model checker for value-passing CCS and the alternation-free fragment of the modal mu-calculus, implemented using the XSB logic programming system [XSB97]. XSB implements tabled (SLG) resolution which effectively computes minimal models of bounded term-depth programs (which include Datalog programs). Furthermore, XSB's evaluation strategy is goal-directed, which enables us to directly implement local model checking algorithms. For normal logic programs (i.e., programs with negated literals on the right-hand side of clauses), XSB computes the *well-founded model*: a three-valued model where each literal is given one of the three truth assignments *true, false* or *unknown*. For instance, consider the program:

```
p :- q, s.
q :- ¬ r.
r :- ¬ q.
s.
```

The well-founded model for the above program is such that p, q and r are *unknown* and s is *true*. While evaluating the well-founded model XSB computes a *residual program* that represents the dependencies between literals with *unknown* values. For the above program, XSB computes the dependencies as

```
p :- q.
q :- ¬ r.
r :- ¬ q.
```

XMC was constructed starting with a straightforward encoding in Horn clauses of the structural operational semantics of value-passing CCS and the natural semantics of the modal mu-calculus. These rules were then subjected to a series of optimizing transformations, yielding a logic program. The XSB system is then used to efficiently evaluate the resulting logic program, over a database of facts representing the process and formula definitions for the given model-checking instance.

In XMC, the ability of XSB to compute minimal models is exploited directly to compute least fixed-point formulas. Formulas with greatest fixed-point operators are transformed using the well known equivalence $\nu X.F(X) \equiv \neg \mu X. \neg F(\neg X)$. For an alternation-free formula, the resultant XSB program is dynamically stratified (i.e., there are no loops through negation in the dynamic call graph), and the well-founded model computed by XSB has no unknown values [SSW96]. The literals encountered while evaluating the XSB program correspond directly to the vertices of the PDG representing the model-checking problem. For formulas without alternation, XSB assigns unique truth values to the vertices of the PDG as and when the PDG is constructed.

For formulas with alternation, however, the resultant evaluation is not dynamically stratified, and hence the well-founded model contains literals with unknown values. That is, while XSB-based evaluation constructs the PDG, it does not label every vertex in the PDG as true or false. For such formulas, the residual program produced by XSB's evaluation captures the subgraph of the PDG induced by vertices that do not have assigned truth values.

We compute the truth values of these remaining vertices by invoking the stable model generator *smodels* [NS96] on the residual program. The algorithm used in *smodels* recursively assigns truth values to literals until all literals have been assigned values, or an assignment is inconsistent with the program rules. When an inconsistency is detected, it backtracks and tries alternate truth assignments for previously encountered literals. By appropriately choosing the order in which literals are assigned values, and the default values, we obtain an algorithm that corresponds to the LAFP algorithm with a naive restore operation. A full implementation of the LAFP algorithm in this framework is currently underway.

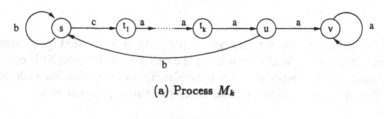

(a) Process M_k

$$\nu X. \mu Y. ([-].(\langle a \rangle \mathrm{tt} \wedge X) \vee Y)$$

(b) Formula F

Benchmark	Tool	Time (sec)
M_{500}, F	CMC	33.84
	FAM	2.88
	LAFP	1.61
M_{1000}, F	CMC	138.51
	FAM	11.64
	LAFP	2.76
M_{1500}, F	CMC	312.10
	FAM	26.61
	LAFP	4.08

(c) Summary of Execution Times

Fig. 2. Experimental evaluation of LAFP.

In order to gauge the performance of our implementation of LAFP, we compared it to the Fixpoint Analysis Machine (FAM) [SCK+95] and a "conventional model checker" (CMC) on a benchmark described in [SCK+95]. The conventional model checker in question is an implementation of the [CKS92] model checking algorithm. The processes and formula comprising the benchmark are shown in Figure 2, along with the corresponding execution times of the three model checking systems. Performance figures for CMC and FAM are from [SCK+95]; these results as well as those for LAFP were obtained on a SUN Sparc-20.

The formula F is a modal mu-calculus formula of alternation depth 2 expressing the property that an a-transition is enabled infinitely often along all infinite paths. It is true for state v of process M_k and false for all other states of M_k. Although the example is fairly simple in structure, it is essentially the only published benchmark for the alternation-depth-n fragment of the modal mu-calculus, $n \geq 2$, of which we are aware.

Note that the CMC and FAM figures reflect the performance of *global* algorithms. Hence, for purposes of comparison, the LAFP results were obtained as the sum of run times for verifying the given formula on each state in the process. For the above examples, the residual programs created by the first phase of XMC-based model checker are relatively small. Therefore, the more expensive (potentially exponential) computation is performed on a very small portion of the state space. This is reflected in the performance of LAFP, which exhibits much slower growth in run times with increase in the size of the system verified, compared to those of the other implementations. We are currently performing a more comprehensive evaluation of the performance of the LAFP algorithm and its implementation.

5 Conclusions

We have presented an abstract model of nested, alternating fixed-point computation, and an algorithm for evaluating PDG fixed points. Careful design of LAFP has resulted in a local algorithm whose asymptotic fixed-point iteration complexity matches that of the best existing global algorithms. Moreover, LAFP has a simple correctness proof and performs extremely well in practice.

It is interesting to note that algorithm LAFP correctly evaluates the input PDG for *any* I, O, and Q satisfying the invariants of given in the proof sketch of Theorem 1. This suggests an *incremental* approach, along the lines of [SS94], for the local computation of alternating fixed points. The incremental version of LAFP would be invoked after LAFP is run on a PDG that subsequently undergoes a set Δ of *changes*, where a change is an inserted or deleted PDG edge. After accounting for the immediate effects of Δ on I, O, and Q, the local fixed-point computation would be restarted. The benefit of this approach is that, in certain cases, the incremental algorithm will terminate much more quickly compared to restarting LAFP from scratch, thereby avoiding significant redundant recomputation. Working out the details of such an incremental algorithm is an important direction for future work, especially in the context of interactive design environments for concurrent systems.

A   Counterexample to the Correctness of [VL94] Restore Strategy No. 4

As mentioned in the Introduction, we have found a counterexample to the correctness of the local model checking algorithm of [VL94], when their "restore strategy" no. 4 is used. The details of the counterexample are as follows; please refer to [VL94] for a description of the algorithm. When procedure AltSolve is used in conjunction with Restore strategy no. 4, it may give an incorrect answer for the following boolean equation system:

$$\mu : \begin{cases} x = u \vee v \\ y = 1 \end{cases}$$
$$\nu : \begin{cases} u = v \wedge y \\ v = u \wedge y \end{cases}$$

This is an alternating equation system with a minimum outer block and a maximum inner block, and it is not difficult to see that the solution should be 1 for every variable. If AltSolve is run with Restore (4) on this example starting with x, the following computation sequence may occur:

- x is set to 0 (default value for a min variable)
- u is set to 1 (as a result of $Expand_1$, default value for a max variable)
- v is set to 1 ($Expand_2$, default value for a max variable)
- y is set to 0 ($Expand_2$, default value for a min variable)
- u is set to 0 ($Update_2$)
- v is set to 0 ($Update_2$)
- y is set to 1 ($Update_1$, here Restore (4) does not change u, v since the right-hand sides of their equations still give value 0 even with y being 1).

AltSolve now terminates with $y = 1, x = u = v = 0$.

References

[And94]   H. R. Andersen. Model checking and boolean graphs. *Theoretical Computer Science*, 126(1), 1994.

[BC96a]   G. S. Bhat and R. Cleaveland. Efficient local model checking for fragments of the modal μ-calculus. In T. Margaria and B. Steffen, editors, *Proceedings of the Second International Workshop on Tools and Algorithms for the Construction and Analysis of Systems (TACAS '96)*, Vol. 1055 of *Lecture Notes in Computer Science*, pages 107–126. Springer-Verlag, March 1996.

[BC96b]   G. S. Bhat and R. Cleaveland. Efficient model checking via the equational μ-calculus. In E. M. Clarke, editor, *11th Annual Symposium on Logic in Computer Science (LICS '96)*, pages 304–312, New Brunswick, NJ, July 1996. Computer Society Press.

[CE81]   E. M. Clarke and E. A. Emerson. Design and synthesis of synchronization skeletons using branching-time temporal logic. In D. Kozen, editor, *Proceedings of the Workshop on Logic of Programs*, Yorktown Heights, volume 131 of *Lecture Notes in Computer Science*, pages 52–71. Springer-Verlag, 1981.

[CES86]   E. M. Clarke, E. A. Emerson, and A. P. Sistla. Automatic verification of finite-state concurrent systems using temporal logic specifications. *ACM TOPLAS*, 8(2), 1986.

[CKS92]   R. Cleaveland, M. Klein, and B. Steffen. Faster model checking for the modal mu-calculus. In G.v. Bochmann and D.K. Probst, editors, *Proceedings of the Fourth International Conference on Computer Aided Verification (CAV '92)*, Vol. 663 of *Lecture Notes in Computer Science*, pages 410–422. Springer-Verlag, 1992.

[Cle90]   R. Cleaveland. Tableau-based model checking in the propositional mu-calculus. *Acta Informatica*, 27(8):725–747, September 1990.

[CW96]   E. M. Clarke and J. M. Wing. Formal methods: State of the art and future directions. *ACM Computing Surveys*, 28(4), December 1996.

[EL86]   E. A. Emerson and C.-L. Lei. Efficient model checking in fragments of the propositional mu-calculus. In *Proceedings of the First Annual Symposium on Logic in Computer Science*, pages 267–278, 1986.

[Koz83]   D. Kozen. Results on the propositional μ-calculus. *Theoretical Computer Science*, 27:333–354, 1983.

[LBC+94]   D. E. Long, A. Browne, E. M. Clarke, S. Jha, and W. R. Marrero. An improved algorithm for the evaluation of fixpoint expressions. In D. Dill, editor, *Proceedings of the Sixth International Conference on Computer Aided Verification (CAV '94)*, Vol. 818 of *Lecture Notes in Computer Science*. Springer-Verlag, 1994.

[Liu92]   X. Liu. *Specification and Decomposition in Concurrency*, Technical Report No. R 92-2005. PhD thesis, Department of Computer Science, Aalborg University, 1992.

[NS96]   I. Niemela and P. Simons. Efficient implementation of the well-founded and stable model semantics. In *Joint International Conference and Symposium on Logic Programming*, pages 289–303, 1996.

[Pra81]   V.R. Pratt. A decidable mu-calculus. In *Proceedings of the 22nd IEEE Ann. Symp. on Foundations of Computer Science*, Nashville, Tennessee, pages 421–427, 1981.

[QS82]   J. P. Queille and J. Sifakis. Specification and verification of concurrent systems in Cesar. In *Proceedings of the International Symposium in Programming*, volume 137 of *Lecture Notes in Computer Science*, Berlin, 1982. Springer-Verlag.

[RRR+97]   Y. S. Ramakrishna, C. R. Ramakrishnan, I. V. Ramakrishnan, S. A. Smolka, T. W. Swift, and D. S. Warren. Efficient model checking using tabled resolution. In *Proceedings of the 9th International Conference on Computer-Aided Verification (CAV '97)*, Haifa, Israel, July 1997. Springer-Verlag.

[RS97]   Y. S. Ramakrishna and S. A. Smolka. Partial-order reduction in the weak modal mu-calculus. In A. Mazurkiewicz and J. Winkowski, editors, *Proceedings of the Eighth International Conference on Concurrency Theory (CONCUR '97)*, volume 1243 of *Lecture Notes in Computer Science*, Warsaw, Poland, July 1997. Springer-Verlag.

[SCK⁺95] B. Steffen, A. Classen, M. Klein, J. Knoop, and T. Margaria. The fixpoint-analysis machine. In I. Lee and S. A. Smolka, editors, *Proceedings of the Sixth International Conference on Concurrency Theory (CONCUR '95)*, Vol. 962 of *Lecture Notes in Computer Science*, pages 72–87. Springer-Verlag, 1995.

[SS94]   O. Sokolsky and S. A. Smolka. Incremental model checking in the modal mu-calculus. In D. Dill, editor, *Proceedings of the Sixth International Conference on Computer Aided Verification (CAV '94)*, Vol. 818 of *Lecture Notes in Computer Science*. Springer-Verlag, 1994.

[SSW96]   K. Sagonas, T. Swift, and D.S. Warren. An abstract machine to compute fixed-order dynamically stratified programs. In *International Conference on Automated Deduction (CADE)*, 1996.

[SW91]   C. Stirling and D. Walker. Local model checking in the modal mu-calculus. *Theoretical Computer Science*, 89(1), 1991.

[VL94]   B. Vergauwen and J. Lewi. Efficient local correctness checking for single and alternating boolean equation systems. In *Proceedings of ICALP'94*, pages 304–315. LNCS 820, 1994.

[Win89]   G. Winskel. A note on model checking the modal ν-calculus. In *Proceedings of ICALP '89*, Vol. 372 of *Lecture Notes in Computer Science*, 1989.

[XSB97]   XSB. The XSB logic programming system v1.7, 1997. Available by anonymous ftp from ftp.cs.sunysb.edu.

Modular Model Checking of Software

Karen Laster and Orna Grumberg

Computer Science Department
The Technion
Haifa 32000, Israel
email: {laster,orna}@cs.technion.ac.il
phone: 972-4-8294327   fax: 972-4-8221128

Abstract. This work presents a modular approach to temporal logic model checking of software.

Model checking is a method that automatically determines whether a finite state system satisfies a temporal logic specification. Model checking algorithms have been successfully used to verify complex systems. However, their use is limited by the high space requirements needed to represent the verified system.

When hardware designs are considered, a typical solution is to partition the design into units running in parallel, and handle each unit separately. For software systems such a solution is not always feasible. This is because a software system might be too large to fit into memory even when it consists of a single sequential unit.

To avoid the high space requirements for software we suggest to partition the program text into *sequentially composed subprograms*. Based on this partition, we present a model checking algorithm for software that arrives at its conclusion by examining each subprogram in separation. The novelty of our approach is that it uses a decomposition of the program in which the interconnection between parts is sequential and not parallel. We handle each part separately, while keeping all other parts on an external memory (files). Consequently, our approach reduces space requirements and enables verification of larger systems.

Our method is applicable to finite state programs. Further, it is applicable to infinite state programs provided that a suitable abstraction can be constructed.

We implemented the ideas described in this paper in a prototype tool called *SoftVer* and applied it to a few small examples. We have achieved reduction in both space and time requirements.

We consider this work as a first step towards making temporal logic model checking useful for software verification.

1 Introduction

This work presents a new modular approach that makes temporal logic model checking applicable to large non-deterministic sequential finite-state programs, written in some high level programming language.

Finite-state programs can be useful for describing, in some level of abstraction, many interesting systems. They can describe the behavior of communication protocols. They can be used to describe expert systems, provided that some of the inputs are mapped into a finite domain. Such programs (written in behavioral Hardware Description Languages) are being used to describe the high level behavior of hardware designs. All these examples are *reactive*, i.e., they continuously interact with their environment. They are also quite complex which makes their verification an important and non-trivial task. Furthermore, even though they are sequential they might be significantly large.

A first step in verification is choosing a specification language. Temporal logics [17], capable of describing behaviors over time, have proven to be most suitable for the specification of reactive systems. When restricted to finite-state systems, propositional temporal logic specifications [7] can be checked by efficient algorithms, called model checking [5, 19, 14, 2]. *Temporal logic model checking* procedures typically receive a system model by means of a state transition graph and a formula in the logic, and determine the set of states in the model that satisfy the formula. Tools based on model checking [15] were successful in finding subtle bugs in real-life designs [16, 6] and are currently in use by the hardware industry in the verification process of newly developed hardware designs [1, 12].

Unfortunately, similar applications of model checking to programs are very limited. One reason for this deficiency arises from the fact that large hardware systems are usually composed of many components working in parallel. Software systems, on the other hand, can be extremely large even when they consist of one sequential component. A useful approach to reducing space requirement is modularity. *Modular model checking* techniques treat each component in separation, based on an assumption about the behavior of its environment [18, 11, 9]. Existing techniques, however, are based on partitioning the system into processes that run in parallel.

Our work applies a modular approach to sequential programs. To do so, we suggest a way of partitioning the program into components, following the program *text*. A given program may have several different partitions. A partition of the program is represented by a *partition graph*, whose nodes are models of the subprograms and whose edges represent the flow of control between subprograms.

Once the program is partitioned, we wish to check each part separately. However, verifying one component in isolation amounts to checking the specification formula on a model in which some of the paths are truncated, i.e. for certain states in the component we do not know how the computation proceeds (since the continuation is in another component). Such states are called *ending states*. We notice, however, that the truth of a formula at a state inside a component can be determined solely by considering the state transition graph of this component, and the set of formulas which are true at the ending states. Moreover, the truth of a formula at an ending state depends only on the paths leaving it, and not on the paths leading to it. This observation is the basis for our algorithm.

We define a notion of *assumption function* that represents partial knowledge about the truth of formulas at ending states. Based on that, we define a *semantics under assumption* that determines the truth of temporal formulas based on a given assumption function. Only minor changes are needed in order to adapt a standard model checking algorithm so that it performs model checking under assumptions.

Given a procedure that performs model checking under assumptions, we develop a *modular model checking algorithm* that checks the program in parts. To illustrate how the algorithm works consider the program $P = P_1; P_2$. We notice that every path of P lies either entirely within P_1 or has a prefix in P_1 followed by a suffix in P_2. In order to check a formula ψ on P, we first model check ψ on P_2. The result does not depend on P_1 and therefore the algorithm can be applied to P_2 in isolation. We next want to model check P_1, but now the result does depend on P_2. In particular, ending states of P_1 have their continuations in P_2. However, each ending state of P_1 is an initial state of P_2 for which we have already the model checking result [1]. Using this result as an *assumption* for P_1, we can now model check P_1 in isolation. Handling loops in the program is more complicated but follows a similar intuition.

The suggested scheme saves significant amounts of space since at any given time the memory contains only the model of the component under consideration, together with the assumption function that maps formulas to the ending states of that component. Often it also saves time, since the model checking task is performed on substantially smaller models.

Our modular algorithm can handle any finite-state while program with non-deterministic assignments. In addition to sequential composition, programs may include choices ("if-then-else") and while loops, nested in any way.

Works discussing model checking of programs written in a high level language are rare. The closest to our work are [8] that verifies concurrent systems written in C, and the SPIN system [10] that validates protocols. However, their approaches are not modular. Another related work is [3], in which they perform model checking on Pushdown Process Systems by considering the semantics of 'fragments', which are interpreted as 'incomplete portions' of the process. The model checking algorithm they propose calculates the *property transformer* of each fragment, which is a function that represents the semantics of a fragment with respect to alternation-free mu-calculus formulas. This algorithm, however, works on all fragments together. It should also be noted that Pushdown Process Systems are suitable for modeling (parallel) processes but they can hardly be considered as a high level programming language.

In contrast, our work applies model checking to programs written in a high level programming language, while exploiting their textual structure in order to reduce space requirements. We consider our work as a first step in making model checking applicable to realistic software systems.

We implemented the ideas described in this paper in a prototype tool called *SoftVer*. We applied the tool to a few small examples, each with different partitions and compared the space and time requirements needed for model checking with the space and time used when the program is unpartitioned. In all cases,

---

[1] The result includes for each sub formula φ of ψ the set of states satisfying φ.

a substantial space reduction has been achieved. Furthermore, in five out of six cases a significant reduction in time has been obtained as well. In the concluding section we summarize these results and explain them.

The paper is organized as follows. In section 2 we introduce the temporal logic CTL and define its semantics under assumptions. Section 3 describes the syntax and semantics of our programming language and Section 4 defines partition graphs. Section 5 gives the modular model checking algorithm. Finally, Section 6 describes the implementation and suggests directions for future research.

2 Basic Definitions

2.1 Kripke Structures

Kripke structures are widely used for modeling finite-state systems. In this paper we use Kripke structures to model the behavior of a finite program.

Definition 1 *A Kripke Structure is a tuple* $M = \langle S, R, I \rangle$ *s.t.* S *is a set of states,* $R \subseteq S \times S$ *is a transition relation and* $I \subseteq S$ *is a set of initial states. A path in* M *from a state* s_0 *is a sequence* $\pi = s_0, s_1, \ldots$ *s.t.* $\forall i[s_i \in S$ *and* $(s_i, s_{i+1}) \in R]$*. A maximal path in* M *is a path which is either infinite, or ends in a state with no outgoing transitions. Let* π *be a maximal path in* M*. We write* $|\pi| = n$ *if* $\pi = s_0, s_1, \ldots, s_{n-1}$ *and* $|\pi| = \infty$ *if* π *is infinite.*

Definition 2 *For a Kripke structure* $M = \langle S, R, I \rangle$ *we define the set of ending states to be:* $end(M) = \{s \in S \mid \neg \exists s'.(s, s') \in R\}$*. We also use* $init(M)$ *to refer to the set* I *of initial states.*

2.2 CTL

For our specification language we use the propositional branching-time temporal logic CTL. It allows us to specify a behavior of a program in terms of its computation tree [4].

We assume a set of *atomic propositions* AP and a labeling function that associates with each state in a structure the set of atomic propositions true at that state. Throughout the paper we assume a fixed labeling function $\mathcal{L} : S \to 2^{AP}$.

We define a CTL formula to be either q for each $q \in AP$, or $\neg f_1$, $f_1 \vee f_2$, $\mathbf{AX} f_1$, $\mathbf{EX} f_1$, $\mathbf{A}(f_1 \mathbf{U} f_2)$, and $\mathbf{E}(f_1 \mathbf{U} f_2)$ where f_1 and f_2 are CTL formulas. Each temporal operator in CTL is constructed of a path quantifier, either $\mathbf{A}$ ("for all paths") or $\mathbf{E}$ ("for some path"), and a temporal operator $\mathbf{X}$ or $\mathbf{U}$. Intuitively, the operator $\mathbf{X}$ means "at the next step", so the formula $\mathbf{AX} q$ states that in all the paths outgoing from a given state, the second state satisfies q. A path satisfies $p \mathbf{U} q$ (p "Until" q) if there exists a state along it that satisfies q and all the states preceding it satisfy p.

CTL formulas are usually interpreted over Kripke structures that have a total transition relation, so that all paths are infinite. We denote the standard semantics for CTL [7, 4] as $M, s \models \psi$ (meaning that the state s in the structure M satisfies ψ). In this paper we introduce an interpretation for CTL over a Kripke structure and an *assumption function* (defined below). The use of assumption functions enables us to give semantics (over infinite paths) in case of incomplete information. When a finite path occurs in a structure, we view it as a prefix of a set of infinite paths with unspecified continuations. The assumption function states which formulas are true over this absent continuation. We use this information only for states in $end(M)$, so the function may be defined only over some subset of S that includes $end(M)$.

Definition 3 *The* closure *of a formula* ψ, $cl(\psi)$, *is the set of all the sub-formulas of* ψ *(including itself).*

Definition 4 *An* assumption function *for a Kripke structure* $M = \langle S, R, I \rangle$ *is a function* $As : cl(\psi) \to (2^{S'} \cup \{\bot\})$ *where* $S' \subseteq S$. *We require that* $end(M) \subseteq S'$ *and that* $\forall \varphi \in cl(\psi)$, *if* $As(\varphi) \neq \bot$ *then* $\forall \varphi' \in cl(\varphi)$, $As(\varphi') \neq \bot$.

For every $\varphi \in cl(\psi)$, if $As(\varphi) \neq \bot$ then $As(\varphi)$ represents the set of all states in S' for which we assume (or know) that φ holds. For every state $s \in S'$ s.t. $s \notin As(\varphi)$ we assume that $\neg\varphi$ holds. When $As(\varphi) = \bot$ it means that we have no knowledge regarding the satisfaction of φ in S'.

Satisfaction of a CTL formula φ in a state $s \in S$ under an assumption function As is denoted $(M, \mathcal{L}), s \models_{As} \varphi$ [2]. We define it so that it holds if either $M, s \models \varphi$ directly (by infinite paths only), or through the assumption. For example, $M, s \models_{As} \mathbf{E}(f \mathbf{U} g)$ if there exists an infinite path from s satisfying f in all states until a state satisfying g is reached, but it is also true if there is a finite path from s in which the last state, say s', satisfies $s' \in As(\mathbf{E}(f \mathbf{U} g))$, and all states until s' satisfy f. Formally:

Definition 5 *Let* $M = \langle S, R, I \rangle$ *be a Kripke structure and* As *an assumption function over* M. *For every* $\varphi \in cl(\psi)$:
If $As(\varphi) = \bot$ *then* $s \models_{As} \varphi$ *is not defined.*
Otherwise, we differentiate between ending states and other states. If $s \in end(M)$ *then* $s \models_{As} \varphi$ *iff* $s \in As(\varphi)$. *If* $s \in S \setminus end(M)$ *then* $s \models_{As} \varphi$ *is defined as follows:*

- $s \models_{As} p$ *iff* $p \in \mathcal{L}(s)$ *for every* $p \in AP$.
- $s \models_{As} \varphi_1 \vee \varphi_2$ *iff* $(s \models_{As} \varphi_1$ *or* $s \models_{As} \varphi_2)$.
- $s \models_{As} \neg\varphi_1$ *iff* $s \not\models_{As} \varphi_1$.
- $s \models_{As} \mathbf{AX}\varphi_1$ *iff* $\forall s'.(s, s') \in R \Rightarrow s' \models_{As} \varphi_1$.
- $s \models_{As} \mathbf{EX}\varphi_1$ *iff* $\exists s'.(s, s') \in R \wedge s' \models_{As} \varphi_1$.
- $s \models_{As} \mathbf{A}(\varphi_1 \mathbf{U}\varphi_2)$ *iff for all (maximal) paths* $\pi = s_0, s_1, \ldots$ *from* s *there is a number* $i < |\pi|$ *s.t. (either* $s_i \models_{As} \varphi_2$ *or* $s_i \in end(M) \wedge s_i \models_{As} \mathbf{A}(\varphi_1 \mathbf{U}\varphi_2))$, *and* $\forall 0 \leq j < i [s_j \models_{As} \varphi_1]$.

---

[2] Since we assume a fixed $\mathcal{L}$, we always omit $\mathcal{L}$. When no confusion may occur we also omit M.

– $s \models_{As} E(\varphi_1 U\varphi_2)$ *iff there exist a (maximal) path* $\pi = s_0, s_1, \ldots$ *from* s *and a number* $i < |\pi|$ *s.t. (either* $s_i \models_{As} \varphi_2$ *or* $s_i \in end(M) \wedge s_i \models_{As} E(\varphi_1 U\varphi_2))$ *and* $\forall 0 \le j < i[s_j \models_{As} \varphi_1]$.

Note that, if the transition relation of M is total then the above definition is equivalent to the traditional definition of CTL semantics, because the assumption function is consulted only on states from which there are no outgoing transitions.

2.3 Model Checking Under Assumptions

The task of model checking is to find all initial states of a given structure that satisfy a formula ψ. We write $M \models_{As} \psi$ iff $\forall s \in I, [M, s \models_{As} \psi]$. From here on we assume that ψ is the formula to be checked on a structure $M = \langle S, R, I \rangle$ (or later, a program).

Definition 6 *Given an assumption function* As *over a structure* M *we define a function* $MC[M, As] : cl(\psi) \to (2^S \cup \{\bot\})$ *so that for any* $\varphi \in cl(\psi)$, *if* $As(\varphi) = \bot$ *then* $MC[M, As](\varphi) = \bot$. *Otherwise,* $MC[M, As](\varphi) = \{s \in S \mid M, s \models_{As} \varphi\}$.

Notice that $MC[M, As]$ results in an assumption function. Given M and As, this function can be calculated using any known model checking algorithm for CTL [5, 19, 2], after adapting it to the semantics under assumptions.

3 The Programming Language

Following we define the syntax and semantics of our programming language NWP (Non-deterministic While-Programs).

Definition 7 *We assume a fixed set of program variables over some finite domain* D. *A program fragment is one of* $x := \{e_1, \ldots, e_k\}$, *skip,* $Prog_1; Prog_2$, *"if* B *then* $Prog_1$ *else* $Prog_2$ *fi" or "while* B *do* $Prog_1$ *od" s.t.* $Prog_1, Prog_2$ *are program fragments,* B *is a boolean expression over program variables and constants,* x *stands for any program variable, and* e *is an expression over program variables and constants. The meaning of* $x:=\{e_1, \ldots, e_k\}$ *is a non-deterministic assignment,* $Prog_1; Prog_2$ *is the sequential composition of* $Prog_1$ *and* $Prog_2$, *and the "if" and "while" structures have the same meaning as in all sequential programming languages.*

A full program is of the form $Prog;fin$ *where* $Prog$ *is a program fragment. The meaning of "fin" is an infinite loop that does not change the values of program variables. We define* E *to be the empty program, such that for every* $P \in NWP$ *it holds that* $P; E = E; P = P$. *The set* NWP *is the set of all full programs.*

From here on we use the word "program" to refer to either a full program, or a program fragment, unless stated otherwise.

The semantics of NWP programs is given by means of Kripke structures. We give here only an informal description, the formal definition can be found in [13].

Let $P \in$ NWP be a program such that $x_1, \ldots, x_n$ are the program variables. An assignment to the program variables is some $\sigma \in D^n$. We create a Kripke structure $struct(P)$ so that each state is a pair (l, σ) where l is a program location and $\sigma \in D^n$ is an assignment to the program variables. Each location is associated with the remaining program to be run from that point on. The transition relation is created in the intuitive way, following the usual semantics of the commands. Evaluating a boolean expression (in an "if" or "while" command) is considered a step in execution. We define the set of initial states $init(P)$ as the set of states with location P. The set of ending states, $end(P)$, is the set of states in $struct(P)$ that have no outgoing transition. If P is a full program then $end(P) = \emptyset$. If P is a program fragment then this is the set of states with the location E (which means that there is nothing more to run).

We add to AP the set $\{at\_l \mid l$ is a location in $P\}$. The new propositions are used to refer to a location in the program within the specification. The labeling function $\mathcal{L} : S \to 2^{AP}$ is extended accordingly.

Figure 1 includes an example of a NWP program, and its structure.

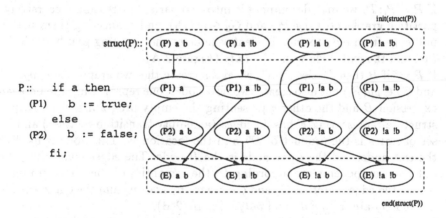

Fig. 1. An example of an NWP program.

4 Partition Graphs

A *Partition Graph* of a program P is a finite graph representing a decomposition of P into several sub-programs while maintaining the original flow of control. The nodes are Kripke structures, each representing a sub-program of P or a boolean expression. A node representing a sub-program P' is of the form $struct(P')$. A node representing a boolean expression B, has the form $\langle S, R, I \rangle$ s.t. $R = \emptyset$ and $S = I = \{(l, \sigma) \mid \sigma \in D^n\}$ where l is the program location of the "if" or "while" command that evaluates B.

There are three types of edges: null-edges, yes-edges, and no-edges, denoted $M_1 \rightarrow M_2$, $M_1 \overset{yes}{\rightarrow} M_2$ and $M_1 \overset{no}{\rightarrow} M_2$ respectively. A null edge $M_1 \rightarrow M_2$, where $M_1 = struct(P_1)$ and $M_2 = struct(P_2)$, means that $init(P_2) = end(P_1)$. This happens when there is no step in the execution between the corresponding sub-programs, for example, when the program to be executed is $P_1; P_2$. Yes-edges and no-edges, called *step-edges*, are edges outgoing from a node representing a boolean expression. Execution from a state in this node continues through the yes-edge or the no-edge, depending on whether the expression evaluates to *true* or *false* in that state. These edges also represent a step in the execution. A partition graph also has two designated nodes: the *entry node*, from which execution starts, and the *exit node*, at which it stops.

The set $pg(P)$ contains all possible partition graphs of P, representing different ways of partitioning P into sub-programs. It is defined recursively, where at each step one may decide to break a given program according to its primary structure, or to create a single node out of it. Figure 2 shows the three different ways in which a program may be decomposed, according to the three structures by which programs are created. We use in_1 (in_2) for the entry node of G_1 (G_2) and out_1 (out_2) for the exit node.

1. If $P = P_1; P_2$ we may decompose it into two parts, by creating (recursively) partition graphs $G_1 \in pg(P_1)$ and $G_2 \in pg(P_2)$, and connecting them with a null edge from out_1 to in_2. The entry node of the resulting graph would be in_1, and the exit node would be out_2 (Figure 2 A).
2. If $P =$ "if B then P_1 else P_2 fi", we again create the two graphs $G_1 \in pg(P_1)$ and $G_2 \in pg(P_2)$ but also create two new nodes, one representing the boolean expression B and the other representing the empty program E. The Kripke structure representing E has no edges (an empty transition relation) and its set of states is the product of D^n and the location E. This node is used as the exit node, and the entry node is the B node. The edges connecting the different components are according to the semantics of the "if" command. Again, the edges entering G_1 and G_2 are to in_1 and in_2 and the edges exiting G_1 and G_2 are from out_1 and out_2. (Figure 2 B).
3. If $P =$ "while B do P_1 od", we create a partition graph $G_1 \in pg(P_1)$ and again a node for B, which is the entry node, and an E node as the exit node. The edges represent the semantics of the "while" loop. (Figure 2 C).

The formal definition of partition graphs and their semantics (given as Kripke structures) can be found in [13]. It is defined so that given any partition graph $G \in pg(P)$, the structure that defines its semantics, denoted $struct(G)$, is identical to $struct(P)$. Informally, $struct(G)$ is created out of the union of all Kripke structures in its nodes (with some adjustment of the program locations). Each step-edge induces a set of transitions from the states in the node representing the boolean expression, to initial states in the node that is pointed at by the edge. A yes-edge (no-edge) creates one transition from each state that satisfies (does not satisfy) the condition into the corresponding state (different location, same assignment to variables). A null-edge $M_1 \rightarrow M_2$ does not create transitions.

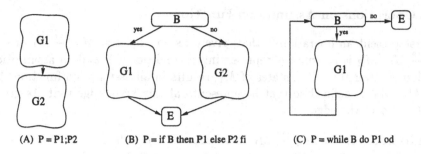

(A) P = P1;P2   (B) P = if B then P1 else P2 fi   (C) P = while B do P1 od

Fig. 2. Creation of partition graphs

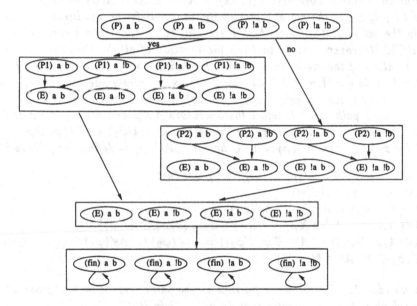

Fig. 3. An example partition graph for the program P;fin, where P is the program from figure 1.

Given a partition graph G we define $init(G)$ to be the set of initial states in $struct(G)$ and $end(G)$ to be the set of ending states in $struct(G)$. Figure 3 gives an example of an actual partition graph.

5 Performing Modular Model Checking

Our algorithm for modular model checking is based on the notion of satisfaction under assumptions. Furthermore, the basic building block in the recursive definition of the algorithm is "model checking under assumptions". We do not give here an explicit algorithm to compute it, we just note that every standard model checking algorithm for CTL can easily be adapted to handle assumptions.

Before we present our modular algorithm we define a few operations on assumption functions that we use in the algorithm.

5.1 Operations on Assumption Functions

We first present an operation T that, given a step-edge $e = M_B \overset{yes}{\to} M_1$ or $e = M_B \overset{no}{\to} M_1$ (M_B is a structure representing a condition B), and an assumption function As over the initial states of M_1, results in an assumption function As' over M_B. As' is defined so that it represents all the knowledge that As gives, translated over the edge.

Definition 8 *Let* $e = M_B \overset{yes}{\to} M_1$ *be an edge in a partition graph* G *s.t.* $M_1 = \langle S_1, R_1, I_1 \rangle$ *and* $M_B = \langle S_B, \emptyset, S_B \rangle$, *and let* $As : cl(\psi) \to (2^{S_1} \cup \{\bot\})$ *be an assumption function over* M_1. $T(e, As) = As'$ *s.t.* $As' : cl(\psi) \to (2^{S_T} \cup \{\bot\})$. *The set* $S_T \subseteq S_B$ *is the set of states in* S_B *that satisfy the condition* B. *This is exactly the set of states from which there will be an edge into a state of* M_1 *in* $struct(G)$. *Moreover, assume that* l *is the location of all the states in* S_B *and* l' *is the location of the states in* I_1. *Then the definition of* $struct(G)$ *is such that from each state* $s = (l, \sigma) \in S_B$ *s.t.* $\sigma \models B$ *there is exactly one transition, into a state* $s' = (l', \sigma)$. *As a result, there is no difference between "for all paths" and "there exists a path" and therefore the operators* $\mathbf{AX}\varphi$ *and* $\mathbf{EX}\varphi$ *are handled in exactly the same way, and so are the operators* $\mathbf{A}(\varphi_1 \, \mathbf{U} \varphi_2)$ *and* $\mathbf{E}(\varphi_1 \, \mathbf{U} \varphi_2)$.

If $As(\varphi) = \bot$ *then* $As'(\varphi) = \bot$. *Otherwise,* $As'(\varphi)$ *is defined as follows* [3]

- *For any* $p \in AP$, $As'(p) = \{s \in S_T \mid p \in \mathcal{L}(s)\}$.
- $As'(\neg\varphi) = S_T \setminus As'(\varphi)$
- $As'(\varphi_1 \vee \varphi_2) = As'(\varphi_1) \cup As'(\varphi_2)$
- $As'(\mathbf{AX}\varphi) = As'(\mathbf{EX}\varphi) = \{(l, \sigma) \in S_T \mid (l', \sigma) \in As(\varphi)\}$
- $As'(\mathbf{A}(\varphi_1 \, \mathbf{U} \varphi_2)) = As'(\mathbf{E}(\varphi_1 \, \mathbf{U} \varphi_2)) = As'(\varphi_2) \cup (As'(\varphi_1) \cap \{(l, \sigma) \in S_T \mid (l', \sigma) \in As(\mathbf{A}(\varphi_1 \, \mathbf{U} \varphi_2))\})$

For a no-edge $M_B \overset{no}{\to} M_1$ *the definition is the same, replacing every use of* S_T *by* S_F *which is the set of states that do not satisfy* B.

An important feature of this operation is that if the original assumption coincides with the truth of formulas in the structure of G then the derived assumption also coincides with the truth of formulas in the structure. The proof of this is omitted due to space restrictions.

5.2 The Compositional Algorithm

Following, we give an algorithm to check a formula ψ on a partition graph G of a full program P. The result is an assumption function over the set of initial states of P that gives, for every sub-formula φ of ψ, the set of all initial states of P satisfying φ. We start with an intuitive description of the algorithm.

The algorithm works on G from the exit node upwards to the entry node. First the structure contained in a leaf node V of G is model checked under an "empty" assumption for $cl(\psi)$, an assumption in which all values are $\emptyset$. Since

---

[3] If $As(\varphi) \neq \bot$ then for all sub-formulas φ' of φ it holds that $As(\varphi') \neq \bot$.

V is a leaf it must represent a full program and therefore all paths in it are infinite, and the assumption function has no influence on the result. The result of the model checking algorithm is an assumption function As' that associates with every sub-formula of ψ the set of all initial states of V that satisfy that sub-formula. Once we have As' on V we can derive a similar function As on the ending states of any node U, preceding V in G (that is, any node U from which there is an edge into V). Next, we model check U under the assumption As. Proceeding this way, each node in G can be checked in isolation, based on assumptions derived from its successor nodes. Special care should be taken when dealing with loops in the partition graph.

We now give an intuitive description of the algorithm CheckGraph (where variable names refer to variables in the algorithm). Given a procedure that properly computes $MC[M, As]$, CheckGraph takes an assumption function As and a partition graph G and performs model checking under assumption resulting in an assumption As'. The answer to the model checking problem is $As'(\psi)$. CheckGraph is able to handle partially defined assumption functions, in which there are some $\perp$ values. For any sub-formula φ s.t. $As(\varphi) = \perp$ we get $As'(\varphi) = \perp$. CheckGraph is defined by induction on the structure of G. The base case handles a single node, that may contain the Kripke structure of any program, by using the given model checking procedure. To model check a partition graph G of $P = P_1; P_2$, as in figure 2 A, CheckGraph first checks G_2 under As (see Figure 4). As_1 is the result of this check (As_1 is over the set $init(G_2)$). It then uses As_1 as an assumption on the ending states of G_1 and checks P_1 w.r.t As_1. The second check returns for all $\varphi \in cl(\psi)$ the set of all initial states of P_1 (also initial states of P) that satisfy φ, which is the desired result.

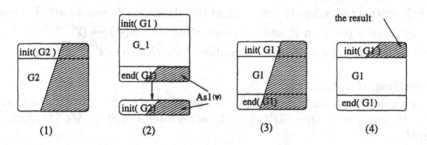

Fig. 4. The operation of the algorithm on sequential composition. The gray area is the set of states that satisfy ψ.

Let G be a partition graph of $P = $ "if B then P_1 else P_2", as in figure 2 B. To check G we first check G_1 and G_2, and then compute 'backwards' over the step-edges (using the function T) to get the result for the initial states of G.

The most complicated part of the algorithm is for the partition graph G of a program $P = $ "while B do P_1 od", as in figure 2 C. We start from the node M_E, for which we have the assumption As. Walking backwards on the no-edge we use the function T to get an assumption $As_{\neg B}$ over the initial states of G that satisfy $\neg B$. We now demonstrate the computation of $\mathbf{E}(\varphi_1 \mathbf{U} \varphi_2)$. We assume that $As'(\varphi_1)$ and $As'(\varphi_2)$ were already calculated. The goal is to mark all states that satisfy $\mathbf{E}(\varphi_1 \mathbf{U} \varphi_2)$ (to create $As'(\mathbf{E}(\varphi_1 \mathbf{U} \varphi_2))$). Standard model checking algorithms would start by marking all states that satisfy φ_2, and then repeatedly move backwards on transitions and mark every state that has a transition into a marked state, and satisfies φ_1 itself. We reconstruct this computation over the partition graph of P. For initial states of G that satisfy B we have no assumption regarding $\mathbf{E}(\varphi_1 \mathbf{U} \varphi_2)$, so we mark all those that satisfy B and φ_2 and keep them in $Init_B$. Together with $As_{\neg B}(\mathbf{E}(\varphi_1 \mathbf{U} \varphi_2))$ we have an initial estimate for $As'(\mathbf{E}(\varphi_1 \mathbf{U} \varphi_2))$ (kept in $As^0(\varphi_k)$). We now want to mark all the fathers in G of these states. Notice that $init(G) = end(G_1)$ so these fathers are inside G_1. Hence we continue from $end(G_1)$ backwards inside G_1 until we arrive at $init(G_1)$. At this point, only the marks on states of $init(G_1)$ are kept (in Tmp). The marks on all other states of G_1 are not preserved. Notice that G_1 itself may consist of more than one node, and the creation of Tmp is done by a recursive call to CheckGraph. From Tmp we can calculate a new estimate for $As'(\mathbf{E}(\varphi_1 \mathbf{U} \varphi_2))$.

The whole process repeats itself since the body of a "while" loop can be executed more than once. Obviously, it is essential that the states satisfying φ_1 and φ_2 be known before this process can be performed. Therefore, we use the $\perp$ value for $\mathbf{E}(\varphi_1 \mathbf{U} \varphi_2)$ when working on the assumptions for φ_1 and φ_2. Only when calculations for all sub-formulas are completed, we may begin calculating the proper result for $\mathbf{E}(\varphi_1 \mathbf{U} \varphi_2)$.

This process stops when the assumption calculated reaches a fix-point ($As^i = As^{i-1}$). Obviously, no new information will be revealed by performing another cycle. The set of states in $init(G)$ that are marked increases with each cycle, until all states that satisfy the formula are marked, and the algorithm stops.

Following is the recursive definition of the algorithm. Given a partition graph $G \in pg(P)$ of a program P, and an assumption $As : cl(\psi) \to (2^{end(G)} \cup \{\perp\})$, CheckGraph$(G, As)$ returns an assumption $As' : cl(\psi) \to (2^{init(G)} \cup \{\perp\})$.

CheckGraph(G,As):

The base case is for a single node M, in which case we return As' s.t. $\forall \varphi \in cl(\psi)$, if $As(\varphi) = \perp$ then $As'(\varphi) = \perp$, otherwise $As'(\varphi) = MC[M, As](\varphi) \cap init(M)$.

The three possible recursive cases are the ones depicted in Figure 2. We assume that in_1 (in_2) is the entry node of G_1 (G_2), M_B is the structure in a "B" node, and M_E is the structure in an "E" node.

- For a sequential composition $P_1; P_2$ (Figure 2 A) perform:
    1. $As_1 \leftarrow$ CheckGraph(G_2, As).
    2. $As' \leftarrow$ CheckGraph(G_1, As_1).
    3. Return(As')
- For a graph of $P =$ "if B then P_1 else P_2 fi" (Figure 2 B) perform:
    1. $As_1 \leftarrow$ CheckGraph(G_1, As).
    2. $As_2 \leftarrow$ CheckGraph(G_2, As).

3. $As_B \leftarrow T(M_B \overset{yes}{\rightarrow} in_1, As_1)$
4. $As_{\neg B} \leftarrow T(M_B \overset{no}{\rightarrow} in_2, As_2)$
5. For every formula $\varphi \in cl(\psi)$, if $As_B(\varphi) = \bot$ then define $As'(\varphi) = \bot$ [4]. Otherwise, $As'(\varphi) = As_B(\varphi) \cup As_{\neg B}(\varphi)$ (Notice that the images of As_B and $As_{\neg B}$ are disjoint).
6. Return As'

- For a graph of $P = $ "while B do P_1 od" (Figure 2 C) perform:
  1. $As_{\neg B} \leftarrow T(M_B \overset{no}{\rightarrow} M_E, As)$
  2. Find an ordering $\varphi_1, \varphi_2, \ldots, \varphi_n$ of the formulas in $cl(\psi)$ such that each formula appears after all of its sub-formulas. Set $As'(\varphi_i) = \bot$ for all i. For $k = 1, \ldots, n$ perform step 3 to define $As'(\varphi_k)$ [5].
  3. Perform one of the following, according to the form of φ_k:

     $\varphi_k \in AP$: $As'(\varphi_k) \leftarrow \{s \in init(G) \mid \varphi_k \in \mathcal{L}(s)\}$

     $\varphi_k = \neg\varphi_l$: $As'(\varphi_k) \leftarrow \{s \in init(G) \mid s \notin As'(\varphi_l)\}$.

     $\varphi_k = \varphi_l \vee \varphi_m$: $As'(\varphi_k) \leftarrow As'(\varphi_l) \cup As'(\varphi_m)$.

     $\varphi_k \in \{\mathbf{AX}\varphi_l, \mathbf{EX}\varphi_l\}$:

     (a) $Tmp \leftarrow$ CheckGraph(G_1, As')

     (b) Let $R_{M_B \overset{yes}{\rightarrow} in_1}$ be the set of transitions induced by the edge $M_B \overset{yes}{\rightarrow} in_1$.
     $As'(\varphi_k) \leftarrow As_{\neg B}(\varphi_k) \cup \{s \in init(G) \mid \forall s' \in init(G_1), (s, s') \in R_{M_B \overset{yes}{\rightarrow} in_1} \Rightarrow (s \models B \wedge s' \in Tmp(\varphi_l))\}$ [6].

     $\varphi_k \in \{\mathbf{A}(\varphi_l\mathbf{U}\varphi_m), \mathbf{E}(\varphi_l\mathbf{U}\varphi_m)\}$:

     (a) Set $i \leftarrow 1$.
     $Init_B \leftarrow As'(\varphi_m) \cap \{s \in init(G) \mid s \models B\}$.
     The initial assumption function is $As^0 \leftarrow As'$.
     Initialize the value for φ_k: $As^0(\varphi_k) \leftarrow As_{\neg B}(\varphi_k) \cup Init_B$.

     (b) do:
     - $Tmp = $ CheckGraph(G_1, As^{i-1})
     - $As_B^i \leftarrow T(M_B \overset{yes}{\rightarrow} in_1, Tmp)$
     - Define As^i so that for all $j < k$, $As^i(\varphi_j) \leftarrow As^0(\varphi_j)$ and $As^i(\varphi_k) \leftarrow As_B^i(\varphi_k) \cup As_{\neg B}(\varphi_k)$
     - $i \leftarrow i + 1$

     as long as $As^i \neq As^{i-1}$.

     (c) $As'(\varphi_k) \leftarrow As^i(\varphi_k)$
  4. Return As'.

Theorem 1 *For any full program P, CTL formula ψ, partition graph $G \in pg(P)$ and empty assumption function $As : cl(\psi) \to \{\emptyset\}$, if $As' = $ CheckGraph(G, As) then for every $\varphi \in cl(\psi)$ and $s \in init(G)$, $s \in As'(\varphi) \Leftrightarrow s \models \varphi$.*

---

[4] Since As_B and $As_{\neg B}$ both originate from the same assumption function As, it holds that $As_B(\varphi) = \bot \iff As_{\neg B}(\varphi) = \bot$.

[5] Notice that when working on φ_k we have already calculated As' for all of its subformulas.

[6] The definition is the same for $\mathbf{AX}\varphi_l$ and $\mathbf{EX}\varphi_l$ because for each state $s \in init(G)$ there is exactly one state $s' \in init(G_1)$ s.t. $(s, s') \in R_{M_B \overset{yes}{\rightarrow} in_1}$.

This theorem states that if we run the algorithm on a full program, with an empty assumption function, the resulting function will give us full knowledge about which formulas in $cl(\psi)$ hold in the initial states of the program according to the standard semantics of CTL.

The space requirements of our modular algorithm will usually be better than that of algorithms that need to have the full model in the direct memory. Our algorithm holds in the direct memory at any particular moment only the model for the subprogram under consideration at that time. In addition, it keeps an assumption function, which at its largest holds the results of performing model checking on this subprogram. This of course is equivalent to any model checking algorithm that must keep its own results.

The time requirements depend on the model checking algorithm used for a single node and on the partition graph. However, experimental results show a save in time as well as space requirements, as described in Section 6.

6   Implementation and Future Research

We implemented the ideas described in this paper in a prototype tool called *SoftVer*. The tool is based on a BDD representation of models and on symbolic model checking [2].

In order to evaluate the effectiveness of partitioning on memory and time requirements, we applied the tool to a few small examples. Each example program has been checked with two different partitionings. The moderate partitioning divided the program into a few components, while the extensive partitioning further divided it into smaller components. For comparison we also checked the unpartitioned full program.

The largest overhead occurs when applying our algorithm to a program in which the body of a while loop is partitioned. Therefore, all our examples include while loops which are divided by both partitionings. Figure 5 gives the space and time used by each partitioning as a percentage of the space and time used by the unpartitioned example.

	SPACE			TIME		
	Ex 1	Ex 2	Ex 3	Ex 1	Ex 2	Ex 3
No Partitioning	100%	100%	100%	100%	100%	100%
Moderate Partitioning	47%	50%	64%	31%	59%	74%
Extensive Partitioning	33%	34%	47%	18%	26%	176%

Fig. 5. Space and time requirements for three examples.

Example 1 is a simulation of the "stop and wait" communication protocol. It consists of a large while loop whose body has two major parts, one for the sender and one for the receiver. The moderate partitioning separates the receiver and the sender into two components. The extensive partitioning further separates different tasks in each of the components. The specification we checked required that the sender does not move to the next message before the current message has arrived at the receiver.

Example 2 is a learning algorithm that learns a single term by examples. As in the previous example, the code is partitioned so that different tasks are put in separate components. The specification required that the algorithm will never give a false negative result, i.e. the algorithm does not make errors on inputs for which the term evaluates to *true*.

Example 3 is the shortest of the three and it performs bubble sort on an array of 5 elements. This program consists of two nested while loops, with a single "if" statement in the body of the inner loop (that compares two adjacent elements). The moderate partitioning breaks the outer loop and the extensive partitioning breaks the inner loop as well. The specification states that the algorithm will terminate, and at that point the array will be sorted.

As can be seen in the table, in all examples space reduction was achieved by both partitionings where further save was obtained with finer ones. More surprisingly, save in time was also obtained in five out of six partitionings. This is explained by the fact that BDD based model checking is polynomial in the size of the BDD representation. Thus, applying the check once to a large model requires significantly more time than applying the check many times to smaller models. The save obtained this way compensates for the overhead of the modular algorithm. In the extensive partitioning of Example 3, however, the resulting components were only slightly smaller than those of the moderate partitioning. Thus, in this case the reduction in component size could not compensate for the additional overhead.

We consider a few directions for future research. One is to extend the language to include procedures and parallel composition. Another is to develop heuristics for optimal partitioning of the program text. Finally, we intend to apply *SoftVer* to large realistic examples.

Acknowledgment: We thank Sergio Campos for sharing with us his knowledge in compiling programs into Kripke structures. Arie Tal is also thanked for his help in the tool development.

References

1. I. Beer, S. Ben-David, C. Eisner, D. Geist, L. Gluhovsky, T. Heyman, A. Landver, P. Paanah, Y. Rodeh, and Y. Wolfstahl. Rulebase: Model checking at IBM. In *Proc. of the 9th International Conference on Computer Aided Verification, LNCS vol. 1254*, pages 480–484. Springer, June 1997.
2. J. R. Burch, E. M. Clarke, K. L. McMillan, D. L. Dill, and L. J. Hwang. Symbolic model checking: 10^{20} states and beyond. *Information and Computation*, 98(2):142–170, June 1992.

3. Olaf Burkart and Bernhard Steffen. Pushdown processes: Parallel composition and model checking. LNCS 836, pages 98–113. Springer, 1994.
4. E. M. Clarke and E. A. Emerson. Synthesis of synchronization skeletons for branching time temporal logic. In *Logic of Programs: Workshop, Yorktown Heights, NY, May 1981*, volume 131 of *Lecture Notes in Computer Science*. Springer-Verlag, 1981.
5. E. M. Clarke, E. A. Emerson, and A. P. Sistla. Automatic verification of finite-state concurrent systems using temporal logic specifications. *ACM Transactions on Programming Languages and Systems*, 8(2):244–263, 1986.
6. E. M. Clarke, O. Grumberg, H. Hiraishi, S. Jha, D. E. Long, K. L. McMillan, and L. A. Ness. Verification of the Futurebus+ cache coherence protocol. *Formal Methods in System Design*, 6(2):217–232, March 1995.
7. E. A. Emerson and J. Y. Halpern. "Sometimes" and "Not Never" revisited: On branching time versus linear time. *Journal of the ACM*, 33:151–178, 1986.
8. P. Godefroid. Model checking for programming languages using VeriSoft. In *Principle of Programming Languages*, January 1997.
9. O. Grumberg and D.E. Long. Model checking and modular verification. *ACM Trans. on Programming Languages and Systems*, 16(3):843–871, 1994.
10. G. Holzmann. *Design and Validation of Computer Protocols*. Prentice-Hall International Editors, 1991.
11. B. Josko. Verifying the correctness of AADL-modules using model checking. In J. W. de Bakker, W.-P. de Roever, and G. Rozenberg, editors, *Proceedings of the REX Workshop on Stepwise Refinement of Distributed Systems, Models, Formalisms, Correctness*, volume 430 of *Lecture Notes in Computer Science*. Springer-Verlag, May 1989.
12. G. Kamhi, O. Weissberg, L. Fix, Z. Binyamini, and Z. Shtadler. Automatic data-path extraction for efficient usage of HDD. In *Proc. of the 9th International Conference on Computer Aided Verification, LNCS vol. 1254*, pages 95–106. Springer, June 1997.
13. Karen Laster and Orna Grumberg. Modular model checking of software. Technical report, Computer Science Dept., Technion. Can be found at: http://www.cs.technion.ac.il/users/orna/.
14. O. Lichtenstein and A. Pnueli. Checking that finite state concurrent programs satisfy their linear specification. In *Proceedings of the Twelfth Annual ACM Symposium on Principles of Programming Languages*, pages 97–107, January 1985.
15. K. L. McMillan. *Symbolic Model Checking: An Approach to the State Explosion Problem*. Kluwer Academic Publishers, 1993.
16. K. L. McMillan and J. Schwalbe. Formal verification of the Encore Gigamax cache consistency protocol. In *Proceedings of the 1991 International Symposium on Shared Memory Multiprocessors*, April 1991.
17. A. Pnueli. A temporal logic of concurrent programs. *Theoretical Computer Science*, 13:45–60, 1981.
18. A. Pnueli. In transition from global to modular temporal reasoning about programs. In K. R. Apt, editor, *Logics and Models of Concurrent Systems*, volume 13 of *NATO ASI series F*. Springer-Verlag, 1984.
19. J.P. Quielle and J. Sifakis. Specification and verification of concurrent systems in CESAR. In *Proceedings of the Fifth International Symposium in Programming*, 1981.

Verification Based on Local States [*]

Michaela Huhn[1] and Peter Niebert[1] and Frank Wallner[2]

[1] Institut für Informatik, Universität Hildesheim,
Postfach 101363, D-31113 Hildesheim, Germany,
{huhn,niebert}@informatik.uni-hildesheim.de

[2] Institut für Informatik, Technische Universität München
D-80290 München, Germany
wallnerf@informatik.tu-muenchen.de

Abstract. Net unfoldings are a well-known partial order semantics for Petri nets. Here we show that they are well suited to act as models for branching-time logics interpreted on *local* states. Such local logics (in particular a *distributed μ-calculus*) can be used to express properties from the point of view of one component in a distributed system. Local logics often allow for more efficient verification procedures because – in contrast to interleaving branching-time logics – they do not refer to the entire space of *global* states. We reduce verification of local properties to standard model checking algorithms known for interleaving branching-time logics. The key is to extract a finite (usually small), local transition system bisimilar to the complete unfolding. The construction is based on the finite prefix of a net unfolding defined by McMillan.

1 Introduction

Model checking is one of the most successful approaches to formal, automated verification of distributed systems. Model checking algorithms decide whether a finite state system meets its specification given in terms of a temporal logic formula. One of the causes of the state explosion problem limiting this approach is the representation of concurrency as interleaving. Recently proposed partial order methods [Pel93, GW91, Val91] avoid the exploration of the entire state space for model checking by reductions according to the *partial order semantics* of the system, where certain interleaving properties are preserved.

Instead of reducing the interleaving model, verification can also be done directly on the partially ordered object: Net unfoldings[3] [NPW80, Eng91] provide a partial order branching time semantics for Petri nets. McMillan [McM92] has shown how to use net unfoldings for *efficient* deadlock detection and reachability analysis of finite-state Petri nets. He described the construction of a "finite prefix" of the (usually infinite) unfolding containing every reachable global state.

---

[*] This work was partially supported by: the SFB 342, Teilprojekt A3 of the DFG; and by the Human Capital and Mobility Cooperation Network "EXPRESS" (Expressivity of Languages for Concurrency).

[3] Also known as (branching) non-sequential processes.

It was already observed by Esparza in [Esp94] that the McMillan prefix can be used for model checking S4 (the modal logic based on the reachability relation of the global state space without *next*-modalities).

We show in this paper that a slight modification of McMillan's construction is a very adequate basis for more expressive branching time logics interpreted on *local states* and that for model checking such logics algorithms known from corresponding interleaving logics can be used. Here we understand a local (prime) configuration as the representation of the *view* of a single component onto the system, taking into account that the individual components have only partial information on a system's global state. Local logics allow to express partial order properties of distributed systems in a natural way, while the expression of properties, that refer to a certain interleaving of concurrent events, is neither impossible nor desired. For the linear time case, such logics have been investigated by Thiagarajan in [Thi94, Thi95] and Niebert [Nie95], local branching time logics were introduced in [LT87, LRT92].

We consider systems – described in terms of Petri nets – composed of sequential, nondeterministic subsystems, which synchronously communicate by means of common actions. As a logic we propose a *distributed μ-calculus*, interpreted solely at the local states of the contributing components. The basic operator is an indexed modality $\langle a \rangle_J$ meaning "*next a for the components $i \in J$*". Using fixpoints, local CTL-operators (cf. Sec.3) or the knowledge operator $\Box_i$ from [LRT92] can be encoded. Thus, the distributed μ-calculus serves as a powerful low-level logic, in which other local branching time logics can be expressed.

Besides considerations of its practical use for specification, the proposed logic is designed (i.e. restricted) in order to stay feasible for automatic verification. For good reasons we do not address the theoretical question of the overall expressiveness of the logic: the reference logics for the comparison with μ-calculi are monadic second order logics, but the monadic second order logic of net unfoldings (or prime event structures) can be shown to have a highly undecidable model-checking problem even for 1-safe Petri nets.

The distributed μ-calculus corresponds directly to the sequential μ-calculus [Koz83] interpreted on the *local configurations* of the system's unfolding. Since the (local) state space of the unfolding is in general infinite, our aim is to extract a *bisimilar, finite-state* representation of the unfolding. Such a representation can be immediately used by proved interleaving model checkers [CS93, CES86], yielding efficient automated verification.

We show that for any local configuration of the system's unfolding we find a bisimilar local configuration in the finite prefix – no matter whether we take McMillan's original definition or the improved prefix construction given in [ERV96]. Thus the local configurations within the finite prefix can serve as the *state space* for the desired finite representation. But the proof does not indicate how to determine the *transitions* needed for the finite bisimilar representation without exploring the complete unfolding. The major problem to solve is to determine those transitions (leading to the direct local successors) that are not already present in the finite prefix but which must exist because the local states of the prefix serve as representatives also for local states in the unfolding far beyond the finite prefix. We show how to find all direct local successors without extending the prefix any further.[4]

Since the resulting local transition system does not contain more states than the prefix contains events, the input for model checkers can be dramatically smaller than the transition system of the global state space. Nevertheless, during the construction of the local transition system we sometimes have to inspect *global* configurations contained in the prefix. Complexity considerations show that the representation of the algorithm given in Sec. 5 can be improved such that it never exceeds the costs of building the global state space times the number of transitions of the original net – which is at the same time the worst case bound of the size of the resulting transition system.

The paper is structured as follows. In Section 2 we introduce basic definitions of our models. In Section 3 we introduce the distributed μ-calculus and its formal semantics, and illustrate its use in specification with examples. In Sections 4 and 5 we show how to use the finite prefix for constructing a finite local transition system on which conventional model checkers apply.

2 Distributed nets and their unfoldings

We begin with the indispensable basic definitions and the class of Petri nets that serve as our system models. For further details on nets, cf. [Rei85].

Petri nets. Let P and T be disjoint, finite sets of *places* and *transitions*, generically called *nodes*. A *net* is a triple $N = (P, T, F)$ with a *flow relation* $F \subseteq (P \times T) \cup (T \times P)$, which we identify with its characteristic function on the set $(P \times T) \cup (T \times P)$. The *preset* $^\bullet x$ and the *postset* $x^\bullet$ of the node x are defined as $^\bullet x := \{y \in P \cup T \mid F(y, x) = 1\}$ and $x^\bullet := \{y \in P \cup T \mid F(x, y) = 1\}$. The preset (postset) of a set X of nodes is given by the union of the presets (postsets) of all nodes in X. We assume $^\bullet x \cup x^\bullet \neq \emptyset$ for every node x.

A *marking* of a net is a mapping $P \to \mathbb{N}$. We call $\Sigma = (N, M_0)$ a *net system* with initial marking M_0 if N is a net and M_0 a marking of N. A marking M *enables* the transition t if $M(p) \geq 1$ for each $p \in {}^\bullet t$. In this case the transition can *occur*, leading to the new marking M', given by $M'(p) = M(p) + F(t, p) - F(p, t)$ for every place p. We denote this occurrence by $M \xrightarrow{t} M'$. If there exists a chain $M_0 \xrightarrow{t_1} M_1 \xrightarrow{t_2} \ldots \xrightarrow{t_n} M_n$ then the sequence $\sigma = t_1 t_2 \ldots t_n$ is called *occurrence sequence* and we write $M_0 \xrightarrow{\sigma} M_n$. M is called a *reachable marking* of Σ if there exists an occurrence sequence σ, such that $M_0 \xrightarrow{\sigma} M$. Two transitions t_1, t_2 are *concurrently enabled* in M if M enables t_1, and t_2 is enabled in M', where $M'(p) = M(p) - F(p, t_1)$ for each p. A system is called *sequential* if no reachable marking concurrently enables two transitions.

---

[4] Since a direct local successor in one component may require an enormous number of causal predecessors in another component, it is not clear in advance when a further extension is sufficient to decide on the existence of a local successor.

We will exclusively regard *1-safe systems*, in which every reachable marking map each place to 0 or 1, and thus can be identified with the set of places it maps to 1, i.e., $M \subseteq P$ for every reachable marking M. Safe net systems can be seen as a synchronization of several finite automata. In the following we will exploit this compositional view by introducing the notion of locations.

Distributed net systems. Let $\{\Sigma_i = (P_i, T_i, F_i, M_i^0) \mid i \in I\}$ be a family of 1-safe, sequential net systems with pairwise disjoint sets P_i of places, indexed by a finite set I of *locations*. The *distributed net system* $\Sigma_I = (N_I, M_0)$ is the union of the *subsystems* Σ_i:

$$P = \bigcup_{i \in I} P_i, \quad T = \bigcup_{i \in I} T_i, \quad F = \bigcup_{i \in I} F_i, \quad M_0 = \bigcup_{i \in I} M_i^0.$$

Clearly, Σ_I is again 1-safe. The intended interpretation of such a system is a collection of sequential, non-deterministic processes with communication capabilities, namely the common transitions. We understand the common execution of a joint transition as a communication event. The *location* $loc(x)$ of a node x is defined by $loc(x) := \{i \in I \mid x \in P_i \cup T_i\}$. A simple distributed net system consisting of two subsystems is depicted in Fig. 1.

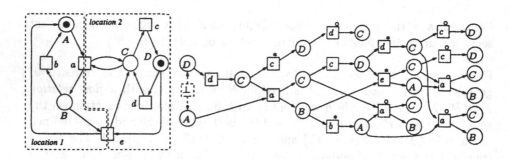

Fig. 1. Distributed net   **Fig. 2.** Branching process

Net unfoldings. In order to define a partial order semantics of the behaviour of a distributed net system, we consider *net unfoldings*, also known as *branching processes*. They contain information about both concurrency and conflict.

Two nodes x_1, x_2 of a net (P, T, F) are *in conflict*, denoted $x_1 \# x_2$, if there exist two distinct transitions t_1, t_2 such that $^\bullet t_1 \cap {}^\bullet t_2 \neq \emptyset$, and $(t_1, x_1), (t_2, x_2)$ belong to the reflexive and transitive closure of F. If $x \# x$, we say x *is in self-conflict*. An *occurrence net* [NPW80] is a net $N = (B, E, F)$ such that (1) for every $b \in B$, $|^\bullet b| \leq 1$, (2) the irreflexive transitive closure $\prec$ of F is well-founded and acyclic, i.e., for every node $x \in B \cup E$, the set $\{y \in B \cup E \mid y \prec x\}$ is finite and does not contain x, and (3) no element $e \in E$ is in self-conflict. The reflexive closure $\preceq$ of $\prec$ determines a partial order, called *causal relation*. In occurrence nets we speak of *conditions* and *events* instead of places and transitions, respectively. $Min(N)$ denotes the minimal elements of N w.r.t. $\preceq$, and $Max(X)$ the causally maximal elements of the set X of nodes.

Given two nets N_1, N_2, the mapping $h : P_1 \cup T_1 \to P_2 \cup T_2$ is called a *homomorphism* if $h(P_1) \subseteq P_2, h(T_1) \subseteq T_2$, and for every $t \in T_1$ the restriction of h to ${}^\bullet t$, denoted $h|_{{}^\bullet t}$, is a bijection between ${}^\bullet t$ and ${}^\bullet h(t)$, and similar for $h|_{t^\bullet}$.

A *branching process* [Eng91] of a net system $\Sigma = (N, M_0)$ is a pair $\beta = (N', \pi)$ where $N' = (B, E, F)$ is an occurrence net and $\pi : N' \to N$ is a homomorphism, such that the restriction of π to $Min(N')$ is a bijection between $Min(N')$ and M_0 and additionally for all $e_1, e_2 \in E$: if $\pi(e_1) = \pi(e_2)$ and ${}^\bullet e_1 = {}^\bullet e_2$ then $e_1 = e_2$. Loosely speaking, we unfold the net N to an occurrence net N', obeying the rules determined by the conditions for π, and labelling each node x of N' with the corresponding node $\pi(x)$ of N. Referring to distributed net systems, the location $loc(x)$ of a node x of N' is given by $loc(x) = loc(\pi(x))$. By E_J we denote the set of J-*events*, i.e., $E_J := \{e \in E \mid J \subseteq loc(e)\}$. For singleton locations $J = \{i\}$ we abbreviate $E_{\{i\}}$ by E_i.

Given two distinct branching processes β_1, β_2 of Σ, we say that β_1 and β_2 are *isomorphic* if there exists a bijective homomorphism $h : N_1 \to N_2$, such that the composition $\pi_2 \circ h$ equals π_1. If h is injective, such that $h|_{Min(N_1)}$ is a bijection between $Min(N_1)$ and $Min(N_2)$, and furtheron $B_1 \subseteq B_2$ and $E_1 \subseteq E_2$, we call β_1 a *prefix* of β_2. Notice that a prefix is uniquely determined by its set of events *or* its set of conditions. In [Eng91] it is shown that a net system has a unique maximal branching process up to isomorphism, which we call the *unfolding* of Σ, and denote by Unf. Fig. 2 shows a prefix of the infinite unfolding of the net system drawn in Fig. 1.

Configurations and Cuts. A *configuration* C of an occurrence net is a causally downward-closed, conflict-free set of events, i.e., for each $e \in C$: if $e' \preceq e$ then $e' \in C$, and for all $e, e' \in C : \neg(e \# e')$.

If $Max(C)$ is a singleton, say $\{e\}$, we speak of the *local configuration of* e and denote it by $\downarrow e$. It is given by the set of all the preceding events, i.e., $\downarrow e = \{e' \in E \mid e' \preceq e\}$. As usual, we identify each finite configuration C with the state of the system that is reached after all the events in C have occurred. A local configuration then defines a *local state*. The set of local configurations of a branching process β is denoted by $\mathcal{C}_{loc}(\beta)$. In order to simplify the handling, we introduce a virtual event symbol $\bot$ that can be seen as initial event with an empty preset and $Min(N)$ as postset. $\downarrow \bot$ then denotes the empty configuration. We extend the set of events of Unf to $E_\bot := E \cup \{\bot\}$ and set $loc(\bot) = I$.

In distributed systems, we define the *i-view* $\downarrow^i C$ of a configuration C as

$$\downarrow^i C := \{e \in C \mid \exists e' \in (C \cap E_i) : e \preceq e'\}$$

The i-view is a configuration: the empty configuration if $C \cap E_i = \emptyset$, and the local configuration of the (unique) maximal i-event in C, otherwise. This follows from the sequentiality of the subsystems. Thus, $\downarrow^i C$ can be understood as the most recent local state of the subsystem $i \in I$ that the whole system is aware of in the global state C. The i-view of the local configuration $\downarrow e$ is written as $\downarrow^i e$.

Two nodes of an occurrence net are *concurrent* if they are neither in conflict nor causally related. A set B' of conditions of an occurrence net is called a *co-set* if any two elements of B' are concurrent. A co-set is called a *cut* if it is a maximal co-set w.r.t. set inclusion. There is a tight interrelation between finite configurations and cuts: the set of conditions

$$Cut(C) = (Min(N) \cup C^{\bullet}) \setminus {}^{\bullet}C$$

where C is a finite configuration, is a cut. The corresponding set of places $\pi(Cut(C))$ is a reachable marking, denoted by $\mathcal{M}(C)$ and called *final state of C*. Notice that for *every* reachable marking M of the system there exist a (not necessarily unique) finite configuration with final state M. Configurations are called $\mathcal{M}$-*equivalent*, denoted by $C =_{\mathcal{M}} C'$, if their final state is equal. Two $\mathcal{M}$-equivalent configurations C, C' have a similar "future", i.e., there exists an isomorphism between the part of *Unf* that lies behind C and that one behind C'. Formally, if $C =_{\mathcal{M}} C'$ then $\beta(C)$ is isomorphic to $\beta(C')$, where $\beta(C) := \{x \in B \cup E \mid \exists b \in Cut(C). \, b \preceq x \, \wedge \, \forall y \in C. \, \neg(x \# y)\}$.

Assume two $\mathcal{M}$-equivalent local configurations $\downarrow e, \downarrow e'$ with $|\downarrow e| < |\downarrow e'|$. The branching process $\beta(\downarrow e)$ can be seen as $\beta(\downarrow e')$ "shifted backward". Any configuration C' containing e' thus can be shifted backward to an $\mathcal{M}$-equivalent configuration C containing e.

In [Esp94] this idea was formalized as follows: let $\mathcal{I}_e^{e'}$ denote the isomorphism from $\beta(\downarrow e')$ to $\beta(\downarrow e)$, and C be a configuration of *Unf*. The (e', e)-*shift of C*, denoted $shift_{(e',e)}(C)$, is defined by

$$shift_{(e',e)}(C) := \begin{cases} C & \text{if } e' \notin C \\ \downarrow e \cup \mathcal{I}_e^{e'}(C \setminus \downarrow e') & \text{if } e' \in C \end{cases}$$

Local successor relation. Let *Act* be a *distributed alphabet* of actions, i.e., $Act = \bigcup_{i \in I} Act_i$ where the Act_i are not necessarily disjoint. We speak of the location of an action, defined as $loc(a) := \{i \mid a \in Act_i\}$. Assume a mapping l from the transitions (and, via π, also from the events) to the actions that respects the distribution of the alphabet: $l(t) = a$ implies $loc(t) = loc(a)$.

Given two configurations C, C' we call C' an *a-successor* of C, written as $C \xrightarrow{a} C'$, if $C' = C \uplus \{e\}$ for some event e mapped to the action a.

This relation works fine for global configurations, but when considering *local* configurations it turns out to be too restrictive. Intuitively, we want to speak of the *local a-successor* of the local state $\downarrow e$, if for some locations that participated in e the next possible action is an a, ignoring the fact that some other locations possibly have to do some preparing steps until a is enabled. By parameterizing the successor relation with sets of locations, we will determine which of the locations may do those preparing steps, and for which locations the a is the immediate next action.

Let C_1, C_2 be configurations, a an action, and J a non-empty set of locations such that $loc(a) \cap J \neq \emptyset$. We call C_2 a *J-local a-successor* of C_1, written as

$C_1 \xrightarrow{a}_J C_2$, if there exists a configuration $C_1' \supseteq C_1$ such that $\downarrow^i C_1 = \downarrow^i C_1'$ for all $i \in J$, and $C_1' \xrightarrow{a} C_2$.

If $J = \{i\}$ is a singleton, we write $\longrightarrow_i$. Note that $\longrightarrow_i$ captures the local transition relation in an adequate way, i.e., $\longrightarrow_i$ in the unfolding of Σ_I corresponds to the $\longrightarrow$ relation in the unfolding of Σ_i.

3 The distributed μ-calculus

In this section we define the syntax and semantics of a version of the μ-calculus [Koz83] that is adequate to describe *local* properties of the components of a distributed system. More precisely, the formulae of the logic are interpreted over the local configurations of the unfolding of a distributed net system. The logic is adapted from a similar linear time logic for Mazurkiewicz traces [Nie95]. We will indicate how the local approach can be used for the specification and verification of distributed systems, and show that our logic naturally can be transferred to the conventional framework of global states.

Syntax. Let (N_I, M_0) be a distributed net system, $Unf = (N', \pi)$ its unfolding, and $l : T \to Act$ a labelling of the transitions of N_I with *actions* taken from the alphabet Act. We identify the corresponding labelling of events with l, i.e., $l(e) = l(\pi(e))$ for e in Unf. The abstract syntax of the logic is given by

$$\varphi ::= p \mid \neg p \mid x \mid \varphi \wedge \varphi \mid \varphi \vee \varphi \mid [a]_J \varphi \mid \langle a \rangle_J \varphi \mid \mu x.\varphi \mid \nu x.\varphi$$

where the atomic propositions p range over the set P of places of the distributed net, x over a set $\mathcal{V}$ of propositional variables, a over Act, and J over $2^I \setminus \emptyset$. For the modal operators $[a]_J$ and $\langle a \rangle_J$, we assume $J \cap loc(a) \neq \emptyset$. The intended meaning of $\langle a \rangle_J \varphi$ is that there exists a *next* local state $\downarrow e$ such that $l(e) = a$ and no event of any of the locations in J will happen before e. The operators μ and ν bind the variables. A formula that does not contain any free variable is *closed*. We use the basic propositions **true** and **false** as abbreviations for $\nu y.y$ and $\mu y.y$, respectively, and define $\langle - \rangle_J \varphi := \bigvee_{a \in Act} \langle a \rangle_J \varphi$ and $[-]_J \varphi := \bigwedge_{a \in Act} [a]_J \varphi$.

We only allow negation of atomic propositions. However, the logic is closed under negation, because every operator has its *dual*, and negations can be drawn inside down to the atomic propositions.

Semantics. The semantics of a formula φ of our logic is a set of local configurations (satisfying it), and is written as $[\varphi]_v^{Unf} \subseteq C_{loc}(Unf)$, where Unf is the unfolding under consideration and $v : \mathcal{V} \to 2^{C_{loc}(Unf)}$ is a valuation function for the variables. Since Unf is clear from the context, we omit this superscript, and if also v is understood, we simply write $[\varphi]$. For $\downarrow e \in [\varphi]$ we also write $\downarrow e \models \varphi$. We inductively define the semantics according to the following rules:

$$[p]_v = \{\downarrow e \mid p \in \mathcal{M}(\downarrow e)\} \qquad [\nu x.\varphi]_v = \bigcup \{A \mid A \subseteq [\varphi]_{v[x:=A]}\}$$
$$[\neg p]_v = \{\downarrow e \mid p \notin \mathcal{M}(\downarrow e)\} \qquad [\mu x.\varphi]_v = \bigcap \{A \mid [\varphi]_{v[x:=A]} \subseteq A\}$$

$$[\varphi \wedge \psi]_v = [\varphi]_v \cap [\psi]_v \qquad [[a]_J \varphi]_v = \{\downarrow e \mid \forall e' \in E. \text{ if } \downarrow e \xrightarrow{a}_J \downarrow e' \text{ then } \downarrow e' \in [\varphi]_v\}$$
$$[\varphi \vee \psi]_v = [\varphi]_v \cup [\psi]_v \qquad [\langle a \rangle_J \varphi]_v = \{\downarrow e \mid \exists e' \in E. \downarrow e \xrightarrow{a}_J \downarrow e' \text{ and } \downarrow e' \in [\varphi]_v\}$$

where $v[y := A](y) = A$, and for $z \neq y$ we have $v[y := A](z) = v(z)$. We say that system Σ satisfies the formula φ, denoted by $\Sigma \models \varphi$, if the empty configuration $\downarrow\perp$ belongs to $[\varphi]$.

Note that a local state $\downarrow e$ may satisfy an atomic proposition p that does not belong to the location of e. Thus, the proposed logic allows to express properties corresponding to the local view that one component has onto other components.

We briefly comment on the assertions expressible by the proposed language. Single-located formulae are simply formulae of the standard μ-calculus, interpreted on the corresponding subsystem. For instance, $\Psi = \nu x.\varphi \wedge [\text{-}]_i\, x$ means that on every path of the i-component φ holds at every local state – 'φ always holds in i'. If we substitute $[\text{-}]_i\, x$ by $([\text{-}]_i\, x \wedge \langle\text{-}\rangle_i\, \text{true})$ in Ψ, we additionally express that the mentioned path is of infinite length since for every local state of i there must exist a successor. 'φ holds in i infinitely often' can be formalized as $\nu y.\mu x.(\varphi \vee [\text{-}]_i\, x) \wedge [\text{-}]_i\, y \wedge \langle\text{-}\rangle_i\, \text{true}$. Notice, however, that this formula may hold even if there exist global runs in which the i-component only executes a finite number of events. It actually states that if i executes infinitely many events in the future then it will satisfy φ infinitely often.

It is useful to translate a local logic reminding of CTL [CES86] to our logic. Localised variants of the two next operators, EX_J and AX_J are already part of the syntax, namely $\langle\text{-}\rangle_J$ and $[\text{-}]_J$. The set of locations specifies, for which components this event is a next step. Similarly we now define the until-operators of CTL with locations:

$$\text{E}(\varphi \text{U}_J\, \psi) := \mu y.\psi \vee (\varphi \wedge \langle\text{-}\rangle_J\, y)$$
$$\text{A}(\varphi \text{U}_J\, \psi) := \mu y.\psi \vee (\varphi \wedge [\text{-}]_J\, y \wedge \langle\text{-}\rangle_J\, \text{true}).$$

Other CTL-like operators, such as $\text{AG}_J, \text{AF}_J, \text{EG}_J, \text{EF}_J$ can in turn be defined using the until-operators in the standard way. $\text{E}(\varphi \text{U}_J\, \psi)$ specifies a J-local chain of events along which φ holds until ψ is satisfied.

The more interesting properties, of course, are expressed by formulae referring to distinct subsystems. If $J = \{i, j, k\}$ then $\nu y.[\text{-}]_i\, y \wedge (p \to \langle a\rangle_J\, \text{true})$ describes that whenever p holds in i then i's next a-action may be a synchronization with j and k, which is also for j and k the next step. Another example referring to several components can be found in the appendix.

It is also possible to refer to conflicts in the causal future of local configurations: $\bigvee_{i \in I}(\langle\text{-}\rangle_i\, p \wedge \langle\text{-}\rangle_i\, \neg p)$ states that there are two next events in conflict which can be distinguished by p. Nevertheless, it is not possible to express that there are two *identically labelled*, but conflicting events if their future cannot be distinguished with the distributed μ-calculus.

As a further example we specify properties of the echo-algorithm as defined in [Wal95] in the distributed μ-calculus. Assume a (strongly connected) network consisting of a set of agents Ag including *initiator* A_0. Each agent A_i communicates exclusively with her direct neighbours, and each agent (but the initiator) behaves identically. At any time the initiator wants to flood the whole network with a *wake-up* signal, each agent – after receiving a wake-up – executes a local computation and sends back an *accept* signal afterwards. Whenever the initiator reaches state *terminated*, she wants to be sure that every agent in the network has executed her local computation: $\Sigma \models \mathsf{AG}_0(terminated \rightarrow \bigwedge_{i \geq 1} accepted_i)$.

Furthermore, no agent shall have finished her local computation, when any of her neighbours is still sleeping: $\Sigma \models \bigwedge_{i \geq 1} \mathsf{AG}_i(accepted_i \rightarrow \bigwedge_{j \in N_i} \neg sleeping_j)$.

4 Transition systems semantics

Now we want to show that the unfolding can be understood as a local transition system $\mathcal{T}_{Unf}$ with transitions labelled by indexed actions a_J, $J \subseteq I$, and with the *local* configurations of *Unf* as set of states. It will be immediate that on $\mathcal{T}_{Unf}$ the distributed μ-calculus corresponds to the standard μ-calculus over the modified action alphabet $\widetilde{Act} = \{a_J \mid a \in Act, J \subseteq I\}$.

μ-calculus and bisimulation. The syntax of the μ-calculus [Koz83] is given by

$$\varphi ::= p \mid \neg p \mid x \mid \varphi \wedge \varphi \mid \varphi \vee \varphi \mid \langle a \rangle \varphi \mid [a]\varphi \mid \mu x.\varphi \mid \nu x.\varphi$$

where $p \in P$, $x \in V$, and $a \in Act_T$. The semantics of the μ-calculus is defined over transition systems $\mathcal{T} = \langle S, s_0, \rightarrow, Act_T, P, I \rangle$ where S is a set of states, Act_T an action alphabet, $s_0 \in S$ the initial state, $\rightarrow \subseteq S \times Act_T \times S$ the transition relation, and $I : S \rightarrow 2^P$ an interpretation mapping the states onto the propositions. As usual, we write $s \xrightarrow{a} s'$ if $(s, a, s') \in \rightarrow$.

The semantics of a μ-calculus formula φ over a given transition system $\mathcal{T}$ is denoted by $[\varphi]_v^\mathcal{T} \subseteq S$, where v is the valuation function for the variables. We write $s \models_\mathcal{T} \varphi$ if $s \in [\varphi]_v$. The semantics is defined inductively by:

$$[p]_v = \{s \mid p \in I(s)\} \qquad [\nu x.\varphi]_v = \bigcup\{A \mid A \subseteq [\varphi]_{v[x:=A]}\}$$
$$[\neg p]_v = \{s \mid p \notin I(s)\} \qquad [\mu x.\varphi]_v = \bigcap\{A \mid [\varphi]_{v[x:=A]} \subseteq A\}$$
$$[\varphi \wedge \chi]_v = [\varphi]_v \cap [\chi]_v \qquad [\langle a \rangle \varphi]_v = \{s \mid \exists s' \in S. \, s \xrightarrow{a} s' \text{ and } s' \in [\varphi]_v\}$$
$$[\varphi \vee \chi]_v = [\varphi]_v \cup [\chi]_v \qquad [[a]\varphi]_v = \{s \mid \forall s' \in S. \text{ if } s \xrightarrow{a} s' \text{ then } s' \in [\varphi]_v\}$$

It is well-known that the distinguishing power of the μ-calculus is limited to standard bisimulation: A relation $\mathcal{R} \subseteq S \times S$ is called a *bisimulation* iff for any $s \, \mathcal{R} \, s'$ it holds that $I(s) = I(s')$ and for all $a \in Act_T$

- if $s \xrightarrow{a} s_1$, then there exists s_1' with $s' \xrightarrow{a} s_1'$ and $s_1 \, \mathcal{R} \, s_1'$, and dually
- if $s' \xrightarrow{a} s_1'$, then there exists s_1 with $s \xrightarrow{a} s_1$ and $s_1 \, \mathcal{R} \, s_1'$.

Two states s and s' are called *bisimilar*, denoted $s \sim s'$, iff there exists a bisimulation $\mathcal{R}$ with $s \, \mathcal{R} \, s'$. We also write $\mathcal{T} \sim \mathcal{T}'$ if for the initial states $s_0 \sim s_0'$. It was shown by Milner [Mil89] (see also [Sti92]) that $s \sim s'$ implies $s \models_\mathcal{T} \varphi \Leftrightarrow s' \models_\mathcal{T} \varphi$ for all closed μ-calculus formulae φ.

The local transition system $\mathcal{T}_{Unf}$. Let *Unf* be the unfolding of a distributed net system Σ. Then the local transition system extracted from *Unf* is given by $\mathcal{T}_{Unf} = \langle \mathcal{C}_{loc}(Unf), \downarrow\perp, \rightarrow, \widetilde{Act}, P, I \rangle$ where $\downarrow e \xrightarrow{a_J} \downarrow e'$ iff $\downarrow e \xrightarrow{a}_J \downarrow e'$, and the interpretation of propositions $I(\downarrow e) = \mathcal{M}(\downarrow e)$ for all $\downarrow e$.

Two events e_1, e_2 are *$\mathcal{M}$-loc-equivalent* iff $\downarrow e_1 =_\mathcal{M} \downarrow e_2$ and $loc(e_1) = loc(e_2)$.

Proposition 1. *Let $\downarrow e_1, \downarrow e_2 \in \mathcal{T}_{Unf}$. If e_1 and e_2 are $\mathcal{M}$-loc-equivalent then $\downarrow e_1 \sim \downarrow e_2$.*

Proof. Let $\mathcal{I}$ be the isomorphism from $\beta(\downarrow e_1)$ to $\beta(\downarrow e_2)$, induced by $\mathcal{M}$-equivalence of $\downarrow e_1$ and $\downarrow e_2$. Clearly, $loc(f) = loc(\mathcal{I}(f))$, and $f \preceq g$ iff $\mathcal{I}(f) \preceq \mathcal{I}(g)$ for all events $f, g \in \beta(\downarrow e_1)$. If furtheron $e_1 \prec f$ and $e_2 \prec \mathcal{I}(f)$, the events f and $\mathcal{I}(f)$ again are $\mathcal{M}$-equivalent, and thus $=_{\mathcal{M}}$ would be a bisimulation. However, it does not necessarily hold that $e_1 \prec f$ iff $e_2 \prec \mathcal{I}(f)$.

The additional *loc*-condition now preserves the desired causality: Let us call e' a *direct successor* of e, iff $e^\bullet \cap {}^\bullet e' \neq \emptyset$. For all e_1, e_1' it holds that if e_1' is a direct successor of e_1 then $loc(e_1) \cap loc(e_1') \neq \emptyset$. Consequently, if e_1' is a direct successor of e_1 then $\mathcal{I}(e_1') \in \beta(\downarrow e_2)$ is a direct successor of e_2 iff $loc(e_2) \cap loc(\mathcal{I}(e_1')) \neq \emptyset$. Thus the set of direct successors is preserved under $\mathcal{M}$-*loc*-equivalence. Since every J-local successor of an event e_1 is a direct successor of e_1 or the J-local successor of a direct successor of e_1, and since every direct successor of e_1 is $\mathcal{M}$-*loc*-equivalent to the corresponding direct successor of e_2, indeed $\mathcal{M}$-*loc*-equivalence is a bisimulation. $\square$

Let φ be a formula of the distributed μ-calculus. Then $\tilde{\varphi}$ denotes the formula where each occurrence of $\langle a \rangle_J$ is substituted by $\langle a_J \rangle$, and similarly $[a]_J$ by $[a_J]$.

Proposition 2. $\downarrow e \models \varphi$ *iff* $\downarrow e \models_{\mathcal{T}} \tilde{\varphi}$ *for any* $\downarrow e \in \mathcal{C}_{loc}(Unf)$.

5 Model checking

In this section we develop the technical tools required to achieve efficient verification techniques for the logic. In fact we will not give an algorithm for the model checking procedure itself. Rather we give a construction, which *reduces* the model checking problem for the distributed μ-calculus to a suitable input for well understood algorithms known from sequential model checking like [CES86, CS93].

As a first step, we will show that there exists a *finite* transition system $\mathcal{T}_{Fin}$ bisimilar to the usually infinite system $\mathcal{T}_{Unf}$. This finite system $\mathcal{T}_{Fin}$ can be defined over the set of local configurations of the *complete finite prefix* introduced by McMillan [McM92]. Secondly, we give an algorithm for constructing $\mathcal{T}_{Fin}$.

The finite prefix. In [McM92], McMillan showed how to construct a finite prefix of the unfolding of a finite-state net system in which every reachable marking is represented by some cut. We will use a slight modification of this prefix to obtain a finite transition system with local states, bisimilar to $\mathcal{T}_{Unf}$.

Let $Unf = (N', \pi)$ be the unfolding of a net system. A *cut-off event* is an event $e \in E_\perp$ whose local configuration's final state coincides with the final state of a smaller local configuration with the same location, formally:

$$\exists\, e' \in E_\perp : |\downarrow e'| < |\downarrow e| \text{ and } e, e' \text{ are } \mathcal{M}\text{-}loc\text{-equivalent.}$$

In McMillan's standard definition $\mathcal{M}$-equivalence suffices.[5] Notice that in general for each cut-off event e there may be several corresponding $\mathcal{M}$-loc-equivalent events e'. In the sequel, we fix one of them and refer to it as $corr(e)$. The prefix Fin is then defined as the unique prefix of Unf with $E_{Fin} \subseteq E_{\perp}$ as set of events, where E_{Fin} is characterised by

$$e \in E_{Fin} \quad \text{iff} \quad \text{no event } e' \prec e \text{ is a cut-off event.}$$

It is easy to prove that Fin is finite for net systems with finitely many reachable markings. Usually, the prefix Fin is much smaller than the state space of the system. However, it can also be larger. In [ERV96] it is shown how to improve McMillan's construction such that the finite prefix never exceeds the size of the full state space (up to a constant). The main idea is to determine cut-off events not by comparing the size of the local configurations of events (which does not produce any cut-off event when the sizes are equal), but other well-founded partial orders instead. In the prefix generated by the refined algorithm, if e and e' are two different non-cut-off events, then they are not $\mathcal{M}$-loc-equivalent.

The number of location sets occurring at events can grossly be bounded by the number of transitions in the original net. Therefore, the number of non-cut-off events never exceeds the number of reachable states times the number of transitions of the original net, and so the prefix can never be substantially larger than the state space.

The finite, local transition system $\mathcal{T}_{Fin}$. Now we show that there exists a finite transition system $\mathcal{T}_{Fin} \sim \mathcal{T}_{Unf}$, such that the states of $\mathcal{T}_{Fin}$ are at most the local configurations of the finite prefix.

Observe that the modified McMillan construction in fact guarantees that for each local configuration $\downarrow e$ in Unf there exists an $\mathcal{M}$-loc-equivalent corresponding configuration $\downarrow e'$ in Fin, i.e., $\downarrow e \sim \downarrow e'$ in $\mathcal{T}_{Unf}$, and $e' \in E_{Fin}$. The only reason for $e \notin E_{Fin}$ can be that e supersedes a cut-off belonging to Fin and therefore itself is a cut-off. By induction it is possible to find a corresponding event for e within E_{Fin}.

For the following, we select for each equivalence class of bisimilar configurations $\downarrow e$ in Unf a unique representative $\downarrow corr(e)$ in Fin which is minimal w.r.t. the size of $|\downarrow corr(e)|$. (In case of using the improved prefix [ERV96], $corr(e)$ is selected from the non-cut-off events in E_{Fin} and thus uniquely determined.)

If we have two bisimilar states $\downarrow e_1 \sim \downarrow e_2$ in $\mathcal{T}_{Unf}$ we can replace each transition $\downarrow e \xrightarrow{a_J} \downarrow e_1$ by $\downarrow e \xrightarrow{a_J} \downarrow e_2$ for any source state $\downarrow e$ and obtain a transition system $\mathcal{T}'_{Unf}$ bisimilar with $\mathcal{T}_{Unf}$ on all states and with the same state space.

Since we have selected for all local configurations $\downarrow e$, $\downarrow e'$ bisimilar representatives $\downarrow corr(e)$ and $\downarrow corr(e')$ in Fin, we can (imaginarily) "bend" all the transitions $\downarrow e \xrightarrow{a_J} \downarrow e'$ in $\mathcal{T}_{Unf}$ to transitions $\downarrow corr(e) \xrightarrow{a_J} \downarrow corr(e')$ in Fin (possibly merging infinitely many transitions into one). Since $corr(e)$ is unique and

---

[5] The cut-off events from the unfolding of the distributed net system of Fig. 1 are tagged by "o" in Fig. 2 whereas the cut-offs due to McMillan's original definition are tagged by "*".

minimal, afterwards all local states $\downarrow e$ reachable from $\downarrow\bot$ via transitions are non-cut-offs. Now we discard all cut-off events (whether contained in *Fin* or not). We call the resulting transition system $\mathcal{T}_{Fin}$. Observe that $\mathcal{T}_{Fin}$ is even smaller than *Fin* itself, since cut-offs are discarded. We obtain:

Proposition 3. $\mathcal{T}_{Fin} \sim \mathcal{T}_{Unf}$.

Theorem 4. *For any closed formula φ of the distributed μ-calculus it holds that* $\downarrow\bot \models \varphi$ *iff* $\downarrow\bot \models_{\mathcal{T}_{Fin}} \tilde{\varphi}$.

Theorem 4 is an immediate consequence of Proposition 2 and Proposition 3. Thus we can reduce the model checking problem of the distributed μ-calculus for some distributed net system to the model-checking problem of the standard μ-calculus over $\mathcal{T}_{Fin}$. Observe that $\mathcal{T}_{Fin}$ is not bigger than the global state space (i.e. the product of the local state spaces) times the number of transitions of the distributed net system – and often much smaller.

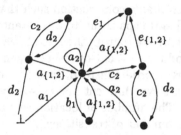

The figure depicts $\mathcal{T}_{Fin}$ of the prefix drawn in Fig. 2.

An algorithm to compute $\mathcal{T}_{Fin}$. By now we know that $\mathcal{T}_{Fin}$ exists, the question remains, how we can compute it. We propose an algorithm that takes *Fin* as input and moreover uses the structural information, which the algorithm computing *Fin* has built up:

- a function *corr* mapping all $\mathcal{M}$-*loc*-equivalent events onto a unique representative non-cut-off event. The codomain of *corr* is called $E_{Rep} \subset E_{Fin}$, the set of representative events. The state space of $\mathcal{T}_{Fin}$ is formed by the local configurations of these representatives.
- a function *shift**, which maps any configuration $C = C_1$ of *Unf* containing some cut-off to a configuration *shift*$^*(C) = C' = C_n$ not containing a cut-off, hence being present in *Fin*. This function works by repeatedly applying $C_{i+1} := shift_{(e_i, corr(e_i))}(C_i)$ with e_i being a cut-off in *Fin* contained in C_i. *shift** terminates, because the sequence $C_1, C_2, ..$ decreases in the underlying (well-founded) order (e.g. contains less and less events in the case of the McMillan order). Obviously this function implies the existence of an isomorphism $\mathcal{I}$ between $\beta(C)$ and $\beta(shift^*(C))$, which is the composition of the isomorphisms $\mathcal{I}^{e_i}_{corr(e_i)}$ induced by the chosen cut-off events. Moreover, *shift*$^*(\downarrow e)$ is strictly smaller than $\downarrow e$ (in the underlying order) for any $e \in \beta(C)$, and hence for any e, for which $C \xrightarrow{a}_J \downarrow e$.

The most important part of the algorithm is the recursive procedure *successors* which, when called *from the top level* with a triple $(\downarrow e, J, a)$, returns the a_J-successors for $\downarrow e$ in $\mathcal{T}_{Fin}$. More generally, *successors* performs depth-first search through triples (C, J, a), where C is an arbitrary, not necessarily local configuration not containing a cut-off, J is a non-empty subset of locations, and a is

type Vertex = { C: Configuration; J: LocationSet; a: ActionLabel;
pathmark: **bool** ; *(* for depth first search *)* }

$prefix\_successors(C, J, a) = \{\downarrow corr(e) \mid e \in E_{Fin} \wedge C \xrightarrow{a}_J \downarrow e\}$

$inheritable\_extension(C, e, J, a) = (\forall i \in J.\ (\downarrow e \setminus C) \cap E_i = \emptyset)$
(* predicate ensuring, that joining $\downarrow e$ to C adds no i-events for $i \in J$ *)

$compatible\_cutoffs(C) = \{e \mid e$ is cut-off and $\downarrow e \cup C$ is a configuration in $Fin\}$

proc $successors(C, J, a)$: ConfigurationSet;
{ **var** result: ConfigurationSet; *(* result accumulator for the current vertex *)*
  Vertex v := findvertex(C,J,a); *(* lookup in hash table, if not found then *)*
                                 (* create new vertex with pathmark = false *)
  if v.pathmark **then return** $\emptyset$; **fi** *(* we have closed a cycle *)*
  result := $prefix\_successors(C, J, a)$; *(* directly accessible successors *)*
  v.pathmark:=**true**; *(* put vertex on path *)*
  for $e_c \in compatible\_cutoffs(C)$ **do**
      (* find successors outside the prefix behind e_c *)
      if $inheritable\_extension(C, e_c, J, a)$ **then**
          result := result $\cup$ $successors(shift^*(C \cup \downarrow e_c), J, a)$;
      fi
  od ;
  v.pathmark:=**false**; *(* take vertex from path *)*
  return result;
}

proc $ComputeT_{Fin}$;
{ InitializeTransitionSystem(ts,Fin) *(* extract state space from Fin *)*
  for $e \in E_{Rep}, a \in Act, \emptyset \neq J \subseteq I$ **do**
    for $\downarrow e' \in successors(\downarrow e, J, a)$ **do**
      add transition $\downarrow e \xrightarrow{a_J} \downarrow e'$
    od
  od
}

Fig. 3. The conceptual algorithm to compute T_{Fin}

an action. It determines the subset of events in E_{Rep} that represent the J-local a-successors of C. Formally, $e \in successors(C, J, a)$ iff there exists $\downarrow e'$ in Unf, which is M-loc-equivalent to $\downarrow e$, and $C \xrightarrow{a}_J \downarrow e'$.

The procedure works as follows. Assume there exists at least one e' anywhere in Unf with $C \xrightarrow{a}_J \downarrow e'$; then there are two possibilities:
(1) One of these e' lies in the prefix. This is easy to determine. The corresponding event $corr(e') \in E_{Rep}$ is given back by $prefix\_successors(C, J, a)$.
(2) There exist such events e', but none of them lies in the prefix. The reason for $e' \notin E_{Fin}$ is the existence of a cut-off $e_c \in E_{Fin}$, such that $e_c \preceq e'$. So we can

do a case analysis over the *compatible* cut-offs. A cut-off e_c is compatible with C if it is not in conflict with C, i.e., $\downarrow e_c \cup C$ is a configuration in *Fin*. If there is a compatible e_c, such that $(\downarrow e_c \setminus C) \cap E_i = \emptyset$ for all $i \in J$ then for at least one of them, we have $(C \cup \downarrow e_c) \xrightarrow{a}_J \downarrow e'$. In this case we inherit the transition $C \xrightarrow{a}_J \downarrow e'$.

In the second case, we loop over all compatible cut-offs e_c looking at the configuration $C_c := C \cup \downarrow e_c$. If the J-local a-successors of C_c are J-local a-successors of C (determined by *inheritable_extension*(C, e_c, J, a)) we want to search for the *successors*(C_c, J, a). But if any J-local a-successor e' of C_c exists, then there also exists a bisimilar e'' for $C^* := shift^*(C_c)$ (by the isomorphism), where moreover $\downarrow e''$ is smaller than $\downarrow e'$. So *successors* is recursively called with (C^*, J, a). Note that C^* contains no cut-off.

Hence we apply depth-first search with respect to triples (C, J, a). Cycles may occur (if we hit a triple (C, J, a) with pathmark= true), at which we break off to ensure termination. Note that the search space is limited by the fact that C is represented in *Fin* and does not contain cut-offs.

It remains to show that the termination is correct: Assume a J-local a-successor e' of C exists. Then we choose from all these suitable successors a minimal one named $e_{\min}$. Whenever a configuration $(C \cup \downarrow e_c)$ is shifted with $shift^*$ to obtain a configuration C' for the next call of *successors*, also $e_{\min}$ is shifted to a strictly smaller $e'_{\min}$. Thus in case we hit a configuration C twice, when searching for J-local a-successors, $e_{\min}$ is mapped by the various $shift^*$s to a strictly smaller event $e^*_{\min}$ which contradicts the minimality of $e_{\min}$. Thus whenever a configuration is investigated a second time for J-local a-successors, we know that there cannot be one.

The main procedure *Compute$\mathcal{T}_{Fin}$* thus only has to loop about all possible triples $(\downarrow e, J, a)$ with $e \in E_{Rep}$ to check for transitions $\downarrow e \xrightarrow{a_J} \downarrow e'$ in $\mathcal{T}_{Fin}$ and to insert the results of *successors*. Concluding the above discussion, we obtain:

Theorem 5. *The algorithm Compute$\mathcal{T}_{Fin}$ computes $\mathcal{T}_{Fin}$.*

Note that at top level, *successors* is only called with local configurations C, but the extension of C with cut-offs requires that we can also handle some global configurations. Further note that we present the algorithm in Fig. 3 with emphasis on understandability, not efficiency: many vertices (C, J, a) will be explored very often, leading to an unsatisfying runtime. However it is very easy to modify the algorithm so that every vertex is explored *at most once*, essentially by storing intermediate results with the vertices in the hash-table. Then the runtime of the algorithm is proportional to the size of the search space. Since we have to deal with some global configurations, in principle the search space can grow to the size of the global state space times the number of the transitions of the original net, but no larger.

Experiments suggest that in many cases the number of *visited* global states will remain small compared to the number of *all* global states existing.

Heuristic improvements. Apart of the improvements mentioned above, the algorithm also allows for several *heuristic improvements* to save unnecessary computation. For instance, it is impossible that a state $\downarrow e$ has any a_J-successor if the J-places in $\mathcal{M}(\downarrow e)$ are not contained in ${}^\bullet t$ for any a-labelled transition t of the original net, and thus $successors(\downarrow e, J, a)$ need not to be called. Moreover, the algorithm can be combined with *on-the-fly* algorithms (sometimes called *local model checking*), by only calling $successors$, when the model checker needs to find the a_J-successors of some state.

6 Conclusion

We introduced a distributed version of the μ-calculus and showed its use in describing branching time properties of distributed algorithms based on local states. We reduced the model checking problem for the distributed μ-calculus to the well-investigated model checking problem of sequential logics over transition systems.

How expensive is all this? The *computation* of $\mathcal{T}_{Fin}$ can be as costly as generating the global state space (although often it will be much cheaper), the *resulting system $\mathcal{T}_{Fin}$* is typically much smaller than the global transition system. The transformation of the formulae is for free. So the cost of computing $\mathcal{T}_{Fin}$ does not affect the runtime of the standard model checker in the next phase. It is necessary to investigate really meaningful examples, to give a concise answer on the benefits of the proposed approach. First experiments with a prototype implementation indicate that $\mathcal{T}_{Fin}$ and the number of global states visited during its computation indeed are very small.

Independently, Penczek [Pen97] suggested a model checker for a future fragment of his event structure logic DESL. Instead of using net unfoldings, Penczek relies on partial order methods in the generation of a finite representation of the event structure. The causal future operators of DESL as considered in [Pen97] can easily be treated by the algorithm we proposed here by changing the modalities and the successor relation accordingly. At the price of the restriction to free-choice systems, in [Pen97] also an *immediate conflict* operator is handled.

Acknowledgment. We thank P.S. Thiagarajan for discussions on location based logics. Burkhard Graves has helped our understanding of the subtleties of *Fin*. Special thanks to Javier Esparza, whose contribution to this work in its initial phase was very important.

References

[CES86] E.M. Clarke, E.A. Emerson, and A.P. Sistla, *Automatic verification of finite-state concurrent systems using temporal logic specifications*, ACM Transactions on Programming Languages and Systems 8 (1986), no. 2, 244–263.

[CS93] Rance Cleaveland and Bernhard Steffen, *A linear time model-checking algorithm for the alternation-free modal mu-calculus*, Formal Methods in system Design 2 (1993), 121–147.

[Eng91] J. Engelfriet, *Branching processes of Petri nets*, Acta Informatica 28 (1991), 575–591.

[ERV96] J. Esparza, S. Römer, and W. Vogler, *An Improvement of McMillan's Unfolding Algorithm*, Tools and Algorithms for the Construction and Analysis of Systems TACAS '96 (Passau, Germany) (T. Margaria and B. Steffen, eds.), LNCS, vol. 1055, Springer, 1996, pp. 87–106.

[Esp94] J. Esparza, *Model checking using net unfoldings*, Science of Computer Programming **23** (1994), 151–195.

[GW91] P. Godefroid and P. Wolper, *A Partial Approach to Model Checking*, Proceedings of the 6th IEEE Symposium on Logic in Computer Science (Amsterdam), July 1991, pp. 406–415.

[HNW96] M. Huhn, P. Niebert, and F. Wallner, *Put your model checker on diet: verification on local states*, Technical Report TUM-I9642, Technische Universität München, December 1996.

[Koz83] Dexter Kozen, *Results on the propositional μ-calculus*, TCS **27** (1983), 333–354.

[LRT92] K. Lodaya, R. Ramanujam, and P.S. Thiagarajan, *Temporal logics for communicating sequential agents: I*, Int. Journal of Foundations of Computer Science **3** (1992), no. 2, 117–159.

[LT87] K. Lodaya and P.S. Thiagarajan, *A modal logic for a subclass of event structures*, Automata, Languages and Programming (T. Ottmann, ed.), LNCS, vol. 267, Springer, 1987, pp. 290–303.

[McM92] K.L. McMillan, *Using unfoldings to avoid the state explosion problem in the verification of asynchronous circuits*, Proceedings of the 4th Workshop on Computer Aided Verification (Montreal), 1992, pp. 164–174.

[Mil89] R. Milner, *Communication and concurrency*, Prentice Hall, 1989.

[MT89] M. Mukund and P.S. Thiagarajan, *An axiomatization of event structures*, Foundations of Software Technology and Theoretical Computer Science (C.E. Veni Madhavan, ed.), LNCS, vol. 405, Springer, 1989, pp. 143–160.

[Nie95] Peter Niebert, *A ν-calculus with local views for systems of sequential agents*, MFCS, LNCS, vol. 969, 1995.

[NPW80] M. Nielsen, G. Plotkin, and G. Winskel, *Petri nets, event structures and domains*, Theoretical Computer Science **13** (1980), no. 1, 85–108.

[Pel93] Doron Peled, *All from one, one for all: on model checking using representatives*, Computer Aided Verification CAV, LNCS, 1993.

[Pen97] W. Penczek, *Model-checking for a subclass of event structures*, TACAS, 97, to appear.

[Rei85] W. Reisig, *Petri Nets*, EATCS Monographs on Theoretical Computer Science, vol. 4, Springer, 1985.

[Sti92] Colin Stirling, *Modal and temporal logics*, Handbook of Logic in Computer Science (S. Abramsky, D. Gabbay, and T. Maibaum, eds.), Oxford University Press, 1992.

[Thi94] P.S. Thiagarajan, *A Trace Based Extension of PTL*, Proceedings of the 9th IEEE Symposium on Logic in Computer Science, 1994.

[Thi95] P.S. Thiagarajan, *A Trace Consistent Subset of PTL*, Proceedings of CONCUR '95 (Philadelphia, P.A., USA) (I. Lee and S.A. Smolka, eds.), LNCS, vol. 962, Springer, 1995, pp. 438–452.

[Val91] A. Valmari, *Stubborn Sets for Reduced State Space Generation*, Advances in Petri Nets 1990 (G.Rozenberg, ed.), LNCS, vol. 483, 1991, pp. 491–515.

[Wal95] Rolf Walter, *Petrinetzmodelle verteilter Algorithmen - Beweistechnik und Intuition*, Ph.D. thesis, Humboldt-Universität zu Berlin, Institut für Informatik, 1995, edition VERSAL, W. Reisig (Hrsg.), Dieter Bertz Verlag.

Exploiting Symmetry in Linear Time Temporal Logic Model Checking: One Step Beyond

K. Ajami[*]   S. Haddad[**]   J-M. Ilié[*]

* LIP6 - CNRS ERS 587	** LAMSADE - CNRS URA 825
Univ. Pierre & Marie Curie,	Univ. Paris Dauphine
Tour 65-66, Bureau 204,	
4, place Jussieu,	Pl. du Maréchal De Lattre de Tassigny,
75252 Paris Cedex 05	75775 Paris

e.mail: Khalil.Ajami@lip6.fr,   e.mail: haddad@lamsade.dauphine.fr
Jean-Michel.Ilie@lip6.fr

Abstract. Model checking is a useful technique to verify properties of dynamic systems but it has to cope with the state explosion problem. By simultaneous exploitation of symmetries of both the system and the property, the model checking can be performed on a reduced quotient structure [2,6,7]. In these techniques a property is specified within a temporal logic formula (CTL*) and the symmetries of the formula are obtained by a syntactical checking. We show here that these approaches fail to capture symmetries in the LTL path subformulas. Thus we propose a more accurate method based on local symmetries of the associated Büchi automaton. We define an appropriate quotient structure for the synchronized product of the Büchi automaton and the global state transition graph. We prove that model checking can be performed over this quotient structure leading to efficient algorithms.

Topic: Formal Methods.
Keywords: Temporal Logic, LTL, Symmetries, Büchi automata, Model Checking, Verification.

1. Introduction

Checking system correctness can be performed by the specification and the verification of temporal logic formulas over a state transition graph which models the system behavior. The well-known combinatorial explosion problem in space and time requires the development of efficient techniques in order to reduce the size of the graph to be built, with respect to some desired properties.

One of the most promising technique has been initiated by Emerson & al [6,7]. It exploits the symmetries of both the system and formula. Such a technique builds a quotient graph in which each node represents an equivalent class of states. The relation is induced by a subgroup of permutations preserving the state graph and the formula. In practice, the permutations act on a set of system processes with identical behavior. Previous works have been already developed focusing on the safeness properties [1,14,17,19]. Other developments include model checking algorithms [2,13], model checking under fairness constraints [8] and application to system bisimulation [16]. Looking carefully at the technique described in [6,7], it appears that currently, the

CTL* model checking can make profit from the symmetries but in a restrictive way. Roughly speaking, two kinds of symmetries are detected: propositional symmetries (e.g. contain subformulas like $f = V_{i \in I} f_i$ where f_i is a propositional formula involving the process i) and global symmetries with respect to a group of symmetries acting on the structure representing the formula (Büchi automata for linear temporal formulas like $f = V_{i \in I} F f_i$).

The aim of this paper is to generalize the previous methods showing how local symmetries can be exploited inside path subformulas of a CTL* formula. In this work, we limit the presentation to the case of LTL formulas. The general framework for branching time model checking can be developed using the iterated method of [10]. Unlike the approach presented in [6,7], *the considered Büchi automaton is not necessarily globally symmetric with respect to a predefined symmetry group.* The starting point of our method is the analysis of any Büchi automaton associated with a LTL formula to be verified (see for instance [11]). Then we relate two states of the Büchi automaton if they represent the same current and future behavior up to a permutation of processes. Given a permutation, this state relation can be computed in polynomial time. Similarly, in the system model, two states are related by a permutation with respect to their current value of the system variables. By applying these relations on the synchronized product of the Büchi automaton and the global state transition graph, we define an appropriate quotient structure. Then we prove that model checking over this quotient is equivalent to model checking over the synchronized product. However, the general computation of permutations wipes out the benefit of having a quotient structure (exponential complexity of computation). Therefore, we propose an alternative approach which computes, in polynomial time, an intermediate size structure. Such a structure has the same equivalence property as the quotient one and leads, in practical cases, to significant savings of space (even exponential).

The next sections are organized as follows: part 2 presents the model of computation and briefly recalls the temporal logic used to specify properties, it also presents the representation of a linear temporal logic formula by means of a Büchi automaton; part 3 presents the definition of system symmetries while part 4 presents the symmetries reflected in a temporal logic formula; part 5 is the analysis of the model checking using symmetries and the proof of its validity; part 6 contains the operational model checking approach using symmetries; part 7 contains our conclusion and perspectives.

2. Model of Computation and Temporal Logic

We can apply our work on any system where symmetries are defined within a group of permutations. So, let us consider a simple model of system.

2.1. The Model

We deal with finite state concurrent systems composed of many processes. Processes are identified by indices. They may share global variables but differ from local ones. The structure of such a system is defined as follows:

Definition 2.1.1: Finite State Concurrent System
We present a finite state system using the temporal structure $M = (S, \Delta, I, V, D, L, S_0)$ where:
- S is the finite set of the states; $S_0 \subseteq S$ is the set of initial states;

- $\Delta \subseteq S \times S$ is the possible changes between states;
- I is the set of process indices;
- V is the set of system variables; it is composed of two distinct subsets, V_G, the set of global variables and V_L the set of local variables.
- D is the definition domain of variables.
- L is the state labeling function, $L: S \times (V_G \cup V_L \times I) \rightarrow D$ such that:

    (i) $L(s,v_g)$ is the value of variable v_g of V_G in state s;

    (ii) $L(s,v_l,i)$ is the value of variable v_l of V_L of process i in state s.

Atomic propositions are built from the association of a value to a variable.

Remark:
The structure of a system depends only on the value of the variables i.e. two different states must have at least one variable with different values.

Definition 2.1.2: Global and Local Atomic propositions
A global atomic proposition, is a pair $(v_g, d) \in V_G \times D$ whereas a local atomic proposition is a triplet $(v_l, i, d) \in V_L \times I \times D$ that depends on a process i.

We define $AP = \{p \mid p \in V_G \times D \cup V_L \times I \times D\}$ the set of atomic propositions built on the global and local variables.

We define *prop*: $S \rightarrow 2^{AP}$ such that *prop(s)* is the set of propositions associated with s.

Definition 2.1.3: Atomic propositions holding in a state
Global (respectively local) atomic propositions hold at state s of S (noted $\models$) as follows: $s \models (v_g, d) \Leftrightarrow L(s, v_g) = d$; (respectively $s \models (v_l, i, d) \Leftrightarrow L(s, v_l, i) = d$).

In the following we recall some notions of temporal logic used to specify system properties. The translation of linear temporal formulas to Büchi automata is also presented.

2.2. Temporal Logic

In a propositional Temporal Logic, the non temporal portion of the logic is propositional logic. Thus formulas are built up from atomic propositions, which intuitively express, atomic facts about the underlying state of the concurrent system, truth-functional connectives and the temporal operators. Furthermore, when defining a system of temporal logic, two possible views of the system, can be considered, regarding the nature of time. One is that the course of time is linear: at each moment there is only one possible future moment. The other is that time has a branching tree-like nature: at each moment, time may split into alternate courses representing different possible futures. In linear time, one reasons about sets of infinite sequences, while in branching time, one reasons about the possible futures of the current state leading to branching tree like structure.

In our work we are mainly interested by the linear time temporal logic formulas. However, the notion of branching time temporal remains the general framework in which our model checking can be extended. We use here two kinds of operators, temporal operators presented later and path quantifiers using the two symbols, A, E, to indicate respectively all or some paths.

2.2.1. Linear Temporal Logic (LTL)

A well-formed linear-time temporal logic, dealing with our system, is constructed from the set of atomic propositions AP, the standard boolean operators V (Or), $\neg$ (Not), and the temporal operators X (neXttime) and U (strong Until). Precisely, formulas are defined inductively as follows: (1) Every member of AP is a formula; (2) if φ and ψ are formulas then so are $\neg\varphi, \varphi\vee\psi, X\varphi, \varphi \ U \ \psi$.

An interpretation for a linear-time temporal logic formula is an infinite word $\xi = x_0 x_1 \ldots$ over an alphabet 2^{AP}. For more precision, the elements of 2^{AP} are interpreted as assigning truth values to the elements of AP: elements in the set are assigned *true*, elements not in the set are assigned *false*. We note ξ_i the suffix of ξ starting at x_i. The semantics of LTL is defined in the following:

- $\xi \vDash \alpha$ iff $\alpha \in x_0$, for $\alpha \in AP$.
- $\xi \vDash \neg\varphi$ iff $\neg(\xi \vDash \varphi)$.
- $\xi \vDash \varphi\vee\psi$ iff $(\xi \vDash \varphi$ or $\xi \vDash \psi)$.
- $\xi \vDash X\varphi$ iff $\xi_1 \vDash \varphi$.
- $\xi \vDash \varphi \ U \ \psi$ iff $\exists i \geq 0$ such that $\xi_i \vDash \psi$ and $\xi_j \vDash \varphi \ 0 \leq \forall j < i$.

As some abbreviations, one can introduce additional linear operators: the *eventuality* operator F where $F\varphi = true \ U \ \varphi$, the *always* operator G where $G\varphi = \neg F\neg\varphi$.

2.2.2. From LTL to Büchi automata

A Büchi automaton is a finite automaton which accepts infinite sequences. A sequence is accepted if, and only if, it is recognized by the automaton and meets infinitely often one of the accepting states (called also designated states).

It has been shown that any LTL formula can be translated to a Büchi automaton in order to perform efficient model checking. Indeed, Büchi automata are strictly more expressive than LTL formulas and equivalent to linear-time Mu-calculus [5,18,21].

Definition 2.2.3: Büchi automata

A Büchi automaton [6] is a tuple $A=(AP, B, \rho, B_0, E, F)$ where:

- B is a set of states. Each state b of B is defined by the set $Atom(b) \subseteq AP$.

- $\rho: B \to 2^B$ is a nondetermistic transition function.

- $B_0 \subseteq B$ is a set of starting states.

- $E: B \to 2^{AP}$.

- $F \subseteq B$ is a set of accepting states.

3. Symmetries on Models

Given a permutation $\pi: I \to I$ on the set of process indices, we want to determine whether two states of the state transition graph are symmetric up this permutation. Effectively, a permutation is said to be a symmetry if and only if it preserves the possible changes between states. We define the symmetries on the model represented by the structure $M=(S, \Delta, I, V, D, L, S_0)$.

Definition 3.1: Symmetry on a State Transition Graph

A permutation π on I, is a symmetry iff:

(1) For each state $s \in S$, there is a unique state s' denoted $\pi(s)$ which satisfies:

    (i) $\forall v_g \in V_G, L(\pi(s), v_g) = L(s, v_g)$;

    (ii) $\forall i \in I, \forall v_l \in V_L, L(\pi(s), v_l, i) = L(s, v_l, \pi(i))$.

(2) Permutation π satisfies the following condition:

$$(\forall s_1 \in S), (\forall s_2 \in S), ((s_1 \rightarrow s_2) \in \Delta \Leftrightarrow (\pi(s_1) \rightarrow \pi(s_2)) \in \Delta).$$

The group of symmetries defined on M is called the automorphisms group of M and denoted $Aut(M)$.

4. Symmetries on Formulas

In [7], the symmetries of a temporal logic formula to be verified are obtained by a syntactical checking while in [6], they result from the analysis of the corresponding Büchi automaton. By looking carefully at this method, it appears that symmetries of a CTL* formula are obtained in a restrictive way. Roughly speaking, many techniques are proposed based on the detection of a group of symmetries:

(1) *State symmetries* obtained from (sub)formulas like $V_{i \in I} f_i$ where f_i is propositional involving process i. Effectively, the symmetries resulting from formulas like $f = EF(V_{i \in I} f_i)$, $f = EF(\Lambda_{i \in I} f_i)$ constitute the group $Sym(I)$, the group of all the permutations between the elements of I. Those computed for formula like $f = EF f_i$ constitute the group $Stab(i)$ (the group of all the permutation between the elements of $I \setminus \{i\}$).

(2) The former approach fails to capture *Path symmetries* in LTL subformulas like $f = V_{i \in I} F f_i$, $f = \Lambda_{i \in I} F f_i$. Thus, the method of [6] introduces a complementary framework by detecting a group of symmetries acting on the states of Büchi automaton.

All these approaches are inefficient for formulas like $f = \Lambda_{i,j \in I}^{i<j} (f_i U f_j)$ because the group of symmetries is reduced to the identity. However, the former formula contains local symmetries that can be reflected in some states of its büchi automaton.

In this section, we propose a more accurate method based on the exploitation of local symmetries computed for some states of the automaton. Hence, we show that the existence of a group is not required to exploit symmetries.

We compute, the symmetries on a Büchi automaton, $A = (AP, B, \rho, B_0, E, F)$. The states equivalence can be detected using the relation defined as follows:

Definition 4.1: Permutation on a set of atomic propositions
Let π be a permutation on I. Let AP_1 be a set of atomic propositions, there is a set AP_2 denoted $\pi(AP_1)$ which satisfies:

$$\pi(AP_1) = AP_2 = \{ (v_g, d') | \forall (v_g, d) \in Atom(b), \exists (v_g, d') \in Atom(b') where (d' = d) \} \cup$$
$$\{ (v_l, j, d') | \forall i \in I, \forall (v_l, i, d) \in Atom(b), \exists j \in I, \exists (v_l, j, d') \in Atom(b') where (d' = d) \}$$

Definition 4.2: Equivalence of two states of a Büchi automaton
A relation $\mathcal{R}_\pi$ is the coarsest relation that defines the equivalence of two states of a Büchi automaton. It fulfills the following two requirements: $\forall b, b' \in V, b \mathcal{R}_\pi b'$ iff:

(1) There is a permutation π that satisfies the two conditions:

(i) $b \in \mathcal{F} \Leftrightarrow b' \in \mathcal{F}$; (ii) $Atom(b') = \pi(Atom(b))$.

(2) $\forall b_1 [b \rightarrow b_1], \exists b'_1 [b' \rightarrow b'_1] | (b_1 \mathcal{R}_\pi b'_1)$.

Generally, $\mathcal{R}_\pi$ is not an equivalence relation. It can be computed in a polynomial time using a fixed-point computation starting with condition (1) and by applying (2).

Example 1: *Let us consider the following Büchi automaton representing the formula* $f = [(p_1 U p_3) \vee (p_2 U p_3)] \wedge (p_1 U p_2)$ *for a system of three processes* P_1, P_2, P_3, *where* p_1, p_2, p_3 *are three atomic propositions.*

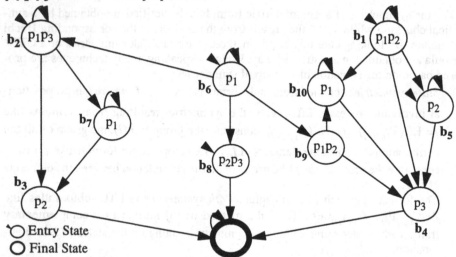

Figure 1: Büchi automaton of the formula f

In this automaton, the only global symmetry group acting on the states is the identity. However, one can observe that states b_7 *and* b_{10} *are symmetrical with respect to definition 4.1 (permutation* π *such that* $\pi(1)=1, \pi(2)=3, \pi(3)=2$ *is used). Similarly, other symmetries can be detected between* b_3 *and* b_4, b_5 *and* b_{10}, b_1 *and* b_9 *etc. Conversely,* b_7 *and* b_6 *are identically labelled but not symmetrical.*

In the next section, we show how to perform an efficient model checking using the Büchi automaton representation and the proposed symmetries.

5. Analysis of Model Checking using symmetries

Classically, model checking is realized by (1) considering the Büchi automaton, $A_{\neg f}$ of the negation of formula f to be verified; (2) building the synchronized product of this automaton and the one which models the behavior of the system; (3) searching in the synchronized product a sequence which has an accepting state repeated infinitely often in order to prove that the negation of the formula holds. The meaning of such algorithm is that one must verify that any behavior of the system validates the formula. This algorithm can work in an "on-the-fly" fashion [11] so as to avoid the construction of the whole graph of the strongly connected components.

5.1. Synchronized Product

The synchronized product of M and A_{-f} is noted $M \times A_{-f}$ and is defined as follows:

Definition 5.1.1: Synchronized Product
The synchronized product of $M=(S, \Delta, I, V, D, L, S_0)$ and $A_{-f}=(AP, B, \rho, B_0, E, F)$
is the automaton $M \times A_{-f}=(AP, \Theta, \Gamma, \Theta_0, \Phi)$ defined below:

- $\Theta = \{ (s,b) \mid s \in S \land b \in B \land (E(b) \subseteq prop(s)) \}$;
- $\Theta_0 = \{ (s,b) \in \Theta \mid s \in S_0 \land b \in B_0 \}$;
- $((s_i, b_i) \rightarrow (s_j, b_j)) \in \Gamma$ iff $(s_i \rightarrow s_j) \in \Delta \land (b_i \rightarrow b_j) \in \rho$.
- $\Phi = \{ (s,b) \in \Theta \mid s \in S \land b \in F \}$.

By means of such a product, a formula f holds through M, if and only if there is no path, in $M \times A_{-f}$, in which an accepting state is repeated infinitely often. Classically, the satisfaction of a formula is expressed as follows:

$$M \models \neg f \Leftrightarrow \exists p = (s_0, b_0) \ldots (s_l, b_l) \ldots (s_m, b_m) \ldots (s_n, b_n) \text{ in } M \times A_{-f} \text{ where } l \leq m < n$$

such that: (1) $b_m \in F$; (2) $(\forall i, j \in I, i \neq j, ((s_i, b_i) = (s_j, b_j) \Leftrightarrow \{i,j\} = \{l,n\}))$

5.2. Quotient Structure

In order to reduce the size of the synchronized product structure, we only consider canonical representatives of the symmetrical states instead of all the states.
Consequently, we build a graph of representatives with respect to a symmetry relation, $\mathcal{R}$ defined on $M \times A_{-f}$ as follows:

Definition 5.2.1: Symmetry Relation, $\mathcal{R}$ Defined on $M \times A_{-f}$
$\forall s, s' \in S, \forall b, b' \in V$ such that $s \models Atom(b)$ and $s' \models Atom(b')$,
$(s,b) \mathcal{R}(s', b')$ iff $\exists \pi \in Aut(M)$ such that $b \mathcal{R}_\pi b'$ and $\pi(s) = s'$.

Observe that $\mathcal{R}$ is an equivalence relation since it is defined on the group $Aut(M)$. Therefore, we can define the quotient structure of the synchronized product $M \times A_{-f}$ denoted $\overline{M \times A_{-f}} = (M \times A_{-f})/\mathcal{R}$ as follows:

Definition 5.2.2: The Quotient Structure $\overline{M \times A_{-f}}$
The quotient structure $\overline{M \times A_{-f}}$ is defined by means of the representatives of the state orbits of $M \times A_{-f}$. The orbit of $(s,b) \in \Theta$ is defined by the set:
$\theta(s,b) = \{ (s', b') \mid \exists \pi \in Aut(M), (\pi(s) = s') \land (b \mathcal{R}_\pi b') \text{ where, } s' \models Atom(b') \}$.
From each orbit $\theta(s,b)$, we pick an arbitrary representative denoted $(\overline{s,b})$.

The representative can be efficiently implemented by defining a canonical representation based on a lexicographical order [1].

5.3. Model Checking Correctness

In this section we validate our approach by showing that the model checking based on the proposed quotient synchronized product is equivalent to the one performed by means of the ordinary structure. Intuitively, we prove that the existence of an accepting state repeated infinitely often in the quotient structure is equivalent to the existence of an accepting state repeated infinitely often in the ordinary synchronized product. Hence, we can prove the satisfaction of temporal logic formulas by using our approach of symmetry.

We start our proof by the correspondence between both the quotient and the ordinary structures of the synchronized product.

Let $M \times A_{\neg f}$ represents the structure resulting from the synchronized product of the state transition graph and the automaton and let $\overline{M \times A_{\neg f}} = (M \times A_{\neg f})/\mathcal{R}$ be its quotient structure with respect to the relation $\mathcal{R}$ introduced in definition 5.2.1. For each symbolic path in the quotient structure there is an ordinary path in the synchronized product such that the corresponding states of the two paths are symmetrical with respect to $\mathcal{R}$:

Lemma: Correspondence Lemma

$$\exists (\overline{s_0, b_0}), \dots, (\overline{s_n, b_n}) \in \overline{M \times A_{\neg f}} \Leftrightarrow \exists (s'_0, b'_0), \dots, (s'_n, b'_n) \in M \times A_{\neg f} \text{ such that}$$

$$0 \leq \forall i \leq n, (s'_i, b'_i) \mathcal{R} (s_i, b_i)$$

Proof:

the $\Leftarrow$ direction is immediate from the definition of quotient structure.

For the $\Rightarrow$ direction, we proceed by induction on, n, the length of the path:

(i) $n=0$, This case is very simple since for any (s'_0, b'_0) such that $(s'_0, b'_0) \mathcal{R} (s_0, b_0)$, the lemma is proved.

(ii) We assume that the lemma is proved for a given length equal to n and we verify that it is proved for a length equal to $n+1$. Let us consider $(\overline{s_0, b_0}), \dots, (\overline{s_n, b_n})$ in $\overline{M \times A_{\neg f}}$, and let us recall that by assumption, we have $(s'_0, b'_0), \dots, (s'_n, b'_n)$ in $M \times A_{\neg f}$ such that $0 \leq \forall i \leq n, (s'_i, b'_i) \mathcal{R} (s_i, b_i)$. Let us consider an edge $(\overline{s_n, b_n}) \to (\overline{s_{n+1}, b_{n+1}})$ of $\overline{M \times A_{\neg f}}$, thus, $\exists (s''_n, b''_n) \to (s''_{n+1}, b''_{n+1})$ in $M \times A_{\neg f}$ such that $(s''_n, b''_n) \mathcal{R} (s_n, b_n)$ and $(s''_{n+1}, b''_{n+1}) \mathcal{R} (s_{n+1}, b_{n+1})$. We have already $(s'_n, b'_n) \mathcal{R} (s_n, b_n)$. So, $(s'_n, b'_n) \mathcal{R} (s''_n, b''_n)$ and from the definition of the relation $\mathcal{R}$: $\exists \pi, s'_n = \pi(s''_n)$ and $b'_n \mathcal{R}_\pi b''_n$. Hence, there is a state $s'_{n+1} = \pi(s''_{n+1})$ and an automaton state b'_{n+1} such that $b'_{n+1} \mathcal{R}_\pi b''_{n+1}$ where $s'_{n+1} = \pi(s''_{n+1}) \models \pi(Atom(b''_{n+1})) = Atom(b'_{n+1})$. Therefore, (s'_{n+1}, b'_{n+1}) is a state of $M \times A_{\neg f}$ and since, there is an arc $(s''_n, b''_n) \to (s''_{n+1}, b''_{n+1})$, the arc $(s'_n, b'_n) \to (s'_{n+1}, b_{n+1})$ is an arc of the same structure also.

From this lemma, we now prove the equivalence of the existence of paths verifying the formula, in both the quotient and the ordinary synchronized product:

Theorem: The two following statements are equivalent:

(i) There is a path $(\overline{s_0,b_0})\ldots(\overline{s_l,b_l})\ldots(\overline{s_m,b_m})\ldots(\overline{s_n,b_n})$ in $\overline{M\times A_{-f}}$ where $l\leq m<n$

such that: (1) $\overline{b_m}\in F$; (2) $\forall i\neq j, ((\overline{s_i,b_i})=(\overline{s_j,b_j}))\Leftrightarrow(\{i,j\}=\{l,n\})$.

(ii) There is a path $(s'_0,b'_0)\ldots(s'_l,b'_l)\ldots(s'_m,b'_m)\ldots(s'_n,b'_n)$ in $M\times A_{-f}$ where

$l\leq m<n$ such that: (1) $b_m\in F$; (2) $\forall i\neq j, ((s'_i,b'_i)=(s'_j,b'_j))\Leftrightarrow(\{i,j\}=\{l,n\})$.

Proof:

(1) (i) $\Rightarrow$ (ii): Let us consider $(\overline{s_0,b_0})\ldots(\overline{s_l,b_l})\ldots(\overline{s_m,b_m})\ldots(\overline{s_n,b_n})$ the shortest path

that verifies (i1) in $\overline{M\times A_{-f}}$. From the correspondence lemma there is a corre-

sponding path $(s'_0,b'_0),\ldots,(s'_l,b'_l),\ldots,(s'_m,b'_m),\ldots,(s'_n,b'_n)$ in $M\times A_{-f}$. We

prove that it verifies the following two statements:

(ii1) $b'_m\in F$, effectively, symmetries built on the automaton preserve accepting states;

(ii2) Two directions have to be proved. The $\Rightarrow$ direction is straightforward since

$(s'_i,b'_i)=(s'_j,b'_j)\Rightarrow((\overline{s_i,b_i})=(\overline{s_j,b_j}))$, consequently we deduce from (i2 that

$\{i,j\}=\{l,n\}$. For the $\Leftarrow$ direction, we have $\{i,j\}=\{l,n\}$, so from (i2),

$(\overline{s_i,b_i})=(\overline{s_j,b_j})$. By assumption, $\{i,j\}=\{l,n\}$, so, $(\overline{s_l,b_l})=(\overline{s_n,b_n})$ from (i2). The

proof is now made by contradiction assuming that $(s'_l,b'_l)\neq(s'_m,b'_m)$. In this

case, $(s'_l,b'_l)\,\mathcal{R}(s'_m,b'_m)$ since their representatives are equals. Consequently,

from the correspondence lemma, we have an infinite path in which there is an in-

finite number of subpaths of the form

$(s'_{n+k(n-l)},b'_{n+k(n-l)})\ldots(s'_{n+(k+1)(n-l)},b'_{n+(k+1)(n-l)})$ where $k=0,1,\ldots$ and

for $l\leq\forall i\leq n$, $(s'_{i+k(n-l)},b'_{i+k(n-l)})\,\mathcal{R}(s'_i,b'_i)$. Because we deal with finite state

transition graph, this infinite path must contain a circuit. Let us consider

$(s'_0,b'_0),\ldots,(s'_x,b'_x),\ldots,(s'_y,b'_y)$ the shortest path that meets twice the same

state where: $(s'_x,b'_x)=(s'_y,b'_y)$ and $x\geq l, y\geq n$. To simplify the proof we consid-

er $x<y$ and we denote $f(x)=x-k(n-l)$, $f(y)=y-k(n-l)$ such that $f(x),f(y)\in[l,n]$.

Since $((s'_x,b'_x)=(s'_y,b'_y))\Rightarrow((\overline{s_x,b_x})=(\overline{s_y,b_y}))\Rightarrow(\overline{s_{f(x)},b_{f(x)}})=(\overline{s_{f(y)},b_{f(y)}})$

we have two cases. In the first one: $f(x),f(y)$ are from $[l,m[$ or $]m,n]$. By considering

$(s'_0,b'_0),\ldots,(s'_l,b'_l),\ldots,(s'_{f(x)},b'_{f(x)}),(s'_{f(y)+1},b'_{f(y)+1}),\ldots,(s'_m,b'_m),(s'_n,b'_n)$

$(s'_0,b'_0),\ldots,(s'_l,b'_l),\ldots,(s'_m,b'_m),(s'_{f(x)},b'_{f(x)}),(s'_{f(y)+1},b'_{f(y)+1}),\ldots,(s'_n,b'_n)$

with respect to the position of $f(x)$, $f(y)$ in the domain, we have a shortest path than

$(s'_0,b'_0),\ldots,(s'_l,b'_l),\ldots,(s'_m,b'_m),(s'_n,b'_n)$ that verifies the two conditions

(ii1) and (ii2) which is opposite to the initial assumption. In the second case: $f(x)$

is from $[l,m[$ and $f(y)$ from $]m,n]$. By considering the following path that verify

(ii1) and (ii2), $(s'_0,b'_0),\ldots,(s'_{f(x)},b'_{f(x)}),\ldots,(s'_m,b'_m),\ldots,(s'_{f(y)},b'_{f(y)})$, we

have a shortest path than $(s'_0,b'_0),\ldots,(s'_l,b'_l),\ldots,(s'_m,b'_m),(s'_n,b'_n)$ which is

contradictory with the initial assumption. Consequently $(s'_l,b'_l)=(s'_m,b'_m)$.

(2) (ii) $\Rightarrow$ (i): Let us consider the set of paths:

$\Pi=\{(s_0,b_0)...(s_l,b_l)...(s_m,b_m)...(s_n,b_n)$ such that $(s_l,b_l)\ \mathcal{R}\ (s_m,b_m)$ and $b_m\in F\}$.

$\Pi\neq\varnothing$ from the assumption (i1). Let us consider $\pi=(s_0,b_0)...(s_n,b_n)$ one of the shortest path of Π. From the correspondence lemma, $\exists\overline{\pi} = (\overline{s'_0,b'_0})...(\overline{s'_n,b'_n})$ a representative path where $(s_i,b_i)R(s'_i,b'_i)$. Consequently, $\overline{\pi}$ verifies (i1) $(\overline{s'_l,b'_l}) = (\overline{s'_n,b'_n})$ and (i2) $b'_m\in F$. We have to prove that, $\forall\{i,j\}\neq\{l,n\}\Rightarrow(\overline{s'_i,b'_i})\neq(\overline{s'_j,b'_j})$. We suppose that $\exists\{i,j\}\neq\{l,n\},(\overline{s'_i,b'_i}) = (\overline{s'_j,b'_j})$, hence, either, $(s'_i,b'_i) = (s'_j,b'_j)$ which is impossible from (ii2), or, $(s'_i,b'_i)\,\mathcal{R}(s'_j,b'_j)$. Hence, three cases can appear. in the first one we have $(i<j\leq l)\vee(l\leq i<j<m)\vee(m<i<j<n)$: by considering the path $(s_0,b_0)...(s_i,b_i)(s_{j+1},b_{j+1})...(s_n,b_n)$ we have a shortest path than π belonging to Π which is opposite to the initial assumption. In the second case we have $i<l<j<m<n$: by considering $(s_0,b_0)...(s_i,b_i)(s_{j+1},b_{j+1})...(s_n,b_n)(s_{l+1},b_{l+1})...(s_j,b_j)$ we have a shortest path than π belonging to Π which is opposite to the initial assumption. In the last case we have $l<j<m<j<n$: by considering $(s_0,b_0)...(s_i,b_i)...(s_m,b_m)...(s_j,b_j)...(s_n,b_n)$ we have also a shortest path than π belonging to Π which is contradictory for the initial assumption. Consequently, $\forall\{i,j\}\neq\{l,n\}\Rightarrow(\overline{s'_i,b'_i})\neq(\overline{s'_j,b'_j})$.

5.4. Consistent Graph

The quotient structure is the smallest structure that can be built to perform model checking using symmetries. In the worst case, $\{\mathcal{R}_\pi\}_\pi$ requires an exponential time construction therefore, we propose a new approach based on the construction of an intermediate structure, called *consistent graph* which does not require the computation of all the relations induced by the symmetries.

In such a graph, (1) reachability is preserved with respect to the ordinary synchronized product; (2) the transition relation of the ordinary synchronized product is preserved accordingly to the symmetry relation $\mathcal{R}$ in the consistent graph; (3) the transition relation of the consistent graph product is preserved accordingly to the symmetry relation $\mathcal{R}$ in the ordinary synchronized. Hence, All paths are preserved with respect to $\mathcal{R}$.

Such a consistent graph will be used in section to propose an efficient model checking in polynomial time.

Definition 5.4.1: Consistent Graph

Let $G=M\times A_{-f}=(AP, \Theta, \tau, \Theta_0, \Phi)$ and let $G' = (AP',\Theta',\tau',\Theta'_0,\Phi')$ we call G' consistent with G iff:

(1) $\forall(s,b)\in\Theta$ such that (s,b) is reachable from $(s_0,b_0)\in\Theta_0$, $\exists(s',b')\in\Theta'$ reachable from $(s'_0,b'_0)\in\Theta'_0$ such that $(s',b')\,\mathcal{R}(s,b)$.

(2) $\forall(s,b)\in\Theta$ such that (s,b) is reachable from $(s_0,b_0)\in\Theta_0$, $\forall(s',b')\in\Theta'$ reachable from $(s'_0,b'_0)\in\Theta'_0$ such that $(s',b')\,\mathcal{R}(s,b)$:

if $(s,b) \to (s_1,b_1) \in \tau$ then $\exists (s'_1,b'_1) \in \Theta'$ where $(s'_1,b'_1) \mathcal{R}(s_1,b_1)$
such that $(s',b') \to (s'_1,b'_1) \in \tau'$.

(3) $\forall (s,b) \in \Theta$ such that (s,b) is reachable from $(s_0,b_0) \in \Theta_0$, $\forall (s',b') \in \Theta'$
reachable from $(s'_0,b'_0) \in \Theta'_0$ such that $(s',b') \mathcal{R}(s,b)$:

if $(s',b') \to (s'_1,b'_1) \in \tau'$ then $\exists (s_1,b_1) \in \Theta$ where $(s_1,b_1) \mathcal{R}(s'_1,b'_1)$
such that $(s,b) \to (s_1,b_1) \in \tau$.

The following lemma highlights the correspondence between the quotient structure $\overline{M \times A_{\neg f}}$ and the graph consistent with $M \times A_{\neg f}$.

Lemma: Consistent Graph Correspondence

$\exists (\overline{s_0, b_0}), \ldots, (\overline{s_n, b_n}) \in \overline{M \times A_{\neg f}} \Leftrightarrow \exists (s'_0, b'_0), \ldots, (s'_n, b'_n) \in G'$ consistent with $G = M \times A_{\neg f}$ such that $0 \le \forall i \le n,\, (s'_i, b'_i) \mathcal{R}(s_i, b_i)$.

Proof: It is similar to the one used for the correspondence lemma (section 5.3).

Hence, we can prove the model checking equivalence between the quotient structure and the graph consistent with the ordinary structure using correspondence lemma of the consistent graph.

Theorem: The two following statements are equivalent:

(i) There is a path $(\overline{s_0, b_0}) \ldots (\overline{s_l, b_l}) \ldots (\overline{s_m, b_m}) \ldots (\overline{s_n, b_n})$ in $G = \overline{M \times A_{\neg f}}$ where $l \le m < n$ such that:

(1) $\overline{b_m} \in F$; (2) $\forall i \ne j,\, ((\overline{s_i, b_i}) = (\overline{s_j, b_j})) \Leftrightarrow (\{i,j\} = \{l,n\})$.

(ii) There is a path $(s'_0, b'_0) \ldots (s'_l, b'_l) \ldots (s'_m, b'_m) \ldots (s'_n, b'_n)$ in G' consistent with $G = M \times A_{\neg f}$ where $l \le m < n$ such that:

(1) $b_m \in F$; (2) $\forall i \ne j,\, ((s'_i, b'_i) = (s'_j, b'_j)) \Leftrightarrow (\{i,j\} = \{l,n\})$.

Proof: This proof is similar to the one presented in the theorem of model checking equivalence (section 5.3) using the consistent graph correspondence lemma.

6. Operational Approach

The construction of a quotient structure is performed by checking, for each node built during the synchronized product, whether it is symmetrical with an already computed one. For this, an equivalence test has to be performed in an exponential time $O(n!)$ (in the worst case), where n is the number of processes. Clearly, this would damage the benefit to have a condensed structure.

The following section introduces an operational approach in order to reduce the complexity of the construction algorithms. Nevertheless, the resulting state transition graph may have a larger size than the quotient structure because we compute only a reduced subset of symmetries. However, it is a consistent structure with both the ordinary and the former quotient structure, thus the model checking can be performed equivalently. This section aims at presenting efficient algorithms to compute symmetries and to construct the consistent graph.

6.1. *ij-Symmetry* on Büchi automata

We now define a set of symmetries called the *ij-symmetries* in such a way that it represents a subset of $\mathcal{R}$.

6.1.1. *ij-Symmetry* Definition

Let $A=(AP, B, \rho, B_0, E, F)$. A relation $\mathcal{R}_{i,j}$ is a coarse relation that defines the equivalence of two states of a Büchi automaton with respect to two given processes. It fulfills the following definition:

$\forall b, b' \in B, b\mathcal{R}_{i,j} b'$ iff the following two conditions hold:

(1) $\forall b, b' \in B$, they satisfy an *ij-permutation*, $\pi_{i,j}$, such that:

$-b\in F \Leftrightarrow b' \in F$

$-Atom(b') = Atom(\pi_{i,j}(b)) =$

$\{ (v_g, d') | \forall (v_g, d) \in Atom(b), \exists (v_g, d') \in Atom(b') where (d'=d) \} \cup$

$\{ (v_i, j, d') | \forall (v_i, i, d) \in Atom(b), \exists (v_i, j, d') \in Atom(b') where (d'=d) \} \cup$

$\{ (v_i, j, d') | \forall (v_i, j, d) \in Atom(b), \exists (v_i, i, d') \in Atom(b') where (d'=d) \} \cup$

$\{ (v_i, k, d') | \forall (v_i, k, d) \in Atom(b), k \neq i, j, \exists (v_i, k, d') \in Atom(b') where (d'=d) \}$

(2) $\forall b_1 [b \rightarrow b_1], \exists b'_1 [b' \rightarrow b'_1] | (b_1 \mathcal{R}_{i,j} b'_1)$.

From this definition we define an inner symmetry, $\mathcal{R}_{in}$ with respect to I as follows:

$\forall i, j \in I, (b, i)\mathcal{R}_{in}(b', j) \Leftrightarrow b\mathcal{R}_{i,j} b'$ where $\mathcal{R}_{in} = \left(\underset{i,j}{\cup} \mathcal{R}_{i,j} \right)^*$. Hence, the inner symmetries presented by the relation $\mathcal{R}_{in}$ constitutes a subset of the set of symmetries presented by $\mathcal{R}$ such that: $b\mathcal{R}_{in}b' \Rightarrow b\mathcal{R}b'$. Based on $\mathcal{R}_{in}$ the next section proposes an efficient algorithm for the determination of the symmetries which are reflected in a Büchi automaton.

6.1.2. *ij-Symmetry* Computation Algorithms

The computation of the inner symmetry starts from the computation of the *ij-symmetry* presented in the definition 6.1.2.

Let f be a temporal specification formula and let A_{-f} be the representation of its negation in terms of Büchi automaton.

Firstly, we calculate, for a pair (i,j) of process indices, an initial partition of the states of A_{-f} using the definition 6.1.2 of *ij-permutation*. This results in a set of state pairs that verify the *ij-permutation*.

Secondly, we restrain the computed *ij-permutations* to $\mathcal{R}_{i,j}$ symmetry by checking the preservation of the transition relation (using the definition 6.1.2). For each state, we save the set of $\mathcal{R}_{i,j}$ symmetries.

This algorithm is repeated for each pair i,j of process indices.

Let $B=\{b_1 ... b_m\}$ be the states of A_{-f} where $|B|=m$ is the number of states. Let I be the set of process indices such that $|I|=n$. We construct a set of boolean matrices that represent the symmetry relation between the states of B. We note Mat_{ij} the matrix representing the symmetry $\mathcal{R}_{i,j}$ where $Mat_{ij}[b_d, b_k]$ is *true* if b_d, b_k are symmetric. We note Mat the set of all the matrices Mat_{ij}.

In the following, we present the function R_{ij} which compute the *ij-symmetry* in the automaton. This function calls two functions: the first one *ij-permut*(b_1,b_2) which checks the *ij-permutation* for two given states b_1 and b_2. The second one $R_{ij}(b_1,b_2)$ which checks if the two states, b_1, b_2, are *ij-symmetric*. Note that The function $Succ(b)$ computes all the successors of a given state b.

It must be noted that the complexity of the following algorithm is $O(m^5)$ for a given i,j.

Hence, The determination of all the *ij-symmetry* have a complexity of $O(n^2 \times m^5)$ which means a polynomial complexity. Furthermore, the computation of $\mathcal{R}_{in} = \left(\underset{i,j}{\cup} \mathcal{R}_{i,j} \right)^*$ can be restricted to have, also, a polynomial complexity.

Algorithm 1: $R_{ij}()$
Output : A boolean value indicates if the two states are ij -symmetric.
BEGIN
    FOR each b_d from V DO
        FOR each b_k from V DO
            $Mat_{ij}[b_d, b_k]$ = ij-permut(b_d,b_k);
    FOR each b_d from V DO
        FOR each b_k from V DO
            $Mat_{ij}[b_d, b_k]$ = $R_{ij}(b_d, b_k)$;
END;

Algorithm 2: $R_{ij}(b_d, b_k)$
Output : A boolean value indicates if the two states are ij-symmetric.
BEGIN
    Loop = TRUE;
    WHILE Loop DO
    BEGIN
        IF $Mat_{ij}[b_d, b_k]$ THEN
            FOR [each b_d' in Succ(b_d)] AND [each b_k' in Succ(b_k)] DO
                $R_{ij}(b_d', b_k')$;
      ELSE
            Loop = FALSE;
    END;
END. / Algorithm */*

6.2. Construction of the Consistent Graph

We compute the symmetries on the synchronized product in order to build the consistent graph. Such symmetries are symmetries of the model and must be an inner symmetries with respect to the considered Büchi automaton.

Let A_{-f} be a Büchi automaton and let M be the structure of the state transition graph. We define the symmetry on the product $M \times A_{-f}$ as follows:

Definition 6.2.1: Symmetry $\mathcal{R}$ **defined on** $M \times A_{-f}$

$\forall s, s' \in S, \forall b, b' \in B$ such that: $s \models Atom(b)$ and $s' \models Atom(b')$,
$(s, b) \mathcal{R} (s', b') \Leftrightarrow \exists \pi \in Aut(M), \mathcal{R}_\pi \in \mathcal{R}_{in}, b\mathcal{R}_\pi b' \wedge \pi(s) = s'$.

The relation, $\mathcal{R}$, is used to build a reduced graph $G' = (AP', \Theta', \tau', \Theta'_0, \Phi')$ consistent with $M \times A_{-f} = (AP, \Theta, \tau, \Theta_0, \Phi)$. Next we present the corresponding algorithm.

Algorithm 3: Consistent Graph Constructor
BEGIN
    / Symmetry Computation */*
    FOR each i,j from I DO
        Rij();
    Polynomial computation of $\mathcal{R}_{in}$;
    FOR each equivalence class of $\mathcal{R}_{in}$ of A_{-f} states DO

        Choose a representative $\hat{b}$;

    / Consistent Graph Construction: */*
    FOR each (s_0, b_0) from Θ_0 such that $s_0 \models \hat{b}_0$ DO
        - Compute the symbolic representative $Rep(s_0, \hat{b}_0)$ using the $\{\mathcal{R}_{i,j}\}_{i,j}$
        symmetries verified for $\hat{b}_0$ (i.e. $\{Mat_{i,j}[\hat{b}_0, \hat{b}_0] = TRUE\}_{i,j}$);
        - $\Theta' = \Theta' \cup Rep(s_0, \hat{b}_0)$;
        - $Push(Rep(s_0, \hat{b}_0))$;
    END; / FOR */*

    WHILE Stack is not empty DO BEGIN
        rs = Pop();
        FOR each arc $(rs \rightarrow (s, b)) \in \rho$ DO BEGIN
            - Compute Rep(s,b);
            - IF Rep(s,b) is not in Θ' THEN
            BEGIN
                - $\Theta' = \Theta' \cup Rep(s,b)$;
                - $Push(Rep(s,b))$;
            END; / IF */*
            - $\rho' = \rho' \cup (rs \rightarrow Rep(s,b))$;
        END; / FOR */*
    END; / WHILE */*
END. / ALGORITHM */*

The complexity of our model checking using symmetries is strongly dependent on the complexity of the former algorithm. Therefore we can deduce its polynomial complexity.

7. Conclusion and Perspectives

We have described two frameworks for performing efficient LTL model checking. Both of them exploits the existence of symmetries reflected in the system and in the specification formula to be checked. With the first one, we show how to build the most aggregated structure by using the largest available symmetry relation. Such technique could be computed using algorithms which, in the worst case, would have an exponential complexity. The second framework computes a subset of symmetries with polynomial complexity algorithms inducing a less condensed structure.

In comparison, the method proposed in [6,7] can be considered as a restrictive case requiring the definition of a symmetry group.

Using the symmetry approach, two cases appear as the two extreme limits: the best one where the structural symmetries of the system are entirely used, causing a maximal aggregation of states and the worst case in which any set of symmetrical objects is reduced to a singleton, leading the reduced structure to be as large as the ordinary one.

We now aim at extending our methods to deal with specifications having nothing but partial symmetries [12]. In such specifications, runs sometimes depend on the process identities (i.e. static priorities based on identities), and sometimes not.

The implementation of this work is performed under GreatSPN2.0 developed by Chiola & Gaëta from the university of Torino-Italy. It will be integrated into the CPN-AMI tool developed by the group of distributed and cooperative systems of LIP6.

8. References

[1] G. Chiola, C. Dutheillet, G. Franceschinis, S. Haddad, "On Well-formed Colored Nets and their Symbolic Reachability Graph", proc. of 11th International Conference on Application and Theory of Petri Nets, Paris-France, June 1990.

[2] E. Clarke, T. Filkorne, S. Jha, "Exploiting Symmetry In Temporal Logic Model Checking", 5th Computer Aided Verification (CAV), June 1993.

[3] E. Clarke,O. Grumberg, D. Long,"Verification Tools for Finit-State Concurrent Systems", "A Decade of Concurrency-Reflections and Perspectives", LNCS vol 803, 1994.

[4] C. Courcoubetis, M. Vardi, P.Wolper, M. Yannakakis, "Memory Efficient Algorithms for the Verification of Temporal Properties", In proceedings of CAV'90, North Holland, DIMACS 30. 1990.

[5] M. Dam. "Fixed points of Büchi automata", In R. Shymanasundar, editor, Foundations of Software Technology and theoretical Computer Science, volume 652 of LNCS, pages 39-50, Springer-Verlag, 1992.

[6] E.A. Emerson, A. Prasad Sistla, "Symmetry and Model Checking", In Formal Methods and System Design 9, pp 105-131, 1996.

[7] E.A. Emerson, A. Prasad Sistla, "Symmetry and Model Checking", 5th conference on Computer Aided Verification (CAV), June 1993.

[8] E.A. Emerson, A. Parsad Sistla, "Utilizing Symmetry when Model Checking under Fairness Assumptions: An Automata-theoric Approach", 7th CAV, LNCS 939, pp. 309-324, Liège, Belgium, July 1995.

[9] E.A. Emerson, "Temporal and Modal Logic", HandBook of Theoretical Computer Science, Volume B, J. van Leeuwen (eds), 1990.

[10] E.A. Emerson and Chin-Laung Lei, "Modalities for Model Checking: Branching Time Stricks Back", In Proc of 12h Annual Symposium on Principles of Programming Languages, New-Orleans, Louisiana, January 1985.

[11] R. Gerth, D. Peled, M. Vardi, P. Wolper, "Simple On-the-fly Automatic Verification of linear Temporal Logic", Protocol Specification Testing and Verification, 1995, Warsaw, Poland.

[12] S. Haddad, JM. Ilié, B. Zouari, M. Taghelit, "Symbolic Reachability Graph and Partial Symmetries", In Proc. of the 16th ICATPN, Torino, Italy, June 1995.

[13] J-M. Ilié, K. Ajami, "Model Checking through the Symbolic Reachability Graph", in Proc of TapSoft'97 - CAAP, pp 213-224, Lille, France, Springer-Verlag, LNCS 1214, Avril 1997.

[14] K. Jensen, G. Rozenberg (eds), "High Level Petri Nets, Theory and Application", Springer-Verlag, 1991.

[15] Z. Manna, A. Pnueli. "The Temporal Logic of Reactive and Concurrent Systems: Specification", Springer-Verlag, 1992.

[16] F. Michel, P. Azéma, F. Vernadat. "Permutable Agents and Process Algebra", In Proc. of TACAS'96, Passau, Germany, 1996, Springer-Verlag, LNCS 1055.

[17] C. Norris IP and D. Dill, "Better Verification Through Symmetry", In Formal Methods in System Design, Vol 9, August 96, pp 41-76.

[18] D. Park,"Concurrency and Automata on Infinite Sequences", LNCS vol 114, 1984.

[19] K. Schmidt, "Symmetry Calculation", Workshop CSP Warschau 1995.

[20] M.Y. Vardi, "Alternating Automata and Program Verification", Computer Science Today: Recent Trends and Developments.LNCS,Vol.1000, Springer-Verlag 1995.

[21] M. Y. Vardi, "An Automata-theoretic approach to linear temporal logic (banff'94), LNCS, 1043, 1996.

OPEN/CÆSAR: An Open Software Architecture for Verification, Simulation, and Testing

Hubert Garavel

INRIA Rhône-Alpes and DYADE / VASY group
655, avenue de l'Europe
38330 Montbonnot St Martin
France
Tel: +(33) 4 76 61 52 24   Fax: +(33) 4 76 61 52 52
E-mail: hubert.garavel@inria.fr
Web: http://www.inrialpes.fr/vasy

Abstract. This paper presents the OPEN/CÆSAR software architecture, which allows to integrate in a common framework different languages/formalisms for the description of concurrent systems, as well as tools with various functionalities, such as random execution, interactive simulation, on-the-fly and exhaustive verification, test generation, etc.. These principles have been fully implemented, leading to an open, extensible, and well-documented programming environment, which allows tools to be developed in a modular framework, independently from any particular description language.

Introduction

Research in the area of tools and algorithms for the construction and analysis of systems has been and remains particularly active. Despite this intense activity, end-users involved in actual system design do not always receive as much computer-aided assistance as they could expect. Among the many tools developed, only a few are robust enough to be applied to real-life problems. Moreover, in many cases, end-users cannot benefit from all these tools, because they are using a different language than the one supported by the tools.

It seems therefore that a significant part of the effort spent in developing tools is wasted, and that the global productivity of the research community in formal methods and verification could be increased through a better coordination.

A large part of these problems could probably be solved if the whole community and industry adopted a unique language for the specification and design of protocols and concurrent systems. However, this is not the case: even the standardization efforts undertaken within ISO and ITU-T led to three different standards (ESTELLE, LOTOS, and SDL), in addition to the many other formalisms that already exist: CCS, CSP, μCRL, PROMELA, etc. It seems therefore clear that different specification languages will continue to exist (as it is already the case for sequential programming languages); even if the Darwinian selection process exists, it is unlikely that one single language will emerge and remain.

Taking as a fact the coexistence of multiple languages, this paper attempts to lower the corresponding economic cost. It describes a generic architecture allowing the development of tools (e.g., simulation, verification, test generation tools, etc.) that can be applied to programs written in different languages (e.g., LOTOS, SDL, etc.). These ideas have been entirely implemented in a tool environment named OPEN/CÆSAR, which has been used for realistic case-studies [4, 7, 11, 19, 21, 22], some of them in an industrial context.

The work on OPEN/CÆSAR was initiated in 1992 as a follow-up to the design of the CÆSAR compiler [12], a model-checking tool for translating LOTOS programs into Labelled Transition Systems (LTSs or *graphs*, for short), a semantic model on which verification can been performed using behavioural equivalences and/or temporal logic formulas. Because the only functionality provided by CÆSAR was graph generation, and due to state explosion, its applicability was restricted to small-size systems.

The initial goal of the OPEN/CÆSAR project was to extend CÆSAR with additional functionalities (including random execution, interactive simulation, and partial, on-the-fly verification) needed to deal with larger systems. It is worth noticing that this goal was a radical departure from previous approaches, consisting either in:

- Providing an environment dedicated to a given language, by juxtaposition of separate tools, each tool providing a distinct functionality: graphical or syntax-driven editor, code generator, interactive simulator, debugger, on-the-fly property checker, test generator, etc. A certain degree of unification between these tools was often achieved by sharing a compiler front-end, using a common format for abstract syntax trees, and exchanging information via defined interfaces (e.g., files). However, the semantical processing parts remained duplicated between the different tools, possibly limiting interoperability, as each tool could have its own restrictions (accepting only a particular subset of the source language) or give a different interpretation of the source language semantics.

  On the contrary, the OPEN/CÆSAR project targeted at the greatest possible integration between the different functionalities by sharing, not only the compiler front-end, but also all semantic processings, the choice between simulation, verification, etc. being deferred as much as possible.

- Adapting an existing code generator or simulator in order to perform verification. In most cases, this approach faced architectural or performance issues: experience proved that it was very difficult to turn a simulation tool into an efficient verification tool, unless the simulator had been intentionally designed for this purpose from the beginning.

  On the contrary, the OPEN/CÆSAR project had to adapt the model-checking verification capabilities of CÆSAR to simulation and code generation. Not so surprisingly, we found out that going this direction was much easier than going the opposite way, exactly like turning a multi-user operating system into a single-user operating system is much easier than the opposite.

After completion of its initial goals, the aims of the OPEN/CÆSAR project were reviewed and extended toward a new target: the architecture was modified so that other languages/formalisms than LOTOS could be integrated into OPEN/CÆSAR.

This paper describes the technical solutions and achievements of the OPEN/CÆSAR project. It is organized as follows: Section 1 presents the principles of the OPEN/CÆSAR architecture, which is based upon a functional decomposition in three modules: the *graph module*, the *library module*, and the *exploration module*. These modules are described in Sections 2, 3, and 4 respectively. Finally, the conclusion summarizes the benefits of the OPEN/CÆSAR approach and discusses its limitations, leaving room for future research.

1   Architecture

The design of the OPEN/CÆSAR architecture takes its roots in the development of CÆSAR [12], the first model-checking tool for full LOTOS. It was also made possible by the author's prior experience in designing the architecture of VESAR [1], a protocol engineering tool for the ESTELLE language, probably the first commercial tool to integrate simulation, on-the-fly analysis and model-checking capabilities. OPEN/CÆSAR also benefited from ideas implemented in other verification tools, especially XESAR [13] and SPIN [14].

Although these tools support different source languages (LOTOS, ESTELLE, and PROMELA), they offer similar functionalities, among which verification by reachability analysis. The basic idea of the OPEN/CÆSAR architecture was to identify the common functionalities shared by these tools and to organize them into three distinct modules. The OPEN/CÆSAR architecture improves previous tools by enforcing a clear separation between these modules using well-defined APIs (Application Programming Interfaces). The OPEN/CÆSAR architecture is depicted on Figure 1.

The graph module is responsible for encapsulating and hiding all language-dependent aspects. From the outside of this module, the source program can be seen only as an LTS, whatever the source language used. The graph module exports a representation for the states and the labels of the transition system, as well as primitives to handle states and labels. It also provides primitives to compute the transition relation (i.e., the initial state and the successors of a given state). These features are accessed through an API named "caesar_graph.h", which does not depend on any particular source program, nor any particular language.

The mapping between a given source program and this interface is achieved using an OPEN/CÆSAR-*compliant compiler*, which translates the source program into a C program implementing this interface. This C program is compiled separately and linked with the other OPEN/CÆSAR modules. In this approach, the

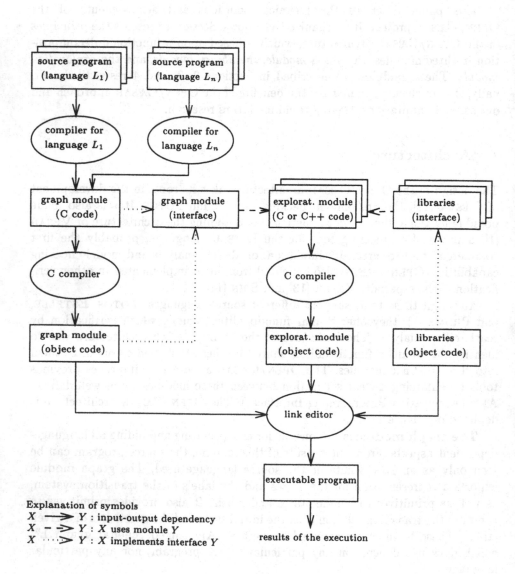

Fig. 1. OPEN/CÆSAR architecture

C language was chosen because efficient compilers for this language are available (C plays the role of a portable assembly language).

A list of available OPEN/CÆSAR-compliant compilers is given in Section 2. The functioning principles and internal details of these compilers are not constrained by the OPEN/CÆSAR architecture, provided that implement the "caesar_graph.h" interface properly.

The library module consists in a set of libraries. Each library provides a coherent set of data structures and associated primitives for handling transition lists, storing visited states during graph traversals (e.g., stacks, tables, bitmap tables), computing hash functions, displaying diagnostics, etc. These libraries are independent from any source program and source language. The available libraries (written in C and pre-compiled) are presented in Section 3, but users can add new libraries to fit their specific needs.

The exploration module can be considered as the "main" program. It contains the core of the verification, simulation, or testing algorithm, and determines how the LTS is to be explored. In most cases, the exploration module is independent from any source program and source language (however, dedicated exploration modules are possible, for instance, to verify a specific property). The exploration module uses the primitives exported by the graph and library modules. It is usually written in C or C++. It can be distributed either in source code form, or in object code form if its algorithms must be kept private. The available exploration modules are listed in Section 4.

Figure 1 illustrates the compiling and linking steps needed to merge the different code fragments (user-written code, library code, and automatically generated code) into a single executable program. Of course, some programming conventions have to be enforced in order to avoid identifier clashes between the different modules. Also, shell-scripts are available for chaining all these steps in a simple, user-friendly way and avoiding unnecessary recompilations.

2   The graph module

As said above, the graph module encapsulates all language-dependent aspects and gives access to them through a language-independent interface. Therefore, the design of such an interface is subject to antagonistic constraints:

- It should be general and abstract enough to accommodate a variety of source languages. This implies not to retain all the particular features of a given language, but to select characteristics shared by several languages. Therefore, the design of the interface relies on the existence of a common semantic model into which different source programs, written in different source languages, can be translated.
- The interface should keep track of the relationship between the semantic model and the corresponding source program, so as to provide enough information for diagnosis: when an error is detected using simulation or verification, the user should be able to understand the reason of the error in terms

of the source program. This is not always easy to implement, especially if the compiler uses sophisticated translation algorithms, involving intermediate forms and optimization techniques.

- As verification algorithms have strong efficiency requirements, the interface should be close enough to existing compilers in order not to introduce unacceptable run-time overhead.

Since 1992, the OPEN/CÆSAR graph module interface has undergone successive revisions to match these constraints. The latest version (September 1996) can be seen as a good compromise between conflicting requirements. We briefly present the main design choices:

- The interface is based upon *interleaving semantics* (which reduces concurrency to sequential composition and non-deterministic choice). Its underlying semantic model is a combination of Labelled Transition Systems and Kripke structures, which was found to be appropriate for various languages and formalisms. This model consists in a set of *states* (with an *initial state*) and a set of *transitions* between states. Depending on the source language considered, there can be additional information attached to each state (these attributes are called *state vectors*) and/or to each transition (these attributes are called *labels*).
- The interface follows the principles of abstract data type specification. It exports two "opaque" types, the *state type* and the *label type*, whose internal representations are left undefined (i.e., up to the compiler) and which can be handled using a set of primitives. There are 13 functions dealing with states and 18 functions dealing with labels.
- As regards states, OPEN/CÆSAR makes the assumption that, for a given system, state vectors can be stored in a fixed-length byte string. This restriction is meant for handling states efficiently [12], for instance when storing them in tables. However, it can be relaxed as the state vector can contain pointers to dynamic data structures (lists, FIFO queues, etc.) allocated in the heap. The functions exported by the interface allow to obtain the size and the alignment (in bytes) of a state, to create and delete a memory cell to store a state, to copy a state to another one, to compare two states, to compute a hash-value on a state, to print a state to a text file, to print the "differences" between two states, etc.

By doing so, the interface provides a somehow "restricted" access to state vectors by converting them to character strings, which can be obtained when printing a state to a file or printing the differences between two states. This approach is justified by the fact that state vectors are highly language- and compiler-dependent (in particular, they often rely upon user-defined types in the source program, for which character strings provide the simplest portable interface).

Notice that, in the case where state vectors contain pointers or, more generally, if their binary representation is not a normal form, some primitives (e.g., comparison and hashing) cannot be simply implemented as bitwise operations between two memory cells. These problems are addressed in the OPEN/CÆSAR architecture.

- Similarly, labels are assumed to be fixed-length byte strings (possibly containing pointers to the heap) and functions are available for obtaining the size and the alignment (in bytes) of a label, for creating and deleting a memory cell to store a label, for copying a label to another one, for comparing two labels, for computing a hash-value on a label, etc.
  State vector restrictions also apply to labels: although label contents depend on the source language, the source program and the compiler, they can be accessed using conversion to character strings. Additional functions are available to decide whether a label is visible or not[1], in how many fields a label is subdivided, from which line of source program a label comes from, etc.

- As regards the transition relation, which is the crucial point of the graph module, OPEN/CÆSAR makes minimal requirements intentionally, in order to give maximal freedom to compiler implementors. Compilers are only required to generate C code for computing the initial state and for enumerating the successors of a given state. For the latter purpose, there are many possible approaches, many of which do not match efficiency or language-independence criteria. The OPEN/CÆSAR interface solves this problem elegantly, by introducing the concept of *callback mechanism*.
  When generating the graph module, an OPEN/CÆSAR-compliant compiler has to produce a *successor enumeration function* $\mathcal{F}$, which iterates over all the successors of a given state S_1. For each transition $S_1 \xrightarrow{L} S_2$, where L is a label and S_2 a successor state, the successor enumeration function $\mathcal{F}$ will make a function call of the form $F(S_1, L, S_2)$, where function F is passed as a parameter to $\mathcal{F}$ and is referred to as the *callback function*. Function F can perform any action, e.g., printing the transition $S_1 \xrightarrow{L} S_2$ to a file, storing S_2 in a state table, etc. It can be either defined by the user in the exploration module, or imported from the library module, which provides several predefined callback functions of general interest. The enumeration of transitions going out of state S_1 is sequential: no direct access to the ith successor is required. The order in which function $\mathcal{F}$ enumerates the successors is left to the compiler. Function F can do side-effects, but it should not invoke function $\mathcal{F}$ recursively (therefore, the iteration mechanism needs not be reentrant). On top of this primitive (but general and efficient) callback mechanism, more elaborated facilities can be developed (see the EDGE library in Section 3).

At the time being, there exist 5 different implementations of OPEN/CÆSAR-compliant compilers, which we briefly review:

1. After designing the OPEN/CÆSAR architecture, the author adapted the CÆSAR compiler [12] accordingly. The core of CÆSAR's compiling algorithms (based upon the translation of LOTOS to an intermediate extended Petri net

---

[1] i.e., the concept of τ-transitions in process algebras

model) was kept unchanged; only the back-end of CÆSAR was modified for compliance with the "caesar_graph.h" interface. In this implementation, each state is a pair $\langle M, C \rangle$ where M is a marking of the Petri net, and C is a context mapping state variables to their values; each transition is generated by the firing of a corresponding transition in the Petri net; each label consists of a gate name followed by a list of exchanged values. The algebraic data types contained in the source LOTOS program can be either translated in C code by the CÆSAR.ADT compiler or implemented manually by the user; in both cases, data structures dynamically allocated in the heap are supported.

2. In 1994, Renaud Ruffiot and the author connected the BCG format for the representation of Labelled Transition Systems [10] to the OPEN/CÆSAR environment. The resulting BCG_OPEN tool enabled the application of all OPEN/CÆSAR tools (see Section 4) to graphs entirely generated and represented in the BCG format. In this implementation (700 lines of C code), each OPEN/CÆSAR state (*resp.* label, transition) is directly mapped to the corresponding BCG state (*resp.* label, transition). The development of BCG_OPEN led to a modification of the "caesar_graph.h" in order to remove some LOTOS-specific aspects.

3. In 1995, Marius Bozga, Jean-Claude Fernandez and Laurent Mounier (VERIMAG, France) developed the EXP.OPEN compiler, which allows to use OPEN/CÆSAR for the compositional verification of networks of communicating automata. The input language accepted by EXP.OPEN consists in a set of automata (entirely generated) connected together using the parallel composition and hiding operators of LOTOS. In their implementation (3,000 lines of C code, including a LEX scanner and a YACC parser), each OPEN/CÆSAR state is a tuple of the individual states of the automata, and transitions are obtained by applying the LOTOS semantics rules for parallel composition and hiding.

4. In 1997, Khalid Laksiouar and Amar Bouali (INRIA Sophia-Antipolis, France) developed the FC2OPEN compiler to connect the FC2 toolset [3] to OPEN/CÆSAR. FC2OPEN takes as input FC2 models, which are either automata or networks of communicating automata connected together by means of so-called *synchronization vectors*. In their implementation (3,000 lines of C++ code), each OPEN/CÆSAR state is either an automaton state or a tuple of local states, and transitions are determined according to the semantics of synchronization vectors.

5. In 1997, Alain Kerbrat, Carlos Rodriguez, and Yves Lejeune (VERIMAG/VERILOG, France) connected VERILOG's OBJECTGEODE tool [2] for SDL to the CÆSAR/ALDÉBARAN toolbox. One aspect of this connection was the developement of a gateway between OBJECTGEODE and OPEN/CÆSAR [17].

3 The library module

OPEN/CÆSAR provides a library of useful, generic facilities. We give an overview of them:

- The EDGE library is built on top of the graph module. It extends the callback mechanism described in Section 2 with higher-level functionalities:

  - The callback mechanism enumerates sequentially the successors of a given state S_1, but does not store them in memory. Moreover, as the callback mechanism is not supposed to be reentrant, it does not allow depth-first traversals algorithms to be programmed recursively. The EDGE library solves this problem by building transition lists, which can be used for programming depth-first traversals. Transition lists are linked lists of tuples $\langle S_1, L, S_2, M \rangle$, where L is a label, S_2 a successor state and M a byte-string in which users can put any information they want. All fields S_1, L, S_2, and M are optional and can be omitted if not relevant to the exploration algorithm under consideration.

  - The order in which the callback mechanism enumerates the successors is left unspecified, but the EDGE library can sort transition lists according to various criteria (e.g., lexicographic order over the L fields). This can be useful, for instance, in an interactive simulator, for displaying to the user an alphabetically-sorted list of transitions.

  - The EDGE library also exports many primitives to create, delete, copy, print, and reverse transition lists; to compute the length and access directly the ith element of transition lists; to access the different tuple fields S_1, L, S_2, and M of a given element. It also provides iterators over transition lists and automatically truncates the transition lists if the available memory is unsufficient to store all successors of a given state.

- The HASH library provides various predefined hash-functions which can be applied to states and labels considered as byte strings. These functions are needed for accessing hash-tables and for Holzmann's algorithm [14]. OPEN/CÆSAR users can add their own hash-functions: see for instance [6], where OPEN/CÆSAR is used for a comparative analysis of various hashing techniques.

- The STACK_1 library is built on top of the EDGE library and provides primitives for managing one or several stacks[2]. Depth-first search algorithms rely on stacks to store the execution path taken from the initial state. These stacks are not merely stacks of states: it is also necessary to store the transitions between states for characterizing an execution path entirely. Also, depth-first search algorithms require to store the list of states remaining to be explored at each stack depth. Therefore, each element in a stack consists of three fields: a *state field* S, a *label field* containing the label of the last transition performed before reaching state S (or a null pointer if S is the initial state), and an *edge field* containing the list of transitions going out of state S that have not been explored yet. For a given stack, the label and edge fields are

---

[2] The number "1" occurring at the end of the name STACK_1 denotes the fact that this library is a particular implementation of the stack, and that alternative implementation could be offered in future versions of OPEN/CÆSAR; this is also the case for the other data structures presented below.

optional: if none of them are present, the stack behaves as a simple stack of states.

The STACK_1 library provides a set of classical primitives for dealing with stacks. These primitives allow to create, delete, copy, and print stacks; to erase the contents of a stack; to check whether a stack is empty; to compute the depth of a stack; to access the fields of the element on top of a stack; to push or pop an element on top of a stack; etc.

There are also specific primitives for depth-first search. They allow to deal with the list of successors of the state on top of the stack and, more specifically to create or delete this list; to check whether it is empty; to compute its length; to remove its first element; to extract its first element and to push it on top of the stack; etc.

The STACK_1 library provides additional features suitable for on-the-fly verification. For instance, when creating a stack, one can specify a maximal depth not to be exceeded, as well as the action to be taken if this maximal depth is reached or when the stack overflows because of a memory shortage (e.g., stopping the exploration, backtracking to the previous state, etc.).

- The TABLE_1 library for managing one or several *state tables*, i.e., tables for storing the states of a program which are visited during a graph traversal. Each element in a given table is a byte string, subdivided into two fields, the *"base"* field and the *"mark"* field. The sizes of these fields is specified when the table is created and it is the same for all the elements in the table. More often than not, base fields contain states of the graph being explored (these states are those produced by the graph module). However, the base fields can be used to store other data. The contents of mark fields (possibly empty) are determined by the user. During graph traversals, mark fields are generally used to store additional attributes attached to states (i.e., base fields). To allow fast access, each table is equipped with an auxiliary hash table that allows to retrieve an element having a given base field.

The primitives offered by the TABLE_1 library allow to create and delete tables; to erase their contents and to print it under various formats; to access the base and mark fields of an element given its index; to put or get an element; to search an element given its base field, optionally inserting it in the table if not already present; to determine if a table is empty or full; etc.

- The BITMAP library provides primitives for managing one or several *bitmap tables* (i.e., large bit arrays) such as those used in Holzmann's bit-space algorithm [14]. In addition to the basic test-and-set primitives, it provides convenient features, such as automatical dimensioning of the table size to the greatest prime number less than the requested size, dump of the bitmap table to a text file under various formats, usage statistics recording and display, etc.

- The DIAGNOSTIC_1 is built on top of the STACK_1 library and provides primitives for dealing with diagnostic sequences (e.g., execution sequences leading to deadlock states). It allows to specify which diagnostic sequences will be displayed to the user and to control the exploration algorithm according to various strategies (for instance, to find the shortest possible diagnostic sequence).

4 The exploration module

On top of the graph and library modules, the exploration module plays the role of the main program: it determines how and why the graph will be explored. There are many different possibilities for exploring a graph G. In an attempt to establish a taxonomy, we list below the essential parameters ("degrees of freedom") that can be tuned by the exploration module:

Definition of states and transitions: it is often the definition exported by the graph module; however, in some cases, this definition has to be modified. For instance, when evaluating temporal logic or μ-calculus formulas on G, or when checking behavioural equivalences (e.g., bisimulation equivalences, preorders, trace inclusion, etc.) between G and some other graph, one often uses "*product states*" of the form (S, S'), where S is a state of G and S' a state of another graph (or observer, or Büchi automaton, or linear trace, etc.) noted G'; the transition relation must also be extended to reflect concurrency and synchronization constraints between G and G'.

Selection of successor states: when at a given state S of G, the exploration program must decide how many successors of S (if any), and which, should be visited. There are several possible answers: *none of them* (i.e., backtracking if some boolean condition is false or if the available memory is exhausted); *one of them* (e.g., chosen randomly in the case of random execution, or by prompting the user in the case of interactive simulation); *all of them* (in the case of reachability analysis); *some of them*, according to various heuristics related to the level of coverage expected. If several successors of S are selected, the order in which they should be enumerated must also be specified.

Storage policy: the exploration program must also decide how many states, and which, should be stored in memory. There are many choices: *only the current state* (e.g., in random execution), *only the states on the path leading from the initial state to the current state* (e.g., in interactive simulation allowing unbounded backtracking facilities), *all the states* (e.g., when constructing the entire graph to perform model-checking at a later stage), *all the states up to a maximal number*, etc.

There are even more sophisticated strategies [16] allowing to discard states stored in memory when some upper limit on the number of states is reached, or when no more memory is available, with again a choice between various replacement policies inspired from garbage collecting (e.g., discarding first the most recent states, the oldest ones, etc.).

Instead of storing states under the exact representation exported by the graph module, it is also possible to store only a "condensed" form of them by using some compression function mapping states to a smaller bit string (typical examples of such functions are hash-functions and cryptographic message digest functions). The classical approach is known as "bitstate hashing" [14], but more elaborate variants exist [15]. Of course, as the compression function is not injective, the exploration algorithm must take into account the fact that two different states may have the same condensed form. Again, the choice of the compression function is left open.

Traversal algorithm: the exploration module has also to decide which type of algorithm should be used (depth-first search, breadth-first search, etc.), as well as many other parameters (for instance, having a maximal exploration depth).

Many exploration modules have been developed within the OPEN/CÆSAR framework[3]; most of them are distributed within the CADP toolbox. We review them briefly:

- DECLARATOR is a debugging tool that exercises all the primitives exported by the "caesar_graph.h" interface. This tool is used to check and validate OPEN/CÆSAR-compliant compilers.
- EXECUTOR is a random execution tool, which produces a random trace starting from the initial state. Various options are available, e.g., to control the seed of the random number generator, to report non-deterministic choices, to display or not invisible transitions, to have an upper limit on the number of transitions fired, etc.
- SIMULATOR is an interactive simulator allowing step-by-step execution (with backtracking) controlled from a command-line interface. XSIMULATOR is a graphical, TCL/TK-based extension of SIMULATOR developed by Mark Jorgensen, Jean-Michel Frume and the author.
- GENERATOR performs reachability analysis to generate exhaustively the LTS (represented in the BCG format) corresponding to a source program. REDUCTOR is similar to GENERATOR, but performs on-the-fly reduction modulo the τ^*a equivalence (which preserves all safety properties).
- TERMINATOR is a deadlock detection tool implementing Holzmann's "bit-state" (or "supertrace") algorithm [14], with various improvements regarding the generation of diagnostic sequences.
- EXHIBITOR searches on-the-fly for execution sequences starting from the initial state and whose labels match a given "pattern". The language used to describe patterns combines boolean operators and (a subset of) regular expressions with an extension to characterize deadlock states. EXHIBITOR implements a depth-first search algorithm and a breadth-first search algorithm, the latter being able to find the shortest sequence(s) matching a given pattern.
- EVALUATOR [9] is an on-the-fly model-checking tool for branching-time μ-calculus developed by Marius Bozga, Jean-Claude Fernandez and Laurent Mounier. It implements two different model-checking algorithms: a global one and a local one.
- ALBATOR is a tool developed by Laurent Mounier and Laurent Aublet-Cuvelier to check on-the-fly whether two LTSs are equivalent modulo strong bisimulation.

---

[3] All these tools have been developed by the author, unless specified otherwise by bibliographic reference or explicit mention of the author(s)

- PROJECTOR [18] is a tool for compositional verification. For each process of the source program, PROJECTOR allows to generate the corresponding LTS in a constrained manner, by taking into account an *interface*, i.e., an LTS expressing (a superset of) the set of execution sequences permitted for this process by its environment.
- TGV [7] is a test generation tool based on verification technology. Given a source program and an automaton formalizing the behavioural part of a test purpose, TGV produces the behaviour description and constraints definitions of a test case in the standard TTCN format.

Concluding remarks and future work

In this paper, we have presented the motivations and achievements of a long-term project, which spanned over the last five years.

We have defined the principles of the OPEN/CÆSAR architecture, a software framework for developing tools that integrate simulation, verification and test generation functionalities in an coherent way. The main principles underlying this architecture are:

Modularity: a clear separation is established between the language-dependent part (definition of states and labels, and computation of the transition relation) and language-independent parts (exploration algorithms themselves). This separation is achieved using the OPEN/CÆSAR API, whose design has been continuously reviewed and improved during the past years. Technically, this interface realizes a good tradeoff between various (conflicting) requirements: expressiveness, language independence, efficiency, portability, genericity, etc.

Reusability: in addition to the modularity principle, the OPEN/CÆSAR also promotes reusability, by providing a library of predefined utilities (thus avoiding to users the tedious process of implementing and debugging data structures such as stacks, state tables, etc.). These libraries are accessible using well-defined interfaces and follow established software engineering methodologies (namely abstract data types and object-orientation).

Orthogonality: within the OPEN/CÆSAR framework, any verification or testing algorithm can be applied to any source language. Thus, in the specialized area of protocol engineering, OPEN/CÆSAR achieves goals similar to those of UNCOL [23], the universal intermediate language, a most inspiring paradigm, discussed but never implemented. This orthogonality property is especially of interest when designing user interfaces: in particular, the EUCALYPTUS graphical user-interface [10] takes advantage of it to present the available operation for each type of source program in a uniform, regular manner.

Openness: as the exploration module can be written in a general-purpose programming language (e.g., C or C++) and relies upon the link edition mechanism offered by the operating system, the user is free to write any possible algorithm. This approach strongly contrasts with more limited solutions in which the user is only given access to a few parameters for controlling the simulation and reachability analysis, but not to a full-fledged programming interface [1, 2].

As time passed, the OPEN/CÆSAR approach proved to be superior, so that industrial tools recently switched to the OPEN/CÆSAR principles by developing a similar API, including a direct connection to OPEN/CÆSAR [17].

Extensibility: the OPEN/CÆSAR environment can be extended in three ways: by adding new connections to source languages, by adding new exploration algorithms, and by adding new libraries to fit specific needs.

The idea of integrating various techniques within a single tool is becoming increasingly popular. Prior to OPEN/CÆSAR, there have been many attempts at turning a simulation tool into a verification or test generation tool. In particular, the SPIN tool [14] allowed to combine simulation and model-checking several years before the first version of OPEN/CÆSAR; however, as SPIN is designed for a single language, PROMELA, its internal architecture remains rather monolithic. Also, some of the OPEN/CÆSAR principles were already present when the author designed the internal architecture of VESAR [1], but not in such a systematic way.

It was the intrinsic merits of OPEN/CÆSAR to formulate the principle of a radical separation between three modules (graph, exploration and libraries), to design and specify the corresponding APIs, and to prove the feasibility of these ideas by providing a complete implementation (the first version of the OPEN/CÆSAR environment was distributed in April 1992 as a part of version R of CADP).

As regards the development of verification tools applicable to different source languages, we can also mention the *Process Algebra Compiler* (PAC) [5], a compiler generation tool for process algebras specified by their BNF syntax and their SOS semantics. The main difference between PAC and OPEN/CÆSAR relies in the fact that PAC provides an implementation for a well-defined class of languages, whereas OPEN/CÆSAR leaves implementation matters to OPEN/CÆSAR compliant compilers. As OPEN/CÆSAR only assumes the existence of states, labels, and transitions, it raises less constraints on the source language, the way it is defined, and the way it is executed: thus, OPEN/CÆSAR can accomodate a wider class of languages (i.e., value-passing process algebras, imperative languages, etc.). Nevertheless, both approaches are not mutually exclusive and could interoperate, as the PAC approach could be used to generate OPEN/CÆSAR compliant compilers automatically.

We believe that the OPEN/CÆSAR environment should be of interest to several categories of people:

Language/compiler designers, who connect their compilers to the OPEN/CÆSAR API can immediately reuse for their language all the existing OPEN/CÆSAR tools available for simulation, verification, and testing. The connection task consists in providing an implementation for the primitives defined in the graph module, which should be straightforward, as all language-dependent features have been gradually lifted out from OPEN/CÆSAR's API. At the time being, five different formalisms are already connected to OPEN/CÆSAR: two standardized high-level languages (LOTOS and SDL), two formalisms for describing networks of communicating finite-state machines (EXP and FC2), and a formalism for representing LTSs (BCG). Our experience indicates that such a connection can be established in 4–6 weeks by a computer-science student without prior knowledge in verification theory.

Algorithm designers, who propose new algorithms for verification and testing will find in OPEN/CÆSAR a rapid prototyping platform for experimenting their ideas. At present, many tools have already been developed within OPEN/CÆSAR, which cover many aspects of protocol engineering (random execution, interactive simulation, reachability analysis, on-the-fly verification of bisimulation and μ-calculus, test generation, etc.) and demonstrate the applicability of OPEN/CÆSAR for a wide spectrum of problems. OPEN/CÆSAR allows to bridge the gap between theoretical research and practical applications by providing a "programming kit" to implement concisely, quickly, and efficiently new algorithms, under a form close to the way these algorithms are specified on paper. It is worth noticing that these algorithms can be written in a fully language-independent way, without the need to develop a compiler from scratch (nor to adapt the code of an existing compiler, if available); yet, they can still be applied to real-life examples, by simply using one of the existing OPEN/CÆSAR-compliant compilers. In this respect, OPEN/CÆSAR could play the role of a common framework for comparing and assessing the performances of different algorithms.

Protocol designers, who are concerned by applicative aspects (but are not interested in developing new languages, compilers, or algorithms) can benefit from a complete set of robust tools, covering almost all aspects of protocol engineering. These tools can easily be accessed from a graphical-user interface [10] and have been field-tested on several real-life applications [4, 11, 19, 21, 22].

Naturally, the design choices of OPEN/CÆSAR induce several limitations and drawbacks. Although these limitations are not considered to be crippling by OPEN/CÆSAR users (especially, industrial users), they leave room for further research and improvements. We briefly discuss the main ones:

- As a counterpart for modularity and reusability, there is a price to pay in terms of performance. For instance, when constructing the state graph of a LOTOS description, the OPEN/CÆSAR GENERATOR tool is slightly less efficient than the dedicated CÆSAR tool. However, this overhead is felt acceptable.
- To achieve language independence, OPEN/CÆSAR operates at the level of a Labelled Transition System model. This creates a gap between the source level program (usually written in a language involving some form of concurrency) and the model of this program, as it is made available by the graph module. There are already some "hook" primitives to keep track of the correspondence between the model and the source program, but they could be enhanced in several ways. For instance, the interface could give more information about the concurrent processes that exist at the source program level, e.g., by indicating in which state a given process is, which processes participate in a given transition, etc. This kind of information is needed by verification algorithms using partial orders and symmetries. Also, it would be desirable to have a more accurate access to the values contained in states and labels (at present, state contents and label contents are represented as

character strings). This would be useful for debugging purpose (for instance, to inspect the value of a variable). However, such facilities are often language-dependant, and require to keep track of the types and functions defined in the source program. A proper treatment of user-defined types and functions[4] would definitely make OPEN/CÆSAR a much more complex system.

- At present, the interface of the graph module allows on-the-fly exploration for a single source program only. This interface could be extended to handle several graphs simultaneously. However, we have not found yet a practical situation where such an enhancement would be needed. Even algorithms for computing bisimulations on-the-fly between two graphs [8] assume that one graph is small enough for being generated exhaustively, so that only one graph remains to be explored on-the-fly.
- When computing the transition relation, OPEN/CÆSAR only gives access to the successors of a given state, but not to the predecessors. Although this is a limitation for some verification algorithms (e.g., [20]), it is justified, as the computation of state predecessors for high-level languages is undecidable in the general case (because of user-defined data types, user-defined functions over these data types, assignment to variables and boolean conditions).
- OPEN/CÆSAR's graph module interface deals with states one by one. This interface remains to be extended in order to deal with symbolic methods (e.g., methods based upon binary decision diagrams or polyhedra) that deal with sets of states, for which they often provide a more efficient representation than lists of isolated states.
- Finally, it is planned to extend the graph module interface with a notion of quantitative time. This is needed for applying OPEN/CÆSAR to timed languages (e.g., the forthcoming ISO standard Extended-LOTOS) that rely upon timed Labelled Transition Systems.

OPEN/CÆSAR can be obtained free of charge as a component of the CADP toolset. See the CADP Web page (http://www.inrialpes.fr/vasy/cadp.html) for further information.

References

1. B. Algayres, V. Coelho, L. Doldi, H. Garavel, Y. Lejeune, and C. Rodriguez. VESAR: A Pragmatic Approach to Formal Specification and Verification. *Computer Networks and ISDN Systems*, 25(7):779–790, February 1993.
2. B. Algayres, Y. Lejeune, and F. Hugonnet. GOAL: Observing SDL behaviors with GEODE. In *Proc. 7th SDL Forum (Oslo, Norway)*, September 1995.
3. A. Bouali, A. Ressouche, V. Roy, and R. de Simone. The Fc2Tools set: a Toolset for the Verification of Concurrent Systems. In *Proc. CAV '96*, LNCS 1102, 1996.
4. G. Chehaibar, H. Garavel, L. Mounier, N. Tawbi, and F. Zulian. Specification and Verification of the PowerScale Bus Arbitration Protocol: An Industrial Experiment with LOTOS. In *Proc. FORTE/PSTV'96*. Chapman & Hall, 1996. Full version available as INRIA Research Report RR-2958.

---

[4] Such an approach has already been investigated in the context of the BCG format.

5. R. Cleaveland, E. Madelaine, and S. Sims. A Front-End Generator for Verification Tools. In *Proc. TACAS'95 Tools and Algorithms for the Construction and Analysis of Systems (Aarhus, Denmark)*, May 1995. Also available as INRIA Research Report RR-2612.
6. B. Cousin and J. Helary. Performance Improvement of State Space Exploration by Regular and Differential Hashing Functions. In *Proc. CAV'94*, LNCS 818, 1994.
7. J-Cl. Fernandez, Cl. Jard, Th. Jéron, L. Nedelka, and C. Viho. An Experiment in Automatic Generation of Test Suites for Protocols with Verification Technology. *Science of Computer Programming*, 29(1–2):123–146, July 1997.
8. J-Cl. Fernandez and L. Mounier. "On the Fly" Verification of Behavioural Equivalences and Preorders. In *Proc. CAV'91*, July 1991.
9. J-Cl. Fernandez and L. Mounier. A Local Checking Algorithm for Boolean Equation Systems. Rapport SPECTRE 95-07, VERIMAG, Grenoble, March 1995.
10. H. Garavel. An Overview of the Eucalyptus Toolbox. In *Proc. COST 247 Int. Workshop on Applied Formal Methods in System Design (Maribor, Slovenia)*, 1996.
11. H. Garavel and L. Mounier. Specification and Verification of various Distributed Leader Election Algorithms for Unidirectional Ring Networks. *Science of Computer Programming*, 29(1–2):171–197, July 1997.
12. H. Garavel and J. Sifakis. Compilation and Verification of LOTOS Specifications. In *Proc. PSTV '90 (Ottawa, Canada)*. North-Holland, 1990.
13. S. Graf, J-L. Richier, C. Rodríguez, and J. Voiron. What are the Limits of Model Checking Methods for the Verification of Real Life Protocols? In *Proc. 1st Workshop on Automatic Verification Methods for Finite State Systems*, LNCS 407, 1989.
14. G. J. Holzmann. *Design and Validation of Computer Protocols*. Prentice Hall, 1991.
15. G. J. Holzmann. State Compression in SPIN: Recursive Indexing and Compression Training Runs. In *Proc. 3rd SPIN Workshop (Twente Univ., The Netherlands)*, 1997.
16. Cl. Jard and Th. Jéron. Bounded-Memory Algorithms for Verification On-the-Fly. In *Proc. CAV '91*, LNCS 575, July 1991.
17. A. Kerbrat, C. Rodriguez, and Y. Lejeune. Interconnecting the ObjectGEODE and CÆSAR/ALDEBARAN Toolsets. In *Proc. 8th SDL Forum*, 1997.
18. J-P. Krimm and L. Mounier. Compositional State Space Generation from Lotos Programs. In *Proc. TACAS'97*, LNCS 1217, 1997.
19. R. Mateescu. Formal Description and Analysis of a Bounded Retransmission Protocol. In *Proc. COST 247 Int. Workshop on Applied Formal Methods in System Design (Maribor, Slovenia)*, 1996. Also available as INRIA Research Report RR-2965.
20. R. Paige and R. E. Tarjan. Three Partition Refinement Algorithms. *SIAM Journal of Computing*, 16(6):973–989, December 1987.
21. Ch. Pecheur. Specification and Verification of the CO4 Distributed Knowledge System Using LOTOS. In *Proc. 12th IEEE Int. Conf. on Automated Software Engineering ASE-97*, 1997. Extended version available as INRIA Research Report RR-3259.
22. M. Sighireanu and R. Mateescu. Validation of the Link Layer Protocol of the IEEE-1394 Serial Bus ("FireWire"): an Experiment with E-LOTOS. In *Proc. 2nd COST 247 Int. Workshop on Applied Formal Methods in System Design (Zagreb, Croatia)*, 1997. Full version available as INRIA Research Report RR-3172.
23. T. B. Steel. A First Version of UNCOL. In *Proc. Western Joint Computer Conf.*, pages 371–378, May 1961.

Practical Model-Checking Using Games

Perdita Stevens * and Colin Stirling **

Department of Computer Science
University of Edinburgh
The King's Buildings
Edinburgh EH9 3JZ

Abstract. We describe how model-checking games can be the foundation for efficient local model-checking of the modal mu-calculus on transition systems. Game-based algorithms generate winning strategies for a certain game, which can then be used interactively to help the user understand why the property is or is not true of the model. This kind of feedback has advantages over traditional techniques such as error traces. We give a proof technique for verifying such algorithms, and apply it to one which we have implemented in the Edinburgh Concurrency Workbench. We discuss its usability and performance.

1 Introduction

The *modal mu-calculus* (see e.g. [9]) is an expressive logic which can be used to describe properties of systems modelled as labelled transition systems (LTSs). The problem of *model-checking* the mu-calculus on transition systems is that of deciding whether an LTS satisfies a formula. Many model-checking algorithms have been developed and implemented in tools. One such tool is the Edinburgh Concurrency Workbench ([7]), in which users design modular systems using the Calculus of Communicating Systems (CCS). The semantics of a CCS process is given by an LTS, and for model-checking purposes we will think of the LTS as the basic notion; of course feedback to the user is all in terms of CCS derivatives. We are mostly interested in local, on-the-fly algorithms; our algorithm will not require global information about the LTS, so we are free to calculate parts of the LTS as required, and in some cases we will be able to check properties of infinite-state LTSs.

Previous work on model-checking has concentrated mostly on the worst-case time complexity of the algorithm in question. This is not our focus here, and indeed, the algorithm we have implemented does not have the best known worst-case time complexity. Instead, we are concerned with two aspects of the needs of users of model-checking tools.

Firstly, and most importantly, we consider the feedback given to users. Any model-checking algorithm can tell the user whether a formula does or does not

---

* Perdita.Stevens@dcs.ed.ac.uk, supported by EPSRC GR/K68547
** Colin.Stirling@dcs.ed.ac.uk

hold of a process; however, for a user trying to design a system which should meet a specification given in the mu-calculus, this is not sufficiently helpful. It can be hard to debug such a system, that is, to work out why its properties are not as required and alter it so that they are. Moreover it is not always obvious how an algorithm can provide output that helps. If the system is supposed to satisfy "can do an a-action" ($\langle a \rangle \mathbf{T}$) and does not, the tool need only show the user the possible first actions of the process to demonstrate what went wrong. But if the user expects the model to satisfy a more complex property such as "there is some path on which P holds infinitely often" – in mu-calculus

$$\nu X. \mu Y. (P \wedge \langle - \rangle X) \vee \langle - \rangle Y$$

– and it does not, then it is much less clear what good diagnostics are: in particular, the tool can't give any particular path through the system, and expect it to be helpful to the user. Presumably, however, the user has some path in mind; if the user somehow gives the path, we may expect to be able to convince her/him that P does not hold infinitely often on that path. We will return to this example to show the user playing against the tool's winning strategy.

Secondly, we are interested in the performance of our algorithm on the examples that arise in practice. This can be strongly affected by common characteristics of practical systems; we shall describe some improvements we have made which have no impact on the worst-case complexity of the algorithm, yet have dramatic effects on the practical performance. This is an area which has not been much addressed in the local model-checking literature. Improving performance necessitates experimentation; it is important to be able to try out variations on an algorithm to see whether they are practical improvements, whilst remaining confident that the algorithm is correct. Therefore we need to have a flexible proof technique which will work for a wide family of algorithms; we need to be able to make changes to our algorithm and prove them correct without needing to re-prove correctness from scratch. One of our contributions here is such a framework; we shall discuss variants on the algorithm as we go.

2 Background and plan

The syntax of the modal mu-calculus we use (positive form) is:

$$\Phi ::= \mathbf{T} \mid \mathbf{F} \mid Z \mid \Phi_1 \wedge \Phi_2 \mid \Phi_1 \vee \Phi_2 \mid [K]\Phi \mid \langle K \rangle \Phi \mid \nu Z. \Phi \mid \mu Z. \Phi$$

where Z ranges over a family of propositional variables, and K over subsets of the set of labels: $-K$ denotes K's complement. [9] provides a tutorial introduction to the mu-calculus and its use: here we assume familiarity with it. We write $\sigma Z. \Phi$ for "either $\mu Z. \Phi$ or $\nu Z. \Phi$". A *closed* formula contains no free variables.

Recently Stirling ([8]) has developed a theory of model-checking games in which the truth of a formula at a state is equivalent to the existence of a (history-free) winning strategy for a certain game. This can be seen as a reformulation of tableau-based approaches such as [10]: a (history-free) winning strategy looks very much like a successful (canonical) tableau. The work is also related to [2] and methods in [3]. The history-free winning strategy, whose size is linear in the size of the problem, that is, in the product of the number of states of the model and the number of subformulae of the formula, should be generated by the model-checking algorithm.[1] Given a tool which takes advantage of this, the user can use the strategy as an *interactive* diagnostic tool to correct wayward intuitions and debug the model. As we shall show, expecting the opposite answer to the one the tool gave corresponds naturally to expecting to be able to beat the tool when it follows its winning strategy. Losing repeatedly to the tool and observing how this happens, the user can locate the problem with the model.

On the theoretical side, we also find thinking in terms of games helpful: it seems to expose the structure and duality of the problem well. An alternative approach is via Boolean graphs [1] or equation systems [5]: indeed Mader has demonstrated the equivalence of Boolean equation systems and the model-checking problem.

We first briefly describe the basic model-checking game, and we introduce *open games* which are a formalisation of the idea of exploring parts of the game-tree separately; a particular case of an open game is the basic model-checking game. Using open games to prove correctness, we describe our implementation of a game-based algorithm in the Edinburgh Concurrency Workbench (CWB). This includes features to allow the user to use the winning strategy interactively, as described. We discuss the usability and performance of the new algorithm, which is encouraging. Finally we mention future work.

Most proofs and some details are omitted for reasons of space.

2.1 The games

We wish to establish whether a process P satisfies a closed Φ of the modal mu-calculus. We assume all bound variables in Φ are distinct, renaming them if necessary to ensure this: the assumption is used in Rule 6 of Figure 1.

The *model-checking game* $\mathcal{G}(P,\Phi)$, is played by ∀belard (or Player I, or Opponent) and ∃loise (or Player II, or Player). ∀belard attempts to show that P fails to have the property Φ whereas ∃loise tries to show that P does have Φ. We write Player A and Player B for "a player" and "the other player" when it doesn't matter which is which.

A *play* of $\mathcal{G}(P_0,\Phi_0)$ is a finite or infinite length sequence of the form $(P_0,\Phi_0)\ldots(P_n,\Phi_n)\ldots$ where each Φ_i is a subformula of Φ_0 and each P_i is a derivative of P_0. (We call such a pair a *configuration* of the game.)

Suppose a play (so far) is $(P_0,\Phi_0)\ldots(P_j,\Phi_j)$. The moves are given in Figure 1: note that the form of the available moves, and which player chooses, are determined by the form of Φ_j. Each time the current game configuration is

---

[1] Somewhat surprisingly, it is not easy to construct a history-free winning strategy from the information calculated by an algorithm (even the obvious variant on this one) which does not explicitly record a strategy. The relationship between proving that a strategy exists and finding it deserves further investigation.

1. if $\Phi_j = \Psi_1 \wedge \Psi_2$ then ∀belard chooses Φ_{j+1} to be either Ψ_1 or Ψ_2, and P_{j+1} is P_j.
2. if $\Phi_j = \Psi_1 \vee \Psi_2$ then ∃loise chooses Φ_{j+1} to be either Ψ_1 or Ψ_2, and P_{j+1} is P_j.
3. if $\Phi_j = [K]\Psi$ then ∀belard chooses a transition $P_j \xrightarrow{a} P_{j+1}$ with $a \in K$ and Φ_{j+1} is Ψ.
4. if $\Phi_j = \langle K \rangle \Psi$ then ∃loise chooses a transition $P_j \xrightarrow{a} P_{j+1}$ with $a \in K$ and Φ_{j+1} is Ψ.
5. if $\Phi_j = \sigma Z.\Psi$ then Φ_{j+1} is Z and P_{j+1} is P_j.
6. if $\Phi_j = Z$ and Z is bound by $\sigma Z.\Psi$ then Φ_{j+1} is Ψ and P_{j+1} is P_j.

Figure 1. Rules for the next move in a game play

$(P, \sigma Z.\Psi)$, at the next step this fixed point is abbreviated to Z, and each time the configuration is (Q, Z) the fixed point subformula it identifies is, in effect, unfolded once as the formula becomes Ψ.[2]

The conditions for winning a play are given in Figure 2. ∀belard wins if a blatantly false configuration is reached, or if ∃loise is stuck, and dually for ∃loise. The remaining condition identifies who wins an infinite length play. We call variables bound by ν ∃loise-variables and variables bound by μ ∀belard-variables, and the notion of subsuming is:

Definition *Suppose $\sigma X.\Psi$ and $\sigma Y.\Psi'$ are subformulae of a formula Φ. X subsumes Y if $\sigma Y.\Psi'$ is a subformula of $\sigma X.\Psi$.*

We omit the easy proof that X in winning condition 3 is indeed unique, so that the condition is well-defined.

A *strategy* π for Player A is a set of rules telling Player A how to move: that is, it is a partial function from plays[3] to configurations, which given a play $p \in \text{dom } \pi$ ending in a configuration (Q, Ψ) from which Player A must move, returns a non-empty set of legal next configurations. If every such set is a singleton, we say that π is *deterministic* (and in this case we will usually think of $\pi(p)$ as a configuration, rather than as a singleton set of configurations). We call π *history-free* if $\pi(p)$ is determined solely by the final configuration (Q, Ψ) of p, irrespective of the rest of the play. A play q *follows* π if for every proper prefix p of q ending in an A-choice, $p \in \text{dom } \pi$ and the next configuration of q after p is in $\pi(p)$. π is *complete* if whenever p is a play following π and ending in a configuration from which Player A must choose, $\pi(p)$ is defined. Otherwise it is partial. π is a *winning strategy* if it is complete and B does not win any play which follows π. A history-free complete strategy may be regarded as a partial function from configurations to configurations.

The basic theorem we exploit is from [8]:

---

[2] As there are no choices here it doesn't matter who "chooses" – we say that the Referee moves.
[3] Plays are just sequences of moves, which need not yet be decided.

∀belard wins

1. The play is $(P_0, \Phi_0) \ldots (P_n, \Phi_n)$ and $\Phi_n = \mathbf{F}$.
2. The play is $(P_0, \Phi_0) \ldots (P_n, \Phi_n)$ and $\Phi_n = \langle K \rangle \Psi$ and $\{Q : P \xrightarrow{a} Q$ and $a \in K\} = \emptyset$.
3. The play $(P_0, \Phi_0) \ldots (P_n, \Phi_n) \ldots$ has infinite length and the unique variable X which occurs infinitely often and which subsumes all other variables that occur infinitely often identifies a least fixed point subformula $\mu X. \Psi$.

∃loise wins

1. The play is $(P_0, \Phi_0) \ldots (P_n, \Phi_n)$ and $\Phi_n = \mathbf{T}$.
2. The play is $(P_0, \Phi_0) \ldots (P_n, \Phi_n)$ and $\Phi_n = [K] \Psi$ and $\{Q : P \xrightarrow{a} Q$ and $a \in K\} = \emptyset$.
3. The play $(P_0, \Phi_0) \ldots (P_n, \Phi_n) \ldots$ has infinite length and the unique variable X which occurs infinitely often and which subsumes all other variables that occur infinitely often identifies a greatest fixed point subformula $\nu X. \Psi$.

Figure 2. Winning conditions

Theorem 2.1. $P \models \Phi$ *iff* ∃*loise has a winning strategy for* $\mathcal{G}(P, \Phi)$.

In fact, the strategy can be required to be deterministic and history-free, but this will follow from what we prove here so we don't need to quote it. The proof follows closely the soundness and completeness proofs from [10]: indeed winning strategies and successful tableaux are closely related.

3 Techniques: indexes and open games

In this section we introduce the definitions and basic results which will enable us to prove our algorithm (and others in the same family) correct.

When we have to think about the play that lead to a configuration, we are often only interested in the positions at which fixed points are unwound (indeed, it is this that leads to the equivalent formulations such as MC games and Boolean equation systems). This motivates:

3.1 Indexes

Fix a "root" formula with fixed point variables $X_1, \ldots X_n$. We have a natural partial order on the variables, given by $X \leq Y$ if X subsumes Y. Now given a play p with final configuration (P, Φ), the *index of p* written index(p), or the *index of* (P, Φ) *with respect to p* is a map i from the fixed point variables $\{X_1, \ldots X_n\}$ to natural numbers, in which $i(X)$ is the number of times in the play p the fixed point X has been unwound *since any other fixed point which subsumes X was last unwound.* We think of i as being a concise description of the features of p that we may have to care about. We will write **0** for the everywhere-zero index.

Let (Q, Ψ) be any legal next configuration after (P, Φ). Then, of course, the index of (Q, Ψ) relative to the extended path, $\text{index}(p(Q, \Psi))$, can be determined from i and Φ without further reference to the play: it is i itself unless Φ was a fixed point variable X (that is, Rule 6 was applied), in which case it is i modified by adding 1 to $i(X)$ and setting $i(Y)$ to 0 for any $Y \neq X$ subsumed by X. Let us denote this new index by $\text{next}(i, \Phi)$.

It is useful to think of the index as being part of the configuration of the game (writing (P, Φ, i)). The index is determined by the play that led to (P, Φ) and by the initial index, which in the case of the standard model-checking game is **0**.

Given a transition system, any index which can arise in a legal play from the root is called *reachable*. If i is a reachable index then j is reachable from i if there is some play pq such that $\text{index}(p) = i$ and $\text{index}(pq) = j$. Note that any reachable index has the property that its non-zero entries are those corresponding to the variables on some prefix of a single branch of the partial order on variables; if i is reachable and $i(X) \neq 0$ and $i(Y) \neq 0$ then either X subsumes Y or vice versa.

We shall need a notion of the leading difference of two different indexes i and j, which should be the outermost variable X such that $i(X) \neq j(X)$. However, this is not yet well-defined: for example, considering the formula

$$\nu X.(\nu Y.[a]X) \wedge (\mu Z.[a]X)$$

indexes $\{X \mapsto 1, Y \mapsto 1, Z \mapsto 0\}$ and $\{X \mapsto 1, Y \mapsto 0, Z \mapsto 1\}$ may both arise as indexes for $[a]\,X$; is their leading difference Y or Z? Either may be chosen, but (for example to make $\leq_A$ below transitive) we need to make consistent choices.

Let us fix a total order on the variables compatible with the natural partial order (that is, if X subsumes Y then $X \leq Y$), and so we can implement the index as an array of natural numbers (from outermost variables on the left to innermost on the right) as an array of natural numbers. We can implement the unwinding of a variable by incrementing its entry and zeroing every entry to the right of that one. For every such entry is either one that we must zero because its variable is subsumed by the one unwound, or must in fact be already 0. We define:

Definition *The* leading difference *of two different indexes i and j is the least variable X such that $i(X) \neq j(X)$.*

Notice that if i is reachable from j then regardless of which order on variables we choose the leading difference of i and j will be the same.

3.2 The open game

Given a root configuration, i.e. a transition system and formula we wish to check, we will need to consider *open games*, in which play proceeds as in the standard model-checking game, except that certain plays are made to terminate earlier than they would in the standard game, and that we may start from some position which is notionally part way through the standard model-checking game. The idea is to have a disciplined way of exploring what may happen in a limited part of the standard game, as a proof technique for proving the correctness of algorithms which generate winning strategies for the standard game.

An *assumption* (the motivation for the terminology will become clearer later) is a triple (P, Φ, i), where (P, Φ) is a configuration as usual, and i is an index.

A *decision for player A* is either (P, Φ, i) where Φ is not a formula from which A must move, or else $((P, \Phi, i), (Q, \Psi))$ where (Q, Ψ) is a configuration which A may choose from the A-choice point (P, Φ). With a slight abuse of terminology we will sometimes talk about (P, Φ, i) as the decision in this case too, and refer to (Q, Ψ) as the move which justifies the decision (P, Φ, i).

Let Γ be a set of assumptions, (P, Φ) a configuration, i an index. The game $G(\Gamma, (P, \Phi, i))$ begins at configuration (P, Φ) and proceeds with moves as described above. As described, we maintain the index recording how many times each fixed point has been unwound; but in $G(\Gamma, (P, \Phi, i))$ the index is initialised to i, not to the everywhere-0 index. The winning conditions are as before, with the addition of the extra rule that if play reaches a configuration (Q, Ψ) with index k, where $(Q, \Psi, j) \in \Gamma$ and $j \neq k$, then play terminates. The winner is A, the player for whom $j <_A k$, according to:

Definition $i <_A j$, where A is a player and i and j are indexes, means that either:

1. The leading difference of i and j corresponds to a variable X which belongs to player A, and $i(X) < j(X)$, or
2. The leading difference of i and j corresponds to a variable X which belongs to player B, and $i(X) > j(X)$.

We write $i \leq_A j$ for $i <_A j$ or $i = j$.

(Recall that we say maximal fixed points belong to ∃loise and minimal fixed points to ∀belard.) Given the total order on variables which made "leading difference" well defined, $\leq_A$ is a total order: it is "partially reversed lexicographic order" in the sense that B variables are compared "upside down". We will of course get different total orders depending on which order on variables we choose. (But again, if j is reachable from i then $i <_A j$ in every possible order or none.)

Of course $<_B$ is just the reverse of $<_A$: $i <_A j$ iff $j <_B i$. (But it's convenient to have separate symbols for the two related orders.)

The relationship between open games and the standard games is that $G(\emptyset, (P, \Phi, 0))$ is the standard model-checking game starting at (P, Φ). We say that σ *A-wins* game G if σ is a winning strategy for player A for G.

Lemma 3.1. σ *A-wins* $G(\Gamma \cup \{(P, \Phi, i)\}, (P, \Phi, i)) \Rightarrow \sigma$ *A-wins* $G(\Gamma, (P, \Phi, i))$

Lemma 3.2. $(\sigma$ *A-wins* $G(\Gamma, (P, \Phi, i)) \wedge i \leq_A j) \Rightarrow \sigma$ *A-wins* $G(\Gamma, (P, \Phi, j))$.

This lemma can be strengthened for particular classes of formulae (by a weaker relationship between i and j): for example the whole algorithm specialises in the case of model-checking a non-alternating formula to one which does not have to store indexes with decisions at all. However, we defer discussion of this to the full paper. For now we will say that an A-decision (P, Φ, i) applies at (P, Φ, j) exactly when $i \leq_A j$.

Lemma 3.3. *If σ A-wins $G(\Gamma \cup \{(D, \Phi, j)\}, (C, \Psi, i))$ and for some $k \leq_A j$ τ A-wins $G(\Gamma, (D, \Phi, k))$, then we can construct σ' such that σ' A-wins $G(\Gamma, (C, \Psi, i))$. If $\sigma = \tau$ then $\sigma' = \sigma = \tau$ will do.*

4 A practical algorithm

The core of the final algorithm is shown in Figure 3.

In brief, we explore depth first, maintaining a *playList* which records the sequence of configurations which lead from the root to the *current node* (empty if the current node *is* the root), along with, for each choice-point, which choices remain unexplored. We consider whether to stop exploring at the current node, which we do if winning conditions 1 or 2 apply, or if we hit a repeat – that is, the configuration of the current node already appears on the *playList* – or if there is some "applicable decision" (see below). If none of these conditions apply, we add the current node to the *playList*, and choose some so-far unexplored successor to be the new current node. If one of the stopping conditions does apply, then for the appropriate player, say A, we retrace our steps along the *playList*, or *backtrack for Player A*, adding decisions for A in a way to be described. Notionally we are trying to build an A-winning strategy. As we backtrack, of course, we remove entries from the end of the *playList*, so the *playList* records a "straight" path from the root to the current node. When we backtrack for Player A to a B-choice-point n, we see whether the *playList* entry records any unexplored B-choices; notionally, we must see whether Player B could have made a better choice than the one that has just led to an A-win. If there are any unexplored B-choices, we must explore one, replacing the record for n on the *playList* having altered it to reflect the fact that one fewer B-choices remain unexplored. Eventually we either backtrack for B through n in which case n will get decided for B, or run out of unexplored B-moves in which case we may mark n as decided for A: Player B has tried all the possibilities and none succeeded.

The application of a decision as a stopping condition is the reuse of previously calculated information.

At any stage in the execution of the algorithm we have a single set of current assumptions for each player, say $\Gamma_\forall$ and $\Gamma_\exists$. Each assumption set will be a subset of the positions on the current *playList*; since we stop exploring any time we encounter a repeat, this implies in particular that for any configuration (Q, Ψ) and player A, there will be at most one k such that $(Q, \Psi, k) \in \Gamma_A$, though the same configuration may appear once in each assumption set.

Moreover at each step for each player A we have a collection of decisions Δ_A. More precisely, for each configuration (P, Φ) and player A we have a stack (possibly empty) of decisions for A at (P, Φ) with different indexes, where if

```
function explore (config as (state, formula)) index playList
-- take the first case which applies:
case:
-- first dispose of trivial cases
  (formula is T) then
     backtrack Eloise playList config
  (formula is F) then
     backtrack Abelard playList config
-- then see if any decision can be used
  (there is a valid decision, (config, i, playerA) say,
   which is applicable at index) then
     backtrack playerA playList config
-- then see if this is a repeat
  (config is in playList with index i: repeat won by playerA) then
     record that (config, i) used as an assumption for playerA
     backtrack playerA playList config
-- otherwise we have to try to keep playing
  (there are no legal next moves for the player who chooses a move
   from this config, say playerA) then -- A can't go, so B wins
     backtrack playerB playList config
  (else if none of the above apply) then
     pick a next move, say to config2
     create index2, index = index2 unless we just unwound a fixpoint
     record that we've played through (config, index)
     create r, a new entry for play list recording untaken choices
     explore config2 index2 (r::playList)
end case

function backtrack playerA playList whereWeCameFrom
  case
    (playList is []) then
       playerA -- playList was empty, we're done
    (playList is (h::t)) then
       if ((config recorded in h) is a playerB choicept & h shows a
           non-empty list (h'::t') of unexplored pl.B choices) then
         alter h to give t' as the unexplored playerB choices
         explore h' playList
       else
         add decision for playerA at h justified by whereWeCameFrom
         if (h was used as an assumption for playerB)
         then (forget all decisions which may have relied on h)
         backtrack playerA t (config recorded at h)
  end case
```

Figure 3. The core of the algorithm

$d_{n+1} = (P, \Phi, i)$ is a decision above $d_n = (P, \Phi, j)$ in the stack, then $i <_A j$. The decision at the top of the stack is the best decision in the sense that when we ask whether any decision applies at our current node, we only have to examine this top element; if it does not apply, neither does any other decision in the stack. If the configuration is an A-choice point, then the "best" move for A to make is that justifying the top decision. Given the current collection of A-decisions Δ_A, the collection of these best moves for each configuration forms a history-free partial strategy (for any of the relevant games), which we call σ_A.

The reader may wonder why we keep decisions other than the top ones at all: the reason is that we may have to *invalidate* sets of decisions, when assumptions on which they rely are removed from the current assumption set. These decisions are then removed from the stacks, which may cause lower decisions to be exposed as the new top decisions, changing the current strategy σ_A.

We do not wish to maintain a complete dependency graph of assumptions and the decisions that rest on them: we use a simple "time-stamping" mechanism instead. (This design decision will doubtless surprise some readers. There are various reasons for it: simplicity, space, and experience with profiling earlier algorithms which suggested that in fact, checking the dependencies in detail was in practice costing more time than it saved. Nevertheless, it would be interesting to return to this topic and see whether we can do better.) At each step of the algorithm we increment the "time" on a single global "clock". When we add a configuration to the *playList* we stamp it with the time when it was added. When we add a decision to $\Delta_\exists$ or $\Delta_\forall$ we stamp it with the time when it was added. Also, for a given decision d we will want to talk about *playList*(d), being the value of *playList* at the time when the decision d was added. (The algorithm does not need to record this path, it's for purposes of proof only.) Then at any stage, given a decision $d \in \Delta_A$ we can define the current *branching time* of d as the time-stamp on the earliest element of *playList* which is not a member of *playList*(d). The idea is that if d depends directly or indirectly on another decision, that decision must have been added before the branching time of d. (Care is needed, to ensure that if d depended on an assumption which was later discharged and turned into a decision d', we record properly the fact that d depends on d' and on any decisions on which d' depends, even though d' was added after d.)

Because a decision which currently does not contribute to σ_A may later do so, our invariant has to refer to more general strategies than σ_A. Suppose that at some stage in the execution of the algorithm we have an A-decision $d = (P, \Phi, k) \in \Delta_A$, and let $\Delta_d \subseteq \Delta_A$ and $\Gamma_d \subseteq \Gamma_A$ be the sets of A-decisions and A-assumptions respectively which were time-stamped before the branching time of d. That is, Δ_d is the set of current A-decisions which were added before the branching time, and Γ_d is the set of assumptions which were *played through* (not necessarily used as assumptions) before then, in other words, the current A-assumptions which appear on *playList*$(d) \cap$ *playList*. Then we will define a (partial, non-deterministic) strategy τ_d of $G(\Gamma_d, d)$ by saying that a play $p = p_1 \ldots p_n$ (where each $p_i = (P_i, \Phi_i)$) of $G(\Gamma_d, d)$ follows τ_d iff there is some sequence $k_1, \ldots, k_n$ of indexes satisfying:

- $(P_1, \Phi_1, k_1) = d$
- $\forall i : 0 < i < n \ (P_i, \Phi_i, k_i) \in \Delta_d$; moreover if (P_i, Φ_i) is an A-choice point then the justifying move for this decision is (P_{i+1}, Φ_{i+1}).
- $\forall i : 0 < i < n \ k_{i+1} \leq_A \text{next}(k_i, \Phi_i)$

Very roughly, the intuition behind this is that play may move up the stack of decisions to a decision which is at least as safe as the starting point, but never down. A play following τ_d is a path through the part of the game tree which has been decided by the algorithm, following the justifying moves, with the modification that we are allowed to jump to another equally safe branch if it is valid at the present position to reuse the calculation it represents.

Our algorithm will maintain the invariant:

(I) for every Player A decision $d \in \Delta_A$, τ_d is a winning strategy for $G(\Gamma_d, d)$.

Therefore if the algorithm terminates by adding a decision for player A at the root configuration (P, Φ), then since $\Gamma_{(P,\Phi,0)} \subseteq \Gamma_A \subseteq playList = \emptyset$, $\Gamma_{(P,\Phi,0)}$ must then be empty, so I gives that $\tau_{(P,\Phi,0)}$ is a winning strategy for the standard model-checking game $G(\emptyset, (P, \Phi, 0))$ starting at the root. To get a deterministic history-free strategy, observe that σ_A is a substrategy of $\tau_{(P,\Phi,0)}$, in the sense that the plays following σ_A are exactly the plays following $\tau_{(P,\Phi,0)}$ which always follow the move prescribed by the top decision on the stack. Moreover completeness of σ_A follows from completeness of $\tau_{(P,\Phi,0)}$, which gives the result. Thus we have to show

1. that the algorithm does indeed maintain I
2. that it terminates with no assumptions, making a decision at the root.

We start with no decisions or assumptions for either player. This establishes the invariant. In what follows we will use primes to denote the old values of things, for example defining the new A-assumption set Γ_A in terms of the old one Γ'_A.

Here we omit the proofs that the invariant is maintained, but we give the relevant settings of assumption and decision sets, and have presented all the important ingredients of the proof.

Exploring Exploring doesn't change the decision sets or the assumption sets, so there's nothing to prove about the invariant. What it does do is to set up the recorded structure so that when we backtrack along the *playList* we always are moving backwards along a real play. Moreover, because we always stop playing and start backtracking when we encounter a repeat configuration, and because we never explore a branch more than once, for finite LTSs termination is automatic.

Stopping the play Play stops when we encounter (a) a position where winning conditions 1 or 2 apply, or (b) a repeat of a configuration on the *playList*, or (c) a current applicable decision. Suppose play stops at (Q, Ψ, j).

(a) If the winning condition says that A wins, we add a decision, setting $\Delta_A = \Delta'_A \cup \{(Q, \Psi, j)\}$. Backtrack for A.

(b) If we stop because of a repeat – say (Q, Ψ, i) occurs on the *playList*– we determine for which player, say A, $i <_A j$. We add an assumption, setting $\Gamma_A = \Gamma'_A \cup \{(Q, \Psi, i)\}$. Backtrack for A.

(c) If there is some $(Q, \Psi, m) \in \Delta_A$ with $m \leq_A j$, backtrack for A.

Backtracking: building the strategies, adding decisions As we have seen, when the algorithm backtracks for player A from (Q, Ψ, j) we know that there is either an assumption $(Q, \Psi, m) \in \Gamma_A$ with $m <_A j$, or some decision $(Q, \Psi, m) \in \Delta_A$ such that $m \leq_A j$.

If (Q, Ψ, j) is the initial position, Γ_A is empty and we must have a decision which applies at the root (in fact, it's easy to see that we must have a decision *at* the root itself), so we're done: we return the answer A and the current A-strategy σ_A. Otherwise, we backtrack to the end of the old *playList*, say to (P, Φ, i).

(a) If (P, Φ, i) is a B-choice point and there are any unexplored B-choices, then we pick one and play to it, returning (P, Φ, i) to the end of the *playList* after updating the record of unexplored moves from (P, Φ, i). We do not alter decisions or assumptions.

(b) Otherwise, we continue to backtrack for A from (P, Φ, i), after having updated decisions and assumptions as follows:

- We add an A decision: $\Delta_A = \Delta'_A \cup \{(P, \Phi, i)\}$; if (P, Φ) is an A-choice point this is justified by move (Q, Ψ).
- If $(P, \Phi, i) \in \Gamma'_A$ we remove (discharge) it: that is, $\Gamma_A = \Gamma'_A \setminus \{(P, \Phi, i)\}$.
- If $(P, \Phi, i) \in \Gamma'_B$ then we must not only remove this assumption, but also remove B-decisions that "may have depended on this assumption". There are various sound ways of doing this: let $\Delta_B \subseteq \Delta'_B$ be the decisions which we decide to keep. We set $\Gamma_B = \Gamma'_B \setminus \{(P, \Phi, i)\}$.

Since in this version of the algorithm we are not keeping full dependency information, we use a time-stamping mechanism to identify which decisions to discard. Specifically, we set Δ_B to be those decisions $d \in \Delta'_B$ whose time-stamps are earlier than the time-stamp t_1 on (P, Φ, i): that is, which were added to Δ_B before we played through (P, Φ, i). (We implement the forgetting of decisions outside Δ_B by unioning the interval $[t_1, now]$ with the set of B-invalid times; then the procedure that looks for decisions discards and ignores any decisions whose time-stamps are invalid times. This simply saves us the time-expensive procedure of going through all our decisions removing invalid ones every time an assumption is removed.) By keeping more information about the dependencies (up to a complete dependency graph) we could of course be less pessimistic; but this approach works surprisingly well in practice.

5 The tool

We have integrated the algorithm described above into the Edinburgh Concurrency Workbench (CWB), which is a well-established and powerful tool for the analysis of concurrent systems expressed in CCS. The CWB is written in Standard ML, and the model-checker is an ML module. ML provides strong type-checking in a convenient high-level functional language, but imposes severe performance penalties. Experience has shown that it is crucial that CWB code be readable: because of the importance of dependability and ease of maintenance, this is even more important than efficiency.

The CWB's WWW home page, from which the current public version can be obtained, is http://www.dcs.ed.ac.uk/home/cwb. The version described here is 7.1beta.

5.1 Interactive diagnostics

We offer the user the chance to play against the CWB, which takes the winning strategy. Of course the user will lose, and the ways in which the CWB defeats the user can help the user to understand the problem, and especially to dispel mistaken intuition. For example, suppose the user believes that the property "there exists an infinite path on which, infinitely often, a is the only action possible", i.e. the formula in the Introduction with $P = \langle a \rangle \mathbf{T} \wedge [-a] \mathbf{F}$, holds of the system A given in CCS in Figure 4. The user must have some path in mind; perhaps the specification should define D as $b.A$, not $b.B$, and the path the user has in mind is that given by following a b transition whenever there is one, and expecting P to be true only at A. In playing against the CWB, the user can test this intuition by trying to follow this path, and will find that A isn't reached infinitely often.[4] Sections from one possible play are shown in figure 5.1.[5] Notice that there are many infinite paths through the system, and the CWB could not (at any rate, without considerable "intelligence"!) tell which one the user had in mind; so no individual error trace suffices as a debugging aid.

5.2 Usability

Initial feedback on the usability of the games have been encouraging. In the light of comments from users, we have made a number of improvements in the interface. For example:

---

[4] Since users cannot be expected to enjoy playing infinite games, a play terminates when it repeats, and the winner is the owner of the outermost variable unwound on the repeat section. Provided that the user is thinking of a *history-free* strategy – and it is difficult to imagine why this would not be so – s/he will get the same information out of this game as out of the original.

[5] We have deleted some blank lines in order to fit the example on the page! The original is more readable.

```
Command: agent A = a.B;
Command: agent B = a.C + b.D;
Command: agent C = a.C + c.B;
Command: agent D = b.B;
Command: prop P = max (X.min (Y.((<a>T & [-a]F) & <->X) | <->Y));
Command: checkprop (A, P);
false
Would you like to play (and lose!) a game against the CWB? (y or n) y
The CWB will choose Abelard's moves.
You can choose Eloise's.
1: Current position:
A
X
The referee unwinds the fixpoint.
2: Current position:
A
Y
The referee unwinds the fixpoint.
3: Current position:
A
(<a>T & [-a]F & <->X) | <->Y
Your turn (playing Eloise)
1:
A
<a>T & [-a]F & <->X
2:
A
<->Y
Which move?
1
4: Current position:
A
<a>T & [-a]F & <->X

[...the play must continue to:]

The referee unwinds the fixpoint.
7: Current position:
B
Y

[... user follows the b-path and chooses disjunct <->Y at B and at D...]

13: Current position:
B
Y
The CWB (playing Abelard) won, because of a repeat
Another game? (y or n) n
```

Figure 4. Playing a game

– Different users, with different problems, need different degrees of automation of the game playing process. Initially, the CWB did not ask users to acknowledge its own moves or the moves of the referee, and it did not ask users to choose a move in circumstances where only one legal move was available. Some users like this, for example, where plays are long and only short sections are of interest. However, sometimes such behaviour is disorienting, and it's easier to follow the game if you take some action on every move, even when it's only an acknowledgement. Therefore the CWB now makes this behaviour configurable (via command "toggle;").

– It's important to be able to examine past portions of the play after the fact. Running the CWB using its Emacs mode is the easiest way to do this.

– We experimented with a graphical user interface for playing games, but in fact for non-trivial examples, this seemed to be less usable than the text version, partly because of the greater ease of finding relevant sections of a long play when running under a powerful editor.

5.3 Implementation and performance

We have done considerable experimentation with correct variants on the algorithm presented, with the aim of finding which theoretical improvements work well in practice. In many cases our major improvements have been achieved by making changes which have no effect on the worst case complexity of the algorithm. For example, when we arrive at a configuration for which there is a decision, but where we cannot prove that it is safe to apply the decision, we must continue to play. Originally, we played using the first move that came to hand, as though we were meeting the configuration for the first time. Later we modified this so that we try first the move that is recorded in the strategy against the decision we weren't allowed to use. Because it often happens that the same strategy will work, even though we didn't have the means to prove it, this often reduces the re-exploration procedure to a process of checking a strategy, rather than finding one. The old strategy *may* not work – so there is no improvement in the worst-case complexity – but in practice, it usually does, so there is a worthwhile improvement in practical performance.

We have already mentioned another example of the same kind: that rather than process decisions every time an assumption is invalidated, we keep a record of which time-stamps correspond to valid decisions, and simply update this record whenever an assumption is invalidated. The check for whether a decision is still valid is made immediately before the decision is used. Because most decisions are never used, this is very helpful.

We use structure-sharing techniques to avoid keeping multiple copies of data structures representing states, formulae etc, and we calculate the game graph and the LTS on the fly as needed. When model-checking a non-alternating formula, we use specialised versions of the decision lookup functions to take advantage of the fact that (as mentioned previously, though proof and detail is omitted) there is no need to store indexes with decisions in this case, as a decision always applies.

We compare the implementation of the new algorithm with the model-checker from the CWB version 7.0, which is an optimised version of a tableau based method. (We ran both in the same executable, so both used the same infrastructure for calculating LTSs etc.)

Practically the game-based implementation vastly outperforms the old tableau-based implementation. We show a few examples. The numbered rows represent that number of parallel copies of a cycler being tested for deadlock-freedom, an alternation-free formula. Peterson uses a complex fairness property with twelve fixed points and two alternations. Where a figure is absent for CWB v7.0 this is because we have not been able to run the example to completion.

We wish to emphasise the *difference* between the figures, not the actual performance, which suffers from inefficiencies elsewhere in the CWB code (and the fact that it's written in ML). Time spent in the model-checking algorithm itself – rather than calculating transitions from CCS terms (on the fly, once only per state) – is given as (MC: n). Times are in user cpu seconds.

Name	Subformulae	States	CWB v7.0 (u-cpu-s)	new CWB (u-cpu-s)
four	4	626	6 (MC: 5)	1 (MC: < 1)
five	4	3126	419 (MC: 413)	9 (MC: 6)
six	4	15626	-	64 (MC: 33)
seven	4	78126	-	371 (MC: 190)
peterson	112	241	-	15 (MC: 14)

6 Conclusions and further work

We have developed and implemented a model-checking algorithm which produces automatically a "proof object" which can interactively help the user to understand and debug systems. The game techniques which we have used seem promising both because of this interaction paradigm and as a way of developing efficient algorithms. In future we intend to gather and build upon information from CWB users about what kinds of interaction are practically useful, and to improve and extend the interface accordingly. We will also continue to investigate variations on the algorithm, with the intention of improving its performance on practical examples further. We should also like to use these game-based techniques to investigate complexity issues, in particular, to compare the problem of finding a winning strategy with the model-checking problem, which can be seen as that of proving that a winning strategy exists without necessarily constructing it. We are in the process of applying similar techniques to classes of infinite state processes, in particular, to well-behaved value-passing CCS processes. This work will be incorporated into a future version of the CWB.

References

1. Andersen, H. (1994). Model checking and boolean graphs. *Theoretical Comp. Science*, **126**, 3-30.

2. Bernholtz, O., Vardi, M. and Wolper, P. (1994). An automata-theoretic approach to branching-time model checking. *Lecture Notes in Computer Science*, **818**, 142-155.

3. Emerson, E., Jutla, C., and Sistla, A. (1993). On model checking for fragments of μ-calculus. *Lecture Notes in Computer Science*, **697**, 385-396.

4. Long, D., Browne, A., Clarke, E., Jha, S., and Marrero, W. (1994) An improved algorithm for the evaluation of fixpoint expressions. *Lecture Notes in Computer Science*, **818**, 338-350.

5. Mader, A. (1996) Verification of Modal Properties Using Boolean Equation Systems. *Doctoral dissertation, Institut für Informatik, Technische Universität München.*

6. Milner, R. (1989) Communication and Concurrency *Prentice Hall*

7. Moller, F. and Stevens, P. (1996). The Edinburgh Concurrency Workbench user manual. http://www.dcs.ed.ac.uk/home/cwb.

8. Stirling, C. (1995). Local model checking games. *Lecture Notes in Computer Science*, **962**, 1-11.

9. Stirling, C. (1996). Modal and temporal logics for processes. *Lecture Notes in Computer Science*, **1043**, 149-237.

10. Stirling, C. and Walker, D. (1991) Local model checking in the modal mu-calculus. *Theoretical Computer Science*, **89**, 161-177.

Combining Finite Automata, Parallel Programs and SDL Using Petri Nets

Bernd Grahlmann

Institut für Informatik,
Universität Hildesheim,
Marienburger Platz 22,
D-31141 Hildesheim,
bernd@informatik.uni-hildesheim.de,
www.informatik.uni-hildesheim.de/~bernd

Abstract. This paper introduces a method to combine finite automata, parallel programs and SDL (Specification and Description Language) specifications. We base our approach on M-nets exploiting the rich set of composition operators available in this algebra of high-level Petri nets. In order to be able to combine different modelling techniques, we rely on compatible interfaces. Therefore,

- we extend an existing semantics, namely the M-net semantics for the parallel programming language B(PN)^2; and
- we present an M-net semantics for finite automata.

Considering the hybrid modelling of an ARQ (Automatic Repeat re-Quest) protocol, we show how the different formalisms fit together as well as the resulting verification possibilities. As a side-effect we describe on-going development of the PEP tool (Programming Environment based on Petri Nets). As a consequence of our approach we are introducing a hierarchical 'programming with nets' method which is currently implemented in the high-level Petri net editor of the tool.

Keywords: B(PN)^2, Finite automata, Hybrid system design, M-nets, Parallel programs, PEP, Petri nets, SDL, Verification.

1 Introduction

So far, the PEP* tool (Programming Environment based on Petri Nets [7, 18]) supports a variety of (high-level) modelling techniques:

- B(PN)^2 (Basic Petri Net Programming Notation) a parallel programming language [8, 5, 13],
- M-nets (Modular multilabelled nets) an algebra of high-level Petri nets [6],
- PFA (Parallel Finite Automata) [16] a collection of FA (Finite Automata).

* The PEP project is financed by the DFG (German Research Foundation). This work has been partially supported by the HCM Cooperation Network EXPRESS (Expressiveness of Languages for Concurrency)

Moreover, we have given a compositional M-net semantics to SDL (Specification Description Language) [9] covering dynamic process creation and termination as well as procedures [14, 15]. However, a hybrid system design approach which combines one or more of these techniques has not been presented so far. Addressing this problem and proposing a solution is the main purpose of this paper.

In contrast to other (even Petri net) tools, the PEP tool has been designed in such a way that Petri nets are the central method into which different kind of systems are translated in order to use Petri net theory for the simulation, the analysis and the verification. Therefore, it is straightforward to realise also the combination of different formalisms using (preferably high-level) Petri nets.

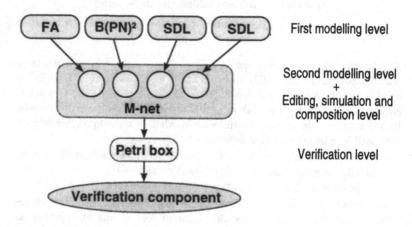

Fig. 1. Abstract presentation of the hybrid modelling.

Fig. 1 shows the abstract idea of our approach. We distinguish two different modelling levels.

1. On the first level, each part (possibly more than one) of the whole system is designed individually using one of the supported modelling formalisms $(B(PN)^2$, FA or SDL).
2. The second level has two purposes:
   (a) A hierarchical description of the system specifies how the individual parts are combined and giving its general functionality.
   (b) It serves as an additional editing and simulation level offering interactive M-net editing, simulation and composition.

The bottom part of the figure shows that the resulting M-nets are unfolded into a special class of low-level Petri nets called *Petri boxes* [4] in order to apply the different verification techniques included in the PEP tool. Currently, PEP includes partial order based model checking [12, 11, 19] and algorithms based on linear programming [23] as well as interfaces to other verification packages [18] such as INA [26], SMV [10, 27] and SPIN [20] providing reduction algorithms based on BDDs, on the stubborn set or sleep set method, and on symmetries.

After choosing a general approach, the next important task is to consider the interfaces in more detail. The interaction facilities of the different formalisms have to be analysed to provide compatible interfaces. This should include:

1. accesses to variables,
2. procedure invocations,
3. process creations,
4. synchronous as well as asynchronous communication via $B(PN)^2$-like channels, and
5. SDL-like send and receive operations.

Assuming that our approach is successful there are a lot of benefits. Users then have the possibility to model each part of a parallel system using the formalism of his/her choice. This is particularly interesting for teams performing distributed or cooperative system design. Apart from personal preferences, gaining expressiveness is an interesting argument. For instance, SDL provides different communication mechanisms from $B(PN)^2$. Obviously, it eases the modelling if all of them may be used. Finally, our approach supports reuse of existing components.

This paper is structured as follows. First, we briefly describe the most relevant aspects of M-nets in section 2. In section 3 we will introduce our running example, a hybrid modelling of an ARQ (Automatic Repeat reQuest) protocol. Thereby, we will give an intuition of the three different modelling formalisms ($B(PN)^2$, FA and SDL). In section 4 we will exploit the interfaces in more detail presenting the different extensions of the semantics. Section 5 illustrates some of the resulting verification possibilities. Before we conclude in section 7 we will present new features of the PEP tool which are closely related to the presented approach in section 6. Finally, a list of references is given. Some of the papers are available at http://www.informatik.uni-hildesheim.de/~pep.

2 M-nets

The class of M-nets forms an algebra of high-level Petri nets. It was introduced in [6] as an abstract and flexible meta-language for the definition of the semantics of concurrent programming languages. The most distinguishing feature of the M-nets is given by the rich set of composition operators they provide. These allow – as composition operators in process algebras usually do – the compositional construction of complex nets from simple ones, thereby satisfying various algebraic properties.

Two kinds of inscriptions are distinguished. Annotations are responsible for the unfolding into low-level Petri nets while labels are used for the composition operations (parallel and sequential composition, choice and iteration as well as synchronisation and restriction). For our purpose it is interesting that

– Places of M-nets are annotated by a *type*, describing the set of allowed tokens. A type may contain natural numbers, the Boolean values, the usual token •, and the special token †, or tuples of these. The label distinguishes entry, internal and exit places.

- Transitions are annotated with occurrence conditions and labelled with (multi) sets of action terms. We will give an example how action terms are used in the synchronisation below.
- For our purpose it is sufficient to annotate arcs with sets of expressions.

We will use Fig. 2 to provide the necessary intuition. Let us first consider the subnet consisting of two internal places Pd and Pe, one transition Tc and two arcs. The *transition rule* for M-nets is explained informally on the example: If Pd is marked with a pair $(3,2)$, the variables in the arc inscriptions (pid and πid) can only be bound to 3 and 2, respectively. Thus, an occurrence of Tc carries the pair $(3,2)$ to Pe. However, Tc can occur in infinitely many modes, because the action term contains variables ($'X$ and X') which are not sufficiently bound. E.g., $X' = 2 \wedge 'X = 3$ is a possible binding.

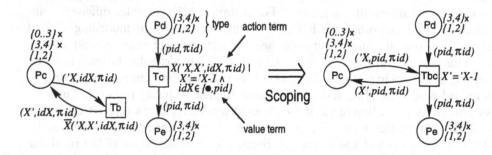

Fig. 2. Scoping example: $N_1 \| N_2$ and $[\ \{X\} : (N_1 \| N_2)\ ]$.

Fig. 2 as a whole depicts how the *scoping* mechanism (first synchronisation and then restriction) may restrict these bindings considering a typical example, namely the access to a local variable within a procedure. Tb is the access transition within the variable net and Tc corresponds to the access of the variable within the procedure. The renaming of the variable idX to pid (according to the $idX \in \{\bullet, pid\}$ part of the value term) ensures that the correct instance of X is accessed. Note that the free variables are bound during the scoping.

3 Hybrid Modelling of the ARQ Example

In this section we will introduce our running example. We will use the description of the hybrid modelling of a simple ARQ communication protocol with alternating acknowledgement to give an overview of the main characteristics of the supported modelling formalisms.

The inner part of Fig 3 shows that the whole ARQ system comprises two different processes (Sender and Receiver) communicating via two SDL signal routes (a and d). Furthermore, the initial number of instances as well as the maximal number are specified (e.g., Sender(1,2)) and the type of the signals is given (e.g., signal ack ($\{0,1\}$)).

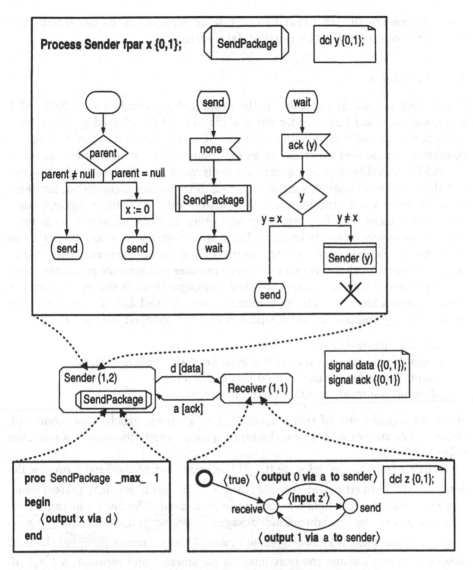

Fig. 3. Hybrid modelling of the ARQ system.

The rest of the figure explains how the three components (one for each process and one for the procedure **SendPackage** belonging to the **Sender** process) are modelled using the editors corresponding to the different formalisms.

The purpose of the ARQ system is to transmit an alternating sequence of 0 and 1 (modelled by a signal type **data** with parameter type {0, 1}). Each **Sender** instance is responsible for the correct transmission of exactly one data package with the label x (which is the formal parameter) via the signal route d to the **Receiver** process. It is intended to introduce failure by letting the **Receiver** process non-deterministically return random acknowledgements via the signal route a to sender (the sender of the last received data package).

3.1 SDL Part

The Sender process is modelled in the graphical representation of SDL. SDL is a quasi-standard language for the specification of distributed systems, especially in the area of telecommunication. An SDL specification describes a *system* consisting of *processes* which are extended communicating finite state machines.

In SDL variables and procedures are declared within the scope of a process, but they are local to process instances – i.e., different instances do not interfere. In addition to the instances which are created automatically at system start, process instances may be created by any other instance of any process type, but can be terminated only by itself. Each process instance is equipped with an input queue. Signals which are transmitted from an instance via signal routes (without delay) or channels (with delay) to another instance are put in the input queue of the receiver. In contrast to other languages there is always one receiver. Neither broadcast nor multiway communication is available. The receiver may be specified by implicit variables whose values are changed automatically

- self: the instance itself,
- sender: the sender instance of the most recently consumed signal,
- parent: the instance that created this one, and
- offspring: the most recently created instance;

or by the signal route (if this is unique). Furthermore, synchronous communication is not supported because the input queue already introduces a potential delay.

Starting from the initial state ($\bigcirc$) the behaviour of the Sender process depends on the implicit parent variable ($\langle$parent$\rangle$). The initial instance (parent=null) sets the value of x to 0 before entering the state send. The Sender instance continues to invoke the procedure SendPackage ($\boxed{\|\text{SendPackage}\|}$) upon receipt ($\boxed{\text{ack (y)}}\langle$) of the corresponding acknowledgement (y$\neq$x). Then it creates ($\boxed{\text{Sender (y)}}$) the next Sender instance (passing the next label as parameter) and terminates ($\times$) afterwards.

3.2 B(PN)^2 Part

The SendPackage procedure is modelled in the parallel programming language B(PN)^2 [8]. Atomic actions (enclosed in action brackets $\langle\rangle$) offer much more expressiveness than the corresponding SDL counterparts. For instance, the action $\langle C1? = {}'x \wedge C2! \geq x' - y'\rangle$ is only executable if the current value of the variable x can be read from the channel $C1$. Furthermore, an occurrence of the action has the effect that the values of the variables x and y are set (non-deterministically) in such a way that the difference is less or equal to a value which can be written (and actually is written upon occurrence of the action) to a second channel (or stack) $C2$. This can not be expressed in SDL and it is very difficult to express it in, for instance, C [22], which is the main language for the implementation of verification algorithms.

As mentioned above, the communication mechanism is also very different. The given action may, for instance, synchronise with an action a_1 of a process Π_1 (via C1) and with b_2 of a process Π_2 (via C2). But, as well also with an action c_1 of the process Π_1 (via C1) and with f_3 of another process Π_3 (via C2).

In [13] the original M-net semantics [5] has been extended by (also recursive) procedures covering severall kind of parameters (value, value-result and reference). In our example, the procedure is declared without any parameter. The maximal number of concurrent instances is restricted to '1' (_max_ 1). The procedure only performs an SDL-like send operation ($\langle$ **output** x **via** d $\rangle$) of the value of the (w.r.t the procedure) global variable x via d (which may be a signal route or a channel). The details of this SDL-like communication mechanism will be explained in section 4.2.

3.3 FA Part

The Receiver process is modelled as an FA [21]. In [16] a special class of $B(PN)^2$ specific FA has been introduced. These FA may consist of

1. a start node (representing the initial state of a process),
2. a set of local nodes,
3. a set of exit nodes (representing that the process has terminated),
4. a set of edges between these nodes, and
5. a labelling function that annotates each edge with a $B(PN)^2$ action.

So far, the PEP tool includes a structure preserving compiler which translates a collection of FA into a $B(PN)^2$ program. This offers an additional nice graphical interface, but it implies a restriction, because not every control structure of an FA may be compiled into a control structure of a $B(PN)^2$ program. In [24] an extension of $B(PN)^2$ (mainly by *GOTOs*) has been proposed which overcomes this restriction. Its implementation would extend the existing possibilities to combine $B(PN)^2$ with FA. In this paper we propose to translate FA directly into M-nets which allows us to use arbitrary control structures without extending other formalisms and without introducing any $B(PN)^2$ specific overhead. Thus, in addition to the nice graphical appearance of FA we may benefit from the extended possibilities to specify control structures.

In our example the FA is very simple. It only consists of one start node, two internal nodes, four arcs and an SDL-like variable declaration (dcl z $\langle\langle 0,1\rangle\rangle$). Starting from the initial state the process first enters the state receive. Then, the process may infinitely often receive ($\langle$ **input** z' $\rangle$) a signal (writing the value to the variable z) and afterwards send (e.g., $\langle$ **output** 0 **via** a **to** sender $\rangle$) randomly either a '1' or a '0' via a (which may be from the point of view of the FA a signal route or a channel) to the sender of the last received signal. This obviously implies that the FA has to be translated in such a way that the handling of the implicit variables (such as sender) as well as of the input queue is done in the same way as in SDL.

4 Extensions of the Semantics

In this section we will first analyse the potential interfaces between the different formalisms in detail. Afterwards, we will give the main ideas for successful extensions. In particular, we will describe different ways to translate an FA or a B(PN)^2 program into an M-net and we will extend the language B(PN)^2 (as well as its semantics) by the introduction of a new communication mechanism.

It is straightforward to compare the existing semantics

1. the original M-net semantics for B(PN)^2 without procedures [5],
2. the M-net semantics for B(PN)^2 with procedures [13], and
3. the M-net semantics for SDL covering dynamic creation and termination of processes as well as procedures [14, 15]

in order to analyse the problems related to interfaces between different formalisms. The most striking difference is the kind of control flow tokens which directly implies differences concerning the types of the places as well as the number of parameters (arity) of the action terms.

In the first semantics it is sufficient to use black tokens ($\bullet$). As a consequence, nearly all places have the type $\{\bullet\}$. Only those places holding the value of a variable have the corresponding type of that variable (e.g., $set1$) as a type. To be precise, this is an abbreviation for a type $set1 \times \{\bullet\}$. Furthermore, action terms have small arities. For instance, the access to a variable x is performed using an action term $x('x,x')$ containing only two parameters, namely for the pre- and the post-value to the variable x.

In the second semantics it is necessary to distinguish different instances of a procedure. As a consequence, everything is extended in order to handle procedure instance identifiers ($pids$):

- $pids$ (which may be bound to $\bullet$ in the global parts) rather than black tokens are passed in the control flow.
- The types of places have one component for the $pids$ which may either be $\{\bullet\}$ for global parts or a set of $pids$ (pid_set) for parts belonging to a procedure.
- Every action term is extended by one parameter for a pid. For instance, $x('x,x',idx)$ is involved in the access to a variable x.

In the third semantics, an additional extension enables the handling of process instance identifiers (πids):

- Tuples (pid, πid) are passed in the control flow. Once more, each of them (pid and πid) may be bound to $\bullet$ in the global parts (outside of a procedure or outside of a process).
- The types of places are extended by one component for the πids (πid_set).

- Every action term is extended by one parameter for a πid. For instance, $x('x,x',idx,\pi id)$ is involved in the access to a variable x.

In summary, this means that:

- As long as we only want to combine FA and $B(PN)^2$ programs without procedures we can choose the first approach.
- If $B(PN)^2$ programs with procedures are involved, we have to translate each component in such a way that it is (at least) compatible with the second approach.
- As soon as SDL is involved we have to switch to the third approach.

4.1 Translating FA

Intuitively, the translation (which is similar to the construction of the semantics of a $B(PN)^2$ program [13]) of an FA into an M-net involves several steps:

1. The FA itself (without any local variable declarations) is compiled into an M-net. This translation is parameterised with the chosen approach as well as with (depending on the chosen approach) a pid_set and a πid_set.
2. All the local declarations are translated (in the same parameterised way) into special variable nets. At the same time initialisation and termination parts are added to the net for the FA itself.
3. The parallel composition of the net for the FA and the variable nets is scoped w.r.t. initialisation, termination and access actions.
4. Depending on the chosen approach the result is integrated into
   (a) the control flow of another net,
   (b) a $B(PN)^2$ or SDL procedure net, or
   (c) an SDL process net.

Let us now consider the first and the last step in some more detail. In principal, the first step translates:

- each node into a place and
- each arc into a transition which is connected via arcs to the places corresponding to the input and the output node, respectively.

All resulting places have the same type which is determined by the parameters of the translation. The inscription of the transition (as well as the arc inscriptions) are constructed in the same way as described in [5, 13, 14], respectively.

Fig. 4 gives two simple examples. In the left part the second approach with a parameter pid_set is chosen. In the right part nearly the same FA is translated using the third approach with parameters pid_set and πid_set. We additionally allowed SDL specific node inscriptions specifying the corresponding states which are compiled into an action term ($q(\text{state1},\text{state2},\bullet,\pi id)$) dealing with the change of the implicit state variable (q).

The application of the steps two and three results in nets which may be characterised by Fig. 5. Two things are important for the subsequent integration into another surrounding net:

1. all input and output places have the same type (*pid_set* or *pid_set* × *πid_set*, respectively) and
2. all remaining action terms (in our example only *q*(state1,state2,•,*πid*)) are compatible with the surrounding net.

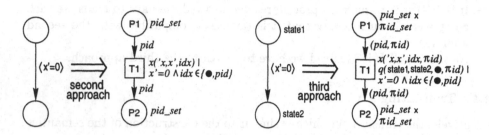

Fig. 4. FA translation example.

Thus, the left net may be inserted in the semantics of a B(PN)^2 program (which has been constructed using the second approach) instead of a block. Therefore, it may, for instance, act as the body of a procedure or just as an arbitrary part of the control flow.

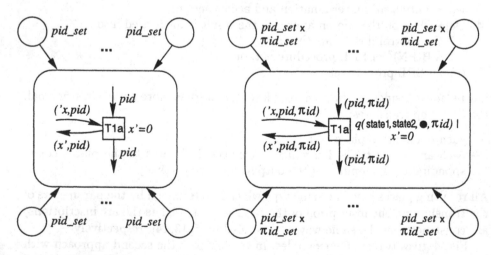

Fig. 5. Simplified representation of the results after the third step.

Due to the fact that an SDL specific FA also performs changes of the implicit state variable (specified by the kind of node and its inscription) the integration of such a net (like the right one) has to obey some further restrictions. Otherwise the surrounding net may, for instance, produce a state **state2** while the FA is specified in such a way that it starts in the initial state. This would cause a deadlock. Nevertheless, if the FA starts in the initial state (expressed by an initial node) and ends in a termination state (expressed by an exit node which may be omitted with the effect that an isolated exit place is added to the net), then the resulting net may be inserted as the body of an SDL process net (as in our running example). An abstract representation of the result of this simple transition substitution (cf. [14]) is shown in Fig. 6.

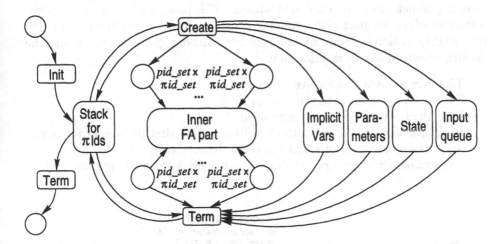

Fig. 6. Abstract view of the FA semantics integration into an SDL process net.

4.2 B(PN)² Extensions

So far, we have only dealt with the first (variable accesses) of the five possible interfaces between the different formalisms mentioned in the introduction. And in addition we will only consider the fifth interface (SDL-like send and receive operations) in more detail because the other three do not demand as sophisticated extensions of the already described semantics as the fifth one. They can be handled in the same way as described in [5, 13, 14], respectively.

As described above, the communication mechanisms provided in SDL and in B(PN)² are completely different. Regarding the fact that SDL is a widely used and standardised [9] language we have chosen to extend B(PN)² (and thus also our FA) by the introduction of SDL-like communication mechanisms rather than extending SDL. To be precise, we basically allow the (standardised) phrase representation of the SDL input and output construct with some additional possibilities.

The receive action (for instance, $\langle$ **input** z' $\rangle$) reads the first value from the input queue into the variable z. Furthermore, the input may be restricted either by a constant (for instance, $\langle$ **input** 0 $\rangle$) or by an additional side condition (for instance, $\langle$ (**input** z') $\wedge$ (z' $\leq$ 'z) $\rangle$).

There are three variants of the send operation specifying the receiver either by its πid (for instance, ⟨ **output** x **to sender** ⟩), or by a channel or signal route (for instance, ⟨ **output** 0 **via** a ⟩), or by both (for instance, ⟨ **output** 0 **via** a **to sender** ⟩). Furthermore, the output may also be restricted or have side effects (for instance, ⟨ **(output** z' **to sender)** ∧ (z' ≤ 'z) ⟩).

The M-net semantics of these new constructs has to take the effects on the implicit variables and the input queue into account which also implies that the resulting M-net has to be combined with an SDL process net. Fig. 7 gives the semantics of the FA part of our running example after the first translation step (the B(PN)^2 action is compiled analogously). Without going too much into the details, we would like to mention that

- **T3** corresponds to the receive arc,
- **T4** and **T5** correspond to the send arcs,
- **P4** is the isolated exit place mentioned above,
- *in?(sig,sender',πid)* accesses the input queue (the first parameter is the signal, the second the sender and the third the receiver),
- *a!(0,πid,sender')* accesses the signal route a (with the same parameters).

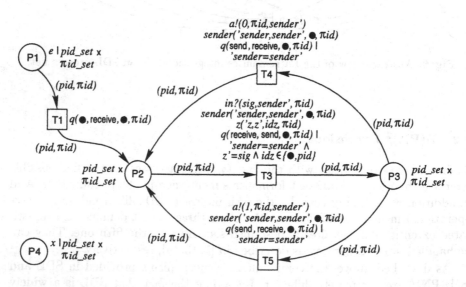

Fig. 7. M-net semantics of the FA part.

5 Verification Results

In [15] we have verified the ARQ protocol applying all kinds of verification techniques which are available in the PEP tool as well as compositional and interactive methods. In contrast to this paper in [15] the whole ARQ system has been modelled in SDL. In order to see the influences of a hybrid modelling using also B(PN)^2 and FA parts we have performed the same verifications.

It turned out that we were able to make the same verifications which was our minimal aim. Moreover, the different verifications have been speeded up by 10–30 % which is a nice secondary benefit. It is very likely that this is a result of the reduction of SDL specific overhead. For instance, the semantics of the Receiver process modelled as an FA is smaller than its semantics using SDL. In the rest of this section we will briefly summarise some of the results.

After unfolding the M-net semantics of the whole ARQ system into a low-level net, we have been able to apply a variety of (not only state space based) verification techniques:

1. Partial order based model checking [12, 11, 19],
2. Sleep set and bitstate techniques [20],
3. Reachability graph based model checking (using 'stubborn set' and 'symmetric' reduction) [26],
4. BDD based model checking [10, 27], and
5. Linear programming based analysis [23].

Using these techniques, we verified

- the deadlock-freeness of the resulting net,
- reachability properties (such as reachability of all the SDL states),
- safety properties (such as *none of the input queues ever contains more than one signal*),
- liveness properties (such as *it is always possible to reach a certain state*),
- progress properties (such as *a send must not be eventually acknowledged*).

Note that we have been able to specify these properties without referring directly to the Petri net, by using an extension of the reference scheme introduced in [17].

Although the main purpose was to show that in general (i.e., also for more complex** systems) such a wide variety of verification techniques may be applied using our approach, we want to provide an intuition of the efficiency. Therefore, we mention that most of the tests took less than one second (using the most appropriate verification method) on a relatively slow 40 MHz SUN SPARC 10, that 32 MB main memory had always been sufficient, and that the resulting low-level net had approximately 3.500 states.

6 New Features of the PEP Tool

The integration of the presented hybrid modelling approach into the PEP tool has been planned for a long time. A couple of steps towards a smooth integration have already been implemented.

** For the time being, this means systems with a complex control flow but without complex data types. The development of high-level net verification methods may solve this restriction.

1. The compiler from $B(PN)^2$ into M-nets optionally uses the first or the second approach for the generation of the semantics. Furthermore, a flexible macro concept has been introduced which allows to choose, for instance, variable or procedure nets from a library of parameterised macro nets [1].
2. The scoping mechanism has been realised as an external program allowing the different necessary scoping operations.
3. A compiler from FA into M-nets supporting the different approaches has been implemented.
4. The high-level net editor has been extended in several ways:
   (a) The concept of hierarchies has been extended towards the additional handling of special purpose parameterised macro nets.
   (b) The editor allows different views of the whole net or of its parts.
   (c) A component for the interactive composition of nets has been added.

The main task which still remains is the implementation of a convenient graphical top-level modelling support which allows the user to specify the interplay of the different components. This includes specifications such as '$B(PN)^2$ program P_1 is inserted as a procedure for the SDL process Π_1' as well as the automatic calculation of the parameters for the corresponding translations and the automatic generation of a net for the global control flow dealing, e.g., with the initialisation, termination and creation of initial process instances.

Moreover, the support for the 'programming with nets' approach will be improved. The user will have the possibility to construct a system in a compositional way using parameterised macro nets for $B(PN)^2$ as well as SDL parts. In order to insert an SDL process net, (s)he will only have to specify some parameters (such as the number of initial instances or the names and types of the formal parameters). Afterwards (s)he may specify the body of the SDL process as well as global variables, for instance. Furthermore, the level of abstraction (whether the real M-net or just an abstract Icon is displayed) may be chosen by the user as well. We will adapt ideas from the COOs [25] and the METAFrame [2] approach.

7 Conclusion

We have presented a new approach to combine different modelling techniques (finite automata, parallel programs and SDL specifications) which allow the user to profit at the same time from the advantages of all these formalisms. These are in particular,

1. powerful and efficient modelling of the control flow using finite automata,
2. high expressiveness (including, for instance, non-determinism, multiway synchronous as well as asynchronous communication and change of multiple variables at a time) of atomic actions in $B(PN)^2$,
3. and nice graphical appearance as well as a complementary communication mechanism in SDL.

Considering an ARQ protocol, we have shown that our approach enables the hybrid modelling of parallel systems and the subsequent application of the rich set of verification methods included in the PEP tool [3, 7, 18]. The fact that our approach is based on M-nets (an algebra of high-level Petri nets) at the one hand enabled the composition operations as well as the verification, but on the other hand does not imply that the user has to be familiar with the technicalities of M-nets because they may be hidden using an extension of the reference scheme presented in [17].

As a side effect we have described on-going development of the PEP tool which will not only result in a smooth integration of the presented approach, but also support a new 'programming with nets' technique.

Acknowledgement:

I would like to thank Eike Best and anonymous referees for their comments; Martin Ackermann, Ulf Fildebrandt, Michael Kater, and Stefan Schwoon for their implementations; and Hans Fleischhack for his suggestion to work on the hybrid modelling approach.

References

1. M. Ackermann. *Konzeption eines Compilers für eine parallele Programmiersprache mit Prozeduren.* Diploma thesis, Universität Hildesheim, 1997.

2. M. v. d. Beeck, V. Braun, A. Claßen, A. Dannecker, C. Friedrich, D. Koschützki, T. Margaria, F. Schreiber, and B. Steffen. Graphs in METAFrame: The Unifying Power of Polymorphism, In E. Brinksma, editor, *Proc. of TACAS'97, Enschede*, *LNCS 1217*, 112–129, Springer, 1997.

3. E. Best. Partial Order Verification with PEP. In G. Holzmann, D. Peled, and V. Pratt, editors, *Proc. of POMIV'96, Princeton*, 305–328. Am. Math. Soc., 1996.

4. E. Best, R. Devillers, and J. G. Hall. The Box Calculus: a New Causal Algebra with Multi-Label Communication. In G. Rozenberg, editor, *Advances in Petri Nets 92, LNCS* 609, 21–69. Springer, 1992.

5. E. Best, H. Fleischhack, W. Frączak, R. P. Hopkins, H. Klaudel, and E. Pelz. An M-Net Semantics of B(PN)^2. In J. Desel, editor, *Proc. of STRICT*, Workshops in Computing, 85–100, Springer, 1995.

6. E. Best, H. Fleischhack, W. Frączak, R. P. Hopkins, H. Klaudel, and E. Pelz. A Class of Composable High Level Petri Nets. G. De Michelis and M. Diaz, editors, *Proc. of ATPN'95, Torino, LNCS* 935, 103–118. Springer, 1995.

7. E. Best and B. Grahlmann. *PEP: Documentation and User Guide.* Universität Hildesheim. Available together with the tool via: http://www.informatik.uni-hildesheim.de/~pep.

8. E. Best and R. P. Hopkins. B(PN)^2 – a Basic Petri Net Programming Notation. A. Bode, M. Reeve, and G. Wolf, editors, *Proc. of PARLE, LNCS* 694, 379–390, Springer, 1993.

9. CCITT. *Specification and Description Language*, CCITT Z.100, Geneva, 1992.

10. E. Clarke, K. McMillan, S. Campos, and V. Hartonas-Garmhausen. Symbolic Model Checking. In R. Alur and T. A. Henzinger, editors, *Proc. of CAV'96, New Brunswick, LNCS* 1102, 419–422, Springer, 1996.

11. J. Esparza, S. Römer, and W. Vogler. An Improvement of McMillan's Unfolding Algorithm. In T. Margaria and B. Steffen, editors, *Proc. of TACAS'96, Passau*, *LNCS 1055*, 87–106, Springer, 1996.

12. J. Esparza. *Model Checking Using Net Unfoldings.* In Number 23 in *Science of Computer Programming*, 151–195, Elsevier, 1994.

13. H. Fleischhack and B. Grahlmann. *A Petri Net Semantics for $B(PN)^2$ with Procedures.* Proc. of *PDSE'97*, 15–27, Boston, IEEE Comp. Soc. Press, 1997.

14. H. Fleischhack and B. Grahlmann. *A Compositional Petri Net Semantics for SDL,* Technical report, HIB 18/97, Universität Hildesheim, 1997.

15. H. Fleischhack and B. Grahlmann. *Towards Compositional Verification of SDL Systems.* Proc. of *31st HICSS – Software Technology Track*, 404–414, IEEE Computer Society Press. 1998.

16. B. Grahlmann, M. Moeller, and U. Anhalt. A New Interface for the PEP Tool – Parallel Finite Automata. *Proc. of 2. Workshop Algorithmen und Werkzeuge für Petrinetze*, AIS 22, 21–26. FB Informatik Universität Oldenburg, 1995.

17. B. Grahlmann. The Reference Component of PEP. In E. Brinksma, editor, *Proc. of TACAS'97, Enschede, LNCS 1217*, 65–80, Springer, 1997.

18. B. Grahlmann. The PEP Tool. In O. Grumberg, editor, *Proc. of CAV'97, Haifa, LNCS 1254*, 440–443, Springer, 1997.

19. B. Graves. Computing Reachability Properties Hidden in Finite Net Unfoldings. *Proc. of FST&TCS'97. LNCS*, Springer. 1997.

20. G. Holzmann and D. Peled. The State of SPIN. In R. Alur and T. A. Henzinger, editors, *Proc. of CAV'96, New Brunswick, LNCS 1102*, 385–389. Springer, 1996.

21. J. E. Hopcraft and J. D. Ullmann. *Introduction to Automata Theory, and Languages, and Computation.* Addison Wesley, 1994.

22. B. W. Kernighan and D. M. Ritchie. *The C Programming Language* Prentice Hall, 1988.

23. S. Melzer and J. Esparza. Checking System Properties via Integer Programming. In H. R. Nielson, editor, *Proc. of ESOP'96, LNCS 1058*, 250–264, Springer, 1996.

24. S. Melzer and S. Römer. Synchronisierende Automaten in PEP. *Proc. of 3. Workshop Algorithmen und Werkzeuge für Petrinetze*, Technical Report 341, 52–59. AIFB Universität Karlsruhe, 1996.

25. C. Sibertin-Blanc. Cooperative Nets. In R. Valette, editor, *Proc. of ATPN'94, LNCS 815*, 471–490, Springer, 1994.

26. P. H. Starke. *INA: Integrated Net Analyzer.* Handbuch, cf. http://www.informatik.hu-berlin.de/~starke/ina.html.

27. G. Wimmel. A BDD-based Model Checker for the PEP Tool. *Technical Report, University of Newcastle upon Tyne*, 1997.

MESA: Support for Scenario-Based Design of Concurrent Systems *

Hanêne Ben-Abdallah[1] and Stefan Leue[2]

[1] Faculté des Sciences Economiques et de Gestion, Université de Sfax
Sfax, Tunisia, hanene@swen.uwaterloo.ca
[2] Electrical and Computer Engineering, University of Waterloo
Waterloo, Ontario N2L 3G1, Canada, sleue@swen.uwaterloo.ca

Abstract. The latest ITU-T standard syntax of Message Sequence Charts (MSCs) [16] offers several operators to compose MSCs in a hierarchical, iterating, and nondeterministic way. However, current tools operate on MSCs that describe finite, deterministic behavior. In this paper, we describe the architecture and the partial implementation of MESA, an MSC-based tool that supports early phases of the software development cycle. The main functionalities of MESA are: an environment for the composition of system models through MSCs, syntactic and model-based analysis of an MSC model, and resolution of resource related underspecifications in an MSC model.

1 Introduction

Message Sequence Charts (MSCs) have been extensively used in the development of telecommunication and reactive systems. They have already been adopted within several software engineering methodologies and tools, e.g., [13], [8], [17], [22], [7], [2], and [3]. MSCs are used to document system requirements that guide the system design [22], describe test scenarios (e.g., [17, 7]), express system properties that are verified against SDL specifications [2], visualize sample behavior of a simulated system specification [22, 2, 12], capture early life-cycle requirements [3], and to express legacy specifications in an intermediate representation that helps in software maintenance and reengineering [13].

In this paper we propose the architecture for an MSC-based tool for the requirements and design phases of the life-cycle of reactive systems. In addition, we illustrate how a portion of this architecture has been implemented in the *Message Sequence Chart Editor, Simulator and Analyzer* (MESA) tool. The presented tool has several motivations. One is to serve as an integration platform for various tools, which gives software engineers an access to a wider range of design and analysis techniques that can be more effective due to certain customizations. The integration is facilitated through the standardized syntax of

---

* This work was partly supported by the Information Technology Research Centre of the Province of Ontario and by the National Science and Engineering Research Council of Canada. ObjecTime Limited provided further support.

MSCs by the ITU-T in Recommendation Z.120 [16]. In other words, we view MESA as a front-end to various methods and tools, and hence code synthesis from MSC specifications is an essential objective. We currently envisage synthesis of SDL [14], ROOM [22] and Promela [11], all of which enjoy support by mature, industrial strength CASE tools.

A second motivation for MESA is to extend the usage of MSCs to the requirements specification and design phases. Current tools that use MSCs operate on MSC specifications that describe finite and deterministic system behavior. However, in its recent extension, called high-level MSCs [15], the MSC language offers modular and hierarchical operators to describe parallel, sequential, iterating, and non-deterministic execution of basic MSCs. These operators facilitate the specification of large-scale systems. In addition, MSCs offer essential constructs in a *requirements* language for reactive systems, e.g., distinction between the *system* and its *environment*, communication exchanges, internal actions, and timers along a formal semantics [16, 18]. As a design language, the notion of *processes* in MSCs along the composition operators can be used to reflect a software architecture. However, iteration and nondeterminism in MSCs require additional, explicit information, e.g., underlying network architecture and interprocess synchronization to resolve nondeterminism [5]. For this, an MSC-based tool for the design of reactive systems must offer analysis techniques to detect instances where such additional information is required and prompts the user for it.

In addition to the above type of design-related analysis, a third motivation for the tool is to provide analysis for high-level MSC models. Currently, tools that support analysis of MSCs operate only on basic MSCs. In particular, the MESA tool offers an extension of MSCs with real-time information and supports timing analysis for high-level MSCs. The time extension is based on currently evolving propositions ([16, 3].)

Another motivation for our tool is that we believe that assertional reasoning is crucial for any realistic analysis of a system model. For this, we benefit from the integration features in MESA and use existing model-checkers, more specifically, by synthesizing code that serves as an input to a model checker, e.g., Promela code for the XSPIN tool [12].

Paper organization. Section 2 discusses the suitability of MSCs for requirements specification and design, while Section 3 reviews current usages of MSCs in software engineering tools. Section 4 illustrates the usage of MSCs based on an automatic teller machine (ATM) example. Section 5 presents the architecture of MESA as an MSC-based tool for the requirements and design phases. Section 6 describes the currently implemented version of MESA and its application to the ATM example. Section 7 summarizes the paper and outlines future research directions.

2 Role of MSC-based Tools in the Software Lifecycle

The standard syntax of MSCs is defined by the ITU-T Recommendation Z.120 [16]. A basic MSC (bMSC) essentially consists of a set of processes (called instances in Z.120) that run in parallel and exchange messages in a one-to-one, asynchronous fashion. In addition to exchanging messages, processes can individually execute internal *actions*, use *timers* to express timing constraints, create and terminate process instances. The standard extension of the MSC language, called *High-Level MSCs* (hMSCs) [16], provides for operators to connect *basic* MSCs to describe parallel, sequential, iterating, and non-deterministic execution of basic MSCs. In addition, hMSCs can describe a system in a hierarchical fashion by combining hMSCs within an hMSC.

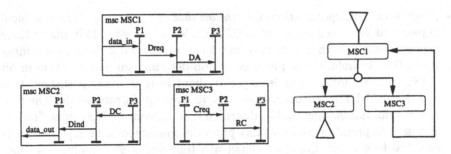

Fig. 1. MSC specification example: basic MSCs (left) and high-level MSC (right)

As an example of an MSC specification, consider Figure 1 which describes a simple connection establishment protocol in a telecommunication system. Process **P1** is a service provider, **P2** is a local and **P3** is a remote protocol machine. The iterating branch describes a repeated request to establish the connection. The non-iterating branch describes a successful connection establishment. The semantics of an MSC essentially consists of sequences (or traces) of messages that are sent and received among the concurrent processes in the MSC. The order of communication events (i.e. message sent or received) in a trace is deduced from the visual flow of control within each process in the MSC along with a causal dependency between the event of sending and receiving a message [18].

Message Sequence Charts offer several advantages to the requirements and design phases of the development of reactive systems. One is the intuitive, graphical notation of MSCs which helps a designer to visualize the system's structure and interfaces. In addition, as a *requirements* specification language an advantage of MSCs is the level of abstraction they offer by merely describing the message flow between processes (which is the core of reactive systems) and abstracting out process behavior. This is to be contrasted to other specification techniques, e.g., SDL and ROOM, which explicitly specify the process behavior and leave the message flow implicit. Another advantage of MSCs as a requirements language is the distinction between the actions of the system and its environment: MSCs visually distinguish between the actions the system produces or initiates from those produced by the environment, which facilitates the identification of the interface between the two system components. For example, in Figure 1 the environment sends a message of type data_in to the system through the process

P1; the system sends a message of type **data_out** to the environment through the process **P1**. As a *design language*, MSCs are suitable through their notions of processes and composition operators which facilitate the description of the system's software architecture.

Due to the focussed expressiveness of MSCs, it is unrealistic to build a CASE tool exclusively on MSCs. A tool based on MSCs should be a front-end to other CASE tools, supporting early life-cycle requirements capture and validation capabilities (see also [3]). In addition, an MSC-based tool should support a number of functionalities including:

- *Analysis* of MSC specifications for *"things that can go wrong"*. The graphical appeal and perceived clarity of MSC specifications contrasts limits in their expressiveness, which in turn may lead to ambiguities due to underspecifications. For example, in the presence of non-determinism and iteration in an hMSC, explicit information is required about inter-process synchronization and the underlying network architecture and queuing strategies [5]. The lack of this information may lead to discrepancies between an MSC specification and its interpretation and thus any potential implementation [5]. Thus, it is essential to support analysis mechanisms that detect such ambiguities and suggest to the designer possible extensions to resolve them. Other analyses include analysis of the consistency of timing constraints attached to an MSC, and semantic analysis that checks safety and liveness properties.
- *Synthesis* of code skeletons in full-fledged specification notations such as SDL, ROOM or Promela, and *testing* notations such as TTCN when testing support is crucial. Code synthesis allows the MSC tool to be integrated with other tools that provide additional functionalities e.g. model-based analysis.
- Means to *simulate* the execution of MSC specifications.
- A GUI-based *editor* to manipulate MSC specifications.

Based on the above tool requirements, we have designed and partly implemented a tool called MESA (*M*essage Sequence Charts *E*ditor, *S*imulator and *A*nalyzer) to support software design for concurrent systems at early life-cycle stages.

3   MSCs in Software Engineering Tools

In our review of current tools (c.f. [4]) that use MSCs, we examined the following set of requirements we find important in the requirements and design phases as previously described: 1) The use of MSCs in the description of reactive systems makes constructs to support *branching* and *iterating* indispensable. 2) Overall compliance with a syntactic convention like Recommendation *Z.120* or the UML [8] notation is desirable. 3) While a translation from MSCs into a different formalism, e.g., for analysis purposes may be necessary, we require that as little *semantic bias* as possible be included. In particular, we criticise the interpretation of MSCs based on SDL, as sometimes proposed, because of SDL's heavily constraining message passing semantics. 4) In a notation that benefits from graphical appeal and visual allusion to such an extent as MSCs, it is mandatory to have semantic assumptions explicitly represented in the specification. Allowing implicit semantic assumptions would defeat the purpose of using MSCs during the requirements and design phases where precise specifications are vital. We call this requirement the *"what-you-see-is-what-you-get"* (WYSIWYG) requirement w.r.t. the semantics given to MSCs as described by their visual representation. 5) A requirements tool needs to provide for means to check the *consistency* of the requirements specified. 6) Executing or simulating MSCs can greatly enhance the debugging of a specification, and thus *simulation* should be provided by an MSC-based tool.

We have analyzed a sizable subset of the tools that support MSC specifications (c.f. [4]). The set of analyzed tools includes:

- The *ObjecTime* toolset by ObjecTime Limited which supports editing of basic MSCs to document requirements on the communication behaviour of an ObjecTime model [22] and to visualize execution traces of an ObjecTime model.
- The SDL based tools *GEODE* [2] by Verilog SA and the *SDT* [1] by Telelogic AB both support editing of basic MSCs as well as a requirements validation check that answers whether at least one execution of the SDL system corresponds to a given bMSC.
- The *MSC Analyzer/POGA* tool by Bell Labs [3] is centered around bMSCs and provides means to analyze an MSC specification syntactically for timing constraints, and analyze it with respect to potential discrepancies between the perceived and the implied event ordering in an MSC. This tool supports the editing of hMSCs, but analysis is focussed on only basic MSCs.
- The *SDE* [13] and *MuSiC++* [20] developed by NTT are closely related tools centered around SDL and providing for MSC editing, analysis and code synthesis. Analyses include an inconsistency check that is based on deadlock detection in bMSCs, and code synthesis that produces SDL code from bMSCs.

From our review of the above tools, we found out that none of them satisfactorily meets the requirements we outlined earlier. In particular, Only the *MSC Analyzer/POGA* tool supports Z.120-style MSC composition. Users are allowed to identify a simple path in the hMSC graph, which is then composed by concatenation to form a large bMSC that in turn is analyzed. Furthermore, while the *SDE* and *MuSiC++* tools provide for a variety of analysis functions, these tools suffer from a heavy bias towards an assumed SDL semantics. For instance, an MSC could be flagged as deadlocking even though it will not deadlock unless one assumes the rather constraining SDL semantics. The SDL-based semantic assumption contradicts our *WYSIWYG* requirement.

4 MSC Specification Example: an ATM System

In the remainder of this paper, we will use an Automated Teller Machine (ATM) example[1] to illustrate the functionalities of MESA. Figures 2, 3 and 4 illustrate

---

[1] A variant of this example was first presented in [6].

the MSC-based specification of the ATM example. All diagrams were generated through the editor component of MESA.

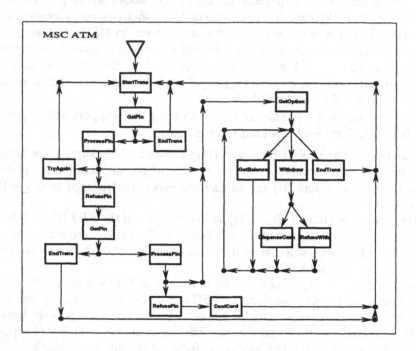

Fig. 2. hMSC for ATM System

Due to space limitations, we briefly review the example; for more detail see [6]. The ATM system consists of three concurrent components: the system's user interface that communicates with potential customers represented by the **User** process, the ATM controller software which is represented by the **ATM** process, and a host computer in a central bank office that is represented by the **Bank** process. Each one of the bMSCs in Figures 3 and 4 represents a scenario or 'use-case' of the system. The hMSC graph in Figure 2 specifies a successor relationship between these scenarios.

5 Architecture of an MSC Requirements and Design Tool

Figure 5 presents a data flow diagram-like view of the architecture of MESA. The four main functions of MESA(editing, syntactic analysis, model-based analysis, and code synthesis) are accessed through the GUI-based editor for hMSCs and bMSCs. Figure 6 shows the hMSC editor displaying the hMSC graph of the ATM example. Double clicking with the mouse on one of the boxes that represents a bMSC opens an editor window for the bMSC that is linked to this box. Figure 7 shows the bMSC editor windows for the **DispenseCash** and **Withdraw** bMSCs.

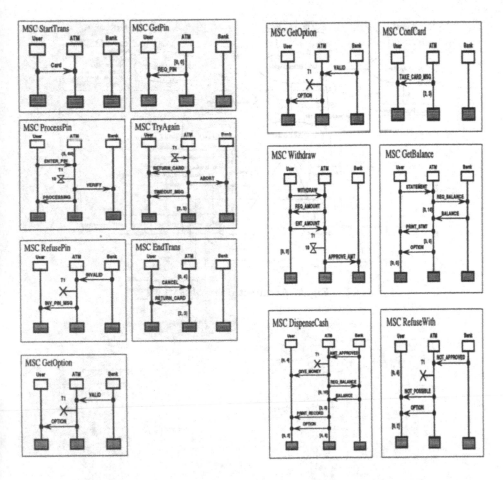

Fig. 3. Part 1 of ATM System (bMSCs)   **Fig. 4.** Part 2 of ATM System (bMSCs)

5.1 Editing

The MESA editor allows the user to textually input, draw and manipulate both
the hMSC and bMSC components of an MSC specification. In addition, it allows
the user to load and store MSC specifications.

Syntactic Checks. There were two design goals for the editing component within
MESA. First, users should be guided in following the graphical syntax of Z.120
[16]. Second, we were interested in leaving users the freedom to choose compliance
with the Z.120 standard to some extent.

Slope of message arrows: Z.120 requires message arrows to be either downwards sloping or horizontal. In [5] we showed that this is a sufficient syntactic
condition to avoid deadlocks in an MSC specification. The MESA editor optionally enforces this rule when drawing message arrows.

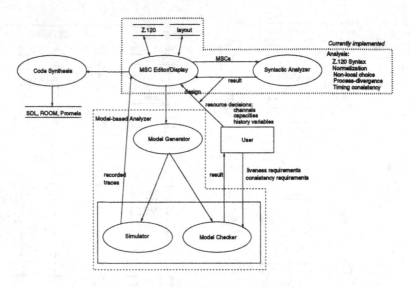

Fig. 5. Architecture of MESA

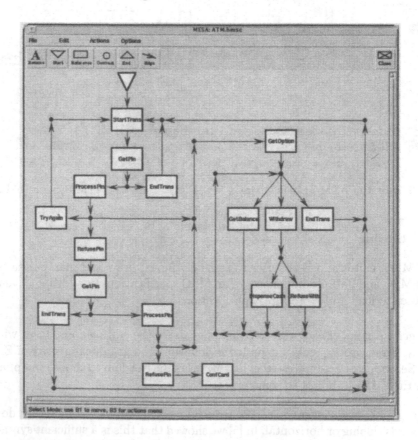

Fig. 6. Snapshot of the hMSC editor

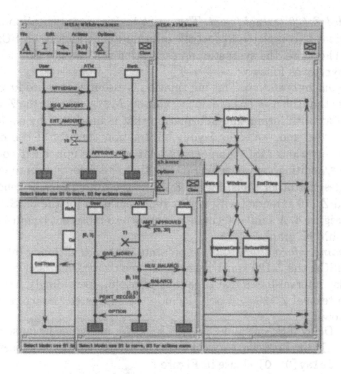

Fig. 7. hMSC and bMSC editors

Graphical well-formedness and compliance with Z.120: MESA checks *bMSCs* for compliance with the following constraints: 1. Each process must be given a unique name within the scope of a bMSC; 2. each message type must always be sent and consumed by the same pair of processes within an MSC specification; 3. a message arrow may not be directed upwards; and 4. two messages may not originate from the exact spot on a process axes to avoid ambiguities in the interpretation of the event ordering. For *hMSCs*, MESA checks the following consistency requirements: 1. All references to bMSCs must be defined; 2. all referenced bMSCs must be legal according to the above bMSC rules; 3. there must be exactly one start node; 4. the hMSC graph must be connected; and 5. the list of process names for each bMSC that is referenced in an hMSC must be identical in all bMSCs. In addition, MESA verifies whether an MSC specification is normalized, i.e. that after a branching in the hMSC graph no two bMSCs have an identical message exchange prefix. Normalization is needed for some analyses [5].

Input and Output Formats. MSC specifications can be stored in three different data formats:

– *Strict Z.120 textual format* [16]. Compliance with the standard textual syntax facilitates sharing of MSC specifications amongst different CASE tools.

– *Extended Z.120 textual fomat.* The strict textual representation of MSCs is insufficient to completely reflect the information content of bMSCs as we use them. Therefore, the syntactic representation that we use extends the strict Z.120 syntax as follows.

1. *Layout information.* This information is essential to reproduce chart layouts that the user has previously chosen. MESA extends the Z.120 textual syntax with formatting information that is bracketed by comment symbols '/*' and '*/'. The layout information consists of the coordinates of the various MSC components relative to the upper left corner of the MESA editing canvas, which means that this information may be meaningless for other tools. Figure 8 shows the automatically generated textual Z.120 extended with layout representation for the bMSC `Withdraw` of Figure 4. A similar technique is chosen to represent layout information for hMSC graphs.

2. *Timing information.* MESA represents two types of timing information in bMSCs: the Z.120 timer-based real-time constraints, and our suggested delay interval-based real-time constraints [6]. Accordingly, MESA extends the textual Z.120 syntax to include the suggested timing constraints as follows:

   • Delay intervals along *process axes*: We introduce a clause `delay [1, u]`[2] in between two consecutive events within a process, c.f. the `delay[0, 0]` clause in Figure 8.

   • Delay intervals along *message arrows*: We extend the Z.120 message clauses with a delay interval. For example, consider the sending of a message of type A to a process P, which is represented by the clause `out A to P;`. To add the timing constraint that this message arrow has been labeled by a `delay [1, u]` clause, we extend this clause to `out A to P delay [1, u];`.

– *Encapsulated Postscript.* To support the use of MSCs in software requirements and design documentation, MESA generates encapsulated postscript code of hMSC graphs and bMSCs.

Graphical Editor. The GUI-based editor (c.f. Figures 6 and 7) provides an icon-based drawing palette with the basic components of the bMSC and hMSC languages. The GUI-based editor is implemented with an object-oriented interface. One mouse click on a drawn object shows a menu of actions associated with the object.

5.2 Syntactic Property Analysis

It is often less expensive to verify properties of a specification syntactically as opposed to analyzing the specification's model. Currently, MESA implements three types of properties that can be efficiently checked syntactically: *process divergence, non-local branching choice* and *timing consistency* (c.f. [5]).

---

[2] 1 and u denote numeric values representing the *lower* and the *upper* bound for the message delivery delay, respectively.

```
msc Withdraw;
inst User, ATM, Bank;
        instance User    /* x=72 length=280*/;
                out WITHDRAW to ATM      /* y=76 */;
                in REQ_AMOUNT from ATM   /* y=110 */;
                out ENT_AMOUNT to ATM    /* y=146 */;
                delay [0, 0];
        endinstance;
        instance ATM     /* x=190 length=280*/;
                in WITHDRAW from User    /* y=76 */;
                out REQ_AMOUNT to User   /* y=110 */;
                in ENT_AMOUNT from User  /* y=146 */;
                set T1 (10)      /* y=187*/;
                out APPROVE_AMT to Bank  /* y=217 */;
        endinstance;
        instance Bank    /* x=304 length=280*/;
                in APPROVE_AMT from ATM  /* y=217 */;
        endinstance;
endmsc;
```

Fig. 8. Z.120 compliant textual syntax of the Withdraw bMSC generated by MESA

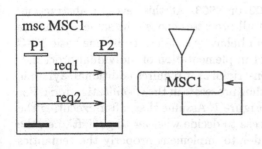

Fig. 9. MSC specification with process divergence

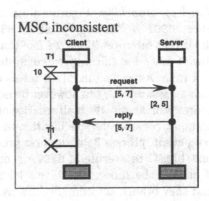

Fig. 10. Timing inconsistent bMSC

Process divergence. When processes iterate in an MSC specification, the asynchronous nature of communication can lead to *process divergence*: a system execution where one process sends a message an unbounded number of times ahead of the receiving process. Since an MSC specification makes no assumption about the speed of its processes, in the absence of a *hand-shake* mechanism, a sender process can run "faster" than a receiver process – possibly flooding the receiver with messages. As an example of process divergence, consider the MSC specification of Figure 9. One possible execution of this MSC specification is the infinite trace !req1 !req2 !req1 !req2 $\cdots$ which is the result of process P1 sending messages without process P2 receiving any one. To handle such a potential execution, the implementation must answer several questions: What is the network architecture between the processes P1 and P2? Is there any queuing mechanism and protocol and if so, what is the capacity of the channels? How are multiple copies of a not-yet received message handled, are they overwritten or are they buffered? Regardless of the answers to the above questions, none of them is based on information explicitly described in the given MSC specification. In addition, different answers may result in different implementations. We view process divergence as potentially *unintended* behavior of the specification that must be detected and brought to the designer's attention. This allows the designer to decide either to modify the specification to resolve the problem (e.g., by adding explicit hand-shakes), or to postpone the problem to the implementation phase. We have syntactically characterized process divergence and developed an algorithm (now implemented in MESA) that runs in a time linear with the number of messages in an MSC specification [5]. The algorithm basically examines the bMSCs involved in a loop and verifies that the processes within the bMSCs communicate through a hand-shake.

Non-local branching. Figure 1 illustrates an example which describes a system where MSC1 is followed by either MSC2 or MSC3. At this level of abstraction, all current interpretations assume that all processes choose the same alternative flow of control so that the overall system behavior is described by one basic MSC at a time. As argued in [5], in terms of implementation of individual processes, such an assumption can however be non-trivial as it requires additional, dynamic information about which alternative other processes in the specification took. For example, consider the specification in Figure 1. Assume that, after executing the Dreq event, process P1 is the first process to decide whether to go 'left', i.e., the next bMSC to execute is MSC2. In order to implement properly the semantics of choice, the processes P2 and P3 must be informed about P1's decision so that they branch accordingly. However, neither the MSC semantics as presented in Annex B of Z.120 [16] nor hMSC graphs provide an explicit way to handle such an information exchange. MESA implements our algorithm to detect non-local branching choices and which executes in a time linear with the number of messages in an MSC specification [5]. The basic idea behind our algorithm is to examine the bMSCs involved in a choice and verify that they all have the same, unique process which sends the first event. In case an MSC specification contains a non-local branching choice, our syntactic analysis produces the bMSCs that are involved in the non-local branching. This allows the user to resolve the choice by modifying the relevant bMSCs.

Timing Analysis. The usage of timing constraints may lead to specifications that have no timed execution, i.e. the specification is timing inconsistent [6]. Consider the bMSC in Figure 10. Obviously, the minimum time that passes from sending message **request** until receiving message **reply** when following the messages and the processing within process **Server** is at least 12 seconds. However, within process **Client** it is assumed that timer T1, which is set to 10 seconds right before sending **request**, is not expiring before **reply** is received. This means that the conjunction of all timing constraints is not satisfiable by any system execution. MESA implements our timing analysis algorithm for branching and iterating MSC specifications in [6] which extends work in [3, 9].

6 Using MESA in the Analysis of the ATM System

The automatic analysis of the ATM example shows that there are no syntactic anomalies and inconsistencies with Z.120 syntax in this specification. This analysis ensures that the subsequent analysis algorithms deliver meaningful results.

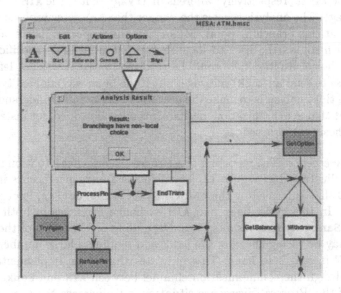

Fig. 11. MESA reporting *Non-local Choice*

Non-local Choice. Figure 11 illustrates how MESA reports the presence of a non-local choice situation in the ATM System. The non-local choice lies in the hMSC branching point that follows the bMSC **ProcessPin:** in **RefusePin** and

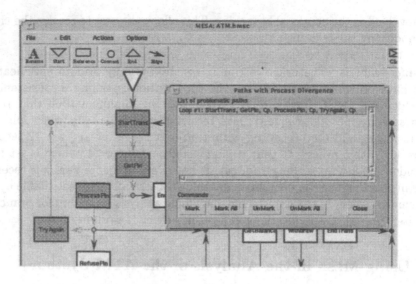

Fig. 12. MESA reporting *Process Divergence*

GetOption it is the **Bank** process which carries out the first action, i.e. sending of **INVALID** or **VALID**, respectively; whereas in **TryAgain** it is the **ATM** that sends the first message. The analysis reveals the danger that processes proceed in different directions at this branching point. MESA tags the respective parts of the hMSC graph which allows the user to localize the potential underspecification. The non-local choice situation here could be resolved in case it was not left up to the **ATM** process to send an **ABORT** message, but if the **Bank** was enabled to do so. The purpose of this analysis is to make the user aware of potential underspecifications, and to hint that synchronization mechanisms must be added, for instance, before code synthesis can proceed.

Process Divergence. The reporting of a Process Divergence situation in the ATM system is illustrated in Figure 12. The Process Divergence occurs in a loop in the hMSC that is formed by the bMSCs **StartTrans**, **GetPin**, **ProcessPin** and **TryAgain**. In this cycle, **User** and **ATM** exchange messages in both directions, while the **Bank** only receives messages. Depending on the speed of the processes, the **ATM** may be racing ahead of the **Bank** and sending a large number of **VERIFY** and **ABORT** messages to **Bank**. This indicates that in an implementation must carefully design the communication channel between **ATM** and **Bank**. A possible remedy of this Process Divergence situation is to increase the level of synchronization between the three processes. For example, the **TryAgain** scenario could be extended so that after sending the **ABORT** message to **Bank** the **ATM** process would only proceed after it had received a **CONFIRM_ABORT** message from **Bank**.

Timing Consistency. In the basic version shown in Figures 2, 3 and 4 all the timing assignments are consistent. But let us assume that we are more concerned about analyzing the timings in the example. Assume that we change the original specification of the ATM system as indicated in Figure 13: the transmission of APPROVE_AMT takes [4,7) seconds, the computations of Bank to determine that the amount cannot be approved take [3,5] seconds, and the transmission of the NOT_APPROVED message consumes [4,7) seconds. The question is now whether these new timing constraints are consistent with the remainder of the timing constraints in the system.

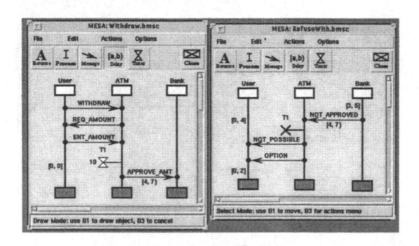

Fig. 13. Altered bMSCs in the ATM example

Timing analysis in MESA shows that these timing constraints are in conflict with the 10 second timer setting of T1 in Withdraw and the pre-expiry reset of this timer in RefuseWith. Figure 14 illustrates how MESA reports the presence of a timing inconsistency by displaying a list of simple loop paths through the hMSC graph that have a timing inconsistency. MESA allows the user to tag some or all of the timing inconsistent loops in order to localize the timing inconsistencies. In Figure 14 we have tagged the loop # 4, which directly connects Withdraw and RefuseWith. For the ATM system, the timing analysis takes about 10 seconds of execution time on a Sun Sparc Ultra 1 –200 MHz system.

7 Conclusion

We have proposed an architecture of a tool for the requirements specification and design of reactive systems based on Message Sequence Charts. We have described the MESA toolset as a partial implementation of this architecture. MESA is designed to be a research testbed for a large variety of algorithms and methods developed around the MSC notation.

Our tool has some similarities with the *MSC Analyzer/POGA* tool [3]. These similarities concern aspects of data formats chosen (Z.120, Postscript), the timing analysis algorithm for *basic* MSCs, and probably aspects of the graphical

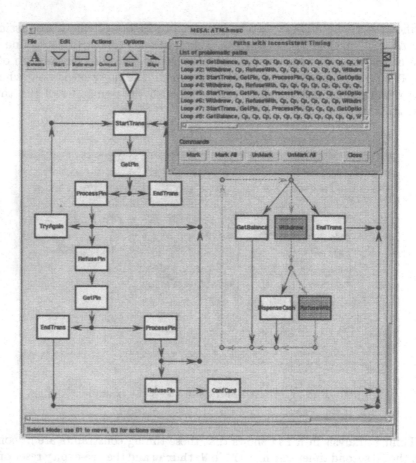

Fig. 14. MESA reporting timing inconsistency in the ATM System

user interface[3]. With respect to analysis algorithms MESA implements the following analyses that the MSC Analyzer/POGA tool does not offer: non-local choice, process divergence, and timing consistency for branching and iterating MSC specifications. In the MSC Analyzer/POGA tool it is necessary to perform manual unfoldings of the hMSC graphs in order to analyze cyclic MSC specifications. MESA performs an exhaustive search for all cyclic paths as well as a complete timing consistency analysis based on the theory discussed in [6].

Currently, we are preparing the public release of version 1.0 of MESA. It consists of those parts marked as "currently implemented" in Figure 5. At the time of writing we have spent approximately 6 man-months on code development for MESA, excluding basic research effort. The tool consists of approximately 15,000 lines of C++ and 3,000 lines of Tcl/Tk code. While the system is currently based on Unix Solaris operating system, we intend to port it to a number of

---

[3] The MSC Analyzer/POGA tool is not publicly available, hence we speculate graphical user interface similarities.

different platforms. Part of the documentation has been done using OMT [21] object modeling diagrams to accommodate the particular needs of the volatile University environment in which this system is being developed. As an "off-the-shelf" component we used the LEDA C++ library [10] for data structures like graphs and strings.

The effectiveness of the practical use of MESA hinges upon the reporting mechanism for analysis results. We are currently working on extending the *timing analysis* reporting such that not only the timing inconsistent loops in the hMSC are displayed, but also events involved in timing inconsistent loops together with the amount of timing inconsistency. To accommodate the *under-specification* of networking resources and branching synchronization mechanism we will allow the user to specify communication channels including capacities and history variables as first suggested in [19]. We are currently developing algorithms to synthesize SDL and ROOM models and we are implementing the synthesis of Promela code as suggested in [19]. Finally, to support *model analysis* and *simulation* capabilities we will pursue two routes: First, the translation into Promela together with the XSPIN model checking tool can accommodate for both features. Ultimately we would like to implement a generic simulator and model checker for MSC specifications based on MESA, which could be more efficient when based directly on the MSC objects.

Acknowledgements

The design of the user interface was based on preliminary work done by Tuan Ngo. Jennifer Hunt was instrumental in the design and implementation of the current version of MESA. She also suggested the extensions to the textual Z.120 syntax.

References

1. Telelogic AB. SDT. In G. von Bochmann, R. Dssouli, and O. Rafiq, editors, *Participant's Proceedings of the 8th International Conference on Formal Description Techniques FORTE'95, List of tools for demonstrations*, page 455, 1995.
2. B. Algayres, Y. Lejeune, F. Hugonment, and F. Hantz. The AVALON project: a validation environment for SDL/MSC descriptions. In O. Faergemand and A. Sarma, editors, *Proceedings of the 6th SDL Forum, SDL'93: Using Objects*, October 1993.
3. R. Alur, G. J. Holzmann, and D. Peled. An analyzer for Message Sequence Charts. In T. Margaria and B. Steffen, editors, *Tools and Algorithms for the Construction and Analysis of Systems, Lecture Notes in Computer Science, Vol. 1055*, pages 35–48. Springer Verlag, 1996.
4. H. Ben-Abdallah and S. Leue. Architecture of a requirements and design tool based on message sequence charts. Technical Report 96-13, Department of Electrical & Computer Engineering, University of Waterloo, October 1996.
5. H. Ben-Abdallah and S. Leue. Syntactic detection of process divergence and non-local choice in message sequence charts. In E. Brinksma, editor, *Tools and Algorithms for the Construction and Analysis of Systems, Lecture Notes in Computer Science, Vol. 1217*, pages 259–274. Springer Verlag, 1997.

6. H. Ben-Abdallah and S. Leue. Timing constraints in message sequence chart specifications. In T. Mizuno, N. Shiratori, T. Higashino, and A. Togashi, editors, *Formal Description Techniques and Protocol Specification, Testing and Verification, FORTE X / PSTV XVII '97*, pages 91 – 106. Chapman & Hall, November 1997.

7. R.J.A. Buhr and C.S. Casselman. *Use Case Maps for Object-Oriented Systems.* Prentice Hall, 1996.

8. Rational Software Corporation. UML notation guide. Research report, 1997. See also http://www.rational.com/uml.

9. R. Dechter, I. Meiri, and J. Pearl. Temporal constraint networks. *Artificial Intelligence*, 49:61–95, 1991.

10. Max Planck Institute for Computer Science. LEDA home-page, 1997. URL http://www.mpi-sb.mpg.de/LEDA/leda.html.

11. G. J. Holzman. *Design and Validation of Computer Protocols.* Prentice-Hall International, 1991.

12. G. J. Holzmann. What's new in SPIN version 2.0. http://netlib.att.com/netlib/spin/index.html, 1996. Version April 17.

13. H. Ichikawa, M. Itoh, J. Kato, A. Takura, and M. Shibasaki. SDE: Incremental specification and development of communications software. *IEEE Transactions on Computers*, 40(4):553–561, Apr. 1991.

14. ITU-T. Recommendation Z.100: Specification and Description Language (SDL). Geneva, Switzerland, 1993.

15. ITU-T. Recommendation Z.120, Annex B: Algebraic Semantics of Message Sequence Charts. ITU - Telecommunication Standardization Sector, Geneva, Switzerland, 1995. To appear.

16. ITU-T. Recommendation Z.120. ITU - Telecommunication Standardization Sector, Geneva, Switzerland, May 1996. Review Draft Version.

17. I. Jacobson and et al. *Object-Oriented Software Engineering - A Use-case Driven Approach.* Addison-Wesley, 1992.

18. P. B. Ladkin and S. Leue. Interpreting Message Flow Graphs. *Formal Aspects of Computing*, 7(5):473–509, 1995.

19. S. Leue and P. B. Ladkin. Implementing and verifying scenario-based specifications using Promela/XSpin. In J.-C. Grégoire, G. J. Holzmann, and D. A. Peled, editors, *Proceedings of the 2nd Workshop on the SPIN Verification System, Rutgers University, August 5, 1996*. American Mathematical Society, DIMACS/32, 1997.

20. NTT Software Corporation, 223-I Yamashita-Cho Naka-Ku, Nakahama-Shi Kanagawa 23I Japan. *MuSiC++ Message Sequence Charts: How To Connect with SDL*, 1995.

21. J. Rumbaugh, M. Blaha, W. Premerlani, F. Eddy, and W. L orensen. *Object-Oriented Modeling and Design.* Prentice Hall International, 1991.

22. B. Selic, G. Gullekson, and P.T. Ward. *Real-Time Object-Oriented Modelling.* John Wiley & Sons, Inc., 1994.

Efficient Modeling of Memory Arrays in Symbolic Ternary Simulation[1]

Miroslav N. Velev*
mvelev@ece.cmu.edu

Randal E. Bryant‡, *
randy.bryant@cs.cmu.edu

*Department of Electrical and Computer Engineering
‡School of Computer Science
Carnegie Mellon University, Pittsburgh, PA 15213, U.S.A.

Abstract. This paper enables symbolic ternary simulation of systems with large embedded memories. Each memory array is replaced with a behavioral model, where the number of symbolic variables used to characterize the initial state of the memory is proportional to the number of distinct symbolic memory locations accessed. The behavioral model provides a conservative approximation of the replaced memory array, while allowing the address and control inputs of the memory to accept symbolic ternary values. Memory state is represented by a list of entries encoding the sequence of updates of symbolic addresses with symbolic data. The list interacts with the rest of the circuit by means of a software interface developed as part of the symbolic simulation engine. This memory model was incorporated into our verification tool based on Symbolic Trajectory Evaluation. Experimental results show that the new model significantly outperforms the transistor level memory model when verifying a simple pipelined data path.

1 Introduction

Ternary simulation, where the "unknown" value X is used to indicate that a signal can be either 0 or 1, has proven to be very powerful for both validation and formal verification of digital circuits [10]. Given that the simulation algorithm satisfies a monotonicity property to be described later, any binary values resulting from simulating patterns with X's would also result when the X's are replaced by any combination of 0's and 1's. Hence, employing X's reduces the number of simulation patterns, often dramatically. However, ternary simulators will sometimes produce a value X, when an exhaustive analysis would determine the value to be binary (i.e., 0 or 1). This has been resolved by combining ternary modeling with symbolic simulation [1], such that the signals can accept symbolic ternary values, instead of the scalar values 0, 1, and X. Each symbolic ternary value is represented by a pair of symbolic Boolean expressions, defined over a set of symbolic Boolean variables, that encode the cases when the signal would evaluate to 0, 1, or X. The advantage of symbolic ternary simulation is that it efficiently covers a wide range of circuit operating conditions with a single symbolic simulation pattern that involves far fewer variables than would be required for a complete binary symbolic simulation.

One of the hurdles in simulation has been the representation of memory arrays. These have been traditionally modeled by explicitly representing every memory bit.

---

1. This research was supported in part by the SRC under contract 97-DC-068.

While this is not a problem for conventional simulation, symbolic simulation would require a symbolic variable to denote the initial state of every memory bit. Furthermore, bit-level symbolic model checking [4][5] would need two symbolic variables per memory bit, in order to build the transition relation. Therefore, in both methods the number of variables is proportional to the size of the memory, and is prohibitive for large memory arrays.

This limitation is overcome in our previous work [11] by replacing each memory array with an Efficient Memory Model (EMM). The EMM is a behavioral model, which allows the number of symbolic variables used to be proportional to the number of distinct symbolic memory locations accessed rather than to the size of the memory. It is based on the observation that a typical verification execution sequence usually accesses only a limited number of distinct symbolic locations. However, it was assumed that the memory address and control inputs can accept only symbolic binary values.

To our knowledge, there has not been previous research on how to define a behavioral memory model for the cases when any of its address or control inputs has the value X in symbolic ternary simulation. Our experiments with Version 2.5 of the Cadence Design Systems VERILOG-XL indicated that a *Read* operation performed with an address containing X's returned the contents of the memory location determined when the X's are replaced by 1's. Also, a *Write* operation performed with an address containing X's did not alter the contents of any memory location. Such behavior might be sufficient in conventional informal logic simulation, where performance is of greater concern than functionality when simulating X values. However, it is not adequate for ternary simulation combined with formal verification, where such behavior might result in false positive verification results. The goal of this work is to enable the EMM to accept symbolic ternary values at its address and control inputs, while providing a conservative approximation of the replaced memory array. Conservative approximation means that false positive verification results are guaranteed not to occur, although false negative verification results are possible.

This paper builds on [11] with the following contributions: 1) an extended EMM which can have symbolic ternary values at its control and address inputs, and 2) an EMM-circuit interface which guarantees that the EMM would behave as a conservative approximation of the replaced memory array. Since symbolic ternary values are a superset of symbolic binary values, the extended EMM defined in this paper is a superset of the one from [11].

Experimental results for the EMM were obtained using the Symbolic Trajectory Evaluation (STE) [10] technique for formal verification. STE is an extension of symbolic simulation that has been used to formally verify circuits, including a simple pipelined data path [3]. Incorporation of the EMM in STE enabled the verification of the pipelined data path with a significantly larger register file than previously possible.

A symbolic representation of memory arrays has been used by Burch and Dill [6]. They apply uninterpreted functions with equality, which abstract away the details of the data path and allow them to introduce only a single symbolic variable to denote the initial state of the entire memory. Each *Write* or *Read* operation results in building a formula over the current memory state, so that the latest memory state is a formula reflecting the sequence of memory writes. In our method, the memory state is represented with a list of entries encoding the sequence of updates of symbolic addresses with symbolic data. Our *Write* operation modifies this list. However, we perform the verification at the circuit level of the implementation and need bit-level data for symbolic word-level memory locations in order to verify the data path. This requires the user to introduce symbolic variables proportional to both the number of distinct symbolic memory locations accessed and the number of data bits per location.

This paper advocates a two step approach for the verification of circuits with large embedded memories. The first step is to use STE to verify the transistor level memory arrays independently from the rest of the circuit. Pandey and Bryant have combined symmetry reductions and STE to enable the verification of very large memory arrays at the transistor level [9][8]. The second step is to use STE to verify the circuit after the memory arrays are replaced by EMMs and is the focus of this work.

In the remainder of the paper, Sect. 2 describes the symbolic domain used in our algorithms. Sect. 3 gives a brief overview of STE. Sect. 4 presents the EMM and Sect. 5 introduces its underlying algorithms. Sect. 6 explains the way to incorporate the EMM into STE. Experimental results and conclusions are presented in Sect. 7.

2 Symbolic Domain

We will consider three different domains - control, address, and data - corresponding to the three different types of information that can be applied at the inputs of a memory array. A control expression c will represent the value of a node in ternary symbolic simulation and will have a high encoding $c.h$ and a low encoding $c.l$, each of which is a Boolean expression. The ternary values that can be represented by a control expression c are shown in Table 1. We would write $[c.h, c.l]$ to denote c. It will be assumed that $c.h$ and $c.l$ cannot be simultaneously **false**. The types **BExpr**, **CExpr** will denote respectively Boolean and control expressions in the algorithms to be presented.

Ternary value	$c.h$	$c.l$
0	false	true
1	true	false
X	true	true

Table 1. 2-bit encoding of ternary logic

The memory address and data inputs, since connected with circuit nodes, will receive ternary values represented as control expressions. Hence, addresses and data will be represented by vectors of control expressions having width n and w, respectively, for a memory with $N = 2^n$ locations, each holding a word consisting of w bits. Observe that an X at a given bit position represents the "unknown" value, i.e., the bit can be either 0 or 1, so that many distinct addresses or data will be represented. To capture this property of ternary simulation, we introduce the type **ASExpr** (address set expression) to denote a set of addresses. Similarly, the type **DSExpr** (data set expression) will denote a set of data. Note that in both cases, a set will be represented by a single vector of ternary values. We will use the notation $\langle a_1, \dots, a_n \rangle$ to explicitly represent the address set expression a, where a_i is the control expression for the corresponding bit position of a. Data set expressions will have a similar explicit representation, but with w bits. Symbolic variables will be introduced in each of the domains and will be used in expression generation.

The symbols $\mathcal{U}_\mathcal{A}$ and $\mathcal{U}_\mathcal{D}$ will designate the universal address and data sets, respectively. They will represent the most general information about a set of addresses or data. Similarly, the symbols $\varnothing_\mathcal{A}$ and $\varnothing_\mathcal{D}$ will denote the empty address and data sets, respectively. In ternary logic, $\mathcal{U}_\mathcal{A}$ and $\mathcal{U}_\mathcal{D}$ can be represented by vectors of control expressions consisting entirely of Xs.

We will use the term *context* to refer to an assignment of values to the symbolic variables. A Boolean expression can be viewed as defining a set of contexts, namely those for which the expression evaluates to **true**.

A symbolic predicate is a function which takes symbolic arguments and returns a symbolic Boolean expression. The following symbolic predicates will be used in our algorithms, where c is of type **CExpr**, and a is of type **ASExpr**:

$$Zero(c) \doteq \neg c.h \wedge c.l, \tag{1}$$

$$Hard(c) \doteq c.h \wedge \neg c.l, \tag{2}$$

$$Soft(c) \doteq c.h \wedge c.l, \tag{3}$$

$$Unique(a) \doteq \bigwedge_{i=1}^{n} \neg Soft(a_i). \tag{4}$$

The predicates *Zero*, *Hard*, and *Soft* define the conditions for their arguments to be the ternary 0, 1, and X, respectively. The predicate *Unique* defines the condition for the address set expression a to represent a *unique* or single address.

The selection operator *ITE* (for "If-Then-Else"), when applied on three Boolean expressions, is defined as:

$$ITE(b, t, e) \doteq (b \wedge t) \vee (\neg b \wedge e). \tag{5}$$

Address set comparison with another address set is implemented as:

$$a_1 = a_2 \doteq \neg \bigvee_{i=1}^{n} [(a_1.h_i \oplus a_2.h_i) \vee (a_1.l_i \oplus a_2.l_i)], \tag{6}$$

where $a_1.h_i$ and $a_1.l_i$ represent the high and low encodings of the control expression for bit i of address set expression a_1. Address set comparison with the universal address set is implemented as:

$$a = \mathcal{U}_\mathcal{A} \doteq \bigwedge_{i=1}^{n} Soft(a_i). \tag{7}$$

Address set selection $a_1 \leftarrow ITE(b, a_2, a_3)$ is implemented by selecting the corresponding bits:

$$a_1.h_i \leftarrow ITE(b, a_2.h_i, a_3.h_i), \quad a_1.l_i \leftarrow ITE(b, a_2.l_i, a_3.l_i), \quad i = 1, \dots, n. \tag{8}$$

Checking whether address set a_1 is a subset of address set a_2 is done by:

$$a_1 \subseteq a_2 \doteq \neg \bigvee_{i=1}^{n} (a_1.h_i \wedge \neg a_2.h_i \vee a_1.l_i \wedge \neg a_2.l_i), \tag{9}$$

and checking address sets a_1 and a_2 for overlap is implemented by:

$$Overlap(a_1, a_2) \doteq \bigwedge_{i=1}^{n} (a_1.l_i \wedge a_2.l_i \vee a_1.h_i \wedge a_2.h_i). \tag{10}$$

Computing $l \in a$, where a is an address set expression and l is a vector of Boolean expressions, is implemented by:

$$l \in a \doteq \bigwedge_{i=1}^{n} ITE(l_i, a.h_i, a.l_i). \tag{11}$$

The definition of symbolic predicates over data set expressions is similar, but over vectors of width w.

Note that all of the above predicates are symbolic, i.e., they return a symbolic Boolean expression and will be true in some contexts and false in others. Therefore, a symbolic predicate cannot be used as a control decision in algorithms. The function $Valid()$, when applied to a symbolic Boolean expression, will return **true** if the expression is valid or equal to **true** (i.e., true for all contexts), and will return **false** otherwise. We can make control decisions based on whether or not an expression is valid.

We will also need to form a data set expression that is the union of two data set expressions, d_1 and d_2. If these differ in exactly one bit position, i.e., one of them has a 0 and the other a 1, then the ternary result will have an X in that bit position and will be an exact computation. However, if d_1 and d_2 differ in many bit positions, these will be represented as Xs in the ternary result and that will not always yield an exact computation. For example, if $d_1 = \langle 0, 1 \rangle$ and $d_2 = \langle 1, 0 \rangle$, the result will be $\langle X, X \rangle$ and will not be exact, as it will also contain the data set expressions $\langle 0, 0 \rangle$ and $\langle 1, 1 \rangle$, which are not subsets of d_1 or d_2. We define the operation *approximate union* $d_1 \tilde{\cup} d_2$ of two data set expressions as:

$$[d_1 \tilde{\cup} d_2]_i \doteq [d_1.h_i \vee d_2.h_i, d_1.l_i \vee d_2.l_i], \quad i = 1, \dots, w. \tag{12}$$

Finally, we will define the operation *data merge*, $\tilde{\bigcup}_{l \in a} d$, where l is a vector of symbolic variables, a is an address set expression, and d is a data set expression, as:

$$[\tilde{\bigcup}_{l \in a} d]_i \doteq [\exists_l (l \in a) \wedge d.h_i, \exists_l (l \in a) \wedge d.l_i], \quad i = 1, \dots, w. \tag{13}$$

We have used Ordered Binary Decision Diagrams (OBDDs) [2] to represent the Boolean expressions in our implementation. However, any representation of Boolean expressions can be substituted, as long as function $Valid()$ can be defined for it.

3 STE Background

STE is a formal verification technique based on symbolic simulation. For the purpose of this paper, it would suffice to say that STE is capable of verifying circuit properties, described as *assertions*, of the form $A \overset{\text{LEADSTO}}{\Rightarrow} C$. The *antecedent* A specifies constraints on the inputs and the internal state of the circuit, and the *consequent* C specifies the set of expected outputs and state transitions. Both A and C are formulas that can be defined recursively as:

1) *a simple predicate*: (**node** $n = b$), or (**node_vector** $N = a$), or (**node_vector** $N = d$), where b, a, and d are of types **BExpr**, **ASExpr**, and **DSExpr**, respectively, and in the last two cases each node of the node vector N gets associated with its corresponding bit-level control expression of the given address-set or data-set expression;

2) *a conjunction of two formulas*: $F_1 \wedge F_2$ is a formula if F_1 and F_2 are formulas;

3) *a domain restriction*: $(b \rightarrow F)$, where b is of type **BExpr**, is a formula if F is a formula, meaning that F should hold for the contexts in which b is **true**;

4) *a next time operator*: NF is a formula if F is a formula, meaning that F should hold in the next time period;

5) *a memory array indexing predicate*: $(mem[a] = d)$, where mem is a memory name, a is of type **ASExpr**, and d is of type **DSExpr**.

A shorthand notation for k nested next time operators is N^k. A formula is said to be *instantaneous* if it does not contain any next time operators. Any formula F can be rewritten into the form $F_0 \wedge NF_1 \wedge N^2F_2 \wedge \ldots \wedge N^kF_k$, where each formula F_i is instantaneous. For simplicity in the current presentation, we will assume that the antecedent is free of self inconsistencies, i.e., it cannot have a node asserted to two complementary logic values simultaneously.

STE maintains two global Boolean expressions OK_A and OK_C, which are initialized to be **true**. The STE algorithm updates the circuit node values and the global Boolean expressions at every simulation time step. The antecedent defines the stimuli and the consequent defines the set of acceptable responses for the circuit. The expression OK_A maintains the condition under which the circuit node values are compatible with the values specified by the antecedent. The expression OK_C maintains the condition under which the circuit node values belong to the set of acceptable values specified by the consequent. The Boolean expression $\neg OK_A \vee OK_C$ defines the condition under which the assertion holds for the circuit.

4   Efficient Modeling of Memory Arrays

The main assumption of our approach is that every memory array can be represented, possibly after the introduction of some extra logic, as a memory with only write and read ports, all of which have the same numbers of address and data bits, as shown in Fig. 1.

The interaction of the memory array with the rest of the circuit is assumed to take place when a port Enable signal is not 0. In case of multiple port Enables not being 0 simultaneously, the resulting accesses to the memory array will be ordered according to the priority of the ports.

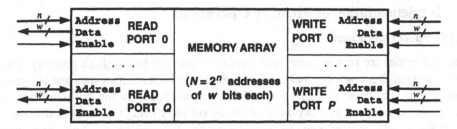

Fig. 1. View of a memory array, according to our model

During symbolic simulation, the memory state is represented by a list containing entries of the form $\langle h, s, a, d \rangle$, where h and s are Boolean expressions denoting the set of contexts for which the entry is defined, a is an address expression denoting a memory location, and d is a data expression representing the contents of this location. The context information is included for modeling memory systems where the *Write* operation may be performed conditionally on the value of a control signal c. The Boolean expression h represents the contexts $Hard(c) \wedge Unique(a)$, when the control signal was 1 and the address a was unique. Under contexts h the location a is definitely overwritten with data d. The Boolean expression s represents the contexts $Soft(c) \vee Hard(c) \wedge \neg Unique(a)$, when the control signal was an X, or it was a 1 and the address was not unique. Under contexts s the location a is uncertainly overwritten with data d. Initially the list is empty. The type **List** will be used to denote such memory lists.

The list interacts with the rest of the circuit by means of a software interface developed as part of the symbolic simulation engine. The interface monitors the memory input lines. Should a memory input value change, given that its corresponding port Enable value c is not 0, a *Write* or a *Read* operation will result, as determined by the type of the port. The Address and Data lines of the port will be scanned in order to form the address set expression a and the data set expression d, respectively. A *Write* operation takes as arguments both a and d, while a *Read* operation takes only a. Both of these operations will be presented in the next section.

After completing a *Write* operation, the software interface checks every read port of the same memory for a possible on-going read (as determined by the port Enable value being different from 0) from an address that overlaps the one of the recent write. For any such port, a *Read* operation is invoked immediately. This guarantees that the EMM will behave as a conservative approximation of the replaced memory array.

A *Read* operation retrieves from the list a data set expression rd that represents the data contents of address a. The software interface completes the read by scheduling the Data lines of the port to be updated with the data set expression $ITE(Hard(c), rd, ITE(Soft(c), (rd \stackrel{\cup}{} d), d))$. The data set expression d is the one that the Data lines will otherwise have.

5 Implementation of Memory Operations

5.1 Support Operations

The list entries are kept in order from *head* (low priority) to *tail* (high priority). The initial state of every memory location is assumed to contain arbitrary data and is represented with the universal data set $\mathcal{U}_D$. Entries in the list from low to high priority model the sequence of memory writes with the tail entry being the result of the latest memory update. Entries may be inserted at the tail end only, using procedure *InsertTail*(), and may be deleted using procedure *Delete*().

5.2 Implementation of Memory *Read* and *Write* Operations

The *Write* operation, shown as a procedure in Fig. 2, takes as arguments a memory list, a control expression denoting the contexts for which the write should be performed, and address set and data set expressions denoting the memory location and its desired contents, respectively. As the code shows, the write is implemented by simply inserting an element into the *tail* (high priority) end of the list, indicating that this entry should overwrite any other entries for this address. An optimized implementation of the *Write* operation will be presented after introducing the *Read* operation.

> **procedure** *Write*(**List** *mem*, **CExpr** *c*, **ASExpr** *a*, **DSExpr** *d*)
> /* Write data *d* to location *a* under control *c* */
> $\quad h \leftarrow Hard(c) \wedge Unique(a)$
> $\quad s \leftarrow Soft(c) \vee Hard(c) \wedge \neg Unique(a)$
> $\quad InsertTail(mem, \langle h, s, a, d \rangle)$

Fig. 2. Implementation of the *Write* operation

Two implementations of the *Read* operation are shown in Figures 3 and 4 as functions which, given a memory list and an address set expression, return a data set expression indicating the contents of this location. The purpose of both implementations is to construct a data set expression giving the contents of the memory location denoted by its argument address set expression. They do this by scanning through the list from lowest to highest priority. For each list entry, a Boolean expression *hard_match* is built that indicates the contexts for which the entry is hard (definite) and its (unique) address equals the read address *a*. Under these contexts, that element's data *ed* is selected. Else, under the contexts expressed by the Boolean expression *soft_match*, the approximate union of the element's data and the previously formed data is selected. Finally, under the contexts when both *hard_match* and *soft_match* are false, the previously formed data is kept.

Both implementations of the *Read* operation use $\mathcal{U}_D$ as the default data set expression. The contexts for which *Read* does not find a matching address in the list are those for which the addressed memory location has never been accessed by a write. The data set expression $\mathcal{U}_D$ is then returned to indicate that the location may contain arbitrary data.

function *Read*(**List** *mem*, **ASExpr** *a*) : **DSExpr**

/* Attempt to read from location *a* */

$\quad l \leftarrow GenVectorBoolVars()$

$\quad address\_containment \leftarrow l \in a$

$\quad rd \leftarrow \mathcal{U}_{\mathcal{D}}$

$\quad$**for each** $\langle eh, es, ea, ed \rangle$ **in** *mem* from head to tail **do**

$\quad\quad match \leftarrow l \in ea \wedge address\_containment$

$\quad\quad hard\_match \leftarrow match \wedge eh$

$\quad\quad soft\_match \leftarrow match \wedge es$

$\quad\quad rd \leftarrow ITE(hard\_match, ed, ITE(soft\_match, (ed \,\tilde{\cup}\, rd), rd))$

$\quad rd \leftarrow \underset{l \in a}{\tilde{\cup}} rd$

$\quad$**return** *rd*

Fig. 3. First implementation of the *Read* operation

The difference between the two implementations is in the precision of the data retrieved from non-unique addresses. While the second implementation will return $\mathcal{U}_{\mathcal{D}}$ for the contexts when the read address *a* is non-unique, the first implementation will try to extract finer data for the contents of the locations contained in *a*. It does so by building a table of data set expressions at each unique address which is a subset of the read address *a*. This is done by introducing a vector of new Boolean variables *l*, which are used for indexing all the unique addresses that are contained in the read address set expression *a*. After scanning the list, these index address variables are existentially quantified from the bit-level low and high encodings of the retrieved data set expression *rd*. This merges the data set expressions corresponding to the contents of every unique address within *a*.

A useful optimization of the indexing is to introduce as many new variables in *l* as there are non-unique bits (i.e., whose low and high encodings are not complements) in the read address set expression *a*. Then, in forming the Boolean expression *match*, the unique bits of *a* will be required to be equal to the corresponding bits of *ea*. Finally, the existential quantification in $\underset{l \in a}{\tilde{\cup}} rd$ is done only over the index variables used.

The second implementation of *Read* is designed to be precise only in the contexts when the argument address is unique, and to return $\mathcal{U}_{\mathcal{D}}$ otherwise. However, because of its fewer calculations, it requires less memory and CPU time. The expression *soft_match* is defined so that for any list entry, whose address overlaps the read address *a*, the approximate union of the entry's data set expression and the previously formed data set expression is selected. Note that in the contexts when the currently examined list element is hard, as determined by *eh*, we require that the element's address does not equal the read address (so that it is a proper subset of it). This ensures that the Boolean expressions for *hard_match* and *soft_match* will not be true simultaneously.

function *Read*(**List** *mem*, **ASExpr** *a*) : **DSExpr**

/* Attempt to read from location *a* */

 rd ← $\mathcal{U}_D$

 if ¬*Valid*(¬*Unique*(*a*)) **then**

  for each ⟨*eh*, *es*, *ea*, *ed*⟩ **in** *mem* from head to tail **do**

   hard_match ← *eh* ∧ (*ea* = *a*)

   soft_match ← (*es* ∨ *eh* ∧ ¬(*ea* = *a*)) ∧ *Overlap*(*ea*, *a*)

   rd ← *ITE*(*hard_match*, *ed*, *ITE*(*soft_match*, (*ed* $\tilde{\cup}$ *rd*), *rd*))

 return *rd*

Fig. 4. Second implementation of the *Read* operation

The difference between the two implementations of *Read*() can be illustrated with the following example. Suppose that the list for memory *mem* was initially empty and then updated with *Write*(*mem*, 1, ⟨0, 0⟩, ⟨1, 1⟩) and *Write*(*mem*, 1, ⟨0, 1⟩, ⟨1, 0⟩). Then *Read*(*mem*, ⟨0, X⟩), will return ⟨1, X⟩ when using the first implementation of the function, but ⟨X, X⟩ when using the second one. The work of the first implementation can be viewed as building a table that maps unique addresses contained in the read address to data set expressions, and then finally merging these data set expressions. In the example, the table will associate address ⟨0, 0⟩ with data ⟨1, 1⟩, and the address ⟨0, 1⟩ with data ⟨1, 0⟩, so that merging the data will give ⟨1, X⟩ as the final result.

procedure *Write*(**List** *mem*, **CExpr** *c*, **ASExpr** *a*, **DSExpr** *d*)

/* Write data *d* to location *a* under control *c* */

 h ← *Hard*(*c*) ∧ *Unique*(*a*)

 s ← *Soft*(*c*) ∨ *Hard*(*c*) ∧ ¬*Unique*(*a*)

 /* Optional optimization */

 overlap ← **false**

 for each ⟨*eh*, *es*, *ea*, *ed*⟩ **in** *mem* **do**

  if *Valid*((*eh* ∨ *es*) ⇒

    (*ea* ⊆ *a*) ∧ [*h* ∨ *s* ∧ *eh* ∧ (*d* = $\mathcal{U}_D$) ∨ *s* ∧ *es* ∧ (*ed* ⊆ *d*)]) **then**

   Delete(*mem*, ⟨*eh*, *es*, *ea*, *ed*⟩)

  else

   if ¬*Valid*(¬(*d* = $\mathcal{U}_D$)) **then**

    overlap ← *overlap* ∨ (*eh* ∨ *es*) ∧ *Overlap*(*ea*, *a*)

 if ¬*Valid*((*h* ∨ *s*) ⇒ ¬*overlap* ∧ (*d* = $\mathcal{U}_D$)) **then**

  /* Perform Write */

  InsertTail(*mem*, ⟨*h*, *s*, *a*, *d*⟩)

Fig. 5. Optimized implementation of the *Write* operation

Based on the definition of the *Read* operation, an optimized version of the *Write* operation can be constructed as shown in Fig. 5. It removes any list elements that for all contexts are either not selected, as determined by both *eh* and *es* being false simultaneously, or are overwritten by the new entry. The latter category can be subdivided into several classes:

1) Entries with a unique address, that are overwritten by a hard write (i.e., *h* is true, which implies that *a* is unique, so that ($ea \subseteq a$) will evaluate to true only for the contexts when *ea* is unique).

2) Entries with a unique address, as determined by *eh* being true, which are overwritten by a soft write (*s* is true) with data equal to $\mathcal{U}_D$. In this case, reading from the current element's address *ea* will select the element's data *ed*, but will later also form the approximate union of the previously formed data with the new element's data $\mathcal{U}_D$. Hence, $\mathcal{U}_D$ will be returned, so that the current element's data will not affect the result.

3) Entries created by a soft write (*es* is true), whose address and data set expressions are subsets of those of the new entry, which is also the result of a soft write (*s* is true). Then, reading from an address, which is a subset of the current element's address *ea*, will select the approximate union of the previously formed data with the current element's data *ed*. However, since ($ea \subseteq a$) and *s* is true, when later scanning the new list element, the approximate union of its data *d* with the previosly formed data will obscure the effect of *ed*.

Another optimization is to form the Boolean expression *overlap* that will express the condition for the new element's address *a* overlapping any other element's address. In the case of no overlap, there is no point in inserting the new element when its data is $\mathcal{U}_D$, as that will be identical with the initial state of location *a*. Finally, when both *h* and *s* are false simultaneously, there is no point in inserting the new entry, as it will never be selected.

Note that these optimizations need not be performed, as they are based on the way that the *Read* operation works. We could safely leave any overwritten element in the list and always insert the new one.

6 Incorporation into STE

Efficient modeling of memory arrays in STE requires that formulas of the form ($b \rightarrow (mem[a] = d)$), where *b* is a Boolean expression, *a* is an address set expression, *d* is a data set expression, and *mem* is a memory array, be incorporated into the STE algorithm. When such formulas occur in the antecedent, they should result in treating *d* as the data of memory location *a*, given contexts *b*, and are processed by procedure *AssertMem*(), presented in Fig. 6. OK_A, the Boolean expression indicating the absence of an antecedent failure, is updated with the condition that either *b* is false, or else the asserted data *d* is neither more general, nor incompatible with the data currently at *a*.

Similarly, when such formulas occur in the consequent, they should result in checking that the data at location *a* is neither more general, nor incompatible with the given data *d* under contexts *b*. These formulas are processed by procedure *CheckMem*() - see Fig. 7.

procedure *AssertMem*(**List** *mem*, **BExpr** *b*, **ASExpr** *a*, **DSExpr** *d*)

/* Determine conditions under which location *a* was asserted to data *d* given contexts *b*, and reflect them on OK_A, the Boolean expression indicating the absence of an antecedent failure */

    $rd \leftarrow Read(mem, a)$

    $OK_A \leftarrow OK_A \wedge (b \Rightarrow (d \subseteq rd))$

    if $\neg Valid(b \Rightarrow (d = rd))$ **then**

        $c.h \leftarrow b$

        $c.l \leftarrow \neg b$

        $Write(mem, c, a, d)$

Fig. 6. Implementation of the STE procedure *AssertMem*

procedure *CheckMem*(**List** *mem*, **BExpr** *b*, **ASExpr** *a*, **DSExpr** *d*)

/* Determine conditions under which location *a* was checked to have data *d* given contexts *b*, and reflect them on OK_C, the Boolean expression indicating the absence of a consequent failure */

    $rd \leftarrow Read(mem, a)$

    $OK_C \leftarrow OK_C \wedge (b \Rightarrow (rd \subseteq d))$

Fig. 7. Implementation of the STE procedure *CheckMem*

7 Experimental Results

Experiments were performed on the pipelined addressable accumulator shown in Fig. 8. The pipeline register Hold separates the execution and the write back stages of the pipeline. The control logic stores the previous address and compares it with the present one at the Addr input. In case of equality, the control signal of the multiplexor is set so as to select the output of the Hold register. Hence, data forwarding takes effect. For a more detailed description of the circuit and its specifications, the reader is referred to [7][11].

For the experiments with the EMM, the dual-ported register file is removed from the circuit. The software interface ensures that a *Read* operation takes place relative to phi1 and a *Write* operation takes place relative to phi2, according to the register file connections shown in Fig. 8.(b).

The specifications necessary for verifying the pipelined addressable accumulator, are presented in (14), (15), and (16). Note that Reg[*i*] and Reg[*j*] in (15) and (16), respectively, are instances of *symbolic indexing* [1]. We construct the antecedents by first defining the operation of the two phase clocks. Shorthand notation for the possible value combinations of the clocks is presented next:

$$Clk01 \doteq (\text{phi1} = 0) \wedge (\text{phi2} = 1),$$
$$Clk00 \doteq (\text{phi1} = 0) \wedge (\text{phi2} = 0),$$
$$Clk10 \doteq (\text{phi1} = 1) \wedge (\text{phi2} = 0).$$

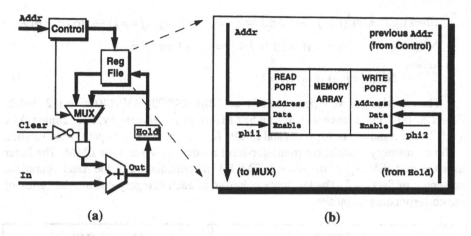

Fig. 8. (a) The pipelined addressable accumulator; (b) the connections of its register file when replaced by an EMM. The thick lines indicate buses, while the thin ones are of a single bit

The clocking behavior of the entire circuit over 4, 8, and 12 time periods, respectively, is described by:

$$Clocks\_4 \doteq Clk01 \wedge \mathbf{N}(Clk00) \wedge \mathbf{N}^2(Clk10) \wedge \mathbf{N}^3(Clk00),$$

$$Clocks\_8 \doteq Clocks\_4 \wedge \mathbf{N}^4(Clocks\_4),$$

$$Clocks\_12 \doteq Clocks\_4 \wedge \mathbf{N}^4(Clocks\_4) \wedge \mathbf{N}^8(Clocks\_4).$$

The first assertion (14) verifies that the Hold register can be initialized with data from the input In of the pipelined addressable accumulator. The next time operator $\mathbf{N}$ positions the constraints on the circuit and the desired responses that should follow relative to the phase clocks, given the timing details of the implementation.

$$Clocks\_8 \wedge \mathbf{N}^2((\texttt{Clear} = 1) \wedge (\texttt{Addr} = i) \wedge (\texttt{In} = a))$$
$$\overset{\text{LEADSTO}}{\Rightarrow} \mathbf{N}^4(\texttt{Out} = a) \wedge \mathbf{N}^5(\texttt{Hold} = a) \qquad (14)$$

The second assertion (15) verifies the adder in the pipelined addressable accumulator. The Hold register and location i of the register file are initialized in such a way, that if the circuit is correct, the second input to the adder will have the symbolic data set expression b, while its external input has data set expression a. The expected response is that the output Out of the adder will get the data set expression $a + b$, and so will the Hold register.

$$Clocks\_12 \wedge \mathbf{N}^2(\texttt{Addr} = k) \wedge \mathbf{N}^5(i == k \rightarrow \texttt{Hold} = b) \wedge$$
$$\mathbf{N}^6((\texttt{Clear} = 0) \wedge (\texttt{Addr} = i) \wedge (\texttt{In} = a) \wedge (i \mathrel{!=} k \rightarrow \texttt{Reg}[i] = b))$$
$$\overset{\text{LEADSTO}}{\Rightarrow} \mathbf{N}^8(\texttt{Out} = a + b) \wedge \mathbf{N}^9(\texttt{Hold} = a + b) \qquad (15)$$

The last assertion (16) verifies that the register file can maintain its state in the pipelined addressable accumulator.

$Clocks\_12 \land \mathbf{N}^2(i \mathrel{!=} j \rightarrow \texttt{Addr} = k) \land \mathbf{N}^5((i \mathrel{!=} j \land j == k) \rightarrow \texttt{Hold} = b) \land$

$\mathbf{N}^6((i \mathrel{!=} j \rightarrow \texttt{Addr} = i) \land ((i \mathrel{!=} j \land j \mathrel{!=} k) \rightarrow \texttt{Reg}[j] = b))$

$$\overset{\text{LEADSTO}}{\Rightarrow} \mathbf{N}^{10}(i \mathrel{!=} j \rightarrow \texttt{Reg}[j] = b) \tag{16}$$

The experiments were performed on an IBM RS/6000 43P-140 with a 233MHz PowerPC 604e microprocessor, having 512 MB of physical memory, and running AIX 4.1.5. Table 2 shows our experimental results for the pipelined data path when verified with two memory models: the transistor-level model (TLM) and the EMM. The latter uses the first (EMM_1) or the second (EMM_2) implementation of the *Read* operation, presented in Section 5. The last three columns of each category contain the ratios of the corresponding quantities.

N	w	CPU Time (s)			TLM / EMM₁	TLM / EMM₂	EMM₁ / EMM₂	Memory (MB)			TLM / EMM₁	TLM / EMM₂	EMM₁ / EMM₂
		TLM	EMM₁	EMM₂				TLM	EMM₁	EMM₂			
16	16	337	45	44	7.5	7.7	1.0	4.2	2.3	1.7	1.8	2.5	1.4
	32	676	88	86	7.7	7.9	1.0	7.3	3.3	2.1	2.2	3.5	1.6
	64	1353	173	169	7.8	8.0	1.0	13.6	5.4	2.9	2.5	4.7	1.9
	128	2716	343	337	7.9	8.1	1.0	26.3	9.5	4.7	2.8	5.6	2.0
32	16	635	51	49	12.5	13.0	1.0	8.2	3.1	1.9	2.6	4.3	1.6
	32	1265	98	93	12.9	13.6	1.1	15.3	4.9	2.5	3.1	6.1	2.0
	64	2538	196	184	12.9	13.8	1.1	29.5	8.6	3.7	3.4	8.0	2.3
	128	5077	392	374	13.0	13.6	1.0	57.7	15.8	6.2	3.7	9.3	2.5
64	16	1227	65	59	18.8	20.8	1.1	16.0	4.7	1.9	3.4	8.4	2.5
	32	2460	126	114	19.5	21.6	1.1	30.7	8.1	2.6	3.8	11.8	3.1
	64	4905	253	224	19.4	21.9	1.1	59.8	14.9	3.8	4.0	15.7	3.9
	128	9853	509	455	19.4	21.7	1.1	118.0	28.6	6.4	4.1	18.4	4.5
128	16	2423	101	87	24.0	27.9	1.2	31.6	7.9	2.3	4.0	13.7	3.4
	32	4867	203	170	24.0	28.6	1.2	61.6	14.5	2.6	4.2	23.7	5.6
	64	9659	405	337	23.8	28.7	1.2	121.1	27.7	4.0	4.4	30.3	6.9
	128	18990	830	691	22.9	27.5	1.2	241.7	54.0	6.6	4.5	36.6	8.2

Table 2. Experimental results for memories with N addresses of w bits each

As can be seen, both the EMM_1 and the EMM_2 outperform the TLM. In the case of EMM_2, a 8-29× speedup and a 3-37× reduction in memory were obtained, with the EMM_2 advantage increasing with both dimensions of the memory array. EMM_1 has a comparable performance in terms of CPU time, but requires up to 8× more memory. The advantage of EMM_2 over EMM_1 increases with both dimensions of the memory array - the more precise calculations of EMM_1 come at a premium. The asymptotic growth of time and memory is summarized in Table 3.

Criterion	TLM	EMM_1	EMM_2
Time(N)	linear	sublinear	sublinear
Time(w)	linear	linear	linear
Memory(N)	linear	sublinear	sublinear
Memory(w)	linear	linear	sublinear

Table 3. Asymptotic growth comparison of the CPU time and memory as a function of the number of addresses N and data bits w for the three memory models

Hence, the new method for efficient modeling of memory arrays has proven to be extremely promising. It will enable the symbolic ternary simulation of memory arrays far larger than previously possible.

References

1. D. L. Beatty, R. E. Bryant, and C.-J. H. Seger, "Synchronous Circuit Verification by Symbolic Simulation: An Illustration," *Sixth MIT Conference on Advanced Research in VLSI*, 1990, pp. 98-112.
2. R. E. Bryant, "Symbolic Boolean Manipulation with Ordered Binary-Decision Diagrams," *ACM Computing Serveys*, Vol. 24, No. 3 (September 1992), pp. 293-318.
3. R. E. Bryant, D. E. Beatty, and C.-J. H. Seger, "Formal Hardware Verification by Symbolic Ternary Trajectory Evaluation," *28th Design Automation Conference*, June 1991, pp. 297-402.
4. J. R. Burch, E. M. Clarke, K. L. McMillan, and D. L. Dill, "Sequential Circuit Verification Using Symbolic Model Checking," *27th Design Automation Conference*, June 1990, pp. 46-51.
5. J. R. Burch, E. M. Clarke, and D. E. Long, "Representing Circuits More Efficiently in Symbolic Model Checking," *28th Design Automation Conference*, June 1991, pp. 403-407.
6. J. R. Burch, and D. L. Dill, "Automated Verification of Pipelined Microprocessor Control," *CAV '94*, D. L. Dill, ed., LNCS 818, Springer-Verlag, June 1994, pp. 68-80.
7. A. Jain, "Formal Hardware Verification by Symbolic Trajectory Evaluation," Ph.D. thesis, Department of Electrical and Computer Engineering, Carnegie Mellon University, August 1997.
8. M. Pandey, "Formal Verification of Memory Arrays," Ph.D. thesis, School of Computer Science, Carnegie Mellon University, May 1997.
9. M. Pandey, and R. E. Bryant, "Exploiting Symmetry When Verifying Transistor-Level Circuits by Symbolic Trajectory Evaluation," *CAV '97*, O. Grumberg, ed., LNCS 1254, Springer-Verlag, June 1997, pp. 244-255.
10. C.-J. H. Seger, and R. E. Bryant, "Formal Verification by Symbolic Evaluation of Partially-Ordered Trajectories," *Formal Methods in System Design*, Vol. 6, No. 2 (March 1995), pp. 147-190.
11. M. Velev, R. E. Bryant, and A. Jain, "Efficient Modeling of Memory Arrays in Symbolic Simulation,"[2] *CAV '97*, O. Grumberg, ed., LNCS 1254, Springer-Verlag, June 1997, pp. 388-399.

---

2. Available from: http://www.ece.cmu.edu/afs/ece/usr/mvelev/.home-page.html

Translation Validation *

A. Pnueli   M. Siegel   E. Singerman **

Weizmann Institute of Science, Rehovot, Israel

Abstract. We present the notion of *translation validation* as a new approach to the verification of translators (compilers, code generators). Rather than proving in advance that the compiler always produces a target code which correctly implements the source code (compiler verification), each individual translation (i.e. a run of the compiler) is followed by a validation phase which verifies that the target code produced on this run correctly implements the submitted source program.
Several ingredients are necessary to set up the – fully automatic – translation validation process, among which are:
1. A common semantic framework for the representation of the source code and the generated target code.
2. A formalization of the notion of "correct implementation" as a refinement relation.
3. A syntactic simulation-based proof method which allows to automatically verify that one model of the semantic framework, representing the produced target code, correctly implements another model which represents the source.

These, and other ingredients are elaborated in this paper, in which we illustrate the new approach in a most challenging case. We consider a translation (compilation) from the *synchronous* multi-clock data-flow language SIGNAL to *asynchronous* (sequential) C-code.

1 Introduction

In this paper, we present the notion of *translation validation* as a new approach to the verification of translators (compilers, code generators). The idea of translation validation is the following: Rather than proving in advance that the compiler always produces a target code which correctly implements the source code (compiler verification), each individual translation (i.e. a run of the compiler) is followed by a validation phase which verifies that the target code produced on this run correctly implements the submitted source code.

Since compiler verification is an extremely complex task and every change to the compiler (even minor revisions) requires redoing the proof, compiler verification tends to "freezes" the compiler design, and discourages any future improvements and revisions. This drawback is avoided in the translation validation

* This research was done as part of the European Community project SACRES (EP 20897) and was supported in part by the Minerva Foundation and an infrastructure grant from the Israeli Ministry of Sciences and Art.
** Current address: Computer Science Laboratory, SRI International, Menlo Park, California.

approach since it compares the input and the output of the compiler for each individual run independently of *how* the output is generated from the input.

The concept of translation validation is depicted in Fig. 1.

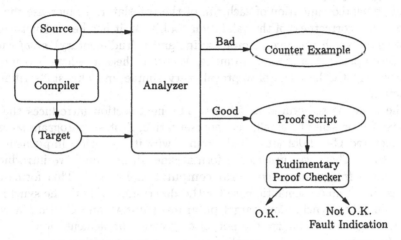

Fig. 1. The concept of Translation Validation

Both the *source* and the *target* programs are fed as inputs to an *Analyzer*. If the analyzer finds that the generated target program correctly implements the source program, it generates a detailed proof script. If the analyzer fails to establish the correct correspondence between source and target, it produces a counter-example. The counter example consists of a scenario in which the generated code behaves differently than the source code. Thus, the counter-example provides an evidence that the compiler is faulty and needs to be fixed.

The following ingredients are necessary to set up the – fully automatic – translation validation process:

1. A common semantic framework for the representation of the source code and the generated target code.
2. A formalization of the notion of "correct implementation" as a refinement relation, based on the common semantic framework.
3. A proof method which allows to prove that one model of the semantic framework, representing the produced target code, correctly implements another model which represents the source.
4. Automation of the proof method, to be carried out by the *analyzer* which, if successful, will also generate a *proof script*; and
5. A rudimentary *proof checker* that examines the proof script produced by the analyzer and provides the last confirmation for the correctness of the translation.

These ingredients are elaborated in this paper, in which we illustrate the new approach in a most challenging case. We consider a translation (compilation) from the *synchronous* multi-clock data-flow language SIGNAL [BGJ91] to *asynchronous* (sequential) C-code.

As part of the Esprit-supported SACRES project (Safety Critical Embedded Systems), the proposed translation validation tool described here is expected to provide repeated validation of each run of the translator. To increase the confidence in the correctness of the validation tool itself, it has been structured into an *analyzer* which produces a proof script and a (rudimentary) *proof checker*. This decomposition enables us to make the proof checker, which is responsible for providing the last seal of approval, very simple and almost "verifiable by inspection".

The paper is structured as follows. The next section introduces the basic notions: We present the small, yet representative, SIGNAL pprogram MUX; give the generated C-code of MUX, and explain why it "correctly implements" the source code. Then, we turn to the formal side. In Section 3 we introduce the *synchronous transition system* (STS) computational model. This formalism is used as the common semantic base for the description of both the synchronous source and the asynchronous target programs (SIGNAL and C resp., in our example). Section 4 formalizes the notion of "correct implementation" by means of a refinement relation. A generalization of the refinement-mapping simulation method is advocated as a proof method for the refinement relation. Automation of this proof method, based on syntactic representation of an appropriate proof rule, is the topic of Section 5, and finally, concluding remarks appear in Section 6. A more detailed discussion of the proof-checker and the decision procedures that were used is saved for the full version.

Related Work

Work in a similar direction was recently reported by Cimatti et al. [C97]. Due to the similarity between the source and target languages, the translation they considered is rather straightforward, and is therefore verified using a much simpler technique than the one we develop here.

Another related work is the "Proof-Carrying Code" mechanism of Necula and Lee, cf. [NL96,N97]. We believe that the translation validation approach may have several advantages over proof-carrying code. The translation validation framework is more general due to its abstract computational model and refinement notions, which the proof-carrying code method does not enjoy. Another important advantage of translation validation is that it is fully automatic, while in proof-carrying code the crucial part of the correctness proof, namely, the verification condition, is generated manually.

2 An Illustrative Example

In this section we first illustrate details of the compilation process by means of an example and then explain the principles which underly the translation validation process.

SIGNAL [BGJ91] is a synchronous programming language used for design and implementation of reactive systems. Statements of SIGNAL are intended to relate clocks (frequencies) as well as values of the various (internal and external) signal flows involved in a given reactive system. Variables (signals) in SIGNAL , as is often the case in synchronous languages, are *volatile*. That is, they only hold values at specific time instances along a computation. Put differently, variables are *absent* almost everywhere along a computation.

Consider the following SIGNAL program:

```
process MUX=
     ( ? integer FB
       ! integer N
     )
       (| N:= FB default (ZN-1)
        | ZN:= N $ 1
        | FB^=when (ZN<=1)
        |)
       where
          integer ZN init 1 ;
end
```

This program uses the integer variable FB as input, the integer variable N as output and the local variable ZN. The body of MUX is composed of three statements which are executed concurrently as follows. An input FB is read and copied to N. If N is greater than 1 it is successively decremented by referring to ZN, which holds the previous value of N (using $ to denote the "previous value" operator) . No new input value for FB is accepted until ZN becomes (or is, in case of a previous non-positive input value for FB) less than or equal to 1. This is achieved by the satatement

```
FB^=when (ZN<=1),
```

which is read "the *clock* of FB is on when ZN ≤ 1", and allows FB to be present only when ZN ≤ 1. A possible computation of this program is:

$$\begin{pmatrix} FB:3 \\ N:3 \\ ZN:1 \end{pmatrix} \rightarrow \begin{pmatrix} FB:\bot \\ N:2 \\ ZN:3 \end{pmatrix} \rightarrow \begin{pmatrix} FB:\bot \\ N:1 \\ ZN:2 \end{pmatrix} \rightarrow \begin{pmatrix} FB:5 \\ N:5 \\ ZN:1 \end{pmatrix} \rightarrow \begin{pmatrix} FB:\bot \\ N:4 \\ ZN:5 \end{pmatrix} \rightarrow \ldots$$

Where $\bot$ denotes the absence of a signal. Note that SIGNAL programs are not expected to terminate.

Let us now consider the C-code obtained by compiling a SIGNAL program. The main-program consists basically of two functions:

- An *initialization* function, which is called once to provide initial values to the program variables.
- An *iteration* function which is called repeatedly in an infinite loop. This function, whose body calculates the effect of one synchronous "step" of the abstract program, is the essential part of the concrete code.

The iteration function obtained by compiling MUX is given below.

```
logical MUX_iterate()
{
10:      h1 = TRUE;
11:      h2 = ZN <= 1;
12:      if (h2)
12.1:        read(FB);
13:      if (h2)
13.1:        N = FB;
         else
13.2:        N = ZN - 1;
14:      write(N);

15:      ZN = N;
         return TRUE;
}
```

Remark 1. The labels are not generated by the compiler but have been added for reference.

The C-code introduces explicit boolean variables to represent the clocks of SIGNAL variables and events. Variable h1 is the clock of N and ZN, and h2 is the clock of FB.

The C program works as follows. If h2, the clock of FB, has the value *true*, a new value for FB is read and assigned to the variable N. If h2 is *false*, N gets the value $ZN - 1$. In both cases the updated value of N is output (at l_4) and also copied into ZN, for reference in the next step .

A computation of this program is given below. We skip some of the intermediate states and use the notation $X : *$ to denote that variable X has an arbitrary value.

$$
\begin{pmatrix} FB:* \\ N:* \\ ZN:1 \\ h1:* \\ h2:* \\ pc:l_0 \end{pmatrix} \rightarrow^* \begin{pmatrix} FB:* \\ N:* \\ ZN:1 \\ h1:* \\ h2:t \\ pc:l_2 \end{pmatrix} \rightarrow^* \begin{pmatrix} FB:3 \\ N:* \\ ZN:1 \\ h1:t \\ h2:t \\ pc:l_3 \end{pmatrix} \rightarrow \begin{pmatrix} FB:3 \\ N:* \\ ZN:1 \\ h1:t \\ h2:t \\ pc:l_{3.1} \end{pmatrix} \rightarrow^* \begin{pmatrix} FB:3 \\ N:3 \\ ZN:1 \\ h1:t \\ h2:t \\ pc:l_5 \end{pmatrix} \rightarrow
$$

$$
\begin{pmatrix} FB:3 \\ N:3 \\ ZN:3 \\ h1:t \\ h2:t \\ pc:l_0 \end{pmatrix} \rightarrow^* \begin{pmatrix} FB:3 \\ N:3 \\ ZN:3 \\ h1:t \\ h2:f \\ pc:l_2 \end{pmatrix} \rightarrow \begin{pmatrix} FB:3 \\ N:3 \\ ZN:3 \\ h1:t \\ h2:f \\ pc:l_3 \end{pmatrix} \rightarrow \begin{pmatrix} FB:3 \\ N:3 \\ ZN:3 \\ h1:t \\ h2:f \\ pc:l_{3.2} \end{pmatrix} \rightarrow^* \begin{pmatrix} FB:3 \\ N:2 \\ ZN:3 \\ h1:t \\ h2:f \\ pc:l_5 \end{pmatrix} \rightarrow \dots
$$

Note the introduction of the variable *pc* which is the *program counter* pointing to the location of the statement which is next to be executed. When comparing this computation to the computation of the SIGNAL program, one finds that the location l_5 is of particular interest: at this location the values of the concrete variables FB, N, and ZN, whose absence or presence is determined by the variables h1 and h2, *coincide* with the values of the corresponding abstract variables.

Taking into account that h1 is the clock of N and ZN and that h2 is the clock of FB, we have an accurate state correspondence between the computation of the SIGNAL program and the following computation of the C-code, where we restrict our observations to subsequent visits at location l_5:

$$
\begin{pmatrix} \text{FB}:3 \\ \text{N}:3 \\ \text{ZN}:1 \\ \text{h1}:t \\ \text{h2}:t \\ \text{pc}:l_5 \end{pmatrix} \rightarrow^* \begin{pmatrix} \text{FB}:3 \\ \text{N}:2 \\ \text{ZN}:3 \\ \text{h1}:t \\ \text{h2}:f \\ \text{pc}:l_5 \end{pmatrix} \rightarrow^* \begin{pmatrix} \text{FB}:3 \\ \text{N}:1 \\ \text{ZN}:2 \\ \text{h1}:t \\ \text{h2}:f \\ \text{pc}:l_5 \end{pmatrix} \rightarrow^* \begin{pmatrix} \text{FB}:5 \\ \text{N}:5 \\ \text{ZN}:1 \\ \text{h1}:t \\ \text{h2}:t \\ \text{pc}:l_5 \end{pmatrix} \rightarrow^* \begin{pmatrix} \text{FB}:5 \\ \text{N}:4 \\ \text{ZN}:5 \\ \text{h1}:t \\ \text{h2}:f \\ \text{pc}:l_5 \end{pmatrix} \rightarrow^* \ldots
$$

The central observation is that there exists a *designated control location* in the C-code (l_5 in our example) where the variables of the concrete (target) system correspond to their abstract (source) counterparts. This is a general pattern for programs generated by the SACRES compiler. Intuitively, the generated C-code correctly implements the original SIGNAL program if the sequence of states obtained at the designated control location corresponds to a possible sequence of states in the abstract system.

In the rest of the paper, we show how this approach can be put on formal grounds and yield a fully automatic translation validation process.

3 The Computational Model

In this section, we present *synchronous transition systems* (STS), which is the computational model on which the process of translation validation is based.

We assume a vocabulary of typed variables $\mathcal{V}$. Some of the variables are identified as *persistent* while the others are identified as *volatile*. The volatile variables are intended to represent *signals* in the sense of the language SIGNAL. The domains of volatile variables contain the designated element $\perp$ to indicate absence of the respective signal.

A *state* s is a type-consistent interpretation of $\mathcal{V}$, assigning to each variable $v \in \mathcal{V}$ a value $s[v]$ over its domain. We denote by Σ the set of all states over $\mathcal{V}$.

Definition 1. *The following components define a* synchronous transition system (STS) $A = (V, \Theta, \rho, E)$ (cf. [PS97]):

- $V \subseteq \mathcal{V}$: A finite set of *system variables*.
- Θ : An *initial condition*. A satisfiable assertion characterizing the initial states of system A.
- ρ : A *transition relation*. This is an assertion $\rho(V, V')$, which relates a state $s \in \Sigma$ to its possible successors $s' \in \Sigma$ by referring to both unprimed and primed versions of the system variables. An unprimed version of a system variable refers to its value in s, while a primed version of the same variable refers to its value in s'. If $(s, s') \models \rho(V, V')$, we say that state s' is a ρ-successor of state s.
- $E \subseteq V$: A set of *externally observable variables*.

Next, we define a *computation* of an STS.

Definition 2. *Let $A = (V, \Theta, \rho, E)$ be an* STS. *The infinite sequence $\sigma = s_0, s_1, s_2, \ldots$, where $s_i \in \Sigma$ for each $i \in \mathbf{N}$, is a computation of A if it satisfies the following requirements:*

$$\text{Initiation}: \quad s_0 \models \Theta$$
$$\text{Consecution}: (s_i, s_{i+1}) \models \rho \quad \text{for each } i \in \mathbf{N}.$$

We denote by $\|A\|$ the set of computations of the STS A.

3.1 STS representation of the SIGNAL program

The SIGNAL program MUX is represented by the STS $A = (V, \Theta, \rho, E)$, where

$$V = \{\text{FB}, \text{N}, \text{ZN}, \text{x.N}\}$$

$$\Theta = (\text{FB} = \perp \wedge \text{N} = \perp \wedge \text{ZN} = \perp \wedge \text{x.N} = \perp)$$

$$\rho = \left\{ \begin{array}{l} \left\{ \begin{array}{l} \wedge \text{N}' = \left(\begin{array}{l} \text{if } \text{FB}' \neq \perp \text{ then } \text{FB}' \\ \text{else if } \text{ZN}' \neq \perp \text{ then } \text{ZN}' - 1 \\ \text{else } \perp \end{array} \right) \\ \wedge \text{x.N}' = \text{if } \text{N}' \neq \perp \text{ then } \text{N}' \text{ else } \text{x.N} \\ \wedge \text{ZN}' = \left(\begin{array}{l} \text{if } \text{N}' = \perp \text{ then } \perp \\ \text{else if } \text{x.N} = \perp \text{ then } 1 \\ \text{else } \text{x.N} \end{array} \right) \\ \wedge \text{ZN}' \leq 1 \leftrightarrow \text{FB}' \neq \perp \end{array} \right\} \\ \vee \ (\text{FB}' = \perp \wedge \text{N}' = \perp \wedge \text{ZN}' = \perp \wedge \text{x.N}' = \text{x.N}) \end{array} \right\}$$

$$E = \{\text{FB}, \text{N}, \text{ZN}\}$$

Two points here require further explanation:

- Besides maintaining all variables occurring in the SIGNAL-program as volatile variables, the STS-encoding of SIGNAL-programs introduces persistent *memorization variables* for those variables occurring in \$-expressions. In our example, there is only one memorization variable, namely, x.N.
- The second disjunct of ρ guarantees the stutter robustness of A. That is, at any step, the system may choose to take a stutter (idling) step in which all signals are set to $\perp$ and all memorization variables retain their previous values.

3.2 STS representation of the C program

The representation of the C code is less straightforward than that of the SIGNAL program. So, we first present the STS and then follow with detailed explanations.

The C code is described by STS C presented below. The predicate $pres(U) = \bigwedge_{v \in U}(v' = v)$ in this presentation expresses that the variables in set $U \subseteq V$ remain unchanged during the current transition, cf. [MP91].

$C = (V, \Theta, \rho, E)$ where

$V = \{\text{FB}, \text{N}, \text{ZN}, \text{x.N}, \text{h1}, \text{h2}, pc\}$

$\Theta = (\text{FB} \neq \bot \wedge \text{N} \neq \bot \wedge \text{ZN} = 1 \wedge \text{x.N} = \bot \wedge pc = l_0)$

$$\rho = \begin{cases}
\vee\ (pc = l_0 \wedge \text{h1}' = true \wedge pc' = l_1 \wedge pres(V \setminus \{pc, \text{h1}\})) \\
\vee\ (pc = l_1 \wedge \text{h2}' = (\text{ZN} \leq 1) \wedge pc' = l_2 \wedge pres(V \setminus \{pc, \text{h2}\})) \\
\vee\ (pc = l_2 \wedge \text{h2} \wedge pc' = l_{2.1} \wedge pres(V \setminus \{pc\})) \\
\vee\ (pc = l_2 \wedge \neg\text{h2} \wedge pc' = l_3 \wedge pres(V \setminus \{pc\})) \\
\vee\ (pc = l_{2.1} \wedge \text{FB}' \neq \bot \wedge pc' = l_3 \wedge pres(V \setminus \{pc, \text{FB}\})) \\
\vee\ (pc = l_3 \wedge \text{h2} \wedge pc' = l_{3.1} \wedge pres(V \setminus \{pc\})) \\
\vee\ (pc = l_3 \wedge \neg\text{h2} \wedge pc' = l_{3.2} \wedge pres(V \setminus \{pc\})) \\
\vee\ (pc = l_{3.1} \wedge \text{N}' = \text{FB} \wedge pc' = l_4 \wedge pres(V \setminus \{pc, \text{N}\})) \\
\vee\ (pc = l_{3.2} \wedge \text{N}' = \text{ZN} - 1 \wedge pc' = l_4 \wedge pres(V \setminus \{pc, \text{N}\})) \\
\vee\ (pc = l_4 \wedge \text{x.N}' = \text{N} \wedge pc' = l_5 \wedge pres(V \setminus \{pc, \text{x.N}\})) \\
\vee\ (pc = l_5 \wedge \text{ZN}' = \text{N} \wedge pc' = l_0 \wedge pres(V \setminus \{pc, \text{ZN}\}))
\end{cases}$$

$E = \{\text{FB}, \text{N}, \text{ZN}\}$

Some remarks are in order.

Input for FB: Being at location $l_{2.1}$, we allow FB to take an arbitrary non-bottom value, which corresponds to a new input for FB from the environment. If h2 is false and we proceed directly from l_2 to l_3, the value of FB remains unchanged as stated by the $pres(V \setminus \{pc\})$ clause.

Output of N: The explicit writing of N at location l_4 in the C-program has been removed; instead, the memorization of N is introduced.

The observation point: As explained above, entering location l_5 means that the mux_iterate function has cumulatively computed one transition of the abstract system. The values of the persistent variables FB, N, and ZN are considered to be present only when being at location l_5 and if their respective clock expressions have the value *true*. This will become apparent when we define the refinement mapping from STS C to STS A. All other persistent variables are considered internal.

Memorization of N: The generated C-code does not use any memorization variables but rather encode memorization by means of scheduling. In order to match the abstract memorization variables we augment the STS-encoding of the generated C-program with memorization variables which have the same name as their abstract counterparts. The general pattern for memorization is that all variables which are memorized in the abstract system, are memorized in the concrete system *directly before entering the observation location*, i.e. the location where the state correspondence is to be established.

In our example, the value of N is copied to a memorization variable x.N, at location l_4, just before the observation location l_5.

4 Correct Implementation: Refinement

In this section, we consider the notion of *correct implementation* which is the relation that should hold between a source code and its correct translation. We suggest that the appropriate relation is that of *refinement* adapted to our special circumstances that involve a translation from a synchronous language such as SIGNAL into an asynchronous language such as C.

In general, we consider refinement between an *abstract system A* and a *concrete system C*. System A can be viewed as a specification or a high-level description of the application we wish to construct, while C is a description closer to the final implementation. An elaborate development process may progress through several refinement steps, each making the representation more concrete. In many cases, the abstract system is described in a more declarative style while the concrete system is presented in a more operational/imperative style.

In order to make the implementation refinement relation maximally effective, we should make it as liberal as possible, provided the *essential* features of the system are preserved.

4.1 Refinement between Systems

Consider the two systems $A = (V_A, \Theta_A, \rho_A, E_A)$ and $C = (V_C, \Theta_C, \rho_C, E_C)$, to which we refer as the *abstract* and *concrete* systems, respectively.

We assume that $E_A \subseteq E_C$. That is, the abstract observable variables are a subset of the concrete observable variables.

For $T \in \{A, C\}$, we denote by Σ_T, the set of T-states, i.e., the set of states obtained by assigning values to the variables V_T. We denote by Σ_T^E the set of states which only assign values to the variables in $E_T \subseteq V_T$.

For a state $s \in \Sigma_T$, we denote by s^E the restriction of s to the subset of observable T-variables, i.e., to E_T. This restriction can be lifted point-wise to a computation $\sigma \in \|T\|$, denoted by σ^E, and then to the complete set of computations $\|T\|$, denoted by $\|T\|^E$.

For the two systems A and C, we define an *interface mapping* to be a function

$$\mathcal{I}: \ \Sigma_C \mapsto \Sigma_A^E,$$

mapping each concrete state $s \in \Sigma_C$ to an abstract observable state $\mathcal{I}(s) \in \Sigma_A^E$.

An interface mapping $\mathcal{I}$ is said to be a *clocked mapping* if, for each observable variable $x \in E_A$ (which also belongs to E_C since $E_A \subseteq E_C$) and every concrete state $s \in \Sigma_C$,

$$\mathcal{I}(s)[x] = s[x] \quad \text{or} \quad \mathcal{I}(s)[x] = \bot.$$

That is, the effect of the mapping $\mathcal{I}$ on a variable x which is observable in both systems is either to preserve its value $(\mathcal{I}(s)[x] = s[x])$ or to declare it absent at the current abstract state $(\mathcal{I}(s)[x] = \bot)$.

We can point-wise lift the interface mapping $\mathcal{I}$ to a concrete computation $\sigma \in \|C\|$, denoted by $\mathcal{I}(\sigma)$, and then to the complete set of concrete computations $\|C\|$, denoted by $\mathcal{I}(\|C\|)$.

Definition 3. *For systems A and C with $E_A \subseteq E_C$, and a clocked interface mapping $\mathcal{I}$ from C to A, we say that C refines A relative to $\mathcal{I}$ if $\mathcal{I}(\|C\|) \subseteq \|A\|^E$.*

That is, C refines A relative to $\mathcal{I}$ if applying the mapping $\mathcal{I}$ to any concrete computation $\sigma \in \|C\|$, we obtain an abstract computation restricted to the observable variables E_A.

Definition 4. *For systems A and C, we say that C refines A if there exists a clocked interface mapping $\mathcal{I}$ from C to A such that C refines A relative to $\mathcal{I}$.*

We write $C \sqsubseteq A$ to denote the fact that system C refines system A. In the next section we investigate a proof method which allows to establish that $C \sqsubseteq A$ indeed holds for some given $A, C \in$ STS.

4.2 Proving Refinement by the Method of Refinement Mapping (Simulation)

As proof method for the refinement notion introduced above we employ a generalization of the well-established concept of simulation with refinement mapping [AL91]. Refinement mappings define a correspondence between the variables of a concrete system and the variables of an abstract system such that observations are preserved. Refinement mappings, or more generally *simulation techniques* (see, e.g., [Jon91,LV91]), are the means to inductively prove a semantically defined notion of containment between observable behaviors.

Note that, while we employed the notion of clocked interface mapping in the definition of refinement, requiring mapping of concrete states only to the observable part of the abstract state, a general refinement mapping is expected to yield a mapping of a concrete state to a full abstract state. Thus, a refinement mapping can be viewed as one of the many possible extensions of an interface mapping.

We define a *refinement mapping from C to A* to be a function $f : \Sigma_C \longrightarrow \Sigma_A$, mapping concrete to abstract states. A refinement mapping f is called a *clocked refinement mapping* if it satisfies

$$f(s)[x] = s[x] \quad \text{or} \quad f(s)[x] = \bot, \qquad \text{for every } s \in \Sigma_C \text{ and } x \in E_A.$$

From now on, we restrict our attention to clocked refinement mappings, which preserve the observables up to stuttering.

The proposed proof method for refinement is based on finding an inductive refinement mapping as defined below. In the definition, we denote by Σ_C^r the set of all reachable states of system C, i.e., all states appearing in some computation of C.

Definition 5. *A clocked refinement mapping $f : \Sigma_C \longrightarrow \Sigma_A$ is called* **inductive** *if it satisfies the requirements of*

- *Initiation: $s \models \Theta_C$ implies $f(s) \models \Theta_A$, for all $s \in \Sigma_C$, and*
- *Propagation: $(s, s') \models \rho_C$ implies $(f(s), f(s')) \models \rho_A$, for all $s, s' \in \Sigma_C^r$.*

The use of an inductive refinement mapping as a proof method is stated in the next theorem.

Theorem 1. *If $f : \Sigma_C \longrightarrow \Sigma_A$ is an inductive (clocked) refinement mapping from C to A, then $C \sqsubseteq A$.*

5 Automating the Translation Validation Process

The proof method presented in the previous section was based on an inductive refinement mapping formulated in semantic terms. Among other things, it assumed an available characterization of the set of reachable concrete states Σ_C^r which is very difficult to compute for even the simplest systems.

In the quest for automating the process, we present in this section a *syntactical representation* of the notions of refinement mapping, and its associated proof method. In this, we follow the ideas in [Lam91,KMP94] and adapt them to deal with the particular notion of refinement needed for our case. Then, we describe how the main components used in the proof can be computed, so that the translation validation process can be carried out fully automatically.

5.1 Syntactic Representation and Proof Rules

Consider two STSs A and C with $E_A \subseteq E_C$, to which we refer as the *abstract* and the *concrete* system, respectively. Let $\alpha : V_A \longrightarrow \mathcal{E}(V_C)$ be a *substitution* that replaces each abstract variable $v \in V_A$ by an expression $\mathcal{E}_v$ over the concrete variables V_C. Such a substitution α induces a mapping between states, denoted by $\overrightarrow{\alpha}$. Let s_C be some state in Σ_C; we refer to s_C as a *concrete state*. The abstract state $s_A \stackrel{\text{def}}{=} \overrightarrow{\alpha}(s_C)$ corresponding to s_C under substitution α assigns to each variable $v \in V_A$ the value of expression $\mathcal{E}_v$ evaluated in s_C. In this way, refinement mappings can be syntactically defined by means of an appropriate substitution α.

Now we show how to syntactically formulate the requirements of initiation, propagation, and preservation of observation (the requirement that $\overrightarrow{\alpha}$ is a clocked refinement mapping) for such a state function $\overrightarrow{\alpha}$. For an expression or state formula φ over V_A, we define the formula (resp. expression) $\varphi[\alpha]$ over V_C obtained from φ by replacing each occurrence of $v \in V_A$ by $\mathcal{E}_v$. In the case that φ contains a primed variable v', this variable is replaced by $\mathcal{E}_v'$ obtained by replacing all occurrences of variables $v \in V_C$ in $\mathcal{E}_v$ by their primed versions.

Given a concrete state s_C and substitution α, we have that the value of any φ evaluated over $\vec{\alpha}(s_C)$ is the same as the value of $\varphi[\alpha]$ evaluated over s_C. This holds, since in both cases φ is evaluated using for $v \in V_A$ its value in $\vec{\alpha}(s_C)$ which is the same as the value of $\mathcal{E}_v$ evaluated over s_C. In particular, for a state formula φ over V_A we have $\vec{\alpha}(s_C) \models \varphi$ iff $s_C \models \varphi[\alpha]$. This equivalence allows to write the proof obligations of Definition 5 as stated in the following syntactical proof rule REF for proving refinement of STS-systems.

Definition 5 imposed the requirement of inductiveness only with respect to *reachable* C-states. Since these are difficult to characterize precisely, rule REF makes the stronger requirement which is that the mapping be inductive with respect to all states satisfying some C-invariant *inv*. If *inv* is indeed a C-invariant then all C-reachable states must satisfy *inv* and, therefore, inductiveness over all *inv*-states clearly implies inductiveness over all reachable states.

For assertion *inv* and substitution $\alpha : V_A \longrightarrow \mathcal{E}(V_C)$

R1. $\Theta_C \rightarrow inv$ *inv* holds initially

R2. $inv \wedge \rho_C \rightarrow inv'$ *inv* is propagated

R3. $\Theta_C \rightarrow \Theta_A[\alpha]$ Initiation

R4. $inv \wedge \rho_C \rightarrow \rho_A[\alpha]$ Propagation

R5. $inv \rightarrow (v[\alpha] = v \vee v[\alpha] = \bot)$ for all $v \in E_A$

$$C \sqsubseteq A$$

Rule REF: Proving Refinement

Two existential quantifications are hidden in this rule: "find an invariant *inv* and a substitution α, s.t. ...". Generally, finding *inv* and α is left to the ingenuity of the verifier. In order for rule REF to be useful in a fully automatic translation validation process, an appropriate invariant of the concrete system and a suitable substitution have to be generated automatically.

5.2 Generating *inv* and α

In general, there is no chance of developing an algorithm which, presented with arbitrary systems A and C, can automatically construct the needed invariant *inv* and refinement substitution α as well as automatically verify the validity of the premises in rule REF. The reason that this is possible in the case of translation validation applied to the language SIGNAL is that we rely on some very strong assumptions about the connections between A and C, based on the fact that C was produced as a result of translation of system A by a code generator of a very specific structure and mode of operation.

The general structure of the main loop in the C-code is illustrated in the figure below.

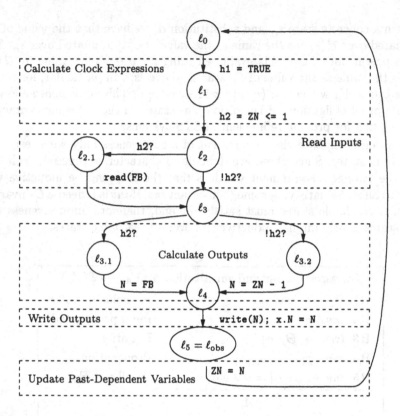

As we see in the figure, the body of the infinitely repeated loop consists of the following stages:

1. *Calculation of clock expressions.* This stage assigns values to the boolean auxiliary variables h_i, $i = 1, \ldots, k$. Each of these variables is associated with an abstract observable variable, and is used to represent the "existence"/"absence" of it.
2. *Reading inputs.* This stage reads the inputs of program, sometimes conditioned on the values of the appropriate clock variables.
3. *Calculating outputs.* This stage calculates the value of output variables.
4. *Writing outputs.* This stage write to external files (or channels) the computed values of output variables.
5. *Update "previous" expressions.* This stage updates the values of (usually local) variables defined by expressions containing the *previous* operator ($).

We use this special structure for the construction of the invariant *inv* and the substitution α. We start by noting that using the *program counter* variable pc, which is always a member of V_C, we can present the refinement substitution α as follows:

1. For each memorization variable $x.v \in V_A$, we include in α the substitution

$$x.v \quad \longrightarrow \quad x.v.$$

2. For every other variable $v \in V_A$, we include in α the substitution

$$v \quad \longrightarrow \quad \textbf{if } pc = \ell_{\text{obs}} \wedge clk(v) \textbf{ then } v \textbf{ else } \bot,$$

where $clk(v)$ is the clock expression for v, indicating whether a new value had been assigned to v in the current iteration.

The detailed algorithm for computing the clock expressions above, and the accumulative invariant inv, which is omitted here for lack of space, is described in the full version of this paper. The construction is based on viewing the main loop of the C-code (procedure MUX-iterate, in our example) as a (cyclic) directed graph, in which ℓ_0 and ℓ_{obs} are two of the nodes, and every edge e is labeled by either a *guard* $\gamma(e)$ or an action which can be a *read* into an input variable, a *write* out of an output variable, or an assignment to a (local or output) variable. For an edge labeled by an action, we can take its guard to be *true*.

The clock expression $clk(v)$ is computed by considering the guards along paths leading to assignments to v. For the MUX-example, the clock expressions obtained are

$$clk(\text{FB}) = \text{h2}$$
$$clk(\text{N}) \;\; = \text{h2} \vee \neg\text{h2} \; (= \textit{true})$$
$$clk(\text{ZN}) = \text{h2} \vee \neg\text{h2} \; (= \textit{true})$$

Based on this, the identification of the observation point as l_5 and the general "skeleton" of α given above, we obtain the following refinement substitution

$$\alpha: \quad \begin{pmatrix} \text{FB} \\ \text{N} \\ \text{ZN} \\ \text{x.N} \end{pmatrix} \quad \longrightarrow \quad \begin{pmatrix} \text{if } \text{h2} \wedge pc = l_5 \text{ then } \text{FB else } \bot \\ \text{if } pc = l_5 \text{ then } \text{N else } \bot \\ \text{if } pc = l_5 \text{ then } \text{ZN else } \bot \\ \text{x.N} \end{pmatrix}$$

The invariant inv is computed by taking the initial values of variables, and then adding the cumulative effect of the actions that are executed along paths. For the MUX-example, we obtain the following proposal for an invariant

$$inv = \begin{pmatrix} \wedge \; \text{FB} \neq \bot \; \wedge \; \text{N} \neq \bot \; \wedge \; \text{ZN} \neq \bot \\ \wedge \; pc \in \{l_0, l_1, l_2, l_{2.1}, l_3, l_{3.1}, l_{3.2}, l_4, l_5\} \\ \wedge \; pc \in \{l_1, l_2, l_{2.1}, l_3, l_{3.1}, l_{3.2}, l_4, l_5\} \rightarrow \text{h1} \\ \wedge \; pc \in \{l_2, l_{2.1}, l_3, l_{3.1}, l_{3.2}, l_4, l_5\} \quad \rightarrow \text{h2} = (\text{ZN} \leq 1) \\ \wedge \; pc \in \{l_4, l_5\} \wedge \text{h2} \qquad\qquad \rightarrow \text{N} = \text{FB} \\ \wedge \; pc \in \{l_4, l_5\} \wedge \neg\text{h2} \qquad\qquad \rightarrow \text{N} = \text{ZN} - 1 \\ \wedge \; pc = l_{2.1} \qquad\qquad\qquad\qquad \rightarrow \text{h2} \\ \wedge \; pc = l_{3.1} \qquad\qquad\qquad\qquad \rightarrow \text{h2} \\ \wedge \; pc = l_{3.2} \qquad\qquad\qquad\qquad \rightarrow \neg\text{h2} \\ \wedge \; pc \neq l_5 \qquad \rightarrow \quad \text{ZN} = (\text{if x.N} = \bot \text{ then } 1 \text{ else x.N}) \\ \wedge \; pc = l_5 \qquad\qquad\qquad\qquad \rightarrow \text{x.N} = \text{N} \end{pmatrix}$$

We have verified all the premises of rule REF, using the TLV proof system of [PS96]. The script files, which are omitted here for lack of space, will appear in the full version of this paper.

6 Conclusions

We introduced the new approach of *translation validation*, described the main components of the construction together with the underline theory, and presented an illustrative example of the method by validating a compilation from a synchronous language to an asynchronous one.

The concept of translation validation is general, and the interest is obviously not limited to translations from SIGNAL to C. We believe that the main ideas presented in this paper can serve as a basis to the translation validation for a large family of source and target languages.

Our intuition is based on the following. First, the STS computational model is very general and can model both synchronous and asynchronous languages. Second, the existence of designated control location(s) in the STS computations of the source and target programs, that can serve as an observation point(s) for comparing the values of a set of externally observable variables (input/output variables, for example), is a reasonable thing to expect for. Otherwise, in what sense could one say that the target program correctly implements the submitted source code? Finally, our notion of refinement via an interface mapping and the associated proof method, based on syntactic representation of the refinement mapping, is again of a general kind.

The approach described here seems to work in all cases that the source and the target programs each consist of a repeated execution of a single loop body, and the correspondence between the executions is such that a single loop iteration in the source corresponds to as single iteration in the target. This seems to be a characteristic of most code generators for synchronous languages such as Esterel [BG], Lustre [CHPP87], and Statecharts [H87], as well as for languages such as Unity [CMB88].

It is clear that a translation validation "tool-set" should be tailored for the particular translator (compiler) involved. The construction can be carried out by following (and modifying) the guidelines of the framework presented here. (In some cases, it may be useful to augment the translator as to make it easier to identify the observation points.) We suspect that in some cases the construction would turn out to be simpler than what was called for in the example presented here. This is so because most of the difficulties we had faced were due to the fact that SIGNAL is a *synchronous* language while C in *asynchronous*.

References

[AL91]   M. Abadi and L. Lamport. The existence of refinement mappings. *Theoretical Computer Science*, 82(2), 1991.

[BG]   G. Berry and G. Gonthier. The Synchronous Programming Language Esterel, Design, Semantics, Implementation. Technical Report 327, INRIA.

[BGJ91] A. Benveniste, P. Le Guernic, and C. Jacquemot. Synchronous programming with event and relations: the SIGNAL language and its semantics. *Science of Computer Programming*, 16, 1991.

[C97]   A. Cimatti, F. Giunchiglia, P. Pecchiari, B. Pietra, J. Profeta, D. Romano, P. Traverso, and B. Yu. A Provably Correct Embedded Verifier for the Certification of Safety Critical Software. In O. Grumberg, editor, *Proc. 9th Intl. Conference on Computer Aided Verification (CAV'97)*, Lect. Notes in Comp. Sci., vol. 1254, pages 202–213. Springer-Verlag, 1997.

[CHPP87] P. Caspi, N. Halbwachs, D. Pilaud, and J. Plaice. LUSTRE, a Declarative Language for Programming Synchronous Systems. *POPL'87*, ACM Press, pages 178–188, 1987.

[CMB88]   K. M. Chandy and J. Misra. *Parallel Program Design*. Addison-Wesley, 1988.

[H87]   D. Harel. Statecharts: A Visual Formalism for Complex Systems. *Science of Computer Programming*, 8, pages 231–274, 1987.

[Jon91]   B. Jonsson. Simulations between specifications of distributed systems. In J. C. M. Baeten and J. F. Groote, editors, *CONCUR '91*, volume 527 of *LNCS*, 1991.

[KMP94]   Y. Kesten, Z. Manna, and A. Pnueli. Temporal verification of simulation and refinement. In J.W. de Bakker, W.-P. de Roever, and G. Rozenberg, editors, *A Decade of Concurrency*, volume 803 of *Lect. Notes in Comp. Sci.* Springer-Verlag, 1994.

[Lam91]   L. Lamport. The temporal logic of actions. Technical Report 79, DEC, Systems Research Center, December 1991. To appear in Transactions on programming Languages and Systems.

[LV91]   N. Lynch and F. Vaandrager. Forward and backward simulations for timing based systems. In *Real-Time: Theory in Practice*, volume 600 of *LNCS*, 1991.

[MP91]   Z. Manna and A. Pnueli. *The Temporal Logic of Reactive and Concurrent Systems*. Springer Verlag, 1991.

[MP95]   Z. Manna and A. Pnueli. *Temporal Verification of Reactive Systems: Safety*. Springer-Verlag, New York, 1995.

[N97]   G. C. Necula. Proof-Carrying Code. In *POPL'97*, ACM press, pages 106–119, 1997.

[NL96]   G. C. Necula and P. Lee. Safe kernel extensions without run-time checking. In *Second Symposium on Operating Systems Design and Implementations*, Usenix, 1996.

[PS96]   A. Pnueli and E. Shahar. A platform for combining deductive with algorithmic verification. In R. Alur and T. Henzinger, editors, *Proc. 8th Intl. Conference on Computer Aided Verification (CAV'96)*, Lect. Notes in Comp. Sci., pages 184–195. Springer-Verlag, 1996.

[PS97]   A. Pnueli and E. Singerman. Fair synchronous transition systems and their liveness proofs. Technical report, Weizmann Institute of Science, 1997. Sacres Report.

A Verified Model Checker for the Modal μ-calculus in Coq

Christoph Sprenger

Computer Networking Laboratory,
Swiss Federal Institute of Technology, Lausanne, Switzerland
sprenger@di.epfl.ch

Abstract. We report on the formalisation and correctness proof of a
model checker for the modal μ-calculus in Coq's constructive type theory. Using Coq's extraction mechanism we obtain an executable Caml
program, which is added as a safe decision procedure to the system.
We thereby avoid the generation of large proof objects while preserving
the high reliability of the proof environment. An example illustrates the
combination of model checking with deductive techniques.

1 Introduction

There is an obvious advantage in combining theorem proving and model checking techniques for the verification of reactive systems. The expressiveness of
the theorem prover's (often higher-order) logic can be used to accommodate a
variety of program modelling and verification paradigms, so infinite state and
parametrised designs can be verified. However, using a theorem prover is not
transparent and may require a fair amount of expertise. On the other hand,
model checking is transparent, but exponential in the number of concurrent
components. Its application is thus limited to systems with small state spaces.
A combination of the two techniques can therefore alleviate the problems inherent to each of them when used in isolation. Such an integration pays off even
more, when used in combination with *reduction techniques* which transform infinite state or parametrised systems into finite state ones, while preserving the
properties of interest. These are often small enough to be amenable to model
checking. Examples of such techniques are abstract interpretation [7, 15, 11] and
inductive reasoning at the process level [27, 14].

Various model checkers have already been integrated in theorem proving environments [24, 18, 12]. Common to all these cases is that the model checker is
an external program that is invoked as needed and, most importantly, whose
results are trusted. The question of the correctness of the model checker itself
is rarely posed. In this paper, we take the position that this is an important
question, whenever the proof environment we use should be highly *reliable*. This
question gains even more importance in the context of provers based on intu-
itionistic type theory such as Coq [5], Alf [2] and Lego [16], where explicit *proof
objects* (i.e. λ-terms) are constructed during the proof. These proof objects are

then verified by an inference engine implementing the basic proof rules. Since there are only a few rules and the correctness of any proof depends only on the correct implementation of these rules, these systems can be regarded as very reliable.

We see two possibilities for the integration of a model checker into such a framework: (1) we implement it as an external program that generates the necessary proof object and add it as a tactic to the system or (2) we prove the model checker itself formally correct and then consider it as a trusted decision procedure. In both approaches the proof system for the temporal or modal logic is implemented in the prover and is therefore available for deductive proofs.

The first approach has been followed by Yu and Luo [28], the work which is closest to ours. They have implemented a model checker for the modal μ-calculus for Lego in this way. While integrating very smoothly into the prover, this approach has the problem of being inefficient. The size of the generated proof objects grows linearly with the number of applications of proof rules. This generates large proof objects even for quite small examples. The second approach is more efficient, but integrates somewhat less smoothly into the proof environment, as the results produced by the model checker have to be introduced as (safe) axioms into the prover.

Our approach is a compromise between the two. We have formalised the modal μ-calculus, a specification of the model checker in [26] and proved it correct in Coq. Using Coq's program extraction mechanism our proof is then translated into an executable Caml program. Moreover, we also have the possibility to directly run the (proof of the) model checker in Coq itself and generate a proof object. We see our contribution as two-fold. Firstly, the specification and correctness proof of the model checker provides a case study in developing provably correct sequential (functional) programs. To the best of our knowledge, this is the first formally verified model checker. Secondly, the formalisation of the μ-calculus can be used to prove properties of (possibly infinite) transition systems. For finite state systems, the model checker provides a useful decision procedure which relieves the user from tedious details of a proof. Reduction techniques can be used to reduce infinite state systems to finite state, which can then be proved automatically with the model checker. We illustrate this use with an example.

The outline of the rest of the paper is as follows. The next section gives an overview of the Coq system. Section 3 recalls the syntax and semantics of the modal μ-calculus. In section 4 we describe our formalisation of the modal μ-calculus, the proof system underlying the model checker and the correctness proof of the algorithm. Section 5 reports on an example illustrating the combination of deductive proof and automatic proof using the model checker. Finally, section 6 concludes the paper.

2 Overview of Coq

Coq [5] is an interactive proof development system implementing the Calculus of Inductive Constructions (CIC) [22, 25]. The underlying pure Calculus of Constructions [10] is the most powerful system in Barendregt's λ-cube [3]. It combines polymorphic, higher order and dependent types. The additional inductive types provide a powerful and natural mechanism for the definition of data types, specifications and predicates as well as for proofs by structural induction. Formally, CIC is a typed lambda calculus. Its natural deduction style proof rules are used to derive judgements of the form $\Gamma \vdash t : T$ meaning that in context Γ, term t has type T. Since proving T in context Γ involves the explicit construction of a λ-term t inhabiting T, the Curry-Howard correspondence allows us to identify proofs with programs and types with specifications.

2.1 The pure calculus

In Coq the following notation for the basic term and type constructions is used: $[x : A]M$ is the abstraction of $x : A$ from M (usually noted $\lambda x : A . M$), $(M\ N)$ denotes application of M to N and $(x : A)B$ the dependent product of A and B (often noted $\forall x : A . M$ or $\Pi x : A . M$). The function space $A \to B$ is the special case of the product when x does not occur free in B. Function application associates to the left and products to the right. In this paper, we write the dependent product as $\forall x : A . M$ in order to improve readability.

Moreover, there are the three constants Prop, Set and Type, called *sorts*. The pure calculus can be specified as the pure type system [3] with sorts $\mathcal{S} = \{\text{Prop}, \text{Set}, \text{Type}\}$, axioms $\mathcal{A} = \{\text{Prop} : \text{Type}, \text{Set} : \text{Type}\}$ and rules $\mathcal{R} = \mathcal{S} \times \mathcal{S}$.

2.2 Inductive types and recursion

A positive inductive type is specified by an arity, and a set of constructors. An *arity* is a type of the form $\forall x_1 : A_1 \ldots \forall x_n : A_n . s$, where s is a sort. We say the arity is of sort s. Along with each inductive type a *structural induction principle* is automatically generated. For our purpose, the definition of inductive types is best explained with a couple of examples.

Example 1. (Natural numbers) The (data) type of natural numbers is specified by the following inductive definition:

Inductive nat : Set := O : nat | S : nat $\to$ nat.

This type has arity Set and two constructors O : nat and S : nat $\to$ nat. In this case, the induction principle is a term nat_ind of the familiar type:

$$\forall P : \text{nat} \to \text{Prop}. (P\ O) \to (\forall n : \text{nat}. (P\ n) \to (P\ (S\ n))) \to \forall n : \text{nat}. (P\ n)$$

The construct Cases . . . of . . . end defines a function by case analysis; it may be combined with the Fixpoint construct to define primitive recursive functions. For instance, addition on natural numbers can be defined by primitive recursion:

Fixpoint add $[n : \text{nat}]$: nat $\to$ nat :=
  $[m : nat]$Cases n of $O \Rightarrow m \mid (S\ p) \Rightarrow (S\ (\text{add}\ p\ m))$ end.

Note that by emphasising the first argument (named n), the system is able to verify that it becomes structurally smaller in each recursive call, thus guaranteeing its termination.

Example 2. (Predicates) The predicate $\leq$ on natural numbers is defined by:

> Inductive le $[n:\text{nat}]:\text{nat}\rightarrow\text{Prop} :=$
>   le_n: (le n n)
> | le_S: $\forall m:\text{nat}.\,(\text{le } n \text{ } m)\rightarrow(\text{le } n \text{ } (S \text{ } m))$.

In fact, this defines the family of inductive predicates "$n \leq .$", indexed by $n:\text{nat}$, to be greater or equal to n.

Example 3. Logical connectives can be defined as non-recursive inductive types. The types of the constructors take the role of introduction rules, while the induction principle provides the elimination rule. As an example, we take existential quantification:

> Inductive ex$[A:\text{Set}; P: A\rightarrow\text{Prop}]:\text{Prop} :=$
>   ex_intro: $\forall x: A.\,(P \text{ } x)\rightarrow(\text{ex } A \text{ } P)$.

The associated induction principle reminds of the $\exists$-elimination rule known from natural deduction:

> ex_ind : $\forall A:\text{Set}.\,\forall P: A\rightarrow\text{Prop}.\,\forall Q:\text{Prop}.$
> $(\forall x: A.\,(P \text{ } x)\rightarrow Q)\rightarrow(\text{ex } A \text{ } P)\rightarrow Q$

2.3   Program development and extraction

According to Heyting's constructive interpretation of propositions [13], a proof of the formula $\forall x: A.\,(P \text{ } x)\rightarrow\exists y: B.\,(Q \text{ } x \text{ } y)$ is a function taking a value i and a proof of $(P \text{ } i)$ and constructs value o along with a proof that $(Q \text{ } i \text{ } o)$. So, this formula can be understood as the specification of a program with precondition P and input-output relation Q.

Any proof of this specification is a valid implementation. However, from a computational point of view, we are only interested in the input and output values and not in the proofs of P and Q, which are of purely logical content. The two sorts Set and Prop are used to mark terms of computational and of logical content, respectively. The *extraction* function, which we denote by ε, strips off (sub-)terms whose types are of sort Prop, while keeping those with types of sort Set. It also forgets about dependencies of types on terms. Its codomain is the subsystem of CIC without dependent types, called F_{ω}^{ind}. CIC is used as specification language for F_{ω}^{ind} programs. These may then be translated into executable Caml programs[1].

In Coq, there is a type sig isomorphic to ex but whose arity is of sort Set. It replaces ex in specifications. (sig A P) is written as $\{x: A \mid (P \text{ } x)\}$. Extraction

---

[1] provided they are typable in Caml, which is the case for most practical applications

yields the inductive type sig' of arity Set → Set with its only constructor of type $A \to (\text{sig}'\ A)$. This type can be simplified to the isomorphic type $[A : \text{Set}]A$. So, a proof of the specification $\forall x : A.\ (P\ x) \to \{y : B \mid (Q\ x\ y)\}$ extracts to a function $f : A \to B$. The correctness of the extractum is justified by the *realisability* interpretation [20, 21], ensuring in this case that f satisfies $\forall x : A.\ (I\ x) \to (Q\ x\ (f\ x))$.

Decision procedures are specified by a variant of logical disjunction (with arity of sort Set) given by:

> Inductive sumbool $[A : \text{Prop}; B : \text{Prop}] : \text{Set} :=$
> left: $A \to (\text{sumbool}\ A\ B) \mid$ right: $B \to (\text{sumbool}\ A\ B)$

The notation for (sumbool $A\ B$) is $\{A\} + \{B\}$. Its extraction is isomorphic to the type of booleans. For example, $\forall x, y : \text{nat}.\ \{x = y\} + \{\neg x = y\}$ specifies a decision procedure for equality on the natural numbers.

Proof methods. There are two possibilities to prove a program specification. The first one is to use the usual tactics and tacticals provided by Coq. Primitive recursive functions are constructed by structural induction on one of their arguments. More sophisticated pattern matching requires stating and proving specialised induction principles, which are then applied to obtain the desired control structure [23].

The idea of the second method is roughly to give the desired program to the system right from the beginning and then apply a special Program tactic which tries to synthesise the computational parts of the proof and generates the logical lemmas necessary to complete the proof. This is the inverse to the extraction process. However, as extraction is not invertible, the raw F_ω^{ind} program is not sufficient and the tactic needs some hints which are given by annotating the program with specifications [19]. Such annotated programs are called *realizers* and the language of realizers is called Real.

3 The propositional modal μ-calculus

The modal μ-calculus subsumes in expressive power many modal and temporal logics such as LTL and CTL. It is interpreted over labelled transition systems (LTS), which are structures of the form $T = (St, Act, \to)$, where St is a set of states, Act is a set of actions and $\to \subseteq St \times Act \times St$ is the transition relation. We write $s \overset{a}{\to} t$ for $(s, a, t) \in \to$. Assume a countable sets Var of variables and AP of atomic propositions. A *model* is a pair (T, ρ) consisting of a LTS T and an environment ρ which assigns to each variable and atomic proposition a set of states. The abstract syntax of the modal μ-calculus is now defined by

$$\phi ::= X \mid A \mid \neg A \mid \phi \vee \phi \mid \phi \wedge \phi \mid \langle \alpha \rangle \phi \mid [\alpha]\phi \mid \mu X\{U\}.\phi \mid \nu X\{U\}.\phi$$

where $X \in Var$ is a variable, $A \in AP$ is an atomic proposition and $\alpha \in Act$ is an action. The fixed point operators μ and ν are tagged with a finite set U of states. We write σ whenever we mean either of μ or ν. The semantics is then inductively defined as follows:

$$\|X\|\rho = \rho(X)$$
$$\|A\|\rho = \rho(A)$$
$$\|\neg A\|\rho = St \setminus \|A\|\rho$$
$$\|\phi_0 \vee \phi_1\|\rho = \|\phi_0\|\rho \cup \|\phi_1\|\rho$$
$$\|\phi_0 \wedge \phi_1\|\rho = \|\phi_0\|\rho \cap \|\phi_1\|\rho$$
$$\|\langle \alpha \rangle \phi\|\rho = \{s \in S \mid \exists s' \in S. s \xrightarrow{\alpha} s' \wedge s' \in \|\phi\|\rho\}$$
$$\|[\alpha]\phi\|\rho = \{s \in S \mid \forall s' \in S. s \xrightarrow{\alpha} s' \Rightarrow s' \in \|\phi\|\rho\}$$
$$\|\mu X\{U\}.\phi\|\rho = \mu S. (\Psi(S) \setminus U)$$
$$\|\nu X\{U\}.\phi\|\rho = \nu S. (U \cup \Psi(S))$$

where $\Psi(S) = \|\phi\|\rho[S/X]$. The usual $\sigma X.\phi$ is defined as $\sigma X\{\varnothing\}.\phi$. Note that the false (F) and true (T) propositions are definable as $\mu X.X$ and $\nu X.X$, respectively. This presentation of the calculus, where negation occurs only in front of atomic proposition is called positive normal form.

4 Implementation of the model checker

This section describes the formalisation of the μ-calculus in Coq and the implementation and correctness proof of the model checker described in [26].

4.1 Fixed points

Assume an arbitrary type U. Then (Ensemble U) is the type of sets over U (which are implemented as predicates $U \to$ Prop). We abbreviate this type to EnsU. Suppose further that F: EnsU $\to$ EnsU is a monotone function w.r.t. the inclusion ordering. We define the following two operators mu and nu:

Definition mu: (EnsU $\to$ EnsU) $\to$ EnsU :=
[F: EnsU $\to$ EnsU][s: U]$\forall X$: EnsU. (Included $(F\ X)\ X$) $\to$ (In X s).

Definition nu: (EnsU $\to$ EnsU) $\to$ EnsU :=
[F: EnsU $\to$ EnsU][s: U]$\exists X$: EnsU. (Included $X\ (F\ X)$) $\wedge$ (In X s).

According to Tarski's theorem, these two operators define the least and greatest fixed points of F, respectively, as is easily proved in Coq. The next ingredient is Winskel's reduction lemma, which forms the basis for the model checker:

Theorem Reduction_lemma :
(Included P (nu F)) $\leftrightarrow$
(Included P (F (nu [S: EnsU]Union P (F S)))).

It states that a set P is contained in the greatest fixed point of a monotone function exactly if it is contained in a certain kind of unfolding of that fixed point, where P is added to F under the fixed point operator.

4.2 μ-calculus syntax and semantics

Our development of the model checker will be parametrised by a labelled transition system. We assume that the set of states is finite and that we have a function which, for any state s and action a, computes a list of a-successors of s. This is expressed in the following lines:

> Parameter Act, St : Set.
> Parameter Trans: St → Act → St → Prop.
> Axiom finite_state : (Finite (Full_set St)).
> Axiom post_spec :
> $\forall s$: St. $\forall a$: Act. $\{l$: (list St) $|$ $\forall t$: St. (Elem t l) $\leftrightarrow$ (Trans s a t)$\}$.

The inductive type defining the syntax is then defined by:

> Inductive MuForm : Set :=
>   Var: nat → MuForm
> | Lit: (St → bool) → MuForm
> | And: MuForm → MuForm → MuForm
> | Or: MuForm → MuForm → MuForm
> | Box: Act → MuForm → MuForm
> | Dia: Act → MuForm → MuForm
> | Mu: (list St) → MuForm → MuForm
> | Nu: (list St) → MuForm → MuForm.

Variables are encoded in the standard way using de Bruijn indices. The valuation of atomic propositions is directly coded into the syntax in the form of computable predicates of type St → bool. Since this type is closed under negation we can drop negation altogether from the syntax. The fixed point operators are tagged with a list of states.

The type Env of environments is defined as nat → EnsSt, which can be seen as an infinite lists of sets of states. We introduce an operation env_cons : EnsSt → Env → Env with (env_cons R ρ) returning R for O and (ρ j) for $j + 1$. The function recursively computing the semantics of a formula ϕ with respect to environment ρ is defined by:

> Fixpoint Sem [ϕ: MuForm] : Env → EnsSt :=
>   [ρ : Env]Cases ϕ of
>   (Var i)   ⇒ (ρ i)
> | (Lit p)   ⇒ (cf2ens St p)
> | (And ϕ_1 ϕ_2) ⇒ (Intersection St (Sem ϕ_1 ρ) (Sem ϕ_2 ρ))
> | (Or ϕ_1 ϕ_2) ⇒ (Union St (Sem ϕ_1 ρ) (Sem ϕ_2 ρ))
> | (Box a ϕ)   ⇒ (BoxSem a (Sem ϕ ρ))
> | (Dia a ϕ)   ⇒ (DiaSem a (Sem ϕ ρ))
> | (Mu l ϕ)   ⇒ (MuSem l [R: EnsSt](Sem ϕ (env_cons R ρ)))
> | (Nu l ϕ)   ⇒ (NuSem l [R: EnsSt](Sem ϕ (env_cons R ρ)))
>   end.

The function (cf2ens St) transforms a predicate of type St → bool into the set of states (of type EnsSt) verifying the predicate. BoxSem, DiaSem are the predicate transformers defining the semantics of the modalities. In the cases of the fixed point operators, the second argument to MuSem and NuSem is the de Bruijn version of $\lambda S. \|\phi\| \rho[S/X]$ when X is the variable bound to the fixed point operator. Here, env_cons has the effect of shifting the interpretation of free variables by one, accounting for the increased abstraction depth under these operators. For illustration, we give the definitions of DiaSem and NuSem.

Inductive DiaSem [a: Act; R: EnsSt]: EnsSt :=
  dia_intro : $\forall s, t$: St. (Trans s a t) → (In St R t) → (In St (DiaSem a R) s).

Definition NuSem: (list St) → (EnsSt → EnsSt) → EnsSt :=
  [P: (list St)][Φ: EnsSt → EnsSt]
    (nu St [R: EnsSt](Union St (list2ens St P) (Φ R))).

Substitution. We define the type of substitutions Subst to be the functions of type nat → MuForm assigning each variable a μ-calculus formula. Substitution is thus a function subst : MuForm → Subst → MuForm. The following table introduces some notation which is useful in the context of de Bruijn-coded variables:

notation	definition	name
id	[i: nat](Var i)	"identity"
↑	[i: nat](Var (S i))	"shift"
$\phi \cdot \theta$	[i: nat]Cases i of$O$ $\Rightarrow$ ϕ | (S k) $\Rightarrow$ (θ k) end	"cons"
$\theta \circ \theta'$	[i: nat](subst (θ i) θ')	"composition"
$\Uparrow (\theta)$	$O \cdot (\theta \circ \uparrow)$	"lift"

In order to improve readability, we will use the usual notation $\phi[\theta]$ instead of (subst ϕ θ). In subst, the cases of the fixed point operators use 'lift' to push substitution inside, i.e. we have $(\sigma\ l\ \psi)[\theta] =_\beta (\sigma\ l\ (\psi[\Uparrow(\theta)]))$. The 'cons' operator is useful in unfolding fixed point formulas: $\psi[(\text{Nu } l\ \psi) \cdot id]$ corresponds to the unfolding of (Nu l ψ). With these definitions, we can prove:

Lemma 4. $\phi \cdot (\theta \circ \theta') = \Uparrow (\theta) \circ (\phi \cdot \theta')$.

The next lemma establishes a standard semantical correspondence between substitution and environment. It is proved is by structural induction on ϕ.

Lemma Substitution_lemma :
  $\forall \phi$: MuForm. $\forall \rho$: Env. $\forall \theta$: Subst.
    (Sem $\phi[\theta]$ ρ) = (Sem ϕ [i: nat](Sem (θ i) ρ)).

4.3 Correctness assertions

The satisfaction relation sat on states and formulas is defined as:

Inductive sat [s: St; ϕ: MuForm]: Prop :=
    sat_intro: ($\forall \rho$: Env. (In St (Sem ϕ ρ) s)) $\rightarrow$ (sat s ϕ).

We call the proposition (sat s ϕ) a *correctness assertion* and write it as $s \models \phi$. In Coq, we can prove the following lemma:

Lemma 5. *For* $\varphi, \varphi_0, \varphi_1$ *and* $(\sigma \; l \; \psi)$ *closed formulas, we have*

1. $s \models$ (And ϕ_0 ϕ_1) $\leftrightarrow$ $s \models \phi_0 \wedge s \models \phi_1$
2. $s \models$ (Or ϕ_0 ϕ_1) $\leftrightarrow$ $s \models \phi_0 \vee s \models \phi_1$
3. $s \models$ (Dia a ϕ) $\leftrightarrow$ $\exists s'$: St. (Trans s a s') $\wedge$ $s' \models \phi$
4. $s \models$ (Box a ϕ) $\leftrightarrow$ $\forall s'$: St. (Trans s a s') $\rightarrow$ $s' \models \phi$
5. *if* (Elem s l) *then (a)* $\neg(s \models$ (Mu l ψ))*, and (b)* $s \models$ (Nu l ψ)
6. *if* $\neg$(Elem s l) *then for* $\sigma \in \{$Mu, Nu$\}$:
    $s \models (\sigma \; l \; \psi)$ $\leftrightarrow$ $s \models \phi[(\sigma$ (cons s l) $\psi) \cdot id]$

Proof. Items (1)-(5) follow directly from the semantic definition. For (6), we need the Reduction and Substitution Lemmas. In the case of the least fixed point, a dual version of the Reduction Lemma is used. $\qquad\square$

These equivalences, when cast into proof rules, can be used to establish properties of arbitrary (possibly infinite state) transition systems deductively.

4.4 The algorithm

In this section, we describe the specification and correctness proof of Winskel's local model checking algorithm [26] in Coq. It decides the truth or falsity of correctness assertions by exploring the neighbourhood of the state of interest. The idea is to exploit the equivalences of the previous Lemma 5 by considering them as simplification rules (in going from left to right). As our transition system is assumed to be finite, the quantifiers appearing in cases (3) and (4) of the modal operators can be replaced by finite disjunction and conjunction, respectively.

Specification. Given a closed formula ϕ of the μ-calculus and a state s of the transition system, the model checker is supposed to decide whether s satisfies ϕ or it not. This leads us to the following Coq specification:

    MuChk: $\forall \phi$: MuForm. (Closed ϕ) $\rightarrow \forall s$: St. $\{s \models \phi\} + \{\neg(s \models \phi)\}$.

We apply Lemma 5 in order to gradually transform the decision problem into (boolean combinations of) simpler ones. The fixed point operators are dealt with by unfolding them while adding the current state to the tag, whenever it is not already there. In cases 1-4 there is a structural reduction in going from left to right. Case 5 provides the base. In case 6 the reduction is less obvious. This means that the correctness proof will proceed by well-founded induction. However, the proof also requires that we extend our specification to arbitrary formulas, be they open or closed. This leads to the following generalised specification MuChk_plus, using the auxiliary predicates Q and Q^+.

Definition Q: MuForm$\rightarrow$Set :=
  $[\phi: \text{MuForm}]\,\forall s: \text{St}.\,\{s \models \phi\}+\{\neg(s \models \phi)\}$.

Definition Q^+: MuForm$\rightarrow$Set :=
  $[\phi: \text{MuForm}]\,\forall \theta: \text{Subst}.$
    $(\forall i: \text{nat}.\,(\text{Elem}\, i\,(\text{fv}\, \phi))\rightarrow(\text{Closed}\,(\theta\, i)))\rightarrow$
      $(\forall i: \text{nat}.\,(\text{Elem}\, i\,(\text{fv}\, \phi))\rightarrow(Q\,(\theta\, i)))\rightarrow(Q\, \phi[\theta])$.

MuChk_plus: $\forall \phi: \text{MuForm}.\,(Q^+ \phi)$

The first condition in the definition of Q^+ means that the substitute $(\theta\, i)$ for each free variable i of ϕ is a closed formula. The second condition expresses the assumption that we know how to decide the satisfaction problem for these substitutes. Since a closed formula trivially satisfies both of these conditions, Q^+ is equivalent to Q in this case. With these definitions the original specification MuChk reads $\forall \phi: \text{MuForm}.\,(\text{Closed}\, \phi)\rightarrow(Q\, \phi)$.

As we will make extensive use of the proof synthesis method provided by the tactic Program, it is interesting to look at the types extracted from Q and Q^+:

$$\varepsilon(Q) = \text{St}\rightarrow\text{sumbool}$$
$$\varepsilon(Q^+) = \text{Subst}\rightarrow(\text{nat}\rightarrow\varepsilon(Q))\rightarrow\varepsilon(Q)$$

The term $(\forall i: \text{nat}.\,(\text{Elem}\, i\,(\text{fv}\, \phi))\rightarrow(\text{Closed}\,(\theta\, i)))$ in Q^+ is of sort Prop and is therefore eliminated by extraction. Also, in $(\forall i.\,\text{nat}.\,(\text{Elem}\, i\,(\text{fv}\, \psi))\rightarrow(Q\,(\theta\, i)))$ the subterm $(\text{Elem}\, i\,(\text{fv}\, \phi))$ is of sort Prop and thus removed. Extraction also forgets about the dependencies of Q and Q^+ on MuForm. Therefore, both extracted types are of the informative sort Set.

Correctness proof. We prove the generalised specification MuChk_plus by well-founded induction. The well-founded induction principle (WFI) is a theorem part of the Coq library. It is stated in the following.

well_founded_induction:
  $\forall A: \text{Set}.\,\forall R: A\rightarrow A\rightarrow\text{Prop}.\,(\text{well\_founded}\, A\, R)\rightarrow$
    $\forall P: A\rightarrow\text{Set}.\,(\forall x: A.\,(\forall y: A.\,(R\, y\, x)\rightarrow(P\, y))\rightarrow(P x))\rightarrow\forall a: A.\,(P\, a)$

The computational content of the proof of the well-founded induction principle obtained by extraction is a general recursor. Its type is $\forall A, P: \text{Set}.\,(A\rightarrow(A\rightarrow P)\rightarrow P)\rightarrow A\rightarrow P$. Note, however, that by the recursive realisability interpretation [23] any program extracted from a proof by well-founded induction is guaranteed to terminate on arguments satisfying the specified preconditions.

Proof of main theorem MuChk_plus. As we follow basically the proof in [26], we try here to point out the application of the proof method provided by realizers and the Program tactic.

Definition 6. Let $\prec$ be the proper one-step[2] subformula relation on μ-calculus formulas. Then relation $R:$ MuForm$\rightarrow$MuForm$\rightarrow$Prop is defined by:

$$[\phi, \phi': \mathtt{MuForm}](\phi \prec \phi' \vee \exists s: \mathtt{St}. \exists l: (\mathtt{list\ St}). \exists \psi: \mathtt{MuForm}.$$
$$(\neg(\mathtt{Elem}\ s\ l) \wedge \phi \equiv (\sigma\ (\mathtt{cons}\ s\ l)\ \psi) \wedge \phi' \equiv (\sigma\ l\ \psi)))$$

Well-foundedness of R follows from the assumption that the set of states St is finite. By the well-founded induction principle, MuChk_plus follows from:

$$\forall\phi: \mathtt{MuForm}. (\forall\psi: \mathtt{MuForm}. (R\ \psi\ \phi)\rightarrow(Q^+\ \psi))\rightarrow(Q^+\ \phi). \tag{1}$$

The proof proceeds by case analysis on the form of ϕ, which generates eight subgoals, one for each constructor of MuForm. We pick out the case of the greatest fixed point which we state as the lemma:

Lemma chk_Nu_plus:
$\quad \forall l: (\mathtt{list\ St}). \forall \phi: \mathtt{MuForm}.$
$\quad\quad (\forall \psi: \mathtt{MuForm}. (R\ \psi\ (\mathtt{Nu}\ l\ \phi))\rightarrow(Q^+\ \psi))\rightarrow(Q^+\ (\mathtt{Nu}\ l\ \phi)).$

After unfolding the definitions of Q^+ and Q, introducing the hypothesis into the context and pushing substitution inside Nu, we obtain the sequent:

$h:\quad \forall\psi: \mathtt{MuForm}. (R\ \psi\ (\mathtt{Nu}\ l\ \phi))\rightarrow$
$\quad\quad \forall\theta': \mathtt{Subst}.$
$\quad\quad\quad (\forall j: \mathtt{nat}. (\mathtt{Elem}\ j\ (\mathtt{fv}\ (\mathtt{Nu}\ l\ \psi)))\rightarrow(\mathtt{Closed}\ (\theta'\ j)))\rightarrow$
$\quad\quad\quad\quad (\forall j: \mathtt{nat}. (\mathtt{Elem}\ j\ (\mathtt{fv}\ (\mathtt{Nu}\ l\ \psi))\rightarrow(Q\ (\theta'\ j)))\rightarrow(Q\ \psi[\theta']))$
$\theta:\quad \mathtt{Subst}$
$h_0:\quad \forall i_0: \mathtt{nat}. (\mathtt{Elem}\ i_0\ (\mathtt{fv}\ (\mathtt{Nu}\ l\ \phi)))\rightarrow(\mathtt{Closed}\ (\theta\ i_0))$
$h_1:\quad \forall i_0: \mathtt{nat}. (\mathtt{Elem}\ i_0\ (\mathtt{fv}\ (\mathtt{Nu}\ l\ \phi))\rightarrow(Q\ (\theta\ i_0))$
$s:\quad \mathtt{St}$

$=============================$
$\quad \{s \models (\mathtt{Nu}\ l\ (\phi[\Uparrow(\theta)]))\} + \{\neg(s \models (\mathtt{Nu}\ l\ (\phi[\Uparrow(\theta)])))\}$

Note that the extracted type of the induction hypothesis h is MuForm$\rightarrow\varepsilon(Q^+)$. The realizer for this goal depends on two lemmas which are proved in the context above with the additional hypothesis $nel: \neg(\mathtt{Elem}\ s\ l)$. The first one is:

Lemma Q_Nu_cons: $(Q\ (\mathtt{Nu}\ (\mathtt{cons}\ s\ l)\ \phi)[\theta])$
Realizer $(h\ (\mathtt{Nu}\ (\mathtt{cons}\ s\ l)\ \phi)\ \theta\ h_1).$

This is automatically proved by **Program_all** using Definition 6. The second one corresponds to the right hand side of Lemma 5(6):

Lemma Q_Nu_unfold: $(Q\ (\phi[\Uparrow(\theta)]))[(\mathtt{Nu}\ (\mathtt{cons}\ s\ l)\ (\phi[\Uparrow(\theta)])) \cdot id])$

---

[2] i.e. if $\phi \prec \phi'$ then there is no ϕ'' s.t. $\phi \prec \phi'' \prec \phi'$

Using Lemma 4, we first rewrite this to $(Q \ \phi[(\text{Nu } (\text{cons } s \ l) \ (\phi[\Uparrow(\theta)])) \cdot \theta])$. Now, since by Lemma Q_Nu_cons we know how to decide $(\text{Nu } (\text{cons } s \ l) \ (\phi[\Uparrow(\theta)]))$ (which is convertible with $(\text{Nu } (\text{cons } s \ l) \ \phi)[\theta]$) and by hypothesis h_1 we know how to do so for each $(\theta \ i)$, we can use the induction hypothesis h to construct the following realizer

> Realizer $(h \ \phi \ (\text{Nu } (\text{cons } s \ l) \ (\phi[\Uparrow(\theta)])) \cdot \theta$
> $[i : \text{nat}]\text{Cases } i \text{ of } O \Rightarrow \text{Q\_Nu\_cons} \ | \ (S \ j) \to (h_1 \ j) \text{ end})$

Applying the tactic Program_all leaves us with two subgoals which are easily solved. Now, with Lemma 5(5b) and (6) in mind, we are ready to give the realizer for the goal of our original sequent:

> Realizer if (is_elem_spec s l) then true else (Q_Nu_unfold s).

where is_elem_spec : $\forall s : \text{St}. \forall l : (\text{list St}). \{(\text{Elem } s \ l)\} + \{\neg(\text{Elem } s \ l)\}$. The subgoals generated by Program_all are all easily proved using Lemmas 5(5b) and 5(6).

A realizer for the control structure. The steps taken in the beginning of the proof (application of the WFI and case analysis) can be replaced by the following realizer for MuChk_plus:

> Realizer $<Q^+>$rec muchk_plus :: :: $\{R\}$
> $[\phi : \text{MuForm}]$Cases ϕ of
> > (Var i) $\Rightarrow$ (chk_Var_plus i)
> > | (Lit p) $\Rightarrow$ (chk_Lit_plus p)
> > | (constr args) $\Rightarrow$ (chk_constr_plus args muchk_plus)
> > | ...   ...
> end.

The notation $<P>$rec h :: :: $\{R\}$ $[a : A]M$, where h is the name of the induction hypothesis and $M : P$, is syntactic sugar for (well_founded_induction A P $[a : A][h : A \to P]M$). The identifiers chk_*constr*_plus, where *constr* is the name of a recursive constructor of MuForm, denote lemmas proving the different cases for ϕ in subgoal (1).

5 Application

In this section we illustrate a possible combination of theorem proving and model checking with an example. We want to show that a simple synchronous protocol P_n is observationally equivalent to a single buffer cell independently of the capacity n of the channel it uses. The proof uses the specification preorder [17, 9] and a network invariant [27] representing the whole family of (fixed-size) channels in order to reduce the problem to the verification of three preorder relations. These relations can then be established with the model checker by using a μ-calculus formula characterising the specification preorder.

All the notions in this section have been formalised in Coq. We use usual mathematical notation for brevity.

CCS and the specification preorder. We recall the basic definitions. For more detail, we refer the reader to [17,9]. Let $\mathcal{A}$ be a set of *names*, their complements $\overline{\mathcal{A}} = \{\overline{l} \mid l \in \mathcal{A}\}$ and the set of *labels* $\mathcal{L} = \mathcal{A} \cup \overline{\mathcal{A}}$. We set $\overline{\overline{l}} = l$. f Define the set of *actions* by $Act = \mathcal{L} \cup \{\tau\}$, where with τ the *invisible/silent* action. f is a relabelling function if $f(\overline{l}) = \overline{f(l)}$ and $f(\tau) = \tau$. Suppose a set $\mathcal{K}$ of *process constants*. The set $\mathcal{P}$ of processes is defined by the abstract syntax:

$$p ::= nil \mid \perp \mid a.p \mid p_0 + p_1 \mid p_0 \mid p_1 \mid p[f] \mid p \backslash L \mid A$$

where $a \in Act$, f a relabelling function, $L \subseteq \mathcal{L}$ and $A \in \mathcal{K}$. $\perp$ represents the undefined process. Let T be the transition system $(\mathcal{P}, Act, \rightarrow)$, whose transition relation $\rightarrow$ is inductively defined by the rules:

$$a.p \xrightarrow{a} p$$
$$p \xrightarrow{a} p' \quad \Rightarrow \quad p + q \xrightarrow{a} p', \quad q + p \xrightarrow{a} p',$$
$$p \mid q \xrightarrow{a} p', \quad q \mid p \xrightarrow{a} p', \quad p\{f\} \xrightarrow{f(a)} p'\{f\}$$
$$p \xrightarrow{a} p', \ a, \overline{a} \notin L \quad \Rightarrow \quad p\backslash L \xrightarrow{a} p'\backslash L$$
$$p \xrightarrow{a} p', \ A \stackrel{\text{def}}{=} p \quad \Rightarrow \quad A \xrightarrow{a} p'$$

The *partiality* predicate $\uparrow$ is the complement of $\downarrow$ which is defined by: (i) $nil \downarrow$, $a.p \downarrow$, (ii) $p \downarrow, q \downarrow \Rightarrow p + q \downarrow, p \mid q \downarrow$, (iii) $p \downarrow \Rightarrow p\backslash L \downarrow, p[f] \downarrow$, (iv) $A \stackrel{\text{def}}{=} p, p \downarrow \Rightarrow A \downarrow$. Intuitively, $\uparrow$ denotes the underdefined processes.

Definition 7. Let $l \in \mathcal{L}$ and $a \in Act$. Define

1. $\xrightarrow{l} = \xrightarrow{\tau^*} \xrightarrow{l} \xrightarrow{\tau^*}$ and $\xrightarrow{\hat{\tau}} = \xrightarrow{\tau^*}$
2. $p \Uparrow$ iff $\exists p'. p \xrightarrow{\varepsilon} p' \wedge p \uparrow$
3. $p \Uparrow a$ iff $p \Uparrow \vee \exists p'. (p \xrightarrow{\hat{a}} p' \wedge p' \Uparrow)$

$p \Downarrow$ ($p \Downarrow a$) is the complement of $p \Uparrow$ ($p \Uparrow a$). We say that a process p is *totally defined* if for all p' reachable from p: $p \Downarrow$. Otherwise, it is *partially defined*.

Definition 8. Define the *specification preorder* $\trianglelefteq$ as the greatest fixed point of the function F on relations over $\mathcal{P}$ defined by $(p,q) \in F(R)$ iff for all $a \in Act$ s.t. $p \Downarrow a$ we have:

1. $q \Downarrow a$,
2. if $p \xrightarrow{a} p'$ then $\exists q'. q \xrightarrow{\hat{a}} q' \wedge (p',q') \in R$,
3. if $q \xrightarrow{a} q'$ then $\exists p'. p \xrightarrow{\hat{a}} p' \wedge (p',q') \in R$.

Let $\approx$ denote weak bisimulation equivalence [17].

Lemma 9. *If $p \trianglelefteq q$ and p is totally defined, then q is totally defined and $p \approx q$.*

Theorem 10. *([9]) The preorder $\trianglelefteq$ is a precongruence w.r.t. parallel composition, restriction and relabelling, i.e. if $p \trianglelefteq q$ then $p \mid r \trianglelefteq q \mid r$, $p\{f\} \trianglelefteq q\{f\}$ and $p\backslash L \trianglelefteq q\backslash L$.*

Verification of $\trianglelefteq$ using the model checker. It is possible to define a μ-calculus formula characterising the specification preorder. This formula has to be interpreted over pairs of processes. Therefore, we introduce the product transition system $T^\times = (\mathcal{P} \times \mathcal{P}, Act \uplus Act, \longrightarrow_\times)$, where $\longrightarrow_\times$ is defined by the two rules:

$$\frac{p \xrightarrow{a} p'}{(p,q) \xrightarrow{\iota_0(a)}_\times (p',q)} \qquad\qquad \frac{q \xrightarrow{a} q'}{(p,q) \xrightarrow{\iota_1(a)}_\times (p,q')}$$

$\uplus$ denotes disjoint sum with injections ι_0 and ι_1. Next, we define some left and right modalities for the μ-calculus interpreted over the transition system $T^\times$:

$$\langle a \rangle_l \, \phi = \langle \iota_0(a) \rangle \phi \qquad\qquad \langle \tau^* \rangle_l \, \phi = \mu X. \phi \vee \langle \tau \rangle_l X \quad (X \notin FV(\phi))$$
$$\langle\!\langle \ell \rangle\!\rangle_l \, \phi = \langle \tau^* \rangle_l \langle \ell \rangle_l \langle \tau^* \rangle_l \, \phi \quad (\ell \in \mathcal{L}) \qquad \langle\!\langle \tau \rangle\!\rangle_l \, \phi = \langle \tau^* \rangle_l \, \phi$$

Of all these we define "right" versions, but with $\langle a \rangle_r \phi = \langle \iota_1(a) \rangle \phi$. Left and right box modalities, $[a]_\ell$ and $[a]_r$, are similarly defined. We also introduce left/right versions of the partiality predicates:

$$\Uparrow_l = \, \uparrow \times \mathcal{P} \qquad\qquad \Uparrow\!\!\Uparrow_l = \langle\!\langle \tau \rangle\!\rangle_l \Uparrow_l \qquad\qquad \Uparrow\!\!\Uparrow_l (a) = \Uparrow_l \vee \langle\!\langle a \rangle\!\rangle_l \Uparrow\!\!\Uparrow_l$$

Similarly, "right" versions are defined using $\uparrow_r = \mathcal{P} \times \uparrow$. Now, supposing the set Act is finite, the function F from definition 8 can be expressed as the μ-calculus formula:

$$\tilde{F}(X) = \bigwedge_{a \in Act} \Big(\neg \Uparrow\!\!\Uparrow_l(a) \vee \big(\Uparrow\!\!\Uparrow_r(a) \wedge [a]_l \langle\!\langle a \rangle\!\rangle_r X \wedge [a]_r \langle\!\langle a \rangle\!\rangle_l X \big) \Big)$$

We define $\chi_{\trianglelefteq} = \nu X. \tilde{F}(X)$. This formula characterises the specification preorder as is stated in the following result:

Lemma 11. *For Act finite: $p \trianglelefteq q \iff (p,q) \models \chi_{\trianglelefteq}$.*

A simple protocol. A simple protocol P_n is composed of a sender S synchronously transmitting signals over a buffer B^n of size n to a receiver R. With $X \parallel Y \stackrel{\text{def}}{=} (X[out/z] \mid Y[in/z]) \backslash \{z\}$, the definition is:

$$B \stackrel{\text{def}}{=} in.\overline{out}.B \qquad\qquad B^n \stackrel{\text{def}}{=} \parallel_{i=1}^{n} B$$
$$S \stackrel{\text{def}}{=} send.\overline{in}.ack.S \qquad\qquad R \stackrel{\text{def}}{=} out.\overline{recv}.\overline{ack}.R$$
$$E \stackrel{\text{def}}{=} (S \mid R) \backslash \{ack\} \qquad\qquad P_n \stackrel{\text{def}}{=} (E \mid B^n) \backslash \{in, out\}$$

We define a specification of the protocol by $Spec \stackrel{\text{def}}{=} send.\overline{recv}.Spec$. We want to show that the behaviour of the protocol is independent of the size of the buffer.

Theorem 12. *For all $n \geq 1$: $Spec \approx P_n$.*

Proof. The proof is decomposed into the following two steps:

1. find a network invariant J such that for all $n \geq 1$: $J \trianglelefteq B^n$
2. verify that $Spec \trianglelefteq (E \mid J) \backslash \{in, out\}$

The result then follows from Theorem 10 and Lemma 9, a fact which is proved by deduction in Coq. We define the network invariant J as follows:

$$J \stackrel{\text{def}}{=} in.J' \qquad\qquad J' \stackrel{\text{def}}{=} \overline{out}.J + in. \perp$$

Step (1) is proved by an implicit induction on n: (a) $J \trianglelefteq B$ (base case) (b) $J \trianglelefteq B \parallel J$ (inductive step). Both these steps can be proved with the model checker, by using the characteristic formula $\chi_{\trianglelefteq}$. That (a) and (b) imply (1) is proved "by hand" in Coq. Step (2) can be delegated to the model checker as well. $\qquad\qquad\qquad\qquad\qquad\qquad\qquad\qquad\qquad\qquad\qquad\qquad\qquad$ $\square$

As any property, expressed in a version of the modal μ-calculus with weak modalities only, is preserved by weak bisimulation equivalence, we can verify it on the specification $Spec$ and conclude that it also holds for each of the P_n.

6 Conclusions

We have formalised a model checker for the modal μ-calculus and its correctness proof in Coq. From this proof we can extract an executable Caml program, which can be considered as a trusted decision procedure. In this way, we are able to avoid the inefficiency due to the generation of large proof objects, while preserving the high reliability of the proof environment. Further, we have illustrated the combination of theorem proving and model checking with an example.

Our development is parametrised by an arbitrary labelled transition system and by a function computing successor states. This makes it possible to use any formalism for specification whose operational semantics can be given by a LTS with computable successor function. This is in contrast to [28], where (part of) the implementation depends on the particular formalism used, because they use an external program to generate Lego proof terms.

On the other hand, their model checker is more tightly integrated into the proof environment. In our approach, although direct normalisation of the proof inside Coq is possible, it is very inefficient, since a lot of logical information (which is stripped off by extraction) has to be carried around in the process. When using the extracted Caml program, we currently have to introduce the results of model checking by hand as axioms into Coq. A tighter integration would be desirable. Generally speaking, some way of reintroducing the results of extracted programs (together with the guarantees given by the realisability interpretation) into Coq would be needed for a tighter integration of efficient decision procedures. Some techniques currently being developed by B. Barras [4] and aiming at bootstrapping Coq in Coq might provide a solution to this problem in the future.

The efficiency of the algorithm could be improved. No optimisations have been made yet. One obvious optimisation would be to replace the tag lists in the fixed point formulas by a more efficient data structure such as balanced trees. Other optimisations such as the ones proposed in [8] are possible.

As part of future work we plan to investigate the application of abstract interpretation techniques to value-passing process calculi. Another track concerns model checkers for infinite state systems such as the ones proposed by Bradfield and Stirling [6] and Andersen [1]. It would be interesting to see to what extent these techniques could be automated in Coq.

Acknowledgements. I would like to thank the Coq development team at INRIA Rocquencourt for helpful discussions and in particular Hugo Herbelin for inviting me there.

References

1. H. R. Andersen. *Verification of Temporal Properties of Concurrent Systems.* PhD thesis, Computer Science Department, Aarhus University, June 1993.
2. L. Augustsson, T. Coquand, and B. Nordström. A short description of another logical framework. In G. Huet and P. G., editors, *Preliminary Proceedings of Logical Frameworks*, 1990.
3. H. P. Barendregt. Lambda calculi with types. In S. Abramsky, D. M. Gabbay, and T. S. E. Maibaum, editors, *Handbook of Logic in Computer Science*, volume 2: Background: Computational Structures, pages 118–309. Oxford University Press, 1992.
4. B. Barras. Coq en Coq. Technical Report 3026, INRIA, Oct. 1996.
5. B. Barras, S. Boutin, C. Cornes, J. Courant, j.-C. Filiâtre, E. Giménez, H. Herbelin, G. Huet, and al . *The Coq Proof Assistant Reference Manual, Version 6.1.* Projet Coq, INRIA Rocquencourt, CNRS - ENS Lyon, Dec. 1996.
6. J. Bradfield and C. Stirling. Local model checking for infinite state spaces. *Theoretical Computer Science*, 96:157–174, 1992.
7. E. M. Clarke, O. Grumberg, and D. E. Long. Model checking and abstraction. *ACM Transactions on Programming Languages and Systems*, 16(5):1512–1542, Sept. 1994.
8. R. Cleaveland. Tableau-based model checking in the propositional μ-calculus. *Acta Informatica*, 27:725–747, 1990.
9. R. Cleaveland and B. Steffen. A preorder for partial process specifications. In *CONCUR' 90*, volume 458 of *Lecture Notes in Computer Science*. Springer-Verlag, 1990.
10. T. Coquand and G. Huet. The calculus of constructions. *Information and Computation*, 76:95–120, 1988.
11. D. Dams, O. Grumberg, and R. Gerth. Abstract interpretation of reactive systems. *ACM Transactions on Programming Languages and Systems*, 19(2):253–291, 1997.
12. J. Dingel and T. Filkorn. Model checking for infinite state systems using data abstraction, assumption-commitment style reasoning and theorem proving. In *CAV '95*, volume 939 of *Lecture Notes in Computer Science*. Springer-Verlag, 1995.
13. J.-Y. Girard, Y. Lafont, and P. Taylor. *Proofs and Types*, volume 7 of *Cambrdge Tracts in Theoretical Computer Science*. Cambridge University Press, 1989.
14. R. P. Kurshan and K. McMillan. A structural induction theorem for processes. In *8th ACM Symposium on Principles of Distributed Computing*, pages 239–248, 1989.

15. C. Loiseaux, S. Graf, J. Sifakis, A. Bouajjani, and B. S. Property preserving abstractions for the verification of concurrent systems. *Formal Methods in System Design*, 6:11–44, 1995.
16. Z. Luo and R. Pollack. Lego proof development system: User's manual. Technical Report ECS-LFCS-92-211, Department of Computer Science, University of Edinburgh, 1992.
17. R. Milner. *Communication and Concurrency*. Prentice Hall International Series in Computer Science. Prentice Hall, 1989.
18. O. Müller and T. Nipkow. Combining model checking and deduction for I/O-automata. In *TACAS 95*, volume 1019 of *Lecture Notes in Computer Science*, pages 1–16. Springer-Verlag, 1995.
19. C. Parent. *Synthèse de preuves de programmes dans le Calcul des Constructions Inductives*. PhD thesis, Ecole Normale Supérieure de Lyon, Jan. 1995.
20. C. Paulin-Mohring. Extracting F_ω programs from proofs in the Calculus of Constructions. In *Sixteenth Annual ACM Symposium on the Priciples of Programming Languages*, Austin, Texas, Jan. 1989.
21. C. Paulin-Mohring. *Extraction de programmes dans le Calcul des Constructions*. PhD thesis, Université de Paris VII, Jan. 1989.
22. C. Paulin-Mohring. Inductive definitions in the system Coq – rules and properties. Technical Report 92-49, Laboratoire de l'Informatique du Parallélisme, ENS Lyon, France, Dec. 1992.
23. C. Paulin-Mohring and B. Werner. Synthesis of ML programs in the system coq. *Journal of Symbolic Computation*, 11:1–34, 1993.
24. S. Rajan, N. Shankar, and M. K. Srivas. An integration of model checking with automated proof checking. In *CAV '95*, volume 939 of *Lecture Notes in Computer Science*, pages 84–97. Springer-Verlag, 1995.
25. B. Werner. *Une Théorie des Constructions Inductives*. PhD thesis, Université de Paris 7, France, 1994.
26. G. Winskel. A note on model checking the modal μ-calculus. *Theoretical Computer Science*, 83:157–167, 1991.
27. P. Wolper and V. Lovinfosse. Verifying properties of large sets of processes with network invariants. In J. Sifakis, editor, *International Workshop on Automatic Verification Methods for Finite State Systems*, volume 407 of *Lecture Notes in Computer Science*, pages 68–80. Springer-Verlag, 1989.
28. S. Yu and Z. Luo. Implementing a model checker for LEGO. In *Formal Methods Europe*, 1997.

Detecting Races in Relay Ladder Logic Programs

Alexander Aiken*, Manuel Fähndrich*, and Zhendong Su*

EECS Department
University of California, Berkeley**

Abstract. Relay Ladder Logic (RLL) [4] is a programming language widely used for complex embedded control applications such as manufacturing and amusement park rides. The cost of bugs in RLL programs is extremely high, often measured in millions of dollars (for shutting down a factory) or human safety (for rides). In this paper, we describe our experience in applying constraint-based program analysis techniques to analyze production RLL programs. Our approach is an interesting combination of probabilistic testing and program analysis, and we show that our system is able to detect bugs with high probability, up to the approximations made by the conservative program analysis. We demonstrate that our analysis is useful in detecting some flaws in production RLL programs that are difficult to find by other techniques.

1 Introduction

Programmable logic controllers (PLC's) are used extensively for complex embedded control applications such as factory control in manufacturing industries and for entertainment equipment in amusement parks. Relay Ladder Logic (RLL) is the most widely used PLC programming language; approximately 50% of the manufacturing capacity in the United States is programmed in RLL [5].

RLL has long been criticized for its low level design, which makes it difficult to write correct programs [18]. Moreover, validation of RLL programs is extremely expensive, often measured in millions of dollars (for factory down-time) or human safety (for rides). One solution is to replace RLL with a higher-level, safer programming language. An alternative is to provide better programming support directly for RLL. Since there are many existing RLL applications, and many more will be written in this language, we consider the latter approach in this paper.

We have designed and implemented a tool for analyzing RLL programs. Our analyzer automatically detects some common programming mistakes that are

---

* Supported in part by the National Science Foundation, Grant No. CCR-9416973, by NSF Infrastructure Grant No. CDA-9401156, and a gift from Rockwell Corporation. The information presented here does not necessarily reflect the position or the policy of the Government and no official endorsement should be inferred.

** Authors' address: EECS Department, University of California, Berkeley, 387 Soda Hall #1776, Berkeley, CA 94720-1776 Email: {aiken,manuel,zhendong}@cs.berkeley.edu

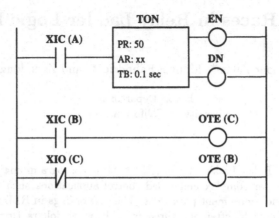

Fig. 1. An example RLL program.

extremely difficult to detect through inspection or testing. The information inferred by the analyzer can be used by RLL programmers to identify and correct these errors. Our most interesting result is an analysis to detect certain race conditions in RLL programs. Tested on real RLL programs, the analysis found several such races, including one known bug that originally costed approximately $750,000 in factory down-time [5].

Our analysis is *constraint-based*, meaning that the information we wish to know about a program is expressed as constraints [16, 2, 3]. The solutions of these constraints yield the desired information. Our analysis is built using a general constraint resolution engine, which allows us to implement the analysis directly in the same natural form it is specified. Constraint-based program analysis is discussed further in Section 2.

Our system has two components: (a) a conservative data and control flow analysis captures information about a program in an initial system of constraints and (b) additional constraints binding program inputs to actual values are added to the initial constraint system, which is then solved to obtain the desired information. Part (a) is done only once, but part (b) is done many times for randomly chosen inputs. Our underlying constraint resolution engine solves and simplifies the initial constraints generated by (a), thereby greatly improving the performance of (b).

Beyond the particular application to RLL programs, this system architecture has properties that may be of independent interest. First, the use of constraints greatly simplifies the engineering needed to factor out the information to be computed once from that which must be reevaluated repeatedly—we simply add new constraints to the initial system. Second, our system is (to the best of our knowledge) a unique blend of conservative program analysis (part (a), which approximates certain aspects of computation) and software testing (part (b), which "executes" the abstraction for concrete inputs). Third, we are able to prove that classes of program errors are detected with high probability, up to the approximations made by the conservative analysis.

We expect that the engineering advantages of using constraints will carry over to other static analysis tools. The latter two results apply directly only if the programming language has a finite domain of values (RLL has only booleans). Thus, our approach is suitable for some other special-purpose languages (e.g., other control languages) but not necessarily for general purpose languages.

1.1 A More Detailed Overview

By any standard RLL is a strange language, combining features of boolean logic (combinatorial circuits), imperative programming (assignment, goto, procedures, conditionals), and real-time computation (timers, counters) with an obscure syntax and complex semantics. Although widely used, RLL is not well-known in the research community. We give a brief overview of RLL together with a more detailed, but still high level, description of our analysis system.

RLL programs are represented as *ladder diagrams*, which are a stylized form of a circuit or data flow diagram. A *ladder diagram* consists of a set of *ladder rungs* with each rung having a set of input instructions and output instructions. We explain this terminology in the context of the example RLL program in Figure 1. In the example, there are two vertical rails. The one on the left supplies power to all crossing rungs of the ladder. The three horizontal lines are the ladder rungs of this program. This example has four kinds of RLL instructions: input (two kinds), outputs, and timer instructions. The small vertical parallel bars | | and |/| represent input instructions, which have a single bit associated with them. The bit is named in the instruction. For example, the | | instruction (an XIC for "Normally Closed Contact" instruction) in the upper-left corner of the diagram reads from the bit named A, and the |/| instruction (an XIO for "Normally Opened Contact" instruction) in the lower-left corner of the diagram reads from the bit named C. The small circles represent output instructions that update the value of their labeled bits. The bits named in input and output instructions are classified into *external* bits, which are connected to inputs or outputs external to the program, and *internal* bits, which are local to the program for temporarily storing program states. External inputs are generally connected to sensors, while external outputs are used to control actuators. The rectangular box represents a timer instruction (a TON for "Timer On-Delay" instruction), where PR (preset) is an integer representing a time interval in seconds, AR (accumulator) keeps the accumulated value, and TB (time base) is the step of each increment of the AR. The timer instructions are used to turn an output on or off after the timer has been on for a preset time interval (the PR value).

Instructions are connected by wires, the horizontal lines between instructions. We say a wire is true if power is supplied to the wire, and the wire is false otherwise.

An RLL program operates by first reading in all the values of the external input bits and executing the rungs in sequence from top to bottom and left to right. Program control instructions may cause portions of the program to be skipped or repeatedly executed. After the last rung is evaluated, all the real output devices connected to the external output bits are updated. Such a three step execution (read inputs, evaluate rungs, update outputs) of the program is called a *scan*. Programs are executed scan after scan until interrupted. Between scans, the input bit values might be changed, either because the inputs were modified by the previous scan (bits can be inputs, outputs, or both) or because of state changes in external sensors attached to the inputs. Subsequent scans use the new input values.

RLL has many types of instructions: relay instructions, timer and counter instructions, data transfer instructions, arithmetic operations, data comparison operations, and program control instructions. Examples of relay instructions are XIC, XIO, and OTE. We briefly describe how these three instructions work for the explanation of our analysis. Let w_1 and w_2 be the wires before and after an instruction respectively. Further, let b be the bit referenced by an instruction.

XIC: if w_1 and b are true, w_2 is true; otherwise, w_2 is false.
XIO: if w_1 is true, and b is false, w_2 is true; otherwise, w_2 is false.
OTE: the bit b is true if and only if w_1 is true.

In this paper, we describe the design and implementation of our RLL program analyzer for detecting *relay races*. In RLL programs, it is desirable that the values of outputs depend solely on the values of inputs and the internal states of timers and counters. If under fixed inputs and timer and counter states, an output x changes from scan to scan, then there is a *relay race on x*. For example, in the program in Figure 1, we will see later that the bit B changes value each scan regardless of its initial value. Relay races are particularly difficult to detect by traditional testing techniques, as races can depend on the timing of external events and the scan rate.

Our analysis generalizes traditional data flow analyses [1]. Instead of data flow equations, set constraints [16, 2, 3] are used. Set constraints are more expressive than data flow equations because the constraints can model not only data flow but also control flow of a program.

Our analysis consists of two steps. In the first step, we generate constraints that describe the data and control flow dependencies of an RLL program. The constraints are generated in a top-down traversal of the program's abstract syntax tree (AST). According to a set of constraint generation rules (see Section 3), appropriate constraints are generated for each AST node. These data and control flow constraints are solved to yield another system of simplified constraints, the *base system*. The base system models where and how a value flows in the program. The base system is a *conservative approximation* of the program: if during program execution, a wire or a bit can be true (false), then true (false) is in the set that denotes the values of the wire or the bit in the base system; however, false (true) may be a value in that set, too.

The second step of the relay race analysis simulates multiple scans and looks for racing outputs. We choose a random assignment of inputs and add the corresponding constraints to the base system. The resulting system is solved; its minimum solution describes the values of the outputs at the end of the scan. Since some output bits are also inputs, the input assignment of the next scan is updated using the outputs from the previous scan. Again, we add this input assignment to the base system and solve to obtain the minimum solution of the outputs after the second scan. If an output changes across scans, a relay race is detected. For example, consider the example program in Figure 1. Since the bottom two rungs do not interfere with the first rung, consider these two rungs only. Assume that B has initial value true. Then C also is true, and so in the last rung, B becomes false. Thus, in the next scan, B is initially false. Thus, C becomes false, which makes B true at the end of this scan. Consequently, we have detected a relay race on B: after the first scan B is false, and after the second scan B is true.

The race analysis is conservative in the sense that it cannot detect all of the relay races in a program. However, any relay races the analyzer detects are indeed relay races, and we can prove that a large class of relay races is detected with high probability.

We have implemented the race analysis in Standard ML of New Jersey (SML) [20]. Our analyzer is accurate and fast enough to be practical—production RLL programs can be analyzed. The relay race analysis not only detected a known bug in a program that took an RLL programmer four hours of factory down-time to uncover, it also detected many previously unknown relay races in our benchmark programs.

The rest of the paper is structured as follows. First, we describe the constraint language used for the analysis (Section 2). The rules for generating the base system come next (Section 3), followed by a description of the relay race analysis (Section 4). Finally, we present some experimental results (Section 5), followed by a discussion of related work (Section 6) and the conclusion (Section 7).

2 Constraints

In this section, we describe the set constraint language we use for expressing our analysis. Our expression language consists of set variables, a least value $\perp$, a greatest value $\top$, constants $\mathbf{T}$ and $\mathbf{F}$, intersections, unions, and conditional expressions. The syntax of the expression language is

$$E ::= v \mid \perp \mid \top \mid c \mid E_1 \cup E_2 \mid E_1 \cap E_2 \mid E_1 \Rightarrow E_2,$$

where c is a constant (either $\mathbf{T}$ or $\mathbf{F}$) and $v \in V$ is a set variable.

The abstract domain consists of four elements: $\emptyset$ (represented by $\perp$), $\{\mathbf{T}\}$ (represented by $\mathbf{T}$), $\{\mathbf{F}\}$ (represented by $\mathbf{F}$), $\{\mathbf{T}, \mathbf{F}\}$ (represented by $\top$) with set inclusion as the partial order on these elements. The domain is a finite lattice with $\cap$ and $\cup$ being the *meet* and *join* respectively. The semantics of the expression language is given in Figure 2.

Conditional expressions deserve some discussion. Conditional expressions are used for accurately modeling flow-of-control (see e.g., [3]). In the context of RLL, they can be used to express boolean relations very directly. For example, we can express the boolean expression $v_1 \wedge v_2$ with the following conditional expression:

$$((v_1 \cap \mathbf{T}) \Rightarrow (v_2 \cap \mathbf{T}) \Rightarrow \mathbf{T}) \cup ((v_1 \cap \mathbf{F}) \Rightarrow \mathbf{F}) \cup ((v_2 \cap \mathbf{F}) \Rightarrow \mathbf{F})$$

$$\rho(\bot) = \emptyset$$
$$\rho(\top) = \{\mathbf{T}, \mathbf{F}\}$$
$$\rho(\mathbf{T}) = \{\mathbf{T}\}$$
$$\rho(\mathbf{F}) = \{\mathbf{F}\}$$
$$\rho(E_1 \cap E_2) = \rho(E_1) \cap \rho(E_2)$$
$$\rho(E_1 \cup E_2) = \rho(E_1) \cup \rho(E_2)$$
$$\rho(E_1 \Rightarrow E_2) = \begin{cases} \rho(E_2) & \text{if } \rho(E_1) \neq \emptyset \\ \emptyset & \text{otherwise} \end{cases}$$

Fig. 2. Semantics of set expressions.

To see this expression does model the $\wedge$ operator, notice that if $v_1 = \mathbf{T}$ and $v_2 = \mathbf{T}$, the above expression simplifies to

$$((\mathbf{T} \cap \mathbf{T}) \Rightarrow (\mathbf{T} \cap \mathbf{T}) \Rightarrow \mathbf{T}) = ((\mathbf{T} \Rightarrow \mathbf{T}) \Rightarrow \mathbf{T}) = \mathbf{T}.$$

One can easily check that the other three cases are also correct.

We use set constraints to model RLL programs instead of boolean logic for two reasons. First, although the core of RLL is boolean logic, other instructions (e.g., control flow instructions) are at best difficult to express using boolean logic. Second, RLL programs are large and complex, so approximations are needed for performance reasons. Set constraints give us the flexibility to model certain instructions less accurately and less expensively than others, thus, making the analysis of RLL programs more manageable.

3 Constraint Generation

In this section, we describe how we use inclusion constraints to model RLL programs. Because of the scan evaluation model of RLL programs, it is natural to express the meaning of a program in terms of the meaning of a single scan. The constraint generation rules model the meaning of a single scan of RLL programs. In the rules set variables denote the values of bits and wires. Thus, a bit or wire may be assigned the abstract values $\emptyset$ (meaning no value), $\{\mathbf{T}\}$ (definitely true), $\{\mathbf{F}\}$ (definitely false) or $\{\mathbf{T}, \mathbf{F}\}$ (meaning either true or false, i.e., no information). Rules have the form

$$E, I \mapsto E', S, v_1, v_2$$

where:

- E and E' are mappings of bits to their corresponding set variables. The operator $+$ extends the mapping such that $(E + \{b, v\})(b') = \begin{cases} v, & \text{if } b' = b \\ E(b'), & \text{otherwise} \end{cases}$
- I is the current instruction;
- S is the set of constraints generated for this instruction;

– v_1 and v_2 are set variables associated with the wires before and after instruction I and are used to link instructions together.

In this section, w_1 and w_2 denote the wires preceding and following an instruction respectively. Furthermore, b denotes the bit referenced by an instruction unless specified otherwise. Figure 3 gives some example inference rules for generating the constraints describing the data and control flow of RLL programs. Below, we explain these rules in more detail.

Contacts

The instruction XIC is called "Normally Closed Contact." If w_1 is true, then b is examined. If b is true, then w_2 is true. Otherwise, w_2 is false. In the rule [XIC], two fresh set variables v_1 and v_2 represent the two wires w_1 and w_2. The set variable v_{ct} represents the referenced bit b. The constraints express that w_2 is true if and only if both w_1 and b are true.
The instruction XIO, called "Normally Opened Contact," is the dual of XIC. The wire w_2 is true if and only if w_1 is true and the referenced bit b is false. The rule for XIO is similar to the rule [XIC].

Energise Coil

The instruction OTE is called "Energise Coil." It is programmed to control either an output connected to the controller or an internal bit. If the wire w_1 is true, then the referenced bit b is set to true. Otherwise, b is set to false. Rule [OTE] models this instruction. The set variables v_1 and v_2 are the same as in the rule [XIC]. The set variable v_{ct} is fresh, representing a new instance[1] of the referenced bit b. The new instance is recorded in the mapping E'. Later references to b use this instance. The constraints express that b is true if and only if w_1 is true.

Latches

The instructions OTL and OTU are similar to OTE. OTL is "Latch Coil," and OTU is "Unlatch Coil." These two instructions appear in pairs. Once an OTL instruction activates its bit b, then b remains true until it is cleared by an unlatch instruction OTU, independently of the wire w_1 which activated the latch. The unlatch coil (OTU) instruction is symmetric. In the rule [OTL], the set variable v'_{ct} represents the value of the b prior to the instruction, while the variable v_{ct} denotes the new instance of b. The constraint expresses that b is true if and only the wire w_1 is true or b is true before evaluating this instruction. The rule for OTU is similar.

Timers

Timers (TON) are instructions that activate an output after an elapsed period of time. Three status bits are associated with a timer: the *done bit* (DN), the *timing bit* (TT), and the *on bit* (EN). The DN bit is true if the wire w_1 has remained true for a preset period of time. The bit remains true unless w_1 becomes false. The TT bit is true if the wire w_1 is true and the

---

[1] Due to the sequential evaluation of rungs, a particular bit can take on distinct values in different parts of a program. An instance of a bit captures the state of a bit at a particular program point.

$$v_1 \text{ and } v_2 \text{ are fresh variables}$$
$$v_{ct} = E(b)$$
$$\frac{S = \{((v_1 \cap \mathbf{T}) \Rightarrow (v_{ct} \cap \mathbf{T}) \Rightarrow \mathbf{T}) \cup ((v_1 \cap \mathbf{F}) \Rightarrow \mathbf{F}) \cup ((v_{ct} \cap \mathbf{F}) \Rightarrow \mathbf{F}) \subseteq v_2\}}{E, XIC(b) \mapsto E, S, v_1, v_2} \quad \text{[XIC]}$$

$$v_1, v_2, \text{ and } v_{ct} \text{ are fresh variables}$$
$$E' = E + \{(b, v_{ct})\}$$
$$\frac{S = \{((v_1 \cap \mathbf{T}) \Rightarrow \mathbf{T}) \cup ((v_1 \cap \mathbf{F}) \Rightarrow \mathbf{F}) \subseteq v_{ct}\}}{E, OTE(b) \mapsto E', S, v_1, v_2} \quad \text{[OTE]}$$

$$v_1, v_2, \text{ and } v_{ct} \text{ are fresh variables}$$
$$v'_{ct} = E(b)$$
$$E' = E + \{(b, v_{ct})\}$$
$$\frac{S = \{((v'_{ct} \cap \mathbf{T}) \Rightarrow \mathbf{T}) \cup ((v_1 \cap \mathbf{T}) \Rightarrow \mathbf{T}) \cup ((v_1 \cap \mathbf{F}) \Rightarrow (v'_{ct} \cap \mathbf{F}) \Rightarrow \mathbf{F}) \subseteq v_{ct}\}}{E, OTL(b) \mapsto E', S, v_1, v_2} \quad \text{[OTL]}$$

$$v_1, v_2, v_{dn}, v_{en}, \text{ and } v_{tt} \text{ are fresh variables}$$
$$E' = E + \{(DN, v_{dn}), (EN, v_{en}), (TT, v_{tt})\}$$
$$\frac{S = \left\{ \begin{array}{r} ((v_1 \cap \mathbf{T}) \Rightarrow \mathbf{T} \cup \mathbf{F}) \subseteq v_{dn}, \\ ((v_1 \cap \mathbf{T}) \Rightarrow (v_{dn} \cap \mathbf{F}) \Rightarrow \mathbf{T}) \cup ((v_1 \cap \mathbf{F}) \Rightarrow \mathbf{F}) \cup ((v_{dn} \cap \mathbf{T}) \Rightarrow \mathbf{F}) \subseteq v_{tt}, \\ ((v_1 \cap \mathbf{T}) \Rightarrow \mathbf{T}) \cup ((v_1 \cap \mathbf{F}) \Rightarrow \mathbf{F}) \subseteq v_{en} \end{array} \right\}}{E, TON \mapsto E', S, v_1, v_2} \quad \text{[TON]}$$

$$B = \text{the set of bits in the program}$$
$$v_1, v_2, nv_b \text{ (for all } b \in B) \text{ are fresh variables}$$
$$R_{fname} = \text{the rungs in the file } fname$$
$$E, R_{fname} \mapsto E', S_0$$
$$E'' = \{(b, nv_b) \mid b \in B\}$$
$$\frac{S = ((v_1 \cap \mathbf{T}) \Rightarrow S_0) \cup \{(v_1 \cap \mathbf{T}) \Rightarrow E'(b) \cup (v_1 \cap \mathbf{F}) \Rightarrow E(b) \subseteq nv_b \mid b \in B\}}{E, JSR_{fname} \mapsto E'', S, v_1, v_2} \quad \text{[JSR]}$$

$$v \text{ is a fresh variable}$$
$$E, R_1 \mapsto E', S_0, v_1, v_2$$
$$E', R_2 \mapsto E'', S_1, v'_1, v'_2$$
$$\frac{S = \{(v_2 \cap \mathbf{T}) \Rightarrow \mathbf{T} \cup (v'_2 \cap \mathbf{T}) \Rightarrow \mathbf{T} \cup (v_2 \cap \mathbf{F}) \Rightarrow (v'_2 \cap \mathbf{F}) \Rightarrow \mathbf{F} \subseteq v\}}{E, R_1 \| R_2 \mapsto E'', S \cup S_0 \cup S_1 \cup \{v_1 = v'_1\}, v_1, v} \quad \text{[PAR]}$$

Fig. 3. Some rules for generating constraints.

DN bit is false. It is false otherwise, i.e., it is false if the wire w_1 is false or the DN bit is true. The EN bit is true if and only if the wire w_1 is true. In the rule [TON], v_{dn}, v_{tt} and v_{en} are fresh set variables representing new instances of the corresponding bits. The constraint for the DN bit is

$$((v_1 \cap \mathbf{T}) \Rightarrow \mathbf{T}) \cup \mathbf{F} \subseteq v_{dn}.$$

The constraint approximates timer operation while ignoring elapsed time. The DN bit can be false (the timer has not reached its preset period), or if the wire w_1 is true, then the DN bit can be true (the timer may have reached its preset period). The constraints for the TT and EN bits are straightforward.

Remark 1. For the relay race analysis, we assume that the DN bit does not change value across scans. This assumption is reasonable since the scan time, compared with the timer increments, is infinitesimal. The DN bit essentially becomes an input bit in the race analysis, and the constraint is accordingly simplified to $E(DN) \subseteq v_{dn}$.

Subroutines
JSR is the subroutine call instruction. If the wire w_1 evaluates to true, the subroutine (a portion of ladder rungs with label *fname* as specified in the JSR instruction) is evaluated up to a return instruction, after which execution continues with the rung after the JSR instruction. If w_1 is false, execution continues immediately with the rung after the JSR instruction. In the rule [JSR], B denotes the set of all bits in a program. IF S is a set of constraints and τ a set expression, then the notation $\tau \Rightarrow S$ abbreviates the set of constraints

$$\{\tau \Rightarrow \tau_0 \subseteq \tau_1 \mid (\tau_0 \subseteq \tau_1) \in S\}$$

The fresh variables nv_b represent new instances of all bits $b \in B$. Constraints S_0 are generated for the ladder rungs of the subroutine together with a modified mapping E'. The constraints

$$\{(v_1 \cap \mathbf{T}) \Rightarrow E'(b) \cup (v_1 \cap \mathbf{F}) \Rightarrow E(b) \subseteq nv_b \mid b \in B\}$$

merge the two instances of every bit b from the two possible control flows. If the wire w_1 (modeled by v_1) is true, then $E'(b)$ (the instance after evaluating the subroutine) should be the value of the current instance, otherwise, $E(b)$ is the value of the current instance.

Parallel Wires
The rule [PAR] describes the generation of constraints for parallel wires. Parallel wires behave the same as the disjunction of two boolean variables, i.e., the wire after the parallel wires is true if any one of the two input wires is true. In the rule $v_1 = v_1'$ is an abbreviation for the two constraints $v_1 \subseteq v_1'$ and $v_1' \subseteq v_1$. The fresh variable v is used to model the wire after the parallel wires. The constraint

$$(v_2 \cap \mathbf{T}) \Rightarrow \mathbf{T} \cup (v_2' \cap \mathbf{T}) \Rightarrow \mathbf{T} \cup (v_2 \cap \mathbf{F}) \Rightarrow (v_2' \cap \mathbf{F}) \Rightarrow \mathbf{F} \subseteq v$$

says that the wire after the parallel wires is true if one of the parallel wires is true. There are other rules for linking instructions together. These rules are similar to [PAR] and are also straightforward.

All solutions of the generated constraints conservatively approximate the evaluation of RLL programs. However, the best approximation is the least solution (in terms of set sizes). We now present a theorem which states that the constraints generated from an RLL program together with constraints for restricting the inputs have a least solution.

Theorem 1 (Existence of Least Solution). *For any RLL program $\mathcal{P}$, let S be the constraint system generated by the rules given in Figure 3. Further let c be an input configuration for $\mathcal{P}$. The constraint system S together with the corresponding constraints of c has a least solution, Sol_{least}.*

Next, we state a soundness theorem of our model of RLL programs, namely that our model is a safe approximation of RLL.

Theorem 2 (Soundness). *Let $\mathcal{P}$ be an RLL program and S be the constraint system generated by the rules given in Figure 3. Further let c be an input configuration for $\mathcal{P}$. The least solution Sol_{least} to the constraint system S together with the constraints restricting the inputs safely approximates the values of the wires and bits in one scan, meaning that if an instance of a bit or a wire is true (false) in an actual scan, then true (false) is a value in the set representing this instance.*

Theorem 1 and Theorem 2 are proven in [21].

4 Relay Race Analysis

In this section, we describe our analysis for detecting relay races in RLL programs. In RLL programs, it is desirable if the values of outputs depend solely on the values of inputs and the internal states of timers and counters. If under fixed inputs and timer and counter states, an output b changes from scan to scan, then there is a relay race on b.

Before describing our analysis, we give a more formal definition of the problem. Consider an RLL program P. Let **IN** denote the set of inputs, and let **OUT** denote the set of outputs[2]. Let C be the set of all possible input configurations. Further, let $\Psi_i : \textbf{OUT} \rightarrow \{\textbf{T}, \textbf{F}\}$ be the mapping from the set of outputs to their corresponding values at the end of the ith scan.

Definition 1. *An RLL program P is race free if for any input configurations $c \in C$, by fixing c, it holds that for all $i \geq 1, \Psi_i = \Psi_1$. Otherwise, we say the program has a race.*

---

[2] Note that **IN** = set of external inputs + internal bits, and **OUT** = set of external outputs + internal bits.

Definition 1 states under what conditions a program exhibits a race. Note that this definition assumes that outputs should stabilize after a single scan.

Definition 2. *Let P be an RLL program. An approximation A of P is an abstraction of P such that, for any configuration c and bit b of P, at the end of any scan, the following condition holds: $P_c(b)$ (the value of b in the program P) is contained in $A_c(b)$ (the value of b in the abstraction A), i.e., $P_c(b) \in A_c(b)$.*

Let A be an approximation of P. Let $\Phi_i : \mathbf{OUT} \to \wp(\{\mathbf{T}, \mathbf{F}\})$ be the mapping from the set of outputs to their corresponding values at the end of the ith scan in A, where $\wp(\{\mathbf{T}, \mathbf{F}\})$ denotes the powerset of $\{\mathbf{T}, \mathbf{F}\}$.

Definition 3. *An approximation A of an RLL program P is race free if for any fixed initial input configuration $c \in C$, and the resulting infinite sequence of abstract scans $S_1, S_2, S_3, \ldots$, there exists $\Psi^* : \mathbf{OUT} \to \{\mathbf{T}, \mathbf{F}\}$ such that $\Psi^*(b) \in \Phi_i(b)$, for all $b \in \mathbf{OUT}$ and $i \geq 1$.*

Lemma 1. *Let P be an RLL program and A an approximation of P. If P is race free, then so is A. In other words, if A exhibits a race, so does P.*

Proof. Since P is race free, by Definition 1, we have $\Psi_i = \Psi_1$ for all $i \geq 1$. Since A is an approximation of P, by Definition 2, $\Psi_i(b) \in \Phi_i(b)$ for all $i \geq 1$. Thus, $\Psi_1(b) \in \Phi_i(b)$ for all $i \geq 1$, and by Definition 3, the approximation A is also race free.

Lemma 1 states that if our analysis detects a race under some input c, then the program will exhibit a race under input c. We now deal with the problem of detecting races in our approximation of RLL programs.

Theorem 3. *For any approximation A of an RLL program P and input $c \in C$, the approximation A races under c if and only if there exists $b \in \mathbf{OUT}$ such that $\bigcap_{i \geq 1} \Phi_i(b) = \emptyset$.*

Proof. Let $b \in \mathbf{OUT}$ be an output such that $\bigcap_{i \geq 1} \Phi_i(b) = \emptyset$. Since A is an approximation of the program P, we have $\Phi_i(b) \neq \emptyset$. Thus, there exist positive integers $i \neq j$ such that $\Phi_i(b) = \{\mathbf{T}\}$ and $\Phi_j(b) = \{\mathbf{F}\}$. Therefore, there does not exist a $\Psi^* : \mathbf{OUT} \to \{\mathbf{T}, \mathbf{F}\}$ such that $\Psi^*(b) \in \Phi_i(b)$ for all $b \in \mathbf{OUT}$ and for all $i \geq 1$. Hence, A has a race under c.

Conversely, suppose for all $b \in \mathbf{OUT}$, we have $\bigcap_{i \geq 1} \Phi_i(b) \neq \emptyset$. Then, let $\Phi(b) = \bigcap_{i \geq 1} \Phi_i(b)$ for all $b \in \mathbf{OUT}$. Clearly there exists a $\Psi^* : \mathbf{OUT} \to \{\mathbf{T}, \mathbf{F}\}$ such that $\Psi^*(b) \in \Phi(b)$ for all $b \in \mathbf{OUT}$. Therefore, A does not race under input c.

In principle, for any given input assignment, it is necessary to simulate scans until a repeating sequence of output configurations is detected, which may require a number of scans exponential in the number of inputs. However, the following lemma shows that two scans are sufficient to uncover the common case.

```
1           for every output b
2               B_sum(b) := {T, F};
3               S_input := random assignment;
4           for Scan := 1 to 2
5               B_current := Sol_least(S_base ∪ S_input);
6               S_input := GetInput(B_current);
7               B_sum := B_sum ∩ B_current;
8               if B_sum(b) = ∅ for some output b
9                   then output b is racing;
```

Fig. 4. Algorithm for detecting races.

Lemma 2. *Let A be an approximation of a program P. If A has a race of bit b under input configuration c, such that $\Phi_i(b) \cap \Phi_{i+1}(b) = \emptyset$ for some scan i, then there exists another input configuration c' such that $\Phi_1(b) \cap \Phi_2(b) = \emptyset$ under c', i.e., it is sufficient to use two scans on every input configuration to uncover the race on b.*

Proof. Let $\Phi_i^c(b)$ denote the value of b at the end of the ith scan starting with input configuration c. Without loss of generality, assume $\Phi_i^c(b) = \{T\}$ and $\Phi_{i+1}^c(b) = \{F\}$. Consider the values of the inputs c_i prior to scan i. Now choose any configuration c', s.t. $c'(b) \subseteq c_i(b)$ for all b. Since our analysis is monotone in the input (Theorem 1), we have $\Phi_1^{c'}(b) = \{T\}$ and $\Phi_2^{c'}(b) = \{F\}$. Hence, the race on bit b can be detected within two scans, starting from a configuration c'.

We have verified experimentally that performing only two scans works well; an experiment in which we performed ten scans per initial input configuration detected no additional races. Theorem 3 and Lemma 2 thus lead naturally to the algorithm in Figure 4 for detecting relay races. The general strategy for the analysis is:

1. Generate the base system using the constraint generation rules presented in Section 3.
2. Add constraints that assign random bits to the inputs.
3. Check whether the program races under this input assignment.
4. Repeat 2.

We make the assumption that all input assignments are possible. In practice, there may be dependencies between inputs that make some input configurations unrealizable. Our analysis can be made more accurate if information about these dependencies is available.

We use the example in Figure 1 to demonstrate how the race detection algorithm works. Consider the last two rungs in the example RLL program in isolation. The base system for these two rungs is given in the top of Figure 5. Assume the bit B is initially true. Adding the constraint $T \subseteq b_{B_0}$ to the base system and solving the resulting system, we obtain its least solution at the end

$$T \subseteq w_0$$
$$((T \cap b_{B_0}) \Rightarrow T) \cup ((F \cap b_{B_0}) \Rightarrow F) \subseteq w_1$$
$$((T \cap w_1) \Rightarrow T) \cup ((F \cap w_1) \Rightarrow F) \subseteq w_2$$
$$((T \cap w_2) \Rightarrow T) \cup ((F \cap w_2) \Rightarrow F) \subseteq b_C$$
$$T \subseteq w_3$$
$$((T \cap b_{B_0}) \Rightarrow F) \cup ((F \cap b_{B_0}) \Rightarrow T) \subseteq w_4$$
$$((T \cap w_4) \Rightarrow T) \cup ((F \cap w_4) \Rightarrow F) \subseteq w_5$$
$$((T \cap w_5) \Rightarrow T) \cup ((F \cap w_5) \Rightarrow F) \subseteq b_{B_1}$$

bit or wire	variable	value after the first scan	value after the second scan
wire preceding XIC(B)	w_0	T	T
wire following XIC(B)	w_1	T	F
wire preceding OTE(C)	w_2	T	F
wire preceding XIO(C)	w_3	T	T
wire following XIO(C)	w_4	F	T
wire preceding OTE(B)	w_5	F	T
first instance of B	b_{B_0}	T	F
last instance of B	b_{B_1}	F	T
the bit C	b_C	T	F

Fig. 5. Base system for the last two rungs of the example program in Figure 1 with the least solutions at the end of the first and the second scans given in the table.

of the first scan (column 3 in Figure 5). We see that at the end of the first scan, the bit B is false. In the second scan, we add the constraint $F \subseteq b_{B_0}$ to the base system. The resulting system is solved, and its least solution is shown in column 4 of Figure 5. We intersect the values of the output bits, i.e., bits B (the last instance) and C, in the least solutions from the first two scans. Since the intersections are empty, we have detected a race.

If our analysis finds a race, then the program does indeed exhibit a race. The absence of races cannot be proven by our analysis due to approximations and due to the finite subspace of input assignments we sample. However, we can analyze the coverage of our random sampling approach using the well-known Coupon Collector's Problem: Consider a hat containing n distinct coupons. In a trial a coupon is drawn at random from the hat, examined, and then placed back in the hat. We are interested in the expected number of trials needed to select all n coupons at least once. One can show that the expected number of trials is $n \ln n + \mathcal{O}(n)$, and that the actual number of trials is sharply concentrated around this expected value (for any constant $c > 0$, the probability that after $n(\ln n + c)$ trials there are still coupons not selected is approximately $1 - e^{-e^{-c}}$). Notice that $1 - e^{-e^{-c}} \approx 0.05$ when $c = 3$, and this probability is independent of n.

Program	Size	#Vars.	Secs/Scan	Ext. Races	Int. Races	#Samples	Time (s)
Mini Factory	9,267	4,227	0.4	55	186	1000	844
Big Bak	32,005	21,596	4	4	6	1000	7466
Wdsdflt(1)	58,561	22,860	3	8	163	1000	7285
Wdsdflt(2)	58,561	22,860	3	7	156	1000	7075

Fig. 6. Benchmark programs for evaluating our analysis.

Theorem 4. *Using the Coupon Collector's problem, after approximately $2^k \ln(2^k + 3)$ random samples, any race depending on a fixed set of k or fewer inputs has been detected with high probability (95%), up to the approximations due to conservative analysis and performing only two scans.*

Note that the expected number of trials depends only on the number of inputs participating in the race, not on the total number of inputs. For example, the number of trials required to find races involving 5 inputs with 95% probability is 200 whether there are 100, 1000, or 10,000 inputs to the program.

5 Experimental Results

We have implemented our analysis using a general constraint solver [13]. Inputs to our analysis are abstract syntax tree (AST) representations of RLL programs. The ASTs are parsed into internal representations, and constraints are generated using the rules in Figure 3. The resulting constraints are solved and simplified to obtain the base system.

5.1 Benchmarks

Four large RLL programs were made available to us in AST form for evaluating our analysis.

- **Mini Factory**
  This is an example program written and used by RLL programmers and researchers working on tools for RLL programming.
- **Big Bak**
  This is a production RLL program.
- **Wdsdflt(1)**
  Another production application, this program has a known race.
- **Wdsdflt(2)**
  This program is a modified version of Wdsdflt(1) with the known race eliminated. The program is included for comparing its results with the results from the original program.

Figure 6 gives a table showing the size of each program as number of lines in abstract syntax tree form, number of set variables in the base system, and the time to analyze one scan. All measurements reported here were done on a Sun Enterprise-5000 with 512MB of main memory (using only one of the eight processors).

Our analysis discovered many relay races in these programs. The results are presented in Figure 6. For each program, we show the number of external racing bits (bits connected to external outputs), the number of internal racing bits (bits internal to the program), the number of samples, and the total analysis time in seconds. By Theorem 4, 1000 trials are sufficient to uncover races involving 7 or fewer inputs.

No relay races were known for the Mini Factory program. Our analysis detected 55 external races, some of which were subsequently verified by running a model factory under the corresponding inputs. Fewer races were found in Big Bak, even though it is a much larger program. Two likely reasons for this situation are that Big Bak uses arithmetic operations heavily (which our analysis approximates rather coarsely) and that Big Bak is a production program and has been more thoroughly debugged than Mini Factory. Our analysis discovered the known relay race in Wdsdflt(1) (fixed in Wdsdflt(2)) among 8 external and 163 internal races. Note that some of the reported races may be unrealizable if they depend on input configurations that cannot occur in practice.

6 Related Work

In this section, we discuss the relationship of our work to work in data flow analysis, model checking, and testing.

Data Flow Analysis Data flow analysis is used primarily in optimizing compilers to collect variable usage information for optimizations such as dead code elimination and register allocation [1]. It has also been applied for ensuring software reliability [14, 15]. Our approach differs from classical data flow analysis in two points. First, we use conditional constraints [3], which are essential for modeling both the boolean instructions and control flow instructions. Second, the use of constraints gives us the flexibility to analyze many input configurations by adding constraints to a base system, instead of performing a global dataflow analysis repeatedly. Our approach is more efficient because the base system can be solved and simplified once and then used repeatedly on different input configurations.

Model Checking Model checking [9, 10] is a branch of formal verification that can be fully automated. Model checking has been used successfully for verifying finite state systems such as hardware and communication protocols [6, 7, 12, 17, 11]. Model checkers exploit the finite nature of these systems by performing exhaustive state space searches. Because even these finite state spaces may be huge, model checking is usually applied to some abstract models of the actual system. These abstract systems are symbolically executed to obtain information about the actual systems. Our analysis for RLL programs is similar to model checking in that our abstract models are finite, whereas RLL programs are in general infinite state systems. Similar to model checking, we make the tradeoffs between modeling accuracy and efficiency. Our abstraction approximates timers, counters, and arithmetic. It is through these approximations that we obtain a simpler analysis that is practical for production codes. On the other hand, due to these approximations our analysis cannot guarantee the absence of errors. However, our approach differs from model checking in the way abstract models are obtained. In model checking, abstract models are often obtained manually, while our analysis automatically generates the model.

Testing   Testing is one of the most commonly used methods for assuring hardware and software quality. The I/O behaviors of the system on input instances are used to deduce whether the given system is faulty or not [19]. Testing is non-exhaustive in most cases due to a large or infinite number of test cases. One distinction of our approach from testing is that we work with an abstract model of the actual system. There are advantages and disadvantages to using an abstract model. A disadvantage is that there is loss of information due to abstraction. As a result, the detection of an error may be impossible, whereas testing the actual system would show the incorrect I/O behavior. Abstract models have the advantage that a much larger space of possible inputs can be covered, which is important if the set of inputs exhibiting a problem is a tiny fraction of all possible inputs. An abstract model is also advantageous when it is very difficult or very expensive to test the actual system. Both of these advantages of abstract modeling apply in the case of detecting relay races in RLL programs. [8] discusses some other tradeoffs of using the actual system and abstract models of the system for testing.

7   Conclusion

In this paper, we have described a relay race analysis for RLL programs to help RLL programmers detect some common programming mistakes. We have demonstrated that the analysis is useful in statically catching such programming errors. Our implementation of the analysis is accurate and fast enough to be practical — production RLL programs can be analyzed. The relay race analysis not only detected a known bug in a program that took an RLL programmer four hours of factory down-time to uncover, it also detected many previously unknown relay races in our benchmark programs.

Acknowledgments

We would like to thank Jim Martin for bringing RLL to our attention and for making this work possible. We would also like to thank Anthony Barrett for information on RLL, providing us with abstract syntax trees of RLL programs, and running some experiments to validate our results. Finally, we thank the anonymous referees for the helpful comments.

References

1. A.V. Aho, R. Sethi, and J.D. Ullman. *Compilers, Principles, Techniques and Tools.* Addison-Wesley, 1986.
2. A. Aiken and E. Wimmers. Type inclusion constraints and type inference. In *Proceedings of the 1993 Conference on Functional Programming Languages and Computer Architecture*, pages 31–41, Copenhagen, Denmark, June 1993.
3. A. Aiken, E. Wimmers, and T.K. Lakshman. Soft typing with conditional types. In *Twenty-First Annual ACM Symposium on Principles of Programming Languages*, pages 163–173, Portland, Oregon, January 1994.
4. Allen–Bradley, Rockwell Automation. *SLC 500 and MicroLogix 1000 Instruction Set.*
5. A. Barrett. Private communication.
6. M. Browne, E.M. Clarke, and D. Dill. Checking the correctness of sequential circuits. In *Proc. IEEE Internat. Conf. on Computer Design*, pages 545–548, 1985.
7. M. Browne, E.M. Clarke, D. Dill, and B. Mishra. Automatic verification of sequential circuits using temporal logic. *IEEE Trans. Comput.*, 35(12):1035–1044, 1986.
8. R.H. Carver and R. Durham. Integrating formal methods and testing for concurrent programs. In *Proceedings of the Tenth Annual Conference on Computer Assurance*, pages 25–33, New York, NY, USA, June 1995.
9. E.M. Clarke and E.A. Emerson. Design and synthesis of synchronization skeletons using branching time temporal logic. In *Proc. Workshop on Logics of Programs*, volume 131, pages 52–71, Berlin, 1981. Springer.
10. E.M. Clarke, E.A. Emerson, and A.P. Sistla. Automatic verification of finite-state concurrent systems using temporal logic specifications. *ACM Transactions on Programming Languages and Systems*, 8(2):244–263, 1986.
11. E.M. Clarke, O. Grumberg, H. Hiraishi, S. Jha, D.E. Long, K.L. McMillan, and L.A. Ness. Verification of the futurebus+ cache coherence protocol. In L. Claesen, editor, *Proceedings of the Eleventh International Symposium on Computer Hardware Description Languages and their Applications*, North-Holland, April 1993.
12. D. Dill and E.M. Clarke. Automatic verification of asynchronous circuits using temporal logic. In *Proceedings of the IEEE*, volume 133, pages 276–282, 1986.
13. M. Fahndrich and A. Aiken. Making set-constraint based program analyses scale. Technical Report UCB/CSD-96-917, University of California at Berkeley, 1996.
14. L.D. Fosdick and L.J. Osterweil. Data flow analysis in software reliability. *ACM Computing Surveys*, 8(3):305–330, September 1976.
15. M.J. Harrold. Using data flow analysis for testing. Technical Report 93-112, Department of Computer Science, Clemson University, 1993.
16. N. Heintze. *Set Based Program Analysis.* PhD thesis, Carnegie Mellon University, 1992.
17. G. Holzmann. *Design and Validation of Computer Protocols.* Prentice-Hall International Editions, 1991.
18. A. Krigman. Relay ladder diagrams: we love them, we love them not. In *Tech*, pages 39–47, October 1985.
19. D. Lee and M. Yannakakis. Principles and methods of testing finite state machines-a survey. In *Proceedings of the IEEE*, pages 1090–1123, August 1996.
20. R. Milner, M. Tofte, and R. Harper. *The Definition of Standard ML.* MIT Press, 1990.
21. Z. Su. Automatic analysis of relay ladder logic programs. Technical Report UCB/CSD-97-969, University of California at Berkeley, 1997.

Verification of Large State/Event Systems Using Compositionality and Dependency Analysis*

Jørn Lind-Nielsen[1], Henrik Reif Andersen[1], Gerd Behrmann[2],
Henrik Hulgaard[1], Kåre Kristoffersen[2], and Kim G. Larsen[2]

[1] Department of Information Technology, Technical University of Denmark
e-mail: {jl,hra,henrik}@it.dtu.dk

[2] BRICS**, Department of Computer Science, Aalborg University
e-mail: {behrmann,jelling,kgl}@cs.auc.dk

Abstract. A state/event model is a concurrent version of Mealy machines used for describing embedded reactive systems. This paper introduces a technique that uses *compositionality* and *dependency analysis* to significantly improve the efficiency of symbolic model checking of state/event models. This technique makes possible automated verification of large industrial designs with the use of only modest resources (less than one hour on a standard PC for a model with 1421 concurrent machines). The results of the paper are being implemented in the next version of the commercial tool visualSTATE™.

1 Introduction

Symbolic model checking is a powerful technique for formal verification of finite-state concurrent systems. The technique has proven very efficient for verifying hardware systems: circuits with an extremely large number of reachable states has been verified. However, it is not clear whether model checking is effective for other kinds of concurrent systems as, for example, software systems. One reason that symbolic model checking may not be as efficient is that software systems tend to be both larger and less regularly structured than hardware. For example, many of the results reported for verifying large hardware systems have been for linear structures like stacks or pipelines (see, e.g., [8]) for which it is known [19] that the size of the transition relation (when represented as an ROBDD) grows linearly with the size of the system. Only recently has the first experiments on larger realistic software systems been reported [3, 20].

This paper presents a technique that significantly improves the performance of symbolic model checking on embedded reactive systems modeled using a

---
* Supported by CIT, The Danish National Center of IT Research
** BRICS (Basic Research in Computer Science) is a basic research center funded by the Danish government at Aarhus and Aalborg

state/event model. The state/event model is a concurrent version of Mealy machines, that is, it consists of a fixed number of concurrent finite state machines that have pairs of input events and output actions associated with the transitions of the machines. The model is synchronous: each input event is reacted upon by all machines in lock-step; the total output is the multi-set union of the output actions of the individual machines. Further synchronization between the machines is achieved by associating a guard with the transitions. Guards are Boolean combinations of conditions on the local states of the other machines. In this way, the firing of transitions in one machine can be made conditional on the local state of other machines. If a machine has no enabled transition for a particular input event, it simply does not perform any state change.

The state/event model is convenient for describing the control portion of embedded reactive systems, including smaller systems as cellular phones, hi-fi equipment, and cruise controls for cars, and large systems as train simulators, flight control systems, telephone and communication protocols. The model is used in the commercial tool visualSTATE™ [18]. This tool assists in developing embedded reactive software by allowing the designer to construct a state/event model and analyze it by either simulating it or by running a *consistency checker*. The tool automatically generates the code for the hardware of the embedded system. The consistency checker is in fact a verification tool that checks for a range of properties that any state/event model should have. Some of the checks must be passed for the generated code to be correct, for instance, it is crucial that the model is deterministic. Other checks are issued as warnings that might be design errors such as transitions that can never fire.

State/event models can be extremely large. And unlike in traditional model checking, the number of checks is at least linear in the size of the model. This paper reports results for models with up to 1421 concurrent state machines (10^{476} states). For systems of this size, traditional symbolic model checking techniques fail, even when using a partitioned transition relation [6] and backwards iteration. We present a *compositional* technique that initially considers only a few machines in determining satisfaction of the verification task and, if necessary, gradually increases the number of considered machines. The machines considered are determined using a *dependency analysis* of the structure of the system.

The results are encouraging. A number of large state/event models from industrial applications have been verified. Even the largest model with 1421 concurrent machines can be verified with modest resources (it takes less than an hour on a standard PC). Compared with the current version of visualSTATE™, the results improve on the efficiency of checking the smaller instances and dramatically increase the size of systems that can be verified.

Related Work

The use of ROBDDs [5] in model checking was introduced by Burch *et al.* [7] and Coudert *et al.* [13]. Several improvements have been developed since, such as using a partitioned transition relation [6, 14] and simplifying the ROBDD representation during the fixed-point iteration [12]. Many of these improvements are implemented in the tool SMV [19]. Other techniques like abstraction [10] and compositional model checking [11] further reduce the complexity of the verification task, but require human insight and interaction.

Several techniques attempt to improve the efficiency of the verification by only considering a subset of the system. For example, [4] presents a conservative technique for showing emptiness of L-processes based on including only a subset of the processes. The technique is based on analyzing an error trace from the verifier, and use this trace to modify the considered subset of L-processes.

A more promising technique, based on ROBDDs, that also exploits the structure of the system is presented in [17]. On the surface this technique is very close to the one presented here and thus we will discuss it in more detail. The technique in [17] uses a partitioned transition relation and a greedy heuristic is used to select subsets of the transition relation. For each chosen subset, a complete fixed-point iteration is performed. If the formula cannot be proven after this iteration, a larger subset is chosen. In case of an invalid formula the algorithm only terminates when the full transition relation has been constructed (or memory or time has been exhausted). To compare this approach with the one presented here, we can consider a subset of the transition relation as being similar to a subset of the machines in the state/event model. The approach of [17] differs from ours in several central aspects:

- In selecting a new machine to include in the transition relation, [17] uses a greedy strategy involving a fixed-point iteration for each of the remaining machines. (If the system only has a single initial state—as in state/event systems—the greedy strategy reduces to selecting an arbitrary machine.) We chose a new machine based on an initial dependency analysis and thus avoids any extraneous fixed-point iterations.
- Due to a central monotonicity result (lemma 1), we can reuse the previously computed portion of the state space instead of having to start from scratch each time a new machine is added.
- In case the property to be verified is invalid, we only include those machines that are actually dependent on each other in the transition relation. In these cases, [17] may have to include all machines to disprove the property.
- Even when all machines are needed, experiments have shown that our technique of including machines one at a time (exploiting the monotonicity property) is *faster* than performing a traditional fixed-point iteration using a partitioned transition relation and early variable quantification. The technique of [17] does not have this property.

The compositional technique presented here shares ideas with partial model checking [1, 2, 16], but explicitly analyzes the structure of the system.

Finally, experiments by Anderson *et al.* [3] and Sreemani and Atlee [20] verified large software systems using SMV. The technique presented here significantly improves on the results we have obtained using SMV and makes it possible to verify larger systems.

Outline

The state/event model is described in section 2. Section 3 explains how the range of consistency checks performed by visualSTATE™ are reduced to two simple types of checks. Section 4 shows how state/event systems are encoded by ROB-DDs. The compositional technique and the dependency analysis is introduced in section 5, and further developed in section 6. The technique is evaluated in section 7 and section 8 draws some conclusions.

2 State/Event Systems

A state/event system consists of n machines $M_1, \ldots, M_n$ over an alphabet of input events E and an output alphabet O. Each machine M_i is a triple (S_i, s_i^0, T_i) of local states, an initial state, and a set of transitions. The set of transitions is a relation

$$T_i \subseteq S_i \times E \times G_i \times \mathcal{M}(O) \times S_i,$$

where $\mathcal{M}(O)$ is a multi-set of outputs, and G_i is the set of guards not containing references to machine i. These guards are generated from the following simple grammar for Boolean expressions:

$$g \quad ::= \quad l_j = p \mid \neg g \mid g \wedge g \mid tt.$$

The atomic predicate $l_j = p$ is read as "machine j is at local state p" and tt denotes a true guard. The global state set of the state/event system is the product of the local state sets: $S = S_1 \times S_2 \times \cdots \times S_n$. The guards are interpreted straightforwardly over S: for any $s \in S$, $s \models l_j = p$ holds exactly when the j'th component of s is p, i.e., $s_j = p$. The notation $g[s_j/l_j]$ denotes that s_j is substituted for l_j, with occurrences of atomic propositions of the form $s_j = p$ replaced by tt or $\neg tt$ depending on whether s_j is identical to p.

Considering a global state s, all guards in the transition relation can be evaluated. We define a version of the transition relation in which the guards have been evaluated. This relation is denoted $s \xrightarrow{e\ o}_i s_i'$ expressing that machine i when receiving input event e makes a transition from s_i to s_i' and generates output o. Formally,

$$s \xrightarrow{e\ o}_i s_i' \Leftrightarrow_{def} \exists g.\ (s_i, e, g, o, s_i') \in T_i \text{ and } s \models g.$$

Two machines can be combined into one. More generally if M_I and M_J are compositions of two disjoint sets of machines I and J, $I, J \subseteq \{1, \ldots, n\}$, we can combine them into one $M_{IJ} = M_I \times M_J = (S_{IJ}, (s_{IJ}^0), T_{IJ})$, where $S_{IJ} = S_I \times S_J$ and $s_{IJ}^0 = (s_I^0, s_J^0)$. The transition relation T_{IJ} is a subset of $S_{IJ} \times E \times G_{IJ} \times \mathcal{M}(O) \times S_{IJ}$, where G_{IJ} are the guards in the composite machine. By construction of T_{IJ}, the guards G_{IJ} will not contain any references to machines in $I \cup J$. To define T_{IJ}, we introduce the predicate $idle$:

$$idle(T_I, s_I, e) = \bigwedge \{\neg g \mid \exists o, s_I'.\ (s_I, e, g, o, s_I') \in T_I\},$$

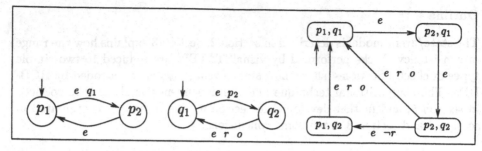

Fig. 1. Two state/event machines and the corresponding parallel combination. The guards, which formally should be of the form $l_j = p$, are simply written as the state p since the location l_j is derivable from the name of the state. The small arrows indicate the initial states. The reference to r is a requirement to a state in a third machine not shown.

which holds for states in which no transitions in M_I are enabled at state s_I when receiving the input event e. The transition relation T_{IJ} is defined by the following inference rules (the symbol $\uplus$ denotes multi-set union):

$$\frac{(s_I, e, g_1, o_1, s_I') \in T_I \quad (s_J, e, g_2, o_2, s_J') \in T_J}{((s_I, s_J), e, g, o_1 \uplus o_2, (s_I', s_J')) \in T_{IJ}} \quad g = g_1[s_J/l_J] \wedge g_2[s_I/l_I]$$

$$\frac{(s_I, e, g_1, o_1, s_I') \in T_I}{((s_I, s_J), e, g, o_1, (s_I', s_J)) \in T_{IJ}} \quad g = g_1[s_J/l_J] \wedge idle(T_J, s_J, e)[s_I/l_I]$$

$$\frac{(s_J, e, g_2, o_2, s_J') \in T_J}{((s_I, s_J), e, g, o_2, (s_I, s_J')) \in T_{IJ}} \quad g = idle(T_I, s_I, e)[s_J/l_J] \wedge g_2[s_I/l_I].$$

The rules show the synchronous behaviour of state/event systems. The first rule represents the case where there exists an enabled transition with input event e in both T_I and T_J and the resulting transition in T_{IJ} represents the synchronization on e. The other two cases occur if no enabled transition exists in either T_I or T_J. The state/event systems in figure 1 shows two machines and the parallel composition of them.

The full combination of all n machines yields a Mealy machine in which the transitions $s \xrightarrow{e \, o} s'$ are defined by

$$s \xrightarrow{e \, o} s' \iff \exists g. \, (s, e, g, o, s') \in \prod_{i=1}^{n} T_i \text{ and } g \text{ is true.}$$

3 Consistency Checks

The consistency checker in visualSTATE™ performs seven predefined types of checks, each of which can be reduced to verifying one of two types of properties. The first type is a *reachability property*. For instance, visualSTATE™ performs a check for "conflicting transitions" i.e., it checks whether two or more transitions can become enabled in the same local state, leading to non-determinism. This can be reduced to questions of reachability by considering all pairs of guards g_1 and g_2 of transitions with the same local state s_i and input event e. A conflict can occur if a global state is reachable in which $(l_j = s_i) \land g_1 \land g_2$ is satisfied.

In total, five of the seven types of checks reduce to reachability checks. Four of these, such as check for transitions that are never enabled and check for states that are never reached, generate a number of reachability checks which is linear in the number of transitions, t. In the worst-case the check for conflicting transitions gives rise to a number of reachability checks which is quadratic in the number of transitions. However, in practice very few transitions have the same starting local state and input event, thus in practice the number of checks generated is much smaller than t.

The remaining two types of consistency checks reduce to a check for absence of *local deadlocks*. A local deadlock occurs if the system can reach a state in which one of the machines idles forever on all input events. This check is made for each of the n machines. In total at least $t + n$ checks have to be performed making the verification of state/event systems quite different from traditional model checking where typically only a few key properties are verified.

We attempt to reduce the number of reachability checks by performing an *implicational analysis* between the guards of the checks. If a guard g_1 implies another guard g_2 then clearly, if g_1 is reachable so is g_2. To use this information we start by sorting all the guards in ascending order of the size of their satisfying state space. In this way the most specific guards are checked first and for each new guard to be checked we compare it to all the already checked (and reachable) guards. If the new guard includes one of them, then we know that it is satisfiable. In our experiments, between 40% and 94% of the reachability checks are eliminated in this manner.

4 ROBDD Representation

This section describes how Reduced Ordered Binary Decision Diagrams (ROB-DDs) [5] are used to represent sets of states and the transition relation. We also show how to perform a traditional forward iteration to construct the set of reachable states from which it is straightforward to check each of the reachability checks.

To construct the ROBDD $\widetilde{T}$ for the transition relation T, we first construct the local transition relations $\widetilde{T}_i$ for each machine M_i. The variables of the ROBDD represents an encoding of the input events, the current states, and the next-states. The variables are ordered as follows: The first $\|E\|$ variables encodes the input events E ($\|X\|$ denotes $\lceil \log_2 |X| \rceil$) and are denoted V_E. Then follows $2\|S_i\|$ variables $V_{i,1}, V'_{i,1}, \dots, V_{i,\|S_i\|}, V'_{i,\|S_i\|}$ encoding the current- (unprimed variables) and the next-states (primed variables) for machine i.

The transition relation $\widetilde{T}_i$ for machine i is constructed as an ROBDD predicate over these variables. The ROBDD for a transition $(s_i, e, g, o, s'_i) \in T_i$ is constructed as the conjunction of the ROBDD encodings of s_i, e, g, and s'_i. (The outputs are not encoded as they have no influence on the reachable states of the system.) The encoding of s_i, e, and s'_i is straightforward and the encoding of the guard g is done by converting all atomic predicates $l_j = p$ to ROBDD predicates over the current-state variables for machine M_j and then performing the Boolean operations in the guard. The encoding of all transitions of machine i is obtained from the disjunction of the encoding of the individual transitions:

$$\tilde{t}_i = \bigvee_{(s_i,e,g,o,s'_i)\in T_i} \tilde{s}_i \wedge \tilde{e} \wedge \tilde{g} \wedge \tilde{s}'_i \,,$$

where $\tilde{e}$ is the ROBDD encoding of input event e and $\tilde{s}_i$ and $\tilde{s}'_i$ are the ROBDD encodings of the current-state s_i and next-state s'_i, respectively.

To properly encode the global transition relation T, we need to deal with situations where no transitions of T_i are enabled. In those cases we want the machine i to stay in its current state. We construct an ROBDD neg_i representing that no transition is enabled by negating all guards in machine i (including the input events):

$$neg_i = \bigwedge_{(s_i,e,g,o,s'_i)\in T_i} \neg(\tilde{s}_i \wedge \tilde{g} \wedge \tilde{e}) \,.$$

The ROBDD equ_i encodes that machine i does not change state by requiring that the next-state is identical to the current-state:

$$equ_i = \bigwedge_{j=1}^{\|S_i\|} V_{i,j} \leftrightarrow V'_{i,j} \,.$$

The local transition relation for machine i is then:

$$\tilde{T}_i = \tilde{t}_i \vee (neg_i \wedge equ_i) \,.$$

The ROBDD $\tilde{T}$ for the full transition relation is the conjunction of the local transition relations:

$$\tilde{T} = \bigwedge_{i=1}^{n} \tilde{T}_i \,.$$

One way to check whether a state s is reachable is to construct the reachable state space R. The construction of R can be done by a standard forward iteration of the transition relation, starting with the initial state s^0:

$$R_0 = \tilde{s}^0$$
$$R_k = R_{k-1} \vee (\exists V, V_E.\ \tilde{T} \wedge R_{k-1})[V/V']$$

where V is the set of current-state variables, V' is the set of next-state variables, and $(\cdots)[V/V']$ denotes the result of replacing all the primed variables in V' by their unprimed versions.

The construction of the full transition relation T can be avoided by using a *partitioned transition relation* [6] together with early variable quantification.

This is done by identifying sets I_j of transition relations that, when applied in the correct order, allows for early quantification of the state variables that no other transition relations depend on. If V_{I_j} are these variables and we have m sets, then we get:

$$R_0 = \tilde{s}^0$$
$$R_k = R_{k-1} \vee (\exists V_E.\exists V_{I_1} . \bigwedge_{i \in I_1} \tilde{T}_i \wedge \ldots \wedge (\exists V_{I_m} . \bigwedge_{i \in I_m} \tilde{T}_i \wedge R_{k-1}))[V/V'].$$

Both approaches have been implemented and tested on our examples as shown in section 7. Here we see that the calculation of the reachable state space using the full transition relation is both fast and efficient for the small examples. However, for models with more than approximately 30 machines, both approaches fail to complete.

5 Compositional Backwards Reachability

The problems of forwards iteration can typically be solved by using a backwards reachability analysis. The verification task is to determine whether a guard g can be satisfied. Instead of computing the reachable state space and check that g is valid somewhere in this set, we start with the set of states in which g is valid and compute in a backwards iteration, states that can reach a state in which g is satisfied. The goal is to determine whether the initial state is among these states. Our novel idea is to perform the backwards iteration in a compositional manner considering only a minimal number of machines. Initially, only machines mentioned in g will be taken into account. Later also machines on which these depend will be included.

Notice that compared to the forwards iteration, this approach has an apparent drawback when performing a large number of reachability checks: instead of just *one* fixed-point iteration to construct the reachable state space R (and then trivially verify the properties), a new fixed-point iteration is necessary for *each* property that is checked. However, our experiments clearly demonstrate that when using a compositional backwards iteration, each of the fixed-point iterations can be completed even for very large models whereas the forwards iteration fails to complete the construction of R for even medium sized models.

To formalize the backwards compositional technique, we need a semantic version of the concept of dependency. For a subset of the machines $I \subseteq \{1, \ldots, n\}$, two states $s, s' \in S$ are *I-equivalent*, written $s =_I s'$, if for all $i \in I$, $s_i = s'_i$ (the primes are here used to denote another state and is not related to the next-states). If a subset P of the reachable states S only is constrained by components in some index set I we can think of P as having I as a *sort*. This leads to the following definition: a subset P of S is *I-sorted* if for all $s, s' \in S$,

$$s \in P \text{ and } s =_I s' \Rightarrow s' \in P.$$

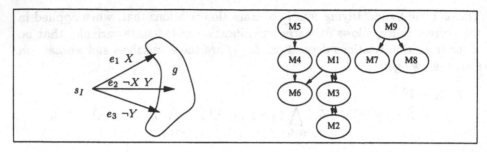

Fig. 2. The left figure is an example showing the effect of $B_I(g)$. If X is the guard $l_j = p$ and Y the guard $l_k = q$ with $j, k \notin I$ then the transitions from s_I seem to depend on machines M_j and M_k outside I. However, the guards X, $\neg X\, Y$, and $\neg Y$ together span all possibilities and therefore, by selecting either e_1, e_2, or e_3, the state s_I can reach g irrespective of the states of the machines M_j and M_k. The right figure illustrates the dependencies between 9 state machines taken from a real example (the example "HI-FI" of section 7). An arrow from one machine M_i to another M_j indicates the existence of a transition in M_i with a guard that depends on a state in machine M_j.

As an example, consider a guard g which mentions only machines 1 and 3. The set of states defined by g is I-sorted for any I containing 1 and 3.[1] Another understanding of the definition is that a set P is I-sorted if it is independent of the machines in the complement $\bar{I} = \{1, \ldots, n\} \setminus I$.

From an I-sorted set g we perform a backwards reachability computation by including states which, irrespective of the states of the machines in $\bar{I}$, can reach g. One backward step is given by the function $B_I(g)$ defined by:

$$B_I(g) = \{s \in S \mid \forall s' \in S.\ s =_I s' \Rightarrow \tag{1}$$
$$\exists e, o, s''.\ s' \xrightarrow{e\ o} s'' \text{ and } s'' \in g\}.$$

By definition $B_I(g)$ is I-sorted. The set $B_I(g)$ is the set of states which independently of machines in $\bar{I}$, by some input event e, can reach a state in g. Observe that $B_I(g)$ is monotonic in both g and I. Figure 2 shows how a state s_I of a machine is included in $B_I(g)$ although it syntactically seems to depend on machines outside I.

By iterating the application of B_I, we can compute the minimum set of states containing g and closed under application of B_I. This is the minimum fixed-point $\mu X.g \cup B_I(X)$, which we refer to as $B_I^*(g)$. Note that $B_{\{1,\ldots,n\}}^*(g)$ becomes the desired set of states which can reach g.

A set of indices I is said to be *dependency closed* if none of the machines in I depend on machines outside I. Formally, I is *dependency closed* if for all $i \in I$, states s', s, s_i, input events e, and outputs o, $s \xrightarrow{e\ o}_i s_i$ and $s' =_I s$ implies $s' \xrightarrow{e\ o}_i s_i$.

---

[1] If the guard is self-contradictory (always false), it will be I-sorted for any I. This reflects the fact that the semantic sortedness is more precise than syntactic occurrence.

The basic properties of the sets $B_I^*(g)$ are captured by the following lemma:

Lemma 1 (Compositional Reachability Lemma). *Assume g is an I-sorted subset of S. For all subsets of machines I, J with $I \subseteq J$ the following holds:*

$$(i). \quad B_I^*(g) \subseteq B_J^*(g)$$

$$(ii). \quad B_J^*(g) = B_J^*(B_I^*(g))$$

$$(iii). \quad I \text{ dependency closed } \Rightarrow B_I^*(g) = B_J^*(g).$$

The results of the lemma are applied in the following manner. To check whether a guard g is reachable, we first consider the set of machines I_1 syntactically mentioned in g. Clearly, g is I_1-sorted. We then compute $B_{I_1}^*(g)$. If the initial state s^0 belongs to $B_{I_1}^*(g)$, then by (i) $s^0 \in B_{\{1,\dots,n\}}^*(g)$ and therefore g is reachable from s^0 and we are done. If not, we extend I_1 to a larger set of machines I_2 by adding machines that are syntactically mentioned on guards in transitions of machines in I_1. We then reuse $B_{I_1}^*(g)$ to compute $B_{I_2}^*(g)$ as $B_{I_2}^*(B_{I_1}^*(g))$ which is correct by (ii). We continue like this until s^0 has been found in one of the sets or an index set I_k is dependency closed. In the latter case we have by (iii) $B_{I_k}^*(g) = B_{\{1,\dots,n\}}^*(g)$ and g is unreachable unless $s^0 \in B_{I_k}^*(g)$.

As an example, assume that we want to determine whether the guard $g = (l_1 = p \wedge l_3 \neq q)$ is reachable in the example of figure 2 (right). The initial index set is $I_1 = \{1,3\}$. If this is not enough to show g reachable, the second index set $I_2 = \{1,3,7,2\}$ is used. Since this set is dependency closed, g is reachable if and only if the initial state belongs to $B_{I_2}^*(B_{I_1}^*(g))$.

The above construction is based on a backwards iteration. A dual version of B_I for a forwards iteration could be defined. However, such a definition would not make use of the dependency information since s^0 is only I-sorted for $I = \{1,\dots,n\}$. Therefore all machines would be considered in the first fixed-point iteration reducing it to the complete forwards iteration mentioned in the previous section.

Seemingly, the definition of $B_I(g)$ requires knowledge of the global transition relation and therefore does not seem to yield any computational advantage. However, as explained below, using ROBDDs this can be avoided leading to an efficient computation of $B_I(g)$. The ROBDD $\widetilde{B}_I(\widetilde{g})$ representing one iteration backwards from the states represented by the ROBDD $\widetilde{g}$ can be constructed immediately from the definition (1):

$$\widetilde{B}_I(\widetilde{g}) = \forall V_{\bar{I}}. \; \exists V_E, V'. \; \widetilde{T} \wedge \widetilde{g}[V'/V] \tag{2}$$

where $\widetilde{g}[V'/V]$ is equal to $\widetilde{g}$ with all variables in V replaced by their primed versions. It is essential to avoid building the global transition relation $\widetilde{T}$. This is done by writing $\exists V'$ as $\exists V_I'.\exists V_{\bar{I}}'$ and $\widetilde{T} = \widetilde{T}_I \wedge \widetilde{T}_{\bar{I}}$ where $\widetilde{T}_I = \bigwedge_{i \in I} \widetilde{T}_i$. This allows us to push the existential quantification of $V_{\bar{I}}'$ to $\widetilde{T}_{\bar{I}}$ since g is I-sorted and thus independent of the variables in $V_{\bar{I}}'$. As $\exists V_{\bar{I}}'.\widetilde{T}_{\bar{I}}$ is a tautology, equation (2) reduces to:

$$\widetilde{B}_I(\widetilde{g}) = \forall V_{\bar{I}}. \; \exists V_E, V_I'. \; \widetilde{T}_I \wedge \widetilde{g}[V'/V]$$

which only uses the local transition relations for machines in I. Each T_i refers only to primed variables in V_i', allowing early variable quantification for each machine individually:

$$\tilde{B}_I(\tilde{g}) = \forall V_{\bar{I}}.\ \exists V_E.\ \exists V_1'.\tilde{T}_1 \wedge (\exists V_2'.\tilde{T}_2 \wedge \cdots \wedge (\exists V_k'.\tilde{T}_k \wedge \tilde{g}[V'/V]) \cdots).$$

This equation efficiently computes one step in the fixed-point iteration constructing $\tilde{B}_I^*(\tilde{g})$.

Notice, that the existential quantifications can be performed in any order. We have chosen the order in which the machines occur in the input, but other orders may exist which improves performance.

6 Local Deadlock Detection

In checking for local deadlocks we use a construction similar to backwards reachability. To make the compositional backwards lemma applicable we work with the notion of a machine being *live* which is the exact dual of having a local deadlock. In words, a machine is live if it always is the case that there exists a way to make the machine move to a new local state. Formally, a global state s is *live* for machine i if there exists a sequence of states $s^1, s^2, \ldots, s^k$ with $s = s^1$ and $s^j \xrightarrow{e\ o} s^{j+1}$ (for some e and o) such that $s_i^k \neq s_i^1$. Machine i is live if all reachable states are live. A simple example of a state/event system with a local deadlock is shown in figure 3.

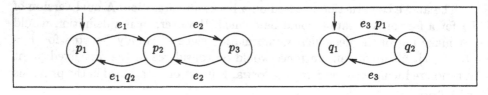

Fig. 3. A state/event system with a local deadlock. The global state $s = (p_2, q_1)$ is not live for the machine to the right since for all input events the guard p_1 remains false. The state s is reachable (e.g., by initially receiving e_1) and thus the machine to the right has a local deadlock.

The check is divided into two parts. First, the set of all live states L_i^* for machine i is computed. Second, we check that all reachable states are in L_i^*. A straightforward but inefficient approach would be to compute the two sets and check for inclusion. However, we will take advantage of the compositional construction used in the backwards reachability in both parts of the check.

Similar to the definition of $B_I(g)$, we define $L_{I,i}(X)$ to be the set of states that are immediately live for machine $i \in I$ independently of the machines outside I or leads to states in X (which are states assumed to be live for machine i):

$$L_{I,i}(X) = \{ s \in S \mid \forall s'.s =_I s' \Rightarrow \tag{3}$$
$$\exists e, o, s''.\ s' \xrightarrow{e\ o} s'' \text{ and } (s_i \neq s_i'' \text{ or } s'' \in X) \}.$$

Notice, that compared to definition (1) the only difference is the extra possibility that the state is immediately live, i.e., $s_i \neq s_i''$. The set of states that are live for machine i independently of machines outside I is then the set $L_{I,i}^*(\emptyset)$ where $L_{I,i}^*(Y)$ is the minimum fixed point defined by $L_{I,i}^*(Y) = \mu X.Y \cup L_{I,i}(X)$.

The three properties of lemma 1 also holds for $L_{I,i}^*(Y)$ when Y is I-sorted. If I is dependency closed it follows from property (iii) of the lemma that $L_{I,i}^*(\emptyset)$ equals $L_{\{1,\ldots,n\},i}^*(\emptyset)$ which is precisely the set of live states of machine i. This gives an efficient way to compute the sets $L_{I,i}^*(\emptyset)$ for different choices of I. We start with I_1 equal to $\{i\}$ and continue with larger I_k's exactly as for the backwards reachability. The only difference is the termination conditions. One possible termination case is if $L_{I_k,i}^*(\emptyset)$ becomes equal to S for some k. In that case it is trivial that the set of reachable states is contained in $L_{I_k,i}^*(\emptyset)$. From the monotonicity property (i) of the lemma it follows that machine i is live and thus free of local deadlocks. The other termination case is when I_k becomes dependency closed. Then we have to check whether there exists reachable states not in $L_{I_k,i}^*(\emptyset)$. This is done by a compositional backwards reachability check with $g = S \setminus L_{I_k,i}^*(\emptyset)$.

7 Experimental Results

The technique presented above has been used on a range of real industrial state/event systems and a set of systems constructed by students in a course on embedded systems. The examples are all constructed using visualSTATE™ [18]. They cover a large range of different applications and are structurally highly irregular.

The examples HI-FI, AVS, FLOW, MOTOR, INTERVM, DKVM, MULTICD, TRAIN1 and TRAIN2 are all industrial examples. HI-FI is the control part of an advanced compact hi-fi system, AVS is the control part of an audio-video system, FLOW is the control part of a flow meter, MOTOR is a motor control, INTERVM and DKVM are advanced vending machines, MULTICD is the control of a multi-volume CD player, and TRAIN1 and TRAIN2 are both independent subsystems of a train simulator. The remaining examples are constructed by students. The VCR is a simulation of a video recorder, CYBER is an alarm clock, JVC is the control of a compact hi-fi system, VIDEO is a video player, and VOLVO is a simulation of the complete functionality of the dashboard of a car. The characteristics of the state/event systems are shown in table 1.

The experiments were carried out on a 166 MHz Pentium PC with 32 MB RAM running Linux. To implement the ROBDD operations, we have constructed our own ROBDD package which is comparable to state-of-the-art packages in terms of performance. In all experiments we limit the total number of ROBDD nodes to one million corresponding to 20 MB of memory. We check for each transition whether the guard is reachable and whether it is conflicting with other transitions. Furthermore, we check for each machine whether it has a local deadlock. The total runtime and memory consumption for these checks are shown in table 2. The total number of checks is far from the quadratic worst-case, which

Table 1. The state/event systems used in the experiments. The last two columns show the size of the declared and reachable state space. The size of the declared state space is the product of the number of local states of each machine. The reachable state space is only known for those systems where the forwards analysis completes.

System	Machines	Local states	Transitions	Declared	Reachable
INTERVM	6	182	745	10^6	15144
VCR	7	46	85	10^5	1279
CYBER	8	19	98	10^3	240
JVC	8	25	106	10^4	352
DKVM	9	55	215	10^6	377568
HI-FI	9	59	373	10^7	1416384
FLOW	10	232	1146	10^5	17040
MOTOR	12	41	295	10^6	34560
AVS	12	66	1737	10^7	1438416
VIDEO	13	74	268	10^8	1219440
VOLVO	20	84	196	10^{11}	$9.2 \cdot 10^9$
MULTICD	28	145	3128	10^{17}	$3.8 \cdot 10^{16}$
TRAIN1	373	931	2988	10^{136}	–
TRAIN2	1421	3204	11166	10^{476}	–

Table 2. The runtime and memory consumptions of the experiments. The second column of the table shows the total number of guards that are checked for reachability after this number has been reduced by the implicational analysis. The forward columns show results using a forward iteration with a full and a partitioned transition relation. The backward columns show the results of a backwards iteration using the full transition relation and the compositional backwards reachability. The visualSTATE column shows the runtimes obtained using an explicit state enumeration as implemented in version 3.0 of visualSTATE™. A "–" denotes that we ran out of memory or the runtime exceeded two hours without finishing.

System	Guards checked	Forward Full Sec	MB	Partitioned Sec	MB	Backward Full Sec	MB	Compositional Sec	MB	visualSTATE Sec
INTERVM	185	1.7	6	6.1	6	6.5	6	22.5	6	22
VCR	50	0.3	6	0.6	5	0.9	6	0.7	7	< 1
CYBER	16	0.2	6	0.3	5	0.2	6	0.2	6	< 1
JVC	22	0.2	6	0.3	5	0.3	6	0.2	6	< 1
DKVM	63	0.8	6	16.0	6	1.7	6	3.4	6	409
HI-FI	120	1.2	6	25.2	6	6.2	6	7.2	6	1200
FLOW	230	1.2	6	3.7	6	8.8	6	10.8	6	22
MOTOR	123	1.0	6	11.6	6	4.9	6	3.2	6	32
AVS	173	8.9	6	126.4	8	9.7	6	13.0	6	3780
VIDEO	122	1.3	6	38.7	6	7.4	6	2.6	6	–
VOLVO	83	4.5	9	1271.3	5	14.3	6	2.6	6	–
MULTICD	199	4.9	6	32.4	5	11.0	6	4.2	6	–
TRAIN1	1335	–	–	–	–	–	–	38.3	9	–
TRAIN2	4708	–	–	–	–	–	–	2918.7	45	–

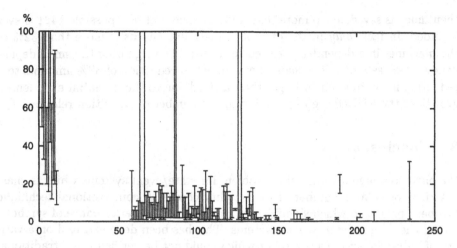

Fig. 4. The fraction of machines actually used in the compositional backwards reachability analysis of the guards of the largest system TRAIN2. For each size of dependency closed set, a line between is drawn between the minimum and maximum fraction of machines used in verifying guards with dependency closed sets of that size. For instance, for the guards with dependency closed sets with 234 machines (the right-most line) only between 1% and 32% of the machines are needed to prove that the guard is reachable.

supports the claim that in practice only very few checks are needed to check for conflicting rules (see section 3).

As expected, the forwards iteration with full transition relation is efficient for smaller systems. It is remarkable that the ROBDD technique is superior to explicit state enumeration even for systems with a very small number of reachable states. Using the partitioned transition relation in the forwards iteration works poorly.

For the two largest systems, only the compositional backwards technique succeeds. In fact, for the four largest systems it is the most efficient and for the small examples it has performance comparable to the full forward technique. This is despite the fact that the number of checks is high and the backward iterations must be repeated for each check. From the experiments it seems that the compositional backwards technique is better than full forwards from somewhere around 20 machines.

In order to understand why the compositional backwards technique is successful we have analyzed the largest system TRAIN2 in more detail, see figure 4. For each guard we have computed the size of its smallest enclosing dependency closed set of machines. During the backwards iterations we have kept track of how many times the set of machines I (used in $B_I^*(g)$) need to be enlarged and how many machines was contained in the set I when the iteration terminated. The dependency closed sets of cardinality 63, 66, 85, 86, 125, 127 all contain at least one machine with a guard that is unreachable. As is clearly seen from the figure, in these cases the iteration has to include the entire dependency closed set in order to prove that the initial state cannot reach the guard. But even then much is saved, as no more than 234 machines out of a possible 1421 is ever included. In fact, *only* in the case of unreachable guards is more than 32% of the machines in a dependency closed set ever needed (ignoring the small dependency closed sets with less than 12 machines). A reduction of 32% amounts to a reduction in runtime much larger than a third due to the potential exponential growth of the ROBDD representation in the number of transition relations $\tilde{T}_i$.

8 Conclusion

We have presented a verification problem for state/event systems which is characterized by a large number of reachability checks. A compositional technique has been presented which significantly improves on the performance of symbolic model checking for state/event systems. This has been demonstrated on a variety of industrial systems several of which could not be verified using traditional symbolic model checking, e.g., using SMV.

We expect that these results can be translated to other models of embedded control systems than the state/event model, as for example StateCharts [15]. Furthermore, the two types of checks are of a general nature. Clearly, reachability is a key property which captures a number of important properties of a system. Moreover, the check for local deadlock shows how properties requiring nesting of fixed points can be checked efficiently with the compositional backwards analysis. Thus, it seems straightforward to implement more general checks as expressed in, for instance, CTL [9].

References

1. H. R. Andersen, J. Staunstrup, and N. Maretti. Partial model checking with ROBDDs. In E. Brinksma, editor, *Proceedings of TACAS'97*, volume 1217 of *LNCS*, pages 35–49. Springer-Verlag, April 1997.
2. H.R. Andersen. Partial model checking (extended abstract). In *Proceedings, Tenth Annual IEEE Symposium on Logic in Computer Science*, pages 398–407, La Jolla, San Diego, 26–29 July 1995. IEEE Computer Society Press.
3. R.J. Anderson, P. Beame, S. M. Burns, W. Chan, F. Modugno, D. Notkin, and J.D. Reese. Model checking large software specifications. In D. Garlan, editor, *SIGSOFT '96. Proceedings of the Fourth ACM SIGSOFT Symposium on the Foundations of Software Engineering*, pages 156–66, San Francisco, 1996. ACM.
4. F. Balarin and A.L. Sangiovanni-Vincentelli. An iterative approach to language containment. In C. Courcoubetis, editor, *CAV'93. 5th International Conference on Computer Aided Verification*, volume 697 of *LNCS*, pages 29–40, Berlin, 1993. Springer-Verlag.
5. R.E. Bryant. Graph-based algorithms for Boolean function manipulation. *IEEE Transactions on Computers*, 8(C-35):677–691, 1986.
6. J. R. Burch, E. M. Clarke, and D. E. Long. Symbolic model checking with partitioned transition relations. In A. Halaas and P. B. Denyer, editors, *Proc. 1991 Int. Conf. on VLSI*, August 1991.

7. J. R. Burch, E. M. Clarke, K. L. McMillan, D. L. Dill, and L. J. Hwang. Symbolic model checking: 10^{20} states and beyond. In *Proceedings, Fifth Annual IEEE Symposium on Logic in Computer Science*, pages 428–439. IEEE Computer Society Press, 1990.

8. J.R. Burch, E.M. Clarke, D.E. Long, K.L. McMillan, and D.L. Dill. Symbolic model checking for sequential circuit verification. *IEEE Transactions on Computer-Aided Design of Integrated Circuits and Systems*, 13(4):401–424, 1994.

9. E.M. Clarke, E.A. Emerson, and A.P. Sistla. Automatic verification of finite-state concurrent systems using temporal logic specifications. *ACM Transactions on Programming Languages and Systems*, 8(2):244–263, 1986.

10. E.M. Clarke, O. Grumberg, and D.E. Long. Model checking and abstraction. *ACM Transactions on Programming Languages and Systems*, 1994.

11. E.M. Clarke, D.E. Long, and K.L. McMillan. Compositional model checking. In *Proceedings, Fourth Annual Symposium on Logic in Computer Science*, pages 353–362, Asilomar Conference Center, Pacific Grove, California, June 5–8 1989. IEEE Computer Society Press.

12. O. Coudert, C. Berthet, and J. C. Madre. Verification of synchronous sequential machines based on symbolic execution. In J. Sifakis, editor, *Automatic Verification Methods for Finite State Systems. Proceedings*, volume 407 of *LNCS*, pages 365–373. Springer-Verlag, 1989.

13. O. Coudert, J. C. Madre, and C. Berthet. Verifying temporal properties of sequential machines without building their state diagrams. In E.M. Clarke and R.P. Kurshan, editors, *CAV'90. Workshop on Computer-Aided Verification.*, pages 75–84, Rutgers, New Jersey, 1990. American Mathematical Society.

14. D. Geist and I. Beer. Efficient model checking by automated ordering of transition relation partitions. In D.L. Dill, editor, *CAV'94. 6th International Conference on Computer Aided Verification*, volume 818 of *LNCS*, pages 299–310, Stanford, 1994. Springer-Verlag.

15. David Harel. STATECHARTS: A visual formalism for complex systems. *Science of Computer Programming*, 8(3):231–274, June 1987.

16. K. J. Kristoffersen, F. Laroussinie, K. G. Larsen, P. Patterson, and W. Yi. A compositional proof of a read-time mutual exclusion protocol. In M. Bidoit and M. Dauchet, editors, *Proceedings of TAPSOFT '97: Theory and Practice of Software Development*, volume 1214 of *LNCS*, pages 565–579. Springer-Verlag, 1997.

17. W. Lee, A. Pardo, J.-Y. Jang, G. Hachtel, and F. Somenzi. Tearing based automatic abstraction for CTL model checking. In *1996 IEEE/ACM International Conference on Computer-Aided Design*, pages 76–81, San Jose, CA, 1996. IEEE Comput. Soc. Press.

18. Beologic® A/S. *visualSTATE™ 3.0 User's Guide*, 1996.

19. K.L. McMillan. *Symbolic Model Checking*. Kluwer Academic Publishers, Norwell Massachusetts, 1993.

20. T. Sreemani and J.M. Atlee. Feasibility of model checking software requirements: a case study. In *COMPASS '96. Proceedings of the Eleventh Annual Conference on Computer Assurance*, pages 77–88, New York, USA, 1996. IEEE.

Tamagotchis Need Not Die – Verification of STATEMATE Designs

Udo Brockmeyer and Gunnar Wittich *

OFFIS, Escherweg 2, 26121 Oldenburg, Germany
email: {Brockmeyer,Wittich}@OFFIS.Uni-Oldenburg.de

Abstract. This paper presents a toolset we built for supporting verification of STATEMATE[1] designs. STATEMATE is a widely used design tool for embedded control applications. Designs are translated into finite state machines which are optimized and then verified by symbolic model checking. To express requirement specifications the visual formalism of symbolic timing diagrams is used. Their semantics is given by translation into temporal logic. If the model checker generates a counterexample, it is retranslated into either a symbolic timing diagram or a stimulus for the STATEMATE simulator.

1 Introduction

Growing complexity and wide usage of embedded systems in safety critical applications raises the demand for proving their correctness. Because verification with theorem provers [16] is a difficult task even for experts, automatic verification techniques, in particular model checking [3,4], are gaining increasing influence in the development of industrial applications.

In this paper we present a toolset we built for the verification of STATEMATE designs [11,12,14]. STATEMATE is a widely used graphical specification tool for embedded control applications. The STATEMATE toolset captures the phases of specification, analysis, design and documentation of real-time embedded systems. To cope with the complexity of real life applications, a system under development (SUD) may be described graphically from three different viewpoints within STATEMATE. They cover the structural (*Module-Charts*), the functional (*Activity-Charts*) and the behavioral (*Statecharts* [10]) aspects of a SUD.

For the verification of STATEMATE designs we use the technique of model checking. Model checking is an automatic method for proving that a given implementation of a design meets its requirement specification represented by a temporal logic formula. To be able to verify STATEMATE designs, we have implemented a set of tools for the translation from STATEMATE into finite state machines required by the model checker [9,19]. The semantical foundation

---

* Part of this work has been funded by the Commission of the European Communities under the ESPRIT project 20897, SACRES and the German BMBF project KORSYS, grant number 01-IS-519-E-0

[1] STATEMATE is a registered trademark of i-Logix Inc.

of this translation can be found in [6]. In our environment we use symbolic timing diagrams [7, 18] for the specification of the intended behavior. Symbolic timing diagrams are a graphical specification formalism. The semantics of these diagrams can be expressed by CTL formulae [17] that are fed into the model checker.

If a design does not meet the requirement specification the model checker generates a counterexample. For debugging purposes this counterexample can be retranslated into a timing diagram and also into a stimulus for the STATEMATE simulator. This visualization of a counterexample is a convenient way to point out the error to the designer.

A work that is closely related to our work can be found in [15]. There a formal semantics for a subset of Statecharts is given which is based on the basic step algorithm as defined in [12]. Also an experimental compiler for connecting a model checker is presented. Our environment supports the synchronous (step) semantics as well as the so called asynchronous (super-step) semantics provided by the STATEMATE simulator and therefore both of the semantics given in [12]. In addition to almost the complete language of Statecharts, including timing aspects, the language of Activity-Charts is covered by our toolset.

As a sample application for the demonstration of our verification environment we have implemented a simplified version of a tamagotchi. With our environment we have proved some interesting properties e.g. the possibility of keeping the tamagotchi alive. Beside this toy example industrial sized applications have been verified with our toolset. Examples for these applications are a central car locking mechanism, provided by our project partner BMW [5], and a aircraft storage management system, provided by our project partner British Aerospace.

This paper is organized as follows. In section 2 we shortly describe symbolic timing diagrams as a visual specification formalism by giving two examples. Section 3 overviews STATEMATE and clarifies its concepts. In section 4 we introduce our sample application. The fifth section covers our verification environment. In section 6 we give some experimental results. Section 7 concludes this paper with an outlook on our future work.

2 Specification with Symbolic Timing Diagrams

In our verification environment symbolic timing diagrams (STD) are used to specify graphically the requirements of reactive systems. STD have a well-defined semantics given by translation into temporal logic. Thus, they are a user-friendly notation with a formal semantics to express the properties that have to be verified. A more detailed description of STD is given in [7, 17, 18].

An advantage of STD is that they are declarative, allowing a designer to specify requirements incrementally. The complete specification is then given as a conjunction of the different STD. When using STD as described above, requirements of reactive systems are described in a compact form. Also, by composing several STD, very complex requirements can be specified in a modular way.

We clarify the concepts by giving two simple but relevant STD specifications for our sample application tamagotchi. The first requirement states that our tamagotchi will always die in the future. We expect this specification not to be valid over the model, inducing the model checker to generate a counterexample. This counterexample is a path on which the tamagotchi never dies. The second requirement says that our tamagotchi will never die. Again, we expect a counterexample for this diagram, giving a path on which the tamagotchi finally dies.

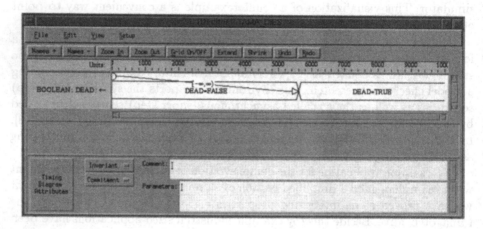

Fig. 1. The STD for property 1

Figure 1 shows the STD for the first property. Every STD describes allowed valuations of visible interface objects of a design over time. The graphical description of every property consists of three parts. On the left side in figure 1 the interface variables which are constrained by an STD are listed together with their data-types. In figure 1, we have just one variable DEAD of type BOOLEAN. An STD consists of symbolic waveforms representing the valuation of interface variables over time. Different phases of the waveforms are annotated with predicates over these variables. Waveforms are worked off from the left side to the right. The valuation of interface variables and thus of predicates is influenced by the dynamic behavior of a design. If a predicate changes from TRUE to FALSE, the next predicate on the right side must evaluate to TRUE. Otherwise, the STD is violated. The conjunction of the predicates in every first phase gives the activation condition of an STD. In figure 1 we have the activation condition that DEAD equals FALSE. The activation mode of an STD is either "initial", meaning it must hold in the initial state of the design, or "invariant", meaning it must hold every time the activation condition becomes TRUE. The activation mode for the diagram in figure 1 is "invariant". The arc in the diagram denotes that the predicate DEAD equals TRUE must eventually become TRUE, thus specifying a liveness property. The informal semantics of this diagram is that whenever DEAD equals FALSE a state will be reached where DEAD equals TRUE.

Figure 2 shows the STD for the second property. This time the only waveform is the one for the BOOLEAN variable ALIVE. The waveform of this "invariant" STD constraints the valuation of ALIVE over time by three predicates. The activation condition is satisfied when ALIVE evaluates to FALSE. When ALIVE becomes TRUE, the STD "steps" into the next phase. The last predicate FALSE cannot be evaluated to TRUE meaning that the STD can only be fulfilled if ALIVE stays TRUE forever, hence this STD specifies a safety property. The informal semantics of this diagram is that once the tamagotchi is alive, it will stay alive.

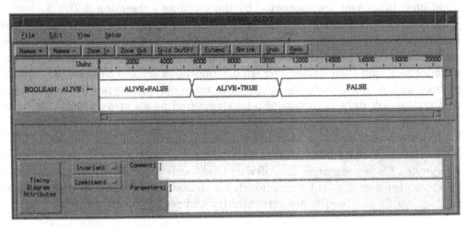

Fig. 2. The STD for property 2

3 Key Features of STATEMATE

In this section an introduction into key features of STATEMATE is given. First, the different languages of STATEMATE are described together with an overview on the available set of tools. In the following subsection interesting points concerning semantical issues are pointed out.

3.1 STATEMATE Toolset

The STATEMATE toolset [11, 12, 14] captures the phases of specification, analysis, design and documentation of real-time embedded systems. To cope with the complexity of real life applications, a system under development (SUD) may be described graphically from three different viewpoints within STATEMATE. They cover the structural, the functional and the behavioral aspects of a SUD.

A designer can create a model of a SUD describing physical components and their interconnections within *Module-Charts*. *Activity-Charts* specify a SUD as a collection of hierarchically and parallelly composed activities and data- and control-flows between activities. This is the method to model a functional decomposition of a SUD. Activities that are not further refined may be described by *Statecharts*. Statecharts essentially represent finite state machines enhanced by concepts of hierarchy, orthogonality and a broadcasting mechanism. Inside a Statechart an arbitrary number of state machines can work in parallel. They communicate via a broadcasting mechanism. A state machine can only be active if and only if its parent is active. Statecharts describe when and how activities in a SUD react to external stimuli. They are intended to implement controller behavior. Designers can use two time concepts in Statecharts. Actions may be scheduled into the future and the reaction on events may be delayed for some amount of time. Within STATEMATE the real-time behavior of a SUD is evaluated relatively to a virtual simulation clock. Several semantics for the above mentioned languages are supported by the tool (see subsection 3.2).

Referenced elements within the three modeling languages have to be defined in a data-dictionary. Three classes of elements exist. Events are instantaneous elements. They live exactly one step before they are consumed. Conditions and data-items retain their values over time. Conditions are the STATEMATE variant of boolean variables. Data-Items can have more complex types like bit, integer and real. Every data-item may also be structured as an array, record, union or as a queue.

Within STATEMATE an interactive analysis can be done on the design with a simulator. A dynamic test tool can be used to check simple properties of the model. Code generators for software and hardware modules are available to produce prototyped code for the model. The remaining tools are for the purposes of documentation, requirement traceability and revision management.

3.2 Semantics of STATEMATE

In the past several semantics for Statecharts have been investigated, for instance [13]. STATEMATE also incorporates several semantics for its languages. We can distinguish between the synchronous simulation semantics or *step semantics*, the asynchronous simulation semantics or *super-step semantics* and the semantics of the generated code for C-, ADA-, VHDL- and Verilog. Informal explanations of these semantics can be found in [12]. Our toolset handles the step and the super-step semantics. A rigorous and formal definition can be found in [6].

In the step semantics the SUD accepts an external stimulus to trigger the modeled reactive system. Then all active components of the design perform exactly one step synchronously to come to a new state configuration and a new valuation of variables. Every step costs a fixed amount of time for every parallel component. After termination of a step, the SUD accepts new stimuli. The step semantics is mainly used for clocked designs.

The basic idea of the super-step semantics is, that after having given an external stimulus to a SUD being in a stable state, it starts a chain of steps until it reaches a stable state again. Stable means, that further steps are impossible without new external stimuli. A large number of reactions are possible until a stable state is reached again. A complete chain is called a super-step, while every single computation is called a step. In contrast to the step semantics, the steps in such a chain do not consume time. All computations between stimulation of such a SUD and returning into a state of equilibrium are performed infinitely fast, hence the virtual simulation clock is not incremented before a super-step has been finished. After completion of a super-step the clock will be advanced to the next relevant point in time. A point in time is relevant, if a scheduled action has to be executed, if a timeout event has expired or if a SUD is triggered again by a new external stimulus. This semantics constraints the interaction of the environment with a SUD to super-step boundaries, but all activities inside a SUD work synchronously and communicate after every step. A prerequisite is, that all activities have completed their actual step. If one activity diverges, e.g. by executing an unbounded loop, then the actual step cannot be terminated and the super-step is unbounded. The super-step semantics is mainly used for asynchronous designs.

This overview shows that the step semantics is much simpler than the super-step semantics. In the step semantics the SUD is stable after every terminated step, time increases uniformly and the environment can influence the valuation of variables on every step. In contrast, the super-step semantics needs additional bookkeeping to indicate stability. Only in a stable state the system can increase timers and can accept new stimuli.

4   A STATEMATE Example

In this section the concepts of STATEMATE are clarified by introducing a tamagotchi as a sample application. The STATEMATE design consists mainly of an Activity-Chart and a set of parallel automata that are described by a Statechart. The Activity-Chart defines the environment and the interface of the application, the Statechart controls the state of the system and reacts on environment actions.

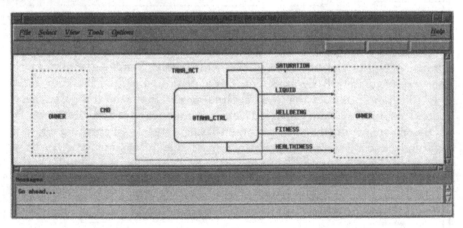

Fig. 3. The Activity-Chart for the tamagotchi

The state of the tamagotchi consists of a set of counters. These counters cover the levels for saturation, liquid, wellbeing, fitness and healthiness. The changes of every counter over time are controlled by the above automata. In every step the counters for saturation, liquid, wellbeing and fitness are decremented by one. The counter for healthiness is decremented depending on the levels for wellbeing and fitness. If the level for wellbeing is zero, the counter for healthiness is decremented by 3; if the level for fitness is zero, it is decremented by 4. If a counter falls below a certain threshold, the tamagotchi outputs a corresponding message. This message is reset when the counter raises again and reaches another threshold. As soon as one of the counters for saturation, liquid or healthiness becomes zero, the tamagotchi dies. To prevent this, the environment (the owner of the tamagotchi) can influence the counters by several actions. In every step one and only one of the actions eat, drink, stroke, play and 'giving an injection' can be performed. These actions increase the corresponding counters by 2,3,15,12 and 7 until upper bounds are reached. The tricky task is that in one step all counters can be decremented, but only one of them can be incremented by an environment action. By interpreting the outputs of the tamagotchi, the next action can be chosen.

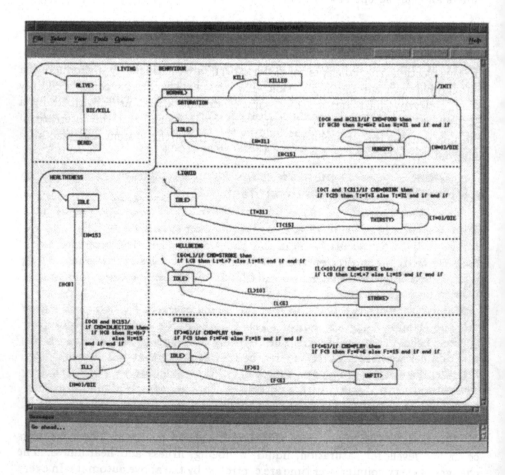

Fig. 4. The Statechart for the tamagotchi

Figure 3 shows the Activity-Chart for our application. It contains the top level activity TAMA_ACT of the system. In this activity there is a control activity TAMA_CTRL. The figure also shows that the environment, the dashed boxes, can influence the system by the input CMD. CMD is defined as an enumeration type describing which of the above actions should be performed in the next step. An idle action is possible, too. The outputs of the system consist of a set of messages to indicate the state of the system.

Figure 4 shows the Statechart implementation of the control activity TAMA_CTRL. The top level state is the parallel composition of two orthogonal automata. The top-left automata LIVING monitors if the remaining system delivers an event DIE showing that one of the critical counters has reached its zero value. It reacts by emitting a KILL event and the remaining system steps into a final state KILLED.

The right automaton BEHAVIOUR is the one which controls the tamagotchi. It consists of two exclusive states, one state for the behavior of the living tamagotchi (NORMAL) and the dead state (KILLED). The state for the behavior itself is the parallel composition of five sub-automata, each controlling one of the counters. Every automata is either in an idling (uncritical) state or in a state in which its counter is below the threshold. On entering the latter one, a corresponding message is generated; on reentering the first one, the message is removed. In every automata there are transitions that are triggered by the input CMD. The effect of executing these transitions is the increment of the corresponding counter. The decrease of the counters is realized by a static reaction associated with the state NORMAL (not visible in the figure). A static reaction of a state is executed as long as the state is active. In our case, the counters are decreased as long as the tamagotchi is alive.

5 The Verification Environment

Figure 5 gives a brief overview over our verification environment. The tools we have built and we concentrate on in this paper are shaded. The unshaded tools are either from our project partners or from other members of our group. After giving a short introduction here, we will explain the separate tools in more detail in the following subsections.

Mainly there are two paths to feed the model checker. The left path starts with the Timing Diagram Editor (TDE)[2], where the user can specify the expected behavior of the design. The resulting diagrams (STD) are translated into computation tree logic (CTL) by the tool std2ctl that was developed by other members of our group. For a more detailed explanation see [7, 17, 18]. The right path of figure 5 starts with STATEMATE. For the extraction of information about a SUD out of STATEMATE, an application procedural interface (API) has been developed in close collaboration with i-Logix which is now delivered together with STATEMATE. The STATEMATE design (STM) is first translated into

---

[2] The timing diagram editor is a product of Abstract Hardware Limited (AHL)

an intermediate language called SMI. We defined SMI as an universal language for the translation of high-level formalisms into finite state machines (FSM)[3] SMI is a tiny, but very powerful language, covering parallelism, nondeterminism and a set of nontrivial data-types like arrays, records and unions. To cope with the problem of complexity, a lot of optimizations can be performed on the SMI code. These optimizers are listed in the box in the middle of the figure. The resulting SMI code is translated into a FSM for model checking. This translation is done using ROBDDs [1, 2]. Together with the computed formula, the FSM is fed into the model checker. Within our environment, we are using two CTL model checkers. The first one is the assumption/commitment style model checker by SIEMENS [9]. Alternatively we use the model checker of the VIS [19] system. If a check fails, i.e. the checked formula is not true, the model checker produces an error-path. This error-path can be retranslated into either a stimulus for the STATEMATE simulator by `err2stm` or a symbolic timing diagram by the tool `err2std` which again was developed by other members of our group.

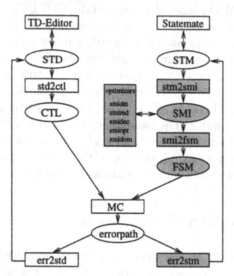

Fig. 5. The verification environment

5.1 Translating STATEMATE into SMI

The compiler `stm2smi` translates STATEMATE designs into the intermediate format SMI. SMI is a simple programming language containing concepts to model hierarchy, parallelism and nondeterminism of STATEMATE designs. The data-types and expression language of SMI is powerful enough to cover a wide range of STATEMATE types. SMI contains statements for null operations, assignments, deterministic branches, nondeterministic branches, while loops, breaks and operators for sequential and parallel compositions. Supported data-types are enumeration, bit, boolean, event, integer, string, array, record and

---

[3] In other projects, we translate VHDL into SMI

union. The expression language contains common boolean and numeric operators and selection on arrays, records and unions.

In the translation process stm2smi performs several tasks. It maps used data-types of a design onto the types of SMI. In addition the state configurations of the Statecharts are encoded by SMI variables. Therefore, stm2smi defines variables to encode data and boolean variables, events and the control information of a design. With every variable in SMI we keep some additional information for back-annotation including the original name, its data-type, its mode (in, out, local) and its origin in a design (data, condition, event, timer, control). These information are mainly used if the model checker produces a counterexample for a given property.

In [6] a compositional semantics for STATEMATE is given. This means, that the semantics of a model contains all possible behaviors of its environment. For the generation of compositional models, some additional variables are introduced. These variables indicate stability and divergence of the model and its environment.

In STATEMATE, all active activities perform a step synchronously, then new stimuli are accepted and the next step is executed. To represent the cyclic behavior of a reactive system modeled as a STATEMATE design, we embed the generated code for a design in a never terminating while loop. The code inside the loop describes one step of the whole system, depending on the valuation of the variables and the state configuration. Depending on the chosen semantics (step, super-step) timers are incremented always or only after the model has reached a stable state again (termination of a super-step). Similar, acceptance of new inputs and setting of auxiliary variables for compositionality depends on the chosen semantics. In the step semantics, after every execution of the body of the loop the model is stable and ready to synchronize.

While translating a SUD a data-flow analysis is performed to compute an interface for a given design. Used objects can be either of mode input, output or local. Only inputs and outputs are included in the generated interface.

The readable format of SMI allows to validate easily the translation process, to perform optimizations, to apply abstractions and it simplifies the generation of ROBDD based finite state machines compared with a direct encoding of STATEMATE designs.

A wide range of STATEMATE concepts for Activity-Charts and Statecharts are supported. Currently, on the graphical level, we disallow the usage of generic charts and combinational assignments in general. In Statecharts, deep-history connectors are not supported. Not supported data-types are real and queue. On the textual level, we do not allow implicit events on structured data. Time units in timeouts and scheduled actions must be constant. The usage of pre-defined functions is limited to a subset.

5.2 Translating SMI into FSMs

The translation of SMI generates functional BDDs instead of relational ones, because they are more efficient during the generation of FSMs and while model checking. For every bit of the state space a characteristic function representing this bit has to be computed. The state space consists of the variables defined in the SMI program. There are no additional variables needed for representing the location within the SMI program because one step of the FSM is one complete run thru the nonterminating outermost loop of the SMI program. For every SMI variable a set of ROBDD variables is needed for the representation. The encoding of the variables is done in the usual way, resulting in a minor overhead representing arrays and records (an array with 3 elements of the subrange 0 to 2 is encoded by $3 * 2 = 6$ bits, but the $3 * 3 * 3 = 27$ possible values of the array can be mapped onto 5 bits). Because we are using functional FSMs we have to add additional input variables to cope with the nondeterminism of SMI. These 'choice' inputs are choosing between the possible runs thru the SMI program and resolve the nondeterminism.

Loops inside the SMI program can be handled in two ways. First, the compiler computes a fixed point for a loop. This technique is capable to detect nonterminating loops, but in practice it is very slow for most applications, because of the necessary usage of the very costly BDD substitution. Alternatively, the compiler unrolls a loop until the condition gets false. This technique cannot handle endless loops and does not stop in these cases. But in practice unrolling is much faster than computing a fixed point, because our technique prevents the usage of BDD substitution.

5.3 Optimizations on the SMI Code

Every compiler produces overhead, resulting in unnecessary instructions and variables. But especially model checking or even the FSM generation can get impossible due to this overhead. A set of optimizers for SMI code were developed to cope with this problem. At present, the following set of optimizations can be performed on SMI code:

smidet (Make SMI more deterministic)
> In some cases unnecessary instructions for nondeterministic executions within the SMI code are produced during the translation from STATEMATE into SMI. These instructions result in additional 'choice' inputs within the FSM. The tool **smidet** detects this overhead and deletes/replaces the instructions in the SMI code.

smired (Reduce SMI)
> With this tool, unused inputs can be determined and eliminated.

smidec (Decompose ASYNC signal)
> Using the super-step semantics of STATEMATE we get a special signal ASYNC that is represented by a very complex ROBDD. The tool **smidec** bypasses this problem by splitting up this signal into a set of signals that can be represented by smaller ROBDDs.

smiopt (Optimize SMI)
> This is the most powerful tool to optimize SMI programs. The tool can be run in order to do one or more of the following tasks:

1. Perform a data flow analysis and delete unused and constant variables
2. Delete code parts that are unused because they can never be taken due to the values of the variables
3. Reduce the SMI program to the set of variables that is needed to verify a given property. This set is computed by building the transitive closure of the data flow graph of the variables used in the property
4. Freeing variables: allows to turn a variable into an input, thus performing a safe abstraction of the original behavior

smidom (Generate an optimized domain for ROBDD generation) The size of the ROBDDs depends very heavily on the ordering of the ROBDD variables. Even though reordering techniques are used during the ROBDD generation, the initial ordering of the ROBDD variables is important. This tool tries to find a good variable ordering for the ROBDDs before any ROBDD is computed. It analyses the data flow within the SMI program and determines the dependencies between the SMI variables and thus between the ROBDD variables. Using special heuristics we developed, the tool produces an initial ordering that is taken by the compiler from SMI to FSM.

	input bits	state bits	time	BDD nodes
tamagotchi	26	75	$0.67s$	2677
+ smidet	11	75	$0.58s$	1801
+ smiopt	11	60	$0.35s$	1741
+ smired	8	60	$0.32s$	1735
+ smidom	8	60	$0.29s$	982

Table 1. Results of the optimizations

Table 1 shows the effect of using the above optimizers on the size of our sample application and the time to generate the FSMs [4]. Each line adds one optimizer to the FSM generation and gives the corresponding results. We see that the number of ROBDD variables and the size of the model decreases dramatically using the optimizers. Other tested case studies gave similar results.

5.4 Retranslation of Error-Paths

The tools err2std and err2stm retranslate a produced error-path into a timing diagram or into a stimuli for the STATEMATE simulator. The STD shows the evaluation of the interesting variables over time, the simulator shows the dynamic behavior of the system until the faulty state is reached. Up to now, only error-paths produced by the the SIEMENS model checker can be retranslated.

6 Experimental Results

In this section we present some results we got applying our tools on some STATEMATE designs. We concentrate on the generation of the FSMs and on

---

[4] All results in this paper have been computed on an Ultra Sparc 1 with 143 MHz

model checking, but omit the translation from STD into CTL, because it is an uncritical task wrt. time/space complexity.

For our tamagotchi, we could generate a FSM out of the STATEMATE design within a few seconds. As expected, the model checker checked both of the two interesting properties presented in section 2 to be false and produced error-paths. The error-path of the first property consists of a 6 step long initial sequence of states followed by a loop sequence of 52 states on which the tamagotchi stays alive. On this loop we can observe every modeled behavior of the tamagotchi (it even gets ill on an intermediate state on the loop) and every input action is performed at least once. The error-path for the second property shows a sequence where the tamagotchi finally dies. On this sequence of length 21 no input actions are performed such that all counters are always decremented until the tamagotchi dies.

An interesting result while model checking the first property of the tamagotchi is the huge amount of time the VIS model checker needed ($8627s$). The reason for this is, that the tamagotchi contains a lot of counters and just a few states and transitions within the automata. Therefore it is dominated by data. When model checking other designs which are dominated by control, meaning that these designs have just a few variables but much more states and transitions, we got results within a few seconds. Two examples for such designs are the well known traffic light controller (TLC) and a controller of the fault tolerant production cell[5] (HDT). A non-trivial example we model checked is a central car locking mechanism (ZV)[6] with 12 Statecharts running in parallel each containing between 3 and 20 states and many transitions [5]. The biggest case study we checked is a storage management systems of an aircraft[7]. Table 2 gives a brief overview over some results we got from our verification environment.

Model	stm2smi in s	optimizers in s	smi2fsm in s	# of bits input/state	# of BDD nodes	MC in s
tama	2.35		0.66	26/75	2177	–
tama (opt)	2.35	0.70	0.35	8/60	982	8627
TLC	1.51		0.23	18/33	2485	5.1
TLC (opt)	1.51	0.60	0.15	11/27	1278	1.8
HDT	15.51		0.26	26/50	2363	10.2
HDT (opt)	15.51	0.60	0.11	10/32	521	2.3
ZV	10.49		45.64	223/327	1147710	–
ZV (opt)	10.49	10.00	13.14	123/279	28602	1785
SMS	20.79		829.84	99/720	21358	–
SMS (opt)	20.79	7.60	786.39	44/643	15249	966

Table 2. Experimental results

---

[5] This case study was provided by our project partner FZI Karlsruhe
[6] This case study was provided by our project partner BMW
[7] This case study was provided by our project partner British Aerospace

The table shows times for the generation and the resulting sizes for five different case studies. Also, the times for model checking of some special verified properties are listed. For every study, the FSM has been computed with and without applying the set of optimizers. We see that the generation of the FSMs could be performed for all studies, but the sizes of the resulting FSMs differ very much depending on the optimizations. While model checking is possible on all optimized FSMs, model checking cannot be performed on the unoptimized FSMs in three cases. The times to generate and optimize SMI are almost linear in the size of STATEMATE design and thus not critical. The critical times result from the translation from SMI into FSMs and especially from the model checking itself. We can observe that the times spent for optimizations are covered by the improved times for model checking, e.g. 0.6s for HDT optimizations leads to 7.9s speedup in model checking. In addition, the table shows, that the time for verifying the tamagotchi is much greater than the times to verify the other studies, although it is a small design.

7 Conclusions and Future Work

In this paper a powerful environment for the verification of STATEMATE designs against symbolic timing diagram specifications has been presented and its usability on a sample application was demonstrated. Also some results on two industrial sized designs were given. Within our environment, almost all features of STATEMATE are supported and we are still working on expanding this set. Even though a set of optimizations can be performed during the verification task, we know that there is still a lot of space for further improvements. We expect to be able to verify much bigger designs in the near future. Even though the STATEMATE concepts of timeouts and scheduled actions are already supported, we still use timing diagrams without time annotations and therefore a normal CTL model checker. We are working on a time annotated extension of timing diagrams [8] in order to perform real-time model checking. Another direction for extending our work is abstraction.

Acknowledgment. We thank our project partners AHL, i-Logix and SIEMENS for providing the tools and for discussions. Furthermore we thank our project partners BMW, British Aerospace and FZI for the case studies. Special thanks to Hans Jürgen Holberg for heavy testing of our toolset and to Werner Damm for constructive critics on this paper. Last but not least we thank the members of our group for helpful discussions and tools.

References

1. S.B. Akers: Binary decision diagrams. In: Transactions on Computers, No. 6 in Vol. C-27, IEEE (1978) 509–516
2. K. S. Brace, Richard L. Rudell and Randal E. Bryant: Efficient implementation of a BDD package. In: Proceedings 27th Design Automation Conference, Orlando, Florida, ACM/IEEE (1990) 40–45

3. J.R. Burch, E.M. Clarke, K.L. McMillan and D.L. Dill: Sequential circuit verification using symbolic model checking. In: Design Automation Conference ACM/IEEE (1990)
4. J.R. Burch, E.M. Clarke, K.L. McMillan, D.L. Dill and Jim Hwang: Symbolic model checking: 10^{20} states and beyond. In: Proceedings of the Fifth Annual IEEE Symposium on Logic in Computer science (1990)
5. W. Damm, U. Brockmeyer, H.J. Holberg, G. Wittich and M. Eckrich: Einsatz formaler Methoden zur Erhöhung der Sicherheit eingebetteter Systeme im KFZ. VDI/VW Gemeinschaftstagung (1997)
6. W. Damm, H. Hungar, B. Josko and A. Pnueli: A Compositional Real-Time Semantics of STATEMATE Designs. In: Proceedings of COMPOS 97, edt. H. Langmaack and W.P. de Roever, Springer Verlag, to appear 1998
7. W. Damm, B. Josko, R. Schlör: Specification and verification of VHDL-based system-level hardware designs. In: E. Börger, editor, Specification and Validation Methods. Oxford University Press, (1995) 331–410
8. K. Feyerabend and B. Josko: A Visual Formalism for Real Time Requirement Specifications, Transformation-Based Reactive Systems Development. In: Proceedings of 4th International AMAST Workshop on Real-Time Systems and Concurrent and Distributed Software, ARTS'97, edt. M. Bertran and T. Rus. Lecture Notes in Computer Science Vol. 1231. Springer Verlag (1997) 156–168
9. T. Filkorn, SIEMENS AG: Applications of Formal Verification in Industrial Automation and Telecommunication. In: Proceedings of Workshop on Formal Design of Safety Critical Embedded Systems, (1997)
10. D. Harel: Statecharts: A Visual Formalism for Complex Systems. In: Science of Computer Programming 8, (1987)
11. D. Harel, H. Lachover, A. Naamad, A. Pnueli, M. Politi, R. Sherman, A. Shtull-Trauring and M. Trakhtenbrot: STATEMATE: A working environment for the development of complex reactive systems. In: IEEE Transactions on Software Engineering, (1990) 403–414
12. D. Harel and A. Naamad: The STATEMATE Semantics of Statecharts. In: ACM transactions on software engineering and methodology, Vol 5 No 4 (1996)
13. D. Harel, A. Pnueli, J.P. Schmidt and R.Sherman: On the Formal Semantics of StateCharts. In: Proceedings of First IEEE, Symposium on Logic in Computer Science, (1987)
14. D. Harel and M. Politi: Modeling Reactive Systems with Statecharts: The STATEMATE Approach. i-LOGIX INC., Three Riverside Drive, Andover, MA 01810, Part No, D–1100–43 (1996)
15. E. Mikk, Y. Lakhnech, C. Petersohn and M. Siegel: On Formal Semantics of Statecharts as Supported by STATEMATE. In: Proceedings of BCS-FACS Northern Formal Methods Workshop, (1997)
16. S. Owre, N. Shankar and J.M. Rushby: A Tutorial on Specification and Verification Using PVS. In: Computer Science Laboratory, SRI Int., (1993)
17. R. Schlör: Symbolic Timing Diagrams: A visual formalism for specification and verification of system-level hardware designs. In: Dissertation (to appear), Universität Oldenburg, (1998)
18. R. Schlör and W. Damm: Specification and Verification of System-Level Hardware Designs using Timing Diagrams. In: EDAC-EUROASIC, (1993)
19. VIS: A system for Verification and Synthesis. The VIS Group. In Proceedings of the 8th International Conference on Computer Aided Verification, Springer Lecture Notes in Computer Science, Vol. 1102, Edited by R. Alur and T. Henzinger, New Brunswick, NJ (1996) 428–432

Modeling and Verification of sC++ Applications

Thierry CATTEL[1]

[1] Computer Networking Laboratory, Swiss Federal Institute
CH-1015 Lausanne, Switzerland
cattel@epfl.ch

Abstract - *This paper presents a means to model and verify concurrent applications written in sC++. sC++ is an extension of C++ that adds concurrency to the language by unifying the object and task concepts into a single one, the active object. The management of active objects is the same as the management of usual C++ passive objects. The difference is that active objects have their own behaviour and that they may either accept method calls or call other objects'methods. They are also capable to await simultaneously several non deterministic events including timers expiration. We show how to systematically model sC++ programs into Promela, a formal language supported by SPIN, a powerful and widely available model-checker. We present a classical example of a concurrent problem and give details about a tool that automatically produces the model from a program, verifies it and allows its debugging.*

1 Introduction

For representing concurrency in software engineering, all the existing analysis methods, including the object oriented paradigm [2] use dataflow diagrams that model data exchange between potentially autonomous items. Applications such as protocols, process control systems, distributed applications, are concurrent by nature and are better modelled and structured if they are modelled with explicit concurrency. The first troubles appear at the implementation of such systems because the available environments are seldom as clear, simple and powerful as the concepts used during analysis. In other words, if concurrency is easily designed with the available analysis tools, it is less easily implemented with the available programming support. This is without mentioning the overhead due to some solutions, for example Unix processes. Concurrent applications development is also more difficult to master and flaw detection before real exploitation is highly desirable. This is usually achieved using formal methods and abstracting the real system into a mathematical model which is submitted to proofs or model-checking. The development process for modeling and verification may proceed either in a bottom-up or a top-down fashion. In the bottom-up way, the verification phase is done a posteriori. The system is already built and one extracts a model that is submitted to verification[3][7]. If a bug is found, it needs to be fixed and the implementation to be modified. In the top-down approach, the verification is done a priori. The model is elaborated and verified before the implementation. This reduces the impact of possible bugs in the development cycle. These two approaches may combine with refinement techniques, but they usually rely on different formalism: one for the model and one for the implementation, the gap between both being often large. Between these two extremes, one can imagine having the same language for modeling and implementation, the modeling language being strictly included into the implementation language. This would simplify the developers work and require reduced skills. This supposes that one either creates a special instance of the verification tool for the language used or that bridges with existing tools are built, thus hiding the modeling language. This is the approach that will be presented in this paper. We use sC++, a minimal concurrent extension of C++ [14] as modeling and implementation language, and SPIN as verification tool. We show how to systematically translate a sC++ program into Promela (SPIN's language) and how to directly perform the verification and debugging onto the initial sC++ program using an adapted version of SPIN. We illustrate the approach with the readers and writers problem.

2 sC++

sC++ is an extension of C++ that provides the possibility to develop executable concurrent programs and distributed applications. It is supported by a set of development tools, including a compiler, which is an extension of *gcc*, code generators, and debuggers. It also exists an implementation in sC++ of an Object Request Broker that allows for developing distributed applications compliant with Corba [14].

Regarding the language itself, it is fairly simple for a programmer already knowing C++, since it possesses only few extra keywords with special semantics. sC++ adds concurrency to the language by unifying the object and task concepts into a single one, the active object. Fig.1 shows an example of active class declaration:

```
1. active class C{
2.    private:   void m1(){}
3.              @C(){...}
4.    public:   C(){...}
5.              ~C(){...}
6.              T1 rdv1(T2 t2, T3 &t3){...}
7.              void rdv2(){}
8. };
```

FIGURE 1. Active class declaration

The only syntactic differences with an usual C++ passive object are the extra keyword *active* and the optional method prefixed with @.

The instances of an active class are active objects, whose public methods, when called by other objects, have a special semantics. A call from an object to another active object's method defines a synchronization and a possibly bidirectional data exchange between both objects. It is a rendez-vous in the sense that the caller is blocked if the callee is not ready to accept the call and the callee is blocked if it is ready to accept the call but no call has been initiated. Besides, the rendez-vous is characterized by the atomic execution of the method called, during which bidirectional data exchange may occur thanks to the usual return value and parameters passed by value or reference.

If a method has no parameter and no code, it only has a synchronizing role. As a consequence of atomicity, the synchronizing methods of an active object are always executed in mutual exclusion. The private methods or the public ones called by the object itself have exactly the same semantics as for passive objects.

The optional private method (called *the body*) prefixed with @ has the same name as the class and cannot be called. It defines the behaviour of the active object and allows an object to accept calls for its methods or to call other objects'methods. For instance the body of Fig.2 contains an infinite loop during which the object successively accepts calls for its methods *rdv1*, calls method *m* of object *o* and accepts calls for *rdv2*. Note for instance that when the object tries to call object *o*'s method *m*, it will block until the rendez-vous is possible; notice also that possible calls from outside to *rdv1* and *rdv2* will be differed until the body accepts them:

```
1. @C(){    for(;;){ accept rdv1; o->m(); accept rdv2; }    };
```

FIGURE 2. An active object's behaviour

Constructors are non-synchronizing public methods, executed before the body is created, but destructors are considered as any other public synchronizing methods. In particular destructors may be explicitly accepted by the object, which is useful for controlling the object's death.

When no body is defined for an active object, an implicit one is defined that accepts calls at any time for all its public methods including the destructor. In other words, an active object without a body behaves as a Hoare monitor [11].

The management of active objects is the same as the management of usual C++ passive objects. They may either be declared directly or through the use of pointers and the *new* statement. They may be destructed explicitly with the *delete* statement or implicitly when the block in which they are contained is exited (Fig.3). They naturally are ready to die (they accept their destructor) if their body finishes.

```
2. {  C c1; C* c2=new C;
3.    c1.rdv2(); c2->rdv2();
4.    delete c2; }/* c1 is implicitly destructed */
```

FIGURE 3. A block with active objects creation and destruction

Here we need to say something about scheduling. Conceptually, scheduling should be very unconstrained and be as if every active object had its own processor. The code of the synchronizing method should be atomically executed only during a rendez-vous, and the control given back to both the caller and the callee. Also, an active object should be thought as running as soon as it is created. In the current mono-processor implementation of the language, after a rendez-vous, the caller gets the processor and only after synchronizations does the control change of active object. This means that an object looping on some pure computations monopolizes the processor, but it is easy to have instead a pre-emptive scheduling based on time sharing. In practice this has a consequence for application startup. If one wants that the application objects begin to execute only when they are all created, one needs either to add special synchronizations for startup or manage that the main creates all the objects before attempting any possible synchronization with some of them, otherwise the control could possibly be transferred to the already created objects; this is done anyhow but only when the main finishes. One also has to be careful of possible situations of deadlocks.

Objects may explicitly suspend their execution until a given date with the statement *waituntil*. When the execution of an object reaches such a statement, its execution is suspended at least until the date mentioned as parameter. The function *now()* provides the current time (Fig.4).

```
1. const int DELAY=...;...;
2. waituntil(now()+DELAY);
```

FIGURE 4. Timeout statement

Active objects are also capable to await simultaneously several non deterministic events including timer expirations. Instead of serializing the calls to its methods, as it appeared on Fig.2, the active object can accept them nondeterministically and at the same time it can attempt to call some other object or execute a timeout with the *waituntil* statement. This is achieved thanks to the *select* statement (Fig.5).

```
1. select{ accept  rdv1;...;
2. ||        o->m();...;
3. ||        accept rdv2;...;
4. ||        waituntil(now()+DELAY);...;
5. }
```

FIGURE 5. Simultaneous events awaiting

Conceptually, the occurrence order of the branches inside the *select* is not meaningful, but in the current implementation, the first enabled branch of the *select* is the one to be executed. Once more, it is easy to change this and execute nondeterministically a branch among the enabled ones. Each branch of a *select* must begin with an event, namely a synchronizing method call or acceptance or a *waituntil* statement. These events may be conditioned by a boolean expression, called a guard, using the *when* statement as in the following example (Fig.6):

```
1. select{ when(C1) accept  rdv1;...;
2. ||        when(C2) o->m();...;
3. ||        when(C3) waituntil(now()+DELAY);...;
4. }
```

FIGURE 6. Guarded synchronizations

Inheritance may be defined between active classes but we do not detail this point here, see [14]. We conclude with a very simple but complete example that illustrates some aspects of the language. It is a system of three processes accessing a critical section protected by a two entries semaphore.

```
1. #include <scxx.h>
2. active class Semaphore{
3.    int n;
4.    @Semaphore(){
5.       for(;;){  select{ when(n>0) accept P;
6.                 ||            accept V;
7.                 }
8.       }
9.    }
10. public:
11.    Semaphore(int N){n=N;}
12.    void P(){n--;}
13.    void V(){n++;}
14. };
```

```
15.active class User{
16.    Semaphore *s;
17.    int pid;
18.    @User(){ for(;;){s->P(); /* critical section */ s->V(); } }
19. public:
20.    User(int i,Semaphore *sem){pid=i;s=sem; }
21.};
22.main(){
23.    Semaphore s(2);User u1(1,&s);User u2(2,&s);User u3(3,&s);}
```

FIGURE 7. Mutual exclusion with a semaphore in sC++

3 Promela/SPIN

SPIN [12] is a powerful verification system that supports the design, verification and debugging of asynchronous process systems. SPIN focuses on proving correctness of process interactions that can be modelled in Promela, the language of SPIN, with rendez-vous primitives, asynchronous message passing through buffered channels and shared variables. Systems specification may be expressed thanks to boolean assertions or linear temporal logic (LTL) formulae. The model-checker may address real-sized problems of several millions states, thanks to several optimizations of depth-first search; first, memory management techniques based on state compression and bit-state-hashing, second, partial order reductions. When errors are found, traces are produced that are used to guide a graphical debugger, quite useful to identify the flaws.

Fig.9 shows problem of Fig.7, modelled in Promela. Active objects are declared with the *proctype* clause and may have parameters (Fig.9 lines 4,12). They are instantiated with the *run* statement (line 17). We have modelled the synchronizing methods *P* and *V* with synchronous channels (lines 1-2). For the moment forget that *P* is an array of three channels. Since no data is exchanged during the synchronization, these channels should convey no value, but one value at least is required, so we exchange a bit that represent the synchronization event. The nondeterministic choice and the loop around is done with the *do :: od* construct. Each branch corresponds to a *select*'s branch of the sC++ code, which is limited to the rendez-vous on *P* and *V*. The rendez-vous are *atomic* (lines 5 and 8) and are composed of the related synchronisation (lines 6 and 9) and method code execution (lines 7 and 10). By convention, we code a call by an emission on the related channel and an acceptance by a reception. We now have to explain why *P* is an array. In the sC++ program of Fig.7, the execution of method *P* of object *Semaphore* is guarded by the condition *(n>0)*. Unfortunately, there exists no dedicated construct in Promela for modeling guards – even the *atomic* statement cannot solve the problem without introducing extra deadlocks – but this can be done using a trick. The boolean type and associated constants exist but as in C, they are related to the integer type. In other words, *true* is 1, and *false* is 0.

```
1. chan R[3] = [0] of {...};
2. sender: R[cond1]!msg;...
3. receiver: R[2-(cond2)]?msg;...
```

FIGURE 8. Guarded Rendez-vous

For modeling a guarded rendez-vous *R (Fig.8)*, we declare two dummy channels *R[0]* and *R[2]* that are used to deflect handshake attempts that should fail. The handshake can only successfully complete on *R[1]* if both *cond1* at the sender side and *cond2* at the receiver side hold.

On our example, only the reception, i.e. the *accept* in the sC++ program, is guarded (Fig.9, line 6), the emission being guarded by *true* (line 13).

The global variable *in_CS* (lines 3, 14) is used for the verification of the assertion (line 14) that at most *N* (here 2) users may have the critical section at the same time, if the semaphore was initialized with *N*.

```
1. chan P[3] = [0] of {bit};
2. chan V    = [0] of {bit};
3. int in_CS=0;
4. proctype Semaphore(int n){
5.    do :: atomic{
6.          P[2-(n>0)]?true;
7.          n-- }
8.       :: atomic{
9.          V?true;
10.         n++}
11.   od }
12.proctype User(int pid){
13.   do :: P[true]!true;
14.         in_CS++; assert(in_CS <= 2); in_CS--;
15.         V!true
16.   od }
17.init{ run Semaphore(2); run User(1);run User(2);run User(3) }
```

FIGURE 9. Mutual exclusion with a semaphore in SPIN

4 Modeling of sC++ Applications

We now show how to model sC++ programs in Promela in a systematic way. Obviously we cannot treat sC++ in its totality, this would suppose treating also all C++, which would be very heavy and certainly lead to inefficient models thus making verification of any kind impracticable because of state explosion. We are first interested in checking somewhat abstract designs and thus we do not need all the power of C++. In particular we only consider active classes. Passive classes, inheritance and generics are only structuring facilities that are not essential for our purpose. We also only consider basic types, such as integers and arrays but no structure, no type definition and no pointer, excepts pointers of active objects that are necessary to pass references between active objects for them to communicate. Some instructions are necessary (*for*, *if*), if they are not (*while*, *switch*, *goto*) we drop them. We also forget compilation directives and suppose that all the methods are defined inside the class. For similar reasons, we only take into account the useful subset of Promela. Besides syntactic limitations evoked above, we still restrict the scope of our translation to the salient points. In particular we only consider direct object creation and thus forget the *new* and *delete* statements. We consider only explicit bodies but implicit constructors and destructors for active classes.

For synchronizations, we only treat methods with no returned type and no reference parameters. Nevertheless we'll treat an explicit constructor with parameters, an implicit body and a complete rendez-vous with bidirectional data exchange on an example.

We formalize the systematic modeling of the considered subset of sC++ in Promela, following the usual practice of defining a denotational semantics[15]. This semantics is defined thanks to a set of semantic functions from abstract syntactic constructions of the source language sC++ to semantics values that are in fact abstract syntactic constructions of the target language Promela. As parameter and result of the semantic functions we also sometimes need particular structures, called environments, that memorize the context of evaluation of a particular construction.

Fig. 10 shows the abstract syntactic domains of sC++ with abstract syntactic variables in font courier that are to be used below for the semantics definition. Fig. 11 shows sC++ related production rules, with an usual BNF syntax. The keywords of the language are in bold, ::= is the derivation symbol, I is the alternative, + and * when used as exponents means one, resp. zero, or more repetitions, the square brackets indicate optional constructions, the parenthesizes factorisation and ε the empty string.

$P \in Program_s$ $X \in Main_s$ $H \in Branch_s$ $I \in Identifier_s$

$D \in Declaration_s$ $K \in Block_s$ $S \in Synchro_s$ $N \in Natural_s$

$A \in ActiveClass_s$ $B \in Body_s$ $E \in Expression_s$

$M \in Method_s$ $C \in Command_s$ $T \in Type_s$

FIGURE 10. sC++ abstract syntactic domains

$Program_s ::= Declaration_s^* ActiveClass_s^* Main_s$

$Declaration_s ::= Type_s [*]Identifier_s[[Natural_s]]$

$ActiveClass_s ::=$ **active class** $Identifier_s \{Declaration_s^* Method_s^* Body_s \}$

$Method_s ::= [Type_s] [\sim] Identifier_s ((Type_s Identifier_s)^*) Block_s$

$Main_s ::= [$**void**$]$ **main**$() Block_s$

$Block_s ::= \{Declaration_s^* Command_s^+ \}$

$Body_s ::= @ Identifier_s () Block_s$

$Command_s ::= Identifier_s = Expression_s \mid Identifier_s++ \mid Identifier_s-- \mid$
    if $Expression_s Command_s^+ \mid$ **if** $Expression_s Command_s^+$ **else** $Command_s^+ \mid$
    for $(Command_s ; Expression_s ; Command_s) Block_s \mid$
    return $Expression_s \mid$ **assert** $Expression_s \mid$ **printf** $String_s \mid$
    select$\{ Branch_s^+ \} \mid Synchro_s$

$Branch_s ::= [$**when**$(Expression_s)] Synchro_s Command_s^*$

$Synchro_s ::=$ **accept** $Identifier_s \mid Identifier_s \rightarrow Identifier_s(Expression_s^*) \mid$
    waituntil$(Expression_s)$

$Type_s :: =$ **int** $\mid$ **void** $\mid Identifier_s$

$Expression_s ::= ...$

FIGURE 11. sC++ abstract production rules

$Program_p$ $Init_p$ $Type_p$ $Natural_p$

$Declaration_p$ $Block_p$ $Expression_p$ $String_p$

$Proctype_p$ $Command_p$ $Identifier_p$

FIGURE 12. Promela abstract syntactic domains

Program$_p$ ::= Typedef* Declaration$_p$* Proctype$_p$* Init$_p$
Typedef ::= **#define** Identifier$_p$ Expression$_p$ | **typedef** Identifier$_p$ {Declaration$_p$$^+$}
Declaration$_p$ ::= Type$_p$ Identifier$_p$[[Natural$_p$]] [= Expression$_p$] |
   chan Identifier$_p$[[Natural$_p$]] = [Natural$_p$] **of** {Type$_p$$^+$}
Proctype$_p$ ::= **proctype** Identifier$_p$ ((Type$_p$ Identifier$_p$)*) Block$_p$
Init$_p$ ::= **init** Block$_p$
Block$_p$ ::= { Declaration$_p$* Command$_p$$^+$ }
Command$_p$ ::= Identifier$_p$: Command$_p$ |
   Identifier$_p$ = Expression$_p$ | Identifier$_p$++ | Identifier$_p$-- |
   goto Identifier$_p$ | **if** (::Command$_p$)$^+$ **fi** | **do** (::Command$_p$)$^+$ **od** |
   Expression$_p$! Expression$_p$$^+$ | Expression$_p$? Identifier$_p$$^+$ |
   assert Expression$_p$ | **printf** String$_p$ | **skip** | **break** |
   atomic{ Command$_p$$^+$} | **run** Expression$_p$(Expression$_p$*)
Type$_p$ :: = **byte** | **int** | **bit** | Identifier$_p$
Expression$_p$ ::= ...

FIGURE 13. Promela abstract production rules

The result of semantic functions are on the one hand values of Promela abstract syntactic domains (Fig.12-13) and values of semantic domains, called environments (Fig.14) defined as abstract data types with the usual manipulations operations (application, projections,...) that are not detailed here.

The environment is composed of four structures. *Active*, given a type name indicates if it corresponds to an active class or not. *Class*, given an object identifier and the identifier of the class in which the object is declared gives the object's class name. *Param* gives for a given method of a given class, the list (possibly empty) of the parameter identifiers and eventually, *Code* gives the executable code of such a method (the instructions but not the possible declarations).

   Environment = Active × Class × Params × Code
      active, class, params, code: *projections*   (): *application*
   Active = Type$_s$ → Boolean
   Class = Identifier$_s$ × Identifier$_s$ → Identifier$_s$
   Params = Identifier$_s$ × Identifier$_s$ → Identifier$_s$*
   Code = Identifier$_s$ × Identifier$_s$ → Command$_s$*

FIGURE 14. Semantic domains

The semantic function *model* (Fig.15) defines the modeling of a sC++ program into Promela. It is defined thanks to auxiliary functions. The function *build* builds the environment of a sC++ program. The function *creat* creates preliminary definitions for objects; for passive objects it is their declaration, for active objects it is in particular the structures used for synchronizations. The function *trans* is the core of the translation, it does the actual creation of active objects and translate the instructions. The function *destr* generates the instructions that calls the active object destruction, which is implicit each time a block is finished for the active objects created directly (without *new*) in the block. These functions have a sC++ program fragment as parameter and possibly the program environment and the identifier of the class inside which the code is currently analysed. We use the traditional special brackets ‖ ‖ in denotational definitions (introduced by the special equal $\equiv$) to separate the syntactic and the semantic worlds. For instance, $trans\|P\|_{E,C} \equiv \ldots$ represents $trans(P,E,C) \equiv \ldots$

$model$: $\text{Program}_s \rightarrow \text{Program}_p$

$build$: $\text{Program}_s \rightarrow \text{Environment}$

$creat$: $\text{Program}_s \times \text{Environment} \rightarrow \text{Program}_p$

$trans,destr$: $\text{Program}_s \times \text{Environment} \times \text{Identifier}_s \rightarrow \text{Program}_p$

FIGURE 15. Semantic functions

4.1 Semantics

For simplicity, we also consider that methods have different names in all the classes of the program and that method parameters and local variables have different names inside a given class. Also, local method parameters cannot be active objects. Our semantics is easily extended to take into account these restrictions and some optimizations such as rendez-vous with no data exchange, but this implies make the presentation heavier, in particular by the introduction of extra structures. We also omit the definition of *build* and the semantics of expressions or things that are rather «stable» under the translation.

Semantic equations

First a program is modelled in its environment. In order to have bounded dynamic object creation to keep the space finite and tractable, for each class we will have a maximum instance number. First are declared the possible global objects and the structures necessary for the active classes. Then the active classes are translated. Finally the main program is translated but preceded by the actual active object creations and followed by their destruction in reverse order.

$model\|P\| \equiv trans\|P\|_{E,prog}$ where $E=build\|P\|$ and $build\|P\| \equiv \ldots$

$trans\|D_1...D_d \ A_1...A_a \ X\|_{E,C} \equiv$

   #define NBMAXINST 8

   $creat\|D_1\|_E \ldots creat\|D_d\|_E \quad creat\|A_1\|_E \ldots creat\|A_a\|_E$

   $trans\|A_1\|_{E,C} \ldots trans\|A_a\|_{E,C}$

   init{ **int i**

        $trans\|D_1\|_{E,C} \ldots trans\|D_d\|_{E,C}$

        $trans\|X\|_{E,C}$

        $destr\|D_d\|_{E,C} \ldots destr\|D_1\|_{E,C} \}$

The object declaration is the usual one for passive objects and a reference (byte) for active objects which is an index in a array of all the instances of the class. A pointer to an object is exactly the same thing (we show here only array declarations, scalar definitions are easily obtained removing the indices). The declaration for an active class concern the channels, grouped in a *typedef*, used for implementing the possibly guarded rendez-vous on synchronizing methods, including the destructor (*dest*). We need two channels ($\_c$, $\_r$) to implement a synchronizing method call which needs to be atomic. If the method has no parameter we need to exchange a minimal value, for instance *true* of type *bit*. The class is represented by array of instances (*inst*) and an instance number (*instnb*) which is to be incremented at each object creation.

$creat\|T \ I \ [N]\|_E \equiv$ if active(E)(T) **byte** I[N] else $creat\|T\|_E$ I[N]

$creat\|T \ ^*I \ [N]\|_E \equiv$ if active(E)(T) **byte** I else error

creat‖**active class** I {$D_1...D_d$ $M_1...M_m$ B}‖$_E$ ≡
    typedef I{   *creat*‖M_1‖$_E$ ... *creat*‖M_d‖$_E$
                      chan dest_c[3] = [0] **of** {**bit**}
                      chan dest_r = [0] **of** {**bit**} }
    I I_inst[NBMAXINST]
    byte I_instnb=0
creat‖**void** I (T_1 $I_1...T_n$ I_n) K‖$_E$ ≡
    chan I_c[3] = [0] **of** {**bit** *creat*‖T_1‖$_E$ ... *creat*‖T_n‖$_E$}
    chan I_r = [0] **of** {**bit**}

The actual active object creation, given here only for arrays, consists in incrementing the instance number of the class, store it in the instance reference array and finally *run* the process that implements the class body (*proc*) with its instance reference as parameter. Note that nothing needs to be done for pointers.

trans‖T I [N]‖$_{E,C}$ ≡
    if ¬ active(E)(T) ε **else**
        i=0
        do :: (i<=N-1)
                atomic{   class(E)(I,C) [i]=class(E)(I,C) **_instnb**
                            class(E)(I,C) **_instnb++**
                            run class(E)(I,C) **_proc**(class(E)(I,C) [i])}
                i++
        :: **else break**
        od
trans‖T *I [N]‖$_{E,C}$ ≡ ε

An active class is implemented as a Promela *proctype*. It corresponds to a collection of instances that are distinguished owing to a byte parameter (*this*). The class variables are declared and run (if active), declarations for each method are done (parameters and local variables), finally the body of the active class is translated. The code of the class is achieved with an acceptance of the class destructor, the execution of which ends the class instance execution. This *accept* statement will be executed if the object naturally reaches its body end. The object can also explicitly accept its destruction, in which case a jump will be done to an ultimate *skip* statement labelled with *end*.

trans‖**active class** I {$D_1...D_d$ $M_1...M_m$ B}‖$_{E,C}$ ≡
        proctype I_proc(**byte this**){
            creat‖D_1‖$_E$ ... *creat*‖D_d‖$_E$
            trans‖D_1‖$_{E,I}$ ... *trans*‖D_d‖$_{E,I}$
            trans‖M_1‖$_{E,I}$ ... *trans*‖M_m‖$_{E,I}$
            trans‖B‖$_{E,I}$
            trans‖**accept** ~I‖$_{E,I}$
        end_I: skip}
trans‖**void** I($D_1...D_n$){$D_{n+1}...D_m$ $C_1...C_c$}‖$_{E,C}$ ≡
    creat‖D_1‖$_E$ ... *creat*‖D_n‖$_E$ *creat*‖D_{n+1}‖$_E$ ... *creat*‖D_m‖$_E$

The translation of a body is its block's which is the declaration of local variables, the instructions translation and the possible destruction of active objects in reverse order of the creation. The translation of the *main* is the translation of its block.

$trans‖@ I() K‖_{E,C} \equiv trans‖K‖_{E,C}$

$trans‖\{D_1...D_d \ C_1...C_c\}‖_{E,C} \equiv$
  $creat‖D_1‖_E ... creat‖D_d‖_E$
  $trans‖D_1‖_{E,C} ... trans‖D_d‖_{E,C}$
  $trans‖C_1‖_{E,C} ... trans‖C_c‖_{E,C}$
  $destr‖D_d‖_{E,C} ... destr‖D_1‖_{E,C}$

$trans‖\textbf{void main}()\{K\}‖_{E,C} \equiv trans‖K‖_{E,main}$

We now come to the instructions. The *select* statement naturally becomes the Promela *if :: fi*. The guarded synchronizations are the most interesting (other ones are obtained setting the guard to *true*). By convention, the calls are implemented as an emission on the first rendez-vous channel associated to the method (*_c*) and the acceptances are receptions. For the guard translation, we use the trick mentioned above. The end of the rendez-vous is implemented by a synchronisation on the second channel (*_r*). For the acceptance, the method code is inserted between both rendez-vous. Note the usage of the environment to retrieve an object's class and a method's parameters and code. Note also that an acceptance for the class destructor is closed by a jump to the *end* label.

$trans‖\textbf{select}\{B_1...B_b\}‖_{E,C} \equiv \textbf{if} :: trans‖B_1‖_{E,C} \ ... \ :: trans‖B_b‖_{E,C} \textbf{ fi}$

$trans‖S \ C_1...C_c‖_{E,C} \equiv trans‖S‖_{E,C} trans‖C_1‖_{E,C} ... trans‖C_c‖_{E,C}$

$trans‖\textbf{when}(E_0) \ I_1\text{->}I_2(E_1...E_n)‖_{E,C} \equiv$
  $class(E)(I_1,C)\_\textbf{inst}[I_1].I_2\_\textbf{c}[trans‖E_0‖_{E,C}]!\textbf{true} \ trans‖E_1‖_{E,C}... trans‖E_n‖_{E,C}$
  $class(E)(I_1,C)\_\textbf{inst}[I_1].I_2\_\textbf{r?true}$

$trans‖\textbf{when}(E) \ \textbf{accept} \ I‖_{E,C} \equiv$
  $\textbf{C\_inst[this]}.I\_\textbf{c}[2\text{-}trans‖E‖_{E,C}]\textbf{?true } params(E)(I,C)$
  $trans‖code(E)(I,C) ‖_{E,C}$
  $\textbf{C\_inst[this]}.I\_\textbf{r!true}$

$trans‖\textbf{when}(E) \ \textbf{accept} \ {\sim}I‖_{E,C} \equiv$
  $\textbf{C\_inst[this].dest\_c}[2\text{-}trans‖E‖_{E,C}]\textbf{?true}$
  $trans‖code(E)({\sim}I,C) ‖_{E,C}$
  $\textbf{C\_inst[this].dest\_r!true}$
  $\textbf{goto end\_C}$

A guarded timeout is translated as the guard itself. A *waituntil* without guard is just a *skip* statement, since our models are only qualitative.

$trans‖\textbf{when}(E_1) \ \textbf{waituntil}(E_2) ‖_{E,C} \equiv trans‖E_1‖_{E,C}$

$trans‖\textbf{waituntil}(E)‖_{E,C} \equiv \textbf{skip}$

Other instructions translate naturally. For instance *if* statements and loops. We also give some optimizations for never ending loops with a *select* as outmost statement.

$trans‖\textbf{assert}(E)‖_{E,C} \equiv \textbf{assert}(trans‖E‖_{E,C})$

$trans‖\textbf{if} \ E \ C_1 \ \textbf{else} \ C_2‖_{E,C} \equiv \textbf{if} :: trans‖E‖_{E,C} \ trans‖C_1‖_{E,C} :: \textbf{else} \ trans‖C_2‖_{E,C} \textbf{ fi}$

$trans‖\textbf{for}(C_1;E;C_2)B‖_{E,C} \equiv$
  $trans‖C_1‖_{E,C}$
  $\textbf{do} :: trans‖E‖_{E,C} \ trans‖B‖_{E,C} \ trans‖C_2‖_{E,C} :: \textbf{else break od}$

$trans‖\textbf{for}(;;)\textbf{select}\{B_1...B_b\}‖_{E,C} \equiv$
  $\textbf{do} :: trans‖B_1‖_{E,C} \ ... \ :: trans‖B_b‖_{E,C} \textbf{ od}$

Finally, destruction of active objects are the counterpart of their creation with rendez-vous on the channels associated to the class destructor.

$destr\|T\ I\ [N]\|_{E,C}\ \equiv$

    if $\neg$ active(E)(T) ε **else**

      i=N-1

      do :: (i>=0)

          class(E)(I,C)_**inst[**I(i)**].dest_c[true]!true**

          class(E)(I,C)_**inst[**I(i)**].dest_r?true**

          i--

        :: else break

      od

$destr\|T\ {}^*I\|_{E,C}\ \equiv\ \varepsilon$

We finish this section showing the modeling of a simple class with a constructor with parameters, a method with bidirectional data exchange and an implicit body (Fig.16).

```
1. active class C{
2.     int n;
3.     C(int N){n=N;}
4.     int M(int v1, int &v2){ v2=v2+n*v1; return v1; }
5. };
6. void main(){
7.     int j;
8.     j=0;
9.     C c(10);
10.    c.M(3,j);}
```

FIGURE 16. Constructor with parameters, complete RDV and implicit body

For the method M, notice that the initial value of the reference parameter is sent at the begining of the call (Fig.17, lines 27 and 12) and received at its end (lines 28 and 14).

```
1. #define NBMAXINST 3
2. byte c;
3. typedef C{ chan M_c[3]     = [0] of {bit,int,int}
4.            chan M_r        = [0] of {bit,int,int}
5.            chan dest_c[3]  = [0] of {bit}
6.            chan dest_r     = [0] of {bit} }
7. C C_inst[NBMAXINST]
8. byte C_instnb=0
9. proctype C_proc(byte this;int N){
10.   byte n; int v1;int v2;
11.   n=N;
12.   do :: C_inst[this].M_c[2-(true)]?true,v1,v2;
13.       v2=v2+n*v1;
14.       C_inst[this].M_r!true,v1,v2;
15.    :: C_inst[this].dest_c[2-(true)]?true;
16.       C_inst[this].dest_r!true;
17.       goto end;
18.   od;
19.end_C:skip}
```

```
20.init{int i;
21.       int M_ret;
22.       int j;
23.       atomic {
24.           c = C_instnb;
25.           C_instnb++ ;
26.           run C_proc(c,10)};
27.       j=0;
28.       C_inst[c].M_c[true]!true,3,j;
29.       C_inst[c].M_r?true,M_ret,j;
30.       C_inst[c].dest_c[true]!true;
31.       C_inst[c].dest_r?true;}
```

FIGURE 17. Modelling in Promela

4.2 The readers writers example

We now illustrate the application of our translation semantics on the classical mutual exclusion example of the readers writers example. Readers and writers processes attempt to access a critical resource with, for instance, the following rules. As many readers may read the data at the same time, provided no writer is writing and only one writer may access the data if no reader is reading. For the implementation of this example, we declare three classes, *SharedData*, *Reader* and *Writer*, one instance for the first class and two instances for each of the following grouped in an array. We also need two counters *nbwriters* and *nbreaders*, for the readers and writers for verifying by assertions, that the rules will hold.

```
1. int nbwriters;int nbreaders;
2. SharedData shData; Reader reader[2]; Writer writer[2];
```

The class *SharedData* manages the critical resource thanks to four methods, two for requesting the resource in read or write mode and two for releasing it (we only show what is related to the reading, what is related to writing is similar).

```
3. active class SharedData {
4.    int readersCounter;int writersCounter;
5.    void BeginRead() { nbreaders++; }
6.    void EndRead() { nbreaders--; } ...
7.    @SharedData() {
8.       readersCounter=0;writersCounter=0;
9.       for(;;){
10.          select{ accept EndRead; readersCounter--;
11.          ||       when(writersCounter==0)
12.                      accept BeginRead;readersCounter++;
13.          || ...
14.          ||       when((readersCounter==0)&&
15.                        (writersCounter==0))
16.                      accept ~SharedData;
17.          }
18.       }
19. }};
```

The *Reader* and *Writer* classes possess a reference on a *SharedData* object, initialized with the method *minit*, and request the critical data through it, conforming to a simple and natural protocol (we only show the *Reader* class code).

```
20.active class Reader {
21.    SharedData *sData;
22.    void minit (SharedData *SD) { sData = SD; }
23.    @Reader() {
24.       accept minit;
25.       for (;;) {
26.          select{ sData->BeginRead();
27.                  assert(nbwriters==0);
28.                  sData->EndRead();
29.          ||      accept ~Reader;
30.          }
31.       }
32.    }
33.};
```

Finally the main function initializes the counters and the active objects.

```
34.void main() {
35.    int p;
36.    nbwriters=0;nbreaders=0;
37.    for (p=0; p<=1; p++){
38.       reader[p]->minit(shData);writer[p]->minit(shData);
39.    }
40.}
```

We give the translation of some of the interesting part of this program. First, the declarations of passive and active objects:

```
1. #define NBMAXINST 3
2. int nbwriters;int nbreaders;
3. byte shData; byte reader[2];byte writer[2];
```

Then, the channels, instance reference array and counter for class *SharedData*:

```
4. typedef SharedData{  chan BeginRead_c[3]  = [0] of {bit}
5.                      chan BeginRead_r     = [0] of {bit}
6.                      chan EndRead_c[3]    = [0] of {bit}
7.                      chan EndRead_r       = [0] of {bit}
8.                      ...
9.                      chan dest_c[3]       = [0] of {bit}
10.                     chan dest_r          = [0] of {bit} }
11.SharedData SharedData_inst[NBMAXINST]
12.byte SharedData_instnb=0
```

The declarations are analogous for class *Reader* (similar for *Writer*), note data passed through method *minit*:

```
13.typedef Reader{ chan minit_c[3]  = [0] of {bit,int}
14.                chan minit_r     = [0] of {bit}
15.                chan dest_c[3]    = [0] of {bit}
16.                chan dest_r       = [0] of {bit} }
17.Reader Reader_inst[NBMAXINST]
18.byte Reader_instnb=0
```

For the process implementing *SharedData* behaviour, we only show the translation of acceptance of *EndRead*, a method with some code and the acceptance of the destructor:

```
19.proctype SharedData_proc(byte this){
20.    int readersCounter;int writersCounter;
21.    readersCounter=0;writersCounter=0;
22.    do :: SharedData_inst[this].EndRead_c[2-(true)]?true;
23.        nbreaders--;
24.        SharedData_inst[this].EndRead_r!true;
25.        readersCounter--
26.        ...
27.        :: SharedData_inst[this].dest_c[2-((readersCounter==0)
28.                                    &&(writersCounter==0))]?true;
29.        SharedData_inst[this].dest_r!true;
30.        goto end_SharedData;
31.    od;
32.end_SharedData:skip}
```

We now show the creation of readers, their initialization with the call to *minit* method and their destruction:

```
33.init{int i; ...
34.    i=0;
35.    do :: (i<=2-1);
36.        atomic {
37.            reader[i] = Reader_instnb;
38.            Reader_instnb++ ;
39.            run Reader_proc(reader[i]) };
40.            i++
41.        :: else;break
42.    od;
43.    ...
44.    int p;
45.    nbwriters=0;nbreaders=0;
46.    p=0;
47.    do :: (p<=1);
48.        Reader_inst[reader[p]].minit_c[true]!true,shData;
49.        Reader_inst[reader[p]].minit_r?true;
50.        Writer_inst[writer[p]].minit_c[true]!true,shData;
51.        Writer_inst[writer[p]].minit_r?true;
52.        p++
53.        :: else;break
54.    od;
55.    ...
56.    i=2-1;
57.    do :: (i>=0);
58.        Reader_inst[reader[i]].dest_c[true]!true;
59.        Reader_inst[reader[i]].dest_r?true;
60.        i--
61.        :: else;break
62.    od;
63.    ...}
```

4.3 Implementation

The semantics presented above has been implemented in Prolog[1]. Apart from translating some sC++ code into Promela, the translator generates a correspondence table that is used for debugging. This table implements a function that relates the line number of the produced code to the line number of the source code. This table is used by a modified version of XSPIN[6] (the graphical interface of SPIN). This allows to do simulations and debugging directly on the sC++ code. When loaded a sC++ program is translated in two files. A first one contains the Promela code and this is the actual file that is used to perform the simulation and verification. The second one contains the table which is used each time a display operation is done in the simulator.

5 Conclusion

This paper presented the key points of the formalization of modeling sC++ programs into Promela and illustrated it through a simple but complete example.

The approach this formalization supports has several advantages. The language itself is to some extent more supple that other similar languages, for it unifies the task and object concept and it possesses symetrical select statements (with acceptances and calls). Beside using a single language for both implementation and verification, once it is clear that one focuses on process interactions and works on some abstraction of the problem under study, the full power of the language is not needed and thus the approach may be fully automatized. We presented only part of the translation without optimizations, but the tool could implement a more complete translations with lots of optimizations. Nevertheless, the produced models are easily readable and tunable if necessary.

If we use the approach in a top-down way, from the beginning we build sC++ programs that are verifiable and already executable. Of course these programs cannot contain all the details, they are a kind of abstraction of the final system, otherwise their verification leads to intractable state explosion. For getting a real system, we only need to add details to it. Thus, the task of the developer is reduced. Obviously, at a given point the program gets too complicated and cannot be verified any more with our method because of state explosion. At this point we can use other tools[13] developed around sC++ that rely on random walk techniques[16].

If we use the approach in a bottom-up way, we always need to make an abstraction effort, but this is partially done by simply deleting lines in the original code, all the tedious work of representing synchronizations through channels and managing the various variables is taken in charge by the tool. Also the intricate semantics of objects death is done automatically, but could be present as an option if objects death is not the key point of verification.

Naturally, for being really useful in practice on real applications, the tool should take into account applications scattered in several files, and treat methods defined outside their classes. This could be included in future extensions of the tool. However, taking into account more sophisticated data types (usual passive C++ classes) and inheritance is a bit in contradiction with the scope of this work, mostly focused on interactions between processes.

This approach has been inspired of bottom-up[3][5][7]as well as top-down[4][8][9][10] experiences. It may easily be adapted for other input languages such as Ada, or Java.

6 References

1. N. Begat, Réalisation d'un interface entre sC++ et SPIN, IIE, Evry, France, engi neer report, in french, 1996.
2. G. Booch, J. Rumbaugh, I. Jacobson The UML User Guide, Add. Wesley, 1998.
3. T. Cattel, Modeling and Verification of a Multiprocessor Realtime OS Kernel, FORTE'94, Berne, 1994.
4. T. Cattel, Using Concurrency and Formal Methods for the Design of Safe Process Control. PDSE/ICSE-18 Workshop, Berlin, March 1996
5. J. Daems, Aide à l'engagement de centrales d'alarmes, EPFL engineer report, in french, 1995
6. G. Duval, Réalisation d'un debugger pour SPIN, report of Maîtrise d'informatique, Université de Besançon, France, in french, 1994.
7. G. Duval, J. Julliand, Modeling and Verification of the RUBIS Micro-Kernel with SPIN, Proc. First SPIN Workshop, INRS Quebec, Canada, Oct. 1995.
8. G. Duval, T. Cattel, Specifying and Verifying the Steam Boiler Controler with SPIN. Springer-Verlag, LNCS vol. 1165, 1996.
9. G. Duval, T. Cattel, From Architecture down to Implementation of Safe Process Control Applications. HICSS-30 Wailea, Maui, Hawaii, U.S.A. 1997.
10. G. Duval, Specification and Verification of an Object Request Broker, submitted to ICSE, Kyoto, Japan, 1998.
11. C.A.R. Hoare, Monitors: An Operating System Structuring Concept, Communications of the ACM, 12(10), October 1974.
12. G.J. Holzmann, The Model Checker SPIN, IEEE Transactions on software engineering, vol. 23, no.5, May 1997.
13. J. Madsen, Validation and Testing of sC++ applications, IEEE conference Engineering of Computer Based Systems, Monterey, California, U.S.A. 1997.
14. C. Petitpierre, sC++, A Language Adapted to Interactive Applications, accepted for IEEE Computer Journal, March 1998. http://diwww.epfl.ch/w3lti/
15. K. Slonneger, B.L. Kurtz, Formal Syntax and Semantics of Programming Languages, Addison-Wesley, 1995.
16. C. West, Protocol validation by random state exploration. PSTV, VI, 1987.

Factotum: Automatic and Systematic Sharing Support for Systems Analyzers

David James Sherman and Nicolas Magnier

Laboratoire Bordelais de Recherche en Informatique
CNRS/Université Bordeaux-1, Bordeaux, France
sherman|magnier@LaBRI.U-Bordeaux.FR

Abstract. Tools for systems analysis often combine different memory-intensive data structures, such as BDDs, tuple sets, and symbolic expressions. When separate packages are used to manipulate these structures, their conflicting resource needs can reduce overall performance despite the individual efficiency of each. *Factotum* is a software system for implementing symbolic computing systems on DAG-based structures that critically rely on sharing of equivalent subterms. It provides an subterm sharing facility that is *automatic* and *systematic*, analogously to the way that automatic memory management is provided by a garbage collector. It also provides a high-level programming interface suitable for use in multithreaded applications. We describe both the theoretical underpinnings and practical aspects of Factotum, show some examples, and report on some recent experiments.

1 Introduction

The size of in-core representations of complex systems is one of the important performance issues for model-checking and other systems analysis tools. *Sharing* of computationally equivalent substructures is a critical need for reasonable performance in these applications: not only does it provide *compact* representations, permitting the entire system being analyzed to be loaded into memory and processed, it is the key to avoiding unnecessary recomputation of equivalent properties.

While automatic garbage collection[McC60,Wil95] has become an accepted practice for managing memory-intensive applications, automatic sharing management is significantly less developed. Sharing of equivalent data structures in memory is well-developed from an algorithmic standpoint, just as explicit allocation and deallocation is an important subject of algorithmic considerations. But uniformly-applied *automatic* detection and maintenance of sharing, analogous to automatic garbage collection, is rarely studied as a general-purpose technique.

Two clear cases where automatic sharing is both critical and well-developed, especially in the context of systems analysis, are *binary decision diagrams*[Ake78] [Bry86,Rau96] and *sharing trees*[ZC95a]. Implementations of binary decision diagrams guarantee, either systematically (for ROBDDs) or at regular intervals (for QROBDDs), that all equivalent subgraphs are fully shared in a DAG structure. The result is a compact and canonical representation of a truth table, that permits efficient calculations that would otherwise explode in time and space. Sharing trees are efficient DAG representations of tuple sets, where maximal prefix and suffix sharing gives a compact and canonical representation that often admits efficient operations.

A third domain in which sharing of equivalent structures has proved important is term rewriting, where sharing induced by the use of congruence closure and its variants can result in exponential speedups at modest (quadratic or linear) cost[Che80,RV90,She94,Mag94,Ver95]. These techniques have not, however, made their way into the mainstream of accepted practice. The same argument can be made for memo functions[Mit68] in functional programming languages[Hug85]; while memoization (also called *tabulation*) is well-known, it is not systematically applied to all functions.

Factotum is an attempt to provide the advantages of automatic uniform sharing to implementors of systems analyzers in general, where computation is performed on labeled tree-like structures with sharing.[1] It grew out of the needs of the Clovis project[2], where decision-diagrams, sharing trees, and memoized function evaluation are needed simultaneously. Factotum is directly inspired by automatic garbage collection, and aims to offer the same kind of freedom from implementation details and the same kinds of guarantees about correctness and global performance.

1.1 Key Observations

The key observation is that the notions of equivalence that permit sharing in the systems cited above are congruences. That is, the addresses of nodes in memory can be considered as names of equivalence classes, and any two nodes with the same label and pairwise equivalent children are also equivalent. Two children are known to be equivalent if they have the same equivalence class name, that is, if their addresses are equal. BDDs and sharing trees use hash tables to discover that an equivalent node already exists and can be shared. While these systems guarantee prefix sharing by construction, suffix sharing is introduced by a *reduce* operation that consults this hash table.

It should consequently be possible to generalize the congruence-based techniques from term rewriting to provide a system of more widespread utility.

Several other observations, based on experience with the systems described above and analysis of their implementation, motivated the design of Factotum.

1. Efficiency in these systems is due to sharing of equivalent nodes.

---

[1] We use the slightly odd term "tree-like" to describe structures that are trees from a naive algorithmic standpoint but are concretely implemented as directed acyclic graphs. Terms (with sharing) are one example.

[2] A collaboration between the LaBRI (Université Bordeaux-1) and the LIP-6 (Université Paris-6) laboratories, concerning modular model-checking of industrial systems.

2. Lack of sharing means a loss of efficiency,[3] but not of correction.
3. Sharing is (re-)established by calls to a *reduce* operation throughout the code.
4. The algorithms for the basic operations are defined at a low level of abstraction.
5. The necessary top-down and bottom-up traversals of the data structures, used to implement basic operations , are defined ad hoc.

1.2   Key claims

The key claims that we make based on these observations are the following.

First, every one of the systems we have studied implements sharing discovery and maintenance in its own way. There is therefore a lot of reimplemention and revalidation, of what is perhaps the least interesting and most fastidious part of the system.

Second, *optimal* algorithms do not necessarily mean *fast* implementations, unless the measure of optimality considers the sequence of operations that will be performed. While one can show that the set operations in [ZC95a] are optimal in the sense that each restores maximal sharing when it is done, this requirement imposes a systematic overhead, and it is not clear whether overall performance might not be improved in some cases by checking for sharing less often. A copying garbage collector can improve overall performance when most objects have short lifetimes[App87,Wil95], simply because it is less eager reclaiming memory; in the same way, a basic sharing service may improve overall performance by checking for sharing less frequently.

Third, and finally, sharing ought to be *automatic* and *systematic*. It should be available without the need for algorithmic support in the application code, and it should be available for all objects manipulated by the system.

The Factotum system aims to provide just such an automatic and systematic sharing service, validated once and for all, where the sharing policy can be fine-tuned for overall performance, and where the structures in memory are manipulated using high-level tools. Factotum makes it possible to integrate, in the same application, different system representations and analysis techniques while guaranteeing overall correctness and performance.

1.3   Outline of the paper

In the first part of what follows, section 2, we give a brief overview of the Factotum system and its basic concepts. Section 3 gives the theoretical foundations and underlying semantics of the system, using the *RWS calculus*. Some concrete and intuitive examples of Factotum use are shown in section 4, while section 5 reports on our initial experiments. We conclude in section 6.

---

[3] Perhaps catastrophically.

2 Factotum Concepts

Factotum is conceived as a programmer's toolbox, providing an integrated set of operations on tree-like structures with sharing. The tools provided by Factotum are normally used by higher-level application code to perform some kind of symbolic computation, such as set-based or term-rewriting calculations.

The applications programmer attaches labels to the tree-like structures provided by Factotum, and assigns an *application-specific* semantics to these labeled structures. Factotum does its best to provide an efficient in-core representation, including maintaining and introducing sharing of equivalent structures. This approach maintains a clear separation between *mechanism* and *policy*: Factotum provides the means to perform operations and some basic guarantees, while the client decides what operations to perform and what the result means.[4] Structures with different semantics can be freely mixed in memory.

The runtime system is automatically initialized at the first use of a Factotum object. Memory and sharing management take place automatically during the course of the computation.

The sharing subsystem in Factotum works independently from the garbage collector to share nodes in memory when possible and convenient. It can, like the garbage collector, intervene at any moment during the computation. Sharing is transparent: the application cannot detect the presence (or absence) of sharing for a given node. Whether it is possible to share two given nodes is determined by node equivalencies indicated by the application code, and observed congruence between existing nodes. The fact that two nodes can be shared does not mean that they are, or will be. The sharing subsystem determines when it is advisable to share nodes based on its own internal policies and its own history of sharing.

2.1 Names and Cursors

The basic Factotum objects that the applications programmer manipulates are Names, that contain fixed references to nodes in memory, and Cursors, that encapsulate an arbitrary exploration below a fixed reference. Figure 1 summarizes the relations between nodes in memory and the objects that refer to them.

A cursor encapsulates an arbitrary tree-like inspection of a structure in memory. A Cursor object always refers to some node in memory, and, like Name objects, can inspect or modify the label, arity, and children of the node. A cursor can also be moved up, down, right, and left in the tree, relative to its current position. A cursor is restricted to the subtree rooted at the node at which the cursor was created.

However, the meaning of cursor movement operations is not clear when nodes may be arbitrarily shared. Figure 2 shows the confusion in the definition of the parent and sibling relations between nodes that arises in the presence of uniform sharing.

---

[4] This is a longstanding distinction, of which the X Window System remains one of the most popular proponents. An interesting recent discussion of the difference between *strategy*, *policy*, and *mechanism* can be found in [WJNB95].

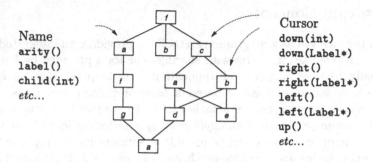

Fig. 1. **Name** and **Cursor** objects are the two ways to refer to nodes in memory

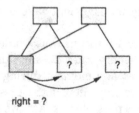

right = ?

Fig. 2. Ambiguity in the right-sibling relation due to sharing

The solution is that *every cursor remembers the history of its descent* in the data structure. It is in this way that a cursor is said to encapsulate its exploration. Since the parent relations between nodes are established relative to the unique history of a cursor, there is no ambiguity in the choice of the parent and siblings of a node in a given context.

This solution also has two further practical consequences. First, since these relations are defined relative to the stored histories of cursors, the data structure in memory has *no provision for storing parent and sibling pointers*. This greatly reduces the physical size of the objects in memory, allowing us to store larger structures, and greatly reduces the need for costly pointer update when nodes are added and deleted. Second, the encapsulation of the state of a cursor lends itself to mutithreaded applications, where only the global data structure in memory is shared between processes.

2.2 Mementos

The state of a cursor can be stored and restored at a later time by a memento object. The state encapsulated in such a memento is defined by the cursor history and the node the cursor presently refers to. A memento is stored and discarded by the application program, and can be applied an arbitrary number of times.

Among other things, mementos provide an *undo* facility. When a memento is applied, any modifications to the cursor since the creation of the memento are forgotten, and any nonpersistent modifications to the subject data structure are abandoned.

2.3 Coupled Traversals

An important observation is that most interesting analyzer operations are *simultaneous*, or parallel, traversals of different structures. Consider the case of set difference in sharing trees[ZC95a]. The basic algorithm is to trace the paths in the minuend and the subtrahend, and only include in the result those paths that are in the one but not the other. Another example is tree pattern-matching[HO82], which compares a pattern term to a subject term, and responds with a match when the two agree. In both cases the intuitively satisfying solution is to define traversals with several cursors moving together. Factotum provides specialized support for these kinds of applications: *coupled traversals*.

In a coupled traversal, a vector of cursors is moved in parallel. The first component, the *independent cursor*, is moved by the traversal as it would be normally. The other components, the *dependent cursors*, try to follow the independent cursor to nodes in their own data structure with the same labels. The traversal also maintains a vector of status registers; dependent cursors that were not able to follow the independent cursor are marked *invalid*, and remain so until the traversal brings them back up to a point where they agree with the independent cursor again.

Oftentimes we want to detect the disagreement of a dependent cursor, make some change to the data structure, and retry the move to bring the cursor back to a valid state. The `retry` operation of the traversal does exactly that.

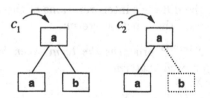

Cursor c_1	status	Cursor c_2	status
down 1	valid	down(a)	valid
up	valid	up	valid
down 2	valid	down(b)	invalid
		add_child	invalid
		set_label(b)	invalid
		retry	valid

Fig. 3. Coupled traversal of two structures

Figure 3 shows an example of two coupled cursors c_1 and c_2, where the second lacks a child labeled **b**. The figure shows the sequence of operations emitted by the traversal, intermixed with the client operations that add the necessary child when the dependent cursor becomes invalid.

3   Underlying Semantics

Factotum is more than a simple memory manager, since it constantly *improves* the representation in memory of the data it manages. Three natural questions immediately impose themselves: What improvements to the data structure in memory are permitted? Who can perform them? What justifies that they are correct?

In short, we need to characterize the *permissible transformations* of the data structures in memory, and define an *underlying semantics* that justifies the improvements. This underlying semantics must admit sharing from congruence, so that we can respond to the requirements evoked in sections 1.1 and 1.2.

3.1   The RWS Calculus

Let Name be a primitive domain of variables, and Sig be a domain of shallow terms of depth at most two over some alphabet Σ with rank function ρ and the variables in Name. We write, for example, $X, Y, Z \in$ Name and $a, g(X), f(X_1, X_2) \in$ Sig. The RWS calculus[She90,She94] uses three tables to define the state of a rewriting system:

> *bind* : Name $\rightarrow$ Sig $\cup \{$Nil$\}$
> *reduce* : Name $\rightarrow$ Name $\cup \{$Nil$\}$
> *index* : Sig $\rightarrow$ Name $\cup \{$Nil$\}$

Formally, congruence is defined by the following.

Definition 1. *Let E be a binary relation on elements of* Name. *Two variables* $X, Y \in$ Name *are congruent under E if bind $X = f(X_1, ..., X_{\rho f})$; bind $Y = f(Y_1, ..., Y_{\rho f})$; and X_i E Y_i for all i from 1 to ρf.*

For any binary relation E on elements of Name, we can define *congruence under E.*

Let *reduce** be the closure of *reduce*. Of the different interpretations of these tables, the useful one in this context is given by the function *rterm*:

Definition 2. *Function* rterm : Name $\rightarrow \Sigma^{terms}$ *produces the term given by following reduce entries as far as possible for each subterm:*
$$\text{rterm } X = \frac{f(\text{rterm } X_1, \ldots, \text{rterm } X_{\rho f})}{\text{where bind reduce* } X = f(X_1, \ldots, X_{\rho f})}.$$

It is useful to consider an example of how we can use these tables. Suppose we want to represent all of the pertinent information about the state of an ordinary term-rewriting system, with labeled terms and the usual sort of rewriting rules. Consider an initial term $f(d, h(b))$ subject to the rules $\{b \rightarrow a, h(a) \rightarrow c, d \rightarrow g(h(a))\}$. The left half of figure 4 on page 9 shows the contents of the three tables after rewriting this term, and the right half gives a schematic interpretation of the table contents. Note that $X_2 = c$, $X_2 = h(a)$, and $X_2 = h(b)$ are logical consequences of the table contents. The three tables represent a state of knowledge about a rewriting system. The RWS calculus allows transformations between such states by means of a set of *logically permissible transformations*, the rules shown in figure 5 on page 9. In the figure, by a slight abuse of notation, only the change to the tables is shown under the bar. The calculus guarantees that any sequence of applications of these rules gives a state that is a logical consequence of the initial state and the axioms used by the Reduction (2) rule.

3.2 Practical consequences

The data structures in memory manipulated by Factotum are a concrete representation of the *bind*, *reduce*, and *index* tables: *bind* is the memory, *reduce* is the set of indirection pointers, and *index* is the hash table used by the Sharer. We now describe the practical consequences of this choice of underlying semantics for the Factotum system.

The client code can build and replace nodes, thanks to the Construction and Reduction rules. These operations are performed using the higher-level interface described in section 2. Replacement is either explicit, following an indication by the client that two nodes are equivalent; or implicit, that is, induced by the modification of the label or the children associated with a node.

Factotum *systematically* uses the Collapsing, Rebinding, and Sharing I rules, to provide the most up-to-date information to the client code. By using these rules it thus makes improvements to the memory contents that persist after the client request.

The sharing subsystem *can* use the Add Index, Sharing II, and Indexing rules to improve sharing in the heap. Its strategy for applying these rules is completely internal, and transparent for the client.

Factotum therefore guarantees to the client that the result of its actions is correct for the equational semantics of the client operations.

4 Examples

To illustrate the ease with which the client programmer manipulates Factotum structures, we include in this section a short example of an operation on shared structures and the C++ code used to perform it. Other examples can be found in [She97a] and [She97b].

Consider the calculation of set difference in sharing trees[ZC95a]. Figure 6 shows an example of such a calculation. The intuition behind the algorithm is: traverse the first set, and try to follow in the second; as long as they agree, do not include anything in the result; at any point where they differ, copy the unsubtracted subtree from the minuend to the result, and go on to the next branch. (The "copy" should of course be shared with the original.) Using Factotum, we write the following code for set difference.

bind	reduce	index
$X_0 = f(X_1, X_2)$	$X_2 = X_5$	$a = X_4$
$X_1 = d$	$X_3 = X_4$	$h(X_3) = X_2$
$X_2 = h(X_3)$	$X_1 = X_7$	$h(X_4) = X_2$
$X_3 = b$		
$X_4 = a$		
$X_5 = c$		
$X_6 = h(X_4)$		
$X_7 = g(X_6)$		

$X_0 : f$

$X_1 : d \cdots\!\!\blacktriangleright X_7 : g \quad X_2 : h \cdots\!\!\blacktriangleright X_5 : c$

$X_6 : h$

$X_3 : b$

$X_4 : a$

$h(X_3)$

$h(X_4)$

$a()$

bind and reduce index

Fig. 4. Table contents representing $f(d, h(b))$ under rewriting. Solid lines are pointers, dotted lines are indirection pointers.

$$\text{Construction} \qquad \frac{X \text{ is not reachable from } X_0, \text{ nor from } \alpha}{bind[X \leftarrow \alpha]} \qquad (1)$$

$$\text{Reduction} \qquad \frac{rterm\ X = \alpha, rterm\ Y = \beta, \Gamma \models \alpha \to \beta}{reduce[X \leftarrow Y]} \qquad (2)$$

$$\text{Collapsing} \qquad \frac{reduce\ (reduce\ X) \neq \text{Nil}}{reduce[X \leftarrow reduce\ (reduce\ X)]} \qquad (3)$$

$$\text{Rebinding} \qquad \frac{bind\ X = \alpha, reduce\ X = Y, bind\ Y = \beta \neq \text{Nil}}{bind[X \leftarrow \beta]} \qquad (4)$$

$$\text{Sharing I} \qquad \frac{bind\ X = f(X_1, \ldots, X_i, \ldots, X_{\rho f}), reduce\ X_i = Y \neq \text{Nil}}{bind[X \leftarrow f(X_1, \ldots, Y, \ldots, X_{\rho f})]} \qquad (5)$$

$$\text{Add Index} \qquad \frac{bind\ X = \alpha}{index[\alpha \leftarrow X]} \qquad (6)$$

$$\text{Sharing II} \qquad \frac{bind\ X = bind\ Y \neq \text{Nil}}{reduce[X \leftarrow Y]} \qquad (7)$$

$$\text{Indexing} \qquad \frac{Y = index\ (bind\ X) \neq \text{Nil}}{reduce[X \leftarrow Y]} \qquad (8)$$

Fig. 5. Permissible transformations in the RWS calculus, where $X, Y \in$ Name, α and β are terms, and Γ is a set of axioms (rewriting rules).

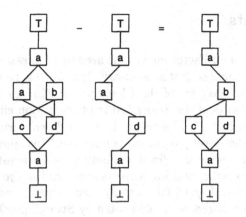

Fig. 6. Set difference in sharing trees

```
DFTraversal t(&minuend, &subtrahend, &result);
t.start();
while(!t.at_end())
  {
    if (t.status(&subtrahend) == valid)
      { // both agree so far; include nothing yet.
        t.next();
      }
    else
      { // disagreement; copy out unsubtracted part.
        if (t.status(&result) == invalid)
          { // result needs a path to here.
            add_spine(minuend, result);
          }
        result.replace(minuend.get());
        t.validate(&result);
        t.next_branch();
      }
  }
```

The auxiliary function add_spine copies the path from the root; once the spine is copied, we simply share the rest of the subtree from the minuend, and go on to the next branch of the subtrahend.

We claim that this code sufficiently high-level to be intuitive, and straightforward to validate. No explicit treatment of suffix sharing is necessary; it is handled by Factotum.

5 Experiments

The initial motivation for Factotum was the need to seamlessly integrate different representations of complex systems—n-ary decision diagrams,[5] sharing trees, functional evaluation—as part of the Clovis project. In this section we present some preliminary results of the associated implementation effort.

Our first experiments with Factotum have chiefly concerned the testing and validation of the higher-level programming interface. This approach permitted us to establish that the system as defined was useful, before investing in its in-depth optimization. Our experimental implementation uses the *cgc* lightweight generational garbage collector[cgc97] for memory management, and the fast dynamic hash tables of Larson[Lar88] as implemented by Strandh[Str92].

MEC[ABC94] is a model-checking program that computes the synchronization product of automata. These synchronization products can be computed by operations on explicit representations of automata, or using tuple-set operations [ZC95b]. In our first experiment we implemented a collection of tuple set operations inspired by Paquay's sharing trees implementation of MEC[Paq96]. An example of this experiment is the set difference example from section 4. A useful observation is that the systematic and transparent nature of sharing can be assumed in the application code, leading to more efficient algorithms. This can be seen in the example, where a difference between the two sets requires a copy of the unsubtracted subtree. Instead of a copy of this subtree, the line

```
result.replace(minuend.get());
```

shares the current node in `result` with the current subtree in `minuend`, taking constant time.

Toupie[RC93] is an interpreter of the propositional μ-calculus extended to finite symbolic domains, used to solve constraints and to describe properties of finite-state machines. In addition to the usual features of constraint languages, Toupie provides universal quantification and permits the definition of relations as fixpoints of equations. Its interest for this study is that its execution motor is based on n-ary decision diagrams, which critically need subtree sharing for efficiency, and memoization of function results.

The data structures and operations used for the Clovis project are directly inspired by Toupie. An important complication is that our variable domains are extended to arbitrary-precision integers and character strings. The former are necessary to adequately deal with nonbounded *counters* that arise in the modeling of systems described by VHDL specifications. The latter are simply convenient. In both cases, the liberty with which Factotum lets application programs define the labels on nodes greatly simplifies their coding. Rather than forcing us to inject the variable domains onto integer intervals, Factotum permits us to attach arbitrary labels, while retaining the performance advantages of direct access when such an injection is possible.

---

[5] Intuitively, BDDs extended to finite domains.

Clovis requires both decision diagrams for representing relations, and symbolic expressions extracted from VHDL programs or used for representing constraints. Both types of data structures are implemented using Factotum. The key challenges for a high-performance implementation of Clovis are, first, defining Toupie-like operators so that sharing is efficiently maintained; and second, making sure that the effects of memoization are obtained by proper sharing of common subexpressions.

A correct response to the first challenge is not a problem: using coupled traversals, we define standard operations for set union, intersection, and difference; constraint operations for join and selection (or cofactoring); and a parallel assignment used for stepwise simulation. Of particular practical interest is the tuning of the sharing strategy for overall efficient operation, a problem which is still under investigation.

The second challenge, concerning subterm sharing in symbolic expressions, resembles the use of sharing in term-rewriting to obtain the result of memoization that we described in chapter 6 of [She94]. The key idea seems to be that each projection of a relation on a set of variables be represented by an expression (subtree) that can be shared each time it appears, so the effect of its evaluation is available whenever the same projection appears in another expression. Work on these aspects continues.

6 Conclusions

The Factotum system provides an automatic and systematic sharing service for systems analysis applications that critically rely on sharing for good performance. It integrates congruence-based sharing techniques and high-level tools for manipulating structures in memory, and makes it possible to fine-tune sharing policy for overall efficiency. Existing sharing-aware applications, such as BDDs and tuple set operations using sharing trees, can clearly benefit from Factotum. But Factotum specifically aims at symbolic applications in general where validated automatic and systematic sharing provides a real advantage compared to explicit ad hoc hashing and memoization techniques.

The theoretical foundations of Factotum are provided by the RWS calculus, that gives an underlying equational semantics to the data structures in memory. This semantics is able, by design, to take into account shallow term equivalency and tabulation information stored in the data structures. Use of the RWS calculus lets Factotum guarantee that the results of its transformations, including persistent sharing improvements to the representation in memory, respect the equational semantics of the client operations.

Factotum provides a practical high-level programming interface for system implementors. Name are Cursor objects encapsulate fixed references (or roots) and arbitrary explorations below a fixed node, respectively. These objects protect the application code from address modifications induced by garbage collection and sharing, and provide a sophisticated programming interface suitable for multithreaded applications. Factotum also provides support for *coupled traversals*, which generalize a great many application-level operations.

Our experiments to-date have concentrated on validating the semantic model and programming interface, by reimplementation of the key parts of the existing tools MEC and Toupie. Further experiments are under way as part of the Clovis project.

A good deal of future work can already be foreseen. The next clear step is in-depth optimization of the Factotum code, based on back-to-back tests with existing systems. Experiments in related systems, such as the different approximations to congruence closure used in the *eqc* equational programming system, have shown that good results can be obtained with low-order constant overhead[She94,Mag94]; consequently we expect positive results from this engineering effort. A further step is the definition of adaptive strategies for the sharing subsystem, based on static or dynamic analysis of a given application, that evolve good performance without the hard-coding of application-specific strategies. This study must necessarily wait for the development of a body of Factotum examples.

Exploitation of the Factotum model in multithreaded and distributed applications is a further topic for research. The latter is of particular importance for analysis of industrial systems, where problem sizes are already beyond the capacity of monoprocessor machines.

References

[ABC94]   André Arnold, Didier Bégay, and Paul Crubillé. *Construction and Analysis of Transition Systems with MEC*. Number 3 in AMAST Series in Computing. World Scientific Publishers, 1994.

[Ake78]   B. Akers. Binary decision diagrams. *IEEE Transactions on Computers*, 27(6):509–516, 1978.

[App87]   Andrew Appel. Garbage collection can be faster than stack allocation. *Information Processing Letters*, 25(4), 1987.

[Bry86]   R. Bryant. Graph based algorithms for boolean fonction manipulation. *IEEE Transactions on Computers*, 35(8):677–691, 1986.

[cgc97]   The CGC copying garbage collector. At ftp://ftp.labri.u-bordeaux.fr/, September 1997. Part of the *eqc* equational programming project.

[Che80]   Leslie Paul Chew. An improved algorithm for computing with equations. In *21st Annual Symposium on Foundations of Computer Science*, 1980.

[HO82]   Christoph Hoffmann and Michael J. O'Donnell. Pattern matching in trees. *Journal of the ACM*, pages 68–95, 1982.

[Hug85]   John Hughes. Lazy memo functions. In *Functional Programming Languages and Computer Architectures*. Springer-Verlag, 1985.

[Lar88]   Per-Ake Larson. Dynamic hash tables. *Communications of the ACM*, 31(4):446–457, April 1988.

[Mag94]   Nicolas Magnier. Recalculs dans les systèmes de réécriture et programmation équationnelle. Technical Report 974-94, Laboratoire Bordelais de Recherche en Informatique, 1994.

[McC60]   J. McCarthy. Recursive functions of symbolic expressions and their computation by machine. *Communications of the ACM*, 3(4):185–195, 1960.

[Mit68]   D. Mitchie. 'Memo' functions and machine learning. *Nature*, pages 19–22, 1968.

[Paq96]   Renaud Paquay. Implémentation du logiciel de vérification de modèle MEC avec les arbrés partagés. Master's Thesis, University Notre-Dame de la Paix, Namur, Belgium, 1996.

[Rau96]   A. Rauzy. An introduction to binary decision diagrams and some of their applications to risk assessment. In O. Roux, editor, *Actes de l'école d'été, Modélisation et Vérification de Processus Parallèles, MOVEP'96*, 1996. Also Technical Report 1121-96, Laboratoire Bordelais de Recherche en Informatique.

[RC93]   Antoine Rauzy and Marc-Michel Corsini. First experiments with Toupie. Technical Report 581-93, Laboratoire Bordelais de Recherche en Informatique, 1993.

[RV90]   I. V. Ramakrishnan and R. Verma. Nonoblivious normalization algorithms for nonlinear systems. In *Proceedings of the International Conference on Automata, Languages, and Programming*, 1990.

[She90]   David J. Sherman. Lazy directed congruence closure. Technical Report 90-028, University of Chicago Department of Computer Science, 1990.

[She94]   David J. Sherman. *Run-time and Compile-time Improvements to Equational Programs*. PhD thesis, University of Chicago, Chicago, Illinois, 1994.

[She97a]   David J. Sherman. Factotum: Automatic and systematic sharing support for symbolic computation. Technical Report 1174-97, Laboratoire Bordelais de Recherche en Informatique, September 1997.

[She97b]   David J. Sherman. On referential transparency in the presence of uniform sharing. Technical Report 1179-97, Laboratoire Bordelais de Recherche en Informatique, October 1997.

[Str92]   Robert Strandh. A dynamic hash library. Available at ftp://ftp.labri.u-bordeaux.fr/, March 1992. Based on Larson, CACM 31(4).

[Ver95]   Rakesh M. Verma. A theory of using history for equational systems with applications. *Journal of the ACM*, 42(5):984–1020, 1995.

[Wil95]   Paul R. Wilson. Garbage collection. *ACM Computing Surveys*, 1995. Available at file://ftp.cs.utexas.edu/pub/garbage/bigsurv.ps.

[WJNB95]   Paul R. Wilson, Mark S. Johnstone, Michael Neely, and David Boles. Dynamic storage allocation: A survey and critical review. Technical report, University of Texas, 1995. Available at file://ftp.cs.utexas.edu/pub/garbage/allocsurv.ps.

[ZC95a]   D. Zampunieris and B. Le Charlier. Efficient handling of large sets of tuples with sharing trees. In *Proceedings of Data Compression Conference, DCC'95*, October 1995. Also Research Paper RP-94-004, Facultés Universitaires Notre-Dame de la Paix, Namur, Belgium.

[ZC95b]   Didier Zampuniéris and Baudouin Le Charlier. An efficient algorithm to compute the synchronized product. In *Int'l Workshop MASCOTS*, 1995.

Model Checking via Reachability Testing for Timed Automata

Luca Aceto[1] *, Augusto Burgueño[2] ** and Kim G. Larsen[1]

[1] BRICS***, Department of Computer Science, Aalborg University,
Fredrik Bajers Vej 7-E, DK-9220 Aalborg Ø, Denmark.
Email: {luca,kgl}@cs.auc.dk, Fax: +45 98 15 98 89
[2] ONERA-CERT, Département d'Informatique,
2 av. E. Belin, BP4025, 31055 Toulouse Cedex 4, France.
Email: a.burgueno@acm.org, Fax: +33 5 62 25 25 93

Abstract. In this paper we develop an approach to model-checking for timed automata via reachability testing. As our specification formalism, we consider a dense-time property language with clocks. This property language may be used to express safety and bounded liveness properties of real-time systems. We show how to automatically synthesize, for every formula φ, a *test automaton* T_φ in such a way that checking whether a system S satisfies the property φ can be reduced to a reachability question over the system obtained by making T_φ interact with S.

1 Introduction

Model-checking of real time systems has been extensively studied in the last few years, leading to both important theoretical results, setting the limits of decidability [3, 10], and to the emergence of practical tools as HyTech [9], Kronos [18] and UPPAAL [6], which have been successfully applied to the verification of real sized systems [5, 12].

The main motivation for the work presented in this paper stems from our experience with the verification tool UPPAAL. In such a tool, real-time systems are specified as networks of timed automata [3], which are then the object of the verification effort. The core of the computational engine of UPPAAL consists of a collection of efficient algorithms that can be used to perform reachability analysis over a model of an actual system. Any other kind of verification problem that the user wants to ask UPPAAL to perform must be encoded as a suitable reachability question. A typical example of such a problem is that of *model checking*. Experience has shown that it is often convenient to describe desired system properties as formulae of some real-time variant of standard modal or

---

* Partially supported by the Human Capital and Mobility project EXPRESS.
** Partially supported by Research Grant of the Spanish Ministry of Education and Culture and by BRICS. This work was carried out while the author was visiting Aalborg University.
*** Basic Research in Computer Science.

temporal logics (see, e.g., [4, 11, 15]). The model-checking problem then amounts to deciding whether a given system specification has the required property or not.

The way model-checking of properties other than plain reachability ones may currently be carried out in UPPAAL is as follows. Given a property φ to model-check, the user must provide a *test automaton* T_φ for that property. This test automaton must be such that the original system has the property expressed by φ if, and only if, none of the distinguished reject states of T_φ can be reached when the test automaton is made to interact with the system under investigation.

As witnessed by existing applications of this approach to verification by model-checking (cf., e.g., [13]), the construction of a test automaton from a temporal formula or informally specified requirements is a task that, in general, requires a high degree of ingenuity, and is error-prone. It would therefore be useful to automate this process by providing a compilation procedure from formulae in some sufficiently expressive real-time logic into appropriate test automata, and establishing its correctness once and for all. Apart from its practical and theoretical interest, the existence of such a connection between specification logics and automata would also free the average user of a verification tool like UPPAAL from the task of having to generate ad hoc test automata in his/her verifications based on the model-checking approach. We envisage that this will help make the tool usable by a larger community of designers of real-time systems.

In this paper we develop an approach to model-checking for timed automata via reachability testing. As our specification formalism, we consider a dense-time property language with clocks, which is a fragment of the one presented in [15]. This property language may be used to express safety and bounded liveness properties of real-time systems. We show how to automatically synthesize, for every formula φ, a so-called *test automaton* T_φ in such a way that checking whether a system S satisfies the property φ can be reduced to a reachability question over the system obtained by making T_φ interact with S. More precisely, we show that S satisfies property φ iff none of the distinguished reject nodes of the test automaton can be reached in the combined system $S \parallel T_\varphi$ (Thm. 5.2). This result is obtained for a model of timed automata with urgent actions and the interpretation of parallel composition used in UPPAAL.

The property language we consider in this paper only allows for a restricted use of the boolean 'or' operator, and of the diamond modality of Hennessy-Milner logic [8]. We argue that these restrictions are necessary to obtain testability of the property language, in the sense outlined above (Propn. 5.4). Indeed, as it will be shown in a companion paper [1], the property language presented in this study is remarkably close to being completely expressive with respect to reachability properties. In fact, a slight extension of the property language considered here allows us to reduce any reachability property of a composite system $S \parallel T$ to a model-checking problem of S.

Despite the aforementioned restrictions, the testable property language we consider is both of practical and theoretical interest. On the practical side, we have used the property language, and the associated approach to model-checking via reachability testing it supports, in the specification and verification in UP-PAAL of a collision avoidance protocol. This protocol was originally analyzed in [13], where rather complex test automata were derived in an ad hoc fashion from informal specifications of the expected behaviour of the protocol. The verification we present here is based on our procedure for the automatic generation of test automata from specifications. This has allowed us to turn specifications of the expected behaviour of the protocol into automata, whose precise fit with the original properties is guaranteed by construction. On the theoretical side, we have shown that the property language is powerful enough to permit the definition of *characteristic properties* [19], with respect to a timed version of the ready simulation preorder [16], for nodes of deterministic, τ-free timed automata. (This result is omitted from this extended abstract for lack of space, but see [2].)

This study establishes a connection between a property language for the specification of safety and bounded liveness properties of real-time systems and the formalism of timed automata. Our emphasis is on the reduction of the model-checking problem for the property language under consideration to an intrinsically automata-theoretic problem, viz. that of checking for the reachability of some distinguished nodes in a timed automaton. The blueprint of this endeavour lies in the automata-theoretic approach to the verification of finite-state reactive systems pioneered by Vardi and Wolper [20, 21]. In this approach to verification, the intimate relationship between linear time propositional temporal logic and ω-automata is exploited to yield elegant and efficient algorithms for the analysis of specifications, and for model-checking. The work presented in this paper is not based on a similarly deep mathematical connection between the property language and timed automata (indeed, it is not clear that such a connection exists because, as shown in [3], timed Büchi automata are not closed under complementation), but draws inspiration from that beautiful theory. In particular, the avenue of investigation pursued in this study may be traced back to the seminal [20].

The paper is organized as follows. We begin by introducing timed automata and timed labelled transition systems (Sect. 2). The notion of test automaton considered in this paper is introduced in Sect. 3, together with the interaction between timed automata and tests. We then proceed to present a real-time property language suitable for expressing safety and bounded liveness properties of real-time systems (Sect. 4). The step from properties to test automata is discussed in Sect. 5, and its implementation in UPPAAL in Sect. 6. Section 7 is devoted to a brief description of the specification and verification of a collision avoidance protocol using the theory developed in this paper. The paper concludes with a mention of some further results we have obtained on the topic of this paper, and a discussion of interesting subjects for future research (Sect. 8).

2 Preliminaries

We begin by briefly reviewing the timed automaton model proposed by Alur and Dill [3].

Timed Labelled Transition Systems Let $\mathcal{A}$ be a finite set of actions ranged over by a. We assume that $\mathcal{A}$ comes equipped with a mapping $\bar{\cdot} : \mathcal{A} \to \mathcal{A}$ such that $\bar{\bar{a}} = a$ for every $a \in \mathcal{A}$. We let $\mathcal{A}_\tau$ stand for $\mathcal{A} \cup \{\tau\}$, where τ is a symbol not occurring in $\mathcal{A}$, and use μ to range over it. Following Milner [17], τ will stand for an internal action of a system. Let N denote the set of natural numbers and $\mathbb{R}_{\geq 0}$ the set of non-negative real numbers. We use $\mathcal{D}$ to denote the set of delay actions $\{\epsilon(d) \mid d \in \mathbb{R}_{\geq 0}\}$, and $\mathcal{L}$ to stand for the union of $\mathcal{A}_\tau$ and $\mathcal{D}$.

Definition 2.1. A *timed labelled transition system* (TLTS) is a structure $\mathcal{T} = \langle S, \mathcal{L}, s^0, \longrightarrow \rangle$ where S is a set of *states*, $s^0 \in S$ is the initial state, and $\longrightarrow \subseteq S \times \mathcal{L} \times S$ is a transition relation satisfying the following properties:

- (TIME DETERMINISM) for every $s, s', s'' \in S$ and $d \in \mathbb{R}_{\geq 0}$, if $s \xrightarrow{\epsilon(d)} s'$ and $s \xrightarrow{\epsilon(d)} s''$, then $s' = s''$;
- (TIME ADDITIVITY) for every $s, s'' \in S$ and $d_1, d_2 \in \mathbb{R}_{\geq 0}$, $s \xrightarrow{\epsilon(d_1 + d_2)} s''$ iff $s \xrightarrow{\epsilon(d_1)} s' \xrightarrow{\epsilon(d_2)} s''$, for some $s' \in S$;
- (0-DELAY) for every $s, s' \in S$, $s \xrightarrow{\epsilon(0)} s'$ iff $s = s'$.

Following [22], we now proceed to define versions of the transition relations that abstract away from the internal evolution of states as follows:

$$s \xRightarrow{a} s' \quad \text{iff} \quad \exists s''. \; s \xrightarrow{\tau}{}^* s'' \xrightarrow{a} s'$$

$$s \xRightarrow{\epsilon(d)} s' \quad \text{iff} \quad \text{there exists a computation}$$

$$s = s_0 \xrightarrow{\alpha_1} s_1 \xrightarrow{\alpha_2} \ldots \xrightarrow{\alpha_n} s_n = s' \quad (n \geq 0) \text{ where}$$

$$(a) \quad \forall i \in \{1, .., n\}. \; \alpha_i = \tau \text{ or } \alpha_i \in \mathcal{D}$$

$$(b) \quad d = \sum \{d_i \mid \alpha_i = \epsilon(d_i)\}$$

By convention, if the set $\{d_i \mid \alpha_i = \epsilon(d_i)\}$ is empty, then $\sum \{d_i \mid \alpha_i = \epsilon(d_i)\}$ is 0. With this convention, the relation $\xRightarrow{\epsilon(0)}$ coincides with $\xrightarrow{\tau}{}^*$, i.e., the reflexive, transitive closure of $\xrightarrow{\tau}$. Note that the derived transition relation $\xRightarrow{a}$ only abstracts from internal transitions *before* the actual execution of action a.

Definition 2.2. Let $\mathcal{T}_i = \langle \Sigma_i, \mathcal{L}, s_i^0, \longrightarrow_i \rangle$ ($i \in \{1, 2\}$) be two TLTSs. The parallel composition of $\mathcal{T}_1$ and $\mathcal{T}_2$ is the TLTS

$$\mathcal{T}_1 \parallel \mathcal{T}_2 = \langle \Sigma_1 \times \Sigma_2, \mathcal{D} \cup \{\tau\}, (s_1^0, s_2^0), \longrightarrow \rangle$$

where the transition relation $\longrightarrow$ is defined by the rules in Table 1. In Table 1, and in the remainder of the paper, we use the more suggestive notation $s \parallel s'$ in lieu of (s, s').

(1)	$\dfrac{s_1 \xrightarrow{\tau} s_1'}{s_1 \| s_2 \xrightarrow{\tau} s_1' \| s_2}$	(2)	$\dfrac{s_2 \xrightarrow{\tau} s_2'}{s_1 \| s_2 \xrightarrow{\tau} s_1 \| s_2'}$

$$(3) \quad \frac{s_1 \xrightarrow{a} s_1' \qquad s_2 \xrightarrow{\bar{a}} s_2'}{s_1 \| s_2 \xrightarrow{\tau} s_1' \| s_2'}$$

$$(4) \quad \frac{s_1 \xrightarrow{\epsilon(d)} s_1' \qquad s_2 \xrightarrow{\epsilon(d)} s_2'}{s_1 \| s_2 \xrightarrow{\epsilon(d)} s_1' \| s_2'} \qquad \begin{array}{l} \forall t \in [0, d[, a \in \mathcal{A}, s_1'', s_2''. \\ \neg(s_1 \xrightarrow{\epsilon(t)} s_1'' \xrightarrow{a} \wedge s_2 \xrightarrow{\epsilon(t)} s_2'' \xrightarrow{\bar{a}}) \end{array}$$

where s_i, s_i', s_i'' are states of $\mathcal{T}_i$ ($i \in \{1, 2\}$),
$a, \bar{a} \in \mathcal{A}$ and $d, t \in \mathbb{R}_{\geq 0}$.

Table 1: Rules defining the transition relation $\rightarrow$ in $\mathcal{T}_1 \| \mathcal{T}_2$

This definition of parallel composition forces the composed TLTSs to synchronize on actions (all but τ-actions) and delays, but with the particularity that delaying is only possible when no synchronization on actions is. This amounts to requiring that all actions in $\mathcal{A}$ be *urgent*. The reader familiar with TCCS [22] may have noticed that the above definition of parallel composition precisely corresponds to a TCCS parallel composition in which all the actions in $\mathcal{A}$ are restricted upon. The use of this kind of parallel composition yields closed systems, of the type that can be analyzed using UPPAAL [6], and is inspired by the pioneering work by De Nicola and Hennessy on testing equivalence for processes [7].

Timed Automata Let C be a set of clocks. We use $\mathcal{B}(C)$ to denote the set of boolean expressions over atomic formulae of the form $x \sim p$, $x - y \sim p$, with $x, y \in C$, $p \in \mathbb{N}$, and $\sim \in \{<, >, =\}$. A *time assignment*, or *valuation*, v for C is a function from C to $\mathbb{R}_{\geq 0}$. For every time assignment v and $d \in \mathbb{R}_{\geq 0}$, we use $v + d$ to denote the time assignment which maps each clock $x \in C$ to the value $v(x) + d$. For every subset of clocks C', $[C' \rightarrow 0]v$ denotes the assignment for C which maps each clock in C' to the value 0 and agrees with v over $C \backslash C'$. Given a condition $g \in \mathcal{B}(C)$ and a time assignment v, the boolean value $g(v)$ describes whether g is satisfied by v or not.

Definition 2.3. A *timed automaton* is a tuple $A = \langle \mathcal{A}_\tau, N, n_0, C, E \rangle$ where N is a finite set of *nodes*, n_0 is the *initial node*, C is a finite set of *clocks*, and $E \subseteq N \times N \times \mathcal{A}_\tau \times 2^C \times \mathcal{B}(C)$ is a set of *edges*. The tuple $e = \langle n, n_e, \mu, r_e, g_e \rangle \in E$ stands for an edge from node n to node n_e (the *target* of e) with action μ, where r_e denotes the set of clocks to be reset to 0 and g_e is the enabling condition (or *guard*) over the clocks of A.

Example 2.4. The timed automaton depicted in Figure 1 has five nodes labelled n_0 to n_4, one clock x, and four edges. The edge from node n_1 to node n_2, for example, is guarded by $x \geq 0$, implies synchronization on a and resets clock x.

A *state* of a timed automaton A is a pair $\langle n, v \rangle$ where n is a node of A and v is a time assignment for C. The initial state of A is $\langle n_0, v_0 \rangle$ where n_0 is the initial node of A and v_0 is the time assignment mapping all clocks in C to 0.

The operational semantics of a timed automaton A is given by the TLTS $\mathcal{T}_A = \langle \Sigma, \mathcal{L}, \sigma^0, \longrightarrow \rangle$, where Σ is the set of states of A, σ^0 is the initial state of A, and $\longrightarrow$ is the transition relation defined as follows:

$$\langle n, v \rangle \xrightarrow{\mu} \langle n', v' \rangle \text{ iff } \exists r, g. \ \langle n, n', \mu, r, g \rangle \in E \wedge g(v) \wedge v' = [r \to 0]v$$

$$\langle n, v \rangle \xrightarrow{\epsilon(d)} \langle n', v' \rangle \text{ iff } n = n' \text{ and } v' = v + d$$

where $\mu \in \mathcal{A}_\tau$ and $\epsilon(d) \in \mathcal{D}$.

3 Testing Automata

In this section we take the first steps towards the definition of *model checking via testing* by defining *testing*. Informally, testing involves the parallel composition of the tested automaton with a *test automaton*. The testing process then consists in performing reachability analysis in the composed system. We say that the tested automaton fails the test if a special reject state of the test automaton is reachable in the parallel composition from their initial configurations, and passes otherwise. The formal definition of testing then involves the definition of what a test automaton is, how the parallel composition is performed and when the test has failed or succeeded. We now proceed to make these notions precise.

Definition 3.1. A *test automaton* is a tuple $T = \langle \mathcal{A}, N, N_T, n_0, C, E \rangle$ where $\mathcal{A}$, N, n_0, C, and E are as in Definition 2.3, and $N_T \subseteq N$ is the set of *reject nodes*.

Intuitively, a test automaton T interacts with a tested system, represented by a TLTS, by communicating with it. The dynamics of the interaction between the tester and the tested system is described by the parallel composition of the TLTS that is being tested and of $\mathcal{T}_T$. We now define failure and success of a test as follows.

Definition 3.2. Let $\mathcal{T}$ be a TLTS and T be a test automaton.

- We say that a node n of T is reachable from a state $s_1 \parallel s_2$ of $\mathcal{T} \parallel \mathcal{T}_T$ iff there is a sequence of transitions leading from $s_1 \parallel s_2$ to a state whose $\mathcal{T}_T$ component is of the form $\langle n, u \rangle$.
- We say that a state s of $\mathcal{T}$ *fails the T-test* iff a reject node of T is reachable in $\mathcal{T} \parallel \mathcal{T}_T$ from the state $s \parallel \langle n_0, u_0 \rangle$, where $\langle n_0, u_0 \rangle$ is the initial state of $\mathcal{T}_T$. Otherwise, we say that s *passes the T-test*.

In the remainder of the paper, we shall mostly apply test automata to the TLTSs that give operational semantics to timed automata. In that case, we shall use the suggestive notation $A \parallel T$ in lieu of $\mathcal{T}_A \parallel \mathcal{T}_T$.

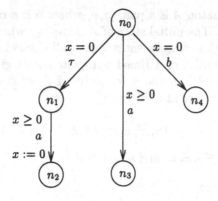

Figure 1: Timed automaton A

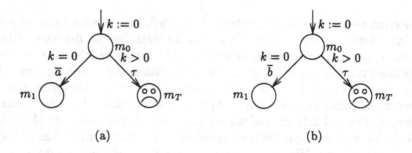

Figure 2: The test automata T_a and T_b

Example 3.3. Consider the timed automaton A of Figure 1 and the test automaton T_b of Figure 2(b). The reject node m_T of the test automaton is reachable from the initial state of $A \parallel T_b$, as follows:

1. first the automaton A can execute the τ-transition and go to node n_1, thus preempting the possibility of synchronizing on channel b with T,
2. now both automata can let time pass, thus enabling the τ-transition from node m_0 in T_b and making m_T reachable.

In this case we say that A fails the test. If we test A using the automaton T_a of Figure 2(a), then in all cases A and T_a must synchronize on a and no initial delay is possible. It follows that the reject node m_T of T_a is unreachable, and A passes the test.

4   The Property Language

We consider a dense-time property language with clocks, which is a fragment of the one presented in [15] and is suitable for the specification of safety and bounded liveness properties of TLTSs.

Definition 4.1. Let K be a set of clocks, disjoint from C. The set SBLL of (safety and bounded liveness) formulae over K is generated by the following grammar:

$$\varphi \quad ::= \quad \mathtt{tt} \quad | \quad \mathtt{ff} \quad | \quad c \quad | \quad \varphi_1 \wedge \varphi_2 \quad | \quad c \vee \varphi \quad | \quad \mathbb{W}\varphi \quad |$$
$$[a]\varphi \quad | \quad \langle a \rangle \mathtt{tt} \quad | \quad x \underline{\text{ in }} \varphi \quad | \quad X \quad | \quad \max(X, \varphi)$$
$$c \quad ::= \quad x \sim p \quad | \quad x - y \sim p$$

where $a \in \mathcal{A}$, $x, y \in K$, $p \in \mathbb{N}$, $\sim \in \{<, >, =\}$, X is a formula variable and $\max(X, \varphi)$ stands for the maximal solution of the recursion equation $X = \varphi$.

A *closed recursive formula* of SBLL is a formula in which every formula variable X appears within the scope of some $\max(X, \varphi)$ construct. In the remainder of this paper, every formula will be closed, unless specified otherwise.

Given a TLTS $\mathcal{T} = \langle S, \mathcal{L}, s^0, \longrightarrow \rangle$, we interpret the closed formulae in SBLL over extended states. An *extended state* is a pair $\langle s, u \rangle$ where s is a state of $\mathcal{T}$ and u is a time assignment for the formula clocks in K.

Definition 4.2. Consider a TLTS $\mathcal{T} = \langle S, \mathcal{L}, s^0, \longrightarrow \rangle$. The satisfaction relation $\models_w$ is the largest relation satisfying the implications in Table 2.

We say that $\mathcal{T}$ weakly satisfies φ, written $\mathcal{T} \models_w \varphi$, when $\langle s^0, u_0 \rangle \models_w \varphi$, where u_0 is the time assignment mapping every clock in K to 0. In the sequel, for a timed automaton A, we shall write $A \models_w \varphi$ in lieu of $\mathcal{T}_A \models_w \varphi$.

The weak satisfaction relation is closed with respect to the relation $\xrightarrow{\tau}{}^*$, in the sense of the following proposition.

Proposition 4.3. *Let $\mathcal{T} = \langle S, \mathcal{L}, s^0, \longrightarrow \rangle$ be a TLTS. Then, for every $s \in S$, $\varphi \in$ SBLL and valuation u for the clocks in K, $\langle s, u \rangle \models_w \varphi$ iff, for every s' such that $s \xrightarrow{\tau}{}^* s'$, $\langle s', u \rangle \models_w \varphi$.*

The reader familiar with the literature on variations on Hennessy-Milner logic [17] and on its real-time extensions [23] may have noticed that our definition of the satisfaction relation is rather different from the standard one presented in the literature. For instance, one might expect the clause of the definition of the satisfaction relation for the formula $\langle a \rangle \mathtt{tt}$ to read

$$\langle s, u \rangle \models_w \langle a \rangle \mathtt{tt} \quad \text{implies} \quad s \xRightarrow{a} s' \text{ for some } s' . \tag{1}$$

Recall, however, that our main aim in this paper is to develop a specification language for timed automata for which the model checking problem can be effectively reduced to deciding reachability. More precisely, for every formula $\varphi \in$ SBLL, we aim at constructing a test automaton T_φ such that every extended state $\langle s, u \rangle$ of a timed automaton satisfies φ iff it passes the test T_φ (in a sense to be made precise in Defn. 5.1). With this aim in mind, a reasonable proposal for a test automaton for the formula $\langle a \rangle \mathtt{tt}$, interpreted as in (1), is the automaton

$$\langle s, u \rangle \models_w \text{tt} \quad \Rightarrow \quad true$$

$$\langle s, u \rangle \models_w \text{ff} \quad \Rightarrow \quad false$$

$$\langle s, u \rangle \models_w c \quad \Rightarrow \quad c(u)$$

$$\langle s, u \rangle \models_w \varphi_1 \wedge \varphi_2 \quad \Rightarrow \quad \forall s'. \ s \xrightarrow{\tau}^* s' \text{ implies } \langle s', u \rangle \models_w \varphi_1 \text{ and } \langle s', u \rangle \models_w \varphi_2$$

$$\langle s, u \rangle \models_w c \vee \varphi \quad \Rightarrow \quad \forall s'. \ s \xrightarrow{\tau}^* s' \text{ implies } c(u) \text{ or } \langle s', u \rangle \models_w \varphi$$

$$\langle s, u \rangle \models_w [a]\varphi \quad \Rightarrow \quad \forall s'. \ s \xRightarrow{a} s' \text{ implies } \langle s', u \rangle \models_w \varphi$$

$$\langle s, u \rangle \models_w \langle a \rangle \text{tt} \quad \Rightarrow \quad \forall s'. \ s \xrightarrow{\tau}^* s' \text{ implies } s' \xrightarrow{a} s'' \text{ for some } s''$$

$$\langle s, u \rangle \models_w \mathbf{V}\varphi \quad \Rightarrow \quad \forall d \in \mathbb{R}_{\geq 0} \ \forall s'. \ s \xRightarrow{\epsilon(d)} s' \text{ implies } \langle s', u + d \rangle \models_w \varphi$$

$$\langle s, u \rangle \models_w x \underline{\text{in}} \ \varphi \quad \Rightarrow \quad \forall s'. \ s \xrightarrow{\tau}^* s' \text{ implies } \langle s', [\{x\} \to 0]u \rangle \models_w \varphi$$

$$\langle s, u \rangle \models_w \text{max}(X, \varphi) \quad \Rightarrow \quad \forall s'. \ s \xrightarrow{\tau}^* s' \text{ implies } \langle s', u \rangle \models_w \varphi\{\text{max}(X, \varphi)/X\}$$

Table 2: Weak satisfaction implications

depicted in Figure 2(a). However, it is not hard to see that such an automaton could be brought into its reject node m_T by one of its possible interactions with the timed automaton associated with the TCCS agent $a + \tau$. This is due to the fact that, because of the definition of parallel composition we have chosen, a test automaton cannot prevent the tested state from performing its internal transition leading to a state where an a-action is no longer possible. (In fact, it is not too hard to generalize these ideas to show that *no* test automaton for the formula $\langle a \rangle \text{tt}$ exists under the interpretation given in (1).) Similar arguments may be applied to all the formulae in the property language SBLL that involve occurrences of the modal operator $[a]$ and/or of the primitive proposition $\langle a \rangle \text{tt}$.

The reader might have also noticed that the language SBLL only allows for a restricted use of the logical connective 'or'. This is due to the fact that it is impossible to generate test automata even for simple formulae like $\langle a \rangle \text{tt} \vee [b]\text{ff}$— cf. Propn. 5.4.

Notation. Given a state $\langle n, v \rangle$ of a timed automaton, and a valuation u for the formula clocks in K, we write $\langle n, v : u \rangle$ for the resulting extended state.

5 Model checking via testing

In Sect. 3 we have seen how we can perform tests on timed automata. We now aim at using test automata to determine whether a given timed automaton weakly satisfies a formula in L. As already mentioned, this approach to model checking for timed automata is not merely a theoretical curiosity, but it is the way in which model checking of properties other than plain reachability ones is routinely carried out in a verification tool like UPPAAL. In order to achieve our goal, we shall define a "compilation" procedure to obtain a test automaton from the formula we want to test for. By means of this compilation procedure, we automate the process of generating test automata from specifications—a task which has so far required a high degree of ingenuity and is error-prone.

Definition 5.1. Let φ be a formula in SBLL and T_φ be a test automaton over clocks $\{k\} \cup K$, k fresh.

- For every extended state $\langle n, v : u \rangle$ of a timed automaton A, we say that $\langle n, v : u \rangle$ passes the T_φ-test iff no reject node of T_φ is reachable from the state $\langle n, v \rangle \parallel \langle m_0, \{k\} \to 0 : u \rangle$, where m_0 is the initial node of T_φ.
- We say that the test automaton T_φ *weakly tests* for the formula φ iff the following holds: for every timed automaton A and every extended state $\langle n, v : u \rangle$ of A, $\langle n, v : u \rangle \models_w \varphi$ iff $\langle n, v : u \rangle$ passes the T_φ-test.

Theorem 5.2. *For every closed formula φ in SBLL, there exists a test automaton T_φ that weakly tests for it.*

Proof. (SKETCH.) The test automata are constructed by structural induction on open formulae. (The UPPAAL implementation of the constructions is depicted in Figures 3 and 4.) It can be shown that, for every closed formula φ, the resulting automaton T_φ weakly tests for φ. The details of the proof will be presented in the full version of the paper.

Corollary 5.3. *Let A be a timed automaton. Then, for every $\varphi \in$ SBLL, there exists a test automaton T_φ with a reject node m_T such that $A \models_w \varphi$ iff node m_T is not reachable in $A \parallel T_\varphi$.*

As remarked in Sect. 4, the property language SBLL only allows for a restricted use of the 'or' operator. This is justified by the following negative result.

Proposition 5.4. *The formula $\langle a \rangle \text{tt} \vee [b] \text{ff}$ is not weakly testable.*

6 Implementation in UPPAAL

The UPPAAL constructs The implementation of testing using the parallel composition operator presented in Sect. 3 requires a model of communicating timed automata with *urgent actions* (cf. rule (4) in Table 1). This feature is available in the UPPAAL model. The test automata are inductively obtained from the formula in a constructive manner, according to the constructions shown in Figures 3 and 4. In these constructions all actions in $\mathcal{A}$ are intended to be urgent. As in UPPAAL it is not possible to guard edges labelled with urgent actions, the theoretical construction for $T_{[a]\varphi}$ used in the proof of Thm. 5.2 is implemented by means of node invariants.

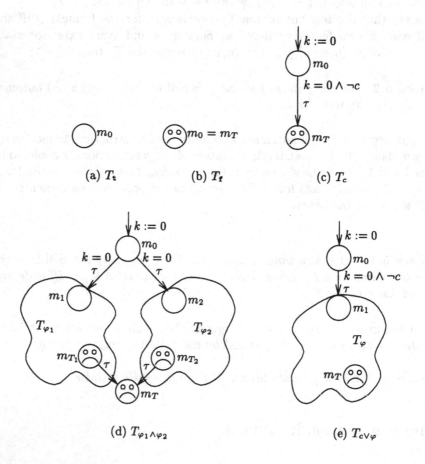

Figure 3: Test automata for SBLL sub-formulae

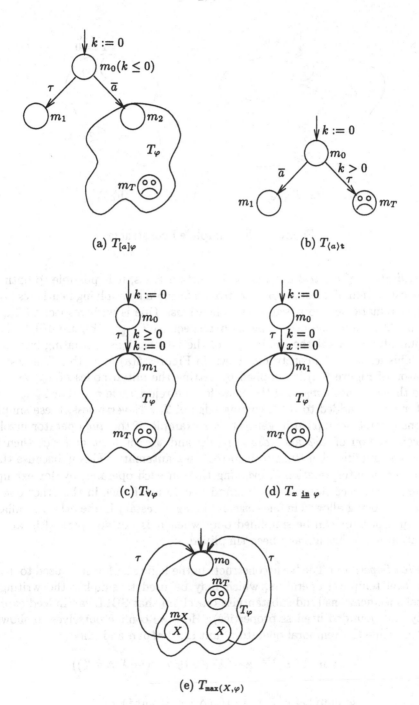

(a) $T_{[a]\varphi}$

(b) $T_{\langle a \rangle t}$

(c) $T_{\forall \varphi}$

(d) $T_{x \underline{\text{in}} \varphi}$

(e) $T_{\max(X,\varphi)}$

Figure 4: Test automata for SBLL sub-formulae (cont.)

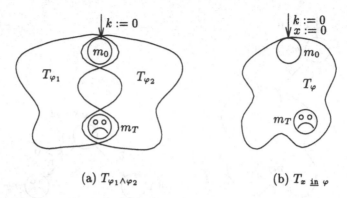

(a) $T_{\varphi_1 \wedge \varphi_2}$ (b) $T_{x \; \underline{\text{in}} \; \varphi}$

Figure 5: New simplified constructs

Simplification of the test automaton In certain cases, it is possible to optimize the construction of a test automaton from a formula by applying heuristics. Here we just remark on two possible simplifications. One is with respect to $T_{\varphi_1 \wedge \varphi_2}$ (Figure 3(d)) and the other one with respect to $T_{x \; \underline{\text{in}} \; \varphi}$ (Figure 4(d)). Both simplifications involve the elimination of the τ-transitions emanating from node m_0. This leads to the constructs shown in Figures 5(a) and 5(b). The test automaton of Figure 5(a) is obtained by setting the initial nodes of T_{φ_1} and T_{φ_2} to be the same node m_0, and the same for the reject node m_T. For $T_{x \; \underline{\text{in}} \; \varphi}$, the reset $x := 0$ is added to the incoming edge of T_φ. Nevertheless, these simplifications cannot be applied in general. For example, if the *and* operator involves the conjunction of $[a]\varphi$ and $\langle a \rangle \text{tt}$, or $[a]\varphi$ and $\mathbb{W}\varphi$, or $\langle a \rangle \text{tt}$ and $\mathbb{W}\varphi$, then the proposed simplification leads to incorrect test automata. This is because there is a different interpretation of evolving time in each operand, by, for example, leading to a reject state in one operand and to a safe one in the other one, or simply not being allowed in one case and being necessary in the other. Similarly, the <u>in</u> operator can be simplified only when it is not an operand in an *and* operation which has already been simplified.

High level operators The basic constructs of the logic SBLL can be used to define high level temporal operators, which may be used to simplify the writing of logical specifications (and substantiate our claim that SBLL can indeed express safety and bounded liveness properties). Here we confine ourselves to showing how to define the temporal operators until, before and inv:

$$\varphi \; \texttt{until} \; c \stackrel{\text{def}}{=} \max(X, c \vee (\varphi \wedge \bigwedge_a [a]X \wedge \mathbb{W}X))$$

$$\varphi \; \texttt{until}_{\leq t} \; c \stackrel{\text{def}}{=} x \; \underline{\text{in}} \; ((\varphi \wedge x \leq t) \; \texttt{until} \; c)$$

$$\texttt{before}_t \; c \stackrel{\text{def}}{=} \text{tt} \; \texttt{until}_{\leq t} \; c$$

$$\texttt{inv} \; \varphi \stackrel{\text{def}}{=} \max(X, \varphi \wedge \bigwedge_a [a]X \wedge \mathbb{W}X) \; .$$

7 Example

Consider a number of stations connected on an Ethernet-like medium, following a basic CSMA/CD protocol as the one considered in [13]. On top of this basic protocol, we want to design a protocol without collisions (applicable for example to real time plants). In particular, we want to guarantee an upper bound on the transmission delay of a buffer, assuming that the medium does not lose or corrupt data, and that the stations function properly. The simplest solution is to introduce a dedicated master station which asks the other stations whether they want to transmit data to another station (see Figure 7). Such a master station has to take into account the possible buffer delays within the receiving stations to ensure that the protocol enjoys the following properties: (1) collision cannot occur, (2) the transmitted data eventually reach their destination, (3) data which are received have been transmitted by a sender, and (4) there is a known upper bound on the transmission delay, assuming error-free transmission.

Modelling and verification of such a protocol in UPPAAL has been presented in [13], where the details of such a modelling may be found. Here we only focus on the external view of the behaviour of the system. The observable actions are: user i sending a message, written send_i!, and user j receiving a message, written recv_j!, for $i, j = \{1, 2, 3\}$. The verification of the protocol presented in *op. cit.* was based on the ad hoc generation of test automata from informal specifications of system requirements. Indeed, some of the test automata that resulted from the informal requirements were rather complex, and it was difficult to extract their semantic interpretation. We now have at our disposal a precise property language to *formally* describe the expected behaviour of the protocol, together with an automatic compilation of such specifications into test automata, and we can therefore apply the aforementioned theory to test the behaviour of the protocol.

One of the requirements of the protocol is that there must be an upper bound on the transmission delay. Assuming that this upper bound is 4, this property can be expressed by means of the following formula in SBLL:

$$\text{inv } \Big([\text{send\_1}!]s \text{ } \underline{\text{in}} \text{ } \mathbb{W}\big([\text{recv\_2}!](s < 4) \wedge [\text{recv\_3}!](s < 4)\big)\Big)$$

This formula states that it invariantly holds that whenever user 1 sends a message, it will be received by users 2 and 3 within 4 units of time. Note that we consider transmission to be error-free, so the message will eventually be received. What we are interested in is the delay expressed by clock s. The test automaton corresponding to this formula is shown in Figure 6. (Note that, although the formula above expresses the required behaviour of the protocol in a very direct way, its encoding as a test automaton is already a rather complex object—which we were glad not to have to build by hand!)

In order to experiment with our current implementation of the test automata construction in UPPAAL, we have also carried out the verification of several other properties of the protocol. For instance, we have verified that, under the assumption that the master waits for two time units before sending out its enquiries, the protocol has a round-trip time bound of 18 time units, and that no faster round-trip exists. However, we have verified that changing the waiting time in the master to zero will allow for faster round-trip times. The details of these experiments will be reported in the full version of this study.

8 Concluding Remarks

As argued in, e.g., [24], efficient algorithms for deciding reachability questions can be used to tackle many common problems related to verification. In this study, following the lead of [20], we have shown how to reduce model-checking of safety and bounded liveness properties expressible in the real-time property language SBLL to checking for reachability of reject states in suitably constructed test automata. This approach allows us to take full advantage of the core of the computational engine of the tool UPPAAL [6], which consists of a collection of efficient algorithms that can be used to perform reachability analysis over timed automata.

The practical applicability of the approach to model-checking that we have developed in this paper has been tested on a basic CSMA/CD protocol. More experimental activity will be needed to fully test the feasibility of model-checking via reachability testing. So far, all the case studies carried out with the use of UPPAAL (see, e.g., [5, 13, 14]) seem to support the conclusion that this approach to model-checking can indeed be applied to realistic case studies, but further evidence needs to be accumulated to substantiate this claim. In this process of experimentation, we also expect to further develop a collection of heuristics that can be used to reduce the size of the test automata obtained by means of our automatic translation of formulae into automata.

In this study, we have shown how to translate the formulae in the property language SBLL into test automata in such a way that model-checking can be reduced to testing for reachability of distinguished reject nodes in the generated automata. Indeed the property language presented in this study is remarkably close to being completely expressive with respect to reachability properties. In fact, as it will be shown in a companion paper [1], a slight extension of the property language considered here allows us to reduce any reachability property for a composite system $S \parallel T$ to a model-checking problem of S.

The interpretation of the formulae in our specification formalism presented in Table 2 abstracts from the internal evolution of real-time processes in a novel way. A natural question to ask is whether the formulae in the property language SBLL are testable, in the sense of this paper, when interpreted with respect to the transition relation $\longrightarrow$. In the full version of this work, we shall show that this is indeed possible if the test automata are allowed to have *committed locations* [5], and the definition of the parallel composition operator is modified to take the nature of these locations into account. We expect, however, that the weak interpretation of the property language will be more useful in practical applications of our approach to model-checking.

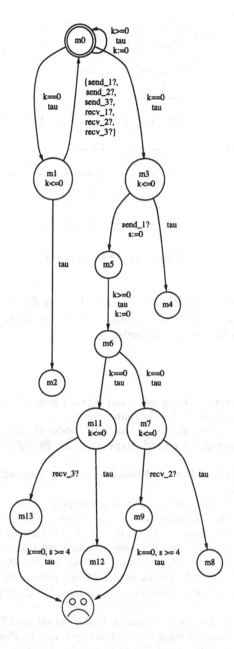

Figure 6: Test automaton for the invariant property

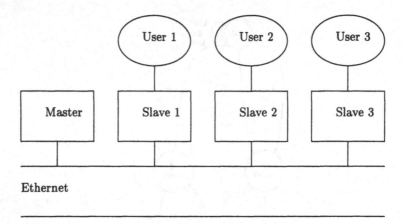

Figure 7: The Ethernet

Acknowledgements. We thank Patricia Bouyer for her help in the implementation of the tool, Kåre Jelling Kristoffersen for his proof-reading, and the anonymous referees for their comments.

References

1. L. Aceto, P. Bouyer, A. Burgueño, and K. G. Larsen. The limitations of testing for timed automata, 1997. Forthcoming paper.
2. L. Aceto, A. Burgueño, and K. G. Larsen. Model checking via reachability testing for timed automata. Research Report RS-97-29, BRICS, Aalborg University, November 1997.
3. R. Alur and D. Dill. A theory of timed automata. *Theoretical Computer Science*, 126:183–235, 1994.
4. R. Alur and T.A. Henzinger. A really temporal logic. *Journal of the ACM*, 41(1):181–204, 1994. Preliminary version appears in Proc. 30th FOCS, 1989.
5. J. Bengtsson, D. Griffioen, K. Kristoffersen, K. G. Larsen, F. Larsson, P. Pettersson, and W. Yi. Verification of an audio protocol with bus collision using UPPAAL. In R. Alur and T. A. Henzinger, editors, *Proc. of the 8th. International Conference on Computer-Aided Verification, CAV'96*, volume 1102 of *Lecture Notes in Computer Science*, New Brunswick, New Jersey, USA, July 31 – August 3 1996. Springer-Verlag.
6. J. Bengtsson, K. G. Larsen, F. Larsson, P. Pettersson, and W. Yi. UPPAAL - a tool suite for automatic verification of real-time systems. In *Proc. of the 4th DIMACS Workshop on Verification and Control of Hybrid Systems*, New Brunswick, New Jersey, 22–24 October 1995.
7. R. De Nicola and M. Hennessy. Testing equivalences for processes. *Theoretical Computer Science*, 34:83–133, 1984.
8. M. Hennessy and R. Milner. Algebraic laws for nondeterminism and concurrency. *Journal of the Association for Computing Machinery*, 32(1):137–161, January 1985.
9. T. A. Henzinger, P.-H. Ho, and H. Wong-Toi. HyTech: the next generation. In *Proc. of the 16th Real-time Systems Symposium, RTSS'95*. IEEE Computer Society press, 1995.

10. T. A. Henzinger, P. W. Kopke, A. Puri, and P. Varaiya. What's decidable about hybrid automata? In *Proc. of the 27th Annual ACM Symposium on Theory of Computing, STOC'95*, pages 373–382, 1995. Also appeared as Cornell University technical report TR95-1541.

11. T. A. Henzinger, X. Nicollin, J. Sifakis, and S. Yovine. Symbolic model checking for real-time systems. *Information and Computation*, 111(2):193–244, 1994.

12. P.-H. Ho and H. Wong-Toi. Automated analysis of an audio control protocol. In P. Wolper, editor, *Proc. of the 7th. International Conference on Computer-Aided Verification, CAV'95*, volume 939 of *Lecture Notes in Computer Science*, pages 381–394, Lige, Belgium, July 1995. Springer-Verlag.

13. H. E. Jensen, K. G. Larsen, and A. Skou. Modelling and analysis of a collision avoidance protocol using SPIN and UPPAAL. In *DIMACS Workshop SPIN '96, 2nd International SPIN Verification Workshop on Algorithms, Applications, Tool Use, Theory*. Rutgers University, New Jersey, USA, 1996.

14. K.J. Kristoffersen and P. Pettersson. Modelling and analysis of a steam generator using UPPAAL. In *Proc. of the 7th Nordic Workshop on Programming Theory*, Göteborg, Sweden, November 1–3 1995.

15. F. Laroussinie, K. G. Larsen, and C. Weise. From timed automata to logic - and back. In J. Wiedermann and P. Hájek, editors, *Proc. of the 20th. International Symposium on Mathematical Foundations of Computer Science, MFCS'95*, volume 969 of *Lecture Notes in Computer Science*, pages 529–539, Prague, Czech Republic, August 28 - September 1 1995. Springer-Verlag.

16. Kim G. Larsen and Arne Skou. Bisimulation through probabilistic testing. *Information and Computation*, 94(1):1–28, September 1991.

17. R. Milner. *Communication and Concurrency*. Series in Computer Science. Prentice Hall International, 1989.

18. A. Olivero and S. Yovine. *Kronos: a tool for verifying real-time systems. User's guide and reference manual*. VERIMAG, Grenoble, France, 1993.

19. B. Steffen and A. Ingólfsdóttir. Characteristic formulae for processes with divergence. *Information and Computation*, 110(1):149–163, April 1994.

20. M. Y. Vardi and P. Wolper. An automata-theoretic approach to automatic program verification. In *Proc. of the 1st. Annual Symposium on Logic in Computer Science, LICS'86*, pages 322–331. IEEE Computer Society Press, 1986.

21. M. Y. Vardi and P. Wolper. Reasoning about infinte computations. *Information and Computation*, 115:1–37, 1994.

22. Y. Wang. Real-time behaviour of asynchronous agents. In J.C.M. Baeten and J.W. Klop, editors, *Proc. of the Conference on Theories of Concurrency: Unification and Extension, CONCUR'90*, volume 458 of *Lecture Notes in Computer Science*, pages 502–520, Amsterdam, The Netherlands, August 27–30 1990. Springer-Verlag.

23. Y. Wang. *A calculus of real time systems*. PhD thesis, Chalmers university of Technology, Göteborg, Sweden, 1991.

24. P. Wolper. Where could SPIN go next? a unifying approach to exploring infinite state spaces. Slides for an invited talk at the *1997 SPIN Workshop*, Enschede, The Netherlands. Available at the URL http://www.montefiore.ulg.ac.be/~pw/papers/psfiles/SPIN4-97.ps.

Formal Design and Analysis of a Gear Controller*

Magnus Lindahl[1]   Paul Pettersson[2]   Wang Yi[2]

[1] Mecel AB, Göteborg, Sweden. E-mail: magnus.lindahl@mecel.se
[2] Department of Computer Systems, Uppsala University, Sweden.
E-mail: {paupet,yi}@docs.uu.se

Abstract. In this paper, we report on an application of the validation and verification tool kit UPPAAL in the design and analysis of a proto-type gear controller, carried out in a joint project between industry and academia. We give a detailed description of the formal model of the gear controller and its surrounding environment, and its correctness formal-ized according to the informal requirements delivered by our industrial partner of the project. The second contribution of this paper is a solution to the problem we met in this case study, namely how to use a tool like UPPAAL, which only provides reachability analysis to verify bounded re-sponse time properties. The advantage of our solution is that we need no additional implementation work to extend the existing model–checker, but simple manual syntactical manipulation on the system description.

1   Introduction

Over the past few years, a number of modeling and verification tools for real-time systems [5, 4, 3] have been developed based on the theory of timed automata [1]. They have been successfully applied in various case-studies [2, 6, 8]. However, the tools have been mainly used in the academic community, namely by the tool developers. It has been a challenge to apply these tools to real-sized industrial case-studies. In this paper we report on an application of the verification tool-kit UPPAAL[1] to a prototype gear controller developed in a joint project between in-dustry and academia. The project has been carried out in collaboration between Mecel AB and Uppsala University.

The gear controller is a component in the real-time embedded system that operates in a modern vehicle. The gear-requests from the driver are delivered over a communication network to the gear controller. The controller implements the actual gear change by actuating the lower level components of the system, such as the clutch, the engine and the gearbox. Obviously, the behavior of the

---

* This work has been supported by ASTEC (Advanced Software TEChnology), NUTEK (Swedish Board for Technical Development) and TFR (Swedish Technical Research Council).
[1] Installation and documentation is available at the UPPAAL home page http://www.docs.uu.se/docs/rtmv/uppaal/.

gear controller is critical to the safety of the vehicle. Simulation and testing have been the traditional ways to ensure that the behavior of the controller satisfies certain safety requirements. However these methods are by no means complete in finding errors though they are useful and practical. As a complement, formal techniques have been a promising approach to ensuring the correctness of embedded systems. The project is to use formal modeling techniques in the early design stages to describe design sketches, and to use symbolic simulators and model checkers as debugging and verification tools to ensure that the predicted behavior of the designed controller at each design phase, satisfies certain requirements under given assumptions on the environment where the gear controller is supposed to operate. The requirements on the controller and assumptions on the environment have been described by Mecel AB in an informal document, and then formalized in the UPPAAL model and a simple linear–time logic based on the UPPAAL logic to deduce the design of the gear controller.

We shall give a detailed description of the formal model of the gear controller and its surrounding environment in the UPPAAL model and its correctness in the UPPAAL logic according to the informal requirements delivered by Mecel AB. Another contribution of this paper is a lesson we learnt in this case study, namely how to use a tool like UPPAAL, which only provides reachability analysis to verify bounded response time properties e.g. *if f_1 (a request) becomes true at a certain time point, f_2 (a response) must be guaranteed to be true within a time bound*. We present a logic and a method to characterize and model–check response time properties. The advantage of this approach is that we need no additional implementation work to extend the existing model–checker, but simple manual syntactical manipulation on the system description.

The paper is organised as follows: In section 2, we present a simple logic to characterize safety and response time properties. Section 3 develops a method to model–check such properties. In Section 4 and 5 the gear controller system and its requirements are informally and formally described. In Section 6 the formal description of the system and its requirements are transformed using the technique developed in section 2 for verification by reachability analysis. Section 7 concludes the paper. Finally, we enclose the formal description of the surrounding environment of the gear controller in the appendix.

2 A Logic for Safety and Bounded Response Time Properties

At the start of the project, we found that it was not so obvious how to formalize (in the UPPAAL logic) the pages of informal requirements delivered by the design engineers. One of the reasons was that our logic is too simple, which can express essentially only invariant properties. After a while, it became obvious that these requirements could be described in a simple logic, which can be model–checked by reachability analysis in combination with a certain syntactical manipulation on the model of the system to be verified. We also noticed that though the logic is so simple, it characterizes the class of logical properties verified in all previous case studies where UPPAAL is applied (see e.g. [2, 6, 8]).

2.1 Timed Transition Systems and Timed Traces

A timed transition system is a labeled transition system with two types of labels: atomic actions and delay actions (i.e. positive reals), representing discrete and continuous changes of real-time systems.

Let Act be a finite set of actions and $\mathcal{P}$ be a set of atomic propositions. We use $\mathbf{R}$ to stand for the set of non-negative real numbers, D for the set of delay actions $\{\epsilon(d) \mid d \in \mathbf{R}\}$, and Σ for the union $Act \cup D$ ranged over by $\alpha, \alpha_1, \alpha_2$ etc.

Definition 1. *A timed transition system over Act and $\mathcal{P}$ is a tuple $\mathcal{S} = \langle S, s_0, \longrightarrow, V \rangle$, where S is a set of states, s_0 is the initial state, $\longrightarrow \subseteq S \times \Sigma \times S$ is a transition relation, and $V : S \to 2^{\mathcal{P}}$ is a proposition assignment function.* □

A trace σ of a timed transition system is an *infinite* sequence of transitions in the form:

$$\sigma = s_0 \xrightarrow{\alpha_0} s_1 \xrightarrow{\alpha_1} s_2 \xrightarrow{\alpha_2} \ldots s_n \xrightarrow{\alpha_n} s_{n+1} \ldots$$

where $\alpha_i \in \Sigma$.

A position i of σ is a natural number. We use $\sigma[i]$ to stand for the ith state of σ, and $\sigma(i)$ for the ith transition of σ, i.e. $\sigma[i] = s_i$ and $\sigma(i) = s_i \xrightarrow{\alpha_i} s_{i+1}$.

We use $\delta(s \xrightarrow{\alpha} s')$ to denote the duration of the transition, defined by $\delta(s \xrightarrow{\alpha} s') = 0$ if $\alpha \in Act$ or d if $\alpha = \epsilon(d)$. Given positions i, k with $i \leq k$, we use $\Delta(\sigma, i, k)$ to stand for the accumulated delay of σ between the positions i, k, defined by $\Delta(\sigma, i, k) = \sum_{i \leq j < k} \delta(\sigma(j))$. We shall only consider *non–zeno* traces.

Definition 2. *A trace σ is non–zeno if for all natural number T there exists a position k such that $D(\sigma, 0, k) > T$. For a timed transition system $\mathcal{S}$, we denote by $Tr(\mathcal{S})$ all non–zeno traces of $\mathcal{S}$ starting from the initial state s_0 of $\mathcal{S}$.* □

Note that the timed transition system defined above can also be represented finitely as a network of timed automata For the definition of such networks, we refer to [7]. Let $\overline{A}$ be a network of timed automata with components $A_1 \ldots A_n$. We denote by $Tr(\overline{A})$ all non–zeno traces of the timed transition system $\overline{\mathcal{S}}$ i.e. $Tr(\overline{A}) = Tr(\overline{\mathcal{S}})$.

2.2 The Logic: Syntax and Semantics

The logic may be seen as a timed variant of a fragement of the linear temporal logic LTL, which does not allow nested applications of modal operators. It is to express invariant and bounded response time properties.

Definition 3. *Assume that $\mathcal{GV}$ ranged over by g is a set of clock constraints as defined in [7] and P is a finite set of propositions ranged over by p, q etc. Let*

$$
\begin{array}{l}
(l, u) \models g \text{ iff } g(u) \\
(l, u) \models p \text{ iff } p \in V(l) \\
(l, u) \models \neg f \text{ iff } (l, u) \not\models f \\
(l, u) \models f_1 \wedge f_2 \text{ iff } (l, u) \models f_1 \text{ and } (l, u) \models f_2 \\
\sigma \models Inv(f) \text{ iff } \forall i : \sigma[i] \models f \\
\sigma \models f_1 \leadsto_{\leq T} f_2 \text{ iff } \forall i : (\sigma[i] \models f_1 \Rightarrow \exists k \geq i : (\sigma[k] \models f_2 \text{ and } D(\sigma, i, k) \leq T))
\end{array}
$$

Table 1. Definition of satisfiability.

$\mathcal{F}_s$ denote the set of boolean expressions over $\mathcal{GV} \cup P$ ranged over by f, f_1, f_2 etc, defined as follows:

$$ f ::= g \mid p \mid \neg f \mid f_1 \wedge f_2 $$

where $g \in \mathcal{GV}$ is a constraint. and $p \in P$ is an atomic proposition. We call $\mathcal{F}_s$ state–formulas, meaning that they will be true of states. □

As usual, we use $f_1 \vee f_2$ to stand for $\neg(\neg f_1 \wedge \neg f_2)$, and tt and ff for $\neg f \vee f$ and $\neg f \wedge f$ respectively. Further, we use $f_1 \Rightarrow f_2$ to denote $\neg f_1 \vee f_2$.

Definition 4. *The set $\mathcal{F}_t$ ranged over by f, f_1, f_2 of trace–formulas over $\mathcal{F}_s$ is defined as follows:*

$$ \varphi ::= Inv(f) \mid f_1 \leadsto_{\leq T} f_2 $$

where T is a natural number.
If f_1 and f_2 are boolean combinations of atomic propositions, we call $f_1 \leadsto_{\leq T} f_2$ a bounded response time formula. □

$Inv(f)$ states that f is an invariant property; a system satisfies $Inv(f)$ if all its reachable states satisfy f. It is useful to express safety properties, that is, bad things (e.g. deadlocks) should never happen, in other words, the system should always behave safely. $f_1 \leadsto_{\leq T} f_2$ is similar to the strong Until-operator in LTL, but with an explicit time bound. In addition to the time bound, it is also an invariant formula. It means that as soon as f_1 is true of a state, f_2 must be true within T time units. However it is not necessary that f_1 must be true continuously before f_2 becomes true as required by the traditional Until-operator.

We shall call formulas of the form $f_1 \leadsto_{\leq T} f_2$ a bounded response time formula. Intuitively, f_1 may be considered as a request and f_2 as a response; thus $f_1 \leadsto_{\leq T} f_2$ specifies the bound for the response time to be T.

We interpret $\mathcal{F}_s$ and $\mathcal{F}_t$ in terms of states and (infinite and non–zeno) traces of timed automata. We write $(l, u) \models f$ to denote that the state (l, u) satisfies the state–formula f and $\sigma \models \varphi$ to denote that the trace σ satisfies the trace–formula φ. The interpretation is defined on the structure of f and φ, given in Table 1. Naturally, if all the traces of a timed automaton satisfy a trace–formula, we say that the automaton satisfies the formula.

Definition 5. *Assume a network of automata $\overline{A}$ and a trace–formula φ. We write $\overline{A} \models \varphi$ if and only if $\sigma \models \varphi$ for all $\sigma \in Tr(\overline{A})$.* □

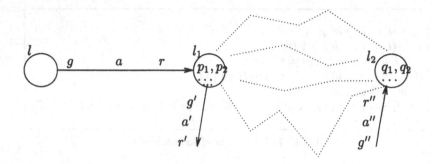

Fig. 1. Illustration of a timed automaton A.

3 Verifying Bounded Response Time Properties by Reachability Analysis

The current version of UPPAAL can only model–check invariant properties by reachability analysis. The question is how to use a tool like UPPAAL to check for bounded response time properties i.e. how to transform the model–checking problem $A \models f_1 \leadsto_{\leq T} f_2$ to a reachability problem. The traditional solution is to translate the formula to a testing automaton t (see e.g. [6]) and then check whether the parallel system $A\|t$ can reach a designated state of t.

We take a different approach. We modify (or rather decorate) the automaton A according to the state-formulas f_1 and f_2, and the time bound T and then construct a state–formula f such that

$$\mathcal{M}(A) \models \mathit{Inv}(\mathsf{f}) \quad \textit{iff} \quad A \models \mathsf{f}_1 \leadsto_{\leq T} \mathsf{f}_2$$

where $\mathcal{M}(A)$ is the modified version of A.

We study an example. First assume that each node of an automaton is assigned implicitly a proposition $at(l)$ meaning that the current control node is l. Consider an automaton A illustrated in Figure 1 and a formula $at(l_1) \leadsto_{\leq 3} at(l_2)$ (i.e. it should always reach l_2 from l_1 within 3 time units). To check whether A satisfies the formula, we introduce an extra clock $c \in C$ and a boolean variable [2] v_1 into the automaton A, that should be initiated with ff. Assume that the node l_1 has no local loops, i.e. containing no edges leaving and entering l_1. We modify the automaton A as follows:

1. Duplicate all edges entering node l_1.
2. Add $\neg v_1$ as a guard to the original edges entering l_1.
3. Add $v_1 := \mathsf{tt}$ and $c := 0$ as reset–operations to the original edges entering l_1.
4. Add v_1 as a guard to the auxiliary copies of the edges entering l_1.
5. Add $v_1 := \mathsf{ff}$ as a reset–operation to all the edges entering l_2.

---

[2] Note that a boolean variable may be represented by an integer variable in UPPAAL.

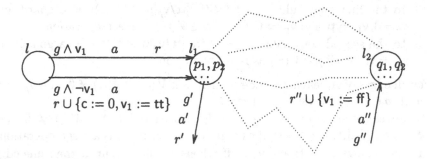

Fig. 2. Illustration of a modified timed automaton $\mathcal{M}(A)$ of A.

The modified (decorated) automaton $\mathcal{M}(A)$ is illustrated in Figure 2. Now we claim that

$$\mathcal{M}(A) \models Inv(v_1 \Rightarrow c \leq 3) \text{ iff } A \models at(l_1) \rightsquigarrow_{\leq 3} at(l_2)$$

The invariant property $v_1 \Rightarrow c \leq 3$ states that either $\neg v_1$ or if v_1 then $c \leq 3$. There is only one situation that violates the invariant: v_1 and $c > 3$. Due to the progress property of time (or non–zenoness), the value of c should always increase. It will sooner or later pass 3. But if l_2 is reached before c reaches 3, v_1 will become ff. Therefore, the only way to keep the invariant property true is that l_2 is reached within 3 time units whenever l_1 is reached.

The above method may be generalized to efficiently model–check response time formulas for networks of automata. Let $\mathcal{A}(f)$ denote the set of atomic propositions occuring in a state–formula f. Assume a network $\overline{A}$ and a response time formula $f_1 \rightsquigarrow_{\leq T} f_2$ For simplicity, we consider the case when only atomic propositions occur in f_1 and f_2. Note that this is not a restriction, the result can be easily extended to the generl case. We introduce to $\overline{A}$:

1. an auxiliary clock $c \in C$ and an boolean variable v_1 (to denote the truth value of f_1) and
2. an auxiliary boolean variable v_p for all $p \in \mathcal{A}(f_1) \cup \mathcal{A}(f_2)$.

Assume that all the booleans of $\mathcal{A}(f_1), \mathcal{A}(f_2)$ and v_1 are initiated to ff.

Let $\mathcal{E}(f)$ denote the boolean expression by replacing all $p \in \mathcal{A}(f)$ with their corresponding boolean variable v_p. As usual, $\mathcal{E}(f)[tt/v_p]$ denotes a substitution that replaces v_p with tt in $\mathcal{E}(f)$. This can be extended in the usual way to set of substitutions. For instance, the truth value of f at a given state s may be calculated by $\mathcal{E}(f)[tt/v_p | p \in V(s)][ff/v_p | p \notin V(s)]$.

Now we are ready to construct a decorated version $\mathcal{M}(\overline{A})$ for the network $\overline{A}$. We modify all the components A_i of $\overline{A}$ as follows:

1. For all edges of A_i, entering a node l_1 such that $V(l_1) \cap \mathcal{A}(f_1) \neq \emptyset$:
   - Make two copies of each such edge.
   - To the original edge, add v_1 as a guard.

- To the first copy, add $\neg \mathcal{E}(f_1) \wedge \mathcal{E}(f_1)[tt/v_p | p \in V(l_1)]$ as a guard and $c := 0, v_1 := tt$ and $v_p := tt$ for all $p \in V(l_1)$ as reset–operations.
- To the second copy, add $\neg v_1 \wedge \neg \mathcal{E}(f_1)[tt/v_p | p \in V(l_1)]$ as a guard and $v_p := tt$ for all $p \in V(l_1)$ as reset–operations.

2. For all edges of A_i leaving a node l_1 such that $V(l_1) \cap \mathcal{A}(f_1) \neq \emptyset$: add $v_p := ff$ for all $p \in V(l_1)$ as reset–operations.

3. For all edges of A_i entering a node l_2 such that $V(l_2) \cap \mathcal{A}(f_2) \neq \emptyset$: add $\neg \mathcal{E}(f_2) \wedge \mathcal{E}(f_2)[tt/v_q | q \in V(l_2)]$ as a guard and $v_1 := ff$ as a reset–operation.

4. Finally, remove $v_p := tt$ and $v_p := ff$ whenever they occur at the same edge [3].

Thus, we have a decorated version $\mathcal{M}(A_i)$ for each A_i of $\overline{A}$. We shall take $\mathcal{M}(A_1) \| \ldots \| \mathcal{M}(A_n)$ to be the decorated version of $\overline{A}$, i.e. $\mathcal{M}(\overline{A}) \equiv \mathcal{M}(A_1) \| \ldots \| \mathcal{M}(A_n)$.

Note that we could have constructed the product automaton of $\overline{A}$ first. Then the construction of $\mathcal{M}(\overline{A})$ from the product automaton would be much simpler. But the size of $\mathcal{M}(\overline{A})$ will be much larger; it will be exponential in the size of the component automata. Our construction here is purely syntactical based on the syntactical structure of each component automaton. The size of $\mathcal{M}(\overline{A})$ is in fact linear in the size of the component automata. It is particularly appropriate for a tool like UPPAAL, that is based on on-the-fly generation of the state–space of a network. For each component automaton A, the size of $\mathcal{M}(A)$ can be calculated precisely as follows: In addition to one auxiliary clock c and $|P(f_1) \cup P(f_2)|$ boolean variables in $\mathcal{M}(A)$, the number of edges of $\mathcal{M}(A)$ is $3 \times |E_A|$ where $|E_A|$ is the number of edges of A (note that no extra nodes introduced in $\mathcal{M}(A)$).

Note also that in the above construction, we have the restriction that f_1 and f_2 contain no constraints, but only atomic propositions. The construction can be easily generalized to allow constraints by considering each constraint as a proposition and decorating each location (that is, the incomming edges) where the constraint could become true when the location is reached. In fact, this is what we did above on the boolean expressions (constraints) $\mathcal{E}(f_1)$ and $\mathcal{E}(f_2)$. Finally, we have the main theoretical result of this paper.

Theorem 1. $\mathcal{M}(\overline{A}) \models Inv(v_1 \Rightarrow c \leq T)$ iff $\overline{A} \models f_1 \leadsto_{\leq T} f_2$ for a network of timed automata $\overline{A}$ and a bounded response time formula $f_1 \leadsto_{\leq T} f_2$. $\quad \square$

4 The Gear Controller

In this section we informally describe the functionality and the requirements of the gear controller proposed by Mecel AB, as well as the abstract behavior of the environment where the controller is supposed to operate.

---

[3] This means that a proposition p is assigned to both the source and the target nodes of the eadge; v_p must have been assigned tt on all the edges entering the source node.

Functionality. The gear controller changes gears by requesting services provided by the components in its environment. The interaction with these components is over the vehicles communication network. A description of the gear controller and its interface is as follows.

Interface: The interface receives service requests and keeps information about the current status of the gear controller, which is either changing gear or idling. The user of this service is either the driver using the gear stick or a dedicated component implementing a gear change algorithm. The interface is assumed to respond when the service is completed.

Gear Controller: The only user of the gear controller is its interface. The controller performs a gear change in five steps beginning when a gear change request is received from the interface. The first step is to accomplish a zero torque transmission, making it possible to release the currently set gear. Secondly the gear is released. The controller then achieves synchronous speed over the transmission and sets the new gear. Once the gear is set the engine torque is increased so that the same wheel torque level as before the gear change is achieved.

Under difficult driving conditions the engine may not be able to accomplish zero torque or synchronous speed over the transmission. It is then possible to change gear using the clutch. By opening the clutch, and consequently the transmission, the connection between the engine and the wheels is broken. The gearbox is at this state able to release and set the new gear, as zero torque and synchronous speed is no longer required. When the clutch closes it safely bridges the speed and torque differences between the engine and the wheels. We refer to these exceptional cases as *recoverable errors*.

Environment. The environment of the gear controller consists of the following three components:

Gearbox: It is an electrically controlled gearbox with control electronics. It provides services to *set* a gear in 100 to 300 ms and to *release* a gear in 100 to 200 ms. If a setting or releasing-operation of a gear takes more than 300 ms or 200 ms respectively, the gearbox will indicate this and stop in a specific error state.

Clutch: It is an electrically controlled clutch that has the same sort of basic services as the gearbox. The clutch can *open* or *close* within 100 to 150 ms. If a opening or closing is not accomplish within the time bounds, the clutch will indicate this and reach a specific error state.

Engine: The engine offers three modes of operation: normal torque, zero torque, and synchronous speed. The normal mode is *normal torque* where the engine gives the requested engine torque. In *zero torque* mode the engine will try to find a zero torque difference over the transmission. Similarly, in *synchronous speed* mode the engine searches zero speed difference between the engine and the wheels[4]. The maximum time bound searching for zero torque is limited

---

[4] Synchronous speed mode is used only when the clutch is open or no gear is set.

to 400 ms within which a safe state is entered. Furthermore, the maximum time bound for synchronous speed control is limited to 500 ms. If 500 ms elapse the engine enters an error state.

We will refer the error states in the environment as *unrecoverable errors* since it is impossible for the gear controller alone to recover from these errors.

4.1 Requirements.

In this section we list the informal requirements and desired functionality on the gear controller, provided by Mecel AB. The requirements are to ensure the correctness of the gear controller. A few operations, such as gear changes and error detections, are crucial to the correctness and must be guaranteed within certain time bounds. In addition, there are also requirements on the controller to ensure desired qualities of the vehicle, such as: good comfort, low fuel consumption, and low emission.

1. **Performance.** These requirements limit the maximum time to perform a gear change when no unrecoverable errors occur.

   (a) A gear change should be completed within 1.5 seconds.
   (b) A gear change, under normal operation conditions, should be performed within 1 second.

2. **Predictability**. The predictability requirements are to ensure strict synchronization and control between components.

   (a) There should not be dead-locks or live-locks in the system.
   (b) When the engine is regulating torque, the clutch should be closed.
   (c) The gear has to be set in the gearbox when the engine is regulating torque.

3. **Functionality.** The following requirements are to ensure the desired functionality of the gear controller.

   (a) It is able to use all gears.
   (b) It uses the engine to enhance zero torque and synchronous speed over the transmission.
   (c) It uses the gearbox to set and release gears.
   (d) It is allowed to use the clutch in difficult conditions.
   (e) It does not request zero torque when changing from neutral gear.
   (f) The gear controller does not request synchronous speed when changing to neutral gear.

4. **Error Detection.** The gear controller detects and indicates error only when:

   (a) the clutch is not opened in time,
   (b) the clutch is not closed in time,
   (c) the gearbox is not able to set a gear in time,
   (d) the gearbox is not able to release a gear in time.

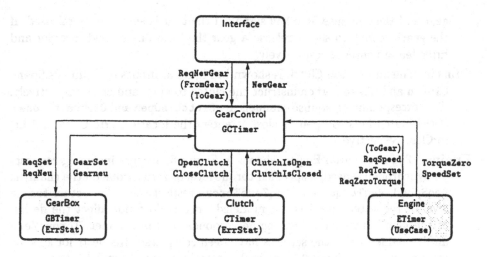

Fig. 3. A Flow-Graph of the Gearbox System.

5 Formal Description of the System

To design and analyze the gear controller we model the controller and its environment in the UPPAAL model [7]. The modeling phase has been separated in two steps. First a model of the environment is created, as its behavior is specified in advance as assumptions (see Section 4). Secondly, the controller itself and its interface are designed to be functionally correct in the given environment. Figure 3 shows a flow-graph of the resulting model where nodes represent automata and edges represent synchronization channels or shared variables (enclosed within parenthesis). The gear controller and its interface are modeled by the automata GearControl (GC) and Interface (I). The environment is modeled by the three automata: Clutch (C), Engine (E), and GearBox (GB).

The system uses six variables. Four are timers that measure 1/1000 of seconds (ms): GCTimer, GBTimer, CTimer and ETimer. The two other variables, named FromGear and ToGear, are used at gear change requests[5]. In the following we describe the five automata of the system.

Environment. The three automata of the environment model the basic functionality and time behavior of the components in the environment. The components have two channels associated with each service: one for requests and one to respond when service have been performed.

Gearbox: In automaton GearBox, shown in Figure 8, inputs on channel ReqSet request a gear set and the corresponding response on GearSet is output if the gear is successfully set. Similarly, the channel ReqNeu requests the neutral

---

[5] The domains of FromGear and ToGear are bounded to $\{0, ..., 6\}$, where 1 to 5 represent gear 1 to gear 5, 0 represents gear N, and 6 is the reverse gear.

gear and the response `GearNeu` signals if the gear is successfully released. If the gearbox fails to set or release a gear the locations named ErrorSet and ErrorNeu are entered respectively.

Clutch: The automaton Clutch is shown in Figure 5. Inputs on channels `Open-Clutch` and `CloseClutch` instruct the clutch to open and close respectively. The corresponding response channels are `ClutchIsOpen` and `ClutchIsClosed`. If the clutch fails to open or close it enters the location ErrorOpen and ErrorClose respectively.

Engine: The automaton Engine, shown in Figure 6, accepts incoming requests for synchronous speed, a specified torque level or zero torque on the channels `ReqSpeed`, `ReqTorque` and `ReqZeroTorque` respectively. The actual torque level or requested speed is not modeled since it does not affect the design of the gear controller[6]. The engine responds on the channels `TorqueZero` and `SpeedSet` when the services have been completed. Requests for specific torque levels (i.e. signal `ReqTorque`) are not answered, instead torque is assumed to increase immediately after the request. If the engine fails to deliver zero torque or synchronous speed in time, it enters location CluthOpen without responding to the request. Similarly, the location ErrorSpeed is entered if the engine regulates on synchronous speed in too long time.

Functionality. Given the formal model of the environment, the gear controller has been designed to satisfy both the functionality requirements given in Section 4, and the correctness requirements in Section 4.1

Gear Controller: The GearControl automaton is shown in Figure 4. Each main loop implements a gear change by interacting with the components of the environment. The designed controller measures response times from the components to detect errors (as failures are not signaled). The reaction of the controller depends on how serious the occurred error is. It either recovers the system from the error, or terminates in a pre-specified location that points out the (unrecoverable) error: COpenError, CCloseError, GNeuError or GSetError. Recoverable errors are detected in the locations CheckTorque and CheckSyncSpeed.

Interface: The automaton Interface requests gears R, N, 1, ..., 5 from the gear controller. A change from gear 1 to gear 2 is shown in Figure 7. Requests and responses are sent through channel `ReqNewGear` and channel `NewGear` respectively. When a request is sent, the shared variables `FromGear` and `ToGear` are assigned values corresponding to the current and the requested new gear respectively.

---

[6] Hence, the time bound for finding zero torque (i.e. 400 ms) should hold when decreasing from an arbitrary torque level.

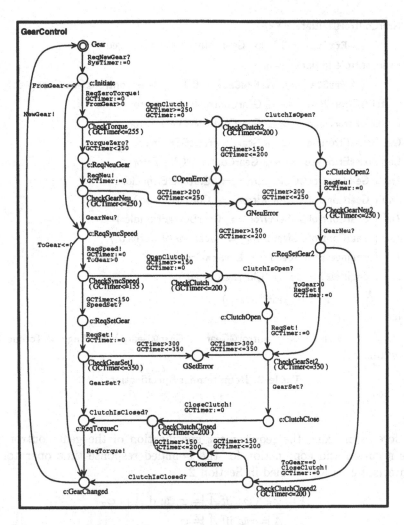

Fig. 4. The Gear Box Controller Automaton.

6 Formal Validation and Verification

In this section we formalize the informal requirements given in Section 4.1 and prove their correctness using the symbolic model-checker of UPPAAL.

To enable formalization (and verification) of requirements, we decorate the system description with two integer variables, ErrStat and UseCase. The variable ErrStat is assigned values at unrecoverable errors: 1 if Clutch fails to close, 2 if Clutch fails to open, 3 if GearBox fails to set a gear, and 4 if GearBox fails to release a gear. The variable UseCase is assigned values whenever a recoverable error occurs in Engine: 1 if it fail to deliver zero torque, and 2 if it is not able to find synchronous speed. The system model is also decorated to enable verification of bounded response time properties, as described in Section 2.

GearControl@Initiate $\leadsto_{\leq 1500}$

$\qquad$ ((ErrStat = 0) $\Rightarrow$ GearControl@GearChanged) $\qquad$ (1)

GearControl@Initiate $\leadsto_{\leq 1000}$

$\qquad$ ((ErrStat = 0 $\wedge$ UseCase = 0) $\Rightarrow$ GearControl@GearChanged) $\qquad$ (2)

Clutch@ErrorClose $\leadsto_{\leq 200}$ GearControl@CCloseError $\qquad$ (3)

Clutch@ErrorOpen $\leadsto_{\leq 200}$ GearControl@COpenError $\qquad$ (4)

GearBox@ErrorIdle $\leadsto_{\leq 350}$ GearControl@GSetError $\qquad$ (5)

GearBox@ErrorNeu $\leadsto_{\leq 200}$ GearControl@GNeuError $\qquad$ (6)

Inv (GearControl@CCloseError $\Rightarrow$ Clutch@ErrorClose) $\qquad$ (7)

Inv (GearControl@COpenError $\Rightarrow$ Clutch@ErrorOpen) $\qquad$ (8)

Inv (GearControl@GSetError $\Rightarrow$ GearBox@ErrorIdle) $\qquad$ (9)

Inv (GearControl@GNeuError $\Rightarrow$ GearBox@ErrorNeu) $\qquad$ (10)

Inv (Engine@ErrorSpeed $\Rightarrow$ ErrStat $\neq 0$) $\qquad$ (11)

Inv (Engine@Torque $\Rightarrow$ Clutch@Closed) $\qquad$ (12)

$$\bigwedge_{i \in \{R,N,1,\ldots,5\}} Poss\ (\ Gear@Gear_i\ ) \qquad (13)$$

$$\bigwedge_{i \in \{R,1,\ldots,5\}} Inv\ (\ (\ GearControl@Gear \wedge Gear@Gear_i\ ) \Rightarrow Engine@Torque\ ) \qquad (14)$$

Table 2. Requirement Specification

Before formalizing the requirement specification of the gear controller we define negation and conjunction for the bounded response time operator and the invariant operator defined in Section 2,

$$\overline{A} \models \varphi_1 \wedge \varphi_2 \text{ iff } \overline{A} \models \varphi_1 \text{ and } \overline{A} \models \varphi_2$$
$$\overline{A} \models \neg\varphi \text{ iff } \overline{A} \not\models \varphi$$

We also extend the (implicit) proposition $at(l)$ to $at(A, l)$, meaning that the control location of automaton A is currently l. Finally, we introduce $Poss(f)$ to denote $\neg Inv(\neg f)$, $f_1 \not\leadsto_{\leq T} f_2$ to denote $\neg(f_1 \leadsto_{\leq T} f_2)$, and $A@l$ to denote $at(A, l)$. We are now ready to formalize the requirements.

6.1 Requirement Specification

The first performance requirement 1a, i.e. that a gear change must be completed within 1.5 seconds given that no unrecoverable errors occur, is specified in property 1. It requires the location GearChanged in automaton GearControl to be reached within 1.5 seconds after location Initiate has been entered. Only scenarios without unrecoverable errors are considered as the value of the variable

`ErrStat` is specified to be zero[7]. To consider scenarios with normal operation
we restrict also the value of variable `UseCase` to zero (i.e. no recoverable errors
occurs). Property 2 requires gear changes to be completed within one second
given that the system is operating normally.

The properties 3 to 6 require the system to terminate in known error-locations
that point out the specific error when errors occur in the clutch or the gear (requirements 4a to 4d). Up to 350 ms is allowed to elapse between the occurrence
of an error and that the error is indicated in the gear controller. The properties 7 to 10 restrict the controller design to indicate an error *only* when the
corresponding error has arisen in the components. Observe that no specific location in the gear controller is dedicated to indicate the unrecoverable error that
may occur when the engines speed-regulation is interrupted (i.e. when location
`Engine@ErrorSpeed` is reached). Property 11 requires that no such location is
needed since this error is always a consequence of a preceding unrecoverable
error in the clutch or in the gear.

Property 13 holds if the system is able to use all gears (requirement 3a).
Furthermore, for full functionality and predictability, the system is required to be
dead-lock and live-lock free (requirement 2a). In this report, dead-lock and live-
lock properties are not specified due to lack of space. However, property 1 (and
2) guarantee progress within bounded time if no unrecoverable error causes the
system to terminate. The properties 12 and 14 specify the informal predictability
requirements 2b and 2c.

A number of functionality requirements specify how the gear controller should
interact with the environment (e.g. 3a to 3f). These requirements have been used
to design the gear controller. They have later been validated using the simulator
in UPPAAL and have not been formally specified and verified.

Time Bound Derivation. Property 1 requires that a gear change should be
performed within one second. Even though this is an interesting property in itself
one may ask for the *lowest* time bound for which a gear change is *guaranteed*. We
show that the time bound is 900 ms for error-free scenarios by proving that the
change is guaranteed at 900 ms (property 15), and that the change is possibly
not completed at 899 ms (property 16). Similarly, for scenarios when the engine
fails to deliver zero torque we derive the bound 1055 ms, and if synchronous
speed is not delivered in the engine the time bound is 1205 ms.

We have shown the shortest time for which a gear change is *possible* in the
three scenarios to be: 150 ms, 550 ms, and 450 ms. However, gear changes involving neutral gear may be faster as the gear does not have to be released (when
changing from gear neutral) or set (when changing to gear neutral). Finally we
consider the same three scenarios but without involving neutral gear by constraining the values of the variables `FromGear` and `ToGear`. The derived time
bounds are: 400 ms, 700 ms and 750.

---

[7] Recall that the variable `ErrStat` is assigned a positive value (i.e. greater than zero)
whenever an unrecoverable error occurs.

GearControl@Initiate $\leadsto_{<900}$

$$((\texttt{ErrStat} = 0 \ \wedge \ \texttt{UseCase} = 0) \ \Rightarrow \ \text{GearControl@GearChanged}) \quad (15)$$

GearControl@Initiate $\not\leadsto_{\leq 899}$

$$((\texttt{ErrStat} = 0 \ \wedge \ \texttt{UseCase} = 0) \ \Rightarrow \ \text{GearControl@GearChanged}) \quad (16)$$

Table 3. Time Bounds

Verification Results. We have verified totally 46 properties of the system[8] using UPPAAL installed on a 75 MHz Pentium PC equipped with 24 MB of primary memory. The verification of all the properties consumed 2.99 second.

7 Conclusion

In this paper, we have reported an industrial case study in applying formal techniques for the design and analysis of control systems for vehicles. The main output of the case-study is a formally described gear controller and a set of formal requirements. The designed controller has been validated and verified using the tool UPPAAL to satisfy the safety and functionality requirements on the controller, provided by Mecel AB. It may be considered as one piece of evidence that the validation and verification tools of today are mature enough to be applied in industrial projects.

We have given a detailed description of the formal model of the gear controller and its surrounding environment, and its correctness formalized in 46 logical formulas according to the informal requirements delivered by industry. The verification was performed in a few seconds on a Pentium PC running UPPAAL version 2.12.2. Another contribution of this paper is a solution to a problem we got in this case study, namely how to use a tool like UPPAAL, which only provides reachability analysis to verify bounded response time properties. We have presented a logic and a method to characterize and model–check such properties by reachability analysis in combination with simple syntactical manipulation on the system description.

This work concerns only one component, namely gear controller of a control system for vehicles. Future work, naturally include modelling and verification of the whole control system. The project is still in progress. We hope to report more in the near future on the project.

References

1. R. Alur and D. Dill. Automata for Modelling Real-Time Systems. *Theoretical Computer Science*, 126(2):183–236, April 1994.

---

[8] A complete list of the verified properties can be found in the full version of this paper.

2. Johan Bengtsson, David Griffioen, Kåre Kristoffersen, Kim G. Larsen, Fredrik Larsson, Paul Pettersson, and Wang Yi. Verification of an Audio Protocol with Bus Collision Using UPPAAL. In Rajeev Alur and Thomas A. Henzinger, editors, *Proc. of 8th Int. Conf. on Computer Aided Verification*, number 1102 in Lecture Notes in Computer Science, pages 244–256. Springer–Verlag, July 1996.

3. Johan Bengtsson, Kim G. Larsen, Fredrik Larsson, Paul Pettersson, and Wang Yi. UPPAAL in 1995. In *Proc. of the 2nd Workshop on Tools and Algorithms for the Construction and Analysis of Systems*, number 1055 in Lecture Notes in Computer Science, pages 431–434. Springer–Verlag, Mars 1996.

4. C. Daws, A. Olivero, S. Tripakis, and S. Yovine. The tool KRONOS. In Rajeev Alur, Thomas A. Henzinger, and Eduardo D. Sontag, editors, *Proc. of Workshop on Verification and Control of Hybrid Systems III*, Lecture Notes in Computer Science, pages 208–219. Springer–Verlag, October 1995.

5. Thomas A. Henzinger, Pei-Hsin Ho, and Howard Wong-Toi. HyTECH: The Next Generation. In *Proc. of the 16th IEEE Real-Time Systems Symposium*, pages 56–65, December 1995.

6. H.E. Jensen, K.G. Larsen, and A. Skou. Modelling and Analysis of a Collision Avoidance Protocol Using SPIN and UPPAAL. In *Proc. of 2nd International Workshop on the SPIN Verification System*, pages 1–20, August 1996.

7. Kim G. Larsen, Paul Pettersson, and Wang Yi. UPPAAL in a Nutshell. To appear in *International Journal on Software Tools for Technology Transfer*, 1998.

8. Thomas Stauner, Olaf Mller, and Max Fuchs. Using hytech to verify an automotive control system. In *Proc. Hybrid and Real-Time Systems, Grenoble, March 26-28, 1997*. Technische Universität München, Lecture Notes in Computer Science, Springer, 1997.

Appendix: The System Description

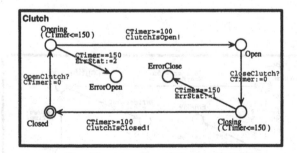

Fig. 5. The Clutch Automaton.

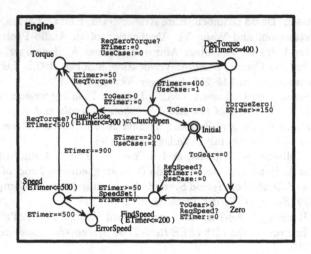

Fig. 6. The Engine Automaton.

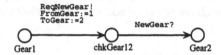

Fig. 7. The Interface Automaton: a gear change.

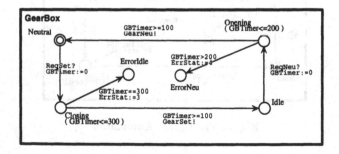

Fig. 8. The Gearbox Automaton.

Verifying Networks of Timed Processes
(Extended Abstract)

Parosh Aziz Abdulla and Bengt Jonsson

Dept. of Computer Systems
Uppsala University
P.O. Box 325, S-751 05 Uppsala, Sweden
{parosh,bengt}@docs.uu.se,
WWW: http://www.docs.uu.se/~{parosh,bengt}

Abstract. Over the last years there has been an increasing research
effort directed towards the automatic verification of infinite state systems, such as timed automata, hybrid automata, data-independent systems, relational automata, Petri nets, and lossy channel systems. We
present a method for deciding reachability properties of networks of
timed processes. Such a network consists of an arbitrary set of identical
timed automata, each with a single real-valued clock. Using a standard
reduction from safety properties to reachability properties, we can use
our algorithm to decide general safety properties of timed networks. To
our knowledge, this is the first decidability result concerning verification
of systems that are infinite-state in "two dimensions": they contain an arbitrary set of (identical) processes, and they use infinite data-structures,
viz. real-valued clocks. We illustrate our method by showing how it can
be used to automatically verify Fischer's protocol, a timer-based protocol
for enforcing mutual exclusion among an arbitrary number of processes.

1 Introduction

The last decade has seen much progress with regard to automated verification of
reactive programs. The most dramatic advances have been obtained for finite-
state programs. However, methods and algorithms are now emerging for the
automatic verification of infinite state programs. There are at least two ways in
which a program can be infinite-state. A program can be infinite-state because
it operates on data structures from a potentially infinite domain, e.g., integers,
stacks, queues, etc. Nontrivial verification algorithms have been developed for
several classes of such systems, notably timed automata [ACD90], hybrid automata [Hen95], data-independent systems [JP93,Wol86], relational automata
([Čer94]), Petri nets ([JM95]), pushdown processes ([BS95]) and lossy channel
systems [AJ96,AK95]. A program can also be infinite-state because it is intended
to run on a network with an arbitrary number of nodes, i.e., the the program is
parameterized with respect to the topology of the network of nodes. In this case,
one would like to verify correctness for any number of components and any interconnection topology. Verification algorithms have been developed for systems

consisting of an unbounded number of similar or identical finite-state processes ([GS92]), and (using a manually supplied induction hypothesis) for more general classes of parameterized systems [CGJ95,KM89].

In this paper, we will present an algorithm for verifying safety properties of a class of programs, which we call *timed networks*. A timed network is a system consisting of an arbitrary set of processes, each of which is a finite-state system operating on a real-valued clock. Each process could roughly be considered as a timed automaton [ACD90] with a single clock. In addition, our model also allows a central finite-state process, called a *controller*. Timed networks embody both of the two reasons for being infinite-state: they use an infinite data structure (namely clocks which can assume values from the set of real numbers), and they are parameterized in allowing an arbitrary set of processes. To our knowledge, this is the first decidability result concerning verification of networks of infinite-state processes.

We present an algorithm for deciding reachability properties of timed networks. Using a standard reduction (described e.g., in [VW86]) from safety properties to reachability properties, we can use this algorithm to decide general safety properties of timed networks. To decide reachability, we adapt a standard symbolic verification algorithm which has been used e.g., in model-checking [CES86]. A rough description of this method is that in order to check whether a state in some set F is reachable, we compute the set of all states from which a state in F is reachable. This computation is performed using a standard fixedpoint iteration, where for successively larger j we compute the set of states from which a state in F can be reached by a sequence of transitions of length less than or equal to j. More precisely, we obtain the $(j + 1)$st approximation from the jth approximation by adding the *pre-image* of the jth approximation, i.e., the set of states from which a state in the jth approximation can be reached by some transition. If this procedure converges, one checks whether the result intersects the set of initial states of the model. The heart of our result is solving the following three problems:

- finding a suitable representation of infinite sets of states,
- finding a method for computing pre-images, and
- proving that the iteration always converges.

To represent sets of states, we use constraints which generalize the notion of regions used to verify properties of (non-parameterized) timed automata [ACD90]. A constraint represents conditions on a potentially unbounded number of processes and their clocks. In contrast to the situation for timed automata [ACD90], where for each program there are finitely many regions, there is in general an infinite number of constraints that can appear in the analysis of a given timed network. To handle this, we introduce an entailment ordering on contraints. The key step in our proof of decidability consists in proving that this relation is a well quasi-ordering, implying that the the above mentioned fixedpoint iteration converges.

Our results also demonstrate the strength and applicability of the general framework described in [AČJYK96,Fin90]. Using that framework, we can conclude the decidability of eventuality properties (of the form $\mathrm{AF}p$ in CTL). for timed networks, and the question of whether or not a timed network simulates or is simulated by a finite-state system. We will not further consider these questions in this paper.

Our model of timed networks is related to other formalisms for timed systems, notably time or timed Petri nets [GMMP91,BD91] and Timed CCS [Yi91]. Our decidability result can be translated to decidability results for variants of these formalisms. It is known that reachability is undecidable for time Petri nets. This is due to the inclusion of *urgency* in the Petri net model. Urgency means that a transition is forced to execute within a specified timeout period. In our model transitions can not be forced to occur; a timeout can only specify that a transition is executed within a specified time period *if* it is executed. Urgency allows the model to test for emptiness of a place, thus leading to undecidability. A similar difference holds in comparison with Timed CCS.

As an illustration of our method, we model Fischer's protocol and show how an automatic verification algorithm would go about verifying mutual exclusion. Several tools for verifying automata with a fixed number of clocks have been used to verify the protocol for an increasing number of processes (e.g., [ACHH92]). Kristoffersen et al. [KLL+97] describes an experiment where the number of processes is 50. In [LSW95], a constraint-based proof methodology is used to perform a manual verification of the protocol.

Outline The rest of the paper is structured as follows. In the next section, we present our model of timed networks. An overview of the reachability algorithm is presented in Section 3. In Section 4, we present our constraint system. In Section 5, we present a procedure for calculating the pre-image of a set of states which are represented by a constraint. In Section 6 we prove that the entailment ordering on the constraint system is a well quasi-ordering, which implies that our algorithm always terminates. An application of the reachability algorithm to the verification of Fischer's protocol is given in Section 7.

2 Timed Networks

In this section, we will define networks of timed processes. Intuitively, a network of timed processes consists of a *controller* and an arbitrarily large set of identical (timed) *processes*. The controller is a finite-state transition system. Each process has a finite-state control part, and an unbounded data structure, namely a real-valued clock[1]. The values of the clocks of the processes are incremented continuously at the same rate. In addition to letting time pass by incrementing the clocks, the network can change its configuration according to a finite number of *rules*. Each rule describes a set of transitions in which the controller and an arbitrary but fixed-size set of processes synchronize and simultaneously change their states. A rule may be conditioned on the control states of the participating

---

[1] The controller could also be equipped with a timer, but this aspect is not central to our result, so we will omit it.

controller and processes, and on conditions on the clock values of the participating processes. If the conditions for a rule are satisfied, the controller and each participating process may change its state and (optionally) reset its clock to 0.

We are interested in verifying correctness of a network regardless of its size. The actual object of study will therefore be a *family* of networks, where the number of processes is not given. A family merely defines the controller and process states together with a set of rules. The parameter (i.e., size) of the network will be introduced later, when we define configurations.

We use $\mathcal{N}$ and $\mathcal{R}^{\geq 0}$ to denote the sets of natural numbers and nonnegative reals respectively. For $n \in \mathcal{N}$, we use $\hat{n}$ to denote the set $\{1, \ldots, n\}$. A *guarded command* is of the form $p(x) \longrightarrow op$, where $p(x)$ is a boolean combination of predicates of the form $k < x$, $k \leq x$, $k > x$, or $k \geq x$ for $k \in \mathcal{N}$, and $op \in \{reset, skip\}$.

Definition 1. *A family of timed networks (timed network for short) is a triple* $\langle C, Q, R \rangle$*, where:*

C *is a finite set of* controller *states.*
Q *is a finite set of* process *states.*
R *is a finite set of* rules. *A rule* r *is of the form*

$$\langle \langle c, c' \rangle, \langle q_1, stmt_1, q'_1 \rangle, \ldots, \langle q_n, stmt_n, q'_n \rangle \rangle$$

where $c, c' \in C$*,* $q_i, q'_i \in Q$*, and* $stmt_i$ *is a guarded command.*

Intuitively, the set C represents the set of states of the controller. The set Q represents the set of states of each of the identical processes. A rule r describes a set of transitions of the network. The rule is enabled if the state of the controller is c, and if there are n processes with states $q_1, \ldots, q_n$, respectively, whose clock values satisfy the corresponding guards. The rule is executed by simultaneously changing the state of the controller to c', changing the states of the n processes to $q'_1, \ldots, q'_n$ respectively, and modifying values of the clocks according to the relevant guarded commands.

Definition 2. *A configuration* γ *of a timed network* $\langle C, Q, R \rangle$ *is a quadruple of form* $\langle I, c, \mathbf{q}, \mathbf{x} \rangle$*, where* I *is a finite index set,* $c \in C$*,* $\mathbf{q}: I \to Q$*, and* $\mathbf{x}: I \to \mathcal{R}^{\geq 0}$*.*

Intuitively, I is the set of indices of processes in the network. The index set does not change when performing transitions. Each element in I will be used as an index to represent one particular process in the network. Thus, we can say that a timed network defines a family of networks parametrized by I^2. The state of the controller is given by c, the states of the processes are given by the mapping $\mathbf{q}$ from indices to process states, and the clock values are given by the mapping $\mathbf{x}$ from indices to nonnegative real numbers.

---

[2] We can extend our model to include dynamic creation and destruction of processes, by allowing the set of indices in a configuration to change dynamically. Our decidability result holds also for such an extension. However, we will not consider that in the present paper.

A timed network changes its configuration by performing transitions. We will define a transition relation $\longrightarrow$ as the union of a *discrete* transition relation $\longrightarrow_D$, representing transitions caused by the rules, and a *timed* transition relation $\longrightarrow_T$ which represents the passage of time. The discrete relation $\longrightarrow_D$ will furthermore be the union of transition relations $\overset{r}{\longrightarrow}_D$ corresponding to each rule r, i.e.,
$$\longrightarrow_D = \bigcup_{r \in R} \overset{r}{\longrightarrow}_D.$$

Definition 3. *Let* $r = \langle \langle c, c' \rangle, \langle q_1, stmt_1, q'_1 \rangle, \ldots, \langle q_n, stmt_n, q'_n \rangle \rangle$ *be a rule where* $stmt_i$ *is of form* $p_i(x) \longrightarrow op_i$ *for* $i = 1, \ldots, n$. *Consider two configurations* $\gamma = \langle I, c, \mathbf{q}, \mathbf{x} \rangle$ *and* $\gamma' = \langle I, c', \mathbf{q}', \mathbf{x}' \rangle$, *with the same index sets, and where the controller states of* γ *and* γ' *are the same as the controller states in the rule* r. *We use* $\gamma \overset{r}{\longrightarrow}_D \gamma'$ *to denote that there is an injection* $h : \hat{n} \to I$ *from indices of the rule* r *to indices of the network such that*

1. $\mathbf{q}(h(i)) = q_i$, *and* $p_i(\mathbf{x}(h(i)))$ *holds for each* $i \in \hat{n}$,
2. $\mathbf{q}'(h(i)) = q'_i$ *for* $i \in \hat{n}$,
3. $\mathbf{q}'(j) = \mathbf{q}(j)$ *for* $j \in (I \setminus range(h))$,
4. $\mathbf{x}'(h(i)) = 0$ *for* $i \in \hat{n}$ *with* $op_i = reset$,
5. $\mathbf{x}'(h(i)) = \mathbf{x}(h(i))$ *for* $i \in \hat{n}$ *with* $op_i = skip$, *and*
6. $\mathbf{x}'(j) = \mathbf{x}(j)$ *for* $j \in (I \setminus range(h))$.

The first condition asserts that r is enabled, i.e., that the process states $q_1, \ldots, q_n$ are matched by the corresponding process states in the configuration γ and that the corresponding guarded commands are enabled. The second condition means that in the transition from γ to γ', the states of processes that are matched (by h) with indices of r are changed according to r. The third condition asserts that the states of the other processes are unchanged. The fourth condition asserts that in the transition from γ to γ', the clock values of processes that are matched (by h) with indices of r are set to 0 if the corresponding guarded command contains *reset*, the fifth asserts that clocks are unchanged if the guarded command contains *skip*. The last condition asserts that clock values of unmatched processes are unchanged.

Let $\gamma = \langle I, c, \mathbf{q}, \mathbf{x} \rangle$ be configuration. For $\delta \in \mathcal{R}^{\geq 0}$, we use $\gamma^{+\delta}$ to denote the configuration $\langle I, c, \mathbf{q}, \mathbf{x}' \rangle$, where $x'(j) = x(j) + \delta$ for each $j \in I$. We say that γ performs a *timed transition* to a configuration γ', denoted $\gamma \longrightarrow_T \gamma'$, if there is a $\delta \in \mathcal{R}^{\geq 0}$ such that $\gamma' = \gamma^{+\delta}$. We use $\gamma \longrightarrow \gamma'$ to denote that either $\gamma \longrightarrow_D \gamma'$ or $\gamma \longrightarrow_T \gamma'$. We use $\overset{*}{\longrightarrow}$ to denote the reflexive transitive closure of $\longrightarrow$.

3 Overview of the Reachability Algorithm

In this section we define the reachability problem, and give an overview of our method for solving it. Given a timed network $\langle C, Q, R \rangle$ together with states $c_{init} \in C$ and $q_{init} \in Q$ which we call *the initial controller state* and *the initial process state* respectively, we define an *initial configuration* γ_{init} of the timed network $\langle C, Q, R \rangle$ as a configuration of the form $\langle I, c_{init}, \mathbf{q}_{init}, \mathbf{x}_{init} \rangle$ where

$q_{init}(j) = q_{init}$ and $x_{init}(j) = 0$ for each $j \in I$. Thus, there is one initial configuration for each possible index set I. We say that a configuration γ is *reachable*
if $\gamma_{init} \xrightarrow{*} \gamma$, for some initial configuration γ_{init}. We say that a set Γ of configurations is *reachable* if there is a reachable $\gamma \in \Gamma$.

We will present an algorithm for deciding whether a set Γ of configurations of
a timed network is reachable. Note that in general, Γ will contain configurations
of networks with infinitely many different sizes, where the size of a configuration
is given by its index set. This means that we ask whether there is *some* size of
the network such that a configuration with this size (as given by its index set)
is reachable. In a typical situation, we are interested in verifying that Γ is an
unreachable set of "bad" configurations, irrespective of the size of the network.
If we include in Γ the bad configurations of all possible network sizes, and if
our analysis finds Γ to be unreachable, this means that we have verified that
the configurations in Γ are unreachable for all possible sizes of the network. For
instance, we can verify correctness of an n-process mutual exclusion algorithm
for all values of n simultaneously.

In Section 4, we will define a class of constraints for representing sets of configurations. A constraint ϕ denotes a (possibly infinite) set $[\![\phi]\!]$ of configurations.
A finite set $\Phi = \{\phi_1, \ldots, \phi_n\}$ of constraints denotes the union of the denotations
of its elements, i.e., $[\![\Phi]\!] = \bigcup_{i=1}^{n} [\![\phi_i]\!]$. Formally, the reachability problem is defined
as follows.

Instance: A timed network $\langle C, Q, R \rangle$, an initial controller state c_{init}, an initial
process state q_{init} and a finite set Φ of constraints.
Question: Does $[\![\Phi]\!]$ contain a reachable configuration?

To check the reachability of Φ we perform a reachability analysis backwards.
Let $pre(\phi)$ denote the set $\{\gamma : \exists \gamma' \in [\![\phi]\!] : \gamma \longrightarrow \gamma'\}$, and $pre(\Phi)$ denote the set
$\{\gamma : \exists \gamma' \in [\![\Phi]\!] : \gamma \longrightarrow \gamma'\}$. Note that $pre(\Phi)$ is equivalent to $\cup_{\phi \in \Phi} pre(\phi)$. Starting from Φ we define the sequence $\Phi_0, \Phi_1, \Phi_2, \ldots$ of finite sets of constraints by
$\Phi_0 = \Phi$ and $\Phi_{j+1} = \Phi_j \cup pre(\Phi_j)$. Intuitively, Φ_j denotes the set of configurations
from which Φ is reachable by a sequence of at most j transitions. Note that the
sequence is increasing i.e., that $[\![\Phi_0]\!] \subseteq [\![\Phi_1]\!] \subseteq [\![\Phi_2]\!] \subseteq \cdots$. In the next paragraph,
we will prove that the iteration converges (using Theorem 4), i.e., that there is
a k such that $[\![\Phi_k]\!] = [\![\Phi_{k+1}]\!]$, implying that $[\![\Phi_k]\!] = [\![\Phi_j]\!]$ for all $j \geq k$. It follows
that Φ is reachable if and only if there is an initial configuration γ_{init} such that
$\gamma_{init} \in [\![\Phi_k]\!]$, which is easily checked since Φ_k is a *finite* set of constraints.

To prove convergence, we introduce, in Definition 6, a quasi-order $\preceq$ on con-
straints by defining $\phi \preceq \phi'$ to denote that $[\![\phi']\!] \subseteq [\![\phi]\!]$. In Theorem 4, we will
show that $\preceq$ is a well quasi-ordering on the set of constraints, i.e., that in any
infinite sequence $\phi_0 \, \phi_1 \, \phi_2 \, \cdots$ of constraints, there are indices $i < j$ such that
$\phi_i \preceq \phi_j$. This implies that any increasing sequence $[\![\Phi_0]\!] \subseteq [\![\Phi_1]\!] \subseteq [\![\Phi_2]\!] \subseteq \cdots$ of
finite sets of constraints will converge, since otherwise we could extract an infi-
nite sequence $\phi_0 \, \phi_1 \, \phi_2 \, \cdots$ of constraints (where ϕ_i is chosen such that $\phi_i \in \Phi_i$
but $[\![\phi_i]\!] \not\subseteq [\![\Phi_{i-1}]\!]$) for which there are no indices $i < j$ such that $\phi_i \preceq \phi_j$.

Summarizing, we have established the following theorem

Theorem 1. *The reachability problem for families of timed networks is decidable*

Proof. Follows from the preceding discussion, using Theorem 2 (decidability of $\preceq$), Theorem 3 (computability of *pre*) and Theorem 4 (well quasi-orderedness of $\preceq$).

The following sections contain the above mentioned definitions and lemmas. In Section 4, we define the constraint system. In Section 5, we show that $pre(\phi)$ can be computed and represented by a finite set of constraints whenever ϕ is a contraint. Finally, in Section 6, we show that the relation $\preceq$ is a well quasi-ordering on the set of constraints.

4 A Constraint System for Timed Networks

In this section we introduce a constraint system for timed networks. Our constraint system generalizes the notion of regions, employed for the analysis of timed automata [ACD90]. We use a representation of constraints, which is similar to a representation of regions used by Godskesen [God94].

For a quasi-order $\sqsubseteq^3$ on some set, we use $a_1 \equiv a_2$ to denote that $a_1 \sqsubseteq a_2$ and $a_2 \sqsubseteq a_1$, and use $a_1 \sqsubset a_2$ to denote that $a_1 \sqsubseteq a_2$ and $a_2 \not\sqsubseteq a_1$. For a real number $x \in \mathcal{R}^{\geq 0}$, let $\lfloor x \rfloor$ denote its integer part, and let $fract(x)$ denote its fractional part.

Definition 4. *Let $\langle C, Q, R \rangle$ be a family of timed networks. Let max be the maximum constant occurring in the guarded commands in R. A constraint ϕ of $\langle C, Q, R \rangle$ is a tuple $\langle c, m, \mathbf{q}, \mathbf{k}, \sqsubseteq \rangle$ where*

- $c \in C$ *is a controller state,*
- *m is a natural number, where $\widehat{m}$ intuitively denotes a set of indices of processes constrained by ϕ,*
- *$\mathbf{q} : \widehat{m} \mapsto Q$ is a mapping from indices to process states,*
- *$\mathbf{k} : \widehat{m} \mapsto \{0, \ldots, max\}$ maps each index to a natural number not greater than max,*
- *$\sqsubseteq$ is a quasi-order on the set $\widehat{m} \cup \{\bot, \top\}$ which satisfies*
  - *the elements $\bot$ and $\top$ are minimal and maximal elements of $\sqsubseteq$, respectively, with $\bot \sqsubset \top$ [4],*
  - *$j \equiv \bot$ or $j \equiv \top$ whenever $\mathbf{k}(j) = max$, for $j \in \widehat{m}$, and*
  - *$\mathbf{k}(j) = max$ whenever $j \equiv \top$, for $j \in \widehat{m}$.*

Intuitively, a constraint denotes a set of configurations of networks in the family. The constraint $\langle c, m, \mathbf{q}, \mathbf{k}, \sqsubseteq \rangle$ represents the set of configurations with controller state c in which each index $j \in \widehat{m}$ represents a process which has control state $\mathbf{q}(j)$, for which $\mathbf{k}(j)$ is either *max* or the integer part of its clock, whichever

---

[3] A quasi-order is a reflexive and transitive relation.
[4] Note that $\bot, \top \notin \widehat{m}$.

is least, for which $j \equiv \perp$ iff the integer part of the clock is at most max and the fractional part of the clock is 0, and for which $j \equiv \top$ iff the clock value is more than max. Furthermore, the fractional parts of the clocks corresponding to indices j with $j \sqsubset \top$ are ordered exactly according to $\sqsubseteq$. This implies, among other things, that for clock values that are larger than max, a constraint gives no information about the difference between the actual clock value and max. The meaning of constraints is made formal in the following definition.

Definition 5. *Let $\phi = \langle c, m, \mathbf{q}, \mathbf{k}, \sqsubseteq \rangle$ be a constraint and let $\gamma = \langle I, c, \mathbf{q}, \mathbf{x} \rangle$ be a configuration[5]. We define $\gamma \in \llbracket \phi \rrbracket$ to mean that there is an injection $h : \hat{m} \mapsto I$ from the indices of ϕ to the indices of γ such that for all $j, j_1, j_2 \in \hat{m}$*

- $\mathbf{q}(h(j)) = \mathbf{q}(j)$,
- $\min(max, \lfloor \mathbf{x}(h(j)) \rfloor) = \mathbf{k}(j)$,
- $j \equiv \perp$ *if and only if* $\mathbf{x}(h(j)) \leq max$ *and* $fract(\mathbf{x}(h(j))) = 0$,
- $j \equiv \top$ *if and only if* $\mathbf{x}(h(j)) > max$, *and*
- *if* $j_1, j_2 \not\equiv \top$ *then* $fract(\mathbf{x}(h(j_1))) \leq fract(\mathbf{x}(h(j_2)))$ *if and only if* $j_1 \sqsubseteq j_2$.

Note that a constraint ϕ defines conditions on states and clock values which should be satisfied by *some* set of processes (those represented by indices in $range(h)$) in the configuration γ in order for γ to be included in $\llbracket \phi \rrbracket$. The constraint puts no requirements on processes whose indices are outside $range(h)$.

Definition 6. *Define the ordering $\preceq$ on constraints by $\phi \preceq \phi' \overset{def}{=} \llbracket \phi' \rrbracket \subseteq \llbracket \phi \rrbracket$.*

Intuitively, $\phi \preceq \phi'$ means that ϕ' is "stronger" than ϕ, or that ϕ' "entails" ϕ. The following theorem shows how to compute $\preceq$.

Theorem 2. *Let $\phi = \langle c, m, \mathbf{q}, \mathbf{k}, \sqsubseteq \rangle$ and $\phi' = \langle c', m', \mathbf{q}', \mathbf{k}', \sqsubseteq' \rangle$ be constraints. We have $\phi \preceq \phi'$ if and only if there is an injection $g : \hat{m} \mapsto \widehat{m'}$ such that*

- $c = c'$,
- *for all $j \in \hat{m}$ we have*
  - $\mathbf{q}'(g(j)) = \mathbf{q}(j)$,
  - $\mathbf{k}'(g(j)) = \mathbf{k}(j)$,
  - $g(j) \equiv' \perp$ *iff* $j \equiv \perp$,
  - $g(j) \equiv' \top$ *iff* $j \equiv \top$,
- *if $j_1, j_2 \in \hat{m}$ then $g(j_1) \sqsubseteq' g(j_2)$ if and only if $j_1 \sqsubseteq j_2$.*

5 Computing *pre*

In this section we show, for a given constraint ϕ, how to compute $pre(\phi)$, defined as $\{\gamma \;:\; \exists \gamma' \in \llbracket \phi \rrbracket : \gamma \longrightarrow \gamma'\}$. Since the transition relation is the union of a discrete and a timed transition relation, we will compute $pre(\phi)$ as $pre_D(\phi) \cup pre_T(\phi)$, where $pre_D(\phi)$ is the set $\{\gamma \;:\; \exists \gamma' \in \llbracket \phi \rrbracket : \gamma \longrightarrow_D \gamma'\}$, and where $pre_T(\phi)$ is the set $\{\gamma \;:\; \exists \gamma' \in \llbracket \phi \rrbracket : \gamma \longrightarrow_T \gamma'\}$.

---

[5] Observe that the controller states are the same in ϕ and γ.

5.1 Computing pre_D

We will compute $pre_D(\phi')$ as $\cup_{r \in R} pre(r, \phi')$, where $pre(r, \phi')$ denotes the set $\{\gamma \ : \ \exists \gamma' \in \llbracket \phi' \rrbracket : \gamma \xrightarrow{r}_D \gamma'\}$ of configurations from which ϕ' is reachable through a single application of r[6].

Let $r = \langle\langle c, c'\rangle, \langle q_1, p_1(x) \longrightarrow op_1, q_1'\rangle, \ldots, \langle q_n, p_n(x) \longrightarrow op_n, q_n'\rangle\rangle$ and let $\phi' = \langle c', m', \mathbf{q}', \mathbf{k}', \sqsubseteq'\rangle$. We will compute a representation of $pre(r, \phi')$ as a finite set of constraints. Each constraint ϕ with $\llbracket \phi \rrbracket \subseteq pre(r, \phi')$ will be obtained from a particular way of matching indices of ϕ' with indices of r. Each such matching gives rise to a set of constraints ϕ with $\llbracket \phi \rrbracket \subseteq pre(r, \phi')$, namely those constraints that are consistent both with the conditions imposed by ϕ' according to Definition 5, and with the conditions imposed by r according to Definition 3.

Let $p(x)$ be a guard and let $\phi = \langle c, m, \mathbf{q}, \mathbf{k}, \sqsubseteq\rangle$ be a constraint. For $j \in \widehat{m}$, we use $\langle\phi, j\rangle \models p(x)$ to mean that p *is satisfied at index* j *in* ϕ. For instance, if $p(x)$ is of form $k \leq x$ for some $k \in \{0, \ldots, max\}$, then $\langle\phi, j\rangle \models p(x)$ iff $\mathbf{k}(j) \geq k$. We can derive analogous expressions for other forms of $p(x)$.

A matching will be represented by a *partial* injection g' from $\widehat{m'}$ to $\widehat{n}$: each index $j \in domain(g')$ of ϕ' is matched with a unique index $g'(j)$ of r (note that $domain(g') \subseteq \widehat{m'}$). Indices in $(\widehat{m'} \setminus domain(g'))$ represent processes which are constrained by ϕ' but are not matched with any index of r. In the indices of ϕ, we must also include the $n - |range(g')|$ indices of r which are not matched with any index of ϕ'. Thus, let $m = m' + (n - |range(g')|)$ be the number of indices of ϕ. Define an *extension* g of g' to be a *surjective* partial injection $g : \widehat{m} \mapsto \widehat{n}$, with domain $domain(g) = domain(g') \cup (\widehat{m} \setminus m')$, such that $g(j) = g'(j)$ for each $j \in domain(g')$.[7] It follows from the definition of extension that $\widehat{m'} \setminus domain(g')$ is not in $domain(g)$ and that g in addition maps each $j \in (\widehat{m} \setminus \widehat{m'})$ to a unique $g(j) \in (\widehat{n} \setminus range(g'))$.

Lemma 1. *If* $\phi' = \langle c', m', \mathbf{q}', \mathbf{k}', \sqsubseteq'\rangle$ *is a constraint and* r *is a rule, as above, then* $pre(r, \phi')$ *is the denotation of the set of constraints of form* $\phi = \langle c, m, \mathbf{q}, \mathbf{k}, \sqsubseteq\rangle$, *for which there is an extension* g *of a partial injection* g' *from* $\widehat{m'}$ *to* $\widehat{n}$, *where* $m = m' + (n - |range(g')|)$, *which satisfies the following conditions*[8].

1. $\mathbf{q}(j) = q_{g(j)}$ *and* $\langle\phi, j\rangle \models p_{g(j)}(x)$ *for each* $j \in domain(g)$,
2. $\mathbf{q}'(j) = q'_{g'(j)}$ *for* $j \in domain(g')$,
3. $\mathbf{q}'(j) = \mathbf{q}(j)$ *for* $j \in \widehat{m'} \setminus domain(g')$,
4. $\mathbf{k}'(j) = 0$ *and* $j \equiv' \perp$ *if* $j \in domain(g')$ *and* $op_{g'(j)} = reset$,
5. *For all* j *such that either* $j \in domain(g')$ *and* $op_{g'(j)} = skip$, *or such that* $j \in \widehat{m'} \setminus domain(g')$,
   we have $\mathbf{k}'(j) = \mathbf{k}(j)$, *and* $j \equiv' \perp$ *iff* $j \equiv \perp$, *and* $j \equiv' \top$ *iff* $j \equiv \top$.

---

[6] In order to be consistent with the notation in Section 2, we use the primed version of the constraint to refer to the constraint after a transition, and an unprimed version of the constraint to refer to the constraint before a transition.

[7] note that $\widehat{m} \setminus \widehat{m'} = \{m' + 1, m' + 2, \ldots, m\}$

[8] Note that we implicitly require the controller states c and c' of r to coincide with the controller states c and c' of ϕ and ϕ', respectively.

6. For each j_1 and j_2 such that for $i = 1, 2$ either $j_i \in domain(g')$ and $op_{g'(j_i)} =$ skip, or $j_i \in \widehat{m'} \setminus domain(g')$,
   we have $j_1 \sqsubseteq' j_2$ if and only if $j_1 \sqsubseteq j_2$.

The above list of conditions captures the semantics of $\xrightarrow{r}_D$, given the correspondences between the indices of r, ϕ' and ϕ which are given by g and g'. Note the close correspondence between the conditions of the lemma and the conditions of transitions in Definition 3. The conditions on controller states are implicitly included by our notation, which requires that the controller states of ϕ and ϕ' be the controller states of r. Condition 1 state that r must be enabled in a configuration satisfying ϕ. Conditions 2 and 3 capture the conditions on states of the processes: after a transition, states of processes with indices in $domain(g')$ are constrained by 2; and processes with indices in $\widehat{m'} \setminus domain(g')$ are unaffected by the rule (condition 3). Condition 4 describes the effect of a *reset* statement: the clock value becomes 0 in ϕ'. Finally, conditions 5 and 6 assert that for indices that correspond to a *skip* statement, or for indices not matched by r (and hence unaffected by the transition), the clock values are unchanged by a transition.

5.2 Computing pre_T

First, we define a relation pre_t which we later use (Lemma 3) to compute pre_T.

Definition 7. *For a constarint $\phi' = \langle c', m', q', k', \sqsubseteq' \rangle$ we define $pre_t(\phi')$ to be the denotation of the set of constraints of form $\phi = \langle c', m', q', k, \sqsubseteq \rangle$ satisfying either of the following two conditions.*

1. *for some $j \in \widehat{m}$ we have $j \equiv' \bot$, there is no $j \in \widehat{m}$ such that $j \equiv' \bot$ and $k'(j) = 0$, and the following three conditions hold.*
   - $k(j) = k'(j) - 1$ *if $j \equiv' \bot$,*
   - $k(j) = k'(j)$ *if $j \not\equiv' \bot$,*
   - $j_1 \sqsubseteq j_2$ *if and only if either*
     (a) $j_2 \equiv' \top$, *or*
     (b) $j_2 \equiv' \bot$ *and $j_1 \not\equiv' \top$, or*
     (c) $j_1 \sqsubseteq' j_2$ *and $\bot \sqsubseteq' j_1, j_2 \sqsubseteq' \top$.*
2. *There is no $j \in \widehat{m}$ such that $j \equiv' \bot$ and the following four conditions hold:*
   - $k = k'$,
   - *whenever $\bot \sqsubseteq' j_1, j_2 \sqsubseteq' \top$ we have $j_1 \sqsubseteq j_2$ if and only if $j_1 \sqsubseteq' j_2$,*
   - *whenever $j \equiv' \top$ we have $j \equiv \bot$ or $j \equiv \top$,*
   - $\sqsubseteq' \neq \sqsubseteq$.

Intuitively, the first case captures the situation where there are indices with fractional parts of some clocks being 0. The second case captures the situation when no clocks have fractional parts equal to 0.

Lemma 2. *There is no infinite sequence $\phi_0, \phi_1, \phi_2, \ldots$ of constraints, such that $\phi_{i+1} \in pre_t(\phi_i)$.*

Definition 8. *For a set of constraints Φ' and a natural number i, we define $pre_t{}^i(\Phi', i)$ inductively as follows.*

- $pre_t{}^0(\Phi') = \Phi'$; and
- $pre_t{}^{i+1}(\Phi') = \{\phi \;:\; \exists \phi' \in pre_t{}^i(\Phi') : \phi \in pre_t(\phi')\}$.

We define $pre_t{}^*(\Phi') = \cup_{i \geq 0} pre_t{}^i(\Phi')$.

Sometimes we write $pre_t{}^*(\phi')$ instead of $pre_t{}^*(\{\phi'\})$

Lemma 3. *If ϕ' is a constraint, then $pre_T(\phi')$ is the denotation of the set of constraints in the set $pre_t{}^*(\{\phi'\})$. In other words*

$$pre_T(\phi') \;=\; [\![pre_t{}^*(\phi)]\!]$$

The computability of pre_T follows from Lemma 3 and Lemma 2.

5.3 Computing *pre*

By combining the rules for computing $pre_D(\phi)$ in Lemma 1 and the rules for computing $pre_T(\phi)$ in Lemma 3, we obtain the following theorem.

Theorem 3. *If ϕ is a constraint, then we can compute a finite set Φ of constraints such that $[\![\Phi]\!] = pre(\phi)$.*

6 The entailment ordering is a well quasi-ordering

In this section, we shall prove that the preorder $\preceq$ on constraints is a well quasi-ordering. We will first review some standard results from the literature concerning well quasi-orderings ([Hig52]), and then apply them to our constraint system.

Definition 9. *Let A be a set. A quasi-order $\preceq$ on A is a binary relation over A which is reflexive and transitive. A quasi-order $\preceq$ is a well quasi-ordering (wqo) if in each infinite sequence $a_0\; a_1\; a_2\; a_3 \cdots$ of elements in A, there are indices $i < j$ such that $a_i \preceq a_j$.*

We shall now restate two standard lemmas, which allow us to lift well quasi-orderings from elements to bags and to sequences. Let A^* denote the set of finite strings over A, and let Let A^B denote the set of finite bags over A. An element of A^* and of A^B can be represented as a mapping $w : \widehat{|w|} \mapsto A$ where $|w|$ is the size of the bag or the length of the sequence. Given a quasi-order $\preceq$ on a set A, define the quasi-order $\preceq^*$ on A^* by letting $w \preceq^* w'$ if and only if there is a monotone[9] injection $h : \widehat{|w|} \mapsto \widehat{|w'|}$ such that $w(j) \preceq w'(h(j))$ for $1 \leq j \leq |w|$. Define the quasi-order $\preceq^B$ on bags of A by $w \preceq^* w'$ if and only if there is a (not necessarily monotonic) injection $h : \widehat{|w|} \mapsto \widehat{|w'|}$ such that $w(j) \preceq w'(h(j))$ for $1 \leq j \leq |w|$.

---

[9] meaning that $h(j_1) \leq h(j_2)$ if and only if $j_1 \leq j_2$

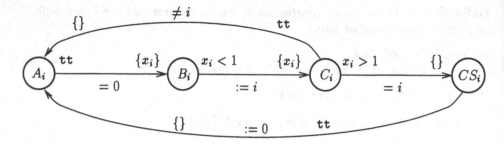

Fig. 1. Fischer's Protocol for Mutual Exclusion.

Lemma 4. *If $\preceq$ is a wqo on A, then $\preceq^*$ is a wqo on A^* and $\preceq^B$ is a wqo on A^B.*

Proof. The proof can be found in [Hig52].

Let ϕ be a constraint $\langle c, m, \mathbf{q}, \mathbf{k}, \sqsubseteq \rangle$. For each $j \in \widehat{m} \cup \{\bot, \top\}$, define the *rank* of j in ϕ to be the number of equivalence classes of $\sqsubseteq$ which are less than or equal (wrp. to $\preceq$) to the equivalence class containing j. In other words, the rank of j is the maximum k such that there is a sequence $\bot \sqsubseteq j_1 \sqsubseteq \cdots \sqsubseteq j_k = j$. Note that the rank of $\top$ is equal to the number of equivalence classes of $\equiv$. Define the rank of ϕ as the rank of $\top$ in ϕ.

Let r be the rank of the constraint $\phi = \langle c, m, \mathbf{q}, \mathbf{k}, \sqsubseteq \rangle$. For $i \in \widehat{r}$, define $\phi[i]$ to be the bag of pairs of the form $\langle q, k \rangle$ such that $u(j) = q$ and $\mathbf{k}(j) = k$ for some j with rank i in ϕ. Define the ordering $\preceq$ on these pairs to be the identity relation on pairs of the form $\langle q, k \rangle$. Since there are finitely many such pairs, $\preceq$ is trivially a well quasi-ordering.

Lemma 5. *Let $\phi = \langle c, m, \mathbf{q}, \mathbf{k}, \sqsubseteq \rangle$ and $\phi' = \langle c', m', \mathbf{q}', \mathbf{k}', \sqsubseteq' \rangle$ be constraints with ranks r and r'. We have $\phi \preceq \phi'$ if and only if $c = c'$, $\phi[0] \preceq^B \phi'[0]$, $\phi[r] \preceq^B \phi'[r']$, and there is a monotonic injection $h : \widehat{(r-1)} \mapsto \widehat{(r'-1)}$ such that $\phi[i] \preceq^B \phi'[h(i)]$ for all $i \in \widehat{(r-1)}$.*

Theorem 4. *The relation $\preceq$ on the set of constraints is a well quasi-ordering.*

Proof. The proof follows from Lemma 5 and repeated application of Lemma 4.

7 Example: Fischer's Protocol

As an illustration of our method, we model Fischer's protocol [SBK92], and show how an automatic verification algorithm would go about verifying mutual exclusion. The purpose of the protocol is to guarantee mutual exclusion in a concurrent system consisting of an arbitrary number of processes, using clocks and a shared variable. Each process has a local clock, and runs a protocol before entering the critical section. Each process has a local control state, which in our model assumes values in the set $\{A, B, C, CS\}$ where A is the initial state and CS represents the critical section. The processes also read from and write to a shared variable whose value is either $\perp$ or the index of one of the processes. A description in a graphical pseudo-code (taken from [KLL+97]) of the behavior of a process with index i is given in Figure 1.

Intuitively, the protocol behaves as follows: A process wishing to enter the critical section starts in state A. If the value of the shared variable is $\perp$, the process can proceed to state B and reset its local clock. From state B, the process can proceed to state C if the clock value is still less than 1. In other words, the clock implements a timeout which guarantees that the process either stays in state B at most one time unit, or gets stuck in B forever. When moving from B to C, the process sets the value of the shared variable to its own index i and again resets its clock. From state C, the process can proceed to the critical section if the clock is strictly more than 1 and if the value of the shared variable is still i, the index of the process. Thus, in state C the clock enforces a delay which is longer than the length of the timeout in state B. Finally, when exiting the critical section, the process resets the shared variable to $\perp$. Processes that get stuck in state C can reenter the protocol by returning to state A. Since we do not intend to model liveness properties, such as e.g., absence of starvation, we do not impose requirements that force processes to change their state[10].

$$
\begin{array}{ll}
initiate : & \langle\langle udf, udf\rangle, \langle A, x \geq 0 \longrightarrow reset, B\rangle\rangle \\
\\
choose_1 : & \langle\langle udf, df\rangle, \langle B, x < 1 \longrightarrow reset, C^\dagger\rangle\rangle \\
choose_2 : & \langle\langle df, df\rangle, \langle B, x < 1 \longrightarrow reset, C^\dagger\rangle, \langle q^\dagger, skip, q\rangle\rangle \\
choose_3 : & \langle\langle df, df\rangle, \langle B^\dagger, x < 1 \longrightarrow reset, C^\dagger\rangle\rangle \\
\\
enter : & \langle\langle df, df\rangle, \langle C^\dagger, x > 1 \longrightarrow skip, CS^\dagger\rangle\rangle \\
\\
fail_1 : & \langle\langle udf, udf\rangle, \langle C, skip, A\rangle\rangle \\
fail_2 : & \langle\langle df, df\rangle, \langle C, skip, A\rangle\rangle \\
\\
exit_1 : & \langle\langle df, udf\rangle, \langle CS^\dagger, skip, A\rangle\rangle \\
exit_2 : & \langle\langle df, udf\rangle, \langle CS, skip, A\rangle, \langle q^\dagger, skip, q\rangle\rangle \\
exit_3 : & \langle\langle udf, udf\rangle, \langle CS, skip, A\rangle\rangle \\
\end{array}
$$

Fig. 2. Rules for Modeling Fischer's protocol

We can model the protocol in our timed networks formalism. The controller state is either udf, indicating that the value of the shared variable is undefined, or df, indicating that the value of the shared variable is defined. The set of

---

[10] In fact, our formalism cannot express such requirements, although they can be added in terms of e.g., fairness constraints.

process states is given by $\{A, B, C, CS, A^\dagger, B^\dagger, C^\dagger, CS^\dagger\}$. The states marked with † correspond to configurations where the value of the shared variable is equal to the index of that particular process.

A straightforward translation of the description in Figure 1 yields the set of rules in Figure 2. We use q to denote an arbitrary process state. We use *skip* to denote the guarded command $0 \leq x \longrightarrow skip$.

Using the method described in this paper, it is possible to verify that there is never more than one process in its critical section, by checking that the set of constraints with $m = 2$ that contain exactly two occurrences of CS or $CS^\dagger$ is unreachable. More details are in the full paper.

References

[ACD90] R. Alur, C. Courcoubetis, and D. Dill. Model-checking for real-time systems. In *Proc. 5th IEEE Int. Symp. on Logic in Computer Science*, pages 414–425, Philadelphia, 1990.

[ACHH92] R. Alur, C. Courcoubetis, T. Henzinger, and P.-H. Ho. Hybrid automata: An algorithmic approach to the specification and verificationof hybrid systems. In Grossman, Nerode, Ravn, and Rischel, editors, *Hybrid Systems*, number 736 in Lecture Notes in Computer Science, pages 209–229, 1992.

[AČJYK96] Parosh Aziz Abdulla, Karlis Čerāns, Bengt Jonsson, and Tsay Yih-Kuen. General decidability theorems for infinite-state systems. In *Proc. 11th IEEE Int. Symp. on Logic in Computer Science*, pages 313–321, 1996.

[AJ96] Parosh Aziz Abdulla and Bengt Jonsson. Verifying programs with unreliable channels. *Information and Computation*, 127(2):91–101, 1996.

[AK95] Parosh Aziz Abdulla and Mats Kindahl. Decidability of simulation and bisimulation between lossy channel systems and finite state systems. In Lee and Smolka, editors, *Proc. CONCUR '95, 6th Int. Conf. on Concurrency Theory*, volume 962 of *Lecture Notes in Computer Science*, pages 333 – 347. Springer Verlag, 1995.

[BD91] B. Berthomieu and M. Diaz. Modeling and verification of time dependent systems using time Petri nets. *IEEE Trans. on Software Engineering*, 17(3):259–273, 1991.

[BS95] O. Burkart and B. Steffen. Composition, decomposition, and model checking of pushdown processes. *Nordic Journal of Computing*, 2(2):89–125, 1995.

[Čer94] K. Čerāns. Deciding properties of integral relational automata. In Abiteboul and Shamir, editors, *Proc. ICALP '94*, volume 820 of *Lecture Notes in Computer Science*, pages 35–46. Springer Verlag, 1994.

[CES86] E.M. Clarke, E.A. Emerson, and A.P. Sistla. Automatic verification of finite-state concurrent systems using temporal logic specification. *ACM Trans. on Programming Languages and Systems*, 8(2):244–263, April 1986.

[CGJ95] E. M. Clarke, O. Grumberg, and S. Jha. Verifying parameterized networks using abstraction and regular languages. In Lee and Smolka, editors, *Proc. CONCUR '95, 6th Int. Conf. on Concurrency Theory*, volume 962 of *Lecture Notes in Computer Science*, pages 395–407. Springer Verlag, 1995.

[Fin90] A. Finkel. Reduction and covering of infinite reachability trees. *Information and Computation*, 89:144–179, 1990.

[GMMP91]   C. Ghezzi, D. Mandrioli, S. Morasca, and M. Pezzè. A unified high-level Petri net formalism for time-critical systems. *IEEE Trans. on Software Engineering*, 17(2):160–172, 1991.

[God94]   J.C. Godskesen. *Timed Modal Specifications*. PhD thesis, Aalborg University, 1994.

[GS92]   S. M. German and A. P. Sistla. Reasoning about systems with many processes. *Journal of the ACM*, 39(3):675–735, 1992.

[Hen95]   T.A. Henzinger. Hybrid automata with finite bisimulations. In *Proc. ICALP '95*, 1995.

[Hig52]   G. Higman. Ordering by divisibility in abstract algebras. *Proc. London Math. Soc.*, 2:326–336, 1952.

[JM95]   P. Jančar and F. Moller. Checking regular properties of Petri nets. In *Proc. CONCUR '95, 6th Int. Conf. on Concurrency Theory*, pages 348–362, 1995.

[JP93]   B. Jonsson and J. Parrow. Deciding bisimulation equivalences for a class of non-finite-state programs. *Information and Computation*, 107(2):272–302, Dec. 1993.

[KLL+97]   K.J. Kristoffersen, F. Larroussinie, K. G. Larsen, P. Pettersson, and W. Yi. A compositional proof of a real-time mutual exclusion protocol. In *TAP-SOFT '97 7th International Joint Conference on the Theory and Practice of Software Development*, Lecture Notes in Computer Science, Lille, France, April 1997. Springer Verlag.

[KM89]   R.P. Kurshan and K. McMillan. A structural induction theorem for processes. In *Proc. 8th ACM Symp. on Principles of Distributed Computing, Canada*, pages 239–247, Edmonton, Alberta, 1989.

[LSW95]   K.G. Larsen, B. Steffen, and C. Weise. Fischer's protocol revisited: a simples proof using modal constraints. In *4th DIMACS Workshop on Verification and Control of Hybrid Systems*, New Brunswick, New Jersey, Oct. 1995.

[SBK92]   F. B. Schneider, Bloom B, and Marzullo K. Putting time into proof outlines. In de Bakker, Huizing, de Roever, and Rozenberg, editors, *Real-Time: Theory in Practice*, volume 600 of *Lecture Notes in Computer Science*, 1992.

[VW86]   M. Y. Vardi and P. Wolper. An automata-theoretic approach to automatic program verification. In *Proc. 1st IEEE Int. Symp. on Logic in Computer Science*, pages 332–344, June 1986.

[Wol86]   Pierre Wolper. Expressing interesting properties of programs in propositional temporal logic (extended abstract). In *Proc. 13th ACM Symp. on Principles of Programming Languages*, pages 184–193, Jan. 1986.

[Yi91]   Wang Yi. CCS + Time = an interleaving model for real time systems. In Leach Albert, Monien, and Rodriguez Artalejo, editors, *Proc. ICALP '91*, volume 510 of *Lecture Notes in Computer Science*. Springer Verlag, 1991.

Model Checking of Real-Time Reachability Properties Using Abstractions*

Conrado Daws and Stavros Tripakis

Abstract. Practical real-time model checking suffers from the *state-explosion* problem: the size of the state space grows exponentially with many system parameters: number of clocks, size of constants, number of system components. To cope with state explosion, we propose to use *abstractions* reducing the state-space while preserving *reachability properties*. Four *exact*, plus one *safe* abstractions are defined. In the main abstraction (*simulation*) a concrete state is mapped to a *symbolic* abstract state (a set of concrete states). The other four abstractions are defined on top of the simulation one. They can be computed on-the-fly in a completely orthogonal manner and thus can be combined to yield better reductions. A prototype implementation in the tool KRONOS has permitted to verify two benchmark examples with a significant scale-up in size.

1 Introduction

Model checking is an approach commonly used for the automatic verification of *reachability properties*. Given a system and a property p, reachability model checking is based on an exhaustive exploration of the reachable state space of the system, testing whether there exists a state where p holds. The main obstacle to this approach is the so-called *state-explosion problem* reflecting the fact that the system's state space is often prohibitively large to be entirely explored.

Abstractions [6,19] have been proven a useful tool in coping with state explosion. Model checking using abstractions consists in exploring a (hopefully much smaller) *abstract* state space rather than the *concrete* one. Since the abstract space contains less information than the concrete, a crucial question is which properties are preserved by the abstraction. *Exact* abstractions imply no information loss: the abstract system satisfies a property iff the concrete one does. *Safe* abstractions ensure only one direction, that is, if a property holds on the concrete system, then it holds also on the abstract one, otherwise no definite conclusion can be made.

In the context of real-time systems modeled as *timed automata*, the state space is infinite, due to continuous variables called *clocks*, used to measure time. An abstraction is provided in [2] which is exact with respect to all properties that can be expressed in the real-time logic TCTL and which also induces a finite

---

* VERIMAG, Centre Équation, 2 avenue de Vignate, 38610 Gières, France. Fax. +33 4 76 63 48 50, e-mail: {Conrado.Daws, Stavros.Tripakis}@imag.fr, internet: http://www.imag.fr/VERIMAG/PEOPLE/Conrado.Daws.

abstract state space called a *region graph*. Unfortunately, the size of the latter is exponential on the number of clocks and on the size of the constants against which the clocks are compared to, in the automaton in question. Therefore, the applicability of region-graph-based approaches remains very limited in practice.

In this paper, we propose five coarser abstractions in order to cope with state-explosion. Four of these are exact with respect to reachability, while the fifth one is safe. The main abstraction is defined on the infinite concrete state space, and is based on the concept of *simulation space*, where abstract states are *symbolic*, that is, predicates characterizing sets of concrete states. The simulation space is obtained as the fix-point of a *successor* (or *post-condition*) operator on symbolic states. The remaining four abstractions are defined on the simulation space, that is, both concrete and abstract states are symbolic. The *extrapolation* abstraction is needed to ensure that the simulation space is finite. The *inclusion* abstraction reduces the number of symbolic states by mapping subsets of concrete states to the same abstract state. The *activity* abstraction reduces the number of clocks by eliminating those which are not active at some point during the exploration. Finally, the *convex-hull* abstraction collapses symbolic states which are associated with the same control location to a single abstract state, the clock part of which is the convex hull of the clock parts of the concrete states. All abstractions are exact, except for the convex-hull one, which is safe.

An important feature of these four abstractions is that they are completely *orthogonal* to each other, that is, they can be composed to yield abstractions which are more powerful in terms of state-space reduction. This results in no loss of information, since the composition of exact abstractions is also exact, while the composition of exact and safe abstractions is safe. Section 3 contains the definitions of the abstractions, as well as some examples.

Section 4 presents our model-checking approach, which consists in generating and exploring *on-the-fly* an abstract state space [1]. This is done using a depth-first or breadth-first search in which the successor operator and storage procedures are parameterized by the abstraction(s) applied.

A prototype implementation of these features has been done on top of the real-time-verification tool KRONOS. Experimental results obtained on two benchmark examples are presented in section 5. Using abstractions, we have been able to verify these examples for a much larger number of components, with respect to previous attempts using explorative-model-checking tools like KRONOS, UPPAAL, HYTECH or RTSPIN. Section 5.2 also compares the results to explorative techniques based on binary decision diagrams (BDDs). Conclusions are presented in section 6.

---

[1] The term on-the-fly is taken to mean two things in this paper: (a) the abstract state space is built dynamically, without having to a-priori generate the simulation space; and (b) The system to be verified is decomposed in a *network* of timed automata which communicate by synchronizing their actions. The global state space is generated directly from these automata, without having to a-priori compute the product automaton.

2 Preliminaries

2.1 Property-preserving abstractions

Abstractions. Let S be a set of *states*, and P be a set of *properties*. An *interpretation function* $\Pi : P \mapsto 2^S$ associates with each property ϕ a set of states satisfying ϕ. Now, consider two sets of states S and S', referred to as the *concrete* and *abstract* state spaces, respectively. An *abstraction* from S to S' is a relation $\alpha \subseteq S \times S'$. Let $\Pi : P \mapsto 2^S$ and $\Pi' : P \mapsto 2^{S'}$ be concrete and abstract interpretation functions, respectively. We say that α is *safe* for P, with respect to Π, Π', iff for each property ϕ over P, for any concrete state $s \in S$ such that $s \in \Pi(\phi)$, there exists an abstract state $s' \in S'$ such that $s' \in \Pi'(\phi)$ and $(s, s') \in \alpha$, that is, s' is related to s by α. α is *exact* iff α and α^{-1} (the inverse relation) are safe.

Composition of abstractions. Given an abstraction α_1 from S to S' and an abstraction α_2 from S' to S'', $\alpha_1 \circ \alpha_2$ is an abstraction from S to S'', where $\circ$ denotes the composition of relations. The following facts can be derived directly from the definitions: (1) if both α_1 and α_2 are exact, then so is $\alpha_1 \circ \alpha_2$; (2) if one of α_1, α_2 is safe while the other one is either exact or safe, then $\alpha_1 \circ \alpha_2$ is safe.

2.2 Timed automata

Clocks, bounds and zones. Let $\mathcal{X} = \{x_1, ..., x_n\}$ be a set of variables called *clocks*, ranging over the positive reals $\mathbb{R}_{\geq 0}$. A *clock valuation* is a function $\nu : \mathcal{X} \mapsto \mathbb{R}_{\geq 0}$, assigning to each clock x a non-negative real value $\nu(x)$. For $X \subseteq \mathcal{X}$, $\nu[X := 0]$ is the valuation ν', such that $\forall x \in X. \nu'(x) = 0$ and $\forall x \notin X. \nu'(x) = \nu(x)$. For every $t \in \mathbb{R}_{\geq 0}$, $\nu + t$ is the valuation ν' such that $\forall x \in \mathcal{X}. \nu'(x) = \nu(x) + t$. A *bound* [11] over $\mathcal{X}$ is a constraint of the form of the form $x_i \# c$ or $x_i - x_j \# c$, where $1 \leq i \neq j \leq n$, $\# \in \{<, \leq, \geq, >\}$ and $c \in \mathbb{N} \cup \{\infty\}$. If we introduce a "dummy" clock variable x_0, taken to represent 0, then bounds can be uniformly written as $x_i - x_j \prec d$, where $0 \leq i \neq j \leq n$, $\prec \in \{<, \leq\}$ and $d \in \mathbb{Z} \cup \{\infty\}$. (For example, $x_1 > 3$ can be written as $x_0 - x_1 < -3$.) A bound $x_i - x_j \prec d$ is *stricter* than $x_i - x_j \prec' d'$ iff either $d < d'$ or $d = d'$ and $\prec = <, \prec' = \leq$. (We assume that $w < \infty$, for any real number w.) For instance, $x_i - x_j < 3$ is stricter than $x_i - x_j \leq 3$, which is stricter than $x_i - x_j < 4$, and so on. For two bounds b and b', $\min(b, b')$ (resp. $\max(b, b')$) is b (resp. b') if b is stricter than b', b' (resp. b) otherwise. A valuation ν satisfies a bound $x_i - x_j \prec d$ iff $\nu(x_i) - \nu(x_j) \prec d$, where, by convention, $\nu(x_0) = 0$.

A *zone* over $\mathcal{X}$ is a conjunction of bounds, $\bigwedge_{0 \leq i \neq j \leq n} x_i - x_j \prec_{ij} d_{ij}$, for $\prec_{ij} \in \{<, \leq\}$ and $d_{ij} \in \mathbb{Z}$. We denote by Z_{ij} the bound $x_i - x_j \prec_{ij} d_{ij}$. A valuation ν satisfies a zone Z iff ν satisfies Z_{ij}, for all $0 \leq i \neq j \leq n$. We often view a zone as the set of valuations satisfying it. Thus, we write $\nu \in Z$, to mean that ν satisfies Z, and $Z = \emptyset$, to mean that no valuation satisfies Z. We also write $Z \cap Z'$ to denote the zone Z'' corresponding to the intersection of Z and Z', that is, such that $Z''_{ij} = \min(Z_{ij}, Z'_{ij})$, for all $0 \leq i \neq j \leq n$. Finally, we write $Z = Z'$ iff Z and Z' represent the same sets of valuations. Notice that $Z = Z'$ does not necessarily imply that Z and Z' are identical. For example, let $Z = 2 < x_1 < 3 \wedge 3 < x_2 < 4 \wedge 0 < x_2 - x_1 < 3$ and $Z' = 2 < x_1 < 3 \wedge 3 < x_2 < 4 \wedge 0 < x_2 - x_1 < 2$. Although the two zones are not syntactically identical, they are semantically equal (i.e., $Z = Z'$), since the bound $x_2 - x_1 < 3$ can be *strengthened* to the (stricter) bound $x_2 - x_1 < 2$. We say that a zone is in *canonical form* iff all its bounds are as strict as possible, that is, none can be strengthened to yield a semantically equal zone. In the sequel we assume that all zones considered are in canonical form. Let $\mathcal{Z}_{\mathcal{X}}$ denote the set of zones over $\mathcal{X}$.

Timed automata. A *timed automaton* (TA) [2, 14] is a tuple $A = (\mathcal{X}, Q, E, q_0, I)$, where: $\mathcal{X}$ is a finite set of clocks; Q is a finite set of *control locations*; E is a finite set of *edges* of the form $e = (q, Z, X, q')$, where $q, q' \in Q$ are the source and target locations, $Z \in \mathcal{Z}_{\mathcal{X}}$ is an enabling guard, and $X \subseteq \mathcal{X}$ is a set of clocks to be reset; q_0 is the initial control location; $I : Q \mapsto \mathcal{Z}_{\mathcal{X}}$ is a function associating with each control location q a *time-progress condition* $I(q)$ (we also write I_q). Figure 1(a) shows an example of a TA, with two clocks x and y, a single location with time progress condition *true* (i.e., $x \geq 0 \wedge y \geq 0$), and two edges a and b.

A *state* of a TA is a pair (q, ν), where $q \in Q$ is a location, and $\nu \in I_q$ is a valuation satisfying the time-progress condition of q. The semantics of A is the smallest set of such states, $\mathcal{S}_A$, such that:

1. $s_0 = (q_0, 0) \in \mathcal{S}_A$, 0 being the valuation assigning zero to all clocks;
2. if $(q, \nu) \in \mathcal{S}_A$ and there exists $e = (q, Z_e, X_e, q') \in E$ such that $\nu \in Z_e$, then $(q', \nu[X_e := 0]) \in \mathcal{S}_A$;
3. if $(q, \nu) \in \mathcal{S}_A$ and there exists $t \in \mathbb{R}_{\geq 0}$ such that $\nu + t \in I_q$, then $(q, \nu + t) \in \mathcal{S}_A$.

Due to the third rule above, $\mathcal{S}_A$ has generally a non-countable number of states.

3 Abstractions for TA

3.1 Simulation

This abstraction consists in mapping sets of concrete states to abstract (symbolic) states. It is based on the concept of *simulation graph*, a reachability graph used in KRONOS for checking safety properties [7] or, more recently, also liveness properties [4].

Consider a TA $A = (\mathcal{X}, Q, E, q_0, I)$, where $\mathcal{X} = \{x_1, ..., x_n\}$. Given a zone $Z \in \mathcal{Z}_{\mathcal{X}}$, a set of clocks $X \subseteq \mathcal{X}$, and an edge $e = (q, Z_e, X_e, q') \in E$, we define the zone operators $\uparrow Z$, $Z[X := 0]$ and $\mathbf{e\text{-}succ}_e(Z)$, such that:

$$\uparrow Z = (\bigwedge_{i \in [0,n], j \in [1,n]} Z_{ij}) \wedge (\bigwedge_{i \in [1,n]} x_i - x_0 < \infty)$$

$$Z[X := 0] = (\bigwedge_{x_i, x_j \notin X} Z_{ij}) \wedge (\bigwedge_{(x_i \in X \vee x_j \in X) \wedge i, j \neq 0} x_i - x_j < \infty) \wedge (\bigwedge_{x_i \in X} 0 \leq x_i - x_0 \leq 0)$$

$$\mathbf{e\text{-}succ}_e(Z) = (Z \cap Z_e)[X_e := 0]$$

Notice that all operators above yield zones. Intuitively, $\uparrow Z \supseteq Z$ is the zone obtained from Z by eliminating all upper bounds of clocks (all bounds Z_{i0} are replaced by the trivial bound ∞), and represents the elapse of time. $Z[X := 0]$ is obtained after resetting all clocks in X to zero. Finally, $\mathbf{e\text{-}succ}_e(Z)$ corresponds to taking the part of Z satisfying the guard of e, then resetting some clocks as specified by e. Figure 2 shows examples of the application of the intersection, time-elapse, and reset operators.

A *symbolic state* S is a pair (q, Z), where $q \in Q$ is a location and $Z \in \mathcal{Z}_\mathcal{X}$ is a zone. We write $(q', \nu) \in (q, Z)$ iff $q' = q$ and $\nu \in Z$. We write $(q, Z) = \emptyset$ iff $Z = \emptyset$. Let $e = (q, Z_e, X_e, q')$ be an edge. We define the post-condition operator **post** as follows:

$$\mathbf{post}_e((q, Z)) = (q', I_{q'} \cap \uparrow \mathbf{e\text{-}succ}_e(Z)) \tag{1}$$

That is, $\mathbf{post}_e(S)$ contains all states that can be reached from some state in S by, first taking a discrete transition by e, then letting some time pass in the new control location, while continuously satisfying its time-progress condition.

The *simulation space* of A is defined to be the smallest set of symbolic states $\mathcal{S}_A^{sim}$ such that:

1. $S_0^{sim} = (q_0, I_{q_0} \cap \uparrow \{0\}) \in \mathcal{S}_A^{sim}$;
2. for any $S_1 \in \mathcal{S}_A^{sim}$ and any $e \in E$, if $S_2 = \mathbf{post}_e(S_1) \neq \emptyset$ then $S_2 \in \mathcal{S}_A^{sim}$.

In other words, $\mathcal{S}_A^{sim}$ is the set of all states obtained from S_0^{sim} by applying the post operator. $\mathcal{S}_A^{sim}$ can be infinite, as in the example of figure 1, where $\mathcal{S}_A^{sim}$ is displayed as a graph, the nodes of which are symbolic states, while the edges show the effect of applying **post**.

The *simulation abstraction* is defined to be the relation $\alpha_{sim} = \{(s, S) \in \mathcal{S}_A \times \mathcal{S}_A^{sim} \mid s \in S\}$.

Regarding the set of properties with respect to which reachability is defined, we consider the set $P = Q \times \mathcal{Z}_\mathcal{X}$, that is, the set of all possible symbolic states. The interpretation function $\Pi : P \mapsto 2^S$ is defined as: $\Pi(q, Z) = \{(q, \nu) \mid \nu \in Z\}$. Similarly, $\Pi^{sim} : P \mapsto 2^{\mathcal{S}_A^{sim}}$ is defined as: $\Pi^{sim}(q, Z) = \{(q, Z') \mid Z' \cap Z \neq \emptyset\}$.

Proposition 31 *The simulation abstraction α_{sim} is exact.*

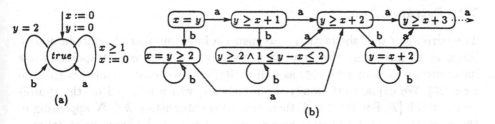

Fig. 1. A timed automaton (a), and its (infinite) simulation space (b).

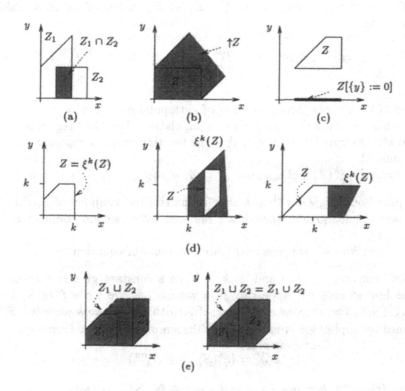

Fig. 2. Zone operations.

3.2 Extrapolation

The purpose of this abstraction is to ensure a finite number of symbolic states, since, as we have seen, the simulation space can be infinite. Extrapolation has been already used in KRONOS, as well as RTSPIN, where it is called *maximization* [20]. We explain informally the main idea, which is based on the (finite) region graph [2]. For any TA A, there is a maximal constant $k \in \mathbb{N}$ appearing in the zones of A (guards or time-progress conditions). In the example of figure 1, k equals 2. Now, consider a valuation ν and a clock x such that $\nu(x) > k$. It is easy to see that for any zone Z of A, the exact value of $\nu(x)$ is insignificant to whether ν belongs to Z or not, that is, for any other ν' which coincides with ν to all clocks but x, such that $\nu'(x) > k$, it holds $\nu \in Z$ iff $\nu' \in Z$. Consequently, once $\nu(x) > k$, $\nu(x)$ can be replaced by a "greater than k" value. We now formalize these notions.

Let $Z = \bigwedge_{0 \leq i \neq j \leq n} x_i - x_j \prec_{ij} d_{ij}$ be a zone over $\mathcal{X} = \{x_1, ..., x_n\}$. For each $k \in \mathbb{N}$, the *extrapolation function* $\xi^k : \mathcal{Z}_\mathcal{X} \mapsto \mathcal{Z}_\mathcal{X}$ is defined as follows (skip on first reading):

$$\xi^k(Z) = \bigwedge_{d_{ij} > k} x_i - x_j < \infty \quad \wedge \quad \bigwedge_{-d_{ij} > k} x_i - x_j < -k \quad \wedge \quad \bigwedge_{|d_{ij}| \leq k} x_i - x_j \prec_{ij} d_{ij} \tag{2}$$

Figure 2(d) presents three examples of extrapolation, for $k = 2$, $\mathcal{X} = \{x, y\}$. (The white region is the zone before extrapolation. The filled region is the part added after extrapolation. Notice that the two rightmost extrapolated zones are unbounded.)

Intuitively, $\xi^k(Z)$ yields a zone $Z' \supseteq Z$, where:

- upper bounds greater than k are eliminated (first conjunct of equation 2);
- lower bounds greater than k are replaced by k (second conjunct of equation 2);
- all other bounds are preserved (third conjunct of equation 2).

Now, consider a TA A and let $k \in \mathbb{N}$ be a constant greater than or equal to the largest constant appearing in a zone of A. We write $\xi^k(q, Z)$ instead of $(q, \xi^k(Z))$. The *extrapolation space* of A with respect to k, denoted $S_{A,k}^{xtr}$, is obtained by applying ξ^k to all states of the simulation space. Formally:

$$S_{A,k}^{xtr} = \{\xi^k(S) \mid S \in S_A^{sim}\}$$

Proposition 32 *For any TA A and any $k \in \mathbb{N}$, $S_{A,k}^{xtr}$ is finite.*

Figure 3(a) shows the effect of applying the extrapolation abstraction for $k = 2$ to the example of figure 1. Notice that the part that changes is the infinite rightmost chain $y \geq x + 3, y \geq x + 4, ...$, which is replaced by a single symbolic state $y > x + 2$.

The *extrapolation abstraction* parameterized by k, is the relation $\alpha_{xtr}^k = \{(S, S') \in S_A^{sim} \times S_A^{xtr} \mid S' = \xi^k(S)\}$.

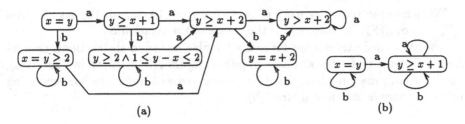

Fig. 3. Applying extrapolation (a) and (optimal) inclusion (b) to the example of figure 1.

The interpretation function Π^{xtr} is defined to be the same as Π^{sim}. Then, it is easy to prove that α^k_{xtr} is exact for any property ϕ such that the maximal constant appearing in ϕ is less than or equal to k. However, this is not generally true for properties involving constants greater than k, since it might be that such a property is reachable in the abstract space, while it is not in the concrete one. In any case, α^k_{xtr} is safe for any property. We now formally present these results.

For $k \in \mathbb{N}$, we define $\mathcal{Z}^k_\chi$ to be the set of all zones Z involving constants less than or equal to k. Let P_k be the set of properties $Q \times \mathcal{Z}^k_\chi$.

Proposition 33 *Let A be a TA and $k \in \mathbb{N}$ be a constant greater than or equal to the largest constant appearing in a zone of A. Then, α^k_{xtr} is exact with respect to P_k. Moreover, for all $m \in \mathbb{N}$, α^m_{xtr} is safe with respect to P.*

Remark 1. For the sake of simplicity, we have defined the extrapolation function with respect to a single constant k. In fact, it is straightforward to adapt the definitions for a set of constants c_{ij}, $0 \le i \ne j \le n$, one for each clock difference $x_i - x_j$. This permits to "optimize" the reduction, since a coarser abstraction is obtained. Preservation results are not affected.

3.3 Inclusion

Although finite, the number of states induced by extrapolation can still be large. This number can be reduced by using the *inclusion* abstraction, the main idea of which is the following. Consider two states S_1 and S_2 in the simulation space, such that S_1 is a subset of S_2. Then, for reachability properties, it is not necessary to examine neither S_1 (since any state belonging to S_1 belongs also to S_2), nor the successors of S_1, since each of them is a subset of the corresponding successor of S_2. Thus, states like S_1 can be eliminated. We formalize this in what follows.

Given a TA A, we say that a total function $\alpha_{inc} : \mathcal{S}^{sim}_A \mapsto \mathcal{S}^{sim}_A$ is an *inclusion abstraction* iff, for any $S \in \mathcal{S}^{sim}$, $\alpha_{inc}(S) \supseteq S$, where $(q, Z) \subseteq (q', Z')$ iff $q = q'$ and $Z \subseteq Z'$. (We regard, again, zones as sets of valuations, so that zone inclusion means set inclusion. $Z \subseteq Z'$ can be implemented by testing that each bound of Z is stricter than or equal to the corresponding bound of Z'.)

We define the *inclusion space* of A with respect to α_{inc} as the set of states $\mathcal{S}^{inc}_{A,\alpha_{inc}} = \alpha_{inc}[\mathcal{S}^{sim}_A]$, where $\alpha[\cdot]$ is the image of the relation α.

The above definitions allow for many possible inclusion abstractions. One inclusion abstraction for the simulation space of figure 1(b) is shown in figure 4(a), where the α_{inc} mapping is depicted by dashed arrowed lines. The corresponding inclusion space is shown in figure 4(b).

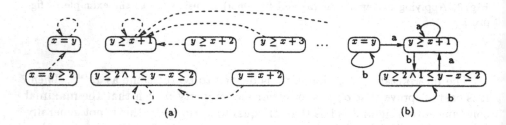

(a)   (b)

Fig. 4. Inclusion abstraction (a) and corresponding inclusion space (b).

An inclusion abstraction $\alpha^\star_{inc}$ is said to be *optimal* iff for any other α'_{inc}, $\alpha^\star_{inc}[\mathcal{S}^{sim}] \subseteq \alpha'_{inc}[\mathcal{S}^{sim}]$ (that is, $\alpha^\star_{inc}$ induces a smaller state space than α'_{inc}). In the case that the simulation space is finite, an optimal inclusion abstraction always exists. (In fact, there may be more than one optimal abstractions, but all of them induce the same inclusion space.) In the case that the simulation space is infinite, an optimal abstraction might still exist, as is the case for the TA of figure 1. The inclusion space induced by this optimal abstraction is shown in figure 3(b). On the other hand, consider a TA similar to the one of figure 1, where the guard $x \geq 1$ is replaced by $x = 1$. In this case, the simulation space as well as any inclusion space are infinite.

The interpretation function Π^{inc} is defined to be the same as Π^{sim}.

Proposition 34 *Any inclusion abstraction is exact.*

3.4 Activity

This abstraction permits to eliminate redundant clocks from a system. It has been introduced in [10] for the case of a single TA and is here generalized to a network of automata. The idea is that a clock should be considered *active* only when it *usefully* counts time, that is, from a point where the clock is reset, up to a point where the clock is tested. In any other case, the clock is inactive and can be ignored. We now formalize these notions.

Consider a TA $A = (\mathcal{X}, Q, E, q_0, I)$, where $\mathcal{X} = \{x_1, ..., x_n\}$. Given a control location $q \in Q$, $\mathsf{clk}(q) \subseteq \mathcal{X}$ is defined as the set of clocks x, such that either x appears in the time-progress condition I_q of q, or there exists an edge $e = (q, Z, X, q')$ in E, such that x appears in the guard Z of e.

Then, the function act : $Q \mapsto 2^X$, associating with each location q the set of active clocks in q, is defined as the least fix-point of the following system of equations (one equation for each location q):

$$\text{act}(q) = \text{clk}(q) \cup \bigcup_{(q,Z,X,q') \in E} \text{act}(q') \setminus X \qquad (3)$$

That is, x is active in q iff either x is in $\text{clk}(q)$, or x is active in a location q' which can be reached from q by a sequence of edges, so that x is never reset along the sequence.

An algorithm to compute act is given in [10]. This algorithm works on the syntactic structure of the automaton, that is, its locations and edges, thus, it is extremely efficient.

Given a symbolic state $S = (q, Z)$, the *projection* of S to active clocks, denoted S/act, is a symbolic state (q, Z'), where Z' is the projection of Z to the set of active clocks of q. Formally:

$$(q, Z)/\text{act} = (q, \bigwedge_{x_i, x_j \in \text{act}(q) \cup \{x_0\}} Z_{ij}) \qquad (4)$$

The *activity space* S_A^{act} of a TA A is the set $S_A^{act} = \{S/\text{act} \mid S \in S_A^{sim}\}$. In other words, S_A^{act} is of *variable dimension*: for each $(q, Z) \in S^{act}$, Z is a zone over $\text{act}(q)$ (if $\text{act}(q)$ is empty, the symbolic state reduces to just the control location q).

The *activity abstraction* is defined to be the relation $\alpha_{act} = \{(S, S') \in S_A^{sim} \times S_A^{act} \mid S' = S/\text{act}\}$.

The interpretation function Π^{act} is defined to be the same as Π^{sim}.

Proposition 35 *The activity abstraction α_{act} is exact for any property $\phi = (q, Z)$, such that the set of clocks appearing in Z is a subset of $\text{act}(q)$.*

Remark 2. The above proposition claims that α_{act} is exact for ϕ if the latter refers to clocks which are active in q. In fact, it is easy to extend the above definitions so that the activity abstraction is exact for any property (q, Z). Indeed, it suffices to add all clocks appearing in Z in the set of clocks initially active in q, $\text{clk}(q)$, and compute the fix-point equations defined in 3 accordingly.

3.5 Convex hull

This abstraction provides a considerable reduction of the state space, permitting to keep a single zone Z with each control location q of the system. In general, there will be many zones $Z_1, ..., Z_n$ associated with a location q, in any of the abstract spaces defined previously. However, $(q, \bigcup_{i=1,...,n} Z_i)$ is not a symbolic state, since the union of two zones is generally a *non-convex* set, that is, cannot be represented as a conjunction of constraints (i.e., a zone). The *convex hull* of two zones is by definition convex, therefore, one can abstract $\bigcup_{i=1,...,n} Z_i$ by $\bigsqcup_{i=1,...,n} Z_i$, where $\sqcup$ denotes the convex hull. On the other hand, convex hulls are generally supersets of unions, meaning that states which are not reachable in the concrete space might be so in the abstract one. This is why this abstraction is not exact, although it is safe. Convex hull abstractions have been used also by [12, 21, 3]. The definitions are given in what follows.

Given two zones Z and Z', the *convex hull* of Z and Z', denoted $Z \sqcup Z'$, is defined as the smallest (with respect to set inclusion) zone Z'' such that $Z \subseteq Z''$ and $Z' \subseteq Z''$. ($Z \sqcup Z'$ can be obtained operationally as follows: $(Z \sqcup Z')_{ij} = \max(Z_{ij}, Z'_{ij})$.) Two examples are shown in figure 2(e).

The *convex-hull space* of a TA A is the set $S^{ch}_A = \{(q, Z) \mid Z = \bigsqcup\{Z' \mid (q, Z') \in S^{sim}_A\}\}$. [2]

The *convex-hull abstraction* is defined to be the relation:
$$\alpha_{ch} = \{((q, Z), (q, Z')) \in S^{sim}_A \times S^{ch}_A \mid Z \subseteq Z'\}.$$
The interpretation function Π^{ch} is defined to be the same as Π^{sim}.

Proposition 36 *The convex-hull abstraction α_{ch} is safe.*

4 Model checking using abstractions

The reachability analysis is implemented in KRONOS as a *breadth-first* (BFS) or *depth-first* (DFS) generation of the abstract state space, starting from an initial state, and checking whether a final state $(\hat{q}, \hat{Z})$ is reachable from an initial state (q_0, Z_0). [3]

Figure 5 shows the DFS procedure. S^α is the set of visited (abstract) states, initialized to $\{(q_0, Z_0)\}$. For each newly-generated state (q, Z), it is checked whether the latter satisfies the property $(\hat{q}, \hat{Z})$, and, if so, a sample trail is returned as output (in this case, by simply running through the DFS stack). Otherwise, (q, Z) is stored to the set of visited states S^α, and the search goes on to explore all successor states which have not been visited yet.

The search is parameterized by an abstraction α, which is either α_{sim}, or $\alpha_{sim} \circ \alpha'$, α' being itself a composition of some of the other four abstractions, $\alpha_{xtr}, \alpha_{inc}, \alpha_{act}, \alpha_{ch}$. The correctness of the method comes from propositions 31, 33, 34, 35, 36, and the fact that composition of abstractions respects property preservation (see section 2.1). Depending on α, the functions post_e, store and visited are modified appropriately, to implement the chosen abstractions. We explain this in what follows.

Extrapolation and Activity. These abstractions are implemented by modifying the successor function post_e. When none of these abstractions is used, then

---

[2] We should note that, in this definition, $\bigsqcup\{Z' \mid (q, Z') \in S^{sim}_A\}$ is actually the *smallest upper bound* of the set $\{Z' \mid (q, Z') \in S^{sim}_A\}$, in the lattice of zones with respect to set inclusion. This is because the set $\{Z' \mid (q, Z') \in S^{sim}_A\}$ may be infinite.

[3] Many interesting properties can be formulated in this way. In particular, this is true for *invariants*, informally stated as "in all reachable states p holds", and *real-time bounded-response* properties informally stated as "p will hold in at most t units of time". We refer the reader to [7] for more details.

```
ReachDFSᵅ ((q, Z), (q̂, Ẑ)) :
  if  (q = q̂ and Z ∩ Ẑ ≠ ∅)  then
    return((q̂, Ẑ) is reachable) ;
    output(DFS stack) ;
  else
    storeᵅ((q, Z), Sᵅ) ;
    for-each  (e ∈ E)  do
      (q', Z') := postₑᵅ(q, Z) ;
      if  (Z' ≠ ∅ and not visitedᵅ(q', Z'))  then
        ReachDFSᵅ((q', Z'), (q̂, Ẑ)) ;
```

Fig. 5. Depth-first reachability using abstractions.

post_e^α is simply post_e, defined in equation 1. When extrapolation is used, then $\text{post}_e^\alpha(q, Z)$ is $\xi^k(\text{post}_e(q, Z))$, where k is found as explained in section 3.2. When activity is used, then $\text{post}_e^\alpha(q, Z)$ is $(\text{post}_e(q, Z))/\text{act}$. When both abstractions are used, both operators are applied (the order does not matter).

Inclusion. This abstraction is implemented by modifying the test $\text{visited}^\alpha(q', Z')$. When inclusion is not used, this test is $(q', Z') \in S^\alpha$. Otherwise, the test becomes $\exists(q', Z'') \in S^\alpha. Z' \subseteq Z''$.

Convex hull. This abstraction is implemented by, first, changing visited as in the case of inclusion, and second, modifying also the storing procedure as follows. When convex hull is used, $\text{store}^\alpha((q, Z), S^\alpha)$ has the following effect: either there is already a state (q, Z'') in S^α, in which case it is replaced by $(q, Z'' \sqcup Z)$; or there is no such state, thus, (q, Z) is added to S^α. When convex hull is not used, (q, Z) is simply added to S^α.

A final comment needs to be made on the incompleteness of the convex-hull abstraction: if a state is reachable in the abstract graph then no conclusion can be made about the concrete graph. A (partial) solution to this is to try to follow the diagnostic trail given by the DFS (i.e., the sequence of transitions fired) using the exact successor function post. This means generating the concrete counterpart of the abstract trail. If the entire transition sequence can be generated then the reachability property indeed holds, otherwise the approximation is too coarse. Notice that this method cannot be generalized, for instance, by simply testing all counter-example trails found in the abstract graph, since their concrete counterparts constitute only a part of the set of trails in the concrete graph.

5   Examples

5.1   The FDDI communication protocol

FDDI (Fiber Distributed Data Interface) [15] is a high-performance fiber-optic token-ring LAN (local-area network). An FDDI network is composed by N identical stations and a ring, where the stations can communicate by *synchronous* messages with high priority or *asynchronous* messages with low priority.

We are interested here in the verification of one aspect of the temporal mechanism of the protocol, namely, the *bounded time for accessing the ring* (BTAR) property, stated as: "the time elapsed between two consecutive receptions of the token by a given station is bounded by c_N". (c_N is a constant depending on the number of stations N).

The system has already been specified and verified with KRONOS, in [8], using a backward fix-point computation, and in [7], using a forward reachability analysis (i.e., exploring the simulation space). In the first case, 8 stations has been the maximum the tool could handle, while in the second, the limit has been 12 stations.

Here we show how enhancing the reachability analysis with abstractions leads to a more efficient verification of this system, both in time and space, thus permitting to verify the property on a system of up to 50 stations.

Specification. The system for N stations is modeled as a TA **FDDI**$_N$ which is obtained as the parallel product of the model of the ring for N stations **Ring**$_N$, and the model of each station, **Station**$_i$, $i = 1, ..., N$. It is worth noting that the size of **FDDI**$_N$ (in locations, transitions and clocks) is linear on the number of stations N. Since the computation of the model of the global system is not costly, on-the-fly verification is not needed in this case. Instead, we apply the reachability analysis to the global model, using the breadth-first-search technique.

Results. Figure 6 shows, in logarithmic scale, the performance results [4]. We can conclude from figure 6(a) that exact abstractions generate an exponential number of symbolic states [5], while their combination with the convex hull abstraction reduces the cost from exponential to polynomial on the number of stations. However, it is important to notice that activity reduces the number of symbolic states generated by half when the convex hull abstraction is not used.

From figure 6(b), we can make the same conclusions about the complexity on the number of stations as those for the size of the state-space generated. However, it turns out that the benefits from the activity abstraction are much more important in terms of time reduction than in terms of state-space size reduction, even when combined with the convex-hull abstraction. The reason for this is that reducing by activity the number of clocks of the system, leads to a more compact representation of zones (i.e. a gain in memory), and to a more efficient computation of the operations on zones. In this case, activity reduces the number of clocks from $2N + 1$, for the original model (2 clocks for each station,

---

[4] The model was verified using the simulation abstraction (denoted "sim" in the figure) alone, or combined with the convex-hull ("ch") or the activity ("act") abstractions. Extrapolation and inclusion have no effect in this case because of the structure of the model.

[5] In this example, the exponential complexity is induced by the temporal aspect of the system, since the size of its control is linear.

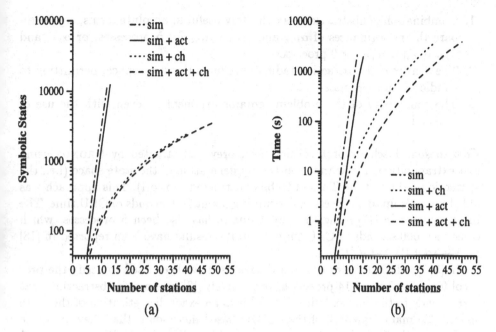

Fig. 6. Results of verification of FDDI protocol using abstractions: state-space size (a) and time (b).

plus a clock for the ring), to $N + 1$, because the clock of the ring and one of the clocks of each station are never active simultaneously. Hence the important gain, both in memory and time, even if the number of symbolic states computed is nearly the same.

5.2 Fischer's mutual-exclusion protocol

This is a real-time mutual-exclusion protocol which has become a benchmark example, thus we ommit its description here (see [9] for more details).

Results. Diagrams (a) and (b) in figure 7 display the results of using abstractions, in linear and logarithmic scale, respectively. [6] Some conclusions coming from these results are the following.

---

[6] "x" stands for extrapolation, "inc" for inclusion. "act" for activity, and "ch" for convex hull. The "+" symbol stands for combination of abstractions. Not all combinations are shown: first, the simulation graph is infinite; second, by definition, convex hull is more general than inclusion; "x+inc+act" turns out to yield exactly the same results as "x+act"; finally, "x+ch" yields almost the same results as "act+ch". Concerning time and memory costs, the largest case treated (9 processes, about 600,000 symbolic states generated) has consumed 2 hours of CPU time and 180 megabytes, on a Sparc-station 20 with 224 megabytes of memory. We should mention that computing the abstractions does not result in a significant time consumption, that is, the overhead is a matter of seconds.

1. Combination of abstractions is definitely useful in absolute terms, e.g., compare the performances of α_{inc} and $\alpha_{xtr} \circ \alpha_{inc}$ for 5 processes, or α_{xtr} and $\alpha_{xtr} \circ \alpha_{inc} \circ \alpha_{act}$ for 6 processes.
2. The convex-hull abstraction radically reduces the state space, permitting to handle up to 9 processes.
3. The complexity of the problem remains exponential, even with the use of convex hull.

Comparison. Fischer's protocol has been previously treated by KRONOS using just extrapolation, and without on-the-fly generation of the state space (i.e., the syntactic product of the TA had to be constructed a priori). This approach was able to handle up to 5 processes, consuming about 140 seconds of CPU time. The limit reported in [17] using the tool UPPAAL has also been 5 processes, which consumed 600 seconds of CPU time. [7] Similar results have been reported in [18] for the tool HYTECH [13].

In [3,5], BDDs (binary decision diagrams) have been used to verify the protocol for up to 10 and 14 processes, respectively. [3] uses a safe abstraction that corresponds to the convex hull, while [5] uses an exact discretization of the state space. The main drawback of these BDD-based methods is that they are quite sensitive to the size of constants: in both case studies above, the values of δ, Δ were assumed to be 1 and 2, respectively. Also, in case the property fails to hold, the BDD encoding the set of reachable states does not contain enough information in order to provide a counter-example, so that some kind of enumerative exploration needs to be also available. (In [5], counter-examples are generated by re-starting the exploration using a BFS, once the BDD is found to intersect the property in question).

Finally, the protocol has been also treated in [18], for up to 7 processes, using a *formula-quotienting* construction, which is not an explorative model-checking approach, thus, cannot be directly compared to ours. [8]

6 Conclusions and perspectives

We proposed abstractions as an efficient way to perform verification of reachability properties. In summary, the simulation abstraction is the formalization of the coarse reachable state space upon which the algorithm is based; extrapolation is in some cases inevitable so that the algorithm terminates; the inclusion, convex-hull and activity abstractions are equally important in practice, since

---

[7] This was on a different machine than ours, and possibly with different constants δ, Δ. We have tried UPPAAL version 2.02, March'97, (command verifyta -S, which enables all state-space reductions) on our machine, for 5 and 7 processes, using the same constants. UPPAAL consumed 485 seconds of CPU time for 5 processes, and hadn't finished for 7 processes after more than 14 hours of CPU time, having consumed 70MB of memory.
[8] In [16], the same approach has been used to verify an acyclic version of the protocol for up to 50 processes.

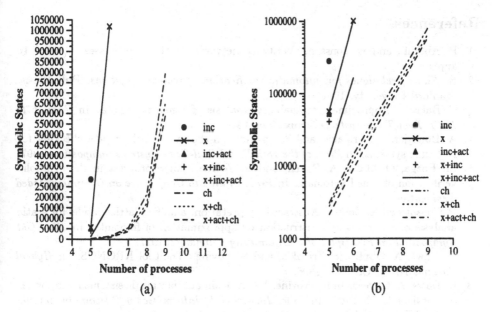

Fig. 7. Results of verification of Fischer's protocol using abstractions.

they reduce the size of the state space: inclusion and convex-hull reduce the *number* of symbolic states generated, whereas as activity also reduces the *size* needed to store each symbolic state.

Apart from convex hull, all other abstractions are exact. The former is still useful, however: If a state is not reachable in the abstract space, it is certainly not reachable in the concrete space either. If a state is reachable in the abstract space, one can always examine the path leading to this state, by re-executing the transitions without applying the abstraction. If the state is indeed reachable then a diagnostic trail is found. Otherwise, the search can continue in the same manner, providing some confidence in the system verified, without, however being definitely conclusive.

Experimental results allow us to infer that our abstractions deal quite well with two factors of exponential growth of the state space, namely, the number of clocks, and the size of constants used in the model. Regarding the third factor of exponential growth, that is, the number of components constituting the system, although these abstractions provide an improvement of performance in absolute terms, they cannot avoid the exponential complexity in general. Notice, however, that this is achieved in the FDDI example, with the help of the convex-hull abstraction.

Regarding perspectives, in the short term, we plan to complete the prototype implementation, namely, by programming variable-dimension structures, and optimal storage techniques. In the long term, compositional methods like the ones in [1, 18], need to be studied more thoroughly.

References

1. P. Abdulla and B. Jonsson. Verifying networks of timed processes. 1997. To appear.
2. R. Alur. *Techniques for automatic verification of real-time systems.* PhD thesis, Stanford University, 1991.
3. F. Balarin. Approximate reachability analysis of timed automata. In *Proc. 17th IEEE Real-Time Systems Symposium,* 1996.
4. A. Bouajjani, S. Tripakis, and S. Yovine. On-the-fly symbolic model checking for real-time systems. In *Proc. of the 18th IEEE Real-Time Systems Symposium,* 1997.
5. M. Bozga, O. Maler, A. Pnueli, and S. Yovine. Some progress in the symbolic verification of timed automata. In *Proc. of the 8th Conference on Computer-Aided Verification,* 1997.
6. P. Cousot and R. Cousot. Abstract interpretation: a unified lattice model for static analysis of programs by construction or approximation of fixpoints. In *4th ACM Symposium on Principles of Programming Languages,* 1977.
7. C. Daws, A. Olivero, S. Tripakis, and S. Yovine. The tool KRONOS. In *Hybrid Systems III.* LNCS 1066, 1996.
8. C. Daws, A. Olivero, and S. Yovine. Verificación automática de sistemas temporizados utilizando KRONOS. In *Proc. Jornadas de Informática y Telecomunicaciones de la IEEE (sección Uruguay),* 1996.
9. C. Daws and S. Tripakis. Model checking of real-time reachability properties using abstractions (full version). Technical Report 97-08, Verimag, october 1997. http://www.imag.fr/VERIMAG/PEOPLE/Conrado.Daws.
10. C. Daws and S. Yovine. Reducing the number of clock variables of timed automata. In *Proc. 17th IEEE Real-Time Systems Symposium, RTSS'96,* 1996.
11. D. Dill. Timing assumptions and verification of finite-state concurrent systems. In *Proc. 1st Intl. Workshop on Computer-Aided Verification,* 1989.
12. N. Halbwachs. Delay analysis in synchronous programs. In *5th Conference on Computer-Aided Verification.* LNCS 697, 1993.
13. T. Henzinger, P. Ho, and H. Wong-Toi. Hytech: The next generation. In *Proc. 16th IEEE Real-time Systems Symposium,* 1995.
14. T.A. Henzinger, X. Nicollin, J. Sifakis, and S. Yovine. Symbolic model checking for real-time systems. *Information and Computation,* 1994.
15. R. Jain. *FDDI handbook: high-speed networking using fiber and other media.* Addison-Wesley, 1994.
16. Kristoffersen, F. Laroussinie, K. Larsen, P. Petterson, and W. Yi. A compositional proof of a real time mutual exclusion protocol. In *Proc. of the 7th Intl. Conf. on the Theory and Practice of Software Development,* 1997.
17. K. Larsen, F. Larsson, P. Pettersson, and W. Yi. Efficient verification of real-time systems: Compact data structures and state-space reduction. In *Proc. of the 18th IEEE Real-Time Systems Symposium,* 1997.
18. K. Larsen, P. Petterson, and W. Yi. Compositional and symbolic model-checking of real-time systems. In *Proc. 16th IEEE Real-Time Systems Symposium,* 1995.
19. C. Loiseaux, S. Graf, J. Sifakis, A. Bouajjani, and S. Bensalem. Property preserving abstractions for the verification of concurrent systems. *Formal Methods in System Design,* 1995.
20. S. Tripakis and C. Courcoubetis. Extending promela and spin for real time. In *TACAS'96.* LNCS 1055, 1996.
21. H. Wong-Toi. *Symbolic Approximations for Verifying Real-Time Systems.* PhD thesis, Stanford University, 1995.

Symbolic Exploration of Transition Hierarchies*

Rajeev Alur**   Thomas A. Henzinger***   Sriram K. Rajamani†

Abstract. In formal design verification, successful model checking is
typically preceded by a laborious manual process of constructing design abstractions. We present a methodology for partially—and in some
cases, fully—bypassing the abstraction process. For this purpose, we provide to the designer abstraction operators which, if used judiciously in
the description of a design, structure the corresponding state space hierarchically. This structure can then be exploited by verification tools, and
makes possible the automatic and exhaustive exploration of state spaces
that would otherwise be out of scope for existing model checkers.

Specifically, we present the following contributions:
- A temporal abstraction operator that aggregates transitions and
  hides intermediate steps. Mathematically, our abstraction operator is
  a function that maps a flat transition system into a two-level hierarchy where each atomic upper-level transition expands into an entire
  lower-level transition system. For example, an arithmetic operation
  may expand into a sequence of bit operations.
- A BDD-based algorithm for the symbolic exploration of multi-level
  hierarchies of transition systems. The algorithm traverses a level-n
  transition by expanding the corresponding level-$(n-1)$ transition
  system on-the-fly. The level-n successors of a state are determined
  by computing a level-$(n-1)$ reach set, which is then immediately
  released from memory. In this fashion, we can exhaustively explore
  hierarchically structured state spaces whose flat counterparts cause
  memory overflows.
- We experimentally demonstrate the efficiency of our method with
  three examples—a multiplier, a cache coherence protocol, and a
  multiprocessor system. In the first two examples, we obtain significant improvements in run times and peak BDD sizes over traditional
  state-space search. The third example cannot be model checked at
  all using conventional methods (without manual abstractions), but
  can be analyzed fully automatically using transition hierarchies.

* This research was supported in part by the Office of Naval Research Young Investi-
gator award N00014-95-1-0520, by the National Science Foundation CAREER award
CCR-9501708, by the National Science Foundation grant CCR-9504469, by the Air
Force Office of Scientific Research contract F49620-93-1-0056, by the Army Research
Office MURI grant DAAH-04-96-1-0341, by the Advanced Research Projects Agency
grant NAG2-892, and by the Semiconductor Research Corporation contract 95-DC-
324.036.
** University of Pennsylvania and Bell Labs, alur@cis.upenn.edu
*** University of California at Berkeley, tah@eecs.berkeley.edu
† University of California at Berkeley, sriramr@eecs.berkeley.edu

1 Introduction

Formal design verification is a methodology for detecting logical errors in high-level designs. In formal design verification, the designer describes a system in a language with a mathematical semantics, and then the system description is analyzed against various correctness requirements. The paradigm is called *model checking* when the analysis is performed automatically by exhaustive state-space exploration. A variety of model checkers, such as COSPAN [HZR96], Murφ [Dil96], SMV [CKSVG96], SPIN [HP96], and VIS [BSVH+96] have been proven effective aids in the design of error-prone system components such as cache coherence protocols [CK96].

As we seek to enhance the applicability of model checking to complex designs, we are faced with the so-called *state-explosion* problem: the size of the state space grows exponentially with the size of the system description, making exhaustive state-space exploration infeasible. Consequently, to use the current tools effectively, one needs to focus on a critical system component. Since the behavior of an individual component typically depends on its interaction with other components, a component cannot be analyzed in isolation; rather, for a meaningful analysis, all relevant aspects of the surrounding system need to be identified. This process, called *abstraction*, is usually performed in an informal, manual fashion, and requires considerable expertise. Indeed, it is not uncommon that a successful verification or falsification run, using a few seconds of CPU time, depends on months of manual labor for constructing abstractions that are neither too coarse to invalidate the correctness requirements, nor too detailed to exhaust the tool capacities.

The goal of our research is to systematize and, whenever possible, automate the construction of useful abstractions. Our approach is to provide the designer, within the system description language, with operators for writing mental design abstractions into the system description. The judicious use of such operators is called *design for verifiability*, because it simplifies—and in some cases, eliminates—the process of "rediscovering" abstractions after the design is completed.

Our abstraction operators are motivated by the two main, orthogonal structuring principles for designs: (1) *spatial aggregation* together with hiding of spatial details, and (2) *temporal aggregation* together with hiding of temporal details. Type-(1) abstractions enable the design of components at different levels of spatial granularity: an ALU can be designed by aggregating gates, then used as an atomic block (after hiding internal gates and wires) in the design of a processor. Type-(2) abstractions enable the design of components at different levels of temporal granularity: an arithmetic operation can be designed by aggregating bit operations, then used as an atomic step (after hiding intermediate results) in the design of an instruction.

Spatial, type-(1) abstractions can be written into a system description using, for aggregation, the *parallel composition* of subsystems and, for hiding, the existential quantification of variables. According operators are provided by most system description languages. They are exploited heavily, both to facilitate the description of complex systems, and to obtain heuristics for coping with state explosion. For instance, in symbolic state-space exploration using BDDs, instead of building a single transition relation for the entire system, one typically maintains a set of transition relations, one for each component [TSL90].

By contrast, most system description languages do not provide operators for defining temporal, type-(2) abstractions. We have introduced such an operator, called **next**, and shown how it facilitates the description of complex systems, in a language called *Reactive Modules* [AH96]. In this paper, we show how the **next** operator can be exploited in symbolic state-space exploration to enhance the power of model checking.

Specifically, if M is a system description, and φ is a condition on the variables of M, then **next** φ **for** M describes the same system at a more abstract temporal level: a single transition of **next** φ **for** M aggregates as many transitions of M as are required to satisfy the condition φ, and hides the intermediate steps. For example, if M is a gate-level description of an ALU, and φ signals the completion of an arithmetic operation, then **next** φ **for** M is an operation-level description of the ALU. Mathematically, the semantics of **next** φ **for** M is defined as a two-level hierarchy of transition systems: each transition of the upper-level (e.g., operation-level) transition system abstracts an entire lower-level (e.g., gate-level) transition system. Then, by nesting **next** operators we obtain multi-level hierarchies of transition systems. The structuring of a state space into a multi-level transition hierarchy makes possible the exhaustive exploration of very large state spaces. This is because after the traversal of a level-n transition, the computed reach set for the corresponding level-$(n-1)$ transition system represents hidden intermediate steps and can be removed from memory.

In Section 2, we briefly review the language of Reactive Modules and give a simple example of a transition hierarchy. In Section 3, we introduce an algorithm for the symbolic exploration of transition hierarchies. In Section 4, we present experimental results that demonstrate the efficiency of our algorithm. For this purpose, we design a system comprising two processors with simple instruction sets, local caches, and shared memory. If we simply put together these components, using parallel composition but no **next** operator, the resulting flat transition system is far beyond the scope of existing model checkers. If, however, we use the **next** operator to aggregate and hide internal transitions between synchronization points before composing the various subsystems, the resulting transition hierarchy can be explored using the search routines of VIS, and correctness requirements can be checked fully automatically. Thus, the description of a design using **next** can eliminate the need for manual abstractions in verification.

Related work. The concept of temporal abstraction is inspired by the notion of *multiform time* in synchronous programming languages [BlGJ91, Hal93], and by the notion of *action refinement* in algebraic languages [AH89]. All of that work, however, concerns only the modeling of systems, and not automatic verification.

Temporal abstraction is implicitly present also in the concept of *stuttering* [Lam83]: a stuttering transition of a system is a transition that leaves all observable variables unchanged. Ignoring differences in the number of stuttering transitions leads to various notions of stutter-insensitive equivalences on state spaces (e.g., weak bisimulation). This suggests the following approach to model checking: for each component system, compute the appropriate stutter-insensitive equivalence, and before search, replace the component by the smaller quotient space. This approach, which has been implemented in tools such as the Concurrency Workbench [CPS93], requires the manipulation of the transition relations for individual components, and has not been shown competitive with simple search (cf. Section 3.1 vs. Section 3.2).

Partial-order methods avoid the exploration of unnecessary interleavings between the transitions of component systems. Gains due to partial-order reduction, in space and time, for verification have been reported both in the case of enumerative [HP94] and BDD-based approaches [ABH+97]. By declaring sequences of transitions to be atomic, the **next** operator also reduces the number of interleavings between concurrent transitions. However, while partial-order reductions need to be "discovered" *a posteriori* from the system description, transition hierarchies are specified *a priori* by the designer, as integral part of the system description.

2 Example: From Bit Addition to Word Addition

2.1 Reactive Modules

We specify systems as Reactive Modules. A formal definition of reactive modules can be found in [AH96]; here we give only a brief introduction. The state of a reactive module is determined by the values of three kinds of variables: the *external variables* are updated by the environment and can be read by the module; the *interface variables* are updated by the module and can be read by the environment; the *private variables* are updated by the module and cannot be read by the environment (this distinction is similar to I/O automata [Lyn96]).

For example, Figure 2 shows a module that adds two words. The environment of the word-adder consists of two modules: a command module, which provides the operands to be added and an instruction that they be added, and a bit-adder, which is called repeatedly by the word-adder. Hence the word-adder has the external variables *addOp1* and *addOp2* of type WORD, which contain the two operands provided by the command module, the external variable *doAdd* of type BOOLEAN, which is set by the command module whenever the two operands should be added, and three output bits of the bit-adder: the sum *bitResult*, the carry-out *cOut*, and the flag *doneBitAdd*, which is set whenever a bit-addition is completed. The word-adder has the interface variables *addResult* of type WORD, which contains the sum, *overflow* of type BOOLEAN, which indicates addition overflow, *doneAdd* of type BOOLEAN, which is set whenever a word-addition is complete, and four input bits for the bit-adder: the operands

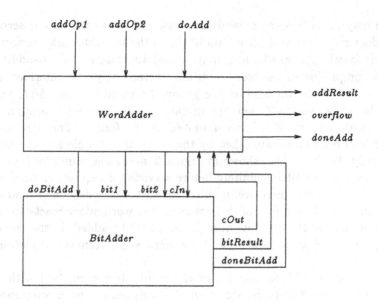

Fig. 1. Word-adder and bit-adder

bit1 and *bit2*, the carry-in *cIn*, and the flag *doBitAdd*, which instructs the bit-adder to perform a bit-addition. The word-adder has the private variables *state* of type FLAGTYPE, which indicates if an addition is being executed, and *bitCount* of type LOGWORD, which tracks the position of the active bits during the addition of two words. We assume that, once a word-addition is requested, the command module keeps the variable *doAdd* true until the word-adder signals completion of the addition by setting *doneAdd* to true.

The state of a reactive module changes in a sequence of rounds. In the first round, the initial values of all interface and private variables are determined. In each subsequent round, the new values of all interface and private variables are determined, possibly dependent on some latched values of external, interface, and private variables from the previous round, and possibly dependent on some new values of external variables from the current round. No assumptions are made about the initial values of external variables, nor on how they are updated in subsequent rounds. However, in order to avoid cyclic dependencies between variables, it is not permitted that within a single round, a module updates an interface variable *x* dependent on the new value of an external variable *y* while the environment updates *y* dependent on the new value of *x*. This restriction is enforced by collecting variables into atoms that can be ordered linearly such that in each round, the variables within an atom can be updated simultaneously provided that all variables within earlier atoms have already been updated. Thus, a round consists of several subrounds—one per atom.

A round of the word-adder consists of four subrounds: first, the command module may provide new operands and issue an add instruction; second, the word-adder may initiate a bit-addition; third, the bit-adder may perform a bit-addition; fourth, the word-adder may record the result of a bit-addition and signal a completion of the word-addition. Accordingly, the interface and private variables of the word-adder are grouped into two atoms: *bit1*, *bit2*, *cIn*, *doBitAdd*, *state*, and *bitCount* are updated in the second subround of each round; *addResult*, *overflow*, and *doneAdd* in the fourth. The first and third subrounds of each round are taken by the command module and the bit-adder, respectively. The bit-adder, shown in Figure 3, needs one round for bit-addition, but can choose to wait indefinitely before servicing a request. A word-addition of two n-bit numbers, therefore, requires at least n rounds—one round for each bitwise addition. In the first of these rounds, the word-adder reacts to the command module, and the first bits may (or may not) be added. In the last of these rounds, the n-th bits are added, and the word-adder signals completion of the addition.

Figure 1 gives a block diagram of the word-adder composed with the bit-adder, and Figures 2 and 3 provide formal descriptions of both components. For each atom, the initial values of the variables and their new values in each subsequent (update) round are specified by guarded commands (as in UNITY [CM88]). In each round, unprimed symbols, such as x, refer to the latched value of the variable x, and primed symbols, such as x', refer to the new value. An atom *reads* the variable x if its guarded commands refer to the latched value of x. The atom *awaits* x if its guarded commands refer to the new value x'. The await dependencies between variables are required to be acyclic. A variable is *history-free* if it is not read by any atom. Since the values of history-free variables at any round do not influence the next round, they do not have to be stored during state-space traversal.

2.2 Flat vs. Hierarchical Models

We discuss two operations for building complex reactive modules from simple ones. The *parallel-composition operator* abstracts spatial complexities of a system by collecting the atoms of several modules within a single module. The *next operator* abstracts temporal complexities of a system by combining several rounds of a module as subrounds of a single round. Intuitively, if M is a reactive module and φ is a condition on the variables of M, then **next** φ **for** M is a module that, in a single round, iterates as many rounds of M as are necessary to make the so-called *aggregation predicate* φ true. Formal definitions of parallel composition and next-abstraction can be found in [AH96].

Consider, for example, the following two modules:

ConcreteAdder = *WordAdder* ‖ *BitAdder*
AbstractAdder = **next** (*doAdd* ⇒ *doneAdd*) **for** *ConcreteAdder*

Each of the two modules is a model for an addition unit that consists of two components, a word-adder composed with a bit-adder. The two models differ

module *WordAdder*
type FLAGTYPE : {IDLE, WORKING};
interface *addResult* : WORD;
    bit1, bit2, cIn, doBitAdd, doneAdd, overflow : BOOLEAN
private *state* : FLAGTYPE;
    bitCount : LOGWORD
external *addOp1, addOp2* : WORD;
    doAdd, doneBitAdd, bitResult, cOut : BOOLEAN
atom controls *state, bitCount, doBitAdd, bit1, bit2, cIn*
  reads *doneBitAdd, bitResult, cOut*
  awaits *addOp1, addOp2, doAdd*
  init
    [] *true* → *state′* := IDLE
  update
    [] (*state* = IDLE) ∧ *doAdd′* →
      state′ := WORKING; *bitCount′* := *false*; *doBitAdd′* := *true*;
      bit1′ := *addOp1′*[0]; *bit2′* := *addOp2′*[0]; *cIn′* := *false*
    [] (*state* = WORKING) ∧ (*bitCount* < WORDLENGTH − 1) ∧ *doneBitAdd* →
      bit1′ := *addOp1′*[*bitCount* + 1]; *bit2′* := *addOp2′*[*bitCount* + 1];
      cIn′ = *cOut*; *bitCount′* = *bitCount* + 1
    [] (*state* = WORKING) ∧ (*bitCount* = WORDLENGTH − 1) ∧ *doneBitAdd* →
      doBitAdd′ = *false*; *state′* := IDLE
endatom

atom controls *addResult, doneAdd, overflow*
  reads *bitCount*
  awaits *bitResult, doneBitAdd, cOut*
  init
    [] *true* → *doneAdd′* := *false*
  update
    [] (*bitCount* < WORDLENGTH − 1) ∧ *doneBitAdd′* →
      addResult′[*bitCount*] := *bitResult′*
    [] (*bitCount* = WORDLENGTH − 1) ∧ *doneBitAdd′* →
      addResult′[*bitCount*] := *bitResult*; *doneAdd′* := *true*; *overflow′* = *cOut′*
endatom
endmodule

Fig. 2. Word-adder

only in their level of temporal granularity. In the flat model *ConcreteAdder*, the addition of two *n*-bit words takes at least *n* rounds. In the hierarchical model *AbstractAdder*, the addition of two *n*-bit words takes a single round. This is because the next-abstracted module combines into a single round as many rounds as are necessary to make either *doAdd* false or *doneAdd* true. In other words, in the flat model, bit-additions are atomic. Thus the flat model is adequate under

```
module BitAdder
interface doneBitAdd, bitResult, cOut : BOOLEAN
external bit1, bit2, cIn, doBitAdd : BOOLEAN
atom doneBitAdd, bitResult, cOut
    awaits bit1, bit2, cIn, doBitAdd
    init
        [] true → doneBitAdd' := false
    update
        [] doBitAdd' →
            bitResult' := bit1' ⊕ bit2' ⊕ cIn';
            cOut' := (bit1'&bit2')|(bit2'&cIn')|(cIn'&bit1');
            doneBitAdd' := true
        [] true → doneBitAdd' := false;
endatom
endmodule
```

Fig. 3. Bit-adder

the assumption that the addition unit is put into an environment that interacts with the addition unit only before and after bit-additions, but does not interrupt in the middle of a bit-addition. By contrast, in the hierarchical model, word-additions are atomic. Therefore the hierarchical model is adequate only under the stronger assumption that the addition unit is put into an environment that interacts with the addition unit only before and after word-additions, but does not interrupt in the middle of a word-addition. While the flat model is adequate in more situations, we will see that the hierarchical model can be verified more efficiently, and therefore should be preferred whenever it is adequate.

3 Symbolic Exploration of Hierarchical State Spaces

The reason why next-abstraction can be exploited by model checking can be seen as follows. If the semantics of a reactive module is viewed as a state-transition graph, with each round corresponding to a transition, then the hierarchical module **next** φ for M may have many fewer states than the flat module M. In particular, the **next** operator removes all states of M in which the aggregation predicate φ is not true; these states are called *transient*. When exploring the state space of the flat module, both transient and nontransient reachable states need to be stored as they are computed. By contrast, when exploring the state space of a hierarchical module, transient states need to be computed in order to find nontransient successor states, but once these states are found, the transient states need not be stored. Moreover, some of the variables that are not history-free in the flat model no longer influence (nontransient) successor states in the hierarchical model, and thus in effect become history-free. This results in further savings in memory for storing states.

The savings are particularly pronounced when hierarchical models are composed. Consider two flat models M and N, and two hierarchical models $M' =$ (**next** φ **for** M) and $N' =$ (**next** ψ **for** N). The hierarchical composition $M' \parallel N'$ is an adequate model for the composed systems if the aggregation predicates φ and ψ characterize the synchronization points of the two components; that is, if M interacts with N whenever φ becomes true, and N interacts with M whenever ψ becomes true. The possible interleavings of transitions of M and N may lead to an explosion of transient states of $M \parallel N$ (states in which either φ or ψ is false), which can be avoided by exploring instead $M' \parallel N'$. In other words, if the interaction between two component systems can be restricted, then some of the state-explosion problem may be avoided. Indeed, as we shall see, in complex systems with many components but well-defined interactions between the components, the computational savings, both in time and memory, can be enormous.

In the following, we first define the transition relations of composite and hierarchical modules from the transition relations of the components. Then we present a nested-search algorithm that explores the state space of a hierarchical module efficiently. The nested-search algorithm uses an implicit, algorithmic representation of the transition relation of a hierarchical module for image computation.

3.1 Explicit Definition of Transition Relations

The state-transition graph of a reactive module can be specified by a symbolic transition relation. Given a module M with variables X, the *symbolic transition relation* of M is a boolean function $T_M(X, X')$. Let $\hat{X}$ and $\hat{X}'$ be two states of M, i.e., valuations to the variables of M. Then the expression $T_M(\hat{X}, \hat{X}')$ evaluates to true iff there is an edge in the state-transition graph from state $\hat{X}$ to state $\hat{X}'$. All modules are built from individual atoms using parallel composition and the **next** operator. It is straightforward to construct the symbolic transition relation of an atom. For complex modules, the symbolic transition relation is defined inductively.

Parallel composition. Consider the module $M = M_1 \parallel M_2$. Let $T_{M_1}(X_1, X_1')$ and $T_{M_2}(X_2, X_2')$ be the symbolic transition relations of M_1 and M_2, respectively. Then the symbolic transition relation of M is given by the conjunction

$$T_M(X, X') = T_{M_1}(X_1, X_1') \wedge T_{M_2}(X_2, X_2').$$

Next abstraction. Consider the module $M = (\textbf{next } \varphi \textbf{ for } N)$. Let $T_N(X, X')$ be the symbolic transition relation of N. For all natural numbers $i \geq 0$, define

- $T_M^0(X, X') = T_N(X, X');$
- $T_M^{i+1}(X, X') = T_M^i(X, X') \vee (\exists Y)(\neg \varphi(Y) \wedge T_N(X, Y) \wedge T_M^i(Y, X')).$

Let $T_M^l = T_M^{l+1}$ be the limit of the fixpoint computation sequence $T_M^0, T_M^1, T_M^2, \ldots$ (finite convergence is guaranteed for finite-state systems). Then the symbolic transition relation of M is given by

$$T_M(X, X') = \varphi(X) \wedge \varphi(X') \wedge T_M^l(X, X').$$

The reachable state set of a module can be computed by iterated application of the transition relation. For this purpose, it is theoretically possible to construct, using the above definitions, a BDD for the symbolic transition relation of a hierarchical module. In practice, however, during the construction the intermediate BDDs often blows up and results in memory overflow. For parallel composition, it is a common trick to leave the transition relation conjunctively decomposed and represent it as a set of BDDs, rather than computing their conjunction as a single BDD [TSL90]. Early quantification heuristics are then used to efficiently compute the image of a state set under a conjunctively partitioned transition relation. For next abstraction, we propose a similar approach.

3.2 Efficient Computation with Implicit Transition Relations

For model checking, it suffices to represent the symbolic transition relation of a module not explicitly, as a BDD, but implicitly, as an algorithm that given a state set, computes the set of successor states. This algorithm can then be iterated for reachability analysis and more general verification problems. Given a module M, the *single-step successor function* of M is a function R_M^1 from state sets of M to state sets of M. Let σ be a set of states of M. Then $R_M^1(\sigma)$ is the set of all states $\hat{X}'$ of M such that there is a state $\hat{X} \in \sigma$ with $T_M(\hat{X}, \hat{X}')$; that is, $R_M^1(\sigma)$ is the image of σ under the transition relation T_M. It is straightforward to compute $R_M^1(\sigma)$ for single atoms. For complex modules, the single-step successor function is computed recursively.

Parallel composition. Consider the module $M = M_1 \parallel M_2$ and a set σ of states of M. Let $R_{M_1}^1(\sigma)$ and $R_{M_2}^1(\sigma)$ be the images of σ for M_1 and M_2, respectively. Then

$$R_M^1(\sigma) = R_{M_1}^1(\sigma) \wedge R_{M_2}^1(\sigma).$$

Next abstraction. Consider the module $M = (\textbf{next } \varphi \textbf{ for } N)$ and a set σ of states of M. Let $R_N^1(\sigma)$ be the image of σ for N. Then $R_M^1(\sigma)$ is computed by the *nested-search* procedure described in Algorithm 3.2.

Algorithm 3.2
　{Given module $M = (\textbf{next } \varphi \textbf{ for } N)$, single-step successor function R_N^1,
　　and state set σ, compute $R_M^1(\sigma)$}
　{We will assume $\sigma \subseteq \varphi$}
　$FirstLevelImage := \{\}$
　$SecondLevelImage := R_N^1(\sigma)$
　$SecondLevelReachSet := \{\}$
　loop
　　$FirstLevelImage := FirstLevelImage \cup (SecondLevelImage \cap \varphi)$
　　$SecondLevelReachSet := SecondLevelReachSet \cup (SecondLevelImage \cap \overline{\varphi})$
　　$SecondLevelImage := R_N^1(SecondLevelReachSet)$

until (*SecondLevelReachSet* does not change)
return (*FirstLevelImage*)

In contrast to a BDD for $T_M(X, X')$, which explicitly represents the transition relation of module M, the recursive algorithm for computing the function R^1_M implicitly represents the same information. In practice, a mixture of explicit symbolic representation of transition relations (for small modules) and implicit image computation (for complex modules) will be most efficient. We report on our experiences with nested search in the following section.

4 Experiments

The aim of our experiments is to investigate the efficiency of the proposed method for the automatic reachability analysis of complex designs. All experimental results reported in this paper were obtained by modeling the systems in Verilog and using the *vl2mv* Verilog compiler along with VIS [BSVH+96]. We implemented a new command in VIS, called *abstract_reach*, based on Algorithm 3.2.

4.1 Multiplier

We model a word-multiplier that functions by repeated addition, using the word-adder described earlier. With help of the **next** operator, we can model the multiplier at various levels of temporal detail. We experiment with two options:

- Model 1: For addition, use the flat module *ConcreteAdder* explained in Section 2. In this model, bit-additions appear as atomic actions of the multiplier.
- Model 2: For addition, use the hierarchical module *AbstractAdder*. In this model, word-additions appear as atomic actions.

We perform reachability analysis with both models. Model 1 is given to VIS directly, and reachability analysis is performed using the *compute_reach* command of VIS. In order to analyze Model 2, we use the *abstract_reach* command with the aggregation predicate $doAdd \Rightarrow doneAdd$. As a result, the states in which *doAdd* is true and *doneAdd* is false become transient states.

We experiment with two 4-bit operands and an 8-bit result. In this case, Model 1 has 68 latches and 1416 gates. After the next abstraction, 24 of these latches become history-free; that is, their values in a state do not influence the next states of Model 2. In particular, the local variables of the adder become history-free, and hence, are represented by trivial functions in the BDD that represents the reachable states. Table 1 shows the peak BDD sizes for both models.

4.2 Cache Coherence Protocol

We describe the various components of a generic cache coherence protocol before discussing our results. Each cache block can be in one of three states: INVALID, READ_SHARED, or WRITE_EXCLUSIVE. Multiple processors can have the same memory location in their caches in the READ_SHARED state, but only one processor can have a given location in the WRITE_EXCLUSIVE state. There is a directory that, for each memory location, has a record of which processors have cached that location and what states (READ_SHARED, WRITE_EXCLUSIVE) these blocks are in. Due to want of space, we will not explain the protocol formally. An example scenario gives the general flavor. Suppose that Processor 1 has a location in WRITE_EXCLUSIVE, and Processor 2 wants to read this location. First Cache 2 records a write miss and communicates that to the directory. The directory then sends a message to Processor 1, requesting it to move the state of the block under consideration from WRITE_EXCLUSIVE to READ_SHARED. Cache 1 acknowledges this request and also sends the latest version of the data in this block to the directory. The directory then services Cache 2 with this data, and Cache 2 gets the block as READ_SHARED. Each of these steps involves a transaction on the bus, which could take an arbitrary number of rounds due to the asynchronous nature of the bus.

We experiment with two levels of temporal granularity. Model 1 is a flat model of the memory system, and Model 2 is a hierarchical model that abstracts temporal detail about the bus. While a bus transaction can consume multiple rounds in Model 1, it is forced to always complete in a single round in Model 2. For our experiments, we choose a 1-bit address bus and 1-bit data bus. In this case, Model 1 has 44 latches, of which 6 latches become history-free in Model 2. The peak BDD sizes during reachability analysis for both models are reported in Table 1.

4.3 Processor-Memory System

Aiming for a more dramatic improvement over flat modeling, we compose several systems whose interactions are limited. We put together two processors, each with an ALU consisting of the adder and multiplier described earlier, and the cache protocol, to obtain a complete processor-memory system. A block diagram of the system is shown in Figure 4. The processors have a simple instruction set: **load/store** register to/from memory, **add** two register operands, **multiply** two register operands, **compare** two registers, and a conditional **branch**. Again we experiment with two models. Model 1 is flat, and Model 2 is constructed by composing next-abstracted versions of the multipliers, adders, and bus protocol.

We choose an 1-bit wide address bus and a 2-bit wide data bus. In this case, Model 1 has 147 latches, of which 36 latches become history-free in Model 2 (15 latches in each multiplier, and 6 in the cache protocol). Here, reachability analysis for Model 1 is beyond the capability of current verification tools. However, fully automatic reachability analysis succeeds for Model 2, which structures the

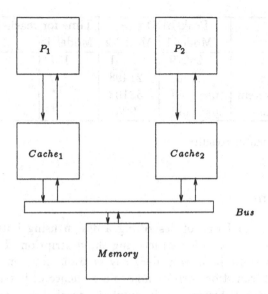

Fig. 4. Processor-Memory System

design using the **next** operator. Consider, for example, the situation where both processors start a multiplication at the same time. In Model 1, there are several transient states due to the interleaving of independent suboperations of the two multipliers. These transient states are entirely absent in Model 2. Indeed, nested search (Algorithm 3.2) is the key to verifying this example: we run out of memory when trying to compute an explicit representation of the transition relation for Model 2.[5]

4.4 Processor-Memory System with Programs

Finally, we add programs to the processors of the processor-memory system. Processor 1 computes $A * B$. Processor 2 computes $C * D$. Processor 1 then adds up both results and computes $A * B + C * D$. The two processors synchronize through a flag in memory. The last entry of the table shows the reachability results for the processor-memory system constrained by these programs. Again, Model 2 completes reachability using *abstract_reach*, whereas Model 1 does not. Thus we are able to verify invariants on Model 2, such as confirming that the results computed by the programs are correct.

---

[5] The transition relation for the multiplier module alone, as computed by VIS, has 7586 BDD nodes and is composed of 6 conjunctive components. Even "and"-ing the components together results in memory overflow.

Example	Peak BDD size		Time for reachability (sec)	
	Model 1	Model 2	Model 1	Model 2
Multiplier	26979	6561	157	122
Cache Coherence	42467	21498	310	227
Proc/Mem System	space out	53103	*	816
with Program	space out	9251	*	153

Table 1. Experimental Results

5 Conclusions

We introduced a formal way of describing a design using both temporal and spatial abstraction operators for structuring the description. The temporal abstraction operator **next** induces a hierarchy of transitions on the state space, where a high-level transition corresponds to a sequence of low-level transitions. We exploited transition hierarchies in symbolic reachability analysis and presented an algorithm for proving invariants of reactive modules using hierarchical search. We tested the algorithm on arithmetic circuits, cache coherence protocols, and processor-memory systems, using an extension of VIS. The experimental results are encouraging, giving fully automatic results even on systems that are amenable to existing tools only after manual abstractions. Transition hierarchies can be exploited to give efficiencies in enumerative reachability analysis as well [AH96]. We are currently building a formal verification tool for reactive modules, called MOCHA, which will incorporate both symbolic and enumerative hierarchical search as primitives.

While the **next** operator is ideally suited for abstracting subsystems that interact with each other at predetermined synchronization points, it does not permit the "out-of-order execution" of low-level transitions. We currently investigate additional abstraction operators, such as operators that permit the temporal abstraction of pipelined designs.

References

[AH89] L. Aceto and M. Hennessy. Towards action refinement in process algebras. In *Proc. of LICS 89: Logic in Computer Science*, pages 138–145. IEEE Computer Society Press, 1989.

[ABH+97] R. Alur, R.K. Brayton, T.A. Henzinger, S. Qadeer, and S.K. Rajamani. Partial-order reduction in symbolic state-space exploration. In *Proc. of CAV 97: Computer-Aided Verification*, LNCS 1254, pages 340–351. Springer-Verlag, 1997.

[AH96] R. Alur and T.A. Henzinger. Reactive modules. In *Proc. of LICS 96: Logic in Computer Science*, pages 207–218. IEEE Computer Society Press, 1996.

[BlGJ91] A. Benveniste, P. le Guernic, and C. Jacquemot. Synchronous programming with events and relations: The SIGNAL language and its semantics. *Science of Computer Programming*, 16:103–149, 1991.

[BSVH+96] R.K. Brayton, A. Sangiovanni-Vincentelli, G.D. Hachtel, F. Somenzi, A. Aziz, S.-T. Cheng, S. Edwards, S. Khatri, Y. Kukimoto, S. Qadeer, R.K. Ranjan, T.R. Shiple, G. Swamy, T. Villa, A. Pardo, and S. Sarwary. VIS: a system for verification and synthesis. In *Proc. of CAV 96: Computer-Aided Verification*, LNCS 1102, pages 428–432. Springer-Verlag, 1996.

[CK96] E.M. Clarke and R.P. Kurshan. Computer-aided verification. *IEEE Spectrum*, 33(6):61–67, 1996.

[CKSVG96] E.M. Clarke, K.L. McMillan, S. Campos, and V. Hartonas-Garmhausen. Symbolic model checking. In *Proc. of CAV 96: Computer-Aided Verification*, LNCS 1102, pages 419–422. Springer-Verlag, 1996.

[CM88] K.M. Chandy and J. Misra. *Parallel Program Design: A Foundation*. Addison-Wesley, 1988.

[CPS93] R.J. Cleaveland, J. Parrow, and B. Steffen. The Concurrency Workbench: a semantics-based tool for the verification of finite-state systems. *ACM Transactions on Programming Languages and Systems*, 15(1):36–72, 1993.

[Dil96] D.L. Dill. The $Mur\phi$ verification system. In *Proc. of CAV 96: Computer-Aided Verification*, LNCS 1102, pages 390–393. Springer-Verlag, 1996.

[Hal93] N. Halbwachs. *Synchronous Programming of Reactive Systems*. Kluwer Academic Publishers, 1993.

[HP94] G.J. Holzmann and D.A. Peled. An improvement in formal verification. In *Proc. of FORTE 94: Formal Description Techniques*, pages 197–211. Chapman & Hall, 1994.

[HP96] G.J. Holzmann and D.A. Peled. The state of SPIN. In *Proc. of CAV 96: Computer-Aided Verification*, LNCS 1102, pages 385–389. Springer-Verlag, 1996.

[HZR96] R.H. Hardin, Z. Har'El, and R.P. Kurshan. COSPAN. In *Proc. of CAV 96: Computer-Aided Verification*, LNCS 1102, pages 423–427. Springer-Verlag, 1996.

[Lam83] L. Lamport. What good is temporal logic? In *Proc. of Information Processing 83: IFIP World Computer Congress*, pages 657–668. Elsevier Science Publishers, 1983.

[Lyn96] N.A. Lynch. *Distributed Algorithms*. Morgan-Kaufmann, 1996.

[TSL90] H.J. Touati, H. Savoj, B. Lin, R.K. Brayton, and A. Sangiovanni-Vincentelli. Implicit state enumeration of finite-state machines using BDDs. In *Proc. of ICCAD 90: Computer-Aided Design*, pages 130–133. IEEE Computer Society Press, 1990.

Static Partial Order Reduction

R. Kurshan[1], V. Levin[1], M. Minea[2], D. Peled[1,2], H. Yenigün[1]

[1] Lucent Technologies, Bell Laboratories, Murray Hill, NJ 07974
[2] Dept. of Computer Science, Carnegie Mellon University, Pittsburgh, PA 15213

Abstract. The state space explosion problem is central to automatic verification algorithms. One of the successful techniques to abate this problem is called 'partial order reduction'. It is based on the observation that in many cases the specification of concurrent programs does not depend on the order in which concurrently executed events are interleaved. In this paper we present a new version of partial order reduction that allows all of the reduction to be set up at the time of compiling the system description. Normally, partial order reduction requires developing specialized verification algorithms, which in the course of a state space search, select a subset of the possible transitions from each reached global state. In our approach, the set of atomic transitions obtained from the system description after our special compilation, already generates a smaller number of choices from each state. Thus, rather than conducting a modified search of the state space generated by the original state transition relation, our approach involves an ordinary search of the reachable state space generated by a modified state transition relation. Among the advantages of this technique over other versions of the reduction is that it can be directly implemented using existing verification tools, as it requires no change of the verification engine: the entire reduction mechanism is set up at compile time. One major application is the use of this reduction technique together with symbolic model checking and localization reduction, obtaining a combined reduction. We discuss an implementation and experimental results for SDL programs translated into COSPAN notation by applying our reduction techniques. This is part of a hardware-software co-verification project.

1   Introduction

One common method for dealing with the intrinsically intractable computational complexity of model-checking asynchronous systems is *partial order reduction*. This reduction technique exploits the common practice of modeling concurrent events in asynchronous systems as an interleaving of the events in all possible execution orders. An important observation about such systems is that the properties one needs to check often do not distinguish among these different orders. The reduction algorithm produces a state graph which contains only a subset of the states and transitions of the original system, but which contains enough information about the modelled system so that it is possible to apply model checking algorithms to it instead of the full state graph. The verified property is guaranteed to be true in the reduced model if and only if it is true in the original model.

Since partial order reduction is naturally defined for asynchronous systems, it has thus far been applied mainly to the verification of software. Traditional partial order reduction algorithms use an explicit state representation and depth first search. In contrast, other techniques for model checking, most notably symbolic model checking based on binary decision diagrams (BDDs), have proved most effective for synchronous systems, in particular for verifying hardware. In this paper we describe a reduction algorithm that was developed to satisfy the following goals:

- Perform efficiently for a system that combines software and hardware, and therefore combine well with symbolic model checking.
- Be independent of the type of search, e.g., be applicable to depth- or breadth-first search without a change.
- Allow a large (in our case, in fact the entire) part of the reduction to be done during compilation of the modelled system.
- Be compatible with existing model checking tools without requiring a change to their search engines.

We show a partial order reduction algorithm that achieves these goals. Our method was motivated by an interest to verify embedded systems containing both hardware and software. In our case, the software was written in the SDL language [13] and was translated into the specification language S/R, which is an automata based language for specifying coordinating processes and used as the input language for the model-checking tool COSPAN [7]. COSPAN runs on synchronous input models and supports a symbolic (BDD-based) state space search.

Previous implementations of partial order reduction algorithms in pre-existing state space search engines required considerable changes in the search mechanism [6, 9]. The alternative was to construct a special tool for performing the search [14]. In [9], a reduction that is based on doing a large part of the calculations at compile time is described. However, some changes are still made to the search engine, controlling the backtracking mechanism in the depth-first search performed in the SPIN [8] model checker.

Since we began with an efficient translator [2] from SDL to S/R, we aimed to investigate whether one could obtain an efficient partial order reduction algorithm with *all* of the reduction-specific calculations taking place at compile time, without changing the search mechanism of the COSPAN verification engine. COSPAN should treat the translated model as a regular model, without having to undergo any changes to implement the reduction. The process is illustrated in Fig. 1. The usual model checking procedure involves translating the source code into some intermediate code, which is then analyzed by the actual model checking algorithms. The reduction usually requires a change to the code of the model checker. In this paper, we suggest a modified partial order reduction that can be applied to the translation. The model checking tool remains unchanged.

A related recent result is the combination of partial order reduction with symbolic model checking reported in [1]. This is based on performing a reduction which uses breadth first search [3]. The method suggested in the present paper is more general in the sense that it is independent of the type of search used (e.g., breadth first or depth first). It can also be applied to existing model checking tools without imposing any changes and hence should be easier to adopt and implement.

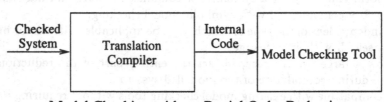

Model Checking without Partial Order Reduction

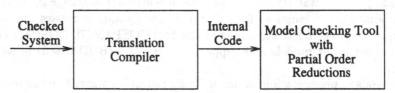

Traditional Model Checking with Partial Order Reduction

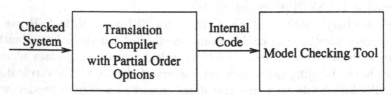

New Scheme for Model Checking with Partial Order Reduction

Fig. 1. Model Checking Scheme

2 A Simplified Search Algorithm

2.1 The Ample Sets Method

The reduction method we describe is applied to systems which are modelled as state-transition graphs. A state transition graph is defined as a tuple $M = (S, S_0, T, L)$, where S is the set of states, S_0 is the initial state set, T is a set of transitions $\alpha \subseteq S \times S$, and $L : S \rightarrow 2^{AP}$ a function that labels each state with some subset of a set AP of atomic propositions. A transition α is *enabled* in state s if there is some state s' for which $\alpha(s, s')$ holds. We denote the set of transitions enabled in s by *enabled(s)*. If for any state s there is at most one state s' with $\alpha(s, s')$, we say that α is *deterministic* and we will write $s' = \alpha(s)$. In the following, we will consider only deterministic transitions. Note that although the transitions are deterministic (a usual practice in modeling concurrency), we can easily model non-deterministic choice (between different transitions that are enabled at the same time).

We introduce the key concept of *independent* transitions. These are transitions whose respective effects are the same, irrespective of their relative order.

Definition 1. Two transitions α and β are *independent* if for every state s the following two conditions hold:
Enabledness: If $\alpha, \beta \in enabled(s)$ then $\beta \in enabled(\alpha(s))$ and $\alpha \in enabled(\beta(s))$
Commutativity: If $\alpha, \beta \in enabled(s)$ then $\alpha(\beta(s)) = \beta(\alpha(s))$.

In other words, a pair of transitions is independent, if at any state executing either of them does not disable the other, and executing both in either order leads to the same state. Two transitions are called dependent if they are not independent.

To construct the reachable state space, model checking algorithms perform a traversal of the state-transition graph (typically depth-first or breadth-first search). The traversal starts from the set of initial states and successively constructs new states by exploring the transitions that are enabled in the current state. Partial order reduction differs from full state exploration in that at each step it considers only a subset of the transitions enabled at the current state s. This set is denoted by *ample(s)*. With a good choice of *ample(s)*, only a small fraction of the reachable state space will be explored. On the other hand, a number of conditions must be enforced on this set to ensure that the truth value of the checked property is preserved in the reduced model. In the following, we give a set of such conditions together with an informal explanation of their role. A complete treatment of these conditions together with a formal proof is given in [12].

Condition **C0** is the simplest and guarantees that if a state has a successor in the original model, it also has a successor in the reduced model.

C0 [Non-emptiness condition] $ample(s) = \emptyset$ if and only if $enabled(s) = \emptyset$.

C1 [Ample decomposition] On any path starting from state s, all the transitions appearing before a transition in $ample(s)$ is executed, are independent of all the transitions in $ample(s)$.

To explain **C1**, note that not every transition sequence in the original model may appear in the reduced model, since the latter is restricted to transitions from $ample(s)$ at each state s. However, **C1** ensures that some transition from $ample(s)$ may be taken in the reduced model without disabling any of the transitions in the original sequence. Consider any transition sequence σ starting in some state s_0. There are two possible cases:

- σ contains a transition $\alpha \in ample(s_0)$, in which case it is of the form $\beta_0\beta_1 \ldots \beta_n\alpha \ldots$. Condition **C1** then implies that α is independent of any $\beta_i, i \leq n$ and commutes with every one of these transitions. Then α can be taken in state s_0 and leaves the sequence $\beta_0\beta_1 \ldots \beta_n \ldots$ still enabled thereafter,
- the sequence does not contain any transitions in $ample(s_0)$. Then an arbitrary transition $\alpha \in ample(s_0)$ can be taken in s_0, it is independent of all transitions in σ and therefore σ is still enabled in $\alpha(s_0)$ in the original model.

In order to be able to use the reduced model instead of the original one in verification, we also need to ensure that the checked property is not sensitive to the paths and states that have been eliminated from the reduced model. We consider as specifications next–time free linear time temporal logic (LTL without the next–time operator) formulas over the set of atomic propositions AP that label the states of the system. We call two paths *stuttering equivalent* if they are identical from the point of view of state labeling, after finite subsequences of successive states with the same labels have been collapsed into one state in each of them. It can be shown [11] that if two state transition graphs have the property that for any infinite path starting from an initial state in one of them there exists a stuttering equivalent infinite path in the other and vice versa, the two models satisfy the same set of next-time free LTL formulas.

We call a transition *invisible* if its execution has no effect on the state labeling. In other words, $\alpha \in T$ is invisible if $\forall s, s', \alpha(s, s') \Rightarrow L(s) = L(s')$. A state s is called *fully expanded* if $ample(s) = enabled(s)$. In this case, all transitions are selected for exploration and no reduction is performed at this point.

C2 [Non-visibility condition] If there exists a visible transition in $ample(s)$ then s is fully expanded.

Revisiting the two cases discussed for condition **C1** it can be seen that in each of these cases, α is an invisible transition (since s_0 is not fully expanded), and therefore the two paths considered will be stuttering equivalent.

Finally, we have to ensure that an enabled transition which does not belong to an ample set will eventually be taken. Otherwise, the constructions outlined in the discussion of **C1** may close a cycle in the reduced state graph while never taking a non-ample transition which is enabled throughout the cycle. Consequently some transitions can be ignored and the truth value of a specification in the two models may no longer be the same. Condition **C3** is introduced to eliminate this problem:

C3 [Cycle closing condition] At least one state along each cycle of the reduced state graph is fully expanded.[3]

As stated in the introduction, our goal was to develop a reduction algorithm which is not restricted to depth-first explicit state search, like the typical one described for instance in [9]. The principles and implementation of this algorithm are described below.

2.2 A Generic Partial Order Reduction

The cycle closing condition **C3** is very natural to check while performing a depth-first search. However, it cannot be checked directly when performing a breadth-first search (which is intrinsic to the symbolic methods), and therefore it seems that significant modifications to the model checking algorithms are needed to accommodate it (*cf* [1]). We show, however, that it is possible to ensure **C3** by performing static checks on the local state-transition graphs of each process. Conceptually, this method is able to perform a reduction (in terms of the number of reached states) at least as good as the traditional dynamic algorithms, although in practice there is a trade-off between the computational cost of the static reduction and computational savings afforded by the reduced model during the dynamic state space search. In fact, the most efficient balance in our algorithm may be achieved with varying degrees of state space reduction.

To describe our algorithm, we first note that both **C2** and **C3** limit the extent to which reduction can be performed: they define cases where a state has to be fully expanded. Moreover, if a cycle contains a visible transition, then **C2** guarantees that the state at which that transition is taken is fully expanded, and therefore **C3** holds for that cycle as well. This suggests that **C2** and **C3** can be combined into a single condition **C2'**:

C2' There exists a set of transitions T which includes all visible transitions, such that any cycle in the reduced state space contains a transition from T. When *ample*(s) includes a transition from T, s is fully expanded.

We call the set of transitions T *sticky transitions*, since intuitively, they stick to all other enabled transitions.

To perform reduction during compilation of the modelled system, our goal is to determine a set T of sticky transitions that breaks all cycles of the reduced state graph, in order to guarantee **C2'**. We assume that the system to be verified is given as a set of component processes. Then, an easy way to find such a set T to look at the static control flow graph of each process of the system. Any cycle in the global state space projects to a cycle (or possibly a self-loop) in each component process. By breaking each local cycle, we are guaranteed to break each global cycle.

This suggests strengthening **C2'** to the following condition **C2''**:

---

[3] There are other stronger and weaker conditions that can be used instead of Condition **C3**. This particular version fits well with our framework.

C2" There is a set of sticky transitions that include all visible transitions. Each cycle in the static control flow of a process of the modelled system contains at least one sticky transition, and if $ample(s)$ includes a sticky transition, then s is fully expanded.

An ideal algorithm would find a minimal set of sticky transitions, in order to maximize the possible reduction. However, this problem is at least as hard as reachability analysis. On the other hand, efficient reduction can still be achieved even without a minimal set. During the state search, priority is given to non-sticky transitions. In this way, full expansion of a state is avoided as much as possible, although eventually no cycle can be closed without performing one full expansion. It is possible therefore that several sticky transitions are delayed until all of them can be taken from the same state, which reduces the effect of selecting too many sticky transitions.

Even with delaying sticky transitions, it is still important that the static analysis generates a small number of sticky transitions, and yet is simple enough not to require excessive overhead. The next section presents such an algorithm which is heuristically likely to generate a smaller number of sticky transitions than required by **C2"**. The set of sticky transitions found by the algorithm guarantees **C2'** and in the worst case it corresponds to **C2"**.

2.3 Finding Sticky Transitions

We assume that the system to be analyzed is given as a set of variables V and a set of processes $\{P_1, P_2, \ldots, P_N\}$. We also assume that, for each process P_i, there exists a variable $cp_i \in V$ called the *control point* (or *program counter*) of process P_i, which always keeps the current local state of the process. A transition of P_i updates cp_i (not necessarily changes its value) and also updates some other variables from V. The state space of the system is simply given by all possible valuations of the variables in V. The state-transition graph of the system is derived from the local state-transition graphs of the processes by using interleaving semantics to model concurrency. A *local* (resp. *global*) cycle is a cycle in the state-transition graph of a process (resp. the system). An *execution* of a cycle is the execution of all the transitions in the cycle starting from a state in the cycle.

An execution of a local cycle of a process P_i restores the value of cp_i. But along the cycle, the values of variables other than cp_i can be changed as well, without necessarily being restored by a complete execution. We call this the side effect of a local cycle on a variable and observe four different types of side effects: (1) *decrementing effect*, if the execution of the cycle always reduces the value of the variable, (2) *incrementing effect* if the execution of the cycle always increases the value of the variable, (3) *complex effect* if the effect of the execution of the cycle on the variable cannot be determined statically, and (4) *no effect* if the variable is not changed by any of the transitions in the cycle.

If the side effect of a local cycle c is incrementing or decrementing over the value of a variable v, it is impossible to have a global cycle in which only c is executed. There must be some other local cycle c' executed in the global cycle to compensate for the side effect of c on v. For every global cycle in which c is executed, c' must be executed as well. Therefore, there is no need to select a sticky transition from both c and c' since neither c nor c' can appear alone in a global cycle.

Let C denote the set of local cycles in the system. We assume the existence of a function $f : C \times V \rightarrow \{-, +, \star, 0\}$ such that for $c \in C$ and $v \in V$, $f(c, v) = -$ ($f(c, v) = +$, $f(c, v) = \star$, $f(c, v) = 0$, respectively) means a decrementing effect (incrementing, complex, no effect, respectively) on v by c. One can always assume $f(c, v) = \star$ if v is updated within c but the side effect is difficult to analyze.

Definition 2. A set of local cycles $H \subseteq C$ *covers* another set of local cycles $G \subseteq C$ if any global cycle that contains (projects to) a local cycle $c \in G$ also has to contain some local cycle $c' \in H$.

In the particular case where G is a singleton set $\{c\}$, we will simply say that H covers c.

We can effectively find a set of cycles that covers a local cycle c by considering the effect of c on some variable v. For a given local cycle c and a variable v, let c_v be the set of local cycles that can compensate the incrementing or decrementing effect of c on v which is formally defined as:

$$c_v = \{c' \in C | \ (f(c, v) = - \ and \ f(c', v) \in \{+, \star\}) \ or$$
$$(f(c, v) = + \ and \ f(c', v) \in \{-, \star\})\}.$$

Since c_v contains *all* cycles that can have the opposite effect on v compared to c, it follows that c_v covers c. This implies that if for some variable v, all cycles in c_v have a sticky transition, there is no need for c to have a sticky transition.

Our goal is to find a subset T of sticky transitions that breaks (when removed from the local process graphs) some set H of local cycles such that H covers the entire set of local cycles C. Then, since every global cycle contains some local cycle $c \in C$, it also has to contain a cycle from H, and with it a sticky transition. Consequently, condition **C2'** holds.

To find such a set, note that trivially H covers H for any $H \subseteq C$. We also have the following lemma:

Lemma 3. *Let $H, G \subseteq C$ and $c \in C$. If H covers G and G covers c, then H covers $G \cup \{c\}$.*

Proof: We need to show that for any global cycle C_1, if C_1 contains a local cycle $g \in G \cup \{c\}$ then it has to contain a local cycle in H. If $g \in G \cup \{c\}$ then we have two cases, either $g \in G$ or $g = c$.
Case (i): If $g \in G$, then since H covers G, C_1 must have a local cycle in H.
Case (ii): If $g = c$, then C_1 has to contain a local cycle $g' \in G$ since G covers c. Furthermore, since C_1 contains $g' \in G$ and H covers G, C_1 contains some cycle in H.
Together, these two cases show that H covers $G \cup \{c\}$.

The Algorithm 1 given in Fig. 2 uses this lemma to compute a set H such that H covers C. It alternates between analyzing the effect of local cycles on variables to increase the covered set G and adding cycles to H if there are still uncovered cycles in C.

Algorithm 1

0. choose $H \subseteq C$, let $G := H$
1. loop
2.   do
3.   let $updated := false$
4. $\forall c \in C \setminus G, \forall v \in V$
5.   if $f(c, v) \in \{-, +\}$ and $c_v \subseteq G$ then
6.   let $G := G \cup \{c\}$
7.   let $updated := true$
8.   while $(updated)$
9.   if $(G = C)$ return H
10.   let $H := H \cup C_{add}$, $G := G \cup C_{add}$ for some $C_{add} \subseteq C \setminus G$, $C_{add} \neq \emptyset$
11. endloop

Fig. 2. An algorithm to find $H \subseteq C$ such that H *covers* C

It is possible not to take a variable v into account during the local cycle analysis by simply assuming that $f(c, v) = \star$ for all local cycles. One can also assume the existence of auxiliary variables to produce the dependency relation between cycles. For example, if there is a variable q of type queue in the system, we can assume that there is also an integer variable q_l, which always keeps the number of elements in this queue variable. It is hard to define the side effect of a push or pop operation on q but they are incrementing and decrementing on q_l respectively. In the extreme case where $\forall c \in C, \forall v \in V, f(c, v) \in \{\star, 0\}$, Algorithm 1 terminates with $H = C$ as the worst case which corresponds to satisfying Condition **C2"** since we have to chose a sticky transition from each local cycle.

The selection of initial set of marked cycles, let's call it C_m, can be arbitrary. A good starting value is given by the sticky transitions which are already required by **C2'**. In particular, C_m can be chosen to be the set of all cycles that include a visible transition.

2.4 The COSPAN Implementation

The static partial order reduction technique explained in this paper has been implemented for SDL and S/R source–target pair of languages. Nevertheless, the method is not specific to this pair of languages. We give the details of this particular implementation in this section.

Our method of applying the reduction entails the modification of the analyzed system such that a transition which is not in the ample set for a given state, is simply not enabled. In other words, the set of enabled transitions at some state in the modified system is exactly an ample set at that state if the original system were analyzed with a modified search algorithm. This property enables us to use any search technique to analyze the modified system. In our case, we are able to use either explicit and symbolic search techniques and also apply localization reduction [10] together with the partial order reduction.

In order to achieve in COSPAN a partial order reduction that is independent of the search control, we exploit the selection mechanism of S/R. The language provides *selection variables*, which are not part of the state, and thus do not incur any memory overhead. When deciding on the successor state, each process chooses non-deterministically among some possible values of its selection variables. The choice of any process can be dependent on the choice of the selections of the other processes (as long as this relationship is acyclic).

In the compilation phase from SDL to S/R, first the visible transitions are tagged as sticky. Algorithm 1 is then executed to find a sufficient set of sticky transitions with the initial selection C_m being the set of local cycles that include a visible transition. Also for each local state of a process, we calculate whether the transitions departing from that local state satisfy Condition **C1**. If the process has only internal transitions (the transitions in which only the local variables are referred), then it is clear that the transitions originating from that local state of the process satisfy **C1** since no other process can refer to those variables. Similarly, when the process has only enabled receiving transitions, the transitions of the process again satisfy **C1**. Although the send transition of another process can change the same message queue from which the receiving transition reads, their execution order does not matter. Depending on the topology of the system, even a send transition of a process can also satisfy **C1**, for example if there is no other process that can send a signal to the same message queue. Note that, the compilation is dependent on the property to be checked (or more precisely, on the set of visible transitions). Therefore, a new compilation is required for each property that impose different visible transitions in the system.

In the current version of our compiler, a process is considered to be ample at a state if it does not have a sticky transition and all of its transitions satisfy **C1** at its current local state. Each process sets a global combinational flag to true or false depending on its ampleness at a global state. From all the ample processes at a state, a process with the least number of outgoing transitions is chosen as the candidate for execution. If more than one process has the least number of transitions, a static priority (index number) is used to chose only one process. If there is no ample process at a state then all the processes are chosen as candidates for execution. A process does not have any enabled transition unless it is selected as one of the candidates for execution. This candidate election mechanism is implemented using the primitives of S/R and is embedded in the source code of the analyzed system without causing any state space overhead.

We added approximately 1000 lines of code to the original compiler (which was around 9000 lines before the addition) to implement the reduction.

3 Experimental Results

This section gives experimental results for our method. The examples specified in SDL are translated into S/R using the compiler incorporating the static partial order reduction approach explained in this paper.

The first example is a concurrent sort algorithm. There are $N + 1$ processes which sort N randomly generated numbers. One of the processes simply generates N random numbers and sends them to the next process on the right. Each process that receives a new number compares it with the current number it has and sends the greater one to the process on the right. The rightmost process receives only one number which is the largest one generated by the leftmost process. The second example is a leader election protocol given in [5]. It contains N processes, each with an index number, that form a ring structure. Each process can only send a signal to the process on its right and can receive a signal from the process on its left. The aim of the protocol is to find the largest index number in the ring. The protocol is verified with respect to all possible initial states. The final example is an asynchronous tree arbiter as taken from [4] whose purpose is to solve the mutual exclusion problem. A resource is arbitrated between N users by a tree of arbiter cells. Each arbiter cell can have at most two children and forwards a request coming from its children to the upper level of the tree. When an arbiter cell receives the grant, it passes the grant to the child that requested the resource. If both of the children are requesting, the grant signal is sent nondeterministically to one of them. When the resource is released, the release information is sent to the root of the tree along the branch connecting the root and the user that released the resource. An acknowledgement is also sent back by the root to the user, using the same branch in the tree. Table 1 gives the measurements we have obtained so far on these examples.

The examples above showed that in case of small state spaces, the symbolic search with partial order reduction is more expensive than an explicit search with partial order reduction. It is even more expensive than a symbolic search on original system without any partial order reduction. As the state space gets bigger, the symbolic search with partial order reduction, starts doing better than the symbolic search without reduction. For large systems, the symbolic search with partial order reduction becomes the fastest of all the alternatives.

The concurrent sort example has an interesting property for the application of Algorithm 1. We have introduced an artificial integer variable for each message queue in the system that is assumed to keep the number of messages in the queue. When Algorithm 1 is executed by taking into account only these artificial variables with $C_m = \emptyset$ initially, it returns $H = \emptyset$. The reason of this is that, even though there are cycles in the local graphs of the processes, the global state space has no cycles and this can be determined by a syntactic analysis.

Since the ample set reduction is applied completely statically, it cannot benefit from all the information available to a dynamic algorithm. For example,

Experiments	No Reduction (*no of states*)	Ample Reduction (*no of states*)
Sort with $N = 2$	191	66
Sort with $N = 3$	4903	553
Sort with $N = 4$	135329	4163
Sort with $N = 5$	3940720	29541
Leader with $N = 2$	383	107
Leader with $N = 3$	11068	490
Leader with $N = 4$	537897	3021
Leader with $N = 5$	26523000	21856
Arbiter with $N = 2$	73	48
Arbiter with $N = 4$	18247	4916
Arbiter with $N = 6$	3272700	358352

Table 1. Experimental Results

Condition **C3** is satisfied by predicting the cycles in the global state space at syntactic level. It is possible that Algorithm 1 will try to break global cycles that can actually never occur. A reduction algorithm that breaks global cycles as they appear during the analysis seems to be more fine tuned for the reduction. However, the produced experimental results are as good as those obtained by dynamic algorithms.

4 Summary

Model checking tools are highly complex and required to have a a good performance. On the other hand, the state space explosion problem forces the tool implementors to incorporate the possible reduction techniques into the tools, making the implementation more complex. Frequently, it is not straightforward to implement a reduction technique on top of the search technique used by a model checker. Until recently [1], there were no implementations that combine partial order reduction and symbolic search techniques although both methods were known for a long time and had good implementations separately.

We have demonstrated a way to compute a partial order reduction of an asynchronous system statically. This facilitates implementation of the reduction into model-checking tools without the need to alter the search algorithms. In particular, our method allows combining partial order reduction with symbolic search. Although our implementation of the method uses SDL and S/R as the source and the target languages, the method itself is not specific to these languages.

Experimental results indicate that for small models, static partial order reduction is faster with an explicit state representation. However, for large models, the symbolic search is not only faster, but completes on models which are computationally infeasible with reduction based on an explicit state search.

References

1. R. Alur, R.K. Brayton, T.A. Henzinger, S. Qadeer, and S.K. Rajamani. Partial order reduction in symbolic state space exploration. In *Proceedings of the Conference on Computer Aided Verification (CAV'97)*, Haifa, Israel, June 1997.
2. E. Bounimova, V. Levin, O. Başbuğoğlu, and K. Inan. A verification engine for SDL specification of communication protocols. In S. Bilgen, U. Çağlayan, and C. Ersoy, editors, *Proceedings of the First Symposium on Computer Networks*, pages 16–25, Istanbul, Turkey, May 1996.
3. C.T. Chou and D. Peled. Formal verification of a partial–order reduction technique for model checking. In *Proceedings of the Second International Workshop on Tools and Algorithms for the Construction and Analysis of Systems*, pages 241–257, Passau, Germany, 1996. Springer–Verlag. Volume 1055 of Lecture Notes in Computer Science.
4. D.L. Dill. *Trace Theory for Automatic Hierarchical Verification of Speed–Independent Circuits*. MIT Press, 1989.
5. D. Dolev, M. Klave, and M. Rodeh. An $O(n \log n)$ unidirectional distributed algorithm for extrema finding in a circle. *Journal of Algorithms*, 3:245–260, 1982.
6. P. Godefroid and D. Pirottin. Refining dependencies improves partial-order verification methods. In *Proc. 5th Conference on Computer Aided Verification*, volume 697 of *Lecture Notes in Computer Science*, pages 438–449, Elounda, June 1993. Springer-Verlag.
7. R. H. Hardin, Z. Har'El, and R. P. Kurshan. COSPAN. In *Proc. CAV'96*, volume 1102, pages 423–427. LNCS, 1996.
8. G.J. Holzmann. *Design and Validation of Computer Protocols*. Prentice-Hall, 1992.
9. G.J. Holzmann and D. Peled. An improvement in formal verification. In *Formal Description Techniques 1994*, pages 197–211, Bern, Switzerland, 1994. Chapman&Hall.
10. R. Kurshan. *Computer-Aided Verification of Coordinating Processes*. Princeton University Press, 1994.
11. L. Lamport. What good is temporal logic. In *IFIP Congress*, pages 657–668. North Holland, 1983. in Computer Science 115.
12. D. Peled. Combining partial order reductions with on-the-fly model checking. *Formal Methods in System Design*, 8:39–64, 1996.
13. *Functional Specification and Description Language (SDL)*, CCITT Blue Book, Recommendation Z.100. Geneva, 1992.
14. A. Valmari. A stubborn attack on state explosion. In *Proc. 2nd Workshop on Computer Aided Verification*, volume 531 of *Lecture Notes in Computer Science*, pages 156–165, Rutgers, June 1990. Springer-Verlag.

Set-Based Analysis of Reactive Infinite-State Systems

Witold Charatonik*   Andreas Podelski

Max-Planck-Institut für Informatik
Im Stadtwald, D-66123 Saarbrücken, Germany
{witold;podelski}@mpi-sb.mpg.de

Abstract. We present an automated abstract verification method for infinite-state systems specified by logic programs (which are a uniform and intermediate layer to which diverse formalisms such as transition systems, pushdown processes and while programs can be mapped). We establish connections between: logic program semantics and CTL properties, set-based program analysis and pushdown processes, and also between model checking and constraint solving, viz. theorem proving. We show that set-based analysis can be used to compute supersets of the values of program variables in the states that satisfy a given CTL property.

1 Introduction

Testing runtime properties of systems with infinite state spaces is generally undecidable. Therefore, the best one can hope for are semi-algorithms implementing a test, or always terminating algorithms implementing a *semi-test* (which either yields yes/don't know answers or, dually, no/don't know answers). Based on the idea that any automated method that sometimes detects programming errors is useful, we investigate semi-tests in this paper.

One way to obtain a semi-test is to apply a test to a finite approximation of the infinite system of interest. An essential part of an automated semi-test computes the approximation from a finite representation of the original system, viz. a program. We will study representations of infinite-state systems by *logic programs*. Logic programs are a uniform and intermediate layer to which diverse formalisms such as finite-state transition systems, pushdown processes and while programs can be mapped. The connection between transition systems and logic via logic programs allows us to establish the correspondence between:

- program semantics and temporal logic properties,
- abstraction and logical implication,
- the *Cartesian* abstraction of set-based analysis and pushdown processes,
- model-checking and first-order, resolution-based theorem proving.

Specifically, we consider the temporal logic CTL [14] (which allows one to express safety, inevitability and other important behavioral properties excluding fairness

---

* On leave from Wrocław University. Partially supported by Polish KBN grant 8T11C02913.

conditions). For a (possibly infinite-state) transition system represented by a logic program, the set of states satisfying a CTL property can be characterized through the semantics of logic programs; see Theorem 2, Section 5.

Now, static program analysis based on abstract interpretation (see, e.g., [10]) may be used to compute a conservative approximation of a CTL property by computing an abstraction of the logic program semantics. The soundness of the abstract-verification method thus obtained holds by the soundness of the abstraction. This is in contrast with the work in, e.g., [22, 11, 23], where the test of a CTL property is applied to an abstraction of the original system.

We use one particular form of static analysis called *set-based analysis*. Here, the abstraction consists of mapping a set of tuples to the smallest Cartesian product of sets containing it (e.g., $\{\langle a, 1\rangle, \langle b, 2\rangle\} \mapsto \{a, b\} \times \{1, 2\}$). The abstract semantics computed by this analysis defines a Cartesian product of sets; each set describes runtime values of a variable at a program point. This set is sometimes called the *type* of the program variable. Now, if the concrete program semantics is used to characterize the set of *correct* input states, the type of an input variable denotes a conservative approximation of the set of all its values in correct input states (where 'correct' refers to states for which a given CTL property is satisfied); see Theorem 3, Section 6.

Logically, the set-based abstraction amounts to replacing a formula, say, $\varphi[x, y]$ with the free variables x and y, by the conjunction $(\exists y\, \varphi)[x] \wedge (\exists x\, \varphi)[y]$ (which is logically implied by φ). Applying this replacement systematically to a program $\mathcal{P}$ yields a new program $\mathcal{P}^\sharp$. This program defines the degree of abstraction of CTL properties in set-based analysis: the full test for the system defined by $\mathcal{P}^\sharp$ is the semi-test for the system defined by $\mathcal{P}$.

The system obtained by the set-based abstraction of a program $\mathcal{P}$ (defined by the program $\mathcal{P}^\sharp$) is not finite-state. Instead, it is a kind of *pushdown process*. Pushdown processes have raised interest as a class of infinite-state systems for which temporal properties are decidable. The systems considered here extend this class by adding parallel composition, tree-like stacks and non-deterministic guesses of stack contents. The latter extension introduces a non-determinism of infinite branching degree. Since set-based analysis here adds no extra approximation, it yields a full test of CTL properties of pushdown processes even with this extension; see Theorem 1, Section 4.

When we use set-based analysis as a verification method, the constraint-solving algorithms which form its computational heart (e.g., [17, 16, 8, 12]) replace the traditional fixpoint iteration of model checking. The constraints used here can be represented by logic programs (see Section 6). Then, constraint-solving (more precisely, testing emptiness of the solution of interest) amounts to first-order theorem proving based on resolution. We are currently working on making the algorithm [7] for computing the greatest solution practical. One algorithm for computing the least solution is already implemented in the saturation-based theorem prover SPASS [29]; due to specific theorem-proving techniques like powerful redundancy criteria, one obtains an efficient decision procedure for the emptiness test, viz. model checking.

Related work. In [25] we present a direct application of the set-based analysis of logic programs to error diagnosis in concurrent constraint programs. The error can be defined as a special case of a CTL property for a transition system that consists of *non-ground* derivations of logic programs.

Our direct inspiration for investigating transition systems specified by *ground* derivations of logic programs was the work on pushdown processes in [2, 5, 28]. Here, we extend the result in [2] about CTL model-checking in DEXPTIME to a more general notion of pushdown processes.

Historically, our work started with the *abstract debugging* scheme of [4]. The invariant and intermittent assertions used there correspond to two special cases of CTL properties. Here, we consider trees instead of numbers for the data domain, an abstract domain of regular sets of trees instead of intervals, and Cartesian instead of convex-hull approximation. Our characterization of CTL properties can be extended to while programs over numeric data by using constraint logic programs (over numbers instead of trees) as an intermediate layer.

In [26], Ramakrishna et al. present an implementation of a model checker for the verification of finite-state systems specified by DATALOG programs (*i.e.*, logic programs without function symbols). The correctness of their implementation (in a logic programming language with tabling called XSB) relies implicitly on the characterization of CTL properties that we formally prove for logic programs with function symbols. In contrast to the work in [26] which applies programming techniques that that are proper to logic programming languages, we view logic programs rather as an automata-theoretic formalism.

Structure of the paper. The first three sections are to give a flavor of our method, which we present in technical terms in the subsequent three sections. Section 2 explains our view of logic programs as an intermediate layer for while programs. For every while program with data structures modeled as trees (e.g., lists), we can find a logic program that represents the same transition system. The purpose of Section 3 is to give the intuition of our characterization of CTL properties (also to readers who are not so familiar with logic programs, to which we do not refer in this section). We show how one can translate a finite transition system to a simple logical formula; the formula belongs to a logic program whose operational semantics is that transition system. We then show how the logical formula must be modified so that a particular solution characterizes a given CTL property; this is the formula that belongs to a *program with oracles*. Section 4 explains our view of logic programs as automata at hand of pushdown processes. Section 5 formally introduces the concepts that we used informally in the previous three sections, and it presents the characterization of CTL properties for monolithic transition systems. Section 6 gives a self-contained account of set-based analysis and presents the results about the conservative approximation of CTL properties that lead to an abstract-verification method. Section 7 gives an extension of these results to multi-processor transition systems defined by logic programs with conjunction (which corresponds to parallel composition); *Basic Parallel Processes* (see, e.g., [15]) are here a special case. Finally, in conclusion, we mention possible directions for future work.

2 While Programs

We consider an imperative programming language with the two data constructors *cons* and *nil* (integers etc. play the role of constant data constructors). For convenience, $cons(x, y)$ is written as $[x|y]$, $cons(x_1, cons(\ldots, x_n, nil)\ldots)$ as $[x_1, \ldots, x_n]$ and *nil* as $[\,]$. We also have the data destructors *hd* and *tl*, where $hd([x|y]) = x$ and $tl([x|y]) = y$. We will neither formally define the language nor present the translation of its programs to monolithic total logic programs. Instead, we present two example programs which will illustrate that such a translation is possible in principle.

The first program consists of one instruction, a while loop, with the program labels p and q before and after the instruction.

$$
\boxed{p} \quad \begin{aligned} &\texttt{while x =/= nil do} \\ &\quad \texttt{i := i+1} \\ \boxed{q}\quad &\quad \texttt{x := tl(x)} \end{aligned}
$$

The program manipulates the two variables x and i. States are thus pairs $\langle p, e \rangle$ formed by the program location p and the environment e which assigns values v_x and v_i to the variables x and i. We write such a state as an atom $p(v_x, v_i)$. The program induces an infinite-state transition system; possible transitions are, for example,

$$
\begin{aligned}
p([a, b], 0) &\longrightarrow p([b], 1), \\
p([b], 1) &\longrightarrow p([\,], 2), \\
p([\,], 2) &\longrightarrow q([\,], 2).
\end{aligned}
$$

Since the transition function must be total, we assume that there exist transitions modeling an explicit exception handling; for example,

$$
\begin{aligned}
p(3, i) &\longrightarrow exception, \\
exception &\longrightarrow exception.
\end{aligned}
$$

We translate the while loop above to the logic program below. Each program location corresponds to a predicate whose arguments correspond to the variables that are visible at that location. We express conditionals through the heads of the clauses. Since our framework requires that the program is total, we add clauses in order to model an exhaustive case statement (in a practical setting, such clauses could be presented implicitly). The transition systems induced by the while program and the logic program coincide.

$$p([x|y], i) \leftarrow p(y, i + 1)$$

$$p([\,], i) \leftarrow q([\,], i)$$

$$p(a, i) \leftarrow exception \text{ (for each other data constructor } a)$$

$$exception \leftarrow exception$$

The CTL property $EF(\{q(v_x', v_i') \mid true\})$ specifies the set of all states at location p from which the location q can be reached. The values v_x for the variable x

in such states are exactly the finite lists. The set of these values can thus be presented as the least solution of the equation $list = cons(T_\Sigma, list) \cup nil$ over sets of trees, or of the program below (and this is also the result of the method presented in this paper).

$$list(cons(x, y)) \leftarrow list(y)$$
$$list(nil)$$

That is, if the while loop is executed with an initial value other than a finite list for x, then it will not reach the program point q (a fact which may be useful for debugging purposes).

The property $EG(\{p(v'_x, i'_x) \mid true\})$ holds for the states $p(v_x, i_x)$ where v_x is an infinite list (which models a circular list). The set of all infinite lists is the greatest solution of the equation $list = cons(T_\Sigma, list)$ over sets of infinite trees, or of the program below interpreted over the domain of infinite trees (again, this is also the result of the method outlined in this paper).

$$list(cons(x, y)) \leftarrow list(y)$$

That is, if the while loop is executed with an initial value other than an infinite list for x, then a program location other than p will be reached or an exception will be raised.

The next example is a program fragment (whose task is to reverse the list x) containing a typographical error ("$[tl(L)]$" instead of "$tl(L)$"). Again, we note p and q the program points before and after the while loop.

```
 p    y := []
      while x =/= nil do
        x := [tl(x)]
        y := [hd(L)|y]
 q
      x:=y
 r
```

We construct the corresponding logic program.

$$init(x) \leftarrow p(x, [])$$
$$p([x|x'],) \leftarrow p([x'], [x|y])$$
$$p([], y) \leftarrow q([], y)$$
$$q(x, y) \leftarrow r(y, y)$$
$$p(a, i) \leftarrow exception \text{ (for each other data constructor } a\text{)}$$
$$exception \leftarrow exception$$

Our method will derive that for any other initial value than the empty list for the variable x the program location q can never be reached.

3 Transition Systems

Abstracting away from the fine structure of states and of transitions, we may present a reactive system with finitely many states as a transition system $\mathcal{S} = \langle S, \tau \rangle$ with the finite set S of states and the non-deterministic transition function $\tau : S \to 2^S$. The state q is a successor state of the state p if $q \in \tau(p)$. We translate $\mathcal{S}$ into a formula $\mathcal{P}_S$ of propositional logic. Here, for each state p, we have a symbol p standing for a nullary predicate (or, a Boolean variable).

$$\mathcal{P}_S = \bigwedge_{p \in S} (p \leftrightarrow \bigvee_{q \in \tau(p)} q) \tag{1}$$

An *interpretation* of $\mathcal{P}_S$ is presented as a set $I \subseteq S$ of states; I specifies the set of all *atoms* p that are valued *true*. A *model* (or, solution) of $\mathcal{P}_S$ is an interpretation under which the formula $\mathcal{P}_S$ holds. Models are partially ordered by subset inclusion. If we require, as usual, that τ is total (i.e., $\tau(s) \neq \emptyset$ for all $s \in S$; thus, every state has at least one successor), then the least model of $\mathcal{P}_S$ is the empty set $\emptyset$ and its greatest model is the set S of all atoms.

We now consider the safety property "P will never happen", written: $AG(S - P)$, or: $S - EF(P)$ in CTL notation, for some property $P \subseteq S$. The set $EF(P)$ of all states from which a state in P is reachable, is exactly the set of atoms in the least model of the following formula.

$$\mathcal{P}_S \wedge P = \bigwedge_{p \notin P} (p \leftrightarrow \bigvee_{q \in \tau(p)} q) \wedge \bigwedge_{p \in P} p \tag{2}$$

The following explanation may help to understand this characterization of $EF(P)$. The formula $\mathcal{P}_S \wedge P$ entails p iff there exists a sequence of implications $p \leftarrow p_1 \leftarrow \ldots \leftarrow p_n$ in $\mathcal{P}_S$ and an implication $p_n \leftarrow true$, which is, p_n is an element of P. The least model of $\mathcal{P}_S \wedge P$ is the set of all entailed atoms ("all atoms that must be true in any model").

Now consider the inevitability property "P will always finally happen", written $AF(P)$, or $S - EG(S - P)$). The set $EG(S - P)$ is the set of atoms in the *greatest* model of the following formula. (The notation $\mathcal{P} \wedge \neg P$ must not be confused with $\mathcal{P} \wedge (S - P)$.)

$$\mathcal{P}_S \wedge \neg P = \bigwedge_{p \notin P} (p \leftrightarrow \bigvee_{q \in \tau(p)} q) \wedge \bigwedge_{p \in P} \neg p \tag{3}$$

This may be explained as follows. The formula above entails $\neg p$ (i.e., it can be valid only if the model does not contain p) iff every maximal sequence of implications of the form $p \to p_1 \to p_2 \to \ldots$ in $\mathcal{P}_S$ is finite and terminates with $p_n \to false$. Thus, an atom p is in the greatest model of $\mathcal{P}_S \wedge \neg P$ iff there exists an infinite sequence of implications avoiding *false*, which is, there exists an infinite sequence of transitions that starts in the state p and avoids the states in P.

The formulas (1), (2) and (3) are the *Clark completion* of logic programs that we formally introduce in Section 5. They are used to define the semantics of program logically.

4 Pushdown Processes

We can model a system consisting of finite-state processes, one of which uses a pushdown stack as a data structure, by a pushdown automaton. In order to describe the ongoing behavior of such a system, we will consider input-less pushdown automata without an acceptance condition. Formally, a pushdown process is a tuple

$$\mathcal{A} = \langle Q, \Sigma, \delta, q^0 \rangle$$

consisting of a finite set of control states Q, the stack alphabet Σ, the non-deterministic transition function

$$\delta \subseteq \ (Q \times \Sigma) \times (Q \times \{\varepsilon\}) \\ \cup (Q \times \{\varepsilon\}) \times (Q \times \Sigma)$$

and the initial control state q^0. The states in the corresponding transition system

$$\mathcal{S}_\mathcal{A} = \langle Q \times \Sigma^*, \tau_\mathcal{A} \rangle$$

are pairs $\langle q, w \rangle$ consisting of the control state $q \in Q$ and the stack contents $w \in \Sigma^*$ (where $w = \varepsilon$ if the stack is empty). The transitions either read one symbol and remove it from the stack or add one.

$$\tau_\mathcal{A}(\langle q, w \rangle) = \{\langle q', w' \rangle \mid w = a.w' \text{ where } a \in \Sigma, \ \langle \langle q, a \rangle, \langle q', \varepsilon \rangle \rangle \in \delta \text{ or}$$
$$w' = a.w \text{ where } a \in \Sigma, \ \langle \langle q, \varepsilon \rangle, \langle q', a \rangle \rangle \in \delta\}$$

Given a pushdown process $\mathcal{A}$, we define the program $\mathcal{P}_\mathcal{A}$ below. We now view Σ as a set of unary function symbols and ε as a constant symbol, and we consider terms over the signature $\Sigma \cup \{\varepsilon\}$.

$$\mathcal{P}_\mathcal{A} = \ \{q(a(x)) \leftarrow q'(x) \mid \langle \langle q, a \rangle, \langle q', \varepsilon \rangle \rangle \in \delta\}$$
$$\cup \{q(x) \leftarrow q'(a(x)) \mid \langle \langle q, \varepsilon \rangle, \langle q', a \rangle \rangle \in \delta\}$$

A program with the first kind of clauses only corresponds to a word automaton. A clause of the form $q(a(x)) \leftarrow q'(x)$ can be read as the instruction: "in state q, reading the word $w = a(x)$ with the first letter a and remaining suffix x, go to state q' and read the suffix x"; q is a final state iff the program contains a clause of the form $q(\varepsilon)$. Here, a word $a_1 a_2 \ldots a_n$ is represented as a unary tree $a_1(a_2(\ldots a_n(\varepsilon) \ldots))$.

The second kind of clause $q(x) \leftarrow q'(a(x))$ can be read as the "push" instruction: "in state q with stack contents w, go to state p' with stack contents $a(w)$."

The next remark is a consequence of the formal definition of the transition system $\mathcal{S}_\mathcal{P}$ induced by a program $\mathcal{P}$, which we defer to the next section.

Remark. The transition system $\mathcal{S}_\mathcal{A}$ of the pushdown process $\mathcal{A}$ and the transition system $\mathcal{S}_{\mathcal{P}_\mathcal{A}}$ induced by the program $\mathcal{P}_\mathcal{A}$ that corresponds to $\mathcal{A}$ coincide.

□

The assumption that the transitions modify the size of the stack by exactly one symbol is not a proper restriction as long as acceptance is considered. If, however, we try to simulate the non-deterministic guessing of a new stack contents via a sequence of transitions that each guess one symbol to be added, then the necessary modification of the transition relation of the pushdown process would not leave the temporal properties invariant (because the guessing sequence can be infinite). Thus, the following generalization seems to be a proper one.

Definition 1 (Generalized pushdown processes). A generalized pushdown process is specified by any monolithic total program over the signature consisting of unary function symbols and one constant symbol.

We may restrict the syntax wlog. to three kinds of Horn clauses.

$$q(a(x)) \leftarrow q'(x)$$
$$q(x) \leftarrow q'(a(x))$$
$$q(x) \leftarrow q'(y)$$

Given the clause $q(x) \leftarrow q'(y)$, every state of the form $\langle q', w' \rangle$ with any stack contents w' can be a successor state of the state $\langle q, w \rangle$. Thus, we here have a non-determinism of branching degree ω.

We will state already here the following theorem, which was shown in [3] for pushdown processes in the restricted sense, i.e., without non-deterministic guesses of stack contents (and hence, with a finite degree of branching).

Theorem 1. Given a generalized pushdown process and a CTL property φ with regular atomic propositions, the set of all states satisfying φ is again regular; its representation in the form of a non-deterministic finite automaton can be computed in single-exponential time (in the number of states).

Proof. The statement is an instance of Theorem 4. $\square$

5 Monolithic Programs

In a *multi-processor* transition system, the states have a structure and the transition function is defined by referring to that structure; we will consider such systems and their modeling through general logic programs in Section 7. In contrast, in a *monolithic* transition system, the transition function is defined directly on the states (i.e., as monolithic items). We can model such a system by a logic program P whose clauses' bodies contain exactly one atom. By extension, we then say that P is a *monolithic program*. Thus, a monolithic program P is given through implications of the form

$$p(t) \leftarrow p'(t')$$

where p and p' are predicates (different from *true*) and t and t' are terms over a given signature Σ of function symbols. When we refer to the logical semantics of P, we use the formula below.

$$P \equiv \bigwedge_p \forall x \ p(x) \leftrightarrow \bigvee_i \exists_{-x} (x = t_i \wedge p'_i(t'_i))$$

Here, p ranges over the set $Pred$ of all predicates defined by the program and i ranges over a suitable index set I_p such that $\{p(t_i) \leftarrow p'(t_i') \mid i \in I_p\}$ are all clauses with the predicate p in the head. As usual, $\exists_{-x}$ stands for the quantification of all variables in t_i and t_i' but x. For technical convenience, we assume that all predicates are unary; the results can easily be extended to the case without this restriction (for example, by extending the signature of function symbols with symbols forming tuples).

We note T_Σ the set of trees (i.e., ground terms) over the signature Σ. We use the same meta variables t, t', etc. for terms and trees. Given the program $\mathcal{P}$ defining the set of predicates $Pred$ and the signature Σ, the *Herbrand base* $\mathcal{B}_\mathcal{P}$ is the set of all *ground atoms* $p(t)$, which are applications of predicates to trees. (Note that $\mathcal{B}_\mathcal{P}$ does not include the propositional constant *true*.)

$$\mathcal{B}_\mathcal{P} = \{p(t) \mid p \in Pred, t \in T_\Sigma\}$$

A *ground clause* of $\mathcal{P}$ is an implication between ground atoms that is entailed by $\mathcal{P}$; thus, it is of the form $p(\sigma(t)) \leftarrow p'(\sigma(t'))$ where $p(t) \leftarrow p'(t')$ is a clause of $\mathcal{P}$ and $\sigma : Var \to T_\Sigma$ is a valuation (extended from variables to terms in the canonical way).

We will always assume that $\mathcal{P}$ is *total*, which means that for all ground atoms $p(t)$ there exists a ground clause of $\mathcal{P}$ of the form $p(t) \leftarrow p'(t')$.

An interpretation I, which we present as a subset of the Herbrand base, (i.e., $I \subseteq \mathcal{B}_\mathcal{P}$), interprets a predicate p as the set $\{t \in T_\Sigma \mid p(t) \in I\}$. A *model* of the program $\mathcal{P}$ is an interpretation under which the formula $\mathcal{P}$ is valid. Models are ordered by subset inclusion. The least model of $\mathcal{P}$, $lm(\mathcal{P})$, and the greatest model of $\mathcal{P}$, $gm(\mathcal{P})$, always exist. The least [greatest] model of a monolithic total program $\mathcal{P}$ is *always* the empty [universal] set, i.e., $lm(\mathcal{P}) = \emptyset$ and $gm(\mathcal{P}) = T_\Sigma$. The models of the programs that we will define next turn out to be more interesting. These programs consists of Horn clauses with additional conjuncts (the "oracles"). Note that $\neg \Gamma_p(t)$ is equivalent to $p(t) \in (\mathcal{B}_\mathcal{P} - \Gamma)$. We always use $\mathcal{P} \wedge \Gamma$ for defining least models, and $\mathcal{P} \wedge \neg \Gamma$ for defining greatest models.

Definition 2 (Programs with oracles). Given a monolithic program $\mathcal{P}$ and a subset Γ of the Herbrand base, we define two kinds of programs with oracles.

$$\mathcal{P} \wedge \Gamma = \mathcal{P} \cup \{p(x) \leftarrow \Gamma_p(x) \mid p \in Pred\}$$
$$\mathcal{P} \wedge \neg \Gamma = \{p(t) \leftarrow p'(t') \wedge \neg \Gamma_p(t) \mid p(t) \leftarrow p'(t') \text{ is a clause in } \mathcal{P}\}$$

The operational semantics of $\mathcal{P}$ can be described as a transition system

$$\mathcal{S}_\mathcal{P} = \langle \mathcal{B}_\mathcal{P}, \tau_\mathcal{P} \rangle$$

whose states are the ground atoms (not (!) including *true*), and whose transition function $\tau_\mathcal{P} : \mathcal{B}_\mathcal{P} \to 2^{\mathcal{B}_\mathcal{P}}$ is defined as follows.

$$\tau_\mathcal{P}(p(t)) = \{p'(t') \mid p(t) \leftarrow p'(t') \text{ is a ground clause of } \mathcal{P}\}$$

Since we have assumed that $\mathcal{P}$ is total, we have that $\tau_P(s) \neq \emptyset$ for all states s ("the transition function τ_P is total"). The fixpoint semantics of P is given through the T_P operator on subsets of the Herbrand base.

$$T_P(I) = \{p(t) \mid p(t) \leftarrow p'(t') \text{ is a ground clause of } \mathcal{P} \text{ and } p'(t') \in I\}$$

We immediately note the connection with the inverse of the transition function (as usual, $\tau_P^{-1}(P) = \{s \in \mathcal{B}_P \mid \tau_P(s) \subseteq P\}$ for subsets P of states).

$$\tau_P^{-1} = T_P$$

In order to define the logic CTL over the transition system $\mathcal{S}_P$ induced by the program $\mathcal{P}$, we first need to fix the set $Prop$ of $atomic\ propositions$. As in the finite-state case, an atomic proposition Γ denotes a set of states, which we also write as Γ. When dealing with algorithmic issues, we will require that Γ can be finitely represented. This is possible, for example, when we require that Γ is a $regular\ atomic\ proposition$, which means that the set

$$\Gamma_p = \{t \in T_\Sigma \mid p(t) \in \Gamma\}$$

is a recognizable set of trees, for each predicate p.

Usually, the denotation of an atomic proposition is described via the detour of a $labeling$ function $L : S \to 2^{Prop}$, where Γ denotes the set $\{s \in S \mid \Gamma \in L(s)\}$. In our setting, the labeling function L is implicit by $L(s) = \{\Gamma \in Prop \mid s \in \Gamma\}$). The finite representation of the sets Γ_p for the atomic propositions occurring in the CTL formula is part of the input. (It is not clear how L could be represented finitely otherwise.)

Given the set $Prop$ of atomic propositions, the set of formulas of the logic CTL and their meaning are defined as in the finite-state case.

$$\varphi ::= \Gamma \mid \neg\varphi \mid \varphi_1 \vee \varphi_2 \mid EX(\varphi) \mid E(\varphi_1 U \varphi_2) \mid A(\varphi_1 U \varphi_2)$$

In addition, we use the following abbreviations: $AX(\varphi) = \neg EX(\neg\varphi)$, $EF(\varphi) = E(true U \varphi)$, $AF(\varphi) = A(true U \varphi)$, $EG(\varphi) = \neg AF(\neg\varphi)$, $AG(\varphi) = \neg EF(\neg\varphi)$.

We write $\mathcal{S}, p \models \varphi$ if the transition system $\mathcal{S}$ with the initial state p satisfies the formula φ. Given $\mathcal{S}$, we simply write φ for the set of all states for which the formula φ is satisfied.

$$\varphi \equiv \{s \mid \mathcal{S}, s \models \varphi\}$$

Theorem 2 (CTL properties and program semantics). Given the transition system $\mathcal{S}_P$ corresponding to the monolithic program $\mathcal{P}$, each set of states denoted by a CTL formula φ can be characterized in terms of subsets of the Herbrand base defined through the semantics of programs with oracles, via the following correspondences.

$$EX(P) = T_P(P)$$
$$AX(S - P) = S - T_P(P)$$
$$EF(P) = lm(\mathcal{P} \wedge P)$$
$$AF(P) = S - gm(\mathcal{P} \wedge \neg P)$$
$$E(S - P_1)UP_2 = lm((\mathcal{P} \wedge \neg P_1) \wedge P_2)$$
$$A(S - P_1)UP_2 = S - (gm(\mathcal{P} \wedge \neg (S - P_2)) \cup lm((\mathcal{P} \wedge \neg P_2) \wedge P_1))$$

These correspondences hold for all subsets of states $P \subseteq \mathcal{B}_P$, which may be defined by atomic propositions Γ or by CTL formulas.

Proof. The first two equalities hold by the definitions of $EX = \tau_{S_P}^{-1}$ and T_P. The next two equalities follow by: (1) the definition of EF [EG] through the least [greatest] fixpoint of EX, (2) the correspondence between the semantics of logic programs defined by the least [greatest] fixpoint and the least [greatest] model (which extend to programs with oracles), and (3) the following identities between fixpoint operators over properties $P \subseteq \mathcal{B}_P$, for any given property $P^0 \subseteq \mathcal{B}_P$.

$$\lambda P. (P^0 \cup EX(P)) = T_{P \wedge P^0}$$
$$\lambda P. ((S - P^0) \cap EX(P)) = T_{P \wedge \neg P^0}$$

The proof of the two remaining equalities uses two basic general facts about the operational semantics and the model-theoretic semantics of a given logic program $\mathcal{P}$. A ground atom $p(t)$ has an execution in S_P that leads to the atom $true$, i.e., $p(t) \in EF(\{true\})$, if and only if $p(t) \in lm(\mathcal{P})$; it has a non-failing execution in S_P i.e., $p(t) \in EG(\mathcal{B}_P \cup \{true\})$ if and only if $p(t) \in gm(\mathcal{P})$. We apply these two facts to programs with oracles instead of $\mathcal{P}$.[1] We note that $E(S - P_1)UP_2$ is the set of all ground atoms $p(t)$ which have an execution that reaches a state in P_2 while avoiding states in P_1, i.e., which reaches $true$ in the program $(\mathcal{P} \wedge \neg P_1) \wedge P_2$. Similarly, a state s is not in $A(S - P_1)UP_2$ if it either has an execution that never reaches a state in P_2, i.e., it has a non-terminating execution in the program $\mathcal{P} \wedge \neg (S - P_2)$, or it has an execution that reaches a state s' in P_1 while avoiding states in P_2 (in the execution up to, and including s'), i.e., it has an execution in the program $(\mathcal{P} \wedge \neg P_2) \wedge P_1$. □

6 Set-based Analysis

In set-based analysis, an abstract semantics of a program is represented as a particular solution of a formula with set-valued variables (often called a set-constraint). The formula is syntactically inferred from the program. The values

---

[1] By our assumptions on *monolithic total* programs $\mathcal{P}$, $EF(\{true\}) = \emptyset$ because $true$ does not appear in the body of a clause in $\mathcal{P}$, and $EG(\mathcal{B}_P) = \mathcal{B}_P$ because the transition function is total.

in the solution are regular sets of trees. Thus, they can be represented through non-deterministic tree automata, which have a linear emptiness test. The algorithmic essence of set-based analysis is the *solving* of the set constraint. This means to compute the particular solution that represents the *set-based* abstract semantics, which again means to compute a non-deterministic tree automaton that represents the solution.

We will give here an introduction to the set-based analysis of logic programs with *uniform programs* (as in [16]). Uniform programs subsume several classes of set constraints used in the set-based analysis of logic and imperative languages (e.g., in [20, 18, 13, 8]) modulo simple translations. Note that we can view any logic program as a formula whose monadic predicate symbols stand for variables ranging over sets of trees, and whose individual variables ranging over trees are all quantified; thus, its free variables are set-valued. We now need to consider general logic programs, which are sets of Horn clauses $p(t) \leftarrow p_1(t_1) \wedge \ldots \wedge p_n(t_n)$ with any number $n \geq 0$ of body atoms. The definitions of the least [greatest] model semantics and fixpoint semantics for monolithic programs in Section 5 carry over directly to the general case (with some extra notational burden). We will discuss the operational semantics in Section 7.

A *uniform program* [16] consists of Horn clauses in one of the following two forms. (In a *linear* term t, each variable occurs at most once.)

- $p(t) \leftarrow p_1(x_1) \wedge \ldots \wedge p_k(x_m)$, where the term t is linear.

- $q(x) \leftarrow p_1(t_1) \wedge \ldots \wedge p_m(t_m)$, where $t_1, \ldots, t_m$ are any terms over Σ.

We derive a uniform program $\mathcal{P}^\sharp$ from any logic program $\mathcal{P}$ in the following way. For every Horn clause

$$p(t) \leftarrow \text{body}$$

where the term t has the n variables $x_1, \ldots, x_n$, we apply renamings x_{ij} to every occurrence of x_i in t in order to obtain a linear term $\tilde{t}$. We introduce n new predicate symbols p_i. Then, $\mathcal{P}^\sharp$ contains the following $n + 1$ clauses for every such Horn clause.

$$p(\tilde{t}) \leftarrow \bigwedge_{i=1}^{n} \bigwedge_j p_i(x_{ij})$$

$$p_1(x_1) \leftarrow \text{body}$$

$$\vdots$$

$$p_n(x_n) \leftarrow \text{body}$$

The program $\mathcal{P}^\sharp$ expresses exactly the so-called set-based abstraction of $\mathcal{P}$ defined in [18] in semantic terms. We can easily translate every uniform program into one whose Horn clauses are in one of the following three forms.

- $p(f(x_1, \ldots, x_n)) \leftarrow p_1(x_1) \wedge \ldots \wedge p_n(x_n)$

    where $n \geq 0$ and $x_1, \ldots, x_n$ pairwise different

- $p(x) \leftarrow p_1(x) \wedge \ldots \wedge p_m(x)$

- $p(x) \leftarrow p'(t)$

A *nondeterministic tree automaton* is a uniform program consisting of the first kind of clauses only. Predicates correspond to states.

The second kind of rules introduces conjunctions of states. An *alternating tree automaton* is a uniform program consisting of the first two kinds of clauses. Note that this is a nice formalization of this concept, without the need to define complicated acceptance conditions.

Finally, the third kind of rule introduces a kind of *push* operation. The rule $p(x) \leftarrow p'(f(x,y))$ can be read as the instruction: "in state p with stack contents t (where t is a tree), go to state p' with stack contents $f(t,t')$ where t' is any tree chosen non-deterministically" (which can be viewed as pushing the context $f(\cdot, t')$ onto the stack).

The following facts hold for the interpretation of programs over finite trees and over infinite trees. The first fact is obvious; the second and third are shown in [16, 6] (the second statement of Fact 2 follows from the form of uniform programs). We call a model $M \subseteq \mathcal{B}_\mathcal{P}$ regular if it can be defined as the least (or, equivalently, as the greatest) model of a tree automaton program; i.e., if all sets $M_p = \{t \in T_\Sigma \mid p(t) \in M\}$ are regular sets of trees (in the standard sense).

Facts about set-based analysis.

1. The uniform program $\mathcal{P}^\sharp$ derived from the logic program $\mathcal{P}$ in the way described above approximates $\mathcal{P}$ in the following sense.

$$lm(\mathcal{P}) \subseteq lm(\mathcal{P}^\sharp)$$

$$gm(\mathcal{P}) \subseteq gm(\mathcal{P}^\sharp)$$

2. The least [greatest] model of a uniform program $\mathcal{P}^\sharp$ is regular; i.e., it can represented by a non-deterministic tree automaton, which again can be represented as a program $\mathcal{P}_{sba}$ (which we define to be the output of the set-based analysis).

$$lm(\mathcal{P}^\sharp) = lm(\mathcal{P}_{sba})$$

$$gm(\mathcal{P}^\sharp) = gm(\mathcal{P}_{sba})$$

   More specifically, if the predicate p is defined by clauses with the heads $p(t_k[x_1, \ldots, x_{n_k}])$ with n_k free variables, then there exist regular sets of trees $T_1^k, \ldots, T_{n_k}^k$ (for each k) such that the set of all p-atoms in the least model [greatest] is a union of *Cartesian products* in the following sense.

$$lm(\mathcal{P}^\sharp) = \bigcup_{p \in Pred} \bigcup_k p(t_k[T_1^k, \ldots, T_{n_k}^k])$$

3. The step $\mathcal{P}^\sharp \mapsto \mathcal{P}_{sba}$ can be computed in single-exponential time. This is also a lower bound for the case of an arbitrary signature; the best known lower bound for the word case is PSPACE.

Theorem 3 (Conservative approximation of CTL properties). Given a transition system specified by a monolithic program $\mathcal{P}$, we can conservatively approximate applications of CTL operators in the following sense.

$$EX(P) \qquad \subseteq T_{\mathcal{P}^\sharp}(P)$$
$$AX(S - P) \quad \supseteq S - T_{\mathcal{P}^\sharp}(P)$$
$$EF(P) \qquad \subseteq lm(\mathcal{P}^\sharp \wedge P)$$
$$AF(P) \qquad \supseteq S - gm(\mathcal{P}^\sharp \wedge \neg P)$$
$$E(S - P_1)UP_2 \subseteq lm((\mathcal{P}^\sharp \wedge \neg P_1) \wedge P_2)$$
$$A(S - P_1)UP_2 \supseteq S - (gm(\mathcal{P}^\sharp \wedge \neg (S - P_2)) \cup lm((\mathcal{P} \wedge \neg P_2) \wedge P_1))$$

Proof. We only need to put together Fact 1 and Theorem 2. □

Theorem 4 (Set-based verification of CTL properties). Given a monolithic uniform program $\mathcal{P}$ and a CTL property φ with regular atomic propositions, the set of all states satisfying φ is again regular; its representation through a non-deterministic tree automaton can be computed in single-exponential time (in the number of predicates of $\mathcal{P}$).

Proof. This follows by Facts 2 and 3 and Theorem 2. □

Set-based abstract verification and types. Theorem 3 suggests the following procedure. Given any monolithic program $\mathcal{P}$ and a CTL property φ built up from regular atomic propositions and the operator EX, EF, EG and EU, we compute a superset $\varphi^\sharp$ of the set of all states satisfying φ in single-exponential time. The set $\varphi^\sharp$ consists of all states that satisfy φ according to the set-based abstract semantics of $\mathcal{P}$.[2]

$$\varphi^\sharp = \{p(t) \in \mathcal{B}_\mathcal{P} \mid \mathcal{S}_{\mathcal{P}^\sharp}, p(t) \models \varphi\}$$

By Fact 2, we know that $\varphi^\sharp$ is a union of Cartesian products of regular sets of trees.

$$\varphi^\sharp = \bigcup_{p \in Pred} \bigcup_k p(t_k[T_1^k, \ldots, T_{n_k}^k])$$

We call the set $T_i = \bigcup_k T_i^k$ the *type* of the variable x_i, for $i = 1, \ldots, n$. If the value for x_i in a ground instance $s \in \mathcal{B}_\mathcal{P}$ of the atom $p(t)$ does not lie in T_i, then the state s does not satisfy φ.

In summary, we obtain an abstract *falsification* procedure for the $\exists$-CTL fragment of CTL, and an abstract *verification* procedure for the $\forall$-CTL fragment.

Set constraints. It is also possible to apply the two approaches in [18] and [25] of set-based analysis of logic programs with least [greatest] models, which infer

---

[2] The set-based abstract semantics of $\mathcal{P}$ is given by the transition system $\mathcal{S}_{\mathcal{P}^\sharp}$ induced by $\mathcal{P}^\sharp$. Here, a state is a conjunction of atoms. Its successor states are obtained by the *simultaneous* rewriting of all its atoms. We ignore the newly introduced predicates; these can be eliminated easily.

a definite [co-definite] set constraint from a logic program and then computes its solution in single-exponential time [17, 8]. We have preferred the formalism of uniform programs for the presentation in this paper because it allows us to greatly simplify the presentation; there is not much difference technically, and no difference at all in the case of unary function symbols (which is relevant for pushdown processes).

7 Parallel Programs

In this section, we will consider transition systems specified by *parallel programs* that consist of Horn clauses of the form

$$p(t) \leftarrow p_1(t_1) \wedge \ldots \wedge p_n(t_n)$$

with any number $n \geq 1$ of body atoms. Operationally, the conjunction of body atoms corresponds to parallel composition. Thus, a parallel program defines a concurrent system, which has, however, only a restricted way of communication (in particular, there is no synchronization between parallelly composed atoms). The logic program P defines a *fair* transition system $\mathcal{S}_P = \langle S_P, \tau_P \rangle$. The states are the *ground queries*, which are nonempty conjunctions of ground atoms.

$$S_P = \{p_1(t_1) \wedge \ldots \wedge p_m(t_m) \mid m \geq 1 \text{ and } p_1(t_1), \ldots, p_m(t_m) \in \mathcal{B}_P\}$$

The one-step transition relation τ_P is defined as usual for ground derivations of logic programs or constraint logic programs [21, 19]. We identify conjunctions modulo commutativity and associativity of conjunction. We give the definition of τ_P in a form that relies on this convention (i.e., every of the conjuncts forming a state can be chosen to be the first in a representation of the state).

$$\tau_P(p_1(t_1) \wedge \ldots \wedge p_m(t_m))$$

$$= p_1(t_1) \wedge \ldots \wedge p_{i-1}(t_{i-1}) \wedge body \wedge p_{i+1}(t_{i+1}) \wedge \ldots \wedge p_m(t_m) \mid$$

$$i \in \{1, \ldots, m\}, \; p_i(t_i) \leftarrow body \text{ is a ground clause of } \mathcal{P}\}$$

The fairness condition of the transition system is related to the fairness of the selection rule which is usually associated with the execution of logic programs. It says that in every execution sequence containing the state $p_1(t_1) \wedge \ldots \wedge p_m(t_m)$, a ground clause with head $p_j(t_j)$ is eventually applied to yield a successor state (for every $j = 1, \ldots, m$).

We require that the program $\mathcal{P}$ is total (which is, there exists a ground clause with the head $p(t)$ for every ground atom $\mathcal{B}_P$), and thus obtain that $\tau_P : S \to 2^S$ is totally defined (even if the fairness condition is taken into account).

In order to define the logic CTL over the transition system $\mathcal{S}_P$ induced by the parallel program $\mathcal{P}$, we will first fix a restricted set $Prop$ of *atomic propositions*. These are of the form $states(\Gamma)$ for some subset Γ of the Herbrand base. It is defined as the set of the states whose conjuncts all lie in Γ.

$$states(\Gamma) = \{p_1(t_1) \wedge \ldots \wedge p_m(t_m) \mid p_1(t_1), \ldots, p_m(t_m) \in \Gamma\}$$

Definition 3 (Restricted CTL formulas). A restricted CTL formula (for a given set of predicates *Pred* and a signature Σ defining the Herbrand base $\mathcal{B}_\mathcal{P}$) is a CTL formula such that either: the atomic propositions P are of the form $P = states(\Gamma)$ where $\Gamma \subseteq \mathcal{B}_\mathcal{P}$ and the quantifiers are only among EX, EF, EG, or: the atomic propositions P are of the form $P = \mathcal{B}_\mathcal{P} - states(\Gamma)$ and the quantifiers are among AX, AF, AG.

Theorem 5 (CTL properties and semantics of parallel programs).
Given the fair transition system $\mathcal{S}_\mathcal{P}$ corresponding to the parallel program $\mathcal{P}$, each set of states φ denoted by a restricted CTL formula φ can be characterized through the semantics of programs with oracles, via the following correspondences (for all subsets of states $\Gamma \subseteq \mathcal{B}_\mathcal{P}$).

$$EF(states(\Gamma)) = states(lm(\mathcal{P} \wedge \Gamma))$$
$$AF(S - states(\Gamma)) = S - states(gm(\mathcal{P} \wedge \neg\ \Gamma))$$
$$EG(states(S - \Gamma)) = states(gm(\mathcal{P} \wedge \neg\ \Gamma))$$
$$AG(S - states(\Gamma)) = S - states(lm(\mathcal{P} \wedge \neg\ \Gamma))$$

Proof. The proof follows the lines of the proof of Theorem 2. □

We can now rephrase Theorem 3 for parallel programs and for restricted CTL formulas with the CTL operators appearing in the statement above. Therefore, we can apply [abstract] set-based verification (in the sense of Theorem 4) also to this setting.

Les us note that parallel programs over nullary predicates represent *Basic Parallel Processes* (see, e.g., [15]). We leave open the question of the connections with other, infinite-state concurrent systems.

8 Conclusion and Future Work

The use of logic programs as specifications of transition systems gives us a new view on accurate and abstract verification of CTL properties for finite and infinite systems. The use of set-based analysis as a method to define an approximation function gives a new view on pushdown processes (namely, as the target of the approximation function) and yields a notion of descriptive types of program variables (wrt. a given CTL property). The use of set-based analysis as an algorithm to compute the conservative approximation of CTL properties gives a new view of model checking of pushdown processes, namely as constraint-solving, viz. theorem proving.

One obvious issue of further research is the extension of our method of abstract verification via set-based analysis to other temporal logics. The extension to the alternation-free mu-calculus seems to be possible directly. The work in [6] is a first step for the extension to the full mu-calculus.

The applications of our method that we have presented in this paper indicate its usefulness for the detection of "simple" programming errors, i.e., for the falsification of programs with respect to behavioral properties. The method may, however, also be useful for the verification of parameterized systems. The idea here is to use logic programs that first non-deterministically guess a parameter (say, the length of the token ring in the example used in [9]) and then simulate the corresponding system.

In the finite-state case, computing the model of a program with oracles is the fixpoint iteration in standard model checking. The programs are Boolean formulas. This is a new view of model checking which may be interesting in connection with BDD's. Also, we need to explore the connection with work in [24] which shows the equivalence of solving Boolean equation systems and model-checking in the modal μ-calculus.

In the finite-state case, programs with oracles are closely related to the product construction of [1]. It may be interesting to explore the connection with the similar product construction of [27] in the infinite-state case.

Acknowledgments. We thank Ahmed Bouajjani, Javier Esparza, David McAllester, Damian Niwiński and Moshe Vardi for fruitful discussions and the anonymous referees for useful remarks.

References

1. O. Bernholtz, M. Y. Vardi, and P. Wolper. An automata-theoretic approach to branching-time model checking. In *Computer Aided Verification, Proc. 6th Int. Workshop*, volume 818 of *LNCS*, pages 142–155, Stanford, California, June 1994. Springer-Verlag. Full version available from authors.
2. A. Bouajjani, J. Esparza, and O. Maler. Reachability Analysis of Pushdown Automata: Application to Model Checking. In *CONCUR'97*. LNCS 1243, 1997.
3. A. Bouajjani and O. Maler. Reachability Analysis of Pushdown Automata. In *Infinity'96*. tech. rep. MIP-9614, Univ. Passau, 1996.
4. F. Bourdoncle. Abstact debugging of higher-order imperative languages. In *Proceedings of the SIGPLAN'93 Conference on Programming Language Design and Implementation (PLDI'93)*, LNCS, pages 46–55. ACM Press, 1993.
5. O. Burkart and B. Steffen. Composition, Decomposition and Model-Checking of Pushdown Processes. *Nordic Journal of Computing*, 2, 1995.
6. W. Charatonik, D. McAllester, D. Niwiński, A. Podelski, and I. Walukiewicz. The Horn mu-calculus. Submitted for publication. Available under www.mpi-sb.mpg.de/~podelski/papers/HornMuCalculus.ps, December 1997.
7. W. Charatonik, D. McAllester, and A. Podelski. Computing the greatest model of the set-based abstraction of logic programs. Presented at the Dagstuhl Workshop on Tree Automata, October 1997.
8. W. Charatonik and A. Podelski. Co-definite set constraints. In T. Nipkow, editor, *Proceedings of the 9th International Conference on Rewriting Techniques and Applications*, LNCS, Tsukuba, Japan, March-April 1998. Springer-Verlag. To appear.
9. E. Clarke, O. Grumberg, and D. Long. Model checking and abstraction. In *Proceedings of the 19th Annual Symposium on Principles of Programming Languages*, pages 343–354. ACM Press, 1992.
10. P. Cousot and R. Cousot. Inductive definitions, semantics and abstract interpretation. In *Proc. POPL '92*, pages 83–94. ACM Press, 1992.

11. D. R. Dams. *Abstract interpretation and partition refinement for model checking.* PhD thesis, Eindhoven University of Technology, 1996.
12. P. Devienne, J.-M. Talbot, and S. Tison. Solving classes of set constraints with tree automata. In G. Smolka, editor, *Proceedings of the Third International Conference on Principles and Practice of Constraint Programming - CP97*, volume 1330 of *LNCS*, pages 68–83. Springer-Verlag, October 1997.
13. P. Devienne, J.-M. Talbot, and S. Tison. Solving classes of set constraints with tree automata. In G. Smolka, editor, *Proceedings of the Third International Conference on Principles and Practice of Constraint Programming - CP97*, volume 1330 of *LNCS*, Berlin, Germany, October 1997. Springer-Verlag.
14. E. Emerson and E. Clarke. Using branching-time temporal logic to synthesize synchronization skeletons. *Science of Computer Programming*, 2(3):241–266, 1982.
15. J. Esparza. Decidability of model checking for infinite-state concurrent systems. *Acta Informatika*, 34:85–107, 1997.
16. T. Frühwirth, E. Shapiro, M. Vardi, and E. Yardeni. Logic programs as types for logic programs. In *Sixth Annual IEEE Symposium on Logic in Computer Science*, pages 300–309, July 1991.
17. N. Heintze and J. Jaffar. A decision procedure for a class of set constraints (extended abstract). In *Fifth Annual IEEE Symposium on Logic in Computer Science*, pages 42–51, 1990.
18. N. Heintze and J. Jaffar. A finite presentation theorem for approximating logic programs. In *Seventeenth Annual ACM Symposium on Principles of Programming Languages*, pages 197–209, January 1990.
19. J. Jaffar and M. J. Maher. Constraint Logic Programming: A Survey. *The Journal of Logic Programming*, 19/20:503–582, May-July 1994.
20. N. D. Jones and S. S. Muchnick. Flow analysis and optimization of lisp-like structures. In *Sixth Annual ACM Symposium on Principles of Programming Languages*, pages 244–256, January 1979.
21. J. W. Lloyd. *Foundations of Logic Programming.* Symbolic Computation. Springer-Verlag, Berlin, Germany, second, extended edition, 1987.
22. C. Loiseaux, S.Graf, J. Sifakis, A. Bouajjani, and S. Bensalem. Property preserving abstractions for the verification of concurrent systems. *Formal Methods in System Design*, 6(1):11–44, 1995.
23. D. E. Long. *Model Checking, Abstraction, and Compositional Verification.* PhD thesis, Carnegie Mellon University, 1993.
24. A. Mader. *Verification of Modal Properties Using Boolean Equation Systems.* Phd thesis, Technische Universität München, 1997.
25. A. Podelski, W. Charatonik, and M. Müller. Set-based error diagnosis of concurrent constraint programs. Submitted for publication. Available under www.mpi-sb.mpg.de/~podelski/papers/diagnosis.ps, 1998.
26. Y. Ramakrishna, C. Ramakrishnan, I. Ramakrishnan, S. Smolka, T. Swift, and D. Warren. Efficient model checking using tabled resolution. In *Computer Aided Verification (CAV'97)*, LNCS 1254. Springer-Verlag, June 1997.
27. M. Y. Vardi. Verification of concurrent programs: The automata-theoretic framework. In *Proceedings of the Second Annual IEEE Symposium on Logic in Computer Science*, pages 167–176, Ithaca, 1987. IEEE Computer Society Press.
28. I. Walukiewicz. Pushdown Processes: Games and Model Checking. In *CAV'96*. LNCS 1102, 1996.
29. C. Weidenbach. Spass version 0.49. *Journal of Automated Reasoning*, 18(2):247–252, 1997.

Deciding Fixed and Non-fixed Size Bit-vectors

Nikolaj S. Bjørner and Mark C. Pichora

Computer Science Department,
Stanford University, Stanford, California 94305
nikolaj|mpichora@cs.stanford.edu

Abstract. We develop a new, efficient, and compact decision procedure for fixed size bit-vectors with bit-wise boolean operations. The algorithm is designed such that it can also decide some common cases of parameterized (non-fixed) size. To handle even more parameterized cases for bit-vectors without bit-wise boolean operations we devise a unification based algorithm which invokes the first algorithm symbolically on parameters of the form $aN + b$, where a and b are integers and N is the only unknown.

Our procedures are designed to be integrated in the Shostak combination of decision procedures. This allows them to be tightly integrated with decision procedures for other theories in STeP's (the Stanford Temporal Prover) simplifier and validity checker.

1 Introduction

Bit-vectors are the natural data-type for hardware descriptions. To handle bit-vectors in computer-aided verification, it is convenient to have specialized decision procedures to solve constraints involving bit-vectors and their operations.

STeP [3], supports the computer-aided verification of reactive, real-time and hybrid systems. STeP provides the capability of verifying properties of parameterized systems with parameterized control and data domains. While model checking techniques are available for finite-state systems, deductive rules for linear-time temporal formulas are available for establishing correctness of very large finite-state and parameterized systems. STeP even supports a diagram-based deductive model checking procedure [18] which can verify infinite-state systems using STeP's deductive tools. The deductive verification methods are based on checking the validity of first-order verification conditions [4] which arise from applications of proof rules.

To verify industrial hardware designs, we are developing a compiler from the Verilog hardware description language to fair transition systems, which are STeP's computational model. Since bit-vectors are pervasive in Verilog we have found it useful to develop the decision procedures for bit-vectors described in

---

* This research was supported in part by the National Science Foundation under grant CCR-95-27927, the Defense Advanced Research Projects Agency under NASA grant NAG2-892, ARO under grant DAAH04-95-1-0317, ARO under MURI grant DAAH04-96-1-0341, and by Army contract DABT63-96-C-0096 (DARPA).

this paper. The presented procedure is easy to integrate tightly with decision procedures for other theories, which fits well into the wide scope of STeP.

1.1 Contributions

This work arose from the need for an efficiently supported theory of bit-vectors to prove basic verification conditions. An algorithm that addresses bit-vectors from a perspective similar to ours has been reported in [11]. In an effort to use that algorithm we found that it had to be extended in a nontrivial way to handle bit-wise boolean operations properly. In contrast, with our algorithm we offer a compact and efficient procedure that readily handles bitwise operations. The key feature of the procedure is that it only splits contiguous bit-vectors on demand. Its performance is often independent of the length of the bit-vectors in the input. We also discuss non-equational bit-vector constraints, which we think have not received proper attention elsewhere.

Legal inputs to the STeP-Verilog verification tool include *parameterized* hardware designs where the bit-vector size is not fixed at verification time. The need then arises for a method that can handle both fixed and non-fixed size bit-vectors. In certain cases our simple procedure for fixed size bit-vectors can be used directly for non-fixed size bit-vectors. To handle more cases, we first present an optimized decision procedure for equations $s = t$, where s and t do not contain bit-wise boolean operations, and then extend it to handle bit-vectors whose sizes are parameterized (still without supporting boolean operations). To our knowledge this is the first reported decision procedure that handles concatenation of a non-trivial class of non-fixed size bit-vectors.

1.2 Bit-vectors

Bit-vector terms are of the form

$$
\begin{array}{lll}
t & ::= & x \mid t[i:j] \mid t_1 \otimes t_2 \mid c_{[m]} \mid t_1 \; op \; t_2 \\
op & ::= & \& \;(\text{bitwise and}) \mid \; \hat{} \;\; (\text{bitwise xor}) \mid \text{``|''} \;(\text{bitwise or}) \\
c & ::= & 1 \mid 0
\end{array}
$$

$t[i:j]$ denotes subfield extraction, and $\otimes$ concatenates two bit-vectors. The constant 0 is synonymous with false and 1 with true. For clarity, a term may be annotated by a length, such that $t_{[m]}$ indicates that t has length m.

Terms are well-formed when for every subterm $t_{[m]}[i:j]$, $0 \le i \le j < m$, and for every $s_{[m]} \; op \; t_{[n]}$, $n = m$. Terms without occurrences of op are called *basic bit-vector terms*.

Bit-vectors can be interpreted as finite functions from an initial segment of the natural numbers to booleans. Hence, if η is a mapping from bit-vector variables $x_{[m]}$ to an element of the function space $\{0, \dots, m-1\} \to \mathcal{B}$ we interpret composite terms as follows:

$$\llbracket x \rrbracket_\eta = \eta(x)$$
$$\llbracket t[i:j] \rrbracket_\eta = \lambda k \in \{0, \ldots, j-i\}.\llbracket t \rrbracket_\eta(i+k)$$
$$\llbracket s_{[m]} \otimes t_{[n]} \rrbracket_\eta = \lambda k \in \{0, \ldots, m+n-1\}.\text{if } k < m \text{ then } \llbracket s \rrbracket_\eta(k) \text{ else } \llbracket t \rrbracket_\eta(k-m)$$
$$\llbracket s_{[m]} \text{ op } t \rrbracket_\eta = \lambda k \in \{0, \ldots, m-1\}.\llbracket s \rrbracket_\eta(k) \llbracket op \rrbracket \llbracket t \rrbracket_\eta(k)$$
$$\llbracket c_{[m]} \rrbracket_\eta = \lambda k \in \{0, \ldots, m-1\}.c = 1$$

Bit-vector terms from the above grammar appear, for instance, throughout the system description and verification conditions from a split-transaction bus design from SUN Micro-systems [13]. A sample proof obligation encountered during STeP's verification of a safety property of the bus (processes are granted exclusive and non-interfering access to the bus) takes the form

$$l\_wires = 4 \wedge request \neq 0_{[8]} \rightarrow$$
$$(request\_h \; \hat{} \; request) \neq 0_{[8]} \tag{1}$$
$$\vee \; (request \neq 0_{[8]}) \wedge request = request\_h$$

where $request$ and $request\_h$ are bit-vector variables of length 8. While this proof obligation is evidently valid, a simple encoding of bit-vectors as tuples causes examination of multiple branches when establishing the verification condition. The procedure developed here avoids this encoding and its potential case splitting. This and similar verification conditions can then be established independently of the bit-vector length (and in a fraction of a second). Thus, our procedure is able to establish this verification condition when the length 8 is replaced by an arbitrary parameter N.

While other logical operations like shifting can easily be encoded in the language of bit-vectors we analyze, the arithmetical (signed, unsigned and IEEE-compliant floating point) operations are not treated in an original way here.

1.3 Alternative approaches

This paper investigates decision methods for bit-vectors that can easily be integrated in the Shostak combination [17], which allows a tight integration of decision procedures for several theories. The strength of this approach is that verification conditions involving a mixture of bit-vector expressions, and uninterpreted function symbols, as in $x[1:6] = y[0:5] \rightarrow R(x[1:5]) = R(y[0:4])$, can be decided efficiently. Our algorithms can then be used in heterogeneous verification conditions. The Shostak combination is also targeted by the procedure in [11]. Naturally, the same verification conditions may be established directly using an axiomatization of bit-vectors and equality. Better than a raw axiomatization, proof assistants like ACL2 and PVS provide sophisticated libraries containing relevant bit-vector lemmas. Although highly useful, libraries do not provide a decision method.

In the symbolic model checking community, BDDs [6] (binary decision diagrams) are used to efficiently represent and reason about bit-vectors. Purely

BDD based representation of bit-vectors requires allocating one variable for every position in a bit-vector. (Just two bit-vector variables each of length 64 require allocation of 128 variables, pushing the limits of current BDD technology). A BMD-based (binary moment diagram) representation [7] optimizes on this while being able to efficiently perform arithmetical operations on bit-vectors. Unfortunately it is nontrivial to combine BMDs efficiently into the Shostak combination.

Since the values of bit-vectors range over strings of 0's and 1's it is possible to use regular automata to constrain the possible values of bit-vectors. Using this approach the MONA tool [2] can effectively represent addition of parameterized bit-vectors using M2L (Monadic Second-Order Logic). The expressive power of M2L also allows a direct and practical decision procedure of fixed size bit-vectors encoded either as tuples of boolean variables or as unary predicates with a constant domain. Furthermore M2L allows quantification over bit-vectors (with non-elementary complexity as the price). The approach based on regular automata, however does not admit an encoding of concatenations of parameterized bit-vectors. For suppose the regular language R_x (say 10*1) encodes evaluations of bit-vector x that satisfy constraint $\varphi(x)$. Then the pumping lemma tells us that the evaluations of y consistent with $\varphi(x) \wedge y = x \otimes x$ is not in general (certainly $\{ww \mid w \in 10^*1\}$ is not) a regular language. Automata with constraints [8] (see chapter 4) is a possible remedy, but this imposes even more challenges in obtaining a direct ground integration with other decision procedures, which we seek here. Our procedure addresses this problem and solves satisfiability of ground equalities, a problem which is "only" NP-complete.

2 A decision procedure for fixed size bit-vectors

We present a normalization function $\mathcal{T}$, which takes a bit-vector term $t_{[m]}$ and a subrange (initially $[0 : m - 1]$) and normalizes it to a bit-vector term $F_1 \otimes F_2 \otimes \ldots \otimes F_n$ where each F_i is of the form

$$F ::= F \ op \ F \mid x \mid c_{[m]} \ .$$

A normalization routine with a similar scope can be found in [5]. In words, $\mathcal{T}$ produces a term without occurrences of subfield extraction where every $\otimes$ is above every op. The translation furthermore maps every original variable $x_{[m]}$ to a concatenation $x_1 \otimes x_2 \otimes \ldots \otimes x_n$, and maintains a decoding of the auxiliary variables into subranges $decode([i_k : j_k])$, such that $i_1 = 0$, $j_n = m - 1$, and $j_k + 1 = i_{k+1}$ for $k = 1 \ldots n - 1$.

The normalization function shown in Figure 3 is designed to satisfy the basic correspondence

$$[\![t_{[n]}]\!]_\eta = [\![\mathcal{T}(t, [0 : n - 1])]\!]_{\eta'}$$

for every η, where η' coincides with η on the free variables in t and, furthermore, if $\mathcal{T}$ rewrites x to $x_1 \otimes \ldots \otimes x_k \otimes \ldots \otimes x_n$, with $decode(x_k) = [i : j]$, then $\eta'(x_k) = \lambda k \in \{0, \ldots, j - i\}.\eta(x)(k + i)$.

Normalization works by recursive descent on the syntax tree of t, pushing a subfield extraction $[i : j]$ downwards. By maintaining only one copy of each variable, the procedure may update a variable occurrence x to a concatenation $x_1 \otimes x_2 \otimes x_3$ globally in the cases where only the subfield $[3 : 5]$ needs to be extracted from $x_{[8]}$. The result of normalizing $x[3 : 5]$ then becomes x_2, such that $decode(x_2) = [3 : 5]$. Since the variable x may occur in a different subterm under the scope of a boolean operator $x \& y$ the cutting of x rewrites this to $(x_1 \otimes x_2 \otimes x_3) \& y$. The auxiliary procedure cut (that takes a term and a cut-point as argument) shown in Figure 1 recursively cuts y in the same proportions as x, and forms the normalized concatenation $x_1 \& y_1 \otimes x_2 \& y_2 \otimes x_3 \& y_3$. It uses a set $parents$ associated with each variable x to collect the maximal boolean subterms involving x that have already been normalized. Initially $parents(x) = \emptyset$ for each variable. Subterms can also be marked. By default (and initially) they are unmarked. To avoid cluttering the pseudocode we have suppressed variable dereferencing. To normalize boolean operators, $\mathcal{T}$ uses the auxiliary procedure $slice$ shown in Figure 2, which aligns the normalized terms s and t into concatenations of equal length boolean subterms. Operator application can then be distributed over each of the equally sized portions. The auxiliary symbol ϵ is used for the empty concatenation.

The proper functioning of $\mathcal{T}$ relies on the precondition that every time $\mathcal{T}(t_{[n]}, [i : j])$ is invoked, then $0 \le i \le j < n$. This ensures that whenever $cut(t_{[n]}, m)$ is invoked then $m < n$.

$$dice(s \text{ op } t, m) =$$
$$\textbf{let}$$
$$\quad (s_1, s_2) = dice(s, m);$$
$$\quad (t_1, t_2) = dice(t, m);$$
$$\textbf{in}$$
$$\quad \textbf{return } (s_1 \text{ op } t_1, s_2 \text{ op } t_2)$$
$$dice(c_{[l]}, m) = \textbf{return } (c_{[m]}, c_{[l-m]})$$
$$dice(x^1_{[m]} \otimes x^2_{[n]}, m) = \textbf{return } (x^1, x^2)$$
$$dice(x, m) =$$
$$\textbf{let}$$
$$\quad [i : j] = decode(x)$$
$$\quad x_1, x_2 \text{ be fresh variables with } \emptyset \text{ parents}$$
$$\textbf{in}$$
$$\quad decode(x_1) := [i : i + m - 1];$$
$$\quad decode(x_2) := [i + m : j];$$
$$\quad x := x_1 \otimes x_2$$
$$\quad \textbf{for each } \text{unmarked } s \in parents(x) \textbf{ do}$$
$$\quad\quad s := s_1 \otimes s_2 \text{ where } (s_1, s_2) = cut(s, m)$$
$$\quad \textbf{return } (x_1, x_2)$$

$$cut(F, m) =$$
$$\quad mark(F);$$
$$\textbf{let}$$
$$\quad (F_1(\overline{x}^1), F_2(\overline{x}^2)) = dice(F, m)$$
$$\textbf{in}$$
$$\quad \textbf{for each } j = 1, 2, x^j \in \overline{x}^j \textbf{ do}$$
$$\quad\quad parents(x^j) := parents(x^j) \cup \{F_j\}$$
$$\quad \textbf{return } (F_1(\overline{x}^1), F_2(\overline{x}^2))$$

Fig. 1. Basic cutting and dicing

Example: As an example of the translation of an bit-vector expression, consider:

$$s : \quad w_{[7]} \quad \& \quad (y_{[7]}[0 : 3] \otimes x_{[3]})$$
$$t : \quad y_{[7]} \quad | \quad (x_{[3]} \otimes 1_{[1]} \otimes w_{[7]}[0 : 2])$$

We first apply $\mathcal{T}(s, [0 : 6])$ which results in cutting y into $y_1 \otimes y_2$, where $decode(y_1) = [0 : 3], decode(y_2) = [4 : 6]$. w is cut similarly. The translation

$apply(op, F(\overline{x}), G(\overline{y})) =$
     for each $x \in \overline{x} \cup \overline{y}$ **do**
         $parents(x) := parents(x) \setminus \{F, G\} \cup \{F(\overline{x}) \; op \; G(\overline{y})\}$
     return $F(\overline{x}) \; op \; G(\overline{y})$

$slice(op, \epsilon, \epsilon) = \epsilon$
$slice(op, F(\overline{x})_{[n]} \otimes s, G(\overline{y})_{[m]} \otimes t) =$
       if $m = n$ **then**
           $apply(op, F(\overline{x}), G(\overline{y})) \otimes slice(op, s, t)$
       else if $m > n$ **then**
           $(G_1(\overline{y}_1), G_2(\overline{y}_2)) := cut(G(\overline{y}), n);$
           $apply(op, F(\overline{x}), G_1(\overline{y}_1)) \otimes slice(op, s, G_2(\overline{y}_2) \otimes t)$
       else
           $(F_1(\overline{x}_1), F_2(\overline{x}_2)) := cut(F(\overline{y}), m);$
           $apply(op, F_1(\overline{x}), G(\overline{y})) \otimes slice(op, F_2(\overline{x}_2) \otimes s, t)$

Fig. 2. Slicing and operator application

$T(s \; op \; t, [i:j]) =$ $slice(op, T(s, [i:j]), T(t, [i:j]))$
$T(s[k:l], [i:j]) =$ $T(s, [k+i:k+j])$
$T(s_{[n]} \otimes t_{[m]}, [i:j]) =$ **if** $n \le i$ **then** $T(t, [i-n:j-n])$ **else**
                         if $n > j$ **then** $T(s, [i:j])$ **else** $T(s, [i:n-1]) \otimes T(t, [0:j-n])$
$T(x_{[m]}, [i:j]) =$ **if** $0 < i$ **then** $T(\text{second}(dice(x, i)), [0:j-i])$ **else**
                         if $j < m-1$ $(i=0)$ **then** $\text{first}(dice(x, j+1))$ **else** x
$T(c_{[m]}, [i:j]) =$ $c_{[j-i+1]}$

Fig. 3. Normalization function T

of t results in further cutting y_1 into $y_3 \otimes y_4$, where $decode(y_3) = [0:2]$, in order to align with $x_{[3]} \otimes 1_{[1]}$. The variable $w_{[7]}$ is also cut into $w_1 \otimes w_2 \otimes w_3$ overing the same intervals as the parts of y, namely $[0:2], [3:3], [4:6]$. The result of translation is then:

$$s : w_1 \; \& \; y_3 \otimes w_2 \; \& \; y_4 \otimes w_3 \; \& \; x \qquad t : y_3 \mid x \otimes y_4 \mid 1_{[1]} \otimes y_2 \mid w_1$$

2.1 Interfacing to the Shostak combination

Shostak's method of combining decision procedures allows integrating decision procedures for theories, such as arrays, linear arithmetic, records, inductive data-types, and sets inside Shostak's congruence closure algorithm [17, 10]. The method requires each decision procedure to provide (1) a canonizer (σ), which satisfies $\sigma(s) = \sigma(t)$ whenever the equality $s = t$ holds in the theory supported by the decision procedure; and (2) a solver, which rewrites an equation $s = t$ to either **false** (if it is unsatisfiable) or into an equivalent form $\exists V_{aux} . \bigwedge_{i=1}^{n} x_i = t_i$, where each x_i is a variable from s or t, each t_i is canonized, and no x_i occurs in t_j or is equal to an x_k, when $k \ne i$. V_{aux} is the collection of auxiliary variables that occur in the t_j's but not in the original equation $s = t$. We will use the equivalent form as a substitution $\theta = [x_i \mapsto t_i \mid i = 1, \ldots, n]$ and call it a *Shostak* *substitution*. The substitution can be used to decide verification conditions of the form $s_1 = t_1 \wedge s_2 = t_2 \to s_3 = t_3$ by extracting θ_1 from $s_1 = t_1$, extracting θ_2 from $\theta_1(s_2 = t_2)$ and check if $\sigma(\theta_2(\theta_1(s_3)))$ is identical to $\sigma(\theta_2(\theta_1(t_3)))$. .

To canonize a term $t_{[m]}$ we first obtain $F^1 \otimes \ldots \otimes F^n = T(t, [0 : m - 1])$. We will identify a free variable x_k in F^i with $x[i : j]$, where $decode(x_k) = [i : j]$. Each F^i is represented in a canonical form (for instance an ordered BDD) based on a total order of the variables. A consecutive pair F^i and F^{i+1} can now be combined whenever F^i is equivalent to the boolean expression obtained from F^{i+1} by replacing each variable $x[k : l]$ by $x[k - n : l - 1]$, where n is the length of F^i.

To decide the satisfiability of an equality $s_{[n]} = t_{[n]}$ and extract a canonized substitution θ we notice that $s = t$ is equivalent to $s \hat{\ } t = 0_{[n]}$. Hence the equality is satisfiable if and only if $T(s \hat{\ } t, [0 : n - 1]) = F^1 \otimes \ldots \otimes F^m$ and $\bigwedge_{i=1}^{m} \neg F^i$ is satisfiable. At this point we can apply the technique used in [11], which extract equalities from BDDs using equivalence preserving transformations of the form $\mathbf{ite}(x, H, G) \equiv (H \vee G) \wedge \exists \delta. x = H \wedge (\neg G \vee \delta)$. This produces a substitution θ_0 with subranges of the original variables in the domain and auxiliary δ's in the range. The resulting Shostak substitution can then be extracted by generating θ as follows:

$$\theta_1 : [x \mapsto \theta_0(x_1) \otimes \ldots \otimes \theta_0(x_n) \mid x_i \in \mathbf{dom}(\theta_0) \wedge x = x_1 \otimes \ldots \otimes x_n]$$

$$\theta_2 : \left[x_k \mapsto x[i : j] \,\middle|\, \begin{array}{l} x = x_1 \otimes \ldots \otimes x_n, \ k \leq n, \\ decode(x_k) = [i : j], \ \forall i : [1..n].x_i \notin \mathbf{dom}(\theta_0) \end{array} \right]$$

$$\theta : [x \mapsto \sigma(\theta_2(\theta_1(x))) \mid x \in \mathbf{dom}(\theta_1)]$$

Example: Continuing with the translated versions of our example terms s and t we will extract a Shostak substitution from the equality constraint $s = t$. We therefore complete the translation to get:

$$s \hat{\ } t : (w_1 \ \& \ y_3) \hat{\ } (y_3 \mid x) \otimes (w_2 \ \& \ y_4) \hat{\ } (y_4 \mid 1_{[1]}) \otimes (w_3 \ \& \ x) \hat{\ } (y_2 \mid w_1)$$

By negating the concatenations, the constraints needed to extract a substitution are obtained. The second constraint is easiest as it simply imposes $w_2 = y_4 = 1_{[1]}$. The conjunction of the first and third constraint is transformed:

$$\neg((w_1 \ \& \ y_3) \hat{\ } (y_3 \mid x)) \ \& \ \neg((w_3 \ \& \ x) \hat{\ } (y_2 \mid w_1)) = 1_{[3]}$$
$$\leftrightarrow \mathbf{ite}(x, w_1 \ \& \ y_3 \ \& \ w_3, \neg y_2 \ \& \ \neg w_1 \ \& \ \neg y_3) = 1_{[3]}$$
$$\leftrightarrow (x = w_1 \ \& \ y_3 \ \& \ w_3) \wedge ((w_1 \ \& \ y_3 \ \& \ w_3) \mid (\neg y_2 \ \& \ \neg w_1 \ \& \ \neg y_3)) = 1_{[3]}$$
$$\leftrightarrow (x = w_1 \ \& \ y_3 \ \& \ w_3) \wedge (w_1 = y_3 \ \& \ w_3) \wedge ((y_3 \ \& \ w_3) \mid (\neg y_2 \ \& \ \neg y_3)) = 1_{[3]}$$
$$\leftrightarrow (x = w_1 \ \& \ y_3 \ \& \ w_3) \wedge (w_1 = y_3 \ \& \ w_3) \wedge (y_3 = w_3) \wedge (w_3 \mid \neg y_2) = 1_{[3]}$$
$$\leftrightarrow (x = w_1 \ \& \ y_3 \ \& \ w_3) \wedge (w_1 = y_3 \ \& \ w_3) \wedge (y_3 = w_3) \wedge \exists \delta. y_2 = w_3 \ \& \ \delta$$

The composition of the extracted equalities gives an idempotent substitution:

$$\theta : [w_1 \mapsto w_3 \ \& \ \delta, \ x \mapsto w_3 \ \& \ \delta, \ y_2 \mapsto w_3 \ \& \ \delta, \ y_3 \mapsto w_3]$$

From this we generate a Shostak substitution, where $V_{aux} = \{w_3, \delta\}$.

$$[x \mapsto w_3 \ \& \ \delta, \quad w \mapsto (w_3 \ \& \ \delta) \otimes 1_{[1]} \otimes w_3, \quad y \mapsto w_3 \otimes 1_{[1]} \otimes (w_3 \ \& \ \delta)] \quad .$$

2.2 Equational running time

For input $s = t_{[n]}$ not involving op subterms (basic bit-vectors) the presented algorithm can be tuned to run in time: $\mathcal{O}(m + n\log(n))$, where m is the number of $\otimes$ and subfield extraction occurrences in s and t. First subfield extraction is pushed to the leaves in time $\mathcal{O}(m)$, then the $\otimes$ subterms are arranged in a balanced tree and $\mathcal{T}$ is applied to the balanced terms while maintaining balance in the tree. The translated equality $s = t$ is processed in a style similar to *slice*, but the auxiliary function *apply* has been replaced by one that builds a graph by connecting vertices representing the equated constants or variables. If some connected component contains two different constants there is a contradiction and the equality is unsatisfiable. Otherwise an equivalence class representative is appointed for each connected component, choosing a constant if one is present, or an arbitrary variable vertex otherwise. The extracted Shostak substitution then maps every variable to a concatenation of equivalence class representatives.

A canonized solution for satisfiable equalities can be extracted in time $\mathcal{O}(n)$ (which is dominated by the running time of $\mathcal{T}$). An algorithm with the same functionality is presented in [11]. That algorithm has running time $\mathcal{O}(m\log(m) + n^2)$, but offers some shortcuts that we don't address. Both procedures may still depend heavily on the parameter n. For instance, the equality

$$0_{[1]} \otimes 1_{[1]} \otimes x_{[m]} = x_{[m]} \otimes 0_{[1]} \otimes 1_{[1]} \tag{2}$$

requires (the maximal) m cuts of x, and is only satisfiable if m is even. The same functionality can, as [11] noticed, be achieved in $\mathcal{O}(m + n)$ time, but at the expense of having this as the minimal running time as well.

Another advantage of our algorithm is that it can be extended (with a few modifications) to the case where bit-vectors of parameterized length are either exclusively on the right or exclusively on the left of every concatenation. This excludes cases like (2), which we will address in Section 3.

2.3 Beyond Equalities

The satisfiability problem for constraints involving disequalities is NP-complete in the case of basic bit-vectors. Membership in NP follows from the fact that we can easily check in polynomial time that a given instantiation of bit-vector variables satisfies prescribed constraints. NP-hardness follows from a reduction from 3-SAT to conjunctions of disequality constraints: take an instance of 3-SAT $\bigwedge_i (l_i \vee k_i \vee m_i)$ where l_i, k_i and m_i are literals over the vocabulary $\mathcal{V}$ of boolean variables. Translate this into $\bigwedge_i (l_i \otimes k_i \otimes m_i \neq 000) \wedge \bigwedge_{x \in \mathcal{V}} (\overline{x} \neq x)$, where for each boolean variable x we associate two bit-vector variables $x_{[1]}$ representing x and $\overline{x}_{[1]}$ representing the negation of x.

We therefore settle here by handling $t \neq s$ as $|(t \mathbin{\char`\^} s)$, and converting $|t_{[n]}$ to $t[0 : 0] \mid \ldots \mid t[n-1 : n-1] = 1_{[1]}$. The connectives $<$ and $\leq$, as well as operations like $+$ and $*$ can be handled similarly, though the advantages of this approach are questionable. Naturally these constraints are only analyzed when all equational constraints have been processed and the resulting Shostak substitutions have been applied to the non-equational constraints.

Verification conditions of the form $f(A) \neq f(B) \wedge f(A) \neq f(C) \rightarrow f(B) = f(C)$, where f is an uninterpreted function symbol, are handled using a complete case analysis on bit-vectors A, B and C (it is valid only when A, B and C are bit-vectors of length 1). Shostak's approach to combining equational theories misses cases like this as it is originally designed for theories admitting infinite models (see for example [15]).

3   Unification of basic bit-vectors

In this section we focus on the problem of finding unifiers for basic bit-vector terms s and t. The restriction to basic bit-vector terms allows us to develop a more efficient procedure and at the same time widen its scope to bit-vectors whose lengths are parameterized.

3.1   *ext*-terms

To more compactly represent solutions to equations like (2) we introduce a new bit-vector term construct $ext(t_{[n]}, m)$ (the extension of t up to length m), which is well-formed whenever $m > 0$. The meaning of ext is given by the equation

$$\llbracket ext(t_{[n]}, m) \rrbracket_\eta = \llbracket \underbrace{t \otimes .. \otimes t}_{k} \otimes t[0:l-1] \rrbracket_\eta \text{ where } (k+1)n \geq m > kn \text{ and } l = m - kn$$

Thus, $ext(t_{[n]}, m)$ repeats t up to the length m. To map ext-terms to terms in the base language we use the unfolding function unf

$$unf(t_{[n]}, m) = \underbrace{t \otimes .. \otimes t}_{k} \otimes T(t, [0:l-1]) \text{ where } (k+1)n \geq m > kn \text{ and } l = m - kn$$

A solution to equation (2) can now be given compactly when m is even as $x = ext(0_{[1]} \otimes 1_{[1]}, m)$.

3.2   Unification with *ext*-terms

To decide the satisfiability of equalities $s = t$ of basic bit-vector terms extended with ext-subterms we will develop a Martelli-Montanari style unification algorithm [14] which takes the singleton set $\mathcal{E}_0 : \{s = t\}$ as input and works by transforming $\mathcal{E}_0$ to intermediary sets $\mathcal{E}_1, \mathcal{E}_2, \ldots$ by equivalence preserving transformations which simplify, delete or propagate equalities. It ultimately produces either FAIL, when $s = t$ is unsatisfiable, or a substitution $\mathcal{E}_{final} : \{x_1 = t_1, \ldots, x_n = t_n\}$.

Since our procedure uses T to decompose terms, every auxiliary variable in $\mathcal{E}_{final}$ furthermore corresponds to a unique disjoint subrange of one of the original variables. The obviously satisfiable conjunction of equalities is equivalent to the original equality.

A canonizer can be obtained by first eliminating the *ext*-terms by using unfold and then using the canonizer of Section 2.1.

Example: Anticipating the algorithm we will present, consider the following equality assertion:

$$y_{[3]} \otimes x_{[16]} \otimes x_{[16]} \otimes z_{[2]} = x_{[16]} \otimes w_{[4]} \otimes 0_{[1]} \otimes x_{[16]} \ .$$

In processing the implied equality $y_{[3]} \otimes x_{[16]} = x_{[16]} \otimes \ldots$ we obtain $x_{[16]} = ext(y_{[3]}, 16)$ as a solution for $x_{[16]}$. Continuing with the remaining equalities we get the intermediate set of equations:

$$x_{[16]} = ext(y_{[3]}, 16), \qquad y_{[3]}[1:2] \otimes y_{[3]}[0:0] \quad = w_{[4]}[0:2],$$
$$z_{[2]} \ = w_{[4]}[3:3] \otimes 0_{[1]}, \quad ext(w_{[4]}[3:3] \otimes 0_{[1]}, 16) = x_{[16]} \ .$$

The two equations involving x are combined to produce the implied constraint

$$ext(y_{[3]}, 16) = ext(w_{[4]}[3:3] \otimes 0_{[1]}, 16) \ .$$

This equality is evidently equivalent to its *unf*-unfolding, but as we will later formulated in a general setting, we can do better and only need to assert:

$$y_{[3]} \otimes y_{[3]}[0:0] = w_{[4]}[3:3] \otimes 0_{[1]} \otimes w_{[4]}[3:3] \otimes 0_{[1]} \ .$$

In fact this implies $y[0:0] = y[1:1] = y[2:2] = w[3:3] = 0_{[1]}$. After propagating the resulting constraints we obtain the final result:

$$w_{[4]} = 0_{[4]}, \qquad x_{[16]} = 0_{[16]}, \qquad y_{[3]} = 0_{[3]}, \qquad z_{[2]} = 0_{[2]} \ .$$

While the full unification algorithm is given in Figure 4 we highlight and explain the more delicate cases below.

$x_{[n]} \otimes s = t_{[m]} \otimes y_{[l]} \otimes u$ when $m + l > n > m$, $x \neq y$. The situation is described in the picture below, which suggests that the equality is equivalent to $x = t \otimes y_1$ and $s = y_2 \otimes u$ for suitable splits y_1 and y_2 of y. We use T to cut y into the appropriate pieces. This replaces y everywhere in $\mathcal{E}$ by $y_1 \otimes y_2$.

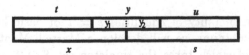

$x_{[n]} \otimes s = t_{[m]} \otimes x_{[n]} \otimes u$ when $n > m$. For example we are given the configuration:

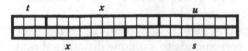

Thus, the original equality constraint is equivalent to $x = t \otimes t \otimes t \otimes t[0:0]$ and $t[1:2] \otimes t[0:0] \otimes u = s$. To more compactly describe the first equality we use the ext-construct to obtain $x = ext(t, 10)$.

$ext(s_{[m]}, l) = ext(t_{[n]}, l)$ The effect of replacing x by s in the variable elimination step may introduce equality constraints between ext-terms. Although the equality constraint is by definition equivalent to $unf(s_{[m]}, l) = unf(t_{[n]}, l)$, we can be even more economical in the unfolding as the following lemma suggests.

Lemma 1. *Assume* $2n \leq l$ *and* $2m \leq l$ *and let* $g = \gcd(m, n)$ *then*

$$ext(s_{[m]}, l) = ext(t_{[n]}, l) \quad \leftrightarrow \quad unf(s, m + n - g) = unf(t, m + n - g)$$

Thus, we will ensure that our algorithm maintains the invariant $2n \leq l$ for every $ext(t_{[n]}, l)$ term, and the equality constraint $ext(s_{[m]}, l) = ext(t_{[n]}, l)$ is replaced by $unf(s, m + n - g) = unf(t, m + n - g)$.

Other simpler cases are summarized in Figure 4. It omits cases that can be obtained using symmetry of equality.

Constructor elimination

R1 $\quad \{s_{[m]} \otimes u = t_{[m]} \otimes v\} \cup \mathcal{E}$ $\quad \rightarrow \quad \{s = t, u = v\} \cup \mathcal{E}$

R2 $\quad \{c_{[m]} \otimes s = c'_{[n]} \otimes t\} \cup \mathcal{E}$ $\quad \rightarrow \quad$ FAIL $\quad\quad\quad\quad$ where $c \neq c'$

R3 $\quad \{c_{[m]} \otimes s = c_{[n]} \otimes t\} \cup \mathcal{E}$ $\quad \rightarrow \quad \{s = c_{[n-m]} \otimes t\} \cup \mathcal{E}$ $\quad$ where $n > m$

R4 $\quad \{x_{[n]} \otimes s = t_{[m]} \otimes y_{[l]} \otimes u\} \cup \mathcal{E}$ $\quad \rightarrow \quad \{x = t \otimes y_1, s = y_2 \otimes u\} \cup \mathcal{E}$
$\quad\quad\quad$ where $m + l > n > m > 0$, $x \neq y$,
$\quad\quad\quad\quad\quad y_1 = \mathcal{T}(y, [0 : m - n - 1]), y_2 = \mathcal{T}(y, [m - n : l - 1])$,

R5 $\quad \{x_{[n]} \otimes s = t_{[m]} \otimes x_{[n]} \otimes u\} \cup \mathcal{E}$ $\quad \rightarrow \quad \{s = wrap(t, n) \otimes u, x = mk\text{-}ext(t, n)\} \cup \mathcal{E}$
$\quad\quad\quad$ where $n > m > 0$

R6 $\quad \{x_{[n]} \otimes s = t_{[m]} \otimes c_{[l]} \otimes u\} \cup \mathcal{E}$ $\quad \rightarrow \quad \{x = t \otimes c_{[m-n]}, s = c_{[l+n-m]} \otimes u\} \cup \mathcal{E}$
$\quad\quad\quad$ where $m + l > n > m \geq 0$

R7 $\quad \{s_{[m]} \otimes t = ext(u_{[l]}, n) \otimes v\} \cup \mathcal{E}$ $\quad \rightarrow \quad \left\{ \begin{array}{l} s_{[m]} = mk\text{-}ext(u, m), \\ t = mk\text{-}ext(wrap(u, m), n - m) \otimes v \end{array} \right\} \cup \mathcal{E}$
$\quad\quad\quad$ where $m < n$

R8 $\quad \{ext(s_{[l_1]}, m) = ext(t_{[l_2]}, m)\} \cup \mathcal{E} \rightarrow \{unf(s, l) = unf(t, l)\} \cup \mathcal{E}$
$\quad\quad\quad$ where $l = l_1 + l_2 - \gcd(l_1, l_2)$

Equality and variable elimination

R9 $\quad \{t = t\} \cup \mathcal{E}$ $\quad\quad\quad\quad\quad\quad\quad \rightarrow \quad \mathcal{E}$

R10 $\quad \{x = s\} \cup \mathcal{E}$ $\quad\quad\quad\quad\quad\quad \rightarrow \quad \{x = s\} \cup \mathcal{E}[x \mapsto s]$

Fig. 4. Rules for unification with ext-terms

The auxiliary function $wrap$ splits the term t at position k and swaps the two pieces. The function $mk\text{-}ext$ produces either an ext-term when the length of t is sufficiently small or unfolds t. It ensures that every $ext(t_{[n]}, m)$ term generated by the algorithm satisfies $2n \leq m$. These are defined more precisely below:

$$wrap(t_{[n]}, m) = \textbf{let } k = m \bmod n \textbf{ in}$$
$$\textbf{if } k = 0 \textbf{ then } t \textbf{ else } T(t, [k : n - 1]) \otimes T(t, [0 : k - 1])$$

$$mk\text{-}ext(t_{[n]}, m) = \textbf{if } 2n \leq m \textbf{ then } ext(t, m) \textbf{ else } unf(t, m)$$

The unification algorithm terminates since the variable elimination step removes duplicate constraints involving x and every other step produces equalities of smaller size (in terms of the number of bitwise comparisons) than the one eliminated. For instance, in the R8 rule we rely on $m \geq 2 \cdot \max(l_1, l_2) > l$.

3.3 Nonfixed size bit-vectors

The most prominent feature of the unification algorithm in Figure 4 is that it can be used to decide bit-vector equality constraints $s = t$, where lengths and projections are not restricted to fixed naturals, but are of the form $aN + b$, where a and b are integers and N is a parameter (where we assume without loss of generality that $N > 0$). This allows us to apply the algorithm in the Shostak combination for deciding verification conditions with non-fixed bit-vector equalities. The unification problem for non-fixed bit-vectors is also reminiscent of the word unification problem, originally solved by Makanin and later solved using a unification procedure in [12]. The main difference is that variables ranging over words in that problem do not have associated size constraints which bit-vectors have. By performing comparisons and arithmetic on these lengths symbolically and allowing admissible answers to be paired with accumulated constraints (as explained later), we can deal with the following example:

Example: By performing the unification of

$$\{w_{[2]} \otimes 0_{[1]} \otimes x_{[N+6]} \otimes y_{[N+7]} = x_{[N+6]} \otimes 1_{[1]} \otimes z_{[3]} \otimes x_{[N+6]}\} \tag{3}$$

we obtain as an intermediate step

$$\left\{ \begin{array}{l} x_{[N+6]} = ext(w_{[2]} \otimes 0_{[1]}, N + 6), \quad y_{[N+7]} = z_{[3]}[2 : 2] \otimes x_{[N+6]} \\ 1_{[1]} \otimes z_{[3]}[0 : 1] = wrap(w_{[2]} \otimes 0_{[1]}, N + 6) \end{array} \right\}$$

and finally two cases:

$$\begin{aligned} x_{[N+6]} &= ext(1_{[1]} \otimes \beta_{[1]} \otimes 0_{[1]}, N + 6), \\ y_{[N+7]} &= \alpha_{[1]} \otimes ext(1_{[1]} \otimes \beta_{[1]} \otimes 0_{[1]}, N + 6), \\ z_{[3]} &= \beta_{[1]} \otimes 0_{[1]} \otimes \alpha_{[1]}, \\ w_{[2]} &= 1_{[1]} \otimes \beta_{[1]} \end{aligned} \quad \text{if } N \equiv 0 \pmod 3$$

$$\begin{aligned} x_{[N+6]} &= ext(\beta_{[1]} \otimes 1_{[1]} \otimes 0_{[1]}, N + 6), \\ y_{[N+7]} &= \alpha_{[1]} \otimes ext(\beta_{[1]} \otimes 1_{[1]} \otimes 0_{[1]}, N + 6), \\ z_{[3]} &= 0_{[1]} \otimes \beta_{[1]} \otimes \alpha_{[1]}, \\ w_{[2]} &= \beta_{[1]} \otimes 1_{[1]} \end{aligned} \quad \text{if } N \equiv 1 \pmod 3$$

When $N \equiv 0 \pmod{3}$, the evaluation of the *wrap* function simplifies the second equation of the intermediate result to $1_{[1]} \otimes z_{[3]}[0:1] = w_{[2]} \otimes 0_{[1]}$. The case that corresponds to $N \equiv 2 \pmod{3}$ requires $1_{[1]} \otimes z_{[3]}[0:1] = 0_{[1]} \otimes w_{[2]}$ which results in an inconsistency. The $\beta_{[1]}, \alpha_{[1]}$ are auxiliary variables that are introduced to represent unknown segments of the bit-vector variables.

Thus, the result produced by the unification algorithm will now be a *set* of constraints, each of the form

$$(ax + b > c, [N \mapsto ax + b] \circ [x_i \mapsto t_i \mid i = 1, \ldots, n])$$

where x is a fresh variable and the first constraint is passed on to decision procedures for linear arithmetic, and the second constraint is a Shostak substitution. We are thus faced with a finitary as opposed to unitary unification problem (see [1] for a survey on unification theory).

The crucial observation that allows lifting the algorithm to parameterized bit-vector expressions is that all operations and tests on the lengths and projections are of the form

$$m + n, \quad m - n, \quad m > n, \quad m \geq n, \quad m = n, \quad m \bmod n.$$

Since terms of the form $aN + b$ are closed under addition and subtraction, the first two operations can be performed directly in a symbolic way.

The comparison $m > n$ is rewritten to $m - n > 0$, $m \geq n$ to $m - n + 1 > 0$, and $n = m$ to $n - m + 1 > 0 \land m - n + 1 > 0$. This reduces the evaluation of comparisons to $aN + b > 0$. Since

$$aN + b > 0 \leftrightarrow (a = 0 \land b > 0 \lor a > 0) \text{ iff}$$
$$(a > 0 > b \lor a < 0 < b) \to N \geq |b| \operatorname{div} |a| \qquad (4)$$

tests can be evaluated using $a = 0 \land b > 0 \lor a > 0$ and accumulating auxiliary lower bounds on N for a separate treatment. Our algorithm then produces answers for all N greater than the largest accumulated lower bound. For values of N smaller than the accumulated bounds we instantiate N and run the fixed size version.

The auxiliary function *wrap* requires us to compute $m \bmod n$. To simplify this case our algorithm will maintain the invariant that $m \bmod n$ is only invoked when n is a constant b', whereas m may be of the form $N + b$. The case $N \geq b' - b$ causes case-splitting on each of the possible solutions $k = 0, \ldots, b' - 1$.

We could represent each case in Presburger arithmetic as $\exists x \geq 0.xb' = N + b - k$ and use a Presburger decision procedure [9] to check satisfiability of conjunctions of such constraints. However, in order to manage these constraints more efficiently we can use the Chinese Remainder Theorem (see [16]). If $\Pi_i p_i^{\alpha_i}$ is a prime factorization of b' (with $p_1, p_2, \ldots$ the sequence of all primes), then

$$N + b \equiv k \pmod{b'} \quad \text{iff} \quad N + b \equiv k \pmod{p_i^{\alpha_i}} \text{ for every } i.$$

Let $D(p, \beta, l)$ be the predicate that $N \equiv l \pmod{p^\beta}$ is true. Let $\mathcal{C}_{\text{mod}} = \bigwedge_i D(p_i, \beta_i, b_i)$ be the conjunction of divisibility constraints imposed on the current system. Only one predicate is needed for each p_i, since:

$$D(p, \beta, l') \wedge D(p, \alpha, l) \wedge \beta \geq \alpha \quad \text{iff} \quad D(p, \beta, l') \wedge l' \equiv l \pmod{p^\alpha} . \tag{5}$$

In order to split on the case $N + b \equiv k \pmod{b'}$ for different values of $k = 0, \ldots, (b' - 1)$ we can form the product of the case splits on $N + b \equiv k_i \pmod{p_i^{\alpha_i}}$ for $k_i = 0, \ldots, (p_i^{\alpha_i} - 1)$ (the product is over $i = 1, 2, \ldots$). The situation is not as bad as it seems, since we can use the existing $\mathcal{C}_{\text{mod}}$ to merge the new constraints in an optimal way:

$$\mathcal{C}'_{\text{mod}} = \bigwedge_i P(i) \quad \text{where} \quad P(i) = \begin{cases} \displaystyle\bigvee_{j=0}^{p_i^{\alpha_i - \beta_i} - 1} D(p_i, \alpha_i, b_i + jp_i^{\beta_i}) & \text{if } \alpha_i \geq \beta_i \\ D(p_i, \beta_i, b_i) & \text{if } \alpha_i < \beta_i \end{cases}$$

The predicate $P(i)$ represents the enumeration of valid congruences modulo a power of p_i. Statement (5) suggests the form of the enumeration for each case in the definition of $P(i)$. Expressing $\mathcal{C}'_{\text{mod}}$ in disjunctive normal form $\bigvee_i \mathcal{C}^i_{\text{mod}}$ the constraints for the different cases are obtained. The value of k for a particular case of $\mathcal{C}_{\text{mod}}$ can be reconstructed using the congruence $k \equiv (\sum_i n_i b_i) - b \pmod{b'}$ where $n_i = z_i \bar{z}_i$, $z_i = \Pi_{j \neq i} p_j^{\alpha_i}$, and $\bar{z}_i$ satisfies $z_i \bar{z}_i \equiv 1 \pmod{p_i^{\alpha_i}}$ (it exists since $\gcd(p_i^{\alpha_i}, z_i) = 1$).

Given expressions s and t our algorithm now engages in the following steps: (1) Apply $\mathcal{T}$ to both s and t, i.e., let $(s, t) := (\mathcal{T}(s, [0 : m - 1]), \mathcal{T}(t, [0 : m - 1]))$. This generates bit-vector expressions without subfield extraction and an assignment to each original variable x to a concatenation $x_1 \otimes x_2 \otimes \ldots \otimes x_n$ of distinct variables, where $decode(x_i)$ cover disjoint intervals of x. Using equivalence (4) the tests in $\mathcal{T}$ are evaluated unambiguously, and possibly generating a new lower bound on N. The cases where N is smaller than this bound are processed later. (2) Every variable $x_{[aN+b]}$ remaining in s or t, where $a > 0$, is replaced by a concatenation of a fresh variables: $x_{[N]}^{(1)} \otimes x_{[N]}^{(2)} \otimes \ldots \otimes x_{[N+b]}^{(a)}$. Constants are cut in a similar way[2]. If b is negative the lower bound $1 - b$ on N is added.

Every variable occurring in s and t now has length $N + k$ or k, where k is an integer. (3) The algorithm in Figure 4 is invoked on the equality $\{s = t\}$. Each comparison accumulates a lower bound on N and each invocation of mod may cause a multi-way case split while accumulating modulus constraints on N. The unification algorithm therefore generates constraints of the form $(\mathcal{E}_1, \mathcal{C}_1), \ldots, (\mathcal{E}_n, \mathcal{C}_n)$, where the $\mathcal{E}_i$ are equalities and $\mathcal{C}_i$ is a conjunction of $N \geq k$ and $D(p_i, \alpha_i, a_i)$ constraints.

We need to ensure that every step is well defined: in particular that $unf(t, m)$ and, as we assumed, $n \bmod m$ are only invoked when m is a constant. This is a consequence of the following invariant:

---

[2] This step is not strictly necessary, but simplifies the further presentation of the algorithm.

Invariant 2 *For every occurrence of* $ext(t_{[aN+b]}, n)$: $a = 0 \land 2b \leq n$.

This holds as ext terms are only generated when $mk\text{-}ext(t_{[aN+b]}, a'N + b')$ is invoked and $2(aN + b) \leq a'N + b'$. Since both a and a' are either 0 or 1, this inequality can only hold if $a = 0$ or N is bounded above by $(b' - 2b)$ div $(2a - a')$. The cases where N is bounded above by a constant are treated separately.

(4) The solved form can now be extracted. For each $(\mathcal{E}, \mathcal{C})$ generated from the previous step let $\mathcal{C}$ be of the form $N \geq k \land \bigwedge_{i=1}^{l} D(p_i, \alpha_i, a_i)$. The Chinese Remainder Theorem tells us how to find n_i such that the constraints can be rewritten to the equivalent form

$$N \geq k \land \exists x. N = Ax + B \text{ where } A = \prod_{i=1}^{l} p_i^{\alpha_i} \ B = \left(\sum_{i=1}^{l} n_i a_i\right) \bmod A$$

Since we extract the Shostak substitution θ from $\mathcal{E}$ as in the fixed-length case the combined constraint returned for this case is

$$(Ax + B \geq k, [N \mapsto Ax + B] \circ \theta).$$

For each k less than the least lower bound accumulated above we instantiate N by k and extract θ_k by running the fixed-size version of the algorithm (that is, running $\{s = t\}[N \mapsto k]$). For these cases the returned constraints have the form

$$(\mathbf{true}, [N \mapsto k] \circ \theta_k).$$

The algorithm now concludes by returning the entire set of the constraints extracted above.

As we have argued above we now have

Theorem 3. *(Correctness) When the non-fixed unification algorithm terminates on the input constraint $s = t$ with a set of constraints $\{(\varphi_i(x), \theta_i) \mid i = 0, \ldots n\}$*

$$\text{then } s = t \quad \leftrightarrow \quad \bigvee_{i=0}^{n} \exists x, V_{\text{aux}}. \varphi_i(x) \land \theta_i.$$

Finally we must ensure that we can make the unification algorithm modified for parameterized lengths terminate. To this end we apply the transformation rules from Figure 4 by preferring the variable and equality elimination rules to the other rules.

We will proceed to prove the termination by induction on the number of distinct non-fixed variables k in $\mathcal{E}$ that participate in some equality where rule R1-R8 can be applied. The base case ($k = 0$) operates only on fixed-size variables, and so it terminates.

Whenever a variable x has been isolated using one of the rules R4-R6, it is eliminated from the rest of $\mathcal{E}$. Indeed it is eliminated as x cannot be a proper subterm of t in the equality constraint $x = t$, since the length of t is the sum of the lengths of its variable and constant subterms, which equals the length of x. Since rules R1-R8 produce equalities between smaller bit-vectors we cannot repeatedly apply these rules without eventually eliminating a non-fixed size variable. Rule R4 may split a non-fixed length variable y into two parts y_1 and y_2, but only one of these parts will have non-fixed length, so the overall number of non-fixed length variables is constant.

We therefore have

Theorem 4. *(Termination) The non-fixed unification algorithm terminates.*

A reduction from the problem of simultaneous incongruences [19] can establish that the unification problem for non-fixed bit-vectors is NP-hard. A more careful analysis of the termination argument can establish that a satisfying unifier can be verified in time polynomial in the constant parameter sizes and number of subterms, hence establishing NP-completeness of the non-fixed bit-vector unification problem.

The unification algorithm finally needs to be supplied also with a canonizer that works on *ext*-terms of non-fixed length to enable an integration with other decision procedures. While simple unfoldings cannot be performed this time our implementation normalizes terms into a concatenation of variables, constants and *ext*-terms whose arguments are fixed size terms in canonical form. The occurrences of *ext* in the resulting expression are then shifted as much as possible to the left. This step cannot be performed unambiguously without asserting congruence constraints on the parameter and hence also leads to case splits.

The table below summarizes a few benchmarks presented to our prototype implementation (coded in SML/NJ, executed on a 200Mhz SUN Ultra II).

1.	equation (3)	satisfiable	0.06 s
2.	$0_{[1]} \otimes 1_{[1]} \otimes 0_{[1]} \otimes x_{[N+7]} \otimes 1_{[1]} \otimes 0_{[1]} \otimes 1_{[1]} \otimes y_{[N+1]}$ $= x_{[N+7]} \otimes x_{[N+7]}$	unsatisfiable	0.06 s
3.	$x_{[N+4]} \otimes 0_{[1]} \otimes 1_{[1]} \otimes 0_{[1]} \otimes y_{[N+9]}$ $= y_{[N+9]} \otimes 1_{[1]} \otimes 0_{[1]} \otimes 1_{[1]} \otimes x_{[N+4]}$	unsatisfiable	0.09 s
4.	$(3) \rightarrow z_{[3]}[0:0] = 0_{[1]} \vee z_{[3]}[1:1] = 0_{[1]}$	valid	0.07 s

4 Conclusion

This paper presented two algorithms: one algorithm handles boolean operations on fixed-size bit-vectors, the other handles equational constraints in the absence of boolean operations on parameterized bit-vectors. A completed picture would combine the algorithms to handle boolean operations on parameterized bit-vectors. Encouraged by the presented results we are currently trying to extend the algorithms to handle parameterized boolean operations, and to address efficient integration of arithmetical operations on bit-vectors. The fixed-size algorithm is presently integrated into STeP's simplifier and validity checker where it has been used in hardware verification. Simultaneously we are experimenting with our prototype implementation of the non-fixed bit-vector decision procedure on verification conditions from parameterized hardware designs.

Acknowledgement: We are grateful for the kind advice from the anonymous referees as well as Michael Colón, Henny B. Sipma and Tomás E. Uribe.

References

1. BAADER, F., AND SIEKMANN, J. Unification theory. In *Handbook of Logic in Artificial Intelligence and Logic Programming*, D. Gabbay, C. Hogger, and J. Robinson, Eds. Oxford University Press, Oxford, UK, 1993.

2. BASIN, D., AND KLARLUND, N. Hardware verification using monadic second-order logic. In *CAV'95* (1995), vol. 939 of *LNCS*, pp. 31–41.

3. BJØRNER, N. S., BROWNE, A., CHANG, E. S., COLÓN, M., KAPUR, A., MANNA, Z., SIPMA, H. B., AND URIBE, T. E. STeP: Deductive-algorithmic verification of reactive and real-time systems. In *CAV'96* (1996), vol. 1102 of *LNCS*, pp. 415–418.

4. BJØRNER, N. S., STICKEL, M. E., AND URIBE, T. E. A practical integration of first-order reasoning and decision procedures. In *CADE'97* (1997), vol. 1249 of *LNCS*, pp. 101–115.

5. BRATSCH, A., EVEKING, H., FÄRBER, H.-J., AND SCHELLIN, U. LOVERT - A Logic Verifier of Register-Transfer Level Descriptions. In *IMEC-IFIP* (1989), L. Claesen, Ed., Elsevier.

6. BRYANT, R. E. Graph-based algorithms for Boolean function manipulation. *IEEE Transactions on Computers C-35*, 8 (1986), 677–691.

7. BRYANT, R. E., AND CHEN, Y.-A. Verification of arithmetic circuits with binary moment diagrams. In *DAC'95* (1995).

8. COMON, H., DAUCHET, M., GILLERON, R., LUGIEZ, D., TISON, S., AND TOMMASI, M. *Tree Automata Techniques and Applications*. Obtainable from http://l3ux02.univ-lille3.fr/tata/, 1998.

9. COOPER, D. C. Theorem proving in arithmetic without multiplication. In *Machine Intelligence*, vol. 7. American Elsevier, 1972, pp. 91–99.

10. CYRLUK, D., LINCOLN, P., AND SHANKAR, N. On Shostak's decision procedure for combinations of theories. In *CADE'96* (1996), vol. 1104 of *LNCS*, pp. 463–477.

11. CYRLUK, D., MÖLLER, O., AND RUESS, H. An efficient decision procedure for the theory of fixed-sized bit-vectors. In *CAV'97* (1997), vol. 1254 of *LNCS*, pp. 60–71.

12. JAFFAR, J. Minimal and complete word unification. *J. ACM 37*, 1 (1990), 47–85.

13. KAMERER, J. Bus scheduler verification using STeP. Unpublished report, 1996.

14. MARTELLI, A., AND MONTANARI, U. An efficient unification algorithm. *ACM Trans. Prog. Lang. Sys. 4*, 2 (1982), 258–282.

15. NELSON, G., AND OPPEN, D. C. Simplification by cooperating decision procedures. *ACM Trans. Prog. Lang. Sys. 1*, 2 (1979), 245–257.

16. NIVEN, I., ZUCKERMAN, H., AND MONTGOMERY, H. *An Introduction to the Theory of Numbers*. John Wiley & Sons, New York, 1991.

17. SHOSTAK, R. E. Deciding combinations of theories. *J. ACM 31*, 1 (1984), 1–12.

18. SIPMA, H. B., URIBE, T. E., AND MANNA, Z. Deductive model checking. In *CAV'96* (1996), vol. 1102 of *LNCS*, pp. 208–219.

19. STOCKMEYER, L. J., AND MEYER, A. R. Word problems requiring exponential time. In *Proc. 5rd ACM Symp. Theory of Comp.* (1973), pp. 1–9.

Experience with Literate Programming in the Modelling and Validation of Systems

Theo C. Ruys and Ed Brinksma

Faculty of Computer Science, University of Twente.
P.O. Box 217, 7500 AE Enschede, The Netherlands.
{ruys,brinksma}@cs.utwente.nl

Abstract. This paper discusses our experience with literate programming tools in the realm of the modelling and validation of systems. We propose the use of literate programming techniques to structure and control the validation trajectory. The use of literate programming is illustrated by means of a running example using Promela and Spin. The paper can also be read as a tutorial on the application of literate programming to formal methods.

1 Introduction

In the past years, we have been involved in several industrial projects concerning the modelling and validation of (communication) protocols [3, 10, 18]. In these projects we used modelling languages and tools - like Promela, Spin [5, 7] and UPPAAL [13] – to specify and verify the protocols and their properties. During each of these projects we encountered the same practical problems of keeping track of various sorts of information and data, for example:

- many documents, which describe parts of the system;
- many versions of the same document;
- consecutive versions of validation models;
- results of validation runs.

The problems of managing such information and data relate to the maintenance problems found in software engineering [15]. This is not surprising as, in a sense, validation using a model checker involves the analysis of many successive versions of the model of a system.

This paper discusses our experience with *literate programming* techniques to help us tackle these information management problems.

Literate Programming. Literate programming is the act of writing computer programs primarily as documents to be read by human beings, and only secondarily as instructions to be executed by computers.

The term "literate programming" was coined by D.E. Knuth, when he described WEB [11, 12] the tool he created to develop the TEX typesetting software.

In general, literate programs combine source code and documentation in a single file. Literate programming tools then parse the file to produce either readable documentation or compilable source code. One of advantages of literate programming is that we are not longer forced to comply with the syntactical order of the programming language. Types, variables and constructs can be introduced at alternative locations where they serve the purpose of the literate document better, e.g. where they are best understood by a human reader. The literate programming tool will reassemble the source parts into their formally correct order.

A literate style of programming has proven very helpful, especially for terse and/or complex programs. In the area of functional programming – where, by nature, programs are often quite terse - the art of writing functional scripts has become quite popular (see for instance [8]). It is remarkable that in the domain of formal methods, which deals with the specification of complex and safety-critical systems, the benefits of literate programming techniques have not yet been acknowledged.

In Sect. 2 we will discuss the application of literate programming in the modelling phase. In Sect. 3 we sketch how the same techniques can be used to structure the validation process. The use of literate programming in the validation trajectory is illustrated by means of a running example using Promela and Spin.[1] The paper is concluded in Sect. 4 where some conclusions and future work are discussed.

2 Literate Modelling

In a way, the literate style of specification has already reached the formal methods community. For example, a Z specification [19] can be considered as a literate specification. The "source code" of a Z specification consists of Z constructions like schema's and constraints, whereas the intertwining documentation (in LATEX) can be regarded as "literate comments". Type checking tools for Z - like fUZZ and ZTC - discard these explaining comments when type checking a Z specification.

The use of literate programming techniques in the modelling phase has several advantages. Several parties are involved in the design of a system, e.g. users, designers, programmers, testers, etc. It is important that they all agree on the same specification of the system. For that reason the specification should be readable and acceptable for all parties. In this way, literate modelling helps to explain formal specifications.

Besides making the documentation more easily accessible, using literate modelling gives us the possibility to annotate the specification or model in a structured way without obscuring the formal specification with too many comments. Common forms of annotations include:

- identifying the *source* of information, which is especially useful when the specification or model is based on different documents from different parties;

---

[1] This document itself is written as a literate specification. This means that not only the document you are reading now, but also the validation results of the running example have been generated from a single source file.

- discussing *modelling choices*, e.g. the abstractions from the design, or assumptions on the environment.

- identifying points of *attention*, e.g. for a future validation phase, or when documents contain contradictory information.

In our modelling work we used the literate programming tool noweb [9, 16, 17] developed by Norman Ramsey. noweb is a literate programming tool like Knuth's WEB, only simpler. Unlike WEB, noweb is independent of the programming language to be literated. noweb has been used in combination with Pascal, C, C++, Modula-2, Icon, ML, Promela and others. A recent book-length example of literate programming using noweb is Fraser and Hanson's book on lcc [4].

2.1 Example – Modelling

To illustrate the use and benefits of literate techniques in the modelling phase, we present an example using noweb. First we give a specification of the specification problem in natural language. Next, we present a literate specification of the model in Promela. In the next section we show how to include validation results into the literate document. Consider the following scheduling problem.

Problem:

Four soldiers who are heavily injured, try to flee to their home land. The enemy is chasing them and in the middle of the night they arrive at a bridge that spans a river which is the border between the two countries at war. The bridge has been damaged and can only carry two soldiers at a time. Furthermore, several landmines have been placed on the bridge and a torch is needed to sidestep all the mines. The enemy is on their tail, so the soldiers know that they have only 60 minutes to cross the bridge. The soldiers only have a single torch and they are not equally injured. The following table lists the crossing times (one-way!) for each of the soldiers:

soldier S_0 5 minutes
soldier S_1 10 minutes
soldier S_2 20 minutes
soldier S_3 25 minutes

Does a schedule exist which gets all four soldiers to the safe side within 60 minutes?

Hint: Before proceeding it may be instructive to try to solve the "soldiers" problem on paper.

During the modelling phase we are not interested in the 60 minutes constraint, but we only want to model how we can get the four soldiers from the unsafe to the safe side of the bridge.

Please note that the specification of the problem is straightforward, and consequently, the noweb specification may be trivial and even overly simple in some places. This is deliberately done to give a better overview of a *complete* literate validation trajectory with noweb. A less trivial example of such trajectory can be found in [2].

```
1       ⟨soldiers.pr 1⟩≡                                                    (20)
            ⟨prelude 2⟩
            ⟨proctypes 8⟩
            ⟨init 27⟩
```

Our Promela specification soldiers.pr consists of a ⟨prelude⟩, some process definitions ⟨proctypes⟩ and an initialization process ⟨init⟩.

In the left margin, noweb identifies the number of the *code chunk*. [2] In the right margin of the definition of a code chunk, between parenthesis, the number of the code chunk is listed, which *uses* this particular code chunk. All code chunks with the same name will be collected by noweb and put in the place where the chunk is used.

```
2       ⟨prelude 2⟩≡                                                        (1)
            ⟨constants 4⟩
            ⟨macros 13⟩
            ⟨types 5⟩
            ⟨channels 3⟩
            ⟨globals 6⟩
```

The Promela ⟨prelude⟩ of the specification consists of constants, macros, types, channels and global variables. These parts will be defined when they are needed in the process definitions of the specification. We start our model of the "soldiers" problem by modelling the bridge.

```
3       ⟨channels 3⟩≡                                                       (2)
            chan unsafe_to_safe = [0] of {soldier, soldier} ;
            chan safe_to_unsafe = [0] of {soldier} ;
```

The bridge is modelled with two channels. The channel unsafe_to_safe models the *unsafe → safe* direction, whereas safe_to_unsafe models the *safe → unsafe* direction.

Every time two soldiers have made it to the safe side, one of the men on the safe side has to go back with the torch. It is clear that it is not very helpful to go back with two men. For that reason, the channel safe_to_unsafe only passes a single soldier.

The four soldiers are identified by integers in the range 0..N-1, where N is defined as follows:

```
4       ⟨constants 4⟩≡                                                      (2)
            #define N            4
```

This means that a soldier can be represented by a byte:

```
5       ⟨types 5⟩≡                                                          (2)
            #define soldier      byte
```

---

[2] In this paper the WEB style of chunk numbering is used. Another popular way of chunk identification is a tag *page.n*, where *n* indicates the *n*-th chunk on page *page*.

```
6       ⟨globals 6⟩≡                                              (2)
        byte     time ;
        byte     val[N] ;
```

The variable time is the number of minutes that have elapsed since the soldiers have started to move. Every time a soldier reaches the other side of the bridge, the variable time is updated.

The array val holds the times it takes the soldiers to cross the bridge. Because Promela doesn't support constant arrays, the array val has to be initialized in the init process:

```
7       ⟨init val 7⟩≡                                             (27)
        val[0] = 5 ; val[1] = 10 ; val[2] = 20 ; val[3] = 25 ;
```

As specified in the problem description, the times for the soldiers to cross the bridge are 5, 10, 20 and 25 minutes, respectively.

```
8       ⟨proctypes 8⟩≡                                            (1)
        ⟨proctype Unsafe 9⟩
        ⟨proctype Safe 25⟩
```

Crossing the bridge is modelled by soldiers that are passed between two processes: Unsafe and Safe. In the beginning, all soldiers are at the Unsafe side, and the goal is to get all soldiers to the Safe side.

In the remainder of this section we only define the chunk ⟨proctype Unsafe⟩. For completeness, we have included the chunks ⟨proctype Safe⟩ and ⟨init⟩ in the Appendix.

```
9       ⟨proctype Unsafe 9⟩≡                                      (8)
        proctype Unsafe()
        {
          ⟨Unsafe: locals 10⟩
          ⟨Unsafe: body 11⟩
        }
```

We model the location of the soldiers by the bit-array here. If here[i] is 1, then soldier i is at the unsafe side of the bridge.

```
10      ⟨Unsafe: locals 10⟩≡                                 (9) 15▷
        bit   here[N] ;
```

Initially, all soldiers are on the unsafe side of the bridge, so the body of Unsafe starts by initializing the array here:[3]

```
11      ⟨Unsafe: body 11⟩≡                                   (9) 12▷
        here[0] = 1 ; here[1] = 1 ; here[2] = 1 ; here[3] = 1 ;
```

---

[3] Note that noweb has added new information in the right margin. The ▷ indicates the next chunk with the same name. Similarly, a ◁ symbol indicates the previous chunk with the same name.

The rest of Unsafe's body is responsible for crossing the bridge.

12   ⟨*Unsafe: body* 11⟩+≡   (9) ◁11
```
      do
   ::  ⟨Unsafe: send two soldiers 14⟩
       ⟨Unsafe: one soldier arrives back 18⟩
      od
```

In every iteration two soldiers are sent to the other side and one soldier is expected back with the torch. In the ⟨*Unsafe: send two soldiers*⟩ part, we need to randomly choose a soldier that is still at the unsafe side. For this purpose we introduce the macro select_soldier(x):

13   ⟨*macros* 13⟩≡   (2) 17▷
```
      #define select_soldier(x)  \
      if                         \
      :: here[0]  -> x=0         \
      :: here[1]  -> x=1         \
      :: here[2]  -> x=2         \
      :: here[3]  -> x=3         \
      fi ;                       \
      here[x] = 0
```

Only the guards for which here[i] is 1 are executable. One of these executable guards is randomly chosen and the variable x gets the number of this soldier. Now we can define the ⟨*Unsafe: send two soldiers*⟩ chunk:

14   ⟨*Unsafe: send two soldiers* 14⟩≡   (12) 16▷
```
      select_soldier(s1) ;
      select_soldier(s2) ;
      unsafe_to_safe ! s1, s2 ;
```

where s1 and s2 are soldiers:

15   ⟨*Unsafe: locals* 10⟩+≡   (9) ◁10
```
      soldier s1, s2 ;
```

16   ⟨*Unsafe: send two soldiers* 14⟩+≡   (12) ◁14
```
      IF all_gone -> break FI ;
```

If there are no soldiers left at the unsafe side, the do-loop of the Unsafe process should be terminated. This break is really needed here, because otherwise the Unsafe process will be blocked (i.e. an invalid endstate in Spin) by select_soldier(s2) if there is only one soldier at the unsafe side.

This last construction uses the following macro definitions:

17   ⟨*macros* 13⟩+≡   (2) ◁13 26▷
```
      #define IF         if ::
      #define FI         :: else fi
      #define all_gone   (!here[0] && !here[1] && !here[2] && !here[3])
```

The IF-FI combination implements a single IF clause and the `all_gone` predicate is *true* when all values in the `here` array are 0.

18   ⟨*Unsafe: one soldier arrives back* 18⟩≡   (12)
```
    safe_to_unsafe ? s1 ;
    here[s1] = 1 ;
    time = time + val[s1] ;
```

The soldier `s1` is the soldier that gets back with the torch. The `time` is updated accordingly to the time it took soldier `s1` to cross the bridge.

The process `Safe` just mirrors the operations of the `Unsafe` process. The body of `Safe` - together with `init` - can be found in the Appendix.

This concludes our literate model of the "soldiers" example. The observant reader will have noticed that the literate style of specification allows us to introduce types, variables, etc. at the location where they are needed, and *not* where the Promela grammar would have forced us to do so.

`noweb` provides index and cross-reference features for code chunks and identifiers. The "soldiers" example only uses cross-references to code chunks. Larger programs or models are easier to understand if identifiers are also cross-referenced.

3 Literate Validation

Although the advantages of literate specification techniques in the modelling phase already proved quite useful in our projects, we have also tried to use literate programming in the validation trajectory.

As mentioned in the introduction, one of the difficulties of using model checkers is the management of all (generated) data during the validation trajectory. It is important that the validation results obtained using the model checker should always be reproducable [6]. Without tool support for the validation phase, one has to resort to general engineering practices and record all validation activities into a log-book.

Recording all this information requires rigorous discipline. The quality of the validation depends on the logging discipline of the validation engineer. Moreover, there remains the problem that after the validation phase one has to compose a coherent validation report from this huge collection of validation data. Experience has shown that this is not easy. In our validation projects, we have profited from literate techniques to help us record the collection of data involved in the validation trajectory:

— *validation models.* As discussed in Sect. 2, literate programming can be used to explicitly specify and annotate a model. Moreover, the *differences* between several validation models can be elegantly presented in a report containing several versions of the model. An example of this can be found in Sect. 3.2 (viz. ⟨*soldiers-60min.pr*⟩) and in [2].

— *validation results.* The results of validation runs, e.g. simulation traces, counter-examples can be included into the literate validation report.

- *directives for the validation runs.* The - often cryptic - directives and options to control validation tools usually end up in a `Makefile`. The rationale behind such directives, however, is usually not recorded. In a literate specification these directives can be annotated together with them. See for instance the code chunks ⟨*directives.dat*⟩ in Sect. 3.2.

Recall that the information above is usually scattered over several files, simulation traces, entries in log-books, etc. When using a literate style of validation, all this information can be collected into a single, literate document. Thus, not only do literate techniques solve the management of validation data, it also releases much of the burden of writing a validation report.

A validation report is especially needed when no 'serious' errors have been found during the validation of a system. A simple "no errors found" doesn't suffice. In such cases, the validation report should describe all the succesful scenarios to identify exactly those parts of the model which have been validated thoroughly. An example of a report of a validation trajectory of a "correct" model can be found in [2].

3.1 Validation Approaches

Before we continue with our (running) example, we discuss the two - extreme - validation approaches that can be followed when using a model checker: the verification approach and the falsification approach.

The purpose of the verification approach is to come up with a correct model on a certain level of abstraction. The verification approach is characterized by the following:

- During the validation phase the model of the system is fixed at a certain level of abstraction.
- All aspects of the model are systematically validated.
- During the validation of a certain aspect of the model, abstractions have to be made of other parts of the model.

The falsification approach aims at finding errors and weaknesses in the (initial) design of a system. The falsification approach focuses its attention on those parts of the system where flaws are most likely to occur. This approach is characterized by the following:

- The validation phase is started with a model on a high level of abstraction.
- During the validation phase, one zooms in at certain aspects of the model using local refinement techniques.
- Only a limited part of the system is validated and no information is obtained about the non-validated components.

Summarizing, the verification approach tries to ascertain the correctness of a detailed model, whereas the falsification approach tries to find errors in a model.

```
⟨Verification approach⟩ ≡
   ⟨Start with detailed model⟩
   ⟨Simulate⟩
while not ⟨convinced by results⟩
do
      ⟨Focus on particular aspects of the model⟩
      ⟨Make abstractions of the other parts as needed⟩
   [ ⟨Introduce errors into the environment⟩   ]
      ⟨Simulate and model check⟩
od
```

Fig. 1. Pseudo-algorithm for the verification approach.

In other words, the verification approach is *specification-driven*, whereas the falsification approach is *error-driven*. Please note that both approaches prescribe extreme methods for validation. In practice, one usually adopts a combination of both approaches. We have used both approaches in our validation work.

Figure 1 presents a pseudo-algorithm for the verification approach whereas Fig. 2 presents a pseudo-algorithm for the falsification approach.

The verification approach starts with a detailed model of the system. Before starting the actual validation loop in the verification approach, the detailed model is simulated to obtain an initial degree of correctness. In general, the state space of such a detailed model will be too large for an exhaustive search by a model checker [5]. In the validation loop of the verification approach, one makes abstractions of parts of the complete model to zoom in on certain aspects of the model. These abstractions are needed to allow an exhaustive search by a model checker. The validation phase is ended when all crucial aspects of the model have been verified.

The falsification approach starts with an abstract model of the system. In the validation loop, the falsification approach tries to find errors by adding details to the model or by introducing errors into the environment. The validation phase of the falsification approach is ended when (enough) errors have been exposed or when resources (e.g. time, money) have run out.

In the ⟨Introduce errors into the environment⟩ step of both approaches, exceptional behaviour of the environment is introduced to validate the robustness of the system. When errors are found in the ⟨Simulate and model check⟩ step, these errors should be corrected, and the simulation and validation step should be started again.

Not surprisingly, the usage of literate programming techniques is different for both approaches. Using the verification approach, the initial model benefits from all annotation facilities of literate programming. Along the validation path, subsequent validation models will be built by making abstractions from the initial model. Using the falsification approach, the initial literate model may only contain annotations identifying the parts (i.e. abstractions) of the system that are *missing*. During the validation trajectory, consecutive validation models

⟨*Falsification approach*⟩≡
  ⟨*Start with abstract model*⟩
  ⟨*Simulate and model check*⟩
  while not ⟨*errors found*⟩ **and** ⟨*resources available*⟩
  do
    (⟨*Zoom in on certain aspects of the model*⟩
    or ⟨*Introduce errors into the environment*⟩)
    ⟨*Simulate and model check*⟩
  od

Fig. 2. Pseudo-algorithm for the falsification approach.

will be constructed by adding details to the initial model. The annotations of the initial model should guide the details to be added.

When errors are found in the model they should be corrected. The literate document (together with dependency rules in a Makefile) will make sure that all previous results will be re-validated. For the verification approach this means that the initial model will be modified, whereas in the falsification approach it does not necessarily mean that the initial abstract model needs to be corrected. For example, an error may be detected in a particular refinement of the previous validation model. Moreover, the purpose of applying the falsification approach is to expose errors, not to come up with a correct model.

3.2 Example – Validation

To illustrate the process of literate validation, we continue our example and try to find a solution which brings the soldiers to the safe side within 60 minutes. The validation of the "soldiers" problem uses the verification approach.

First, we assure ourselves that our original specification soldiers.pr does not contain any errors. This means that we have to check for possible deadlocks (i.e. invalid endstates) in our specification.

The validation results themselves are meaningless if we cannot reproduce them. In the realm of Spin this means that we also have to record:

− the *directives* for the C compiler to build the pan analyser[4] ; and
− the run-time *options* for the pan analyser.

For the verification runs with Spin we use a data file (i.e. directives.dat), which contains for each Promela validation model these directives and options. A simple script is used to translate this data file into a Makefile that drives the complete validation process. For the Promela specification soldiers.pr the directives and options are the following:

---

[4] The pan analyser is the validation program which is *generated* by Spin [5]. It is the program that performs the validation of a system.

19   ⟨*directives.dat* 19⟩≡   24▷

```
soldiers
-D_POSIX_SOURCE -DSAFETY -DNOFAIR -DMEMCNT=22
-c1 -w15 -m1000 -n
```

For this paper, the meaning of the Spin directives is not important. In a validation report, however, an explanation and reasoning behind these directives may be needed. Running the pan analyser produces the following (stripped) output:

```
(Spin Version 3.0.5 -- 5 November 1997)  [run on 07-January-98 17:36:18]

State-vector 52 byte, depth reached 66, errors: 0
    5072 states, stored
     438 states, matched
    5510 transitions (= stored+matched)
       1 atomic steps
hash conflicts: 1432 (resolved)
(max size 2^15 states)

Stats on memory usage (in Megabytes):
0.304   equivalent memory usage for states (stored*(State-vector + overhead))
0.204   actual memory usage for states (compression: 67.14%)
        State-vector as stored = 32 byte + 8 byte overhead
0.131   memory used for hash-table (-w15)
0.024   memory used for DFS stack (-m1000)
0.438   total actual memory usage

        Command being timed: "./soldiers.pan -c1 -w15 -m1000 -n"
        User time (seconds): 0.14
        System time (seconds): 0.03
```

Within 60 minutes. Now we try to find the schedule that get all soldiers to the safe side within 60 minutes. Our idea is to try to verify that "eventually, the time will be be greater than 60". This property can easily be formulated as a Linear Time Logic (LTL) formula: $\diamond(time > 60)$. The LTL property is violated if all soldiers are at the safe side and the time elapsed is less then or equal to 60. To let Spin find a counterexample which violates the property, the LTL property is translated to a Promela never claim which is simply added to our original Promela specification:

20   ⟨*soldiers-60min.pr* 20⟩≡

       ⟨*soldiers.pr* 1⟩
       ⟨*never* 22⟩

We use Spin's -F option to translate the LTL property to a never claim. The claim is the following:

21   ⟨*60min.claim* 21⟩≡

```
! (<> p)
```

where p is defined as follows:

22   ⟨*never* 22⟩≡   (20) 23▷

```
#define p (time > 60)
```

With $\langle 60min.\,claim \rangle$ as input, "Spin -F" generates the following 'never claim':

23    $\langle never\ 22 \rangle +\equiv$ (20) ◁22

```
never {        /* ! (<> p) */
accept_init:
TO_init:       if
               :: (! ((p))) -> goto accept_S1
               fi;
accept_S1:
TO_S1:         if
               :: (! ((p))) -> goto accept_S1
               fi;
accept_all:    skip
}
```

The verification of soldiers-60min.pr involves the following directives and options:

24    $\langle directives.\,dat\ 19 \rangle +\equiv$ ◁19

```
soldiers-60min
-D_POSIX_SOURCE -DNOFAIR -DMEMCNT=22
-a -c1 -w15 -m1000 -n
```

The pan analyser will try to prove that $\diamond(time > 60)$ holds for all possible executions of the model. Running the pan analyser on soldiers-60min.pr produces the following (stripped) output:

```
(Spin Version 3.0.5 -- 5 November 1997)  [run on 07-January-98 17:36:39]

State-vector 56 byte, depth reached 127, errors: 1
      291 states, stored (522 visited)
      230 states, matched
      752 transitions (= visited+matched)
        1 atomic steps
hash conflicts: 79 (resolved)
(max size 2^15 states)

0.336   memory usage (Mbyte)

        Command being timed: "./soldiers-60min.pan -a -c1 -w15 -m1000 -n"
        User time (seconds): 0.04
        System time (seconds): 0.02
```

And we see that Spin has found an error in one of possible executions of the model. We let Spin generate a simulation trace leading to this error.

Running "Spin -M -t" on soldiers-60min.pr results in the Message Sequence Chart (MSC) of Fig. 3. The MSC shows a possible schedule to get all soldiers to the safe side within 60 minutes.

4 Conclusions

In this paper we have discussed our experience with the literate programming tool noweb in validation projects. Using a simple model as a running example,

Spin Version 3.0.5 -- 5 November 1997 -- soldiers-60min.pr -- MSC -- 1

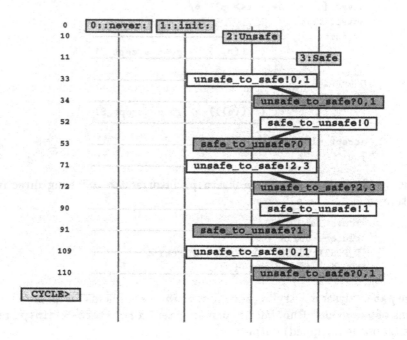

Fig. 3. Schedule to cross the bridge in 60 minutes.

we have introduced the use of literate techniques in the modelling and validation of systems.

The use of literate programming tools in the modelling phase has proven quite valuable. Especially the possibility to annotate the model has proven quite helpful to make the models more accessible and readable for all parties that are involved in the design of a system.

Literate techniques are also useful during the validation trajectory. All details on validation runs can be nicely structured into a validation report. However, essentially, the management of the validation trajectory is nothing more than the management of different versions of the model together with the validation results. For this class of management problems several so-called source-control tools [1] are available. One may argue that the use of literate programming techniques in the validation trajectory implements a source-control system by hand. To a certain degree this is true. When using literate techniques, the validation models are incrementally constructed, which could be automated using source-control tools.

However, a literate style of validation has several advantages over source-control tools alone:

- most source-control systems lack the possibility of annotating and describing modelling and validation choices;
- the management of validation results is more problematic;
- a source-control system typically does not help in composing a validation report.

On the other hand, using literate techniques during the complete validation trajectory may become tedious and time-consuming. Furthermore, it is probably not desirable (and helpful) that all validation results end up in a single document. One may wish to prune the validation tree to only include those results and models that are meaningful. Here, a source-control system could be helpful.

So far, validation activities in our group have been conducted by a single person at a time. As soon as more than one person is working on the validation of the same project, source-control systems are indispensable with respect to the management of the validation process.

The bottom line is that using literate programming techniques alone or using source-control systems alone are both not ideal. A combination of a source-control system and a literate programming tool probably works best to support a structured validation methodology.

In our current approach, all details on validation results of Spin have to be manually included into the literate specification. We are working on enhancements to Spin and XSpin to have these results automatically generated and included into a literate specification. Furthermore, we are trying to combine a source-control system like RCS [20] or PRCS [14] with XSpin.

References

1. Don Bolinger and Tan Bronson. *Applying RCS and SCCS*. O'Reilly & Associates, Inc., Sebastopol, 1995.
2. Pedro R. D'Argenio, Joost-Pieter Katoen, Theo C. Ruys, and G. Jan Tretmans. The Bounded Retransmission Protocol must be on time! (Full Version). CTIT Technical Report Series 97-03, Centre for Telematics and Information Technology, University of Twente, Enschede, The Netherlands, 1997. Also available from URL: http://wwwtios.cs.utwente.nl/~dargenio/brp/.
3. Pedro R. D'Argenio, Joost-Pieter Katoen, Theo C. Ruys, and G. Jan Tretmans. The Bounded Retransmission Protocol must be on time! In Ed Brinksma, editor, *Proceedings of the Third International Workshop on Tools and Algorithms for the Construction and Analysis of Systems (TACAS'97)*, number 1217 in Lecture Notes in Computer Science (LNCS), pages 416–431, University of Twente, Enschede, The Netherlands, April 1997. Springer Verlag, Berlin.
4. Christopher W. Fraser and David R. Hanson. *A Retargetable C Compiler: Design and Implementation*. Addison-Wesley, 1995.
5. Gerard J. Holzmann. *Design and Validation of Computer Protocols*. Prentice Hall, Englewood Cliffs, New Jersey, 1991.

6. Gerard J. Holzmann. The Theory and Practice of a Formal Method: NewCore. In *Proceedings of the IFIP World Congress*, Hamburg, Germany, August 1994. Also available from URL:
   http://cm.bell-labs.com/cm/cs/doc/94/index.html.
7. Gerard J. Holzmann. The Model Checker SPIN. *IEEE Transactions on Software Engineering*, 23(5):279–295, May 1997. See also URL:
   http://netlib.bell-labs.com/netlib/spin/whatispin.html.
8. Johan Jeuring and Erik Meijer, editors. *Advanced Functional Programming – Tutorial Text of the First International Spring School on Advanced Functional Programming Techniques*, number 925 in Lecture Notes in Computer Science (LNCS), Båstad, Sweden, May 1995. Springer Verlag, Berlin.
9. Andrew L. Johnson and Brad C. Johnson. Literate Programming using noweb. *Linux Journal*, pages 64–69, October 1997.
10. Pim Kars. The Application of PROMELA and SPIN in the BOS Project. In Jean-Charles Grégoire, Gerard J. Holzmann, and Doron A. Peled, editors, *Proceedings of SPIN96, the Second International Workshop on SPIN (published as "The Spin Verification System)*, volume 32 of *DIMACS Series in Discrete Mathematics and Theoretical Computer Science*, Rutgers University, New Jersey, August 1996. American Mathematical Society. Also available from URL:
    http://netlib.bell-labs.com/netlib/spin/ws96/Ka.ps.Z.
11. Donald E. Knuth. Literate Programming. *The Computer Journal*, 27(2):97–111, May 1984.
12. Donald E. Knuth. *Literate Programming*. Number 27 in CSLI Lecture Notes. Center for the Study of Language and Information (CSLI), Stanford University, California, 1992.
13. Kim G. Larsen, Paul Pettersson, and Wang Yi. UPPAAL in a Nutshell. *Springer International Journal of Software Tools for Technology Transfer (STTT)*, 1(1/2), October 1997.
14. Josh MacDonald. PRCS – Project Revision Control System. Available from URL:
    http://www.xcf.berkeley.edu/~jmacd/prcs.html.
15. Roger S. Pressman. *Software Engineering – A Practioner's Approach*. McGraw-Hill, New York, third edition, 1992.
16. Norman Ramsey. noweb – homepage. Available from URL:
    http://www.cs.virginia.edu/~nr/noweb/.
17. Norman Ramsey. Literate Programming Simplified. *IEEE Software*, 11(5):97–105, September 1994.
18. Theo C. Ruys and Rom Langerak. Validation of Bosch' Mobile Communication-Network Architecture with SPIN. In *Proceedings of SPIN97, the Third International Workshop on SPIN*, University of Twente, Enschede, The Netherlands, April 1997. Also available from URL:
    http://netlib.bell-labs.com/netlib/spin/ws97/ruys.ps.Z.
19. J.M. Spivey. *The Z Notation – A Reference Manual*. Prentice Hall, New York, second edition, 1992.
20. Walter F. Tichy. RCS – A System for Version Control. *Software, Practice & Experience*, 15(7):637–654, July 1985.

Appendix

The Safe process is defined as follows:

25 ⟨*proctype Safe* 25⟩≡   (8)

```
proctype Safe()
{
  bit      here[N] ;
  soldier s1, s2 ;
  do
  ::  unsafe_to_safe ? s1, s2 ;
      here[s1] = 1 ;
      here[s2] = 1 ;
      time = time + max(val[s1], val[s2]) ;
      IF all_here -> break FI ;
      select_soldier(s1) ;
      safe_to_unsafe ! s1
  od
}
```

where the macro max and all_here are defined as:

26 ⟨*macros* 13⟩+≡   (2) ◁17

```
#define max(x,y)       ((x>y) -> x : y)
#define all_here       (here[0] && here[1] && here[2] && here[3])
```

The init process initializes the array val and starts the processes Unsafe and Safe.

27 ⟨*init* 27⟩≡   (1)

```
init {
  ⟨init val 7⟩
  atomic { run Unsafe() ; run Safe() ; }
}
```

A Proof of Burns N-Process Mutual Exclusion Algorithm Using Abstraction

Henrik E. Jensen[1] and Nancy A. Lynch[2]

[1] Department of Computer Science, Institute for Electronic Systems, Aalborg
University, DK-9220 Aalborg Ø, Denmark.
e-mail: ejersbo@cs.auc.dk
[2] Laboratory for Computer Science, Massachusetts Institute of Technology,
Cambridge, MA 02139 USA.
e-mail: lynch@theory.lcs.mit.edu

Abstract. Within the Input/Output Automata framework, we state
and prove a general abstraction theorem giving conditions for preservation of safety properties from one automaton to another. We use our
abstraction theorem to verify that Burns distributed mutual exclusion algorithm parameterized in the number of processes n satisfies the mutual
exclusion property. The concrete n-process algorithm is abstracted by a
simple 2-process algorithm which is property preserving with respect to
the mutual exclusion property. The condition for property preservation
is proved to be satisfied by use of the LP theorem prover with a minimum of user assistance, and the 2-process abstraction is automatically
verified using the SPIN model checker.

1 Introduction

The majority of existing formal verification methods can be characterized as
being either *theorem proving methods* or *model checking methods*, each of these
having their own well-known advantages and disadvantages. Theorem proving
methods can be applied to arbitrary systems and provide good insight into the
systems at hand, but the methods require intelligent user interaction and are
therefore only computer–assisted in a limited way. Model checking methods on
the other hand are fully automatic, but limited to systems with finite state
models or restricted kinds of infinite state models.

To benefit from the advantages of both methodologies there has recently been
an increasing interest into the development of verification frameworks integrating
theorem proving and model checking approaches, the key idea in this integration
being the use of *abstraction*.

Given a system model, too large to be verified automatically, abstraction
techniques are used to reduce this concrete model to a small (finite-state) abstract model which is *property preserving*. Meaning, that if the abstract model
enjoys a property that implies, by the abstraction relation, the concrete property
of interest, then the concrete model enjoys the concrete property.

The abstract model provides insight, as it captures the essence of the behavior of the concrete model with respect to the property of interest, and as it is finite state it can be verified by model checking methods. Theorem proving methods are used to prove, that the abstract model is indeed property preserving, and as a result no restrictions need to be imposed on the kind of concrete system models to which abstraction is amenable.

We propose a method, in the line of above, in the framework of Lynch and Tuttle's *Input/Output Automata (IOA)* [1,2]. We are interested in verifying safety properties of IOA. Properties are expressed as sets of traces, and hence verifying that an IOA A satisfies a trace safety property P amounts to proving that the set of traces of A is included in the set of traces of P. Given a concrete IOA C together with a safety property P_C, we give a general abstraction theorem stating conditions for an abstract IOA A and an abstract property P_A to be property preserving in the sense of above.

The theorem allows for abstraction of concrete system models regardless of the reason for their large size, being e.g. unbounded data structures or an unbounded number of identical processes (parameterized systems). The theorem states as a condition for property preservation the existence of a *parameterized simulation relation* from the concrete IOA to the abstract one, which allows for the abstraction of just a subset of the concrete behaviors.

We illustrate the use of our theorem on the case study of Burns distributed mutual exclusion algorithm parameterized in the number n of processes. We provide a 2-process abstraction and prove using the Larch Proof Assistant [3] that this abstraction satisfies the conditions for preservation of the mutual exclusion property. We verify, using the SPIN [4] model checker, that the abstraction enjoys the abstract mutual exclusion property, and by our abstraction theorem, the n-process algorithm then enjoys the original property.

Related Work

Property preserving abstraction methods have been studied e.g. in [5–10]. These methods are, like ours, all based on proving the existence of some kind of 'mimicing' relation from concrete system models to abstract ones. Different kinds of relations such as *simulation relations*, *homomorphic functions* [10,8,6,7] and *Galois connections* [9,5] have been considered. Our notion of parameterized simulation relations is a generalization of standard simulation relations.

Fully algorithmic methods have been developed, that use automatic abstraction to construct finite state abstract models of restricted kinds of large concrete models s.t. properties are preserved in both directions between the concrete and abstract models. Almost all existing model checkers for dense reactive systems (real–time/hybrid) are based on automatically constructed strongly preserving abstractions [11–13]. The idea is to let abstract states be *equivalence classes* of concrete states with respect to either some behavioral equivalence on concrete states or with respect to an equivalence on concrete states induced by satisfaction of the same properties in some property language.

Structural induction techniques have, together with model checking techniques, been used to verify parameterized systems. By model checking it is verified that *one* process enjoys the property of interest, and assuming that the property holds for some number n of processes (induction hypothesis) one just needs to prove that the property holds for $n+1$ processes as well. Using a finite representation of n processes assumed to enjoy the considered property, now allows model checking to establish that this representation composed with just one more process satisfies the property, and by induction principle this concludes that the property holds for *any* number of composed processes. Works on such techniques have been reported on in [14, 15].

Outline

This paper is organized as follows. In Section 2 we give some mathematical preliminaries used in the rest of the paper. In Section 3 we give the formal background of the IOA framework, and in Section 4 we present our abstraction theory. In Section 5 we present Burns n-process mutual exclusion algorithm which will serve as case-study for the use of our abstraction theorem. Section 6 describes the property preserving abstraction of Burns algorithm and Section 7 describes how the condition for preservation is proved and how LP is used in the proof. Section 8 describes the model checking of the abstract algorithm in the SPIN tool and Section 9 concludes.

2 Mathematical Preliminaries

Relations

A *relation* over sets X and Y is defined to be any subset of the cartesian product $X \times Y$. If R is a relation over X and Y, then we define the *domain* of R to be $dom(R) = \{x \in X \mid (x,y) \in R \text{ for some } y \in Y\}$, and the range of R to be $ran(R) = \{y \in Y \mid (x,y) \in R \text{ for some } x \in X\}$. If $dom(R) = X$ we say that R is *total* (on X). For $x \in X$, we define $R[x] = \{y \in Y \mid (x,y) \in R\}$.

Sequences

Let S be any set. The set of finite and infinite sequences of elements of S is denoted $seq(S)$. The symbol λ denotes the empty sequence and the sequence containing one element $s \in S$ is denoted by s. Concatenation of a finite sequence with a finite or infinite sequence is denoted by juxtaposition. A sequence σ is a *prefix* of a sequence ρ, denoted by $\sigma \leq \rho$, if either $\sigma = \rho$, or σ is finite and $\rho = \sigma\sigma'$ for some sequence σ'. A set Σ of sequences is *prefix closed* if, whenever some sequence is in Σ, all its prefixes are as well. A set Σ of sequences is *limit closed* if, an infinite sequence is in Σ whenever all its finite prefixes are.

If σ is a nonempty sequence then *first*(σ) denotes the first element of σ, and *tail*(σ) denotes the sequence obtained from σ by removing *first*(σ). Also, if σ is finite, *last*(σ) denotes the last element of σ.

If $\sigma \in seq(S)$, and $S' \subseteq S$, then $\sigma \lceil S'$ denotes the restriction of σ to elements in S', i.e. the subsequence of σ consisting of the elements of S'. If $\Sigma \subseteq seq(S)$, then $\Sigma \lceil S'$ is the set $\{\sigma \lceil S' \mid \sigma \in \Sigma\}$.

Assume $R \subseteq S \times S'$ is a total relation between sets S and S'. If $\sigma = s_0 s_1 s_2 \ldots$ is a nonempty sequence in $seq(S)$ then $R(\sigma)$ is the set of sequences $s_0' s_1' s_2' \ldots$ over $ran(R)$ such that for all i, $s_i' \in R[s_i]$. If $\sigma = \lambda$ then $R(\sigma) = \{\lambda\}$. If $\Sigma \subseteq seq(S)$, then $R(\Sigma) = \bigcup_{\sigma \in \Sigma} R(\sigma)$

Lemma 1. *Let S and S' be sets and let $R \subseteq S \times S'$ be some total relation. For Σ and Σ' non-empty subsets of $seq(S)$, if $\Sigma \subseteq \Sigma'$ then $R(\Sigma) \subseteq R(\Sigma')$.*

Proof. Follows from the fact that the set $R(\sigma)$ is unique for any $\sigma \in seq(S)$. □

3 I/O Automata

As we will only be considering safety issues, we will use simplified versions of standard I/O automata that do not incorporate notions of fairness.

Definition 1. *An I/O automaton A is a tuple $(sig(A), states(A), start(A), trans(A))$ where,*

- *$sig(A)$ is a tuple $(in(A), out(A), int(A))$, consisting of disjoint sets of input, output and internal actions, respectively. The set $ext(A)$ of external actions of A is $in(A) \cup out(A)$, and the set $acts(A)$ of actions of A is $ext(A) \cup int(A)$.*
- *$states(A)$ is a set of states.*
- *$start(A) \subseteq states(A)$ is a nonempty set of start states.*
- *$trans(A) \subseteq states(A) \times acts(A) \times states(A)$ is a state transition relation.*

We let $s, s', u, u', \ldots$ range over states, and $\pi, \pi', \ldots$ over actions. We write $s \xrightarrow{\pi}_A s'$, or just $s \xrightarrow{\pi} s'$ if A is clear from the context, as a shorthand for $(s, \pi, s') \in trans(A)$.

An *execution fragment* $s_0 \pi_1 s_1 \pi_2 s_2 \ldots$ of an I/O automaton A is a finite or infinite sequence of alternating states and actions beginning with a state, and if it is finite also ending with a state, s.t. for all i, $s_i \xrightarrow{\pi_{i+1}} s_{i+1}$. An *execution* of A is an execution fragment α where $first(\alpha) \in start(A)$. A state s of A is *reachable* if $s = last(\alpha)$ for some finite execution α of A. The *trace* of an execution α, written $trace(\alpha)$, is the subsequence consisting of all the external actions occurring in α. We say that β is a trace of A if there is an execution α of A with $\beta = trace(\alpha)$. We denote the set of traces of A by $traces(A)$.

Composition

We can compose individual automata to represent complex systems of interacting components. We impose certain restrictions on the automata that may be composed.

Formally, we define a countable collection $\{A_i\}_{i \in I}$ of automata to be *compatible* if for all $i, j \in I$, $i \neq j$, all of the following hold: $int(A_i) \cap acts(A_j) = \emptyset$, $out(A_i) \cap out(A_j) = \emptyset$, and no action is contained in infinitely many sets $acts(A_i)$.

Definition 2. *The composition* $A = \prod_{i \in I} A_i$ *of a countable, compatible collection of I/O automata* $\{A_i\}_{i \in I}$ *is the automaton with:*

- $in(A) = \bigcup_{i \in I} in(A_i) - \bigcup_{i \in I} out(A_i)$
- $out(A) = \bigcup_{i \in I} out(A_i)$
- $int(A) = \bigcup_{i \in I} int(A_i))$
- $states(A) = \prod_{i \in I} states(A_i)$
- $start(A) = \prod_{i \in I} start(A_i)$
- $trans(A)$ *is the set of triples* (s, π, s') *such that, for all* $i \in I$, *if* $\pi \in acts(A_i)$, *then* $(s_i, \pi, s'_i) \in trans(A_i)$; *otherwise* $s_i = s'_i$

The $\prod$ in the definition of $states(A)$ and $start(A)$ refers to ordinary Cartesian product. Also, s_i in the definition of $trans(A)$ denotes the ith component of state vector s.

Trace Properties

We will be considering properties to be proved about an I/O automaton A, as properties about the ordering, in traces of A, of some external actions from a subset of $ext(A)$.

A *trace property* P is a tuple $(sig(P), traces(P))$ where, $sig(P)$ is a pair $(in(P), out(P))$, consisting of disjoint sets of input and output actions, respectively. We let $acts(P)$ denote the set $in(P) \cup out(P)$. $traces(P)$ is a set of (finite or infinite) sequences of actions in $acts(P)$. We will be considering only *safety* properties, so we assume $traces(P)$ is nonempty, prefix-closed, and limit-closed.

An I/O automaton A and a trace property P are said to be *compatible* if, $in(P) \subseteq in(A)$ and $out(P) \subseteq out(A)$.

Definition 3. *Let A be an I/O automaton and P a trace property such that A and P are compatible. Then A satisfies P if, $traces(A)\lceil acts(P) \subseteq traces(P)$.*

4 Abstraction Theory

Suppose A is an I/O automaton and P is a trace property such that A and P are compatible. We will denote the pair (A, P) a *verification problem*. If (A, P) and (A', P') are two verification problems, we say that (A', P') is *safe* for (A, P) provided that A' satisfies P' implies that A satisfies P. In this section we give a general abstraction theorem, stating when one verification problem is safe for another.

If A and A' are two I/O automata and R is some relation from $ext(A')$ to $ext(A)$, we write, $s \overset{\beta}{\Longrightarrow}_{A'} s'$, when A' has a finite execution fragment α with $first(\alpha) = s$, $last(\alpha) = s'$ and $trace(\alpha)\lceil dom(R) = \beta$.

We now define the notion of a *parameterized simulation relation* between two automata A and A', and we give a soundness result needed for the abstraction theorem.

Definition 4. *Let A and A' be two I/O automata and let R be a relation from $ext(A')$ to $ext(A)$. A relation $f_R \subseteq states(A) \times states(A')$ is a simulation relation from A to A' parameterized by R provided,*

1. *If $s \in start(A)$ then $f_R[s] \cap start(A') \neq \emptyset$.*
2. *If $s \xrightarrow{\pi}_A s'$, $u \in f_R[s]$, and s and u are reachable states of A and A' respectively, then*

   (a) If $\pi \in ran(R)$, then $\exists \pi', u'$ such that $u \xRightarrow{\pi'}_{A'} u'$, $(\pi', \pi) \in R$ and $(s', u') \in f_R$.

   (b) If $\pi \notin ran(R)$, then $\exists u'$ such that $u \xRightarrow{\lambda}_{A'} u'$ and $(s', u') \in f_R$.

We write $A \leq_R A'$ if there is a simulation from A to A' parameterized by R.

Lemma 2. $A \leq_R A' \Rightarrow traces(A)\lceil ran(R) \subseteq R(traces(A')\lceil dom(R))$

Proof. Analogous to proof for standard forward simulation [16]. □

Theorem 1. *Let (A, P) and (A', P') be two verification problems. Also, let R be a relation from $ext(A')$ to $ext(A)$, with $dom(R) = acts(P')$ and $ran(R) = acts(P)$, such that $R(traces(P')) \subseteq traces(P)$. If,*

$$A \leq_R A' \quad and \quad A' \ satisfies \ P'$$

then

$$A \ satisfies \ P$$

Proof. Assume that $A \leq_R A'$ and that A' satisfies P'. From second assumption we have $traces(A')\lceil acts(P') \subseteq traces(P')$ and from Lemma 1 we get $(*)$ $R(traces(A')\lceil acts(P')) \subseteq R(traces(P'))$, as R is total on $acts(P')$. Also, from Lemma 2, and the fact that $dom(R) = acts(P')$ and $ran(R) = acts(P)$, we have that $traces(A)\lceil acts(P) \subseteq R(traces(A')\lceil acts(P'))$ and this together with $(*)$ now gives us that $traces(A)\lceil acts(P) \subseteq R(traces(P'))$ and finally as $R(traces(P')) \subseteq traces(P)$ we get the wanted result, namely $traces(A)\lceil acts(P) \subseteq traces(P)$ i.e. A satisfies P. □

5 Burns N–Process Mutual Exclusion Algorithm

In this section we present Burns n-process distributed mutual exclusion algorithm, which we will verify with respect to the mutual exclusion property using the abstraction approach from the previous section.

The algorithm runs on a shared memory model consisting of n processes $P_1, \ldots, P_n$ together with n shared variables $flag_1, \ldots, flag_n$, each $flag_i$ writable by process P_i and readable by all other processes. Each process P_i is acting on behalf of a user process U_i which can be thought of as some application program. The processes $P_1, \ldots, P_n$ competes for mutual exclusive access to a shared resource by reading and writing the shared variables in a way determined by the algorithm.

We model the algorithm formally as an I/O automaton $BurnsME$, which is the composition of a shared memory automaton M and a set of user automata $U_1, \ldots, U_n$. M models the n processes $P_1, \ldots, P_n$ together with the set of shared variables $flag_1, \ldots, flag_n$, and it is modelled as one big I/O automaton, where the process and variable structure is captured by means of some locality restrictions on transitions. Each state in M consists of a state for each process P_i, plus a value for each shared variable $flag_i$. A state variable v of process P_i in automaton M is denoted $M.v_i$. Similarly, $U.v_i$ denotes a state variable v of automaton U_i. We omit the preceding $U(M)$ and the subscripts i when these are clear from the context.

The inputs to M are (for all $1 \leq i \leq n$) actions try_i, which models a request by user U_i to process P_i for access to the shared resource, and actions $exit_i$, which models an announcement by user U_i to process P_i that it is done with the resource. The outputs of M are $crit_i$, which models the granting from process P_i of the resource to U_i, and rem_i, which models P_i telling U_i that it can continue with the rest of its work.

Each process P_i executes three loops. The first two loops involve checking the flags of all processes with smaller indices, i.e. all $flag_j$, $1 \leq j < i$. The first loop is actually not needed for the mutual exclusion condition, but is important to guarantee progress. The two loops are modelled in M by internal actions $test\text{-}sml\text{-}fst(j)_i$ and $test\text{-}sml\text{-}snd(j)_i$, where j is a parameter denoting the index of the flag to be read by process P_i. In between the first two loops process P_i sets its own $flag_i$ to 1, modelled in M by internal action $set\text{-}flg\text{-}1_i$. If both loops are successfully passed, meaning all the considered flags have value 0, then P_i can proceed to the third loop, which involves checking the flags of all processes with larger indices, i.e. $flag_j$, $i < j \leq n$. This is modelled by internal action $test\text{-}lrg(j)_i$. If process P_i passes all three loops successfully, it proceeds to its critical region. Process P_i keeps the value of its $flag_i$ to 1 from when it starts testing flags with larger indices and until it leaves its critical region.

The User Automata: Each automaton U_i has as single state variable a program counter pc initially having the value rem, indicating that U_i starts in its remainder region ready to make a request for access to the shared resource.

output: try_i
    Pre: $pc = rem$
    Eff: $pc := try$

output: $exit_i$
    Pre: $pc = crit$
    Eff: $pc = exit$

input: $crit_i$
    Eff: $pc := crit$

input: rem_i
    Eff: $pc := rem$

The Shared Memory Automaton: The state of each process P_i in M is modelled by two state variables: a program counter pc initially having the value *rem*, and a set S of process id's initially empty, used to keep track of the indices of all shared flags that have successfully been checked in one of the three loops.

input: try_i
  Eff: $pc := set\text{-}flg\text{-}0$

internal: $set\text{-}flg\text{-}0_i$
  Pre: $pc = set\text{-}flg\text{-}0$
  Eff: $flag_i := 0$
      if $i = 1$ then
        $pc := set\text{-}flg\text{-}1$
      else
        $pc := test\text{-}sml\text{-}fst$

internal: $test\text{-}sml\text{-}fst(j)_i$
  Pre: $pc = test\text{-}sml\text{-}fst$
      $j \notin S$
      $1 \leq j \leq i - 1$
  Eff: if $flag_j = 1$ then
      $S := \emptyset$
      $pc := set\text{-}flg\text{-}0$
      else
        $S := S \cup \{j\}$
        if $|S| = i - 1$ then
          $S := \emptyset$
          $pc := set\text{-}flg\text{-}1$

internal: $set\text{-}flg\text{-}1_i$
  Pre: $pc = set\text{-}flg\text{-}1$
  Eff: $flag_i := 1$
      if $i = 1$ then
        $pc := test\text{-}lrg$
      else
        $pc := test\text{-}sml\text{-}snd$

internal: $test\text{-}sml\text{-}snd(j)_i$
  Pre: $pc = test\text{-}sml\text{-}snd$
      $j \notin S$
      $1 \leq j \leq i - 1$
  Eff: if $flag_j = 1$ then
      $S := \emptyset$
      $pc := set\text{-}flg\text{-}0$
      else
        $S := S \cup \{j\}$
        if $|S| = i - 1$ then
          $S := \emptyset$
          if $i = n$ then
            $pc := leave\text{-}try$
          else
            $pc := test\text{-}lrg$

internal: $test\text{-}lrg(j)_i$
  Pre: $pc = test\text{-}lrg$
      $j \notin S$
      $i + 1 \leq j \leq n$
  Eff: if $flag_j = 1$ then
      $S := \emptyset$
      else
        $S := S \cup \{j\}$
        if $|S| = n - i$ then
          $pc := leave\text{-}try$

output: $crit_i$
  Pre: $pc = leave\text{-}try$
  Eff: $pc := crit$

input: $exit_i$
  Eff: $pc := reset$

internal: $reset_i$
  Pre: $pc = reset$
  Eff: $flag_i := 0$
      $S := \emptyset$
      $pc := leave\text{-}exit$

output: rem_i
  Pre: $pc = leave\text{-}exit$
  Eff: $pc := rem$

The mutual exclusion property for *BurnsME* is a set of trace properties $P_{\{i,j\}}$, one for each subset $\{i,j\}_{i \neq j}$ in the set of process indices $\{1,\ldots,n\}$, such that $sig(P_{\{i,j\}})$ has as its only actions the set of output actions from *BurnsME* with indices i and j, and $traces(P_{\{i,j\}})$ is the set of sequences such that no two $crit_i$, $crit_j$ events occur (in that order) without an intervening $exit_i$ event, and similarly for i and j switched.

6   Abstracting *BurnsME*

To construct a property-preserving abstraction of *BurnsME* we examine the mutual exclusion property as stated in the previous section. The property is the conjunction of properties $P_{\{i,j\}}$, one for each subset $\{i,j\}$ of indices in $\{1,\ldots,n\}$, with each $P_{\{i,j\}}$ saying that processes P_i and P_j can not both be in their critical section at the same time.

The abstraction idea is now as follows. We will construct a single finite-state abstraction which preserves the external behavior of *any* two concrete processes P_i and P_j running in the environment of *all* other processes and users. This abstraction will then preserve the mutual exclusion property between any pair of concrete processes and hence the complete property.

Formally, we construct an abstract automaton *ABurnsME*, which is the composition of a shared memory automaton *AM*, with two user automata AU_0 and AU_1. *AM* models two abstract processes AP_0 and AP_1 together with two shared variables $flag_0$ and $flag_1$. AP_0 and AP_1 are abstract representations of any pair of concrete processes P_i and P_j within the environment of all other concrete processes, such that AP_0 represents *the smaller process* P_i and AP_1 represents *the larger process* P_j for $i < j$.

A state of *AM* consists of a state for each of the abstract processes AP_0 and AP_1 together with values for each of the shared variables $flag_0$ and $flag_1$. A state variable v of process AP_i in automaton *AM* is denoted $AM.v_i$. Similarly, $AU.v_i$ denotes a variable v of automaton AU_i. We omit the preceding $AM(AU)$ and the subscripts i when these are clear from the context.

The interface between AU_0 and AP_0 (AU_1 and AP_1) is identical to the interface between any concrete user automaton U_i and corresponding concrete process P_i, except for a change of indices. Process AP_0 has as actions abstracted versions of all actions actions in any smaller process P_i, and AP_1 has abstracted versions of all actions in any larger process P_j.

The automata AU_0 and AU_1 of *ABurnsME*, are identical to each other and to any concrete user automaton U_i except for a change of indices.

The Abstract Shared Memory Automaton: The state of each of the abstract processes AP_0 and AP_1 is modelled, analogous to the state of concrete processes, by two state variables: a program counter pc, initially *rem* and a set S of indices, initially empty. The transitions for AP_0 are as follows.

input: try_0
  Eff: $pc := set\text{-}flg\text{-}0$

internal: $set\text{-}flg\text{-}0_0$
  Pre: $pc = set\text{-}flg\text{-}0$
  Eff: $flag_0 := 0$
      $pc := test\text{-}sml\text{-}fst$

internal: $set\text{-}flg\text{-}0\text{-}sml_0$
  Pre: $pc = set\text{-}flg\text{-}0$
  Eff: $flag_0 := 0$
      $pc := set\text{-}flg\text{-}1$

internal: $test\text{-}sml\text{-}fail_0$
  Pre: $pc \in \{test\text{-}sml\text{-}fst, test\text{-}sml\text{-}snd\}$
  Eff: $pc := set\text{-}flg\text{-}0$

internal: $test\text{-}sml\text{-}fst\text{-}succ_0$
  Pre: $pc = test\text{-}sml\text{-}fst$
  Eff: $pc := set\text{-}flg\text{-}1$

internal: $set\text{-}flg\text{-}1_0$
  Pre: $pc = set\text{-}flg\text{-}1$
  Eff: $flag_0 := 1$
      $pc := test\text{-}sml\text{-}snd$

internal: $set\text{-}flg\text{-}1\text{-}sml_0$
  Pre: $pc = set\text{-}flg\text{-}1$
  Eff: $flag_0 := 1$
      $pc := test\text{-}lrg$

internal: $test\text{-}sml\text{-}snd\text{-}succ_0$
  Pre: $pc = test\text{-}sml\text{-}snd$
  Eff: $pc := test\text{-}lrg$

internal: $test\text{-}other\text{-}flg_0$
  Pre: $pc = test\text{-}lrg$
      $S = \emptyset$
  Eff: if $flag_1 = 0$ then
      $S := S \cup \{1\}$

internal: $test\text{-}lrg\text{-}fail_0$
  Pre: $pc = test\text{-}lrg$
  Eff: $S := \emptyset$

internal: $test\text{-}lrg\text{-}succ_0$
  Pre: $pc = test\text{-}lrg$
      $S = \{1\}$
  Eff: $pc := leave\text{-}try$

output: $crit_0$
  Pre: $pc = leave\text{-}try$
  Eff: $pc := crit$

input: $exit_0$
  Eff: $pc := reset$

internal: $reset_0$
  Pre: $pc = reset$
  Eff: $flag_0 := 0$
      $S := \emptyset$
      $pc := leave\text{-}exit$

output: rem_0
  Pre: $pc = leave\text{-}exit$
  Eff: $pc := rem$

One of the consequences of AP_0 representing the behavior of *any* smaller process is that AP_0 has two actions for setting its own flag to 0 (1): $set\text{-}flg\text{-}0\text{-}sml_0$ ($set\text{-}flg\text{-}1\text{-}sml_0$) and $set\text{-}flg\text{-}0_0$ ($set\text{-}flg\text{-}1_0$). The first representing that the concrete process P_1 (the one with smallest index) sets its flag to 0 (1), where after it skips the test of flags with smaller indices, as there are none, and sets it program counter to $set\text{-}flg\text{-}1$ ($test\text{-}lrg$). The second representing that any other smaller process sets it flag to 0 (1) and thereafter tests flags with smaller indices, which do exist in this case. AP_0 represents that a smaller process fails or succeeds a test of smaller flags by allowing abstract fail or succeed actions whenever its program counter is $test\text{-}sml\text{-}fst$ or $test\text{-}sml\text{-}snd$. No further preconditions apply to these actions as all information about the actual values of smaller flags have been abstracted away.

In order for AP_0 to succeed its test of flags with larger indices, it must test the flag of abstract process AP_1 as AP_1 represent some larger process. This test is modelled by the action *test-other-flg₀*. Having read this flag successfully (i.e. as 0) AP_0 can now enter its critical region. Also, as long as AP_0 has program counter *test-lrg* it can at any time perform an abstract action *test-lrg-fail*.

Abstract process AP_1 is modelled analogously to AP_0, and its transitions are as follows.

input: *try₁*
Eff: $pc := set\text{-}flg\text{-}0$

internal: *set-flg-0₁*
Pre: $pc = set\text{-}flg\text{-}0$
Eff: $flag_1 := 0$
       $pc = test\text{-}sml\text{-}fst$

internal: *test-other-flg₁*
Pre: $pc \in \{test\text{-}sml\text{-}fst, test\text{-}sml\text{-}snd\}$
       $S = \emptyset$
Eff: if $flag_0 = 0$ then
       $S := S \cup \{0\}$

internal: *test-sml-fail₁*
Pre: $pc \in \{test\text{-}sml\text{-}fst, test\text{-}sml\text{-}snd\}$
Eff: $S := \emptyset$
       $pc := set\text{-}flg\text{-}0$

internal: *test-sml-fst-succ₁*
Pre: $pc = test\text{-}sml\text{-}fst$
       $S = \{0\}$
Eff: $S := \emptyset$
       $pc := set\text{-}flg\text{-}1$

internal: *set-flg-1₁*
Pre: $pc = set\text{-}flg\text{-}1$
Eff: $flag_1 := 1$
       $pc := test\text{-}sml\text{-}snd$

internal: *test-sml-snd-succ₁*
Pre: $pc = test\text{-}sml\text{-}snd$
       $S = \{0\}$
Eff: $pc := test\text{-}lrg$

internal: *test-sml-snd-succ-lrg₁*
Pre: $pc = test\text{-}sml\text{-}snd$
       $S = \{0\}$
Eff: $pc := leave\text{-}try$

internal: *test-lrg-fail₁*
Pre: $pc = test\text{-}lrg$
Eff: $pc := test\text{-}lrg$

internal: *test-lrg-succ₁*
Pre: $pc = test\text{-}lrg$
Eff: $pc := leave\text{-}try$

output: *crit₁*
Pre: $pc = leave\text{-}try$
Eff: $pc := crit$

input: *exit₁*
Eff: $pc := reset$

internal: *reset₁*
Pre: $pc = reset$
Eff: $flag_1 := 0$
       $S := \emptyset$
       $pc := leave\text{-}exit$

output: *rem₁*
Pre: $pc = leave\text{-}exit$
Eff: $pc := rem$

The abstract mutual exclusion property for *ABurnsME* is the one trace property $P_{(0,1)}$ with $sig(P_{(0,1)})$ having as its only actions the output actions of *ABurnsME* and $traces(P_{(0,1)})$ being the set of sequences such that no two *crit₀* and *crit₁* events occur (in that order) without an intervening *exit₀* event, and similarly for 0 and 1 switched.

Now, for any $\{i,j\}$ we define a relation $R_{\{i,j\}}$ from $acts(P_{(0,1)})$ to $acts(P_{\{i,j\}})$. We assume $i < j$.

$$R_{\{i,j\}} = \{(try_0, try_i), (try_1, try_j), (crit_0, crit_i), (crit_1, crit_j),$$
$$(exit_0, exit_i), (exit_1, exit_j), (rem_0, rem_i), (rem_1, rem_j)\}$$

By definition, $R_{\{i,j\}}(P_{(0,1)}) \subseteq P_{\{i,j\}}$. We use $R_{\{i,j\}}$ as parameter to a state relation $f_{R_{\{i,j\}}}$ defined as follows.

Definition 5. $f_{R_{\{i,j\}}}$ *is a relation from states*($BurnsME$) *to states*($ABurnsME$) *such that* $f_{R_{\{i,j\}}}(s,u)$ *iff* :

- $u.AU.pc_0 = s.U.pc_i$ and $u.AU.pc_1 = s.U.pc_j$
- $u.AM.pc_0 = s.M.pc_i$ and $u.AM.pc_1 = s.M.pc_j$
- $u.flag_0 = s.flag_i$ and $u.flag_1 = s.flag_j$
- $u.AM.S_0 = \{1\}$ if $j \in s.M.S_i$ and $u.AM.S_1 = \{0\}$ if $i \in s.M.S_j$

Note, that we use dot notation to denote the value of a given variable in a state.

Theorem 2. *For all* $\{i,j\}$ *subsets of* $\{1,\ldots,n\}$, $f_{R_{\{i,j\}}}$ *is a simulation relation from BurnsME to ABurnsME parameterized by* $R_{\{i,j\}}$.

7 The Simulation Proof

To prove Theorem 2 for *all* $\{i,j\}$ we prove it for *any* $\{i,j\}$ with i and j treated as Skolem constants. The proof follows the line of a standard forward simulation proof [2]. To see that $f_{R_{\{i,j\}}}$ is in fact a parameterized simulation relation we check the two conditions in Definition 4. The start condition is trivial, because the initial states of *BurnsME* and *ABurnsME* have the value of pc set to rem for all processes and users, and they have all flags set to 0 and all sets of indices empty.

Now, for the step condition suppose that $s \in states(BurnsME)$ and $u \in states(ABurnsME)$ s.t. $f_{R_{\{i,j\}}}(s,u)$. We then consider cases based on the type of action π_x performed by s on a transition $s \xrightarrow{\pi_x} s'$. For each action π_x we consider $x = i$, $x = j$ and $x \notin \{i,j\}$. The proof is relatively simple, as the execution fragment corresponding to a certain concrete action π_x for the most cases can be picked to be the abstract version of the concrete action. So the proof is a rather straightforward matching up of concrete actions with their abstract counterparts.

In [17] a framework is introduced for specifying and reasoning about IOA using the Larch tools. The notion of IOA is formalized in the Larch Shared Language (LSL) [18] which is supported by a tool that produces input for LP. LP is a theorem prover for first-order logic designed to assist users who employ standard proof techniques such as proofs by cases, induction, and contradiction.

In [17] LP is used to construct standard simulation proofs, and we use the framework introduced here to (re)do the proof of Theorem 2. Using LP for the simulation proof allows us to disregard many of the routine steps which are needed in the hand proof, as LP carries these out automatically. The main user assistance that LP needs for the proof is the input of the corresponding abstract execution fragment for each concrete action. The rest of the user guidance consists of directing LP to break some proof parts into cases, and directing LP to use whatever information it has already got to try and do some rewriting to complete proof subgoals.

Having proved Theorem 2 now allows us to apply Theorem 1 and conclude that if *ABurnsME* satisfies $P_{(0,1)}$ then *BurnsME* satisfies $P_{\{i,j\}}$ for all $\{i,j\}$ subsets of $\{1,\ldots,n\}$. That *ABurnsME* satisfies $P_{(0,1)}$ is model checked using the SPIN model checker.

8 Model Checking *ABurnsME*

The SPIN verification tool relies on a simple yet powerful modelling language based on processes communicating either on asynchronous channels or via shared variables. As property language SPIN uses Linear Time Temporal Logic (LTL).

We translate the IOA description of *ABurnsME* into a SPIN model and we translate the property $P_{(0,1)}$ into an LTL formula suitable for SPIN. Automaton *ABurnsME* is translated into a SPIN model with two processes implementing the behavior of the composition of AU_0 with AP_0, and AU_1 with AP_1, respectively. Each process has variables representing the program counters and internal index sets of the corresponding IOA. The SPIN processes each execute a loop checking preconditions and performing effects of representations of the actions of their corresponding IOA. For each action, checking preconditions and performing effects is done atomically, i.e. non-interleaved with any other actions, hence preserving the exact IOA semantics.

The property $P_{(0,1)}$ is translated into an LTL property of the SPIN model. From *ABurnsME* it is easy to see, that the property $P_{(0,1)}$ can be stated (equivalently) as a property of states rather than actions. Recall, that $P_{(0,1)}$ is the set of sequences of external actions such that no two $crit_0$ and $crit_1$ events occur (in that order) without an intervening $exit_0$ event, and similarly for 0 and 1 switched. But, if an action $crit_i$, $i \in \{0,1\}$, is performed then $AM.pc_i$ gets the value $crit$ and it can not change until an $exit_i$ action is performed. Consequently, the property $P_{(0,1)}$ can equivalently be stated as an invariant saying that for any state u it is the case that $u.AM.pc_0$ and $u.AM.pc_1$ can not both have the value $crit$. This property is exactly in the form of an LTL property and can be stated in the property language of SPIN without translation.

Using SPIN to analyse the abstracted algorithm with respect to its corresponding abstract property stated in LTL, immediately lead to a successful verification result.

9 Conclusion

In this paper we have presented a general abstraction theorem within the Input/Output Automata framework, which gives conditions for preservation of safety properties from one (abstract) automaton to another (concrete) automaton. The preservation condition is expressed by the requirement of a parameterized simulation relation from the concrete to the abstract automaton.

We have used our abstraction theorem to verify that Burns n-process mutual exclusion algorithm enjoys the mutual exclusion property, by constructing and proving a 2-process property preserving abstraction of the concrete algorithm. We have used the Larch Proof Assistant, LP to prove the conditions for property preservation, and by using the SPIN model checker we have successfully verified the abstraction.

Using our abstraction approach to prove Burns algorithm led to a proof style having the advantages of providing both essential insight into the algorithm and some automatic verification. The insight gained in the case of Burns algorithm is that its essential behavior with respect to the mutual exclusion property can be abstracted to the behavior of just two processes.

In general, our abstraction approach does of course not guarantee the existence of finite state abstractions for any concrete system neither does it provide a method for finding such abstractions. Further case studies needs to be considered to identify classes of systems to which certain specific abstraction techniques/patterns can be applied. The specific approach applied to the Burns algorithm has also been succesfully applied to the Bakery mutual exclusion algorithm, and it seems to be useful in general to many parameterized systems where the property of interest can be stated as a conjunction of equivalent properties over a finite subset of components.

Tool support is essential to assist in the process of finding common abstraction patterns for classes of systems, and we are investigating approaches to further integrate model checking facilities with the Larch tools.

References

1. Nancy Lynch and Mark Tuttle. An Introduction to Input/Output Automata. *CWI-Quarterly*, 2(3)219–246, 1989.
2. Nancy A. Lynch. *Distributed Algorithms.* Morgan Kaufmann Publishers, 1996.
3. S.J. Garland and J.V. Guttag. A Guide to LP, the Larch Prover. Technical Report, Research Report 82, Digital Systems Research Center, 1991.
4. Gerard Holzmann. *The Design and Validation of Computer Protocols.* Prentice Hall, 1991.
5. D. Dams. Abstract Interpretation and Partition Refinement for Model Checking. PhD thesis, Eindhoven University of Technology, 1996.
6. Jürgen Dingel and Thomas Filkorn. Model checking for infinite state systems using data abstraction, assumption-commitment style reasoning and theorem proving. In *Proc. of CAV'95*, Lecture Notes in Computer Science, volume 939, pages 54–69, 1995.
7. E.M. Clarke, O. Grumberg and D.E. Long. Model Checking and Abstraction. In *Nineteenth Annual ACM SIGPLAN-SIGACT Symposium on Principles of Programming Languages*, 1992.
8. R.P. Kurshan. Analysis of Discrete Event Coordination. In J.W. de Bakker, W.-P. de Roever, and G. Rozenberg, editors, *Proceedings of the Workshop on Stepwise Refinement of Distributed Systems: Models, Formalisms, Correctness*, Lecture Notes in Computer Science, volume 430, pages 414–454. Springer Verlag, 1989.

9. C. Loiseaux, S. Graf, J. Sifakis, A. Bouajjani, and S. Bensalem. Property Preserving Abstractions for the Verification of Concurrent Systems. *Formal Methods in System Design*, pages 6:11–44, 1995.

10. Olaf Müller and Tobias Nipkow. Combining Model Checking and Deduction for I/O-Automata. In *Tools and Algorithms for the Construction and Analysis of Systems*, Lecture Notes in Computer Science, volume 1019, pages 1–16. Springer Verlag, 1995.

11. Johan Bengtsson, Kim G. Larsen, Fredrik Larsson, Paul Pettersson, and Wang Yi. Uppaal — a Tool Suite for Automatic Verification of Real–Time Systems. In *Proc. of the 4th DIMACS Workshop on Verification and Control of Hybrid Systems*, Lecture Notes in Computer Science, October 1995.

12. Thomas A. Henzinger, Pei–Hsin Ho, and Howard Wong-Toi. A Users Guide to HYTECH. Technical Report, Department of Computer Science, Cornell University, 1995.

13. Monika R. Henzinger, Thomas A. Henzinger, and Peter W. Kopke. Computing Simulations on Finite and Infinite Graphs. In *36th Annual Symposium on Foundations of Computer Science*, pages 453–462. IEEE Computer Society Press, 1995.

14. Pierre Wolper and Vincianne Lovinfosse. Verifying Properties of Large Sets of Processes with Network Invariants. *International Workshop on Automatic Verification Methods for Finite State Machines*, Lecture Notes in Computer Science, volume 407, 1989.

15. R.P. Kurshan and K. McMillan. A Structural Induction Theorem for Processes. In *Proceedings of the 8th Annual ACM Symposium on Principles of Distributed Computing*, 1989.

16. N. Lynch and M. Tuttle. Hierarchical Correctness Proofs for Distributed Algorithms. In *Proc. of the 6th ACM Symposium on Principles of Distributed Computation*, pages 137–151, 1987.

17. Jørgen Søgaard–Andersen, Stephen J. Garland, John V. Guttag, Nancy A. Lynch, and Anna Pogosyants. Computer-Assisted Simulation Proofs. In Costas Courcoubetis, editor, *Computer-Aided Verification (5th International Conference, CAV'93, Elounda, Greece, June/July 1993)*, Lecture Notes in Computer Science, volume 697, pages 305–319. Springer Verlag, 1993.

18. J.V. Guttag and J.J. Horning. *Larch: Languages and Tools for Formal Specification.* Springer Verlag, 1993.

Automated Verification
of Szymanski's Algorithm[1]

E. Pascal Gribomont and Guy Zenner

University of Liège (Belgium)

Abstract. The algorithm for mutual exclusion proposed by B. Szymanski is an interesting challenge for verification methods and tools. Several full proofs have been described in the literature, but they seem to require lengthy interactive sessions with powerful theorem provers. As far as this algorithm makes use of only the most elementary facts of arithmetics, we conjectured that a simple, non-interactive proof should exist; this paper gives such a proof, describes its development and how an elementary tool has been used to complete the verification.

1 Introduction

Many kinds of hardware and software systems are now tentatively subjected to formal verification. Among the most interesting ones are the algorithms used to ensure mutual exclusion in distributed networks. This is due to both practical and scientific reasons. First, it is of foremost importance to guarantee that concurrently running processes do not interfere in a destructive way; in fact, most of the communication, cooperation and synchronization problems between concurrent processes can be seen as variants of the mutual exclusion problem: this problem therefore deserves much attention. Furthermore, algorithms that solve the mutual exclusion problem ... or are thought to solve it, tend to be rather short but subtle pieces of code. As a result, their formal verification is challenging but still within reach of tools whose practical efficiency decreases badly when the size of the code to be verified increases.

Szymanski's algorithm implements mutual exclusion in a distributed network. Each process owns only three boolean variables, meaning that computations take place within a finite state space; this algorithm can be verified in a fully automated way with model checking methods and tools. The only problem is that the number n of processes is arbitrary. The size of the state space grows exponentially with n, so verification based on model checking is realistic (and very efficient) for small values of n only. Anyway, a general proof, valid for every integer n, would be more useful and more elegant, but can not be devised purely within the model checking paradigm. In fact, Szymanski's algorithm involves

---

[1] *Correspondence to:*
P. Gribomont
Institut Montefiore
ULg, Sart-Tilman, B 28
B – 4000 Liège (Belgium)

Phone: +32 4 366 26 67
Fax: +32 4 366 29 84
e-mail: gribomont@montefiore.ulg.ac.be

each process accessing the state of all other processes. Statements' guards are quantified formulas, and quantified formulas also appear in any useful global invariant. Even if the quantification is bounded (by the number n of processes), using first-order logic seems mandatory.

Our purpose in the sequel of this paper is to show that a particular kind of tautology checking is not impaired by the exponentially growing size of the state space, even in the case of algorithms like Szymanski's, where quantifications in both the guards and the invariant are numerous.

A version of Szymanski's algorithm is introduced in Section 2, a propositional model is built in Section 3, the verification techniques are addressed in Section 4 and the computer-aided verification of the algorithm is described in Section 5. Section 6 outlines comparison with other approaches and gives a conclusion.

2   Szymanski's algorithm, a hybrid version

This algorithm has been first proposed in [28] but has been slightly modified several times. The version considered here is adapted from [22].

There are n concurrent processes, numbered from 1 to n, which switch endlessly between a non critical section and a critical section. The main safety requirement is that at most one process at a time can be within its critical section. (Other requirements, not investigated here, are absence of deadlock, responsiveness and pseudo-linear waiting.)

Each process executes the same code and has only reading access to the variables owned by the other processes. Process p owns three boolean variables a_p, s_p and w_p, which are initially false. An abstract version of the code repeatedly executed by process p is given in Figure 1.

It is convenient to introduce some terminology. Process p can be either in the anteroom (executing lines 1 to 3) or in the doorway (line 4) or in the waiting room (lines 5 to 8) or in the inner sanctum (lines 9 to 13). Now, this abstract, coarse-grained version (atomic version in [22,23]) is interesting since it grasps the essence of the algorithm, without bothering with potential interference problems between processes; it is also easy to guess what the appropriate invariant for this algorithm should be. However, the abstract version should not be implemented as such, with each line being an atomic, uninterruptible piece of code : this would be very unefficient. In fact, each line involving all processes $q \neq p$ should be split into $n - 1$ (or, for line 11, $p - 1$) more elementary statements, to be executed independently or sequentially.

From the point of view of methods and tools, both versions are challenging. The abstract, coarse-grained one involves quantified guards, but the finer-grained version (called "molecular" in [22,23], where both versions are considered) contains more transitions, with a more complex invariant, and gives rise to a more complex proof.

Presenting both versions in a paper of acceptable size is not possible, but we can show how to cope with both kinds of problems by addressing a "hybrid"

1. NCS (Non Critical Section)
2. $a_p := true$
3. await $\forall j \leq n : \neg s_j$
4. $(w_p, s_p) := (true, true)$
5. if $\exists j \leq n : a_j \wedge \neg w_j$
6. then $\quad s_p := false$
7. $\qquad$ await $\exists j \leq n : s_j \wedge \neg w_j$
8. $\qquad\quad s_p := true$
9. $w_p := false$
10. await $\forall j \leq n : \neg w_j$
11. await $\forall j < p : \neg s_j$
12. CS (Critical Section)
13. $(a_p, s_p) := (false, false)$

Fig. 1. Abstract version of Szymanski's algorithm

version. We will split only one quantified statement, which is the crucial "count-down" statement just before the critical section (line 11). A boolean array X_p is introduced to control this; $X_p[q]$ holds as soon as process p has checked $\neg s_q$. This has to be done for all $q < p$, so initially $X_p[q]$ holds only for all $q \geq p$ (deno-ted $X_p = I_p$); when the countdown is completed, $X_p[q]$ holds for all q (denoted $X_p = TR$).

It is also convenient to make explicit the various control points of the system; for each control point ℓ, there is a predicate $at\ \ell$ which is true when the execution is at control point ℓ. The transitions executed by process p in our hybrid version are listed in Figure 2. A transition $(p_i, G \rightarrow S, p_j)$ can be executed by process p when the control state is at p_i and the memory state satisfies the guard G, that is, when formula $(at\ p_i \wedge G)$ is true; the effect of the transition is to alter the memory state according to the assignment S and to transfer the control at point p_j.

The links between control points and program variables are expressed by assertions (1).

$$at\ p_{5,9..13} \Leftrightarrow s_p\,,$$
$$at\ p_{3..13} \Leftrightarrow a_p\,, \tag{1}$$
$$at\ p_{5..9} \Leftrightarrow w_p\,.$$

(The expression $at\ p_{5,9..13}$ stands for the formula $at\ p_5 \vee at\ p_9 \vee at\ p_{10} \vee at\ p_{11} \vee at\ p_{12} \vee at\ p_{13}$.)

The terminology introduced above allows for the following intuitive description [22] of the strategy used in the algorithm to grant passage from one "room" into another, and access to the critical section:

A_0 : When p is in the inner sanctum, the doorway is locked.

$(p_1, true \longrightarrow NCS, p_2)$

$(p_2, true \longrightarrow a_p := true, p_3)$

$(p_3, \forall j \leq n : \neg s_j \longrightarrow skip, p_4)$

$(p_4, true \longrightarrow (w_p, s_p) := (true, true), p_5)$

$(p_5, \exists j \leq n : a_j \wedge \neg w_j \longrightarrow s_p := false, p_7)$

$(p_7, \exists j \leq n : s_j \wedge \neg w_j \longrightarrow skip, p_8)$

$(p_8, true \longrightarrow s_p := true, p_9)$

$(p_5, \neg \exists j \leq n : a_j \wedge \neg w_j \longrightarrow skip, p_9)$

$(p_9, true \longrightarrow w_p := false, p_{10})$

$(p_{10}, \forall j \leq n : \neg w_j \longrightarrow skip, p_{11})$

$(p_{11}, q < p \wedge \neg X_p[q] \wedge \neg s_q \longrightarrow X_p[q] := true, p_{11})$

$(p_{11}, X_p = TR \longrightarrow X_p := I_p, p_{12})$

$(p_{12}, true \longrightarrow CS, p_{13})$

$(p_{13}, true \longrightarrow (a_p, s_p) := false, p_1).$

Fig. 2. Hybrid version of Szymanski's algorithm

A_1 : When p is about to leave the waiting room,
some process has entered the inner sanctum.

A_2 : Once p is in the latter part of the inner sanctum,
the waiting room and the doorway are empty.

A_3 : If p is in its critical section, then no process with smaller index
can be in the doorway, waiting room or inner sanctum.

Four supplementary assertions (2) formalize this:

$$
\begin{aligned}
A_0 : & & at \ p_{8..13} & \Rightarrow \neg at \ q_4 \\
A_1 : & & at \ p_8 & \Rightarrow \exists k \leq n : at \ k_{10} \\
A_2 : & & at \ p_{11..13} & \Rightarrow \neg at \ q_{4..9} \\
A_3 : & ((at \ p_{11} \wedge X_p[q]) \vee at \ p_{12,13}) \wedge q < p & & \Rightarrow \neg at \ q_{4..13}
\end{aligned}
\tag{2}
$$

The countdown for access to the critical section takes place at state p_{11}; the behaviour of array X_p is formalized in assertions (3).

$$
\begin{aligned}
q \geq p & \Rightarrow X_p[q], \\
(q < p \wedge X_p[q]) & \Rightarrow at \ p_{11}.
\end{aligned}
\tag{3}
$$

Assume now that $I(p,q)$ denotes the conjunction of all assertions (1,2,3). As an invariant, the formula $\forall p \forall q \neq p \ I(p,q)$ is a likely candidate. We observe it is true initially, when each process p is at p_1, with a_p, s_p, w_p being false, and $X_p = I_p$. Besides, assertion A_3 expresses that p and q cannot be both at the same time in their critical section: $at \ p_{12} \Rightarrow \neg at \ q_{12}$ is a logical consequence of this assertion.

3 A propositional model

3.1 Introduction

In order to prove that I is an invariant, we have to check that every transition τ respects formula I; this is written $\{I\}\tau\{I\}$. We rely on the classical rule: the triple

$$\{A\}\ \tau\ \{B\}$$

holds if and only if the formula

$$A \Rightarrow wp[\tau; B]$$

is valid. The operator wp (weakest precondition) takes two arguments, a transition τ and a set of states represented by a formula B. The associated value is the set of all states whose τ-successor satisfies B. The operator wp is easily computable and many tools exist which automate this computation (in the sequel, we use our tool CAVEAT [12]). This symbolic computation is based on the identity

$$wp[x := f(x,y)\,;\ B(x,y)] = B(f(x,y),y). \tag{4}$$

The assertion $I \Rightarrow wp[\tau; I]$ is the verification condition associated with τ. It is easy to generate them in a fully automatic way, but less easy to check them for validity. In general, these assertions belong to first order logic, especially when the guards of the transitions are quantified formulas.

3.2 Elimination of explicit quantifiers

Earlier verification of Szymanski's algorithm have been completed with the assistance of an interactive theorem prover for first order logic [22, 23]. Our purpose now is to do it again, but without interactive work. This is possible if we rewrite the problem in the framework of propositional logic. The first step of this rewriting is the elimination of quantifiers. To achieve this, we introduce six auxiliary variables (5); these variables are counters, whose role is to record the number of processes for which some boolean expression is true.

$$
\begin{aligned}
\#(s) &=_{def} |\{j : 1 \le j \le n \wedge s_j\}|; \\
\#(w) &=_{def} |\{j : 1 \le j \le n \wedge s_j\}|; \\
\#(s\overline{w}) &=_{def} |\{j : 1 \le j \le n \wedge s_j \wedge \neg w_j\}|; \\
\#(a\overline{w}) &=_{def} |\{j : 1 \le j \le n \wedge a_j \wedge \neg w_j\}|; \\
\#(X_p) &=_{def} |\{j : 1 \le j \le n \wedge X_p[j]\}|; \\
\#(10) &=_{def} |\{j : 1 \le j \le n \wedge at\ j_{10}\}|.
\end{aligned}
\tag{5}
$$

The range of all these variables is the set $\{0, \ldots, n\}$; for instance, $\#(s)$ is the number of processes whose s-variable is true. With these notations, quantifiers can be eliminated, according to Figure 3. The quantifier-free version of the program is given in Figure 4.

Comment. This translation is not difficult but should be completed with care. For instance, the statement $s_p := \textit{false}$ is adequately translated into the statement

$\exists j \leq n : a_j \wedge \neg w_j$	$\#(a\overline{w}) \geq 1$
$\forall j \leq n : \neg w_j$	$\#(w) = 0$
$\exists q \leq n : at\ q_{10}$	$\#(10) \geq 1$
$\exists j \leq n : a_j \wedge \neg w_j$	$\#(a\overline{w}) \geq 1$
$\longrightarrow$	$\longrightarrow$
$s_p := false$	$(s_p, \#(s)) := (false, \#(s) - 1)$

Fig. 3. Eliminating quantification

$(s_p, \#(s)) := (false, \#(s) - 1)$ only if we already know that s_p is always true before the execution (which is a consequence of the invariant).

The invariant is translated in a similar way (6) and the behaviour of the auxiliary variables is formalized in supplementary assertions (7), added to the invariant.

$$\begin{aligned}
at\ p_{8..13} &\Rightarrow \neg at\ q_4 \\
at\ p_8 &\Rightarrow \#(10) \geq 1 \\
at\ p_{11..13} &\Rightarrow \neg at\ q_{4..9} \\
((at\ p_{11} \wedge X_p[q]) \vee at\ p_{12,13}) \wedge q < p &\Rightarrow \neg at\ q_{4..13} .
\end{aligned} \tag{6}$$

$$\begin{aligned}
\#(s) &\geq 0 \\
\#(w) &\geq 0 \\
\#(s\overline{w}) &\geq 0 \\
\#(a\overline{w}) &\geq 0 \\
\#(10) &\geq 0 \\
at\ p_{3,4,10..13} &\Rightarrow \#(a\overline{w}) \geq 1 \\
at\ p_{10..13} &\Rightarrow \#(s\overline{w}) \geq 1 \\
\#(X_p) &\geq n - p + 1 \\
\neg at\ p_{11} &\Rightarrow \#(X_p) = n - p + 1 \\
at\ p_{10} &\Rightarrow \#(10) \geq 1 .
\end{aligned} \tag{7}$$

3.3 Elimination of implicit quantifiers

We have to prove the triple $\{\forall p \,\forall q \neq p\, I(p, q)\} \tau \{\forall p \,\forall q \neq p\, I(p, q)\}$ for each transition τ. Due to symmetry, we can restrict to transitions executed by a single fixed station p, so 14 transitions have to be considered. The "countdown" transition also refers to some process $q < p$, so we also select a second station $q < p$.

Besides, the assertions of the invariant refer to (at most) two distinct stations, say p' and q'. Instead of proving the original triple (in fact, 14 triples) we can prove the simpler triples

$$\{\forall p \,\forall q \neq p\, I(p, q)\} \ \tau \ \{I(p', q')\} .$$

These stations can be distinct from p and q, or not. We need therefore to evoke at most four distinct stations, say p, q, r and s. As argued in [12], our proof task

$(p_1, true \longrightarrow skip, p_2)$

$(p_2, true \longrightarrow (a_p, \#(a\overline{w})) := (true, \#(a\overline{w}) + 1), p_3)$

$(p_3, \#(s) = 0 \longrightarrow skip, p_4)$

$(p_4, true \longrightarrow (w_p, \quad s_p, \quad \#(w), \quad \#(s), \quad \#(a\overline{w})) :=$
$(true, true, \#(w) + 1, \#(s) + 1, \#(a\overline{w}) - 1), p_5)$

$(p_5, \#(a\overline{w}) \geq 1 \longrightarrow (s_p, \#(s)) := (false, \#(s) - 1), p_7)$

$(p_7, \#(s\overline{w}) \geq 1 \longrightarrow skip, p_8)$

$(p_8, true \longrightarrow (s_p, \#(s)) := (true, \#(s) + 1), p_9)$

$(p_5, \#(a\overline{w}) = 0 \longrightarrow skip, p_9)$

$(p_9, true \longrightarrow (w_p, \quad \#(10), \quad \#(w), \quad \#(a\overline{w}), \quad \#(s\overline{w})) :=$
$(false, \#(10) + 1, \#(w) - 1, \#(a\overline{w}) + 1, \#(s\overline{w}) + 1), p_{10})$

$(p_{10}, \#(w) = 0 \longrightarrow \#(10) := \#(10) - 1, p_{11})$

$(p_{11}, q < p \wedge \neg X_p[q] \wedge s_q \longrightarrow (X_p[q], \#(X_p)) := (true, \#(X_p) + 1), p_{11})$

$(p_{11}, \#(X_p) = n \longrightarrow (X_p, \#(X_p)) := (I_p, n - p + 1), p_{12})$

$(p_{12}, true \longrightarrow skip, p_{13})$

$(p_{13}, true \longrightarrow (a_p, \quad s_p, \quad \#(s), \quad \#(a\overline{w}), \quad \#(s\overline{w})) :=$
$(false, false, \#(s) - 1, \#(a\overline{w}) - 1, \#(s\overline{w}) - 1), p_1).$

Fig. 4. Quantifier-free version of Szymanski's algorithm

can be reduced to checking the following triples:

$$\{\forall p \, \forall q \neq p \, I(p, q)\} \; \tau \; \{I(p, q)\},$$
$$\{\forall p \, \forall q \neq p \, I(p, q)\} \; \tau \; \{I(q, p)\},$$
$$\{\forall p \, \forall q \neq p \, I(p, q)\} \; \tau \; \{I(p, r)\},$$
$$\{\forall p \, \forall q \neq p \, I(p, q)\} \; \tau \; \{I(r, p)\},$$
$$\{\forall p \, \forall q \neq p \, I(p, q)\} \; \tau \; \{I(s, q)\},$$
$$\{\forall p \, \forall q \neq p \, I(p, q)\} \; \tau \; \{I(q, s)\},$$
$$\{\forall p \, \forall q \neq p \, I(p, q)\} \; \tau \; \{I(r, s)\},$$

However, we have assumed $q < p$, but know nothing about the positions of r and s. In the example outlined in [12], that was irrelevant since neither the code nor the invariant involved comparison between these numbers. This is no longer true here, so we have to check every possibility. For instance,

$$\{\forall p \, \forall q \neq p \, I(p, q)\} \; \tau \; \{I(s, q)\}$$

splits into three subcases: $s < q < p$, $q < s < p$ and $q < p < s$; for the last triple, there are 12 subcases. Last, it seems safe to assume that, in the precondition $\forall p \, \forall q \neq p \, I(p, q)$, only the seven instances $I(p, q), \ldots, I(r, s)$ will be needed, so we replace the quantified precondition by the conjunction of these instances.

3.4 Generation of verification conditions

Automating wp-calculus is easy, at least when all statements and assertions are quantifier-free.[2] The tool CAVEAT was used to generate the verification conditions. These conditions still contain predicates, like $q < p$ and $\#(w) = 0$; these predicates will be viewed as atoms by the tautology checker.

3.5 Additional hypotheses

A full reduction of first-order theories to propositional calculus is obviously impossible. Information is lost if, for instance, the predicate $\{\#(w) = 0\}$ is viewed as an atomic proposition ("pseudo-atoms" are surrounded by curly braces). As a consequence, specific axioms are needed to restore this information; they will be used as additional hypotheses in the verification conditions. The axioms maintain the consistency between the original variables like w_p, and the pseudo-atoms like $\{\#(w) = 0\}$, and also between the pseudo-atoms themselves. For instance, the axiom

$$\neg(w_p \wedge \{\#(w) = 0\})$$

was used as an additional hypothesesis for verifying Szymanski's algorithm.

4 Propositional verification techniques

Supplementing the set of additional hypotheses seems a fair price to pay for reducing the first-order validity problem to tautology checking. However, the elimination of implicit quantifiers has strongly increased the size and the number of verification conditions. In fact, even state-of-the-art tautology checkers can barely cope with really big formulas. Fortunately, propositional verification conditions have a very particular structure. If the invariant I is the conjunction $a_1 \wedge \cdots \wedge a_n$, then the condition $I \Rightarrow wp[\tau; I]$ can be written as

$$(a_1 \wedge \cdots \wedge a_n) \Rightarrow (c_1 \wedge \cdots \wedge c_n), \qquad (8)$$

where typically the members of the set of hypotheses $H = \{a_1, \ldots, a_n\}$ are small, while the size n of this set is big. For the propositional model of the hybrid version of Szymanski's algorithm, the average value of n is 130, but it is much higher for the finer-grained, molecular version.

It is often convenient to consider conclusions $c_1, \ldots, c_n$ one at a time, i.e., to split the verification condition (8) into the (conjunctive) set of formulas (9).

$$(a_1 \wedge \cdots \wedge a_n) \Rightarrow c_1,$$
$$\cdots \quad \cdots \qquad\qquad (9)$$
$$(a_1 \wedge \cdots \wedge a_n) \Rightarrow c_n.$$

---

[2] One should be careful to deal with array assignments, though: the usual assignment rule (4) has to be adapted for arrays. However, this induces no trouble in the present framework.

The reason is as follows. When condition (8) happens to be valid, most of the hypotheses have a role in a validity proof, which is therefore lengthy and not easily constructed. However, experimentation shows that, most of the time, each formula of the list (8) admits a short proof, using only a small subset H_j of the big set $H = \{a_1, \ldots, a_n\}$ of hypotheses; it is more efficient to construct n small proofs than to construct a big one.[3]

In order to discover the relevant set H_j of hypotheses, needed to establish conclusion c_j (in fact, as small a superset as possible), we use a three-phased approach. The first phase interleaves simplification and elimination of provably irrelevant hypotheses. A hypothesis h is *provably irrelevant* with respect to a conclusion c if formulas $(h \wedge \varphi) \Rightarrow c$ and $\varphi \Rightarrow c$ are equivalent for every formula φ. Syntactic criteria for simplification and irrelevance detection are developed in [13]. Second, the remaining hypotheses are sorted in a list $h_1, h_2, \ldots$; the idea is that seemingly most relevant hypotheses appear before seemingly less relevant ones. This notion is investigated in [13] so only an elementary example is given here. If c is $c_1 \Rightarrow c_2$, then a hypothesis like $c_3 \Rightarrow c_2$ is potentially useful (say, if $c_1 \Rightarrow c_3$ can be established from other hypotheses) and will therefore appear early in the list. On the contrary, a hypothesis like $c_2 \Rightarrow c_4$ is provably irrelevant, and therefore will not appear at all. (See [13] for more details.)

Comment. The nth step of the sorting procedure select $h_n \in H \backslash \{h_1, \ldots, h_{n-1}\}$ as the most promising hypothesis with respect to the formula

$$(h_1 \wedge \cdots \wedge h_{n-1}) \Rightarrow c$$

and not with respect to c alone.

Last, a tautology checker is iteratively called. The first attempt is to validate the conclusion c; if it fails, $h_1 \Rightarrow c$ is tried, and so on either until a member of the sequence

$$c, \ h_1 \Rightarrow c, \ h_2 \Rightarrow (h_1 \Rightarrow c), \ldots$$

is recognized as valid, or until the set of hypotheses has been exhausted. In the former case, the verification condition is valid.

Comment. The only cause of incompleteness in CAVEAT is the database of additional axioms. If the tautology checker does not provide a positive answer, either the program is not correct with respect to the invariant, or the database of additional axioms is too weak.

5 Automated verification

The proof of correctness of the hybrid version of Szymanski's algorithm with respect to its invariant has been completed with the tool CAVEAT (for Computer Aided VErification And Transformation). The first version of the tool has been presented in [12], but the version used here is rather different.

---

[3] This is usually true for verification conditions, but not for arbitrary propositional formulas.

The first component of CAVEAT is a classical generator of verification conditions. The data file contains the code of the program and the invariant as stated in Section 2, with a slightly different syntax. For the example considered here, the program contains 14 transitions and the invariant, in the form $I(p, q) \wedge \cdots \wedge I(r, s)$, is the conjunction of 66 assertions (after removing repetitions, since some assertions appear both in $I(p, q)$ and $I(p, r)$, for instance). The output file is the list of 14 verification conditions, obtained by weakest-precondition calculus. These are boolean formulas whose atomic propositions are true propositions (like w_p), place predicates (like $at\ q_4$) and pseudo-atoms, like $\{p < q\}$ and $\{\#(s) - 1 \geq 0\}$.

The second component of CAVEAT works with two data files, containing respectively one of the verification conditions (produced by the first component), and the list of additional hypotheses. The component simply inserts this list in the list of hypotheses of the verification condition, and then performs the splitting described in paragraph 4. This splitting allows for further elementary simplifications, so many of the $66 * 14$ produced conditions reduce to true and vanish; CAVEAT has in fact produced 155 conditions; one of them, corresponding to transition

$$(p_5, \neg \exists j \leq n : a_j \wedge \neg w_j \longrightarrow skip, p_9)$$

and to assertion

$$at\ p_{8..13} \Rightarrow \neg at\ q_4$$

is investigated further in the appendix; it contains 145 hypotheses, and the conclusion is

$$\{\#(a\bar{w}) = 0\} \Rightarrow (\neg at\ q_4).$$

The list of additional hypotheses is the same for all verification conditions. For now, they are produced by the user, either from scratch, or by adaptation of some available databases of standard additional hypotheses. In our case, four databases have been used, for shared boolean arrays, identity, comparison operators ($\leq$, $\geq$, ...) and increment/decrement (properties of unary functions $x \mapsto x + 1$ and $x \mapsto x - 1$. For instance, the database for shared boolean arrays (like a, s and w in our example) is

$$\{\#(b) = n\} \Rightarrow b_p,\ b_p \Rightarrow \{\#(b) \geq 1\},$$

whereas

$$\{x \geq 1\} \Rightarrow \neg\{x = 0\}$$

can be found in another database. Further relevant facts are obtained by combining several databases, like

$$\{\#(b) \geq 1\} \Rightarrow \neg\{\#(b) = 0\}.$$

The data file used by CAVEAT in our example contains 84 facts; a sample is given in the appendix.

The third component of CAVEAT applies simplification and elimination rules, in order to suppress as many hypotheses as possible. For the aforementioned example, 90 hypotheses have been eliminated (out of 145); the remaining 55 hypotheses are listed in the appendix.

The fourth component consists in sorting the list of potentially relevant hypotheses, and the last component is the tautology checking itself. Recall that the latter work iteratively. For our example, only two hypotheses (out of 55) were really needed to establish the conclusion; their rank in the sorted list were 2 and 4, so five iterations were needed to validate the condition. (More details are given in the appendix.)

6 Discussion, comparison and conclusion

Szymanski's algorithm has been frequently used as benchmark for computer-aided verification tools. Two earlier successful attempts are [22] and [23]. We were puzzled by the fact that the critical problem in them was associated with the validation of the verification conditions. Clearly, those conditions are consequences of few elementary mathematical facts; the only difficulty is their huge size and number.

In fact, state-of-the-art theorem provers like recent versions of NQTHM or OTTER have been successfully used to prove non trivial mathematical theorems, but such systems are not at their best with very long formulas (see e.g. [9,21, 24,27]). That is the reason why the first version of CAVEAT emphasized propositional reasoning instead of first-order reasoning [12,13]. However, good results were obtained only for "nearly propositional" concurrent systems. In particular, Szymanski's algorithm was outside the practical scope of CAVEAT. To overcome this worrying limitation, we have eliminated the need of true first-order reasoning from CAVEAT; the only link between first-order reasoning and CAVEAT is now the database of additional hypotheses. The database itself is purely propositional; first-order reasoning is required only for its construction and, for now, little help is available to the user. The propositional part of CAVEAT works very efficiently, due to the simplification rules and the elimination rules based on the idea of relevance [13]; we have seen that the size of the formula effectively validated by the tautology checker was far smaller than the verification condition itself, 4 hypotheses instead of 145 in our example. As a result, the validation time needed by CAVEAT is quite short. Naturally, some time has to be spent for the construction of the database of additional hypothesis, but there is an important difference : the user faces only very short formulas, whose validity is trivial, instead of lengthy verification conditions. Besides, using first-order ATP tools is not easy. For instance, the strength of OTTER relies noticeably on an appropriate choice of resolution strategies; if the user is not skilled in this domain, the strength becomes weakness. In this respect, the main advantage of our proof of Szymanski's algorithm is that it relies only on $wp\text{-}sp$ calculus, propositional logic, and the (most elementary) mathematical facts used in Szymanski's algorithm itself.

Validation is not the only difficult step with the assertional approach : the construction of the invariant can also be a problem. For coarse-grained versions of concurrent algorithms, the construction of the invariant is simply a formal traduction of the main idea underlying the algorithm. However, as explicitly stated in [22], and also demonstrated e.g. in [11, 19], the invariant of a reasonably fine-grained version is a complex formula, whose construction can be challenging. Much work has been devoted to invariant construction, adaptation and approximation (see e.g. [2, 3, 5, 8, 10]). Most techniques rely on fixpoint calculus, implemented as weakest-precondition and strongest-postcondition calculi. These are already present in CAVEAT, and a module for invariant adaptation is planned; its purpose will not be the design of an invariant from scratch, but the incremental adaptation of a coarse-grained invariant into a finer-grained one (see [11] for a detailed presentation of this technique).

Another approach for concurrent program verification is model checking. Its main advantage is that little extra-work is required from the user, not even writing an inductive invariant. (See e.g. [4, 6, 14, 17, 25] for presentation and examples.) The problem is, model checking requires a finite, bounded model of programs and properties. Basically, a "parametric" system involving some unspecified integer constant n (the number of processes, for instance) can be investigated fully automatically only if n has been given an explicit numeric value; besides, the verification time may grow exponentially with this value. In spite of several attempts to overcome this limitation, e.g. [16, 30], and the combinatorial explosion [15, 26, 29], we feel this will remain a serious drawback (see also [1]). On the other hand, if we request a formal verification only for some fixed small values of parameters like n, model checking is the most convenient approach.

The approach presented here has also an educational advantage, especially if several versions of the same concurrent program are considered in sequence, coarser-grained version before finer-grained ones. The tool allows the user to understand more easily why some guard or some assertion is needed, for instance; it is also useful to the program designer, who is able to determine how fine-grained his/her algorithm can be implemented without destroying its properties.

Several tools and methods have been proposed which combine the assertional method and model checking, for instance [17, 18, 22]. As far as tautology checking is an elementary kind of model checking, the new version of CAVEAT also belongs in this category.

References

1. K.R. Apt and D.C. Kozen, Limits for Automatic Program Verification, *Inform. Process. Letters* **22** (1986) 307-309.
2. S. Bensalem, Y. Lakhnech and H. Saidi, Powerful techniques for the automatic generation, *Lect. Notes in Comput. Sci.* (1996) 323-335.
3. N. Bjorner, A. Browne and Z. Manna, Automatic Generation of Invariants and Intermediate Assertions, *Lect. Notes in Comput. Sci.* **976** (1995) 589-623.
4. J.R. Burch et al., Symbolic Model Checking: 10^{20} States and Beyond, Proc. 5th. Symp. on Logic in Computer Science (1990) 428-439.

5. E. Clarke, Program invariants as fixed points, Proc. 18th IEEE Symp. on Foundations of Comput. Sci. (1977) 18-29.

6. E. Clarke, E. Emerson and A. Sistla, Automatic Verification of Finite-State Concurrent Systems Using Temporal Logic Specifications, *ACM Trans. Programming Languages Syst.* **8** (1986) 244-263.

7. K.M. Chandy and J. Misra, *Parallel Program Design: A Foundation* (Addison-Wesley, Reading, MA, 1988).

8. P. Cousot and N. Halbwachs, Automatic Discovery of Linear Restraints Among Variables of a Program, Proc. 5th ACM Symp. on Principles of Programming Languages (1978) 84-96.

9. D.M. Goldschlag, Mechanically Verifying Concurrent programs with the Boyer-Moore prover, *IEEE Trans. on Software Engineering* **16** (1990) 1005-1023.

10. S. Graf and H. Saidi, Verifying invariants using theorem proving, *Lect. Notes in Comput. Sci.* **1102** (1996) 196-207.

11. E.P. Gribomont, Concurrency without toil: a systematic method for parallel program design, *Sci. Comput. Programming* **21** (1993) 1-56.

12. E.P. Gribomont and D. Rossetto, CAVEAT: technique and tool for Computer Aided VErification And Transformation, *Lect. Notes in Comput. Sci.* **939** (1995) 70-83.

13. E.P. Gribomont, Preprocessing for invariant validation, *Lect. Notes in Comput. Sci.* **1101** (1996) 256-270.

14. G. Holtzmann, An improved protocol reachability analysis technique, *Software, Practice, and Experience,* **18** (1988) (137-161)

15. C.N. Ip and D.L. Dill, Verifying Systems with Replicated Components in Murφ, *Lect. Notes in Comput. Sci.* **1102** (1996) 147-158.

16. B. Jonsson and L. Kempe, Verifying safety properties of a class of infinite-state distributed algorithms, *Lect. Notes in Comput. Sci.* **939** (1995) 42-53.

17. R.P. Kurshan and L. Lamport, Verification of a Multiplier : 64 Bits and Beyond, *Lect. Notes in Comput. Sci.* **697** (1993) 166-179.

18. D. Kapur and M. Subramanian, Mechanically Verifying a Family of Multiplier Circuits, *Lect. Notes in Comput. Sci.* **1102** (1996) 135-146.

19. L. Lamport, An Assertional Correctness Proof of a Distributed Algorithm, *Sci. Comput. Programming* **2** (1983) 175-206.

20. K. Larsen, B. Steffen and C. Weise, Fisher's protocol revisited : a simple proof using modal constraints, Proc. 4th DIMACS Workshop on Verification and Control of Hybrid Systems. New Brunswick, New Jersey, 22-24 October, 1995.

21. W. McCune, OTTER 3.0 Reference manual and guide, Argonne National Laboratory, 1994.

22. Z. Manna et al., STEP : the Stanford Temporal Prover (Draft), Report No. STAN-CS-TR-94-1518, Stanford University, June 1994.

23. M. Nagayama and C. Talcott, An NQTHM Mechanization of Szymanski's algorithm, Report No. STAN-CS-91-1370, Stanford University, June 1991.

24. D.M. Russinoff, A Verification System for Concurrent Programs Based on the Boyer-Moore Prover, *Formal Aspects of Computing* **4** (1992) 597-611.

25. K. McMillan, *Symbolic Model Checking*, Kluwer Academic Publishers, 1993.

26. A. Parashkevov and J. Yantchev, Space Efficient Reachability Analysis Through Use of Pseudo-root States, *Lect. Notes in Comput. Sci.* **1217** (1997) 50-64.

27. D.M. Russinoff, A Mechanically Verified Incremental Garbage Collector, *Formal Aspects of Computing* **6** (1994) 359-390.

28. B. Szymanski, A simple solution to Lamport's concurrent programming problem with linear wait, Proc. 1988 Int. Conf. on Supercomputing Systems (1988) 621-626.

29. P. Wolper and D. Leroy, Reliable Hashing without Collision Detection, *Lect. Notes in Comput. Sci.* **697** (1993)

30. P. Wolper and V. Lovinfosse, Verifying Properties of large Sets of Processes with Network Invariants, *Lect. Notes in Comput. Sci.* **407** (1990) 68-80.

A   A worked-out example

The verification condition considered here is $(I \wedge D) \Rightarrow wp[\tau; a]$ were I is the invariant, D is the database of additional hypotheses, τ is transition

$$(p_5, \neg\exists j \leq n : a_j \wedge \neg w_j \longrightarrow skip, p_9)$$

and a is the assertion

$$at\ p_{8..13} \Rightarrow \neg at\ q_4 .$$

Comment. The syntax used here is nearly the same as in [22]; it is more readable than CAVEAT syntax, where for instance

$$at\ p_{8..10}$$

becomes

$$at\ 8[p]\ or\ at\ 9[p]\ or\ at\ 10[p] .$$

In the sequel, everything has been translated back into the external syntax.

A.1   The database of additional facts

It contains a set of 84 mathematical facts. All of them are obviously valid; the critical point is not to omit any of them. Here is a small sample:

$$\{\#(w) = 0\} \Rightarrow \neg w_p ,$$
$$\{\#(a\bar{w}) \geq 0\} \Rightarrow \{\#(a\bar{w}) + 1 \geq 1\},$$
$$\{\#(10) \geq 0\} \Rightarrow \{\#(10) - 1 \geq 0\},$$
$$\{\#(X_p) = n\} \Rightarrow X_p[q]) .$$

A.2   Sorting hypotheses

The simplification / elimination phase strongly reduces the number of hypotheses in a verification condition. In our example, 55 hypotheses were maintained; here they are :

$$s_p$$
$$s_q \Rightarrow at\ p_{5,9..13}$$
$$s_r \Rightarrow at\ r_{5,9}$$
$$s_s \Rightarrow (at\ s_{5,9,11,12,13}$$
$$at\ q_{3..13} \Rightarrow a_q$$
$$a_r \Rightarrow at\ r_{3,4,5,7,9}$$
$$a_s \Rightarrow at\ s_{3,4,5,7,9,11,12,13}$$
$$at\ q_{5..9} \Rightarrow w_q$$
$$at\ r_{5,7,9} \Rightarrow w_r$$
$$at\ s_{5,7,9} \Rightarrow w_s$$
$$at\ q_{3,4,10..13} \Rightarrow \{\#(a\bar w) \geq 1\}$$
$$at\ s_{3,4,11,12,13} \Rightarrow \{\#(a\bar w) \geq 1\}$$
$$((at\ s_{11,12,13} \Rightarrow \{\#(s\bar w) \geq 1\}$$
$$at\ r_9 \Rightarrow (\neg at\ q_4)$$
$$\neg at\ q_8$$
$$\neg at\ q_{11,12,13}$$
$$\{\#(a\bar w) \geq 1\} \Rightarrow (\neg\{\#(a\bar w) = 0\})$$
$$X_q[q]$$
$$X_s[s]$$
$$\{\#(a\bar w) \geq 1\} \Rightarrow ((\neg w_p) \vee (\neg w_r))$$
$$\{\#(a\bar w) \geq 1\} \Rightarrow ((\neg w_r) \vee (\neg w_s))$$
$$\{\#(a\bar w) \geq 1\} \Rightarrow ((\neg w_q) \vee (\neg w_s))$$
$$\{\#(s\bar w) \geq 1\} \Rightarrow (s_p \vee s_r)$$
$$\{\#(s\bar w) \geq 1\} \Rightarrow (s_r \vee s_s)$$
$$\{\#(s\bar w) \geq 1\} \Rightarrow (s_q \vee s_s)$$
$$\{\#(s\bar w) \geq 1\} \Rightarrow ((\neg w_p) \vee (\neg w_r))$$
$$\{\#(s\bar w) \geq 1\} \Rightarrow ((\neg w_s) \vee (\neg w_r))$$
$$\{\#(s\bar w) \geq 1\} \Rightarrow ((\neg w_s) \vee (\neg w_q))$$

$$at\ p_{5,9..13} \Rightarrow s_q$$
$$at\ r_{5,9} \Rightarrow s_r$$
$$at\ s_{5,9,11,12,13} \Rightarrow s_s$$
$$a_p$$
$$at\ r_{3,4,5,7,9} \Rightarrow a_r$$
$$at\ s_{3,4,5,7,9,11,12,13} \Rightarrow a_s$$
$$w_p$$
$$w_q \Rightarrow at\ q_{5..9}$$
$$w_r \Rightarrow at\ r_{5,7,9}$$
$$w_s \Rightarrow at\ s_{5,7,9}$$
$$at\ r_{3,4} \Rightarrow \{\#(a\bar w) \geq 1\}$$
$$at\ q_{10..13} \Rightarrow \{\#(s\bar w) \geq 1\}$$
$$at\ q_{8..13} \Rightarrow (\neg at\ r_4)$$
$$at\ r_9 \Rightarrow (\neg at\ s_4)$$
$$\neg at\ q_{10}$$
$$at\ q_{11,12,13} \Rightarrow (\neg at\ r_{4,5,7,9})$$
$$X_p[p]$$
$$X_r[r]$$
$$\{\#(a\bar w) \geq 1\} \Rightarrow ((\neg w_p) \vee (\neg w_q))$$
$$\{\#(a\bar w) \geq 1\} \Rightarrow ((\neg w_r) \vee (\neg w_q))$$
$$\{\#(a\bar w) \geq 1\} \Rightarrow ((\neg w_p) \vee (\neg w_s))$$
$$\{\#(s\bar w) \geq 1\} \Rightarrow (s_p \vee s_q)$$
$$\{\#(s\bar w) \geq 1\} \Rightarrow (s_r \vee s_q)$$
$$\{\#(s\bar w) \geq 1\} \Rightarrow (s_p \vee s_s)$$
$$\{\#(s\bar w) \geq 1\} \Rightarrow ((\neg w_p) \vee (\neg w_q))$$
$$\{\#(s\bar w) \geq 1\} \Rightarrow ((\neg w_r) \vee (\neg w_q))$$
$$\{\#(s\bar w) \geq 1\} \Rightarrow ((\neg w_s) \vee (\neg w_p))$$

The conclusion is

$$\{\#(a\bar w) = 0\} \Rightarrow \neg at\ q_4.$$

The sorting procedure produces this

$$h_1 : at\ q_{3..13} \Rightarrow a_q$$
$$h_2 : at\ q_{3,4,10..13} \Rightarrow \{\#(a\bar w) \geq 1\}$$
$$h_3 : at\ r_9 \Rightarrow (\neg at\ q_4)$$
$$h_4 : \{\#(a\bar w) \geq 1\} \Rightarrow (\neg\{\#(a\bar w) = 0\})$$
$$h_5 : \ldots$$

Hypothesis h_1 seems promising: it could be used to establish a_q, which in turn would refute the antecedent of the conclusion, and therefore validate the conclusion. Hypothesis h_2 is interesting too, also as a helper for refuting the antecedent of the conclusion. Hypothesis h_3 could be used more directly, to establish the consequent of the conclusion. The next hypothesis h_4 allows to conclude. In fact,

$$(h_2 \wedge h_4) \Rightarrow c$$

is propositionally valid.

Formal Verification of SDL Systems at the Siemens Mobile Phone Department

Franz Regensburger * and Aenne Barnard **

Siemens AG

Abstract. In this paper we present the multi process verification of SDL systems at the Siemens mobile phone department. The formal verification is efficiently performed by the model checker tool SVE that is developed at Siemens, too. Several case studies in the area of telecommunication protocols show that model checking techniques have reached a state where they can profitably be integrated in the industrial software development process.

Keywords: formal verification, model checking, SDL, telecommunication protocols.

1 Introduction

Specification of telecommunication software with SDL-like languages has a pretty long tradition at Siemens. Besides the standardised SDL versions SDL-like languages have been used at least for the last 20 years at the departments that develop software for telecommunication.

In the last years formal verification through model checking has gained increasing attention in industries since this kind of formal verification has proved its effectiveness not only in academic case studies.

A research and development group at Siemens ZT AN 1 is working on automatic verification of SDL processes since 1993. In the beginning verification concentrated on the model checking of single SDL processes. However, during the past two years the model checker group at Siemens ZT AN 1 has worked on several case studies in cooperation with the Siemens mobile phone department to extend the application of model checking to multiprocess systems.

This paper reports on the results of joint work between Siemens PN KE as the user of formal verification and Siemens ZT as tool supplier. The case studies show that model checking effectively integrates in the software development process and demonstrably improves software quality.

The paper is organised as follows. After some preliminary remarks in section 2 about the GSM case study and the operating system of a mobile phone designed at Siemens we briefly survey the technical background of the verification tool SVE in section 3. Section 4 explains why the specification language SDL is used at Siemens.

* Franz.Regensburger@mchp.siemens.de
** Aenne.Barnard@pn.siemens.de

Section 5 is devoted to the task of automatic extraction of a verification model from an SDL description. Section 6 shows some examples for system properties formulated in the property language SPL and section 7 shows the usage of the tool SVE in more detail. In section 8 we report time and space complexity for two case studies performed at the Siemens mobile phone department. Section 9 concludes the paper with some remarks about current and future work.

2 Protocol Software for Mobile Phones

For a couple of years mobile phones are getting more and more popular around the world. Besides basic telephone functionality additional features like short messages, faxes or data transfer are standard by now. Although so small and handy every mobile phone contains a lot of software (about 500 000 loc) which is an implementation of the highly complex GSM protocol.

The GSM protocol is organised in an architecture structured into three layers. In the application of formal verification we have mainly concentrated on layer 3. The GSM layer 3 is responsible for linking the mobile to the network if possible. For that it has to trace the surrounding base stations continuously, it has to determine which one of these bases is the best and finally make sure that the mobile is connected to that specific base. In parallel incoming and outgoing calls must be controlled. An implementation of layer 3 has to make sure that these functions synchronise properly without running into life- or deadlocks.

The connection of the processes we concentrated on in our case studies is shown in figure 1. The examples in section 8 correspond to different versions of the depicted scenario. An important process of layer 3 is the mobility manager MM. One of its slave processes is the radio resource manager RR, which is responsible for establishing and maintaining connections. During idle mode (no call is active) RR controls the two slave processes cell selection CS and cell reselection CR.

The process CS establishes the connection to some base station (cell). To do so it first looks for radio waves in the air and then filters out the waves that really correspond to base stations. Among these stations it selects the one, which is the best according to some metrics that considers not only the quality of the signal but also roaming contracts between the net providers. When CS has established the connection it remains in some busy state. At that moment its master RR starts the process CR, which has to maintain the connection established by CS. The processes RR, CS and CR are able to send messages to the lower protocol levels 2 and 1. However, all answers from the lower levels are sent to RR, which routes packages addressed to CS and CR. See section 5.2 for the modelling of the processes and their environment.

The mobile software at Siemens is organised in a multi process single processor architecture, which means all the functions the software performs are split between independent processes but all the processes share a single processor. The processes can communicate with each other by messages. An incoming message is stored temporarily in a queue until the process can respond. Due to our architecture at most one of the processes can use the processor at any time.

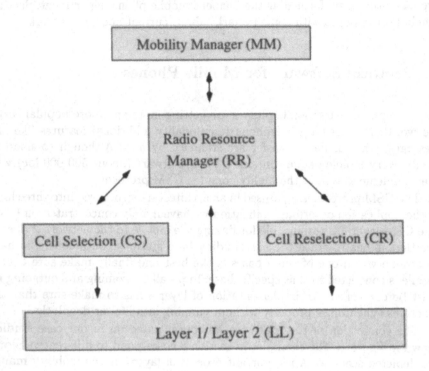

Fig. 1. Processes of GSM protocol layer 3 in idle mode

A process using the processor is called *active*. All the other processes are *inactive*. It is assumed that an active process becomes inactive again after some time. The inactive processes either have messages in their input queue, these processes are called *waiting*, or they do not have any message, these processes are called *idle*. The operating system performs a simple scheduling algorithm that determines which of the waiting processes becomes active next. See section 5.4 for the scheduling algorithm.

At the Siemens mobile phone department, during the design phase each process is understood as a simple state machine that has a number (normally 5-20) of states and sometimes a few very simple local data structures. In each state a process can react to input messages by modifying the values of local data structures and sending messages to other processes. Although this representation of the protocol is still quite abstract, it contains already the basic ideas, how the protocol should work and especially how the interprocess communication works.

3   The SVE System and Its Technical Basis

SVE (System Verification Environment) is a tool for the formal verification of software and hardware systems. It was developed at Siemens ZT AN 1. In SVE system properties are formulated in an application specific language SPL (SDL Property Language) [1] that is automatically translated into the temporal logics (A)CTL and LTL [3]. The system behaviour is modelled as a finite state machine that is automatically derived from an application specific system description, e.g. a SDL system description. The kernel of the SVE system is a BDD-based symbolic model checker, which was developed at ZT AN 1, too. Currently, there exist front ends for various SDL dialects, for control systems and for hardware description languages.

4   Using SDL as a Design Language

At the mobile phone department at Siemens we use SDL (Specification and Description Language) [2] as an input language. In the following we want to explain some of the reasons that lead us towards that decision.

The prime features we expected from our design language were:

- powerful enough to describe our design state machines
- widespread used in telecommunication
- tool support available
- easy to learn and easy to understand
- graphical representation available

At Siemens SDL is used in several departments as a design and as an implementation language. At the mobile phone department it is just used for the design at the moment. In the beginning our design models are very abstract and consist just of a few processes with some few states (see the examples in section 8). Therefore, a much simpler language would have done for the design. However, we plan to extend the use of SDL to the implementation phases as well, which requires a language with the expressiveness of SDL.

Software systems for telecommunication tend to be monsters in terms of size. The code grows over the years and changing the language base by a complete reimplementation is usually impossible. Therefore, the evolution of the languages used for design and implementation should be controlled by some institution like the ITU (International Telecommunication Union). Since SDL was designed especially for telecommunication and is controlled by the ITU it was quite natural to choose SDL.

Despite the standardisation by ITU SDL also has its weak points. The ITU publishes standards for the syntax and the semantics of SDL in working periods of currently 4 years. One goal of these standards is to guarantee portability between SDL tools. However, a recent tool evaluation at Siemens showed that several SDL tools, which officially support SDL/PR 92 or later, are only able to interchange SDL/PR 88 with one another. The situation on the semantic level is even worse. Besides tool incompatibilities there is a widespread practice to use special purpose code generators instead of the generators supplied with the SDL tools.

At the mobile phone department we use the tool Object/Geode from Verilog with SDL/PR 92. Unfortunately the conformance with ITU only holds for the syntactic level. On the semantic level, our developers insisted in slightly changing the semantics of some SDL symbols and the scheduling policy. In section 5 we describe these changes and how we reflected them in the verification models generated by SVE (see especially sections 5.3 and 5.4).

5 Automatic Generation of the Verification Model

In this section we present the automatic generation of the verification model from the SDL input files. SVE has interfaces to various SDL dialects. For the multi process verification presented in this paper we use the phrase language SDL/PR of SDL 92 [2] that is standardised by the ITU (formerly CCITT).

5.1 Supported Sub-Language of SDL

At the mobile phone department at Siemens formal verification is used in the early design phase of a protocol. As a consequence, the SDL systems that need to be verified are on a rather abstract level. Besides message passing the processes just maintain some local variables that play the role of flags. Therefore, it is possible to restrict SDL to a large degree. In the following we enumerate the most important restrictions we imposed on the SDL/PR 92 input language.

Currently, the only data types that need to be supported are enumeration types with equality and inequality as atomic predicates. This is sufficient to model the flags mentioned above. However, the next release will also support finite integer ranges with appropriate arithmetics. Consequently the only tasks that are supported in transitions are assignments to local variables. All other tasks are simply ignored. At the time of this writing we are coding a version of the model generator that supports recursion free procedures and macros, too.

Of course selections and decisions are supported. Conditions that are only composed of atomic predicates about enumeration types are fully supported in their semantics. Selections and decisions that contain other conditions, e.g. informal text, are treated as nondeterministic branchings.

The provided and save directives are fully supported. However, our developers at the mobile phone department use a slightly modified semantics for these constructs.

Since our case studies did not use any of the object oriented features of SDL 92 we completely discarded the entire OO stuff.

Message passing operates on a restricted broadcast mechanism. Every process that mentions a specific signal in its input interface (in the type of some incoming signal route) will receive this signal if the sender is not explicitly mentioned with the send operation. In order to simplify the interpretation of the SDL input we currently do not support the qualification of the receiver via signal route specification with the sending operation.

All the restrictions mentioned above were possible due to the abstract nature of the designs that are written by our developers. With the exception of recursion free procedures these restrictions were not a prerequisite for verification.

However, in order to enable the symbolic execution of transitions described in section 5.5 we had to inhibit procedures with recursion and the join construct. Another restriction vital to our approach was the inhibition of dynamic creation of processes.

5.2 Modelling the Environment

When we talk about multi process verification we actually mean the verification of some processes of a system that are communicating with each other. Due to the inherent complexity of this task we are usually not able to verify all the processes of an entire system at once.

However, we can verify smaller groups of processes which are closely coupled. Especially in the protocol area of telecommunication not all processes need to communicate with each other. Therefore, it is usually not difficult to identify such groups.

Of course, these groups are not isolated but communicate with other groups and perhaps with the environment of the entire system. It is a matter of taste whether the environmental groups and the systems environment are modelled as state machines, or whether their behaviour is modelled using temporal logic.

In practice, it turned out that all the complicated aspects of the environment should be specified via small pseudo SDL processes. Specifying the same behaviour via temporal logic is usually much more difficult and more error prone. Only if the environmental behaviour can be expressed easily by temporal logic, we use temporal formulae and add them as assumptions to our verification model. The fact that engineers have a very natural understanding of state machines but hesitate to use temporal logic was another encouragement to use this technique of environment specification.

Figure 2 shows this kind of modelling for one of our case studies. We concentrated on the processes RR, CS and CR of layer 3 of the GSM handy protocol (see section 2). The processes of layers 1 and 2 are modelled via a single pseudo SDL process LL. User interaction and relevant parts of the mobility manager were subsumed by the pseudo SDL process MM. Minor effects like timer interrupts and reset messages were modelled using temporal formulae that were added as assumptions.

5.3 Priority Queueing

In this subsection we concentrate on the queueing of messages. Standard SDL propagates *infinite* FIFO queues[1], which is obviously not adequate for small

---

[1] in this context infinite means: *there is always an available slot in the input queue.*

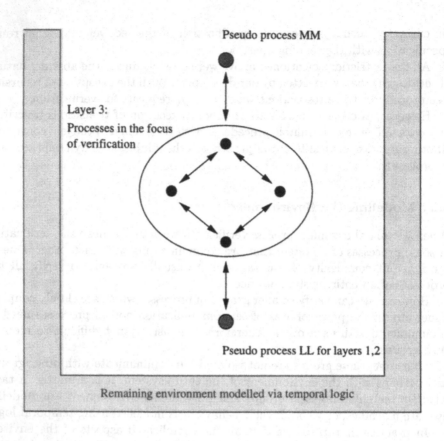

Fig. 2. Verification model for the GSM case study

hardware devices like mobile phones. Even worse, in the case study about mobile phones the system designers decided to use priority queues of a small finite size.

As a consequence our verification model has to perform some kind of overflow detection and should reflect priority queueing. Where the first obligation is not a problem the second one turned out to be hairy. Priority queues can either be coded using one FIFO queue per priority or by using a single sorted queue, where every buffer operation respects sorting. Both approaches tend to be rather space consuming in terms of BDD sizes. In the end we chose sorted queues as representation. For the variable ordering of the buffer bits the bitwise interleaving $b_{(1,1)}, \ldots, b_{(n,1)}, \ldots, b_{(1,m)} \ldots, b_{(n,m)}$ turned out to be best, where $b_{(k,l)}$ denotes bit l of buffer slot k.

5.4 Priority Scheduling

In section 2 we explained that it is assumed that an active process becomes inactive again after some time. This assumption of cooperative processes is technically accomplished in the following way. Whenever a process becomes active it performs exactly one transition from its current SDL state to the next SDL state. When it reaches the next SDL state it becomes inactive again. During the transition it cannot be interrupted in any way no matter how long the execution of the transition may take.

A unique priority is assigned to every process of the system. Therefore, the scheduling algorithm is pretty easy: If more than one process has a message in its queue exactly that one with the highest priority becomes active.

This scheduling strategy together with the cooperative nature of processes influences the verification model to a large degree. One obvious consequence is that the transition of a process from one SDL state to the next one is an indivisible unit in every execution sequence of the system. This fact is heavily exploited as we will see in the next section.

5.5 Symbolic Execution

When coding the verification model one of the main questions is how fine grained the processes should be represented in the finite state machines. One first approach could be to represent every single task on an SDL transition as an execution point in the state machine. Since dealing with multiple processes means building the product automaton of all the automata for the single processes, this approach would yield gigantic BBD representations and therefore is not practicable.

Fortunately, the scheduling policy for the mobile phone operating system allows a far coarser granularity. Since a process cannot be interrupted during the execution of a transition, the verification properties for multi process verification usually do not depend on particular positions within a transition. They rather depend just on the current state, the current input message and the setting of local variables for the various processes.

Therefore, the automatic generation of the verification model performs a detailed analysis of the SDL description for every process. For every combination of state and input we compute every possible thread of execution that can be obtained from the SDL flow charts.

Next, we perform a symbolic execution of these threads. On every thread we accumulate changes in the local variable environment, output directives and logical conditions at branching points that are evaluated according to the actual symbolic variable environment. As a result we obtain the cumulated effect of every thread together with a set of logical conditions enabling the thread.

In the resulting state machine of a single process the abstract states[2] consist of the current SDL state, the local variable environment and the current buffer contents of the process. The abstract states of the state machine are connected through the computed threads above.

After we have computed the state machines for the single processes we finally combine them all with the simple scheduler described above by simply forming

---

[2] we use the term *abstract state* to distinguish the states in the state machine of the verification model from states in the SDL description.

the product automaton. In a last step we perform a complete reachability analysis of the entire system in order to speed up the model checking process, which takes advantage of the precomputed set of reachable states.

With the help of symbolic execution of threads and the ordering of BBD variables described above we are able to build verification models with reasonable space and time complexity[3]. From the above it should be clear that this is only possible due to radical optimisation techniques that are based on the special semantics of the operating system in the mobile phone case studies.

6 The Property Language SPL

In the last section we explained how the SDL input is translated into a verification model. In this section we briefly describe the language that is used to formulate properties about the system.

6.1 Technical Background

The property language SPL (SDL Property Language) [1] is translated into a language of temporal logic, which then in turn is fed to the model checker. Properties are translated into the temporal logic CTL [3] whereas assumptions are translated to LTL [3].

Since the generated verification model is an abstract view of the real system it usually allows more computation sequences than the real system. This is the reason why we restrict our property language to the universal fragment ACTL[4] of the logic CTL [3, 4]. Strictly speaking, the constructs of our property language SPL are defined in a way that their translation to CTL always yields formulae of the fragment ACTL.

6.2 Some Properties Formulated in SPL

Now we are going to give some typical examples for properties and their SPL representations. Representative examples of system properties are:

1. Process p_1 and process p_2 are never in their busy states at the same time.
2. There is never an overflow in the input queues for any of the processes.
3. If process p_1 receives a stop_req this process eventually reaches its idle state

SPL properties look like simple english sentences. Very often a property formulated in natural language can be transformed into a SPL formula quite easily. The properties listed above are expressed in SPL as follows:

1. Property1 is never
   process p_1 state busy and
   process p_2 state busy;

---

[3] see section 8 for more details.
[4] some authors use the notation ∀CTL.

2. Set all_processes is set(p_1,p_2);
   Property2 is
      forall \$procs in all_processes:
         always \$procs.overflow = false;
3. Property3 is
      occurs process p_1 state idle
      after process p_1 event stop_req

Experiences from our case studies show that engineers quickly adopted this style of writing properties. Especially the facility to define parameterised properties (macros) proved to be useful since this allows the engineer to reuse properties.

6.3 Adding Assumptions

Due to abstraction, the verification model normally permits more execution sequences than the real system. Therefore, the model checker sometimes prompts an error trace (counter sequence) to the engineer that is not realistic. In that case the engineer has the option to enrich the property by *assumptions* about the systems behaviour to exclude unrealistic error traces.

Since assumptions usually are only related to some properties and do not apply in general to all properties of the system, the language SPL allows the annotation of assumptions to those properties they are intended for.

As an example for adding assumptions consider property 3 from above. In some rare execution sequences process p_1 never reaches its idle state. Due to abstraction p_1 never becomes active and therefore never gets the chance to perform any actions. We can exclude these traces by formulating the following assumption:

Assumption progress is occurs activeP = p_1 after true

This assumption postulates a fairness constraint[5] for process p_1. By adding this assumption to property 3 we restrict the verification model to those execution sequences for which process p_1 always gets the chance to be active after a finite number of execution steps.

Property3 is
   occurs process p_1 state idle
   after process p_1 event stop_req
   with progress

As another example assume we want to verify that after process p_1 has reached the state connect it will send the message release before it reaches its state idle. One possibility to formulate this in SPL is:

Property CheckRelease is
   occurs process p_1 output release

---
[5] this is translated to gf activeP=p_1 in LTL.

        after process p_1 state connect
        upto process p_1 state idle

The experience of the past years shows that engineers do not like temporal formulae even if they are so simple like the one above. However, they are used to setting flags and testing them somewhere else in their programs. Therefore we support the introduction of history variables (called model variables in SPL). The following SPL property is equivalent to the one above.

    Assumption AsmRelease is
      begin
        dcl MVarWantRelease set(yes,no) init := no
        at process p_1 state connect do MVarWantRelease := yes
        at process p_1 output release do MVarWantRelease := no
      end

    Property CheckRelease2 is
      never (process p_1 state idle and MVarWantRelease = yes)
    with AsmRelease

7 A Survey of the Verification Process

This section is intended to give an overview of the verification process. The following paragraphs should give you an idea how a software engineer interacts with the SVE system during verification. This is accomplished best by looking at the main window of the SVE tool that is shown in figure 3.

First of all the SDL system must be transformed into a system of finite state machines that can be handled by the model checker. This is done by pushing the button **generate a model** in the left column of command buttons. Depending on the size of the SDL system this may take some time. For example, the model generation for one of the GSM case studies (see example 2 in section 8) takes about 6 minutes on a Pentium pro running at 200 MHz.

After model generation has completed the verification model consisting of several BDDs is stored in a file so that it can be reloaded for later verification using button **select a model**. In section 5 we described the automatic model generation in more detail. In contrast to model generation the reloading of a model just takes a few seconds. After the model has been successfully generated the engineer's next task is to formulate some properties in the property language SPL and to store them in an SPL file. In section 6 we described this subject in more detail. In order to check these properties against the verification model one has to load the SPL file using the button **load an SPL file**. During loading the SPL properties are translated into temporal logic and some simple consistency checks are performed, which is usually accomplished in a few seconds.

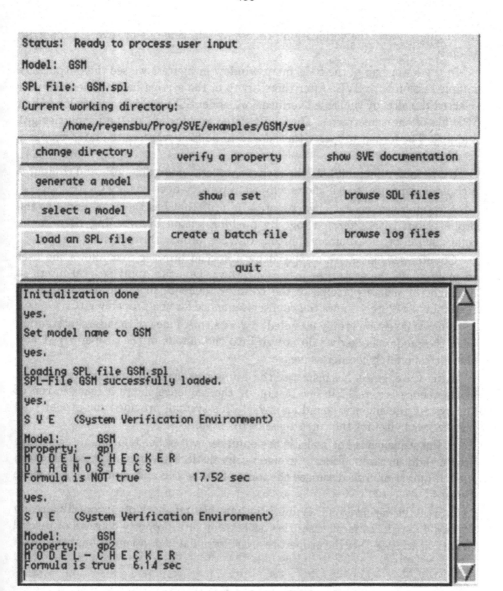

Fig. 3. main window of the SVE system

Now, everything is prepared for the verification of the properties. Pushing button **verify a property** in the middle column of the main window presents a box, which lists all the properties that are defined in the SPL file. From this box the engineer starts the verification process by selecting one or several properties at once.

In the lower half of the SVE main window in figure 3 we see the output of a sample session with SVE. After the startup of the system had finished the user selected the already generated verification model **GSM** and afterwards loaded an SPL file of the same name. Then he started verification of the properties **gp1** and **gp2**. The former property turned out to be false whereas the later property could be proved.

If a property does not hold the model checker starts a diagnosis and computes a counter sequence, which shows why the property does not hold.

A counter sequence is always stored in a file that has the same name as the property but with extension **log**. By pushing button **browse log files** in the right column of the command buttons one can browse through such log files.

Counter sequences are displayed by a special browser that allows the user to manipulate the sequences in various ways. One can apply several filters to highlight or delete portions of the counter sequence in order to enhance its readability. Figure 4 shows the counter sequence for the property **gp1**.

Since this section is only intended to give a rough idea of the users interaction with the model checker we do not go into the details of the property gp1 and the corresponding counter sequence.

After the engineer has inspected the counter sequence he must decide whether the sequence is a realistic one or not. If the sequence shows a realistic run of the system the engineer found an error in his system, provided the property he checked was vital for the correctness of his system.

If the sequence is not realistic the engineer will either reformulate the property or add an assumption to exclude unrealistic behaviour of the verification model. In section 6 we discussed the topic of properties and assumptions in more detail.

In real life verification it is unlikely that the first check of a property already reveals an error. In most cases the verification of a property consists of several iterations where either the properties are reformulated or assumptions are added.

8 Some Remarks on Complexity

There are certain properties of a system that in general have a major influence on the corresponding state space. When doing multiprocess verification, one important factor is the scheduling of the processes. As we discussed in section 5 in detail, we use a rather restricted deterministic scheduling, which limits process interleaving to a large degree.

The next factor that has a major influence on a system's state space is the use of variables and especially the cardinality of their types. Our experience shows that in most cases the variables could be abstracted either to Boolean variables or to enumeration types with cardinality smaller than 10.

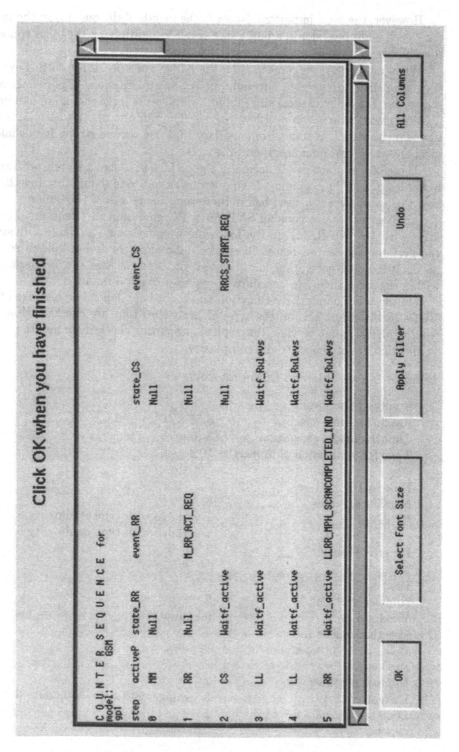

Fig. 4. counter sequence for property gp1

However, the most important factor is the length of the queues. In the worst case, each additional slot in a buffer can result in multiplying the state space by the number of possible messages coming in.

When more messages come in than the buffer can store, the resulting system status is called an *overflow*, normally an erroneous situation. Experiences have shown that if a buffer of short size (about 3 slots) is not large enough to handle all possible states without an overflow, an overflow will also occur when the buffer size is increased. This stems from the fact that one prefers strong handshaking mechanisms in telecommunication protocols.

Therefore, in practice it is normally a good idea to design a system with small buffer lengths in the beginning. If an overflow occurs, one should first investigate how this overflow was caused before increasing the length of the buffer.

At Siemens we are running SVE on a PC environment (Pentium pro 200 MHz with 128 MB RAM). In the following we give some numbers to illustrate the performance we can reach. Of course these numbers do not guarantee that automatic model generation for a system of the same size can be performed within the same time, but certainly they give a rough estimation.

On the other hand, the verification times not only depend on the size of the BDDs involved but also on the type of properties that are checked. However, from a logical point of view the typical properties checked for multi process verification are of almost trivial complexity.

Example 1. Part of layer 3 GSM protocol

Number of processes	3
Reachable state space	8.35×10^7
Time for model generation	3 min
Time for verification of properties	10 s – 30 s

Process 1:	
Number of states	8
Variables	1 variable with type cardinality 8
	1 variable with type cardinality 6
Length of queue	3

Process 2:	
Number of states	9
Variables	no variable
Length of queue	5

Process 3:	
Number of states	2
Variables	3 variable with type cardinality 3
Length of queue	2

Example 2. Part of layer 3 GSM protocol

Number of processes   6
Reachable state space 1.46×10^{13}
Time for model generation   6 min
Time for verification of properties   10 s – 2 min

Process 1:
Number of states   5
Variables   1 variable with type cardinality 2
Length of queue   3

Process 2:
Number of states   6
Variables   1 variable with type cardinality 2
Length of queue   3

Process 3:
Number of states   6
Variables   no variable
Length of queue   2

Process 4:
Number of states   3
Variables   no variable
Length of queue   1

Process 5:
Number of states   2
Variables   no variable
Length of queue   1

Process 6:
Number of states   3
Variables   no variable
Length of queue   1

9 Conclusion

This paper presented the application of model checking to telecommunication protocols for mobile phones. Several case studies have proved that this form of formal verification is learned quickly by engineers and is normally regarded by them as highly capable for finding errors.

So far we have completed a number of case studies to find out if we can apply model checking during our software development in effective and efficient manner. Our main interest at that point was to investigate the capabilities of formal verification. In these case studies we left our concept of applying verification in the early phases, but post verified the design long after the code was implemented. Therefore we were not too surprised not to find big bugs. But besides its capability of finding errors in system designs, we experienced various other positive side effects when using model checking.

The first one is that a programmer using model checking is forced to think about the system in a different way. The normal way of thinking when writing programs is procedural in terms of program steps like *after step 1 is completed step 2 is executed.* When designing system properties, you have to think in a property oriented way like *always when condition 1 holds condition 2 holds as well.* Most of our engineers applying model checking reported that by thinking about the system in terms of properties they learned a lot about their own programs.

Another benefit in the application of model checking is the possibility to investigate how small modifications in the system design (e.g. priority settings) influence the system properties. Without formal verification the effect of such modifications is hard to determine (there might be one rare case where such a modification causes an unwanted effect). When using formal verification, one just starts the model checker again and it will verify if all system properties specified still hold.

In contrast to other model checking case studies performed at Siemens before, we applied model checking to multi process systems. Although multi process systems are more complex than single process systems the model checker SVE worked efficient enough to handle typical system descriptions of the early design phase.

Our future work will concentrate on extending the supported SDL subset to make the application of formal verification more comfortable for the user.

10   Acknowledgement

We like to thank our colleagues Thomas Filkorn and Peter Bader for their comments about various versions of this paper. Also much credit goes to our colleague Peter Warkentin who coded the initial machine for multi process verification and who also implemented some optimisations for the low level BDD representations of our models. Last but not least we like to thank the referees of this paper for their valuable comments and Bernhard Steffen for his persistency.

References

1. P. Bader, T. Filkorn, and J. Bormann. SPL (SDL Property Language): Syntax und Semantik. Siemens ZT AN 1 (internal document), December 1996.
2. Z.100(1993):CCITT specification and description language (SDL). ITU-T, 1993.
3. E.A. Emerson. Temporal and Modal Logic. In *Handbook of Theoretical Computer Science*, chapter 16, pages 996–1072. Elsevier Science Publisher, 1990.
4. D.E. Long. *Model Checking, Abstraction and Compositional Verification.* PhD thesis, Carnegie Mellon University, 1993.

Author Index

Springer
and the
environment

Springer

Lecture Notes in Computer Science

For information about Vols. 1–1308

please contact your bookseller or Springer-Verlag